Not For Tourists Guide to

CHICAGO

Get more on
notfortourists.com

Keep connected with:

Twitter:
twitter/notfortourists

Facebook:
facebook/notfortourists

iPhone App:
nftiphone.com

www.notfortourists.com

Not For Tourists, Inc

Skyhorse Publishing

designed by:
Not For Tourists, Inc
NFT$_{TM}$—Not For Tourists$_{TM}$ Guide to Chicago
www.notfortourists.com

Publisher
Skyhorse Publishing

Co-Founders
Jane Pirone
Rob Tallia

Information Design
Jane Pirone
Rob Tallia
Scot Covey

Director
Stuart Farr

Managing Editors
Craig Nelson
Rob Tallia

City Editor
Aaron Schielke

Sales & Marketing Director
Sarah Hocevar

Production Manager
Aaron Schielke

Printed in China
ISBN# 978-1-61608-527-8 $19.95

10th Edition

Every effort has been made to ensure that the information in this book is as up-to-date as possible at press time. However, many details are liable to change—as we have learned. Not For Tourists cannot accept responsibility for any consequences arising from the use of this book.

Not For Tourists does not solicit individuals, organizations, or businesses for listings inclusion in our guides, nor do we accept payment for inclusion into the editorial portion of our book; the advertising sections, however, are exempt from this policy. We always welcome communications from anyone regarding ANYTHING having to do with our books; please visit us on our website at www.notfortourists.com for appropriate contact information.

www.skyhorsepublishing.com

9 8 7 6 5 4 3 2 1

Dear NFT User,

With the very long Daley era now officially over, Chicago can start a new era with Rahm Emanuel in control. Unfortunately in the current economy, times are still tough. Yet there is good as well as bad—property values, which had ballooned during the real estate boom, are now coming back down to earth, making the market easier than it's been in ages for first-time home buyers. Plus, a certain Chicago connection to the White House seems to be assuring that a fair share of jobs and opportunities will be directed our way.

And life goes on. Neighborhoods evolve, new businesses open while others close, and although for many of us, times are tight, Chicagoans are always looking for new ideas for a memorable night on the town, a great family outing, and affordable options to enjoy the bounty of the city that, despite her shortcomings, is still a great place to live. Yet with so much in flux, how can anyone stay on top of it all? That, dear NFT user, is where we come in. Every year, our staff of local editors revisits every section and every listing from the previous year, updating those that need updating, removing out-of-date info and adding hundreds of new listings; overall we make over 1,000 changes to the book every year, doing our best to make it the most up-to-date and genuinely useful Chicago guidebook ever.

But print publishing has its shortcomings—it can only reflect what was happening in the city at the time of publication, and things are always changing. That's where our website (www.NotForTourists.com/Chicago) and swanky high-falutin' new iPhone application come in. With the website, which was named one of the best Chicago websites by none other than Chicago Magazine (and they should know), information (and your feedback) can be registered instantly. There is even an opportunity to add your favorite places if they have been overlooked. The iPhone app also allows you to give feedback on the spot, and includes a GPS locater, that allows you to find the coffee shops, restaurants, landmarks, "L" stops, etc., closest to you, wherever you are in the city. And while you can't scribble your notes on the webpage or iphone app, we still think they're pretty neat compliments to the book, and we bet you will, too.

Thank you for picking up the Not For Tourist's Guide to Chicago. As the only guidebook of the city written by fellow Chicagoans that includes detailed map-by-map descriptions of every neighborhood in Chicago (as well as Evanston, Oak Park, and Skokie), we hope to worm our way into your heart as your indispensible right hand tool for navigating this dynamic and energetic city that we love.

Cordially Yours,

Jane & Rob

Table of Contents

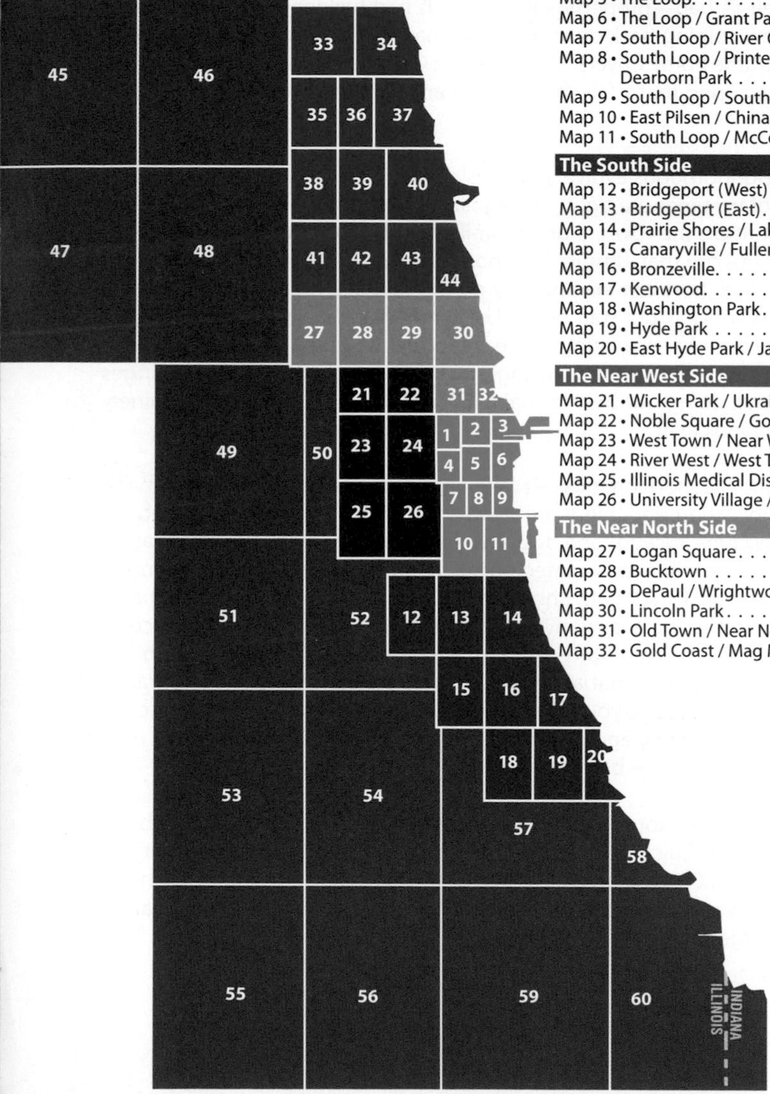

Chicago Neighborhoods

The Greater Loop

The South Side

The Near West Side

The Near North Side

Map 1 • **River North / Fulton Market District**

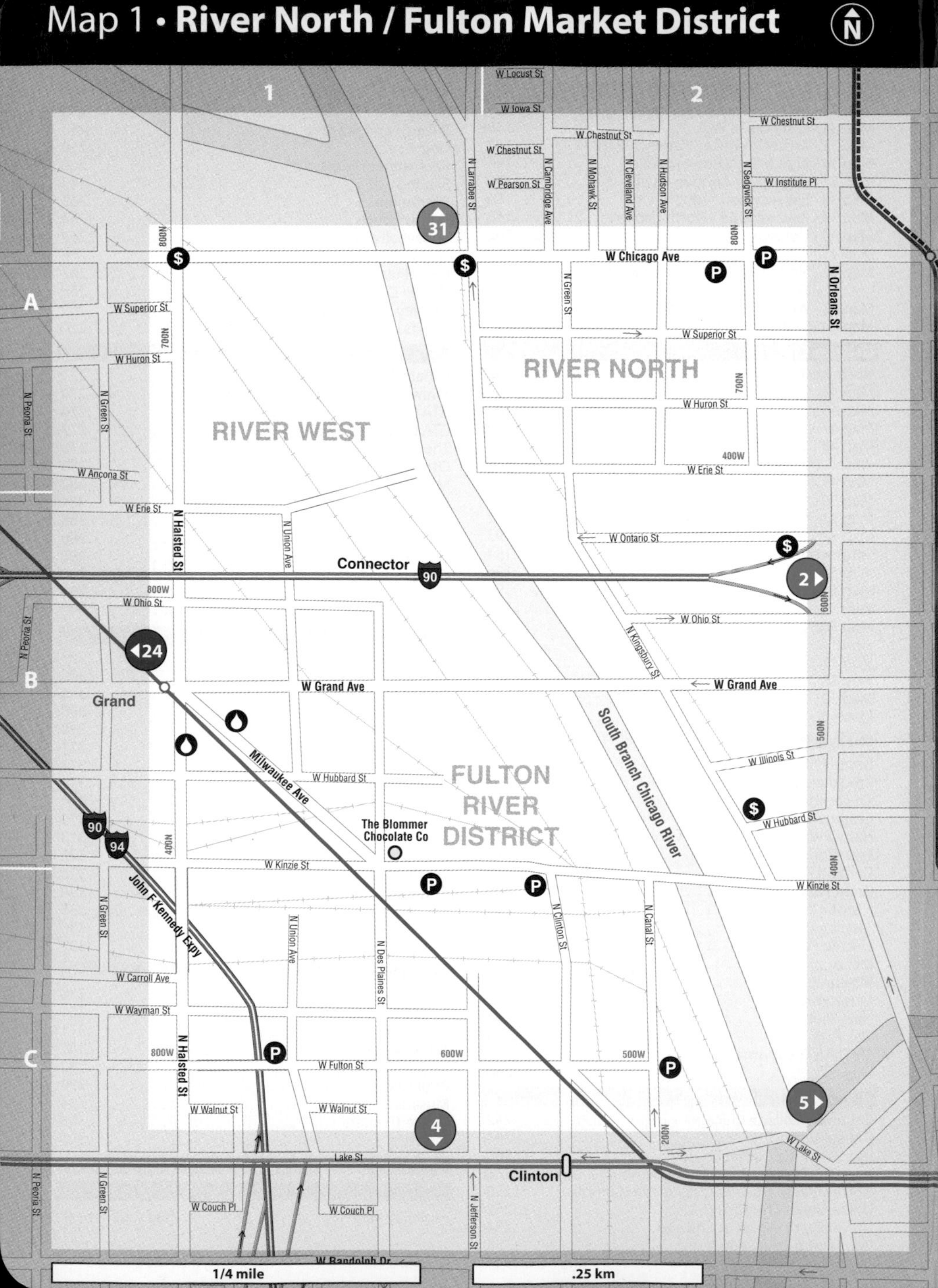

Essentials

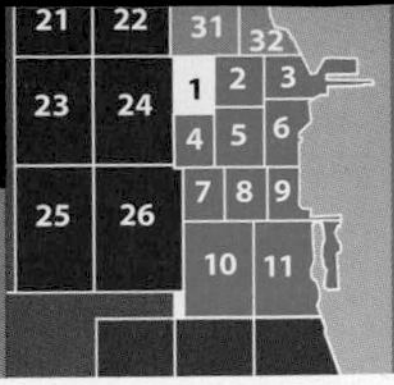

Crisscrossed by rail tracks, I-90/94, and the Chicago River, this area is transitioning from industrial to residential as the loft-conversion craze in River North, Greek Town, and West Loop Gate expands. The Blommer Chocolate Company pumps sweet, chocolate-coated air into the streets all day. Diabetics, beware.

$ Banks

- **Bank of America** • 600 W Chicago Ave
- **Bank of America** • 770 N Halsted St
- **Chase** • 500 N Kingsbury St
- **New Century** • 363 W Ontario St
- **MB Financial** • 306 N Halsted St

Car Washes

- **River West Hand Car Wash** • 478 N Milwaukee Ave
- **We Wash III** • 452 N Halsted St

Landmarks

- **The Blommer Chocolate Co** • 600 W Kinzie St

P Parking

Map 1 • River North / Fulton Market District

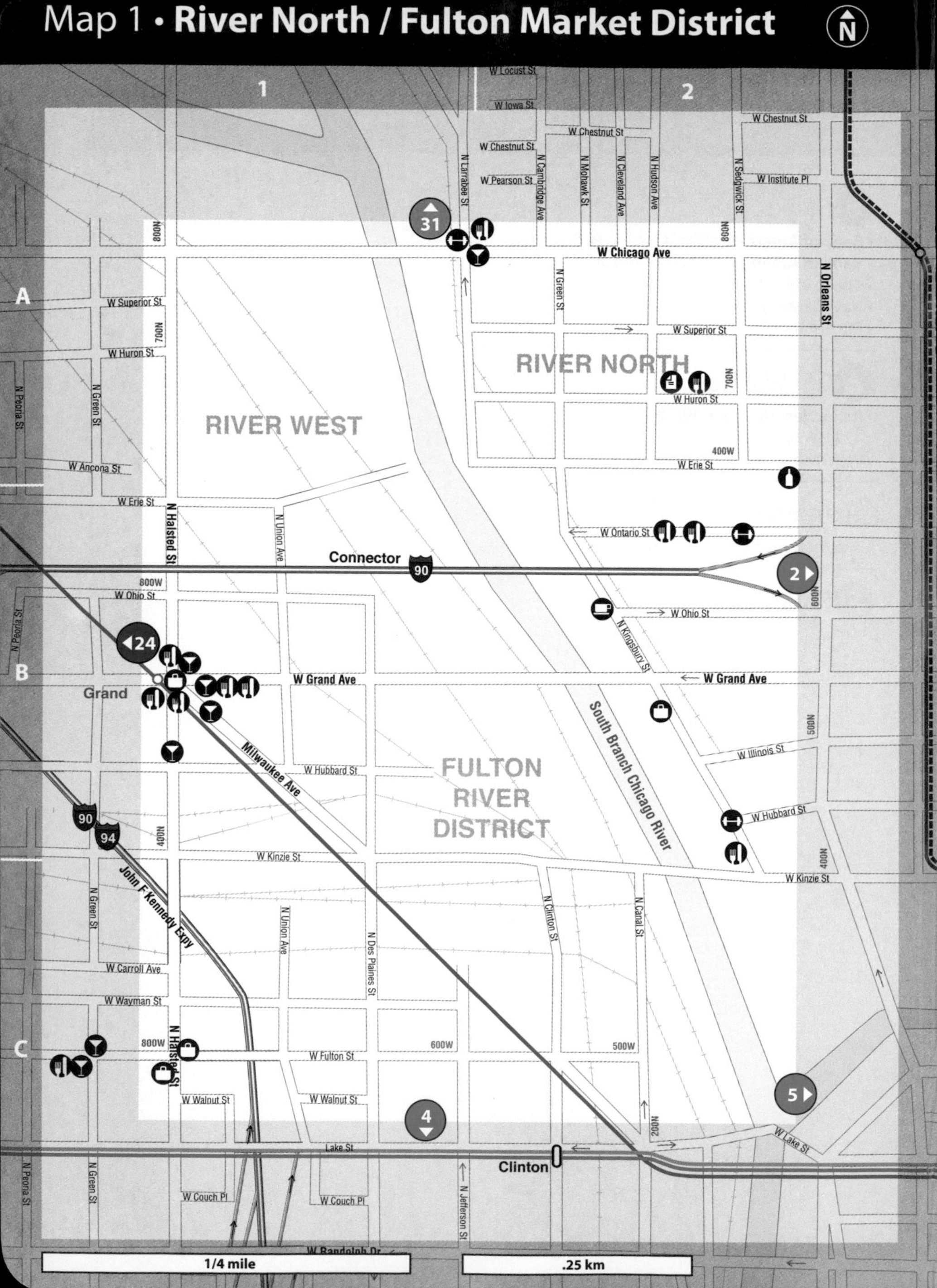

Sundries / Entertainment

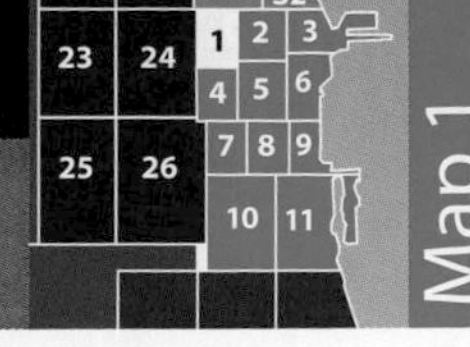

Be seen sipping on sophisticated cocktails at Fulton Lounge or put on your fancy party shoes and head to Lumen. Those looking for a simple, nostalgic night order up a round of Manhattans while popping quarters in the jukebox at The Motel Bar. Impress your date with an alfresco meal at French-Japanese fusion restaurant Japonais.

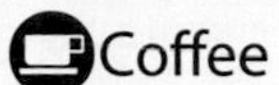

Coffee

- **Caribou Coffee** • 600 N Kingsbury St

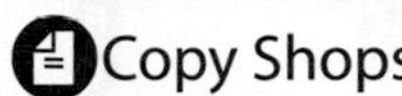

Copy Shops

- **Cushing & Color Chicago** • 420 W Huron St

Gyms

- **David Barton Gym** • 600 W Chicago Ave
- **East Bank Club** • 500 N Kingsbury St
- **Sharper Fitness** • 401 W Ontario St, 4th Fl

Liquor Stores

- **Hart Davis Hart Wine** • 363 W Erie St

Nightlife

- **Emmit's Irish Pub & Eatery** • 495 N Milwaukee Ave
- **Funky Buddha Lounge** • 728 W Grand Ave
- **Lumen 839** • W Fulton St
- **The Motel Bar** • 600 W Chicago Ave
- **Rednofive & Fifth Floor** • 440 N Halsted St
- **Richard's Bar** • 491 N Milwaukee Ave

Restaurants

- **Blue 13** • 416 W Ontario St
- **Carnivale** • 702 W Fulton St
- **Iguana Café** • 517 N Halsted St
- **Japonais** • 600 W Chicago Ave
- **La Scarola** • 721 W Grand Ave
- **Orange** • 730 W Grand Ave
- **Piccolo Sogno** • 464 N Halstead St
- **Publican** • 837 W Fulton Market
- **Reza's** • 432 W Ontario St
- **Scoozi!** • 410 W Huron St
- **Steve's Deli** • 354 W Hubbard St
- **Zealous** • 419 W Superior St

Shopping

- **Doolin's** • 511 N Halsted St
- **L. Isaacson & Stein's Fish Market** • 800 W. Fulton
- **Veruca Salt** • 521 N Kingsbury St

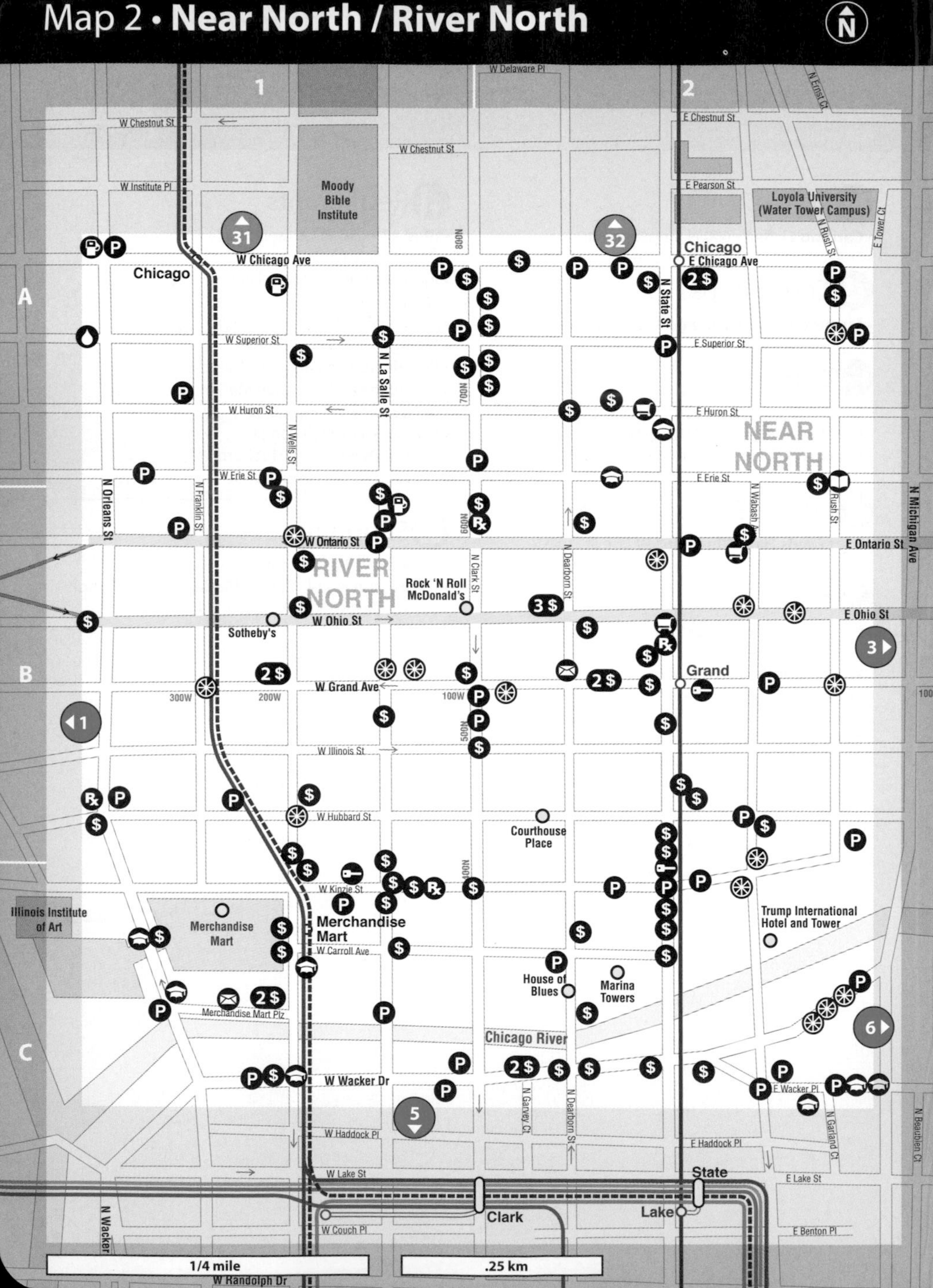
N
1
2
A
B
C
NEAR NORTH
RIVER NORTH
Moody Bible Institute
Loyola University (Water Tower Campus)
Chicago
Rock 'N Roll McDonald's
Sotheby's
Grand
Courthouse Place
Illinois Institute of Art
Merchandise Mart
Trump International Hotel and Tower
House of Blues
Marina Towers
Chicago River
State
Lake
Clark
W Delaware Pl
W Chestnut St
E Chestnut St
W Institute Pl
E Pearson St
W Chicago Ave
E Chicago Ave
W Superior St
E Superior St
W Huron St
E Huron St
W Erie St
E Erie St
W Ontario St
E Ontario St
W Ohio St
E Ohio St
W Grand Ave
W Illinois St
W Hubbard St
W Kinzie St
W Carroll Ave
Merchandise Mart Plz
W Wacker Dr
E Wacker Pl
W Haddock Pl
E Haddock Pl
W Lake St
E Lake St
W Couch Pl
E Benton Pl
W Randolph Dr
N Orleans St
N Franklin St
N Wells St
N La Salle St
N Clark St
N Dearborn St
N State St
N Wabash Ave
N Rush St
N Michigan Ave
N Ernst Ct
E Tower Ct
N Garvey Ct
N Garland Ct
N Beaubien Ct
N Wacker
300W
200W
100W
800N
700N
600N
500N
400N
31
32
3
6
1
5
1/4 mile
.25 km

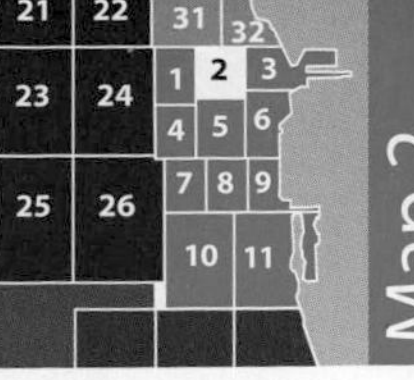

Essentials

Monolithic Merchandise Mart (seriously—it has its own zip code) casts its shadow over River North, helping the area maintain its industrial edge even if all of the former warehouse spaces are now upscale lofts or designer showrooms. A former art gallery haven, only the most successful (and staid) have persevered—edgier artistes have migrated to lower rents on the nearby west side.

Banks

- **Banco Popular** • 415 N La Salle St
- **Bank of America** • 49 E Chicago Ave
- **Bank of America** • 515 N La Salle St
- **Bank of America** • 601 N Dearborn St
- **Bank of America (ATM)** • 59 E Chicago Ave
- **Bank of America (ATM)** • 77 W Wacker Dr
- **Bank of America (ATM)** • CVS • 121 W Kinzie St
- **Bank of America (ATM)** • 320 N Wells St
- **Bank of America (ATM)** • CVS • 344 W Hubbard St
- **Bank of America (ATM)** • 521 N State St
- **Bank of America (ATM)** • 640 N Wells St
- **Charter One** • 33 W Grand Ave
- **Charter One (ATM)** • 35 E Wacker Dr
- **Charter One (ATM)** • 451 N State St
- **Chase** • 230 W Grand Ave
- **Chase** • 340 N State St
- **Chase** • 35 W Wacker Dr
- **Chase** • 71 W Chicago Ave
- **Chase** • 600 • N Dearborn St
- **Chase (ATM)** • 101 E Erie St
- **Chase (ATM)** • 222 Merchandise Mart Plz
- **Chase (ATM)** • 321 N Clark St
- **Chase (ATM)** • Walgreens • 641 N Clark St
- **Citibank** • 400 N Clark St
- **Citibank (ATM)** • 343 N LaSalle St
- **Citibank (ATM)** • 7-Eleven • 418 N State St
- **Citibank (ATM)** • 7-Eleven • 714 N Clark St
- **Fifth Third** • 222 Merchandise Mart Plz
- **Fifth Third** • 42 E Ontario St
- **Fifth Third (ATM)** • 350 N Orleans St
- **Fifth Third (ATM)** • 401 N Wells St
- **Fifth Third (ATM)** • 431 N Wells St
- **First American (ATM)** • 310 W Chicago Ave
- **First American (ATM)** • Renaissance Hotel • 1 W Wacker Dr
- **First American (ATM)** • Hilton Garden Inn Downtown • 10 E Grand Ave
- **First American (ATM)** • 200 W Ohio St
- **First American (ATM)** • 213 W Grand Ave
- **First American (ATM)** • 225 W Wacker Dr
- **First American (ATM)** • Courtyard Marriott • 30 E Hubbard St
- **First American (ATM)** • 30 W Huron St
- **First American (ATM)** • 325 N Wells St
- **First American (ATM)** • House of Blues Hotel Chicago • 333 N Dearborn St
- **First American (ATM)** • 401 N Wells St
- **First American (ATM)** • 50 E Ohio St
- **First American (ATM)** • 640 N La Salle St
- **First American (ATM)** • 70 W Erie St
- **First American (ATM)** • Howard Johnson Inn • 720 N La Salle St
- **First American (ATM)** • Howard Johnson Inn • 721 N Wells St
- **First American (ATM)** • 734 N Clark St
- **First American (ATM)** • 750 N Clark St
- **First American (ATM)** • 750 N Rush St
- **Harris Trust & Savings** • 33 W Ohio St
- **Lakeside** • 55 W Wacker Dr
- **MB Financial (ATM)** • 100 W Grand Ave
- **MB Financial (ATM)** • 615 N Wells St
- **MB Financial** • 1 E Wacker Dr
- **MB Financial** • 33 W Huron St
- **National City Bank** • 16 W Grand Ave
- **National City Bank** • 401 N LaSalle St
- **New Century (ATM)** • 441 N Wabash Ave
- **New Century** • 363 W Ontario St
- **North** • 501 N Clark St
- **North Community** • 448 N Wells St
- **North Community** • 800 N State St
- **Park National** • 801 N Clark St
- **TCF** • 635 N Dearborn St
- **TCF (ATM)** • DePaul University • 333 N State St
- **TCF (ATM)** • 7-Eleven • 343 N La Salle St
- **TCF (ATM)** • 7-Eleven • 418 N State St
- **TCF (ATM)** • 550 N State St
- **TCF (ATM)** • 7-Eleven • 714 N Clark St

Car Washes

- **River North Hand Car Wash** • 356 W Superior St

Car Rental

- **Enterprise** • 10 E Grand Ave • 312-670-7270
- **Enterprise** • 160 W Kinzie St • 312-494-3434
- **Hertz** • 401 N State St • 312-372 7600

Gas Stations

- **BP Connect** • 631 N La Salle Dr
- **Citgo** • 750 N Wells St
- **Shell** • 350 W Chicago Ave

Landmarks

- **Courthouse Place** • 54 W Hubbard St
- **House of Blues** • 329 N Dearborn St
- **Marina Towers** • 300 N State St
- **Merchandise Mart** • 222 Merchandise Mart Plz
- **Rock N Roll McDonald's** • 600 N Clark St
- **Sotheby's** • 215 W Ohio St
- **Trump International Hotel and Tower** • 401 N Wabash Ave

Parking

- **Mac Parking** • 640 N La Salle St

Pharmacies

- **CVS** • 121 W Kinzie St
- **CVS Pharmacy** • 344 W Hubbard St
- **Jewel-Osco** • 550 N State St
- **Walgreens** • 641 N Clark St

Pizza

- **Bella Bacinos** • 75 E Wacker Dr
- **Bella Bacino's** • 75 E Wacker Dr
- **Buca Di Beppo** • 521 N Rush St
- **California Pizza Kitchen** • 52 E Ohio St
- **Delicious** • 308 W Erie St
- **Gino's East** • 633 N Wells St
- **Giordano's** • 730 N Rush St
- **La Madia** • 59 W Grand Ave
- **Lou Malnati's Pizzeria** • 439 N Wells St
- **Pizza Ria** • 405 N Wabash Ave
- **Pizzeria Due** • 619 N Wabash Ave
- **Pizzeria Ora** • 545 N La Salle St
- **Pizzeria Uno** • 29 E Ohio St
- **Rizzata's Pizzeria** • 300 W Grand Ave
- **Rosati's Pizza and California Style Deli** • 126 W Grand Ave

Post Offices

- **US Post Office** • 222 Merchandise Mart Plz
- **US Post Office** • 540 N Dearborn St

Schools

- **Adler School of Professional Psychology** • 65 E Wacker Pl
- **Argosy University** • 350 N Orleans St
- **Associated Colleges of the Midwest** • 205 W Wacker Dr
- **Chicago School of Professional Psychology** • 325 N Wells St
- **Feltre** • 22 W Erie St
- **Frances Xavier Ward Middle** • 751 N State St
- **Illinois Institute of Art** • 350 N Orleans St

Supermarkets

- **Jewel-Osco** • 550 N State St
- **Trader Joe's** • 44 E Ontario St
- **Whole Foods Market** • 30 W Huron St

Map 2 • Near North / River North

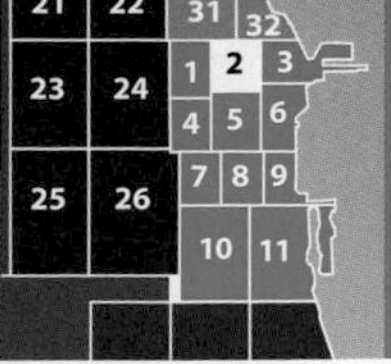

You can find almost every nightlife experience here, from "dress to impress" Enclave to underground karaoke at Blue Frog Bar & Grill to dueling jazz pianists at Redhead Piano Bar. It's also the home of some of Chicago's most renowned restaurants, including Gene & Georgetti's Italian fare, Sunda's snazzy sushi, and Café Iberico's traditional Spanish tapas.

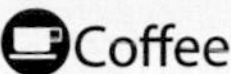

Coffee

- **Cosi** • 55 E Grand Ave
- **Dunkin' Donuts** • 404 N Wabash Ave
- **Dunkin' Donuts** • Merchandise Mart Plz
- **Ohio House Coffee Shop** • 600 N La Salle St
- **Starbucks** • Marriott Courtyard • 30 E Hubbard St
- **Starbucks** • 35 E Wacker Dr
- **Starbucks** • 38 E Ontario St
- **Starbucks** • 414 N Orleans St
- **Starbucks** • 42 E Chicago Ave
- **Starbucks** • 430 N Clark St
- **Starbucks** • 470 Merchandise Mart Plz
- **Starbucks** • Embassy Suites • 600 N State St
- **Starbucks** • 750 N Franklin St
- **Starbucks** • 30 W Erie St

Copy Shops

- **FedEx Kinko's** • 350 N Clark St
- **FedEx Kinko's** • 444 N Wells St ⓐ
- **Icon Printing** • 18 W Hubbard St
- **Office Depot** • 352 W Grand Ave
- **Printwell** • 20 W Hubbard St
- **Quantity Photo & Print** • 119 W Hubbard St
- **The UPS Store** • 40 E Chicago Ave
- **The UPS Store** • 446 N Wells St

Gyms

- **Crunch Fitness** • 350 N State St
- **Crunch Fitness** • 38 E Grand Ave
- **Executive Sports & Fitness Center** • 77 W Wacker Dr
- **Lakeshore Athletic Club** • 441 N Wabash Ave
- **Lawson YMCA** • 30 W Chicago Ave
- **Lifestart** • 10 E Ontario St

Hardware Stores

- **Clark & Barlow Hardware** • 353 W Grand Ave
- **Gordon's Ace Hardware & Paint** • 440 N Orleans St
- **Katonah Architectural Hardware** • 222 Merchandise Mart Plz

Liquor Stores

- **Artisan Cellar** • 222 Merchandise Mart Plz
- **Ben'z Liquors** • 15 E Ohio St
- **Binny's Beverage Depot** • 213 W Grand Ave
- **Copperfield's** • 70 W Huron St
- **Dalal Food & Liquor** • 414 N State St
- **Galleria Market** • 340 W Superior St
- **Hart Davis Hart Wine** • 363 W Erie St
- **Holiday Wines & Spirits** • 6 W Chicago Ave
- **Marina Food & Liquor** • 300 N State St
- **Plaza Market** • 405 N Wabash Ave
- **Rossi's Liquors** • 412 N State St
- **Superior Liquor** • 750 N Clark St
- **White Hen Pantry** • 645 N State St

Nightlife

- **Andy's** • 11 E Hubbard St
- **Bin 36** • 339 N Dearborn St
- **Blue Chicago** • 736 N Clark St
- **Blue Frog Bar & Grill** • 676 N La Salle Dr
- **Bull and Bear** • 431 N Wells St
- **Brehon Pub** • 731 N Wells St
- **Buzz Club** • 308 W Erie St
- **Celtic Crossings** • 751 N Clark St
- **Clark Street Ale House** • 742 N Clark St
- **Enclave** • 220 W Chicago Ave
- **English** • 444 N Lasalle St
- **Green Door Tavern** • 678 N Orleans St
- **Howl at the Moon** • 26 W Hubbard St
- **The Lucky Lady** • 440 N State St
- **Martini Park** • 151 W Erie St
- **Martini Ranch** • 311 W Chicago Ave
- **Ontourage** • 157 W Ontario St
- **Pippin's Tavern** • 806 N Rush St
- **Pops for Champagne** • 601 N State St
- **Redhead Piano Bar** • 16 W Ontario St
- **Rossi's** • 412 N State St
- **Spy Bar** • 646 N Franklin St
- **Social Twenty-Five** • 25 W Hubbard St
- **Sound Bar** • 226 W Ontario St
- **Stay** • 111 W Erie St
- **Streeter's Tavern** • 50 E Chicago Ave
- **Swirl Wine Bar** • 111 W Hubbard St
- **Vision** • 632 N Dearborn St

Pet Shops

- **Pet Stuff** • 509 N La Salle St
- **Petco** • 440 N Orleans St

Restaurants

- **1492 Tapas Bar** • 42 E Superior St
- **A Mano** • 335 N Dearborn St
- **Avenues** • Peninsula Hotel • 108 E Superior St
- **Ben Pao** • 52 W Illinois St
- **Brasserie Jo** • 59 W Hubbard St
- **Brett's Kitchen** • 233 W Superior St
- **Café Iberico** • 739 N La Salle Blvd
- **Castel Gandolfo** • 800 N Dearborn St
- **Chicago Chop House** • 60 W Ontario St
- **Club Lago** • 331 W Superior St
- **Coco Pazzo** • 300 W Hubbard St
- **Crofton on Wells** • 535 N Wells St
- **Cyrano's Bistrot & Wine Bar** • 546 N Wells St
- **David Burke's Primehouse** • 616 N Rush St
- **Dick's Last Resort** • 315 N Dearborn St
- **English** • 444 N Lasalle St
- **Frontera Grill** • 445 N Clark St
- **Fulton's on the River** • 315 N La Salle St
- **Gene & Georgetti** • 500 N Franklin St
- **Gino's East** • 633 N Wells St
- **Ginza Restaurant** • 19 E Ohio St
- **Graham Elliot** • 217 W Huron St
- **Keefer's** • 20 W Kinzie St
- **Kinzie Chophouse** • 400 N Wells St
- **Klay Oven** • 414 N Orleans St
- **Karyn's Cooked** • 738 N Wells St
- **Lawry's The Prime Rib** • 100 E Ontario St
- **Lou Malnati's Pizzeria** • 439 N Wells St
- **Maggiano's Little Italy** • 516 N Clark St
- **The Melting Pot** • 609 N Dearborn St
- **Mr Beef** • 666 N Orleans St
- **Nacional 27** • 325 W Huron St
- **Naha** • 500 N Clark St
- **Osteria Via Stato** • 620 N State St
- **Pizzeria Uno** • 29 E Ohio St
- **Quartino** • 626 N State St
- **Rosebud on Rush** • 720 N Rush St
- **Roy's** • 720 N State St
- **Ruth's Chris Steak House** • 431 N Dearborn St
- **Shanghai Terrace** • Peninsula Hotel • 108 E Superior St
- **Shaw's Crab House & Blue Crab Lounge** • 21 E Hubbard St
- **Smith & Wollensky** • 318 N State St
- **Soupbox** • 50 E Chicago Ave
- **Sullivan's Steakhouse** • 415 N Dearborn St
- **Sunda** • 110 W Illinois St
- **Sushi Naniwa** • 607 N Wells St
- **Tizi Melloul** • 531 N Wells St
- **Topolobampo** • 445 N Clark St
- **Vermillion** • 10 W Hubbard St
- **Wildfire** • 159 W Erie St
- **XOCO** • 449 N Clark St
- **Yolk** • 747 N Wells St
- **Zocalo** • 358 W Ontario St

Shopping

- **Drinks Over Dearborn** • 650 N Dearborn St
- **Elements** • 741 N Wells St
- **Greenheart** • 746 N Lasalle St
- **Jazz Record Mart** • 27 E Illinois St
- **Jonathan Adler** • 676 N Wabash Ave
- **Leaders 1354** • 672 N Wells St
- **Lightology** • 215 W Chicago Ave
- **Montauk Sofa** • 401 N Wells St
- **Orange Skin** • 223 W Erie St
- **Paper Source** • 232 W Chicago Ave
- **P.O.S.H.** • 613 N State St

Video Rental

- **Blockbuster** • 700 N State St
- **Hubbard's Street Books** • 109 W Hubbard St

Map 3 • Streeterville / Mag Mile

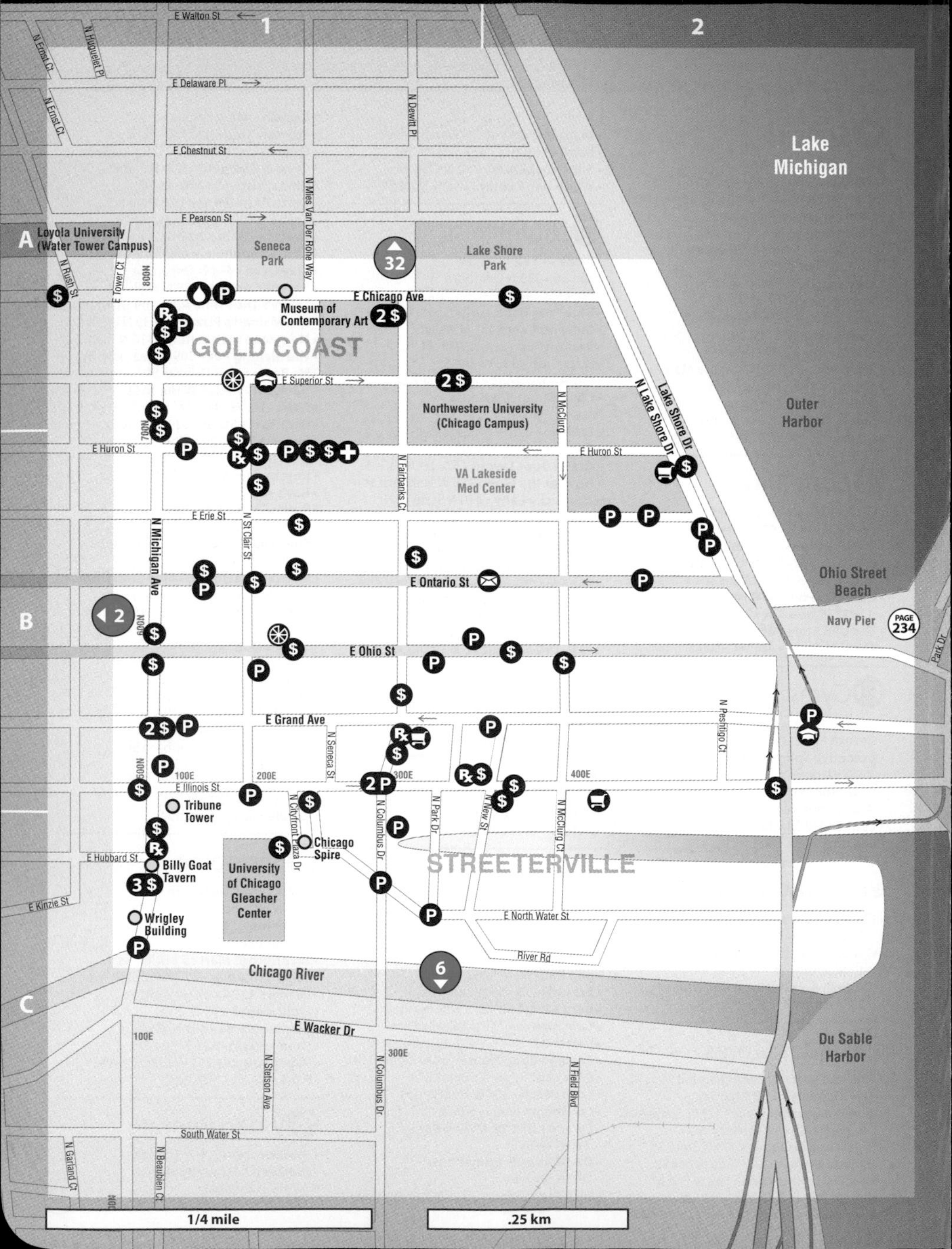

N

1
2
A
B
C

E Walton St
N Ernst Ct
N Huguelet Pl
E Delaware Pl
N Dewitt Pl
E Chestnut St
N Mies Van Der Rohe Way
E Pearson St
Loyola University (Water Tower Campus)
Seneca Park
Lake Shore Park
32
Lake Michigan
N Rush St
E Tower Ct
800N
E Chicago Ave
Museum of Contemporary Art
GOLD COAST
E Superior St
Northwestern University (Chicago Campus)
N McClurg Ct
N Lake Shore Dr
Lake Shore Dr
Outer Harbor
700N
E Huron St
N Fairbanks Ct
VA Lakeside Med Center
E Erie St
N St Clair St
N Michigan Ave
E Ontario St
Ohio Street Beach
Navy Pier
PAGE 234
Park Dr
2
600N
E Ohio St
E Grand Ave
N Peshtigo Ct
N Seneca St
500N
100E
200E
300E
400E
E Illinois St
Tribune Tower
N Cityfront Plaza Dr
N Columbus Dr
N Park Dr
N New St
N McClurg Ct
Chicago Spire
E Hubbard St
Billy Goat Tavern
University of Chicago Gleacher Center
STREETERVILLE
E Kinzie St
Wrigley Building
E North Water St
River Rd
Chicago River
6
E Wacker Dr
100E
300E
N Stetson Ave
N Columbus Dr
N Field Blvd
Du Sable Harbor
South Water St
N Garland Ct
N Beaubien Ct

1/4 mile
.25 km

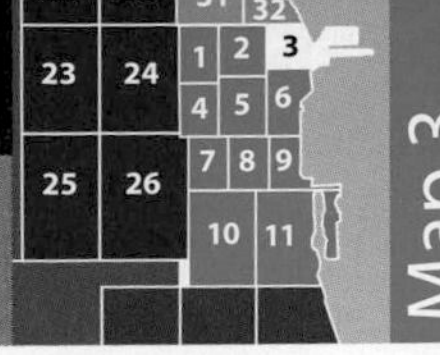

The tiny, densely populated blocks of Streeterville are home to big stores, big restaurants, and big hotels, as well as the maze that is the Northwestern University Medical campus. The hoity-toity residents of the premier high-rises sip on their champagne and laugh at the shopping bag-toting provincials who look like ants so, so far below.

Banks

- **Banco Popular** • 717 N Michigan Ave
- **Bank of America** • 500 N Michigan Ave
- **Bank of America (ATM)** • 474 N Lake Shore Dr
- **Bank of America (ATM)** • 520 N Michigan Ave
- **Bank of America (ATM)** • 600 E Grand Ave
- **Bank of America (ATM)** • 600 N Michigan Ave
- **Bank of America (ATM)** • 800 N Michigan Ave
- **Chase** • 605 N Michigan Ave
- **Chase (ATM)** • Northwestern Hospital 251 E Huron St
- **Chase (ATM)** • Northwestern Hospital • 250 E Superior St
- **Chase (ATM)** • 255 E Grand Ave
- **Chase (ATM)** • Walgreens • 342 E Illinois St
- **Chase (ATM)** • Rehabilitation Institute of Chicago • 345 E Superior St
- **Chase (ATM)** • Walgreens • 430 N Michigan Ave
- **Chase (ATM)** • Walgreens • 757 N Michigan Ave
- **Chase** • 355 E Illinois St
- **Citibank** • 539 N Michigan Ave
- **First American** • Prentice Women's Hospital • 250 E Superior St
- **First American** • 643 N Fairbanks Ct
- **First American (ATM)** • 400 N Michigan Ave
- **First American (ATM)** • 165 E Ontario St
- **First American (ATM)** • 226 E Ontario St
- **First American (ATM)** • 233 E Erie St
- **First American (ATM)** • 247 E Ohio St
- **First American (ATM)** • 393 E Illinois St
- **First American (ATM)** • 401 N Michigan Ave
- **First American (ATM)** • Wrigley Building • 410 N Michigan Ave
- **First American (ATM)** • 541 N Fairbanks Ct
- **First American (ATM)** • 633 N St Clair St
- **First American (ATM)** • 676 N St Clair St
- **Harris Trust & Savings** • 352 E Illinois St
- **Harris Trust & Savings (ATM)** • 455 N Cityfront Plz Dr
- **North** • 360 E Ohio St
- **Northern Trust** • 201 E Huron St
- **Northern Trust (ATM)** • Northwestern Hospital • 251 E Huron St
- **Shore Bank (ATM)** • 700 N Michigan Ave
- **US (ATM)** • 200 E Huron St
- **US (ATM)** • 320 E Superior St
- **US (ATM)** • Northwestern University • 357 E Chicago Ave
- **US (ATM)** • 710 N Lake Shore Dr

Car Washes

- **River North Experts** • 161 E Chicago Ave

Emergency Rooms

- **Northwestern Memorial** • 251 E Huron St

Landmarks

- **Billy Goat Tavern** • 430 N Michigan Ave
- **Chicago Spire** • 455 N Cityfront Plaza Dr
- **Museum of Contemporary Art** • 220 E Chicago Ave
- **Tribune Tower** • 435 N Michigan Ave
- **Wrigley Building** • 400 N Michigan Ave

Parking

Pharmacies

- **Dominick's** • 255 E Grand Ave
- **Walgreens** • 342 E Illinois St
- **Walgreens** • 430 N Michigan Ave
- **Walgreens** • 757 N Michigan Ave
- **Walgreens** • 201 E Huron St

Pizza

- **Gino's East Pizza** • 162 E Superior St
- **Pompei Bakery** • 212 E Ohio St

Post Offices

- **US Post Office** • 227 E Ontario St

Schools

- **Near the Pier Development Center** • 540 N Lake Shore Dr
- **Northwestern University** • 211 E Superior St

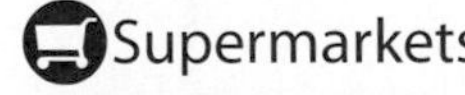

Supermarkets

- **Dominick's** • 255 E Grand Ave
- **Fox & Obel Food Store** • 401 E Illinois St
- **Treasure Island** • 680 N Lake Shore Dr

Map 3 • **Streeterville / Mag Mile**

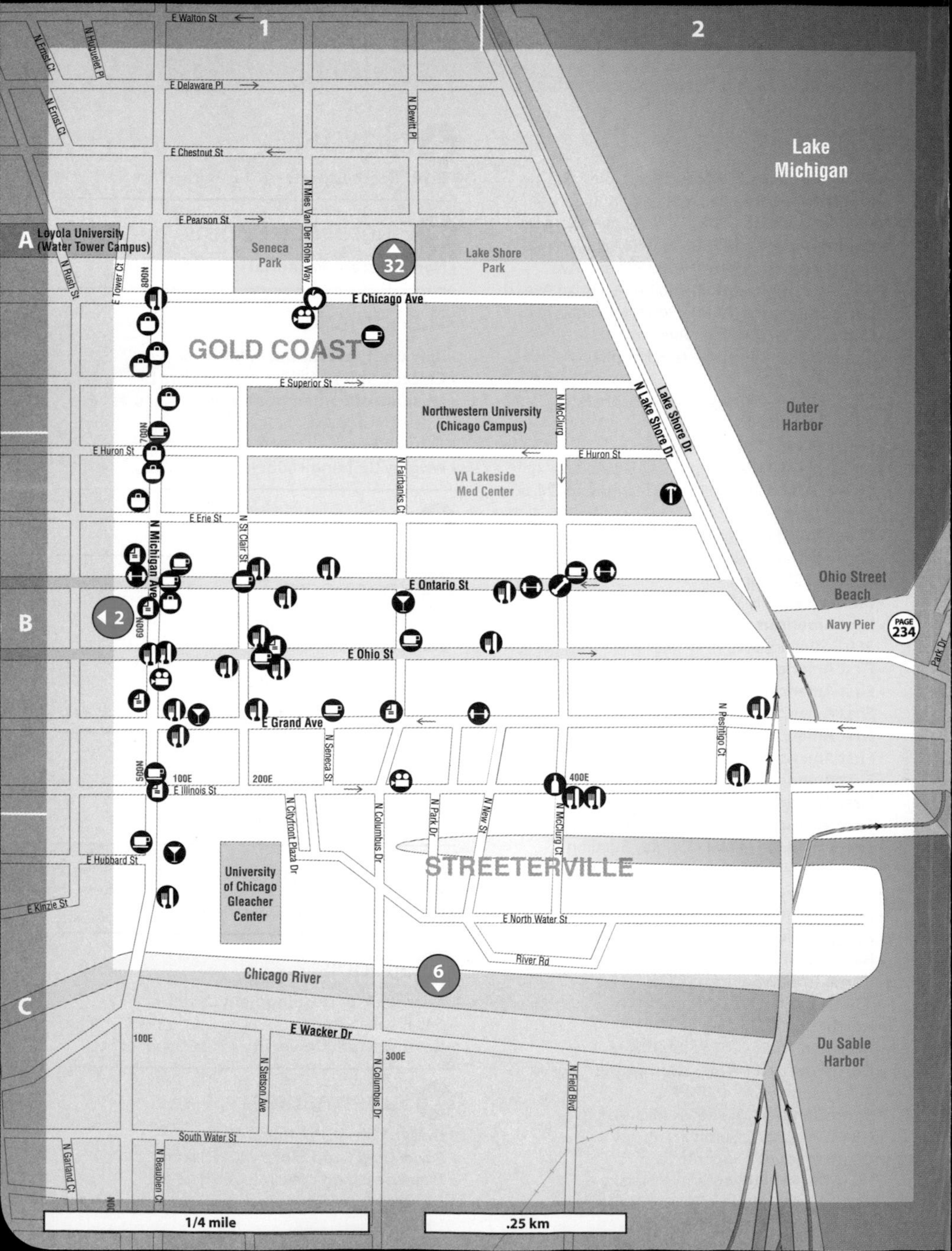

N

1
2
A
B
C
E Walton St
E Delaware Pl
E Chestnut St
E Pearson St
E Chicago Ave
E Superior St
E Huron St
E Erie St
E Ontario St
E Ohio St
E Grand Ave
E Illinois St
E Hubbard St
E Kinzie St
E North Water St
River Rd
E Wacker Dr
South Water St
N Ernst Ct
N Huguelet Pl
N Rush St
N Tower Ct
N Michigan Ave
N St Clair St
N Miles Van Der Rohe Way
N Dewitt Pl
N Fairbanks Ct
N McClurg Ct
N Lake Shore Dr
Lake Shore Dr
N Seneca St
N Cityfront Plaza Dr
N Columbus Dr
N Park Dr
N New St
N Peshtigo Ct
N Stetson Ave
N Field Blvd
N Garland Ct
N Beaubien Ct
Park Dr
800N
700N
600N
500N
100E
200E
300E
400E
Loyola University (Water Tower Campus)
Seneca Park
Lake Shore Park
GOLD COAST
Northwestern University (Chicago Campus)
VA Lakeside Med Center
University of Chicago Gleacher Center
STREETERVILLE
Chicago River
Lake Michigan
Outer Harbor
Ohio Street Beach
Navy Pier
Du Sable Harbor

32
2
6
PAGE 234

1/4 mile
.25 km

Sundries / Entertainment

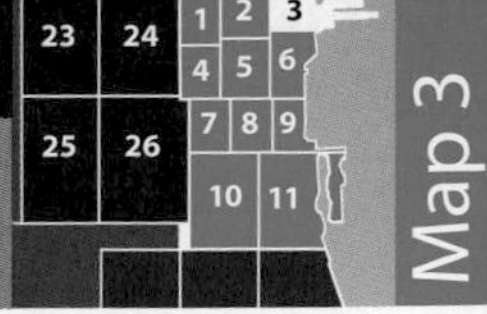

Young singles pose artfully at the Museum of Contemporary Art's First Friday series, featuring a deejay, free finger food, and a cash bar. And speaking of cash, drop a wad of it dining at the posh French food emporium Les Nomades, or Rick Tramanto and Gale Gand's trendsetting Tru. For slumming it, hit the Billy Goat Tavern.

Coffee

- **Argo Tea** • Northwestern Memorial Hospital, 250 E Superior St
- **Dunkin' Donuts** • 200 E Ohio St
- **Einstein Bros Bagels** • 300 E Ohio St
- **Starbucks** • 165 E Ontario St
- **Starbucks** • Marriott Courtyard Chicago, 155 E Ontario St
- **Starbucks** • Northwestern Memorial Hospital, 251 E Huron St
- **Starbucks** • Dominick's • 255 E Grand Ave
- **Starbucks** • Intercontinental Hotel, 444 N Michigan Ave

Copy Shops

- **AlphaGraphics** • 645 N Michigan Ave
- **FedEx Kinko's** • 540 N Michigan Ave
- **Kwik Kopy** • 500 N Michigan Ave
- **Press Type and Copy** • 541 N Fairbanks Ct
- **The UPS Store** • 207 E Ohio St

Farmers Markets

- **Museum of Contemporary Art/Streeterville (Jun–Oct; Tues, 9am–4pm)** • 220 E Chicago Ave

Gyms

- **Holmes Place** • 355 E Grand Ave
- **Lakeshore Athletic Club** • 333 E Ontario St
- **Onterie Fitness Center** • 446 E Ontario St
- **Woman's Athletic Club** • 626 N Michigan Ave

Hardware Stores

- **Streeterville Ace Hardware** • 680 N Lake Shore Dr

Liquor Stores

- **Market Place FoodUncork It** • 393 E Illinois St

Movie Theaters

- **AMC Loews 600** • 600 N Michigan Ave
- **AMC River East 21** • 322 E Illinois St
- **Museum of Contemporary Art Movie Theater** • 220 E Chicago Ave

Nightlife

- **Billy Goat Tavern** • 430 N Michigan Ave
- **Reagle Beagle** • 160 E Grand Ave
- **Timothy O'Toole's Pub** • 622 N Fairbanks Ct

Pet Shops

- **Streeterville Pet Spa and Boutique** • 401 E Ontario St

Restaurants

- **Atrium Wine Bar** • 401 E Illinois St
- **Bandera** • 535 N Michigan Ave
- **Billy Goat Tavern** • 430 N Michigan Ave
- **Boston Blackies** • 164 E Grand Ave
- **Capital Grille** • 633 N St Clair St
- **D4 Irish Pub & Café** • 345 E Ohio St
- **De La Costa** • 465 E Illinois St
- **Emilio's Tapas Sol y Nieve** • 215 E Ohio St
- **Fox & Obel Café** • 401 E Illinois St
- **Grand Lux Café** • 600 N Michigan Ave
- **Heaven on Seven** • 600 N Michigan Ave
- **Indian Garden** • 247 E Ontario St
- **Kamehachi** • 240 E Ontario St
- **Les Nomades** • 222 E Ontario St
- **Nomi** • Park Hyatt • 800 N Michigan Ave
- **Sayat Nova** • 157 E Ohio St
- **Tru** • 676 N St Clair St
- **Volare** • 201 E Grand Ave

Shopping

- **Apple Store** • 679 N Michigan Ave
- **Disney Store** • 717 N Michigan Ave
- **Garrett Gourmet Popcorn** • 625 N Michigan Ave
- **Neiman-Marcus** • 737 N Michigan Ave
- **Niketown** • 669 N Michigan Ave
- **Ralph Lauren** • 750 N Michigan Ave
- **Tiffany & Co** • 730 N Michigan Ave

Map 4 • West Loop Gate / Greek Town

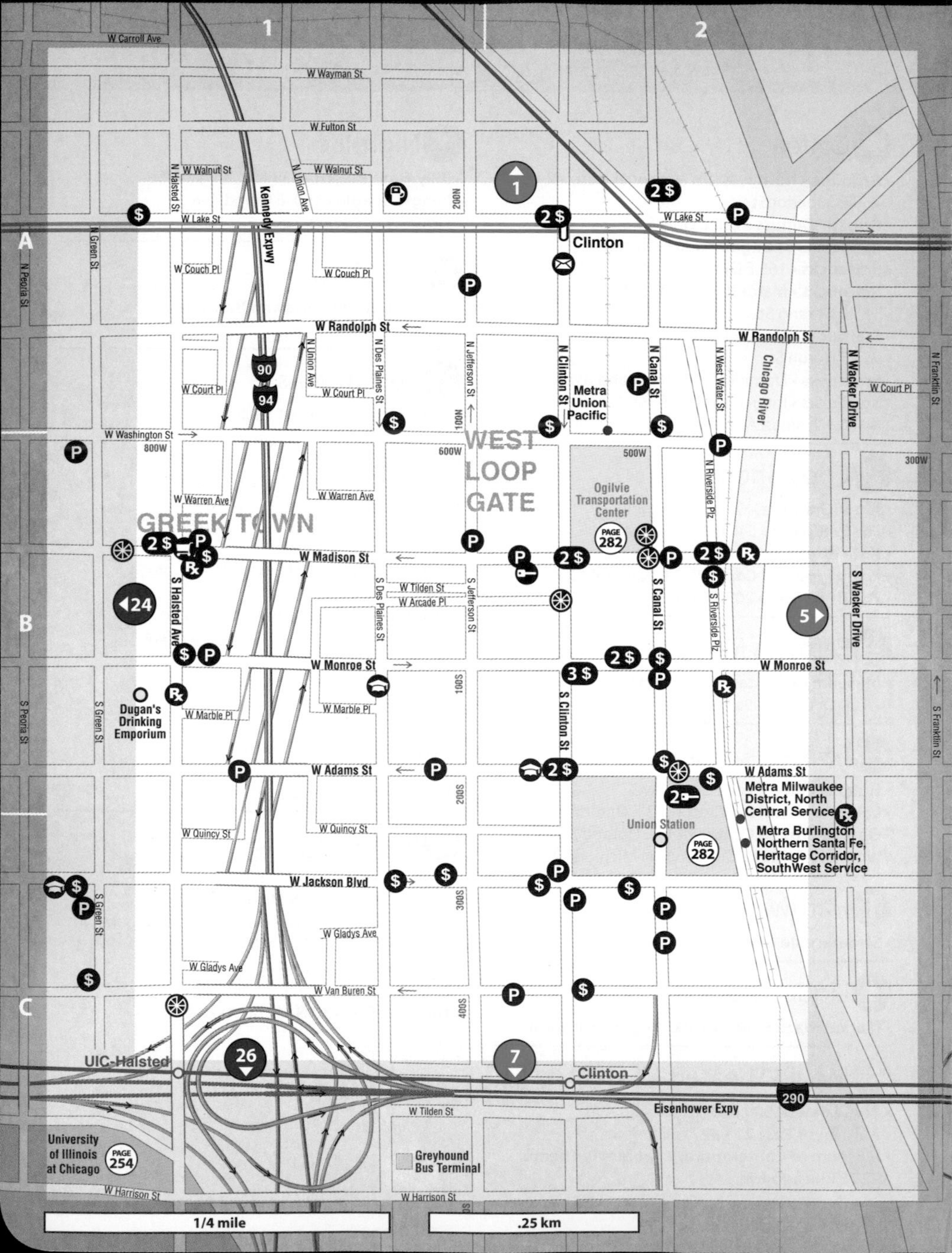

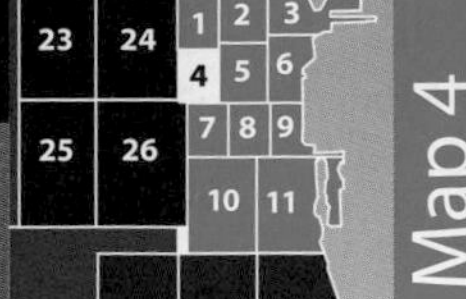

Trains, buses, gyros, and loft spaces define this 'hood. Proximity to the Loop, the Expressway, Union Station, Ogilvie Transportation Center, and the Greyhound Bus Depot may seem just right for hip, urban commuters. Nonetheless, many pockets maintain a gritty vibe (particularly around said Greyhound station—isn't that always the case?).

Banks

- **Bank of America** • 2 N Riverside Plz
- **Bank of America** • 105 N Halsted St
- **Bank of America** • 540 W Madison St
- **Bank of America (ATM)** • 130 S Canal St
- **Bank of America (ATM)** • Amtrack-Union Station • 225 S Canal St
- **Bank of America** • 850 W Jackson Blvd
- **Bank of America (ATM)** • 400 W Madison St
- **Bank of America (ATM)** • 550 W Van Buren St
- **Charter One** • 555 W Jackson Blvd
- **Charter One (ATM)** • 101 S Clinton St
- **Charter One (ATM)** • 627 W Jackson Blvd
- **Charter One (ATM)** • 833 W Van Buren St
- **Chase** • 1 N Halsted St
- **Chase** • 300 S Riverside Plz
- **Chase** • 550 W Adams St
- **Chase (ATM)** • Chicago Union Station • 225 S Canal St
- **Chase (ATM)** • 525 W Monroe St
- **Chase (ATM)** • Chicago-Kent College of Law • 565 W Adams St
- **Chase (ATM)** • 567 W Lake St
- **Citibank** • 500 W Madison St
- **Citibank (ATM)** • 7-Eleven • 567 W Lake St
- **Corus** • 10 S Riverside Plz
- **Fifth Third** • 222 S Riverside Plz
- **Fifth Third** • 100 S Halsted St
- **Fifth Third (ATM)** • Union Station • 225 S Canal St
- **First American (ATM)** • 117 S Clinton St
- **First American (ATM)** • 500 W Monroe St
- **First American (ATM)** • 517 W Jackson Blvd
- **First American (ATM)** • 550 W Washington St
- **First American (ATM)** • Crowne Plaza • 733 W Madison St
- **Harris Trust & Savings (ATM)** • 555 W Madison St
- **Harris Trust & Savings (ATM)** • 626 W Jackson Blvd
- **MB Financial** • 800 W Madison St
- **MB Financial (ATM)** •811 W Lake St
- **New Century (ATM)** • 225 S Canal St
- **New Century (ATM)** • Union Station • 225 S Canal St
- **TCF** • 120 S Riverside Plz
- **TCF (ATM)** • 400 W Madison St
- **US (ATM)** • 111 N Canal St

Car Rental

- **Enterprise** • 555 W Madison St • 312-906-8300
- **Hertz** • 225 S Canal St • 312-928-0538

Gas Stations

- **Fulton & Des Plaines** • 225 N Desplaines St

Landmarks

- **Dugan's** • 128 S Halsted St
- **Union Station** • 210 S Canal St

Parking

- **Central Parking** • 322 S Green St
- **Walker Parking Service** • 850 W Washington Blvd

Pharmacies

- **CVS** • 400 W Madison St
- **CVS** • 130 S Canal St
- **Dominick's** • 1 N Halsted St ㉔
- **Walgreens** • 111 S Halsted St ㉔
- **Walgreens** • 250 S Wacker Dr

Pizza

- **Bacino's** • 118 S Clinton St
- **Giordano's** • 815 W Van Buren St
- **Leona's** • 848 W Madison St
- **Sbarro** • 500 W Madison St

Post Offices

- **US Post Office** • 168 N Clinton St

Schools

- **American Quality** • 850 W Jackson Blvd
- **Chicago-Kent College of Law** • 565 W Adams St
- **Frances Xavier Warde** • 120 S Desplaines St

Supermarkets

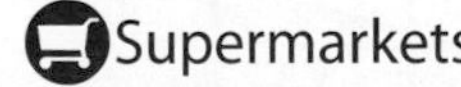
- **Dominick's** • 1 N Halsted St ㉔

Map 4 • West Loop Gate / Greek Town

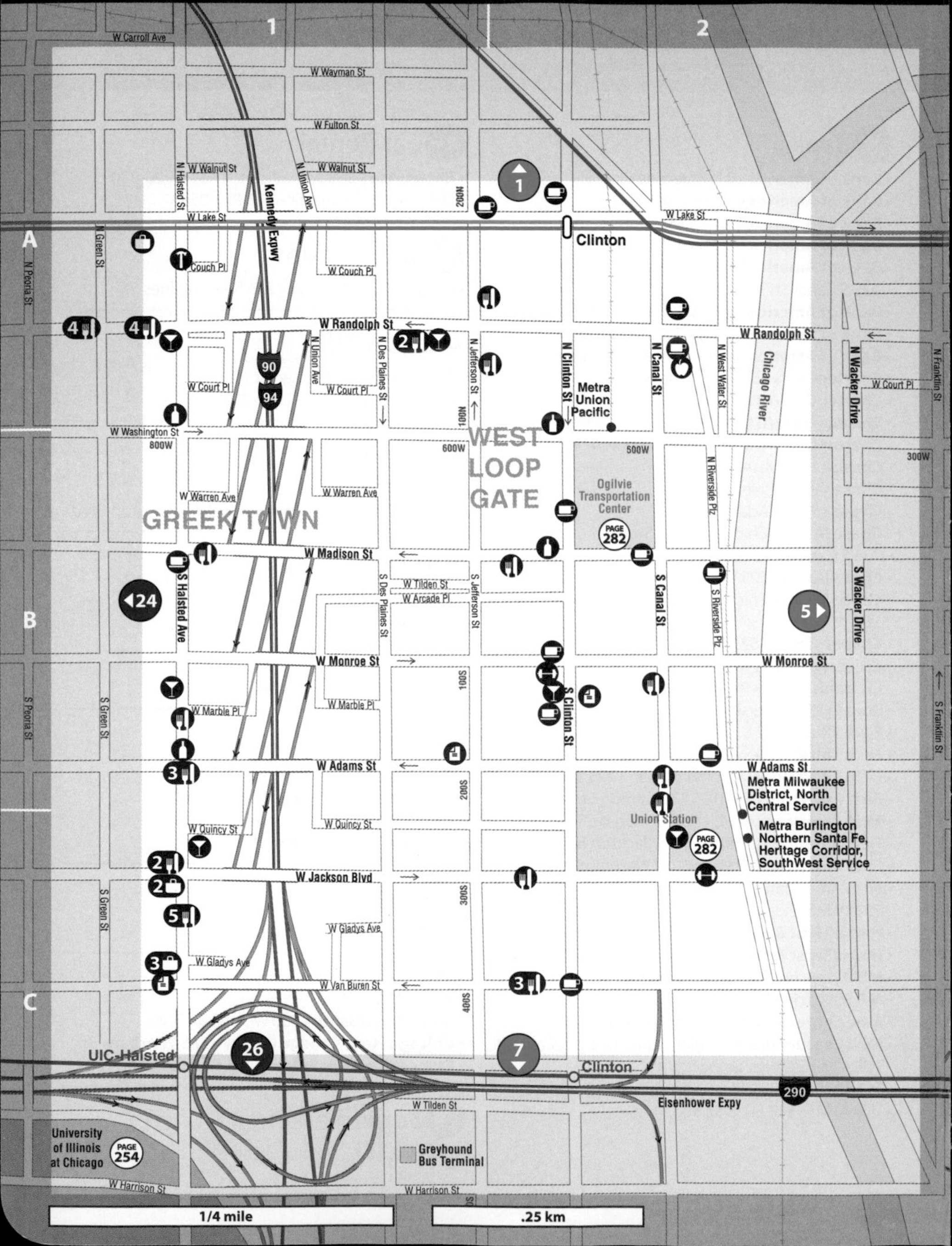
N
1
2
A
B
C
W Carroll Ave
W Wayman St
W Fulton St
W Walnut St
N Halsted St
N Union Ave
Kennedy Expwy
W Lake St
Clinton
N Green St
N Peoria St
W Couch Pl
W Randolph St
N Union Ave
N Des Plaines St
N Jefferson St
N Clinton St
N Canal St
N West Water St
Chicago River
N Wacker Drive
N Franklin St
90
94
W Court Pl
Metra Union Pacific
W Washington St
800W
600W
500W
300W
100N
200N
WEST LOOP GATE
W Warren Ave
N Riverside Plz
Ogilvie Transportation Center
PAGE 282
GREEK TOWN
W Madison St
W Tilden St
W Arcade Pl
S Des Plaines St
S Jefferson St
S Canal St
S Riverside Plz
S Wacker Drive
S Halsted Ave
24
5
W Monroe St
S Green St
S Peoria St
W Marble Pl
S Clinton St
S Franklin St
100S
200S
300S
400S
W Adams St
Metra Milwaukee District, North Central Service
Union Station
Metra Burlington Northern Santa Fe, Heritage Corridor, SouthWest Service
W Quincy St
W Jackson Blvd
W Gladys Ave
W Van Buren St
UIC-Halsted
26
7
Clinton
290
Eisenhower Expy
W Tilden St
University of Illinois at Chicago
PAGE 254
Greyhound Bus Terminal
W Harrison St
1/4 mile
.25 km

Sundries / Entertainment

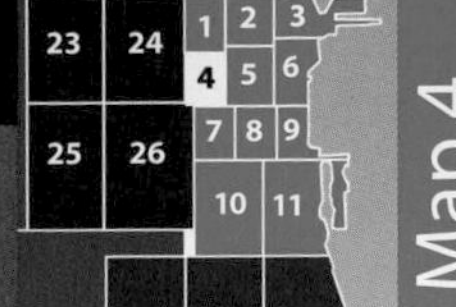

Randolph Street's funky, contemporary restaurant row kicks off here and continues westward while just north on Halsted shouts of "Opaa!" ring out in Greek Town. Go to the Athenian Candle Co to stock up on "Law Be Gone" room spray and "Lover Come Back" floor wash.

Coffee

- **Caribou Coffee** • 222 S Riverside Plz
- **Caribou Coffee** • 500 W Madison St
- **Dunkin' Donuts** • 2 N Riverside Plz
- **Dunkin' Donuts** • 500 W Madison St
- **Dunkin' Donuts** • 555 W Lake St
- **Starbucks** • Dominick's • 1 N Halsted St
- **Starbucks** • 10 S Riverside Plz
- **Starbucks** • 139 S Clinton St
- **Starbucks** • 40 N Clinton St
- **Starbucks** • 400 W Madison St
- **Starbucks** • 550 W Van Buren St
- **Starbucks** • 600 W Lake St

Copy Shops

- **American Color Laboratory** • 611 W Adams St
- **Comet Press** • 812 W Van Buren St
- **FedEx Kinko's** • 127 S Clinton St ㉔

Farmers Markets

- **Riverside Plaza (Jun–Oct; every other Thurs)** • 2 N Riverside Plaza

Gyms

- **Fitness Formula** • 444 W Jackson Blvd
- **Lifestart** • 555 W Monroe St

Hardware Stores

- **Chicago Wholesale Hardware** • 171 N Halsted St

Liquor Stores

- **Bennett Special Wines** • 802 W Washington Blvd
- **Just Grapes (wine only)** • 560 W Washington Blvd
- **Monemvassia Wines** • 801 W Adams St
- **Presidential Market** • 555 W Madison St

Nightlife

- **Dugan's** • 128 S Halsted St
- **Dylan's** • 118 S Clinton St
- **Nara 623** • W Randolph St
- **Snuggery Saloon & Dining Room** • Union Station • 225 S Canal St
- **Spectrum Bar & Grill** • 233 S Halstead St

Restaurants

- **9 Muses** • 315 S Halsted St
- **Athena** • 212 S Halsted St
- **Avec** • 615 W Randolph St
- **Blackbird** • 619 W Randolph St
- **Bombacigno's J & C Inn** • 558 W Van Buren St
- **Dine** • Crowne Plaza Chicago Metro Hotel • 733 W Madison St
- **DeCero** • 814 W Randolph St
- **Girl & The Goat** • 809 W Randolph St
- **Gold Coast Dogs** • Union Station • 225 S Canal St
- **Greek Islands** • 200 S Halsted St
- **J&C Inn** • 558 W Van Buren St
- **Jubilee Juice** • 140 N Halsted St
- **Lou Mitchell's** • 565 W Jackson Blvd
- **Meli** • 301 S Halsted St
- **Mr Greek Gyros** • 234 S Halsted St
- **Nine** • 440 W Randolph St
- **Parthenon** • 314 S Halsted St
- **Pegasus Restaurant and Taverna** • 130 S Halsted St
- **Perez** • 853 W Randolph St
- **Province** • 161 N Jefferson St
- **Red Light** • 820 W Randolph St
- **Robinson's No 1 Ribs** • Union Station • 225 S Canal St
- **Rodity's** • 222 S Halsted St
- **Santorini** • 800 W Adams St
- **Sepia** • 123 N Jefferson St
- **Sushi Wabi** • 842 W Randolph St
- **Takumi** • 555 W Madison St
- **Veerasway** • 844 W Randolph St
- **Vivo** • 838 W Randolph St
- **Wild** • 3130 N Broadway St

Shopping

- **Athenian Candle Co** • 300 S Halsted St
- **Athens Grocery** • 324 S Halsted St
- **Greektown Music** • 330 S Halsted St
- **Northwestern Cutlery** • 810 W Lake St
- **Pan Hellenic Pastry Shop** • 322 S Halsted St

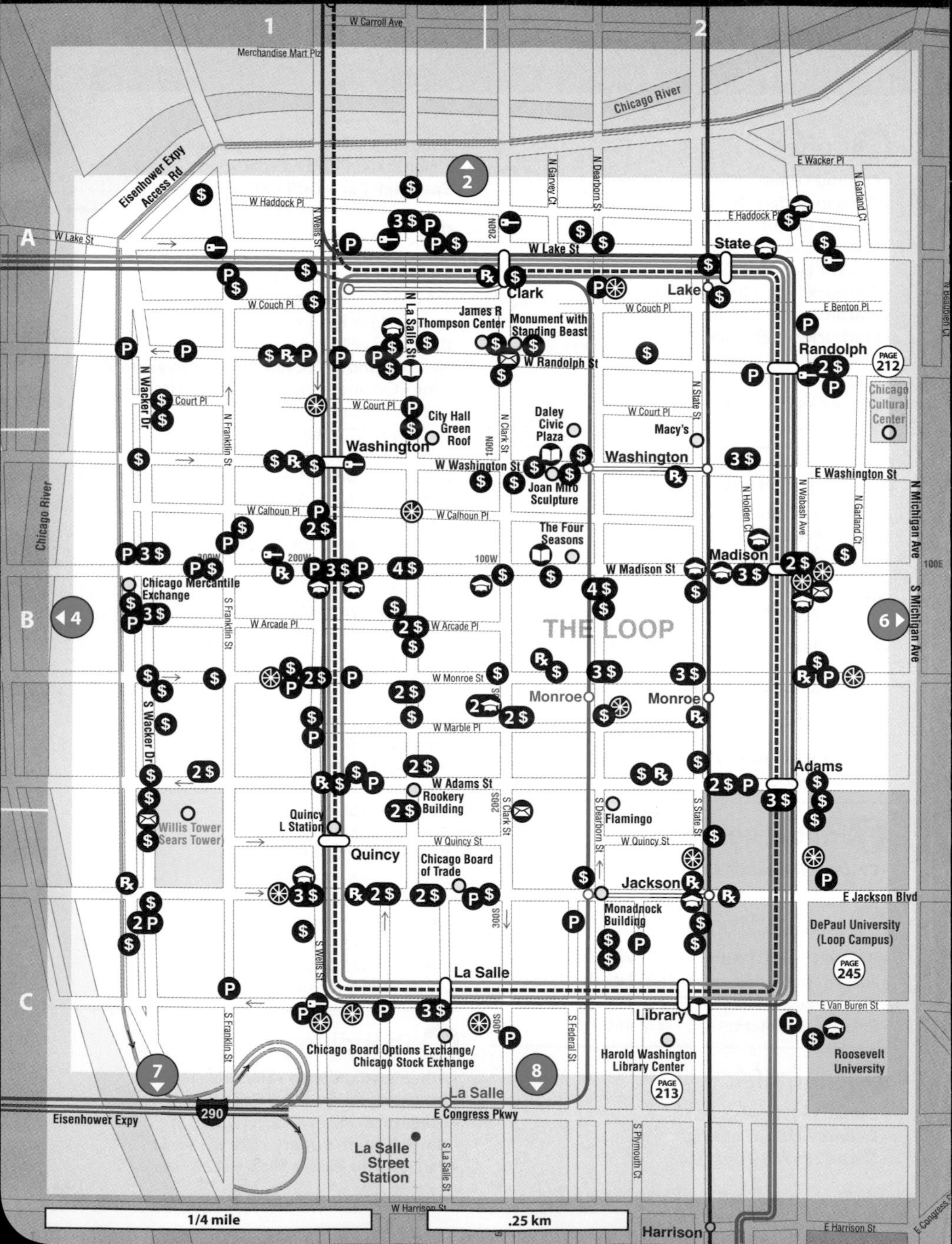

Map 5 • The Loop

THE LOOP

W Carroll Ave
Merchandise Mart Plz
Chicago River
Eisenhower Expy Access Rd
W Haddock Pl
W Lake St
W Couch Pl
E Wacker Pl
E Haddock Pl
N Garland Ct
E Benton Pl
N Wells St
N La Salle St
N Garvey Ct
N Dearborn St
N Clark St
N State St
N Wacker Dr
N Franklin St
W Court Pl
W Randolph St
W Washington St
E Washington St
W Calhoun Pl
W Madison St
W Arcade Pl
W Monroe St
W Marble Pl
W Adams St
W Quincy St
E Jackson Blvd
E Van Buren St
S Wacker Dr
S Franklin St
S Wells St
S Clark St
S Dearborn St
S State St
S Federal St
N Holden Ct
N Wabash Ave
N Michigan Ave
S Michigan Ave
S La Salle St
S Plymouth Ct
E Congress Pkwy
Eisenhower Expy
W Harrison St
E Harrison St
N Beaubien Ct
E Congress Pkwy

State
Lake
Clark
Randolph
Washington
Madison
Monroe
Adams
Quincy
Jackson
La Salle
Library
Harrison

James R Thompson Center
Monument with Standing Beast
City Hall Green Roof
Daley Civic Plaza
Macy's
Chicago Cultural Center
Joan Miro Sculpture
The Four Seasons
Chicago Mercantile Exchange
Rookery Building
Quincy L Station
Willis Tower (Sears Tower)
Flamingo
Chicago Board of Trade
Monadnock Building
DePaul University (Loop Campus)
Chicago Board Options Exchange/ Chicago Stock Exchange
Harold Washington Library Center
Roosevelt University
La Salle Street Station

PAGE 212
PAGE 245
PAGE 213

1/4 mile
.25 km

Essentials

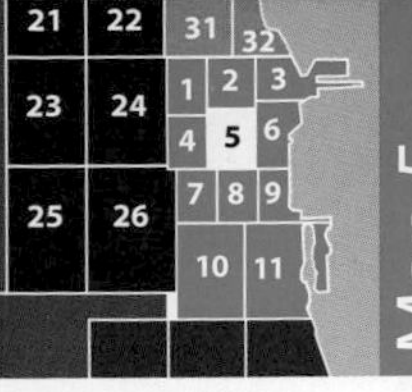

The Loop derives its moniker from the L tracks that lasso the city's heart. This here is the bustling financial and business district, where banks are plentiful and parking is pricey. The intersection of State and Madison is literally ground zero (0 east, 0 west, 0 north, 0 south) for Chicago's easy-to-follow street numbering grid. Watching over it all is North America's tallest building the Sears Tower—no wait, the Willis Tower, but don't ever call it that in public.

$ Banks

- **Amalgamated** • 1 W Monroe St
- **Associated** • 200 N La Salle St
- **Banco Popular** • 415 N La Salle St
- **Bank of America** • 77 S Dearborn St
- **Bank of America** • 100 S Wacker Dr
- **Bank of America** • 105 W Madison St
- **Bank of America** • 120 N La Salle St
- **Bank of America** • 135 S La Salle St
- **Bank of America** • 201 S State St
- **Bank of America** • 203 N La Salle St
- **Bank of America** • 205 W Monroe St
- **Bank of America** • 231 S La Salle St
- **Bank of America** • 33 N Dearborn St
- **Bank of America (ATM)** • 5 S Wabash Ave
- **Bank of America (ATM)** • 18 W Monroe St
- **Bank of America (ATM)** • 20 S State St
- **Bank of America (ATM)** • 24 W Randolph St
- **Bank of America (ATM)** • 55 W Lake St
- **Bank of America (ATM)** • 55 E Monroe St
- **Bank of America (ATM)** • 64 E Madison St
- **Bank of America (ATM)** • Hyatt Center • 71 S Wacker Dr
- **Bank of America (ATM)** • 79 W Monroe St
- **Bank of America (ATM)** • 100 W Lake St
- **Bank of America (ATM)** • 151 W Randolph St
- **Bank of America (ATM)** • 175 N State St
- **Bank of America (ATM)** • 175 W Jackson Blvd
- **Bank of America (ATM)** • 180 N LaSalle St
- **Bank of America (ATM)** • 200 N State St
- **Bank of America (ATM)** • 201 W Madison St
- **Bank of America (ATM)** • CVS • 208 W Washington St
- **Bank of America (ATM)** • 226 W Jackson Blvd
- **Bank of America (ATM)** • 230 W Washington St
- **Bank of America (ATM)** • 233 S Wacker Dr
- **Bank of America (ATM)** • 300 S Wacker Dr
- **Bank of America (ATM)** • 302 W Adams St
- **Charter One** • 150 S Wacker Dr
- **Charter One** • 2 S State St
- **Charter One** • 400 S La Salle St
- **Charter One** • 71 S Wacker Dr
- **Charter One (ATM)** • 200 N Dearborn St
- **Chase** • 10 S Dearborn St
- **Chase** • 120 S La Salle St
- **Chase** • 200 W Jackson Blvd
- **Chase** • 30 S Wacker Dr
- **Chase (ATM)** • 400 S La Salle St
- **Chase (ATM)** • 333 W Wacker Dr
- **Chase (ATM)** • 200 S Wacker Dr
- **Chase (ATM)** • 161 N Clark St
- **Chase (ATM)** • 131 S Dearborn St
- **Chase (ATM)** • Walgreens • 15 W Washington St
- **Chase (ATM)** • 16 W Adams St
- **Chase (ATM)** • 191 N Clark St
- **Chase (ATM)** • Walgreens • 200 W Adams St
- **Chase (ATM)** • Walgreens • 201 W Madison St
- **Chase (ATM)** • Walgreens • 240 W Randolph St
- **Chase (ATM)** • 30 S Dearborn St
- **Chase (ATM)** • Walgreens • 300 S State St
- **Chase (ATM)** • 425 S Wabash Ave
- **Chase (ATM)** • 55 W Monroe St
- **Chase (ATM)** • 66 W Washington St
- **Chase (ATM)** • 70 W Madison St
- **Chicago Community** • 51 W Jackson Blvd
- **Citibank** • 11 S La Salle St
- **Citibank** • 222 W Adams St
- **Citibank** • 69 W Washington St
- **Citibank (ATM)** • 216 W Jackson Blvd
- **Citibank (ATM)** • 209 S La Salle St
- **Citibank (ATM)** • 1 W Monroe St
- **Citibank (ATM)** • 125 S Clark St
- **Citibank (ATM)** • 7-Eleven • 180 N Franklin St
- **Citibank (ATM)** • 25 E Washington St
- **Citibank (ATM)** • 7-Eleven • 29 E Madison St
- **Citibank (ATM)** • 7-Eleven • 318 W Adams St
- **Citibank (ATM)** • 7-Eleven • 33 E Adams St
- **Citibank (ATM)** • 7-Eleven • 343 S Dearborn St
- **Citibank (ATM)** • 7-Eleven • 48 N Wells St
- **Citibank (ATM)** • 7-Eleven • 58 E Lake St
- **Citibank (ATM)** • 69 W Washington St
- **Cole Taylor** • 111 W Washington St
- **Fifth Third** • 1 N Wacker Dr
- **Fifth Third** • 1 S Dearborn St
- **Fifth Third** • 161 N Clark St
- **Fifth Third** • 175 W Jackson Blvd
- **Fifth Third** • Sears Tower • 233 S Wacker Dr
- **Fifth Third** • 57 E Randolph St
- **Fifth Third (ATM)** • 101 N Wacker Dr
- **First** • 161 N Clark St
- **First** • 20 N Wacker Dr
- **First American** • 33 W Monroe St
- **First American** • 50 E Adams St
- **First American (ATM)** • 55 E Adams St
- **First American (ATM)** • 111 W Jackson Blvd
- **First American (ATM)** • 123 N Wacker Dr
- **First American (ATM)** • 145 S Wells St
- **First American (ATM)** • 171 W Randolph St
- **First American (ATM)** • 172 W Adams St
- **First American (ATM)** • 190 S La Salle St
- **First American (ATM)** • 200 W Madison St
- **First American (ATM)** • 208 S Wabash Ave
- **First American (ATM)** • 222 N La Salle St
- **First American (ATM)** • 234 S Wabash Ave
- **First American (ATM)** • 25 E Washington St
- **First American (ATM)** • 303 W Madison St
- **First American (ATM)** • 311 S Wacker Dr
- **First American (ATM)** • 326 S Wells St
- **First American (ATM)** • 60 E Randolph St
- **Harris** • 111 W Monroe St
- **Harris** • 141 W Jackson Blvd
- **Harris** • 99 W Washington St
- **Harris (ATM)** • 115 S La Salle St
- **Harris (ATM)** • 311 W Monroe St
- **Lakeside** • 141 W Jackson Blvd
- **MB Financial** • 1 S Wacker Dr
- **MB Financial** • 2 S La Salle St
- **MB Financial (ATM)** • 223 W Jackson Blvd
- **MB Financial (ATM)**• 216 N Wabash Ave
- **MB Financial (ATM)** • 223 W Jackson Blvd
- **National City Bank** • 1 N Franklin St
- **Northern Trust** • 50 S La Salle St
- **Northern Trust (ATM)** • 10 S La Salle St
- **Northern Trust (ATM)** • 111 S Wacker Dr
- **Northern Trust (ATM)** • 181 W Madison St
- **Shore** • 333 S State St
- **TCF** • 29 E Madison St
- **TCF (ATM)** • DePaul University • 1 E Jackson Blvd
- **TCF (ATM)** • 7-Eleven • 125 S Clark St
- **TCF (ATM)** • Osco • 137 S State St
- **TCF (ATM)** • 7-Eleven • 180 N Franklin St
- **TCF (ATM)** • 7-Eleven • 29 E Madison St
- **TCF (ATM)** • 7-Eleven • 33 E Adams St
- **TCF (ATM)** • 7-Eleven • 343 S Dearborn St
- **TCF (ATM)** • 7-Eleven • 48 N Wells St
- **US** • 209 S La Salle St
- **US** • 25 E Washington St
- **US (ATM)** • 333 S Wabash Ave

Car Rental

- **Avis** • 214 N Clark St • 312-782-6825
- **Enterprise** • 65 E Lake St • 312-251-0200
- **Enterprise** • 201 W Madison St • 312-553-5230
- **Enterprise** • 303 W Lake St • 312-332-7783
- **Enterprise** • 425 S Wells St • 312-939-6001
- **Hertz** • 181 W Washington Blvd • 312-726-1476
- **National/Alamo** • 203 N La Salle St • 312-236-2581
- **Zipcar** • 160 N Wabash Ave

Landmarks

- **Chicago Board of Trade** • 141 W Jackson Blvd
- **Chicago Board Options Exchange** • 400 S La Salle St
- **Chicago Cultural Center** • 78 E Washington St
- **Chicago Mercantile Exchange** • 20 S Wacker Dr
- **Chicago Stock Exchange** • 440 S La Salle St
- **City Hall Green Roof** • 121 N LaSalle St
- **Daley Civic Plaza** • 50 W Washington St
- **Flamingo** • 219 S Dearborn St
- **The Four Seasons** • 70 W Madison St
- **Harold Washington Library Center** • 400 S State St
- **James R Thompson Center** • 100 W Randolph St
- **Joan Miro Sculpture** • 69 W Washington St
- **Macy's** • 111 N State St
- **Monadnock Building** • 53 W Jackson Blvd
- **Monument with Standing Beast** • 100 W Randolph St
- **Quincy L Station** • 220 S Wells St
- **Rookery Building** • 209 S La Salle St
- **Willis Tower (Sears Tower)** • 233 S Wacker Dr

Libraries

- **Harold Washington Public Library** • 400 S State St
- **The Swedenborg Library** • 77 W Washington St, Rm 1700

Parking

Pharmacies

- **CVS** • 137 S State St
- **CVS** • 105 S Wabash Ave
- **Walgreens** • 250 S Wacker Dr
- **CVS** • 175 W Jackson Blvd
- **CVS** • 208 W Washington Blvd
- **Walgreens** • 15 W Washington St
- **Walgreens** • 16 W Adams St
- **Walgreens** • 191 N Clark St
- **Walgreens** • 200 W Adams St
- **Walgreens** • 201 W Madison St
- **Walgreens** • 240 W Randolph St
- **Walgreens** • 300 S State St
- **Walgreens** • 79 W Monroe St

Pizza

- **Bacci Pizzeria** • 120 N Wells St
- **Bonivino Restaurant** • 111 W Van Buren St
- **California Pizza Kitchen** • 30 N La Salle St
- **Exchequer Pub** • 226 S Wabash Ave
- **Giordano's** • 223 W Jackson Blvd
- **Jimmy John's** • 205 W Monroe St
- **Little Pompeii** • 131 S Dearborn St
- **Pizano's Pizza & Pasta** • 61 E Madison St
- **Pizza Broker** • 400 S Financial Pl
- **Reggie's Pizza Express** • 411 S Wells St

Post Offices

- **US Post Office** • 100 W Randolph St
- **US Post Office** • 211 S Clark St
- **US Post Office** • Sears Tower • 233 S Wacker Dr
- **US Post Office** • 5 S Wabash Ave

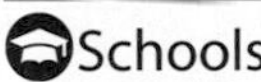

Schools

- **Alternative Safe Schools** • 125 S Clark St
- **Chicago City Colleges** • 226 W Jackson Blvd
- **Chicago School of Massage Therapy** • 18 N Wabash Ave
- **DePaul University** • 1 E Jackson Blvd
- **Harold Washington College** • 30 E Lake St
- **Harrington College of Design** • 200 W Madison St
- **International Academy of Design and Technology** • 1 N State St
- **John Marshall Law** • 315 S Plymouth Ct
- **Keller Graduate School of Management** • 225 W Washington St
- **LINC Alternative High** • 125 S Clark St
- **MacCormac College** • 29 E Madison St
- **Robert Morris College** • 401 S State St
- **School of the Art Institute** • 37 S Wabash Ave

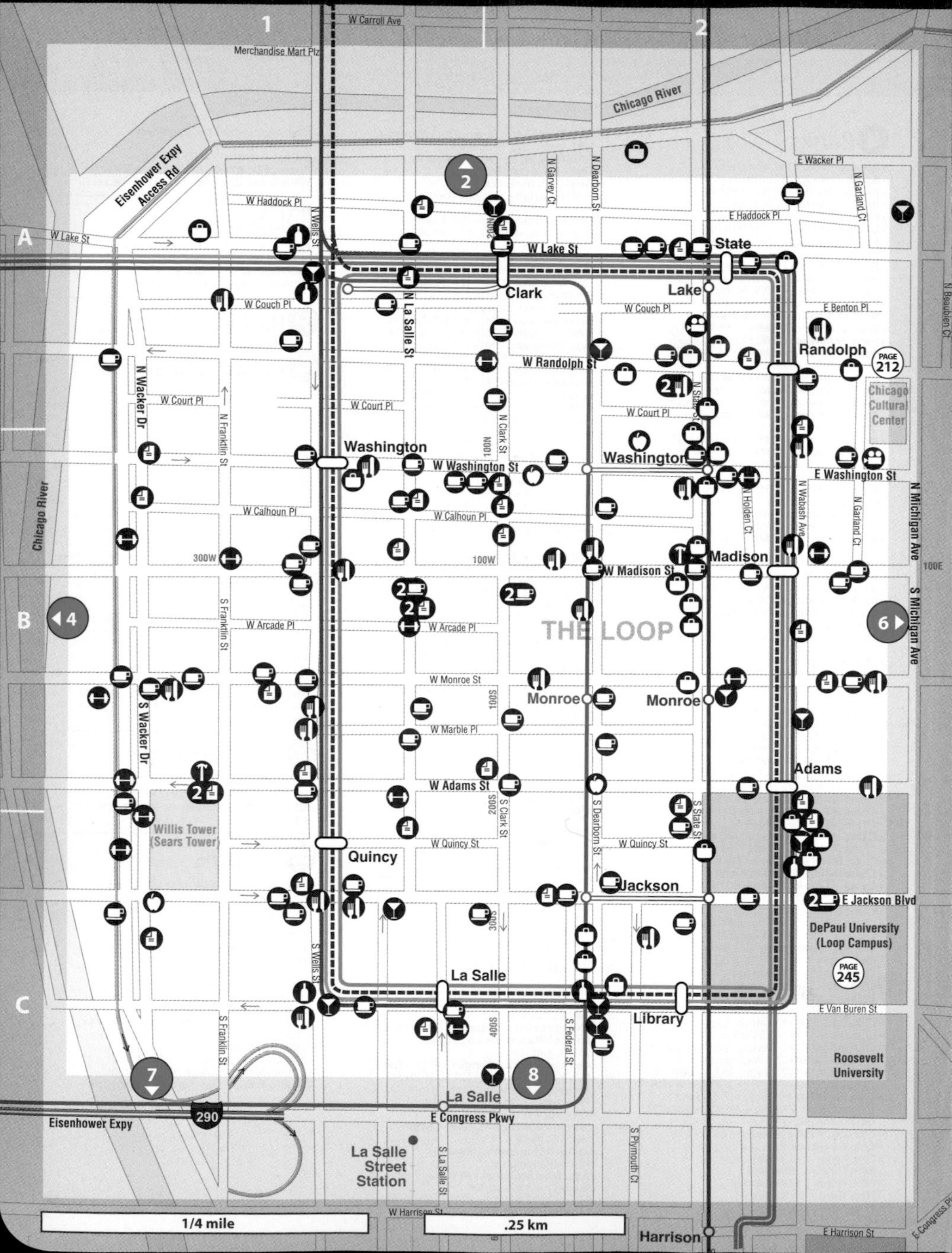

Map 5 • The Loop

N

1
2
A
B
C
W Carroll Ave
Merchandise Mart Plz
Chicago River
Eisenhower Expy Access Rd
E Wacker Pl
N Garvey Ct
N Dearborn St
N Garland Ct
W Haddock Pl
E Haddock Pl
N Wells St
W Lake St
State
Clark
Lake
N La Salle St
W Couch Pl
E Benton Pl
N Beaubien Ct
Randolph
PAGE 212
W Randolph St
Chicago Cultural Center
N Wacker Dr
W Court Pl
N Franklin St
N State St
Washington
W Washington St
E Washington St
N Clark St
100N
Chicago River
W Calhoun Pl
N Holden Ct
N Wabash Ave
N Michigan Ave
300W
100W
Madison
W Madison St
100E
4
6
W Arcade Pl
S Franklin St
THE LOOP
S Michigan Ave
W Monroe St
100S
Monroe
S Wacker Dr
W Marble Pl
Adams
W Adams St
200S
S Clark St
S Dearborn St
S State St
Willis Tower (Sears Tower)
W Quincy St
Quincy
Jackson
E Jackson Blvd
DePaul University (Loop Campus)
300S
PAGE 245
S Wells St
La Salle
E Van Buren St
Library
S Franklin St
400S
S Federal St
Roosevelt University
7
8
La Salle
Eisenhower Expy
290
E Congress Pkwy
La Salle Street Station
S La Salle St
S Plymouth Ct
1/4 mile
.25 km
W Harrison St
Harrison
E Harrison St
E Congress Pkwy

Sundries/ Entertainment

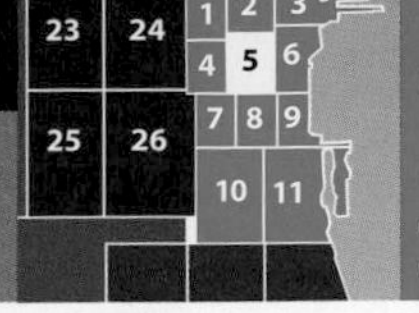

Iconic State Street is finding its footing again with an influx of new retailers and the near completion of the multi-use complex on Block 37 across from Macy's flagship store. Drinks after work range from not that cheap to really expensive, however it's the best place to do "dinner and a show"; start at the famous Italian Village followed by a visit to one several theatres on "Broadway in Chicago."

Coffee

- **Argo Tea** • 1 N Dearborn St
- **Argo Tea** • 140 S Dearborn St
- **Argo Tea** • 16 W Randolph St
- **Caffe Rom** • Hyatt Center • 71 S Wacker Dr
- **Caribou Coffee** • 10 S La Salle St
- **Caribou Coffee** • 200 N La Salle St
- **Caribou Coffee** • 311 W Monroe St
- **Caribou Coffee** • 55 W Monroe St
- **Cosi** • 203 N La Salle St
- **Cosi** • 230 W Monroe St
- **Cosi** • 230 W Washington St
- **Cosi** • 33 N Dearborn St
- **Dunkin' Donuts** • 400 S Financial Pl
- **Dunkin' Donuts** • 166 W Washington St
- **Dunkin' Donuts** • 105 W Madison St
- **Dunkin' Donuts** • 39 W Jackson Blvd
- **Dunkin' Donuts** • 27 W Lake St
- **Dunkin' Donuts** • 100 W Randolph St
- **Dunkin' Donuts** • 125 S Clark St
- **Dunkin' Donuts** • 201 N Clark St
- **Dunkin' Donuts** • 201 W Madison St
- **Dunkin' Donuts** • 205 W Randolph St
- **Dunkin' Donuts** • 215 W Lake St
- **Dunkin' Donuts** • 220 W Washington St
- **Dunkin' Donuts** • 229 W Jackson Blvd
- **Dunkin' Donuts** • 230 S State St
- **Dunkin' Donuts** • 27 W Lake St
- **Dunkin' Donuts** • 31 E Adams St
- **Dunkin' Donuts** • 333 S State St
- **Dunkin' Donuts** • 439 S Dearborn St
- **Dunkin' Donuts** • 6 N Wabash Ave
- **Dunkin' Donuts** • 62 E Jackson Blvd
- **Dunkin' Donuts** • 75 E Washington St
- **Intelligentsia Coffee** • 53 E Randolph St
- **Intelligentsia Coffee** • 53 W Jackson Blvd
- **Lavazza** • 111 W Jackson Blvd
- **Lavazza** • 134 N La Salle St
- **Lavazza** • 27 W Washington St
- **Liberty Coffee and Tea** • 401 S La Salle St
- **Starbucks** • 200 W Madison St
- **Starbucks** • 100 S Wacker Dr
- **Starbucks** • 105 W Adams St
- **Starbucks** • Macy's • 111 N State St
- **Starbucks** • 111 W Washington St
- **Starbucks** • 131 S Dearborn St
- **Starbucks** • 150 N Wacker Dr
- **Starbucks** • CT&T Bldg • 161 N Clark St
- **Starbucks** • 175 W Jackson Blvd
- **Starbucks** • 180 N La Salle St
- **Starbucks** • 200 W Adams St
- **Starbucks** • 209 W Jackson Blvd
- **Starbucks** • Chase Tower • 21 S Clark St
- **Starbucks** • AT&T Bldg • 227 W Monroe St
- **Starbucks** • 231 S La Salle St
- **Starbucks** • Sears Tower • 233 S Wacker Dr
- **Starbucks** • 25 E Washington St
- **Starbucks** • 30 N La Salle St
- **Starbucks** • 303 W Madison St
- **Starbucks** • 311 S Wacker Dr
- **Starbucks** • 39 S La Salle St
- **Starbucks** • 40 W Lake St
- **Starbucks** • 55 E Jackson Blvd
- **Starbucks** • 66 W Washington St
- **Starbucks** • 68 E Madison St
- **Starbucks** • 70 W Madison St

Copy Shops

- **24 Seven Copies** • 222 N La Salle St ㉔
- **Acme Copy** • 218 S Wabash Ave
- **Advance Instant Printing** • 5 S Wabash Ave
- **AlphaGraphics** • 208 S La Salle St
- **Best Imaging** • 20 E Randolph St
- **Copy Corps** • 20 N Clark St
- **Document Technologies** • 105 W Adams St
- **Fastrac Printing** • 220 S State St
- **FedEx Kinko's** • 101 N Wacker Dr
- **FedEx Kinko's** • 111 W Washington St
- **FedEx Kinko's** • 2 N La Salle St
- **FedEx Kinko's** • 200 W Jackson Blvd
- **FedEx Kinko's** • 227 W Monroe St
- **FedEx Kinko's** • 29 S La Salle St ㉔
- **FedEx Kinko's** • 400 S La Salle St
- **FedEx Kinko's** • 55 E Monroe St
- **FedEx Kinko's** • 6 W Lake St
- **Instant Printing** • 180 N La Salle St
- **Instant Printing** • 200 S Clark St
- **Kwik Kopy** • 11 S La Salle St
- **Landmark Document Services** • 200 W Adams St
- **Loop Legal Copier** • 318 W Adams St
- **Record Copy Services** • 30 N La Salle St
- **Reproduction Consultants** • 218 S Wabash Ave
- **Sir Speedy** • 311 S Wacker Dr
- **Staples Copy & Print Centers** • 111 N Wabash Ave
- **The UPS Store** • 27 N Wacker Dr
- **Viking Printing & Copying** • 53 W Jackson Blvd
- **Williams Lea** • 300 W Adams St

Farmers Markets

- **Daley Plaza (May–Sep; Thurs 7 am–3 pm)** • 50 W Washington St
- **Federal Plaza (May–Oct; Tues, 7 am–3 pm)** • Adams St & Dearborn St
- **The Park at Jackson & Wacker (June–Oct; Thurs, 7 am–3 pm)** • 233 S Wacker Dr

Gyms

- **Bally Total Fitness** • 25 E Washington St
- **Buckingham Athletic Club** • 440 S La Salle St
- **Curves (women only)** • 39 S La Salle St
- **Equinox** • 200 W Monroe St
- **Executive Fitness Center** • Palmer House Hilton • 17 E Monroe St
- **Fitness Image Incorporated** • 9 N Wabash Ave, 4th Fl
- **Lifestart** • 1 N Franklin St
- **Lifestart** • 161 N Clark St
- **Lifestart** • 20 N Wacker Dr
- **Lifestart** • 200 S Wacker Dr
- **Metropolitan Fitness Club** • Sears Tower • 233 S Wacker Dr, 67th Fl
- **Women's Workout World (women only)** • 208 S La Salle St
- **World Gym** • 150 S Wacker Dr

Hardware Stores

- **Ace Hardware** • 312 W Adams St
- **Lens Ace Hardware** • 272 W Lake St
- **Sears** • 2 N State St

Liquor Stores

- **Cal's** • 400 S Wells St
- **G&J Gifts & Liquor** • 167 N Wells St
- **Lake-Wells Food And Liquors** • 201 West Lake St
- **Rothschild Liquor Mart** • 55 W Van Buren St, Ste 350
- **Wabash Food & Liquor** • 234 S Wabash Ave

Movie Theaters

- **Chicago Cultural Center** • 78 E Washington St
- **Gene Siskel Film Center** • 164 N State St

Nightlife

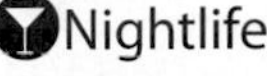

- **Base Bar** • 230 N Michigan Ave
- **Brando's Speakeasy** • 343 S Dearborn St
- **Cal's** • 400 S Wells St
- **Ceres Cafe** • 141 W Jackson Blvd
- **Close Up 2** • 416 S Clark St
- **Exchequer Pub** • 226 S Wabash Ave
- **Jaffa Bakery** • 186 W Van Buren St
- **Manhattans** • 415 S Dearborn St
- **Miller's Pub** • 134 S Wabash Ave
- **Monk's Pub** • 205 W Lake St
- **Petterino's** • 150 N Dearborn St
- **Potter's Lounge** • 17 E Monroe St

Restaurants

- **Atwood Café** • 1 W Washington St
- **Caffe Rom** • Hyatt Center • 71 S Wacker Dr
- **Everest** • 440 S La Salle St
- **Frontera Fresco** • 111 N State St
- **Goodwin's** • 175 N Franklin St
- **Hannah's Bretzel** • 180 W Washington St
- **Heaven on Seven** • 111 N Wabash Ave
- **La Cantina Enoteca** • Italian Village Restaurant Complex • 71 W Monroe St
- **La Rosetta** • 70 W Madison St
- **Miller's Pub** • 134 S Wabash Ave
- **Oasis Café** • 21 N Wabash Ave
- **Plymouth Restaurant** • 327 S Plymouth Ct ㉔
- **Russian Tea Time** • 77 E Adams St
- **Salad Spinners** • 200 W Monroe St
- **Trattoria No 10** • 10 N Dearborn St
- **The Village** • Italian Village Restaurant Complex • 71 W Monroe St
- **Vivere** • 71 W Monroe St
- **Wow Bao** • 175 W Jackson Blvd

Shopping

- **A New Leaf** • 312 S Dearborn St
- **Arts & Artisans** • 35 E Wacker Dr
- **Ashley Stewart** • 7 W Madison St
- **Avenue** • 231 S State St
- **American Music World** • 111 N State St
- **Blick Art Materials** • 42 S State St
- **Borders** • 150 N State St
- **Central Camera Company** • 230 S Wabash Ave
- **Florodora** • 330 S Dearborn St
- **Gallery 37 Store** • 66 E Randolph St
- **Garrett Popcorn Shop** • 26 W Randolph St
- **Kramer's Health Food Center** • 230 S Wabash Ave
- **Loehmann's** • 151 N State St
- **Lush Cosmetics** • Macy's Building • 111 N State St
- **Sears** • 2 N State St
- **Pastoral Artisan Cheese, Bread & Wine** • 53 E Lake St
- **Ulta** • 114 S State St
- **Urban Outfitters** • 20 S State St

Map 6 • The Loop / Grant Park

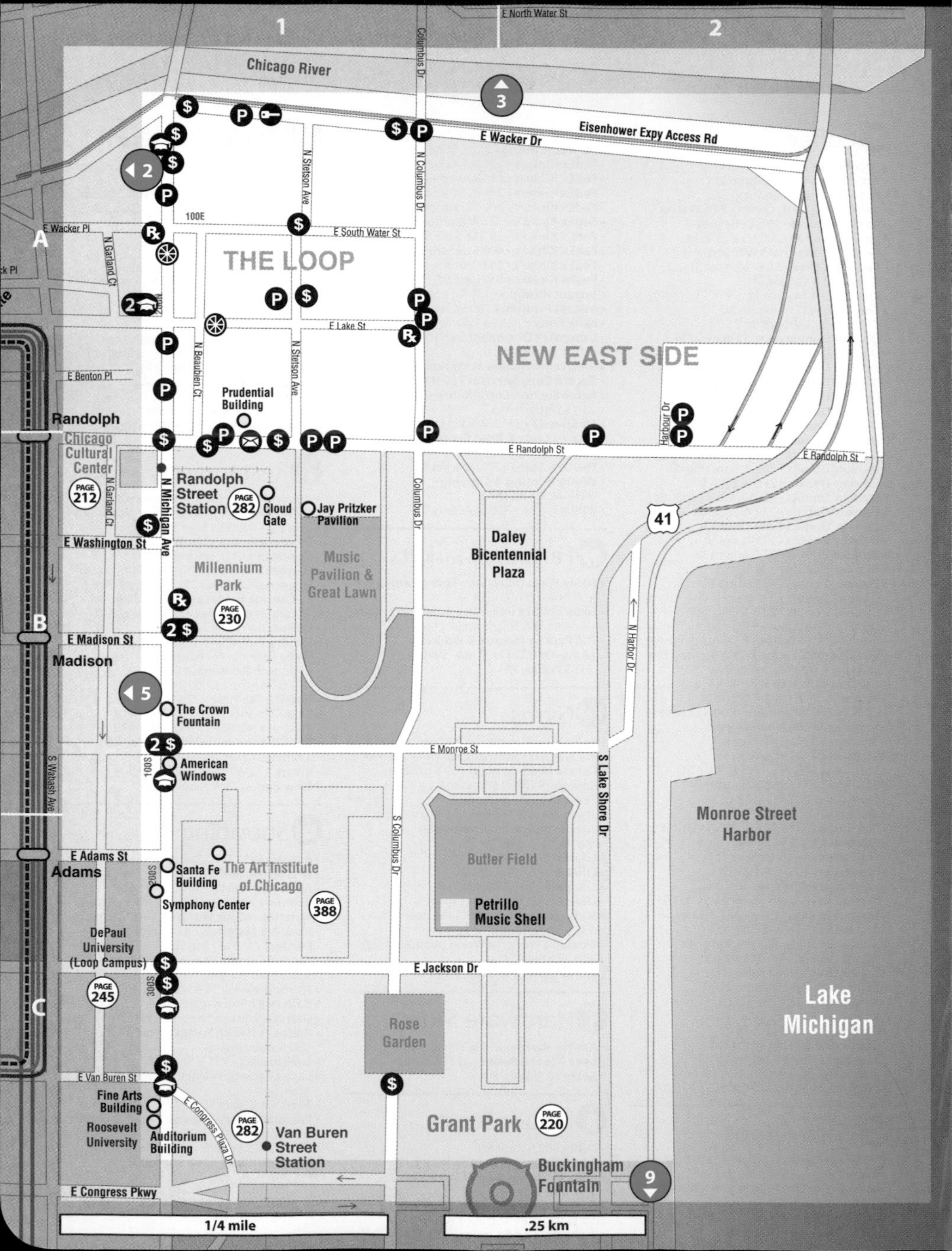

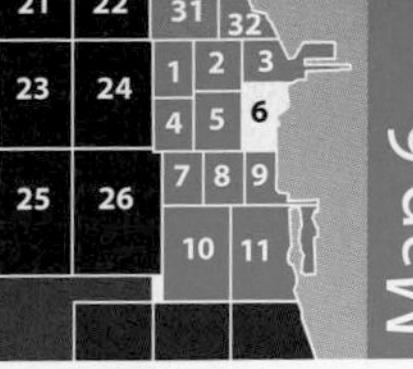

A giant silver bean and 50-foot-tall animated faces...yes, really! Millennium Park is definitely the Chicago show-stopper, with its unique blend of artwork and landscaping. Further down Michigan Avenue, the more traditional Grant Park brings highbrow and lowbrow culture side by side. Tasteful music or Taste of Chicago, there's something for everyone.

Banks

- **Associated** • 130 E Randolph St
- **Associated** • 200 E Randolph St
- **Associated** • 225 N Michigan Ave
- **Bank of America (ATM)** • 122 S Michigan Ave
- **Bank of America (ATM)** • 404 S Michigan Ave
- **Chase** • 150 N Michigan Ave
- **Chase (ATM)** • 151 N Michigan Ave
- **Chase (ATM)** • 11 N Michigan Ave
- **Chase (ATM)** • 30 N Michigan Ave
- **Chase (ATM)** • Walgreens • 300 N Michigan Ave
- **Citibank** • 100 S Michigan Ave
- **Citibank** • 233 N Michigan Ave
- **Citibank (ATM)** • 7-Eleven • 174 N Michigan Ave
- **Citibank (ATM)** • 360 N Michigan Ave
- **Fifth Third** • 400 E South Water St
- **First American (ATM)** • Hard Rock Hotel • 230 N Michigan Ave
- **MB Financial** • 303 E Wacker Dr
- **Midwest Bank & Trust Company** • 300 S Michigan Ave
- **Midwest Bank & Trust Company (ATM)** • 332 S Michigan Ave
- **New Century (ATM)** • 211 N Stetson Ave
- **North Community** • 180 N Michigan Ave
- **TCF (ATM)** • 7-Eleven • 174 N Michigan Ave
- **TCF (ATM)** • 500 S Columbus Dr
- **US** • 360 N Michigan Ave
- **US (ATM)** • 111 E Wacker Dr
- **Washington Mutual** • 206 N Michigan Ave

Car Rental

- **Hertz** • 151 E Wacker Dr

Landmarks

- **America Windows** • Art Institute • 111 S Michigan Ave
- **Art Institute of Chicago** • 111 S Michigan Ave
- **Auditorium Building** • 430 S Michigan Ave
- **Cloud Gate** • 201 E Randolph St
- **The Crown Fountain** • 201 E Randolph St
- **Fine Arts Building** • 410 S Michigan Ave
- **Jay Pritzker Pavilion** • Millennium Park • 201 E Randolph St
- **Prudential Building** • 130 E Randolph St
- **Santa Fe Building** • 224 S Michigan Ave
- **Symphony Center** • 220 S Michigan Ave

Parking

Pharmacies

- **Walgreens** • 30 N Michigan Ave
- **Walgreens** • 300 N Michigan Ave

Pizza

- **Giordano's** • 135 E Lake St
- **Sbarro** • 233 N Michigan Ave

Post Offices

- **US Post Office** • 200 E Randolph St

Schools

- **American Academy of Art** • 332 S Michigan Ave
- **Career Works Alternative** • 200 N Michigan Ave
- **Institute for Clinical Social Work** • 200 N Michigan Ave
- **National-Louis University** • 122 S Michigan Ave
- **Roosevelt University** • 430 S Michigan Ave

Map 6 • The Loop / Grant Park

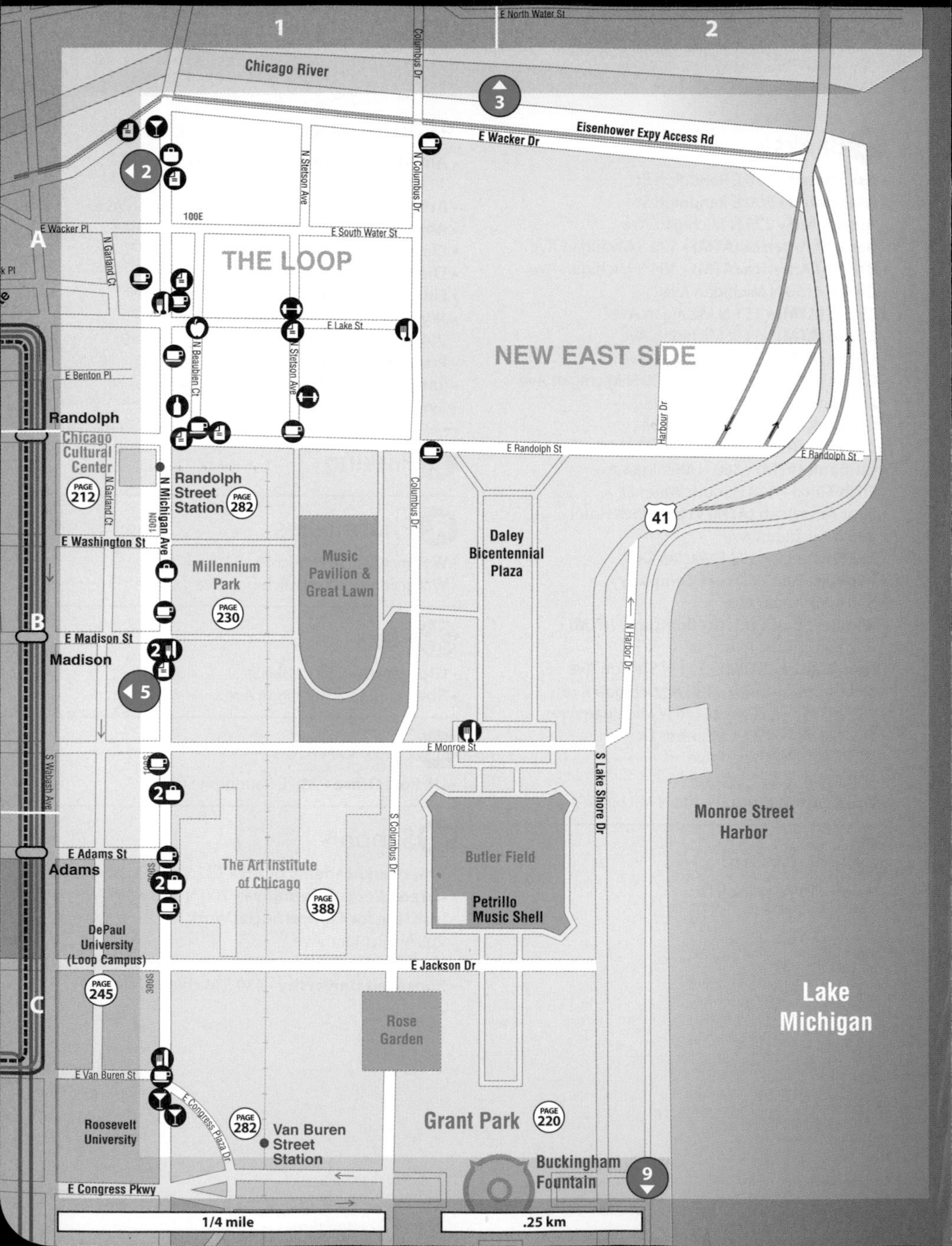

Sundries / Entertainment

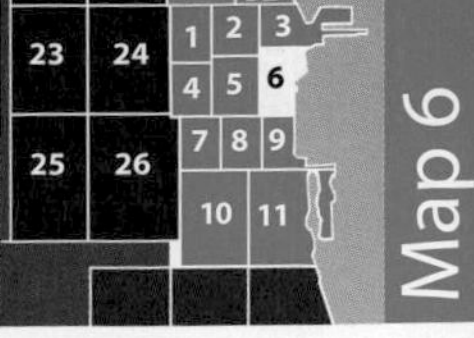

Park Grill's front yard morphs from an ice skating rink in winter to an outdoor café in summer. Take in a free concert at the renowned Pritzker Pavilion, rent a bike and ride along the lakeshore, or paddle in the crowd-pleasing Crown Fountain. For those long winter months the Art Institute's free Thursday nights are ideal, whilst the Symphony Center offers Afterwork Masterworks for commuters.

Coffee

- **Caribou Coffee** • 20 N Michigan Ave
- **Cosi** • 116 S Michigan Ave
- **Cosi** • 233 N Michigan Ave
- **Dunkin' Donuts** • 406 S Michigan Ave
- **Dunkin' Donuts** • 233 N Michigan Ave
- **Dunkin' Donuts** • 300 E Randolph St
- **Dunkin' Donuts** • 303 E Wacker Dr
- **Starbucks** • 151 N Michigan Ave
- **Starbucks** • Millenium Station • 130 E Randolph St
- **Starbucks** • Amoco Bldg • 200 E Randolph St
- **Starbucks** • 202 N Michigan Ave
- **Starbucks** • Illinois Ctr • 225 N Michigan Ave

Copy Shops

- **AlphaGraphics** • 180 N Stetson Ave
- **FedEx Kinko's** • 111 E Wacker Dr
- **FedEx Kinko's** • 130 E Randolph St
- **FedEx Kinko's** • 225 N Michigan Ave
- **FedEx Kinko's** • 34 S Michigan Ave
- **Sir Speedy** • 130 E Randolph St
- **Swift Impressions** • 333 N Michigan Ave

Farmers Markets

- **Prudential Plaza (Jun–Oct; Thurs, 7 am–3 pm)** • E Lake St & N Beaubien Ct

Gyms

- **Curves (women only)** • 180 N Stetson Ave
- **Lakeshore Athletic Club** • 211 N Stetson Ave

Liquor Stores

- **Gourmet Pantry** • 155 N Michigan Ave

Nightlife

- **Houlihan's** • 111 E Wacker Dr
- **Tango Chicago** • 408 S Michigan Ave

Restaurants

- **Aria** • Fairmont Chicago Hotel • 200 N Columbus Dr
- **Artist's Café** • 412 S Michigan Ave
- **China Grill** • Hard Rock Hotel • 230 N Michigan Ave
- **The Gage** • 24 S Michigan Ave
- **The Green at Grant Park** • 352 E Monroe St
- **Park Grill** • 11 N Michigan Ave

Shopping

- **Chicago Architecture Foundation** • 224 S Michigan Ave
- **Arts & Artisans** • 108 S Michigan Ave
- **Museum Shop of the Art Institute** • 111 S Michigan Ave
- **Poster Plus** • 200 S Michigan Ave
- **Precious Possessions** • 28 N Michigan Ave

Map 7 • South Loop / River City

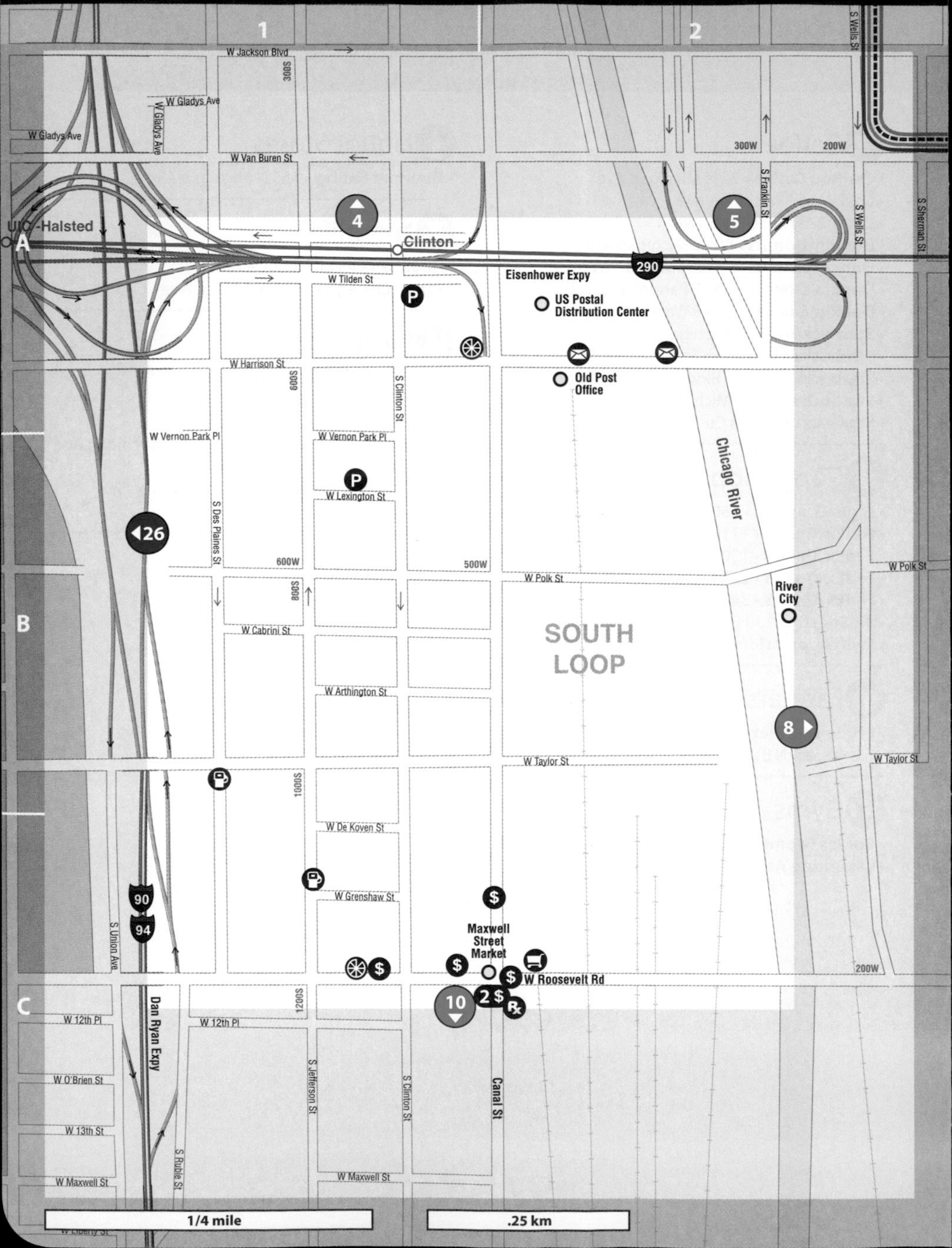

N

1
2
A
B
C

W Jackson Blvd
W Gladys Ave
W Gladys Ave
W Van Buren St
UIC-Halsted
Clinton
Eisenhower Expy
290
W Tilden St
US Postal Distribution Center
W Harrison St
Old Post Office
S Clinton St
W Vernon Park Pl
W Vernon Park Pl
W Lexington St
S Des Plaines St
Chicago River
600W
500W
300W
200W
S Franklin St
S Wells St
S Sherman St
W Polk St
W Polk St
River City
SOUTH LOOP
W Cabrini St
W Arthington St
W Taylor St
W Taylor St
W De Koven St
W Grenshaw St
Maxwell Street Market
W Roosevelt Rd
200W
S Union Ave
90
94
Dan Ryan Expy
W 12th Pl
W 12th Pl
W O'Brien St
W 13th St
W Maxwell St
W Maxwell St
S Ruble St
S Jefferson St
S Clinton St
Canal St
W Liberty St
300S
600S
800S
1000S
1200S
4
5
26
8
10

1/4 mile
.25 km

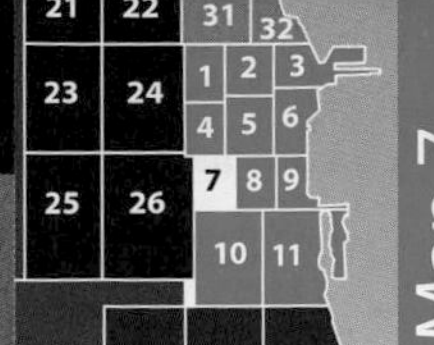

This longtime industrial deadzone is emerging as a bustling business district—including a swanky new Whole Foods—to serve the rampant residential growth in all of the adjacent hoods. River City residents have never had it so good. Seriously, they haven't.

Banks

- **Bank of America** • 430 W Roosevelt Rd
- **Chase** • 1130 S Canal St
- **Chase (ATM)** • Walgreens • 501 W Roosevelt Rd
- **First American** • 1101 S Canal St
- **Harris Trust & Savings** • 522 W Roosevelt Rd
- **South Central** • 525 W Roosevelt Rd

Gas Stations

- **Citgo** • 1004 S Desplaines St
- **Marathon** • 1121 S Jefferson St

Landmarks

- **Maxwell Street Market (Sun, 7 am–3 pm)** • 548 W Roosevelt Rd
- **Old Post Office** • 404 W Harrison St
- **River City** • 800 S Wells St
- **US Postal Distribution Center** • 433 W Harrison St

Parking

Pharmacies

- **Walgreens** • 501 W Roosevelt Rd

Pizza

- **Atinos Pizza** • 570 W Roosevelt Rd
- **Aurelio's Pizza** • 506 W Harrison St

Post Offices

- **US Post Office** • 358 W Harrison St
- **US Post Office** • 433 W Harrison St

Supermarkets

- **Whole Foods** • 1101 S Canal St

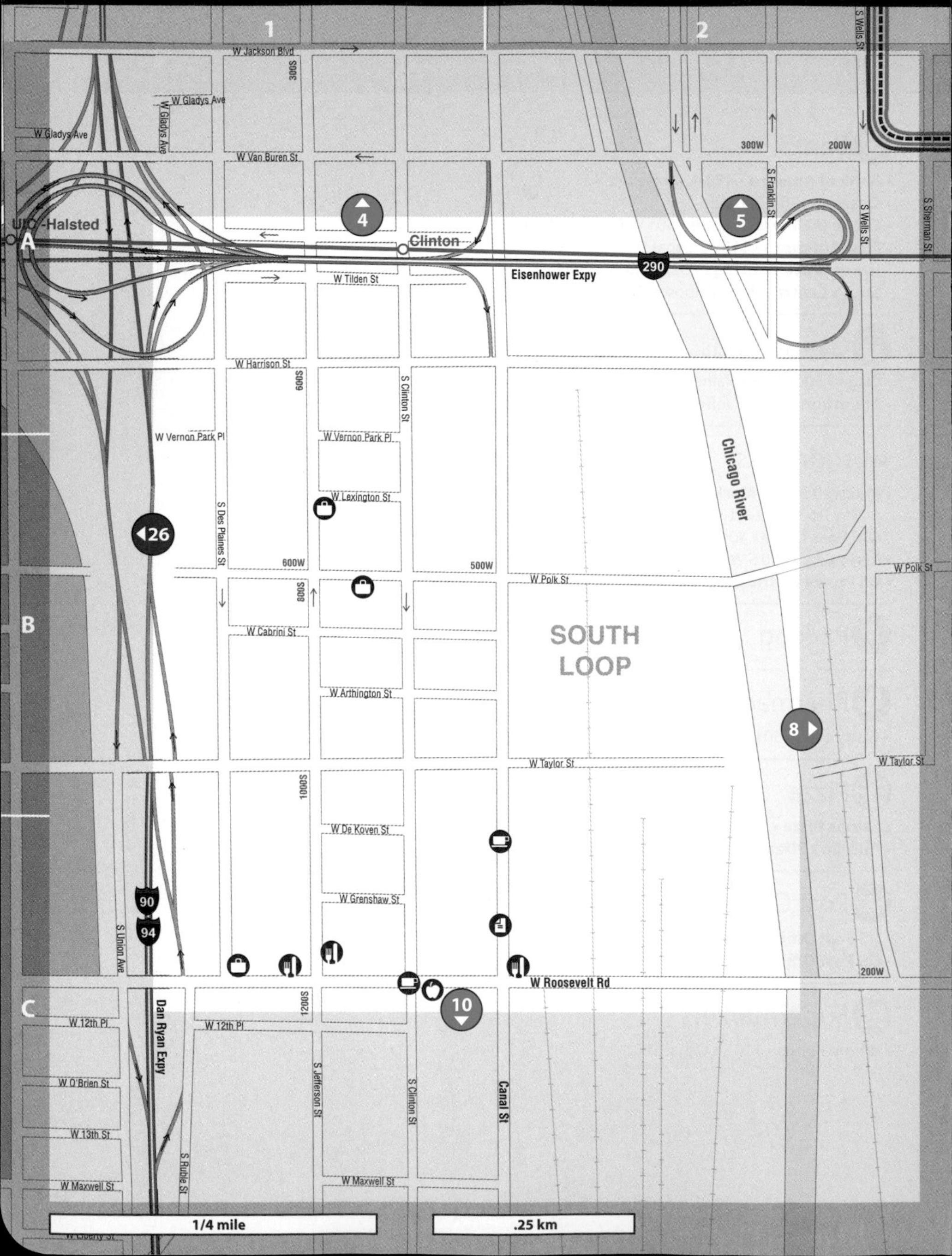

N
1
2
W Jackson Blvd
W Gladys Ave
W Gladys Ave
W Gladys Ave
W Van Buren St
300W
200W
S Wells St
S Franklin St
S Sherman St
UIC-Halsted
A
4
5
Clinton
290
Eisenhower Expy
W Tilden St
W Harrison St
600S
S Clinton St
W Vernon Park Pl
W Vernon Park Pl
W Lexington St
Chicago River
26
S Des Plaines St
600W
500W
W Polk St
W Polk St
800S
B
W Cabrini St
SOUTH LOOP
W Arthington St
8
W Taylor St
W Taylor St
1000S
W De Koven St
W Grenshaw St
90
94
S Union Ave
200W
W Roosevelt Rd
C
10
1200S
W 12th Pl
W 12th Pl
Dan Ryan Expy
W O'Brien St
S Jefferson St
S Clinton St
Canal St
W 13th St
S Ruble St
W Maxwell St
W Maxwell St
1/4 mile
.25 km
W Liberty St

Manny's is essential for folks who enjoy sarcasm with their pastrami; pack a wire—this place is so popular with deal-making politicos that you never know what you'll overhear. The 24-hour White Palace Grill has sopped up late night booze since 1939. Although a shadow of its former self, the Maxwell Sunday Market remains a haven for tube socks, churros, and trashy treasures.

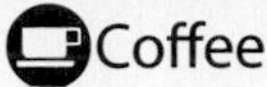

Coffee

- **Dunkin' Donuts** • 500 W Roosevelt Rd
- **Starbucks** • 1101 S Canal St

Copy Shops

- **Staples** • 1130 S Canal St

Farmers Markets

- **Maxwell Street Market (Sun, 7 am–3 pm)** • 548 W Roosevelt Rd

Pet Shops

- **Petsmart** • 1101 S Canal St

Restaurants

- **Bake for Me** • 600 W Roosevelt Rd
- **Manny's Coffee Shop** • 1141 S Jefferson St
- **White Palace Grill** • 1159 S Canal St

Shopping

- **Fishman's Fabrics** • 1101 S Des Plaines St
- **Lee's Foreign Car Service** • 727 S Jefferson St
- **Morris & Sons** • 557 W Polk St

Map 8 • South Loop / Printers Row / Dearborn Park

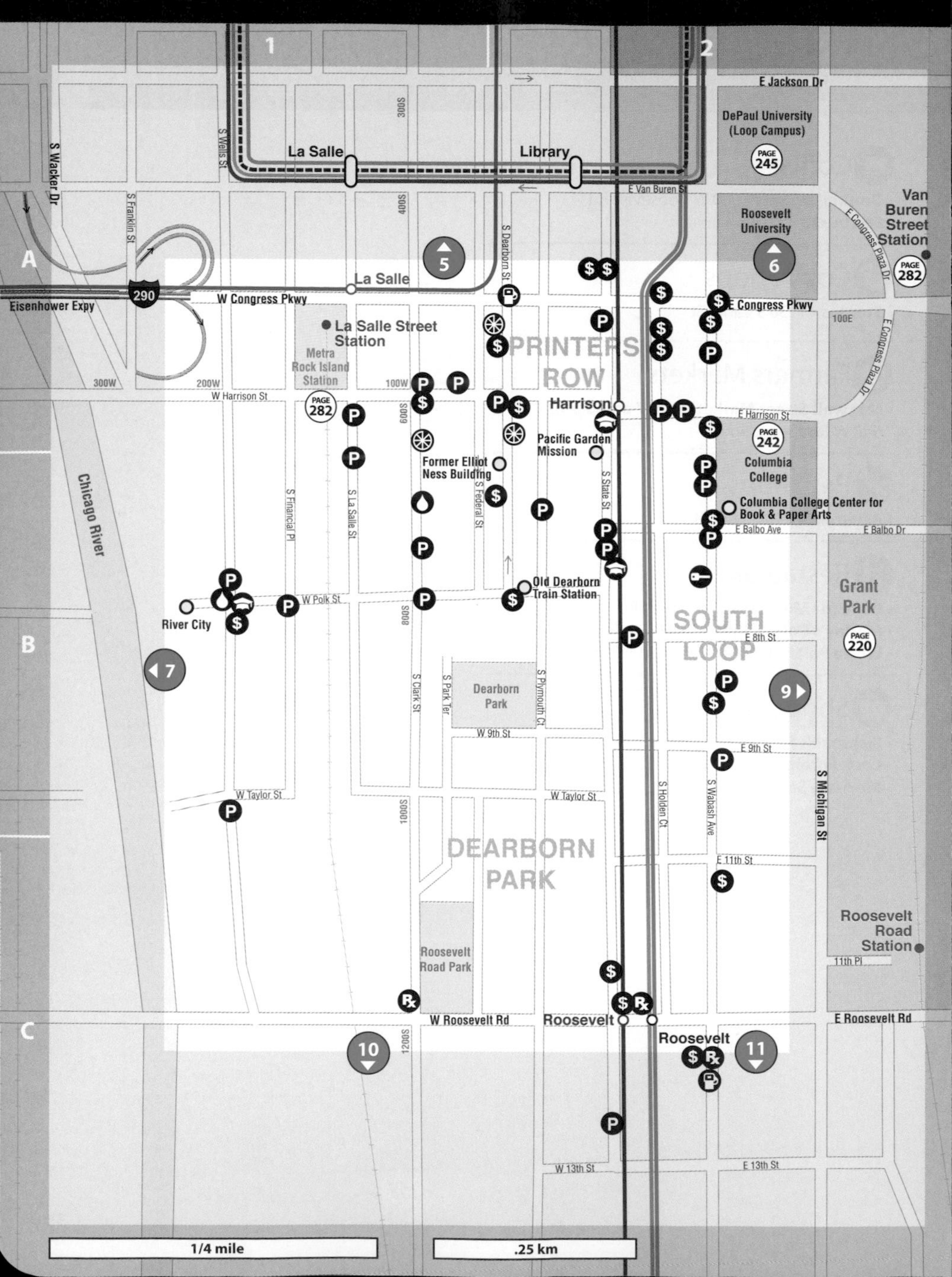

Essentials

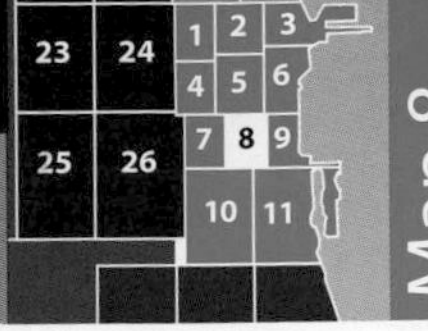

With all the student-friendly dining near the Columbia College campus, the upscale Mercat a la Planxa is a welcome addition, offering elegant tapas and lovely wines. Meanwhile, Epic Burger offers trendy organic burgers for about double the price of Micky D's but exactly none of the growth hormones. As to be expected in a 'hood with such a dense student population, undergrads, grads, and profs alike frequent local watering holes Georges, Kasey's and the South Loop Club.

Banks

- **Bank of America (ATM)** • 50 E Congress Pkwy
- **Bank of America (ATM)** • 1104 S Wabash Ave
- **Bank of America (ATM)** • 623 S Wabash Ave
- **Charter One (ATM)** • 600 S Dearborn St
- **Chase** • 550 S Dearborn St
- **Chase** • 850 S Wabash Ave
- **Chase (ATM)** • 717 S Dearborn St
- **Chase (ATM)** • 1167 S State St
- **Chase (ATM)** • Walgreens • 2 E Roosevelt Rd
- **Chase (ATM)** • 800 S Wells St
- **Chicago Community** • 47 W Polk St
- **Citibank (ATM)** • 7-Eleven • 525 S State St
- **First American (ATM)** • 711 S State St
- **First American (ATM)** • 24 E Congress Pkwy
- **First American (ATM)** • 524 S Wabash Ave
- **First American (ATM)** • 600 S Clark St
- **MB Financial** • 557 S State St
- **MB Financial (ATM)** • 525 S State St
- **TCF** • Jewel • 1224 S Wabash Ave
- **TCF (ATM)** • 7-Eleven • 525 S State St

Car Washes

- **Kendo's Hand Car Wash** • 700 S Clark St
- **River City Car Wash** • 800 S Wells St

Car Rental

- **Budget** • 714 S Wabash Ave • 312-935-3440

Gas Stations

- **BP** • 50 W Congress Pkwy
- **BP** • 1221 S Wabash Ave

Landmarks

- **Columbia College Center for Book & Paper Arts** • 1104 S Wabash Ave
- **Former Elliot Ness Building** • 600 S Dearborn St
- **Old Dearborn Train Station** • 47 W Polk St
- **Pacific Garden Mission** • 646 S State St
- **River City** • 800 S Wells St

Parking

Pharmacies

- **Jewel-Osco** • 1224 S Wabash Ave
- **Target** • 1154 S Clark St
- **Walgreens** • 2 E Roosevelt Rd

Pizza

- **Edwardo's Natural Pizza** • 521 S Dearborn St
- **Pat's Pizzeria** • 638 S Clark St
- **Trattoria Caterina** • 616 S Dearborn St

Schools

- **Daystar Education Association** • 800 S Wells St
- **Jones College Prep** • 606 S State St
- **Renaissance Prep** • 719 S State St

Map 8 • South Loop / Printers Row / Dearborn Park

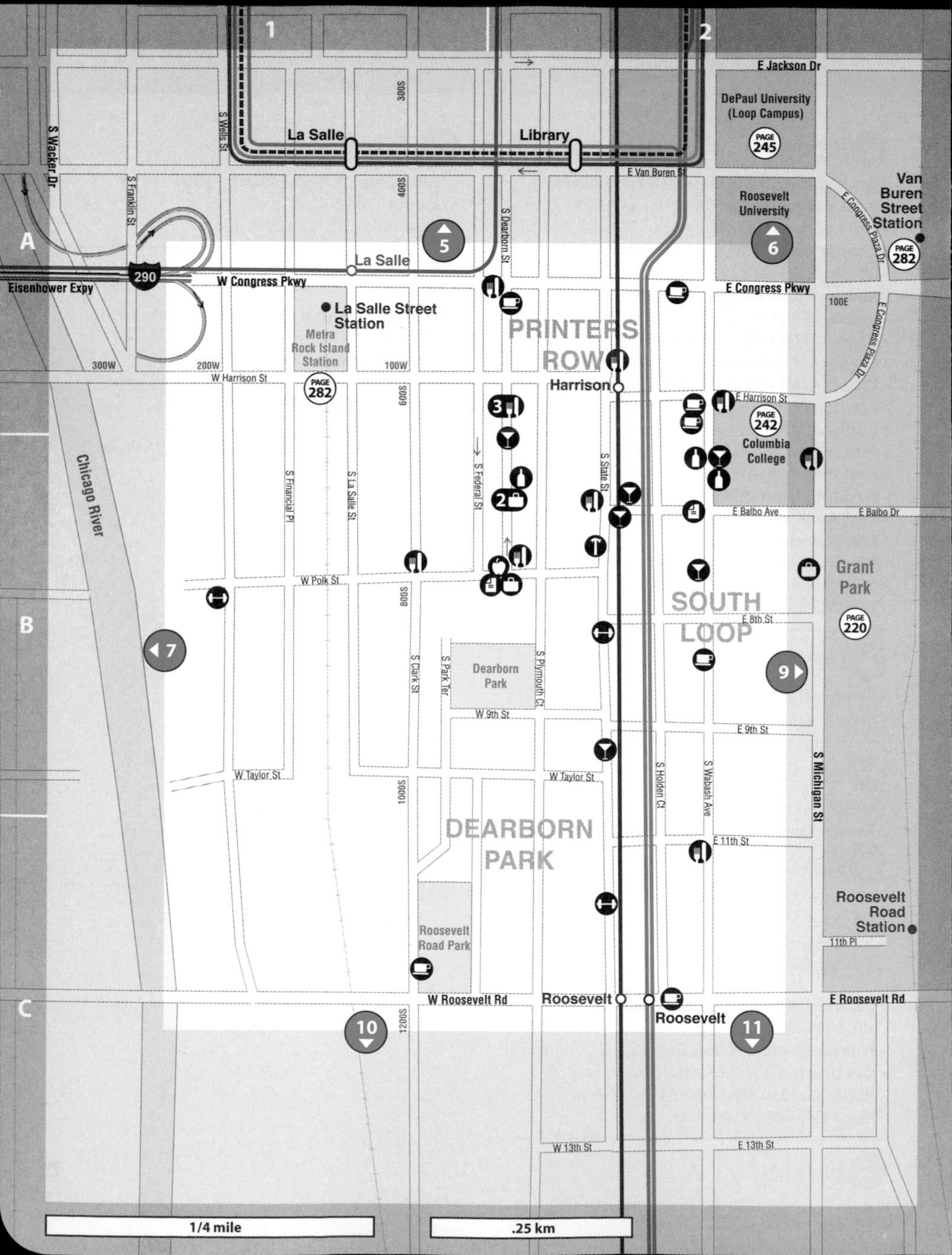

Sundries / Entertainment

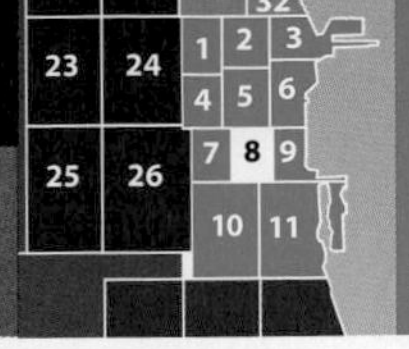

Blackie's is the real deal, the oldest and most racially-mixed bar in the neighborhood. Hackney's bar food is way underrated. Same goes for South Loop Club—sit by a window here to take in the always-interesting street scene at this funky intersection. Meanwhile, restaurateur Shawn McClain (Spring, Green Zebra) gets carnivorous at his latest venture, Custom House.

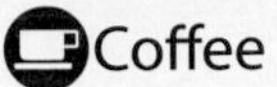

Coffee

- **Cafecito** • 26 E Congress Pkwy
- **Caribou Coffee** • 41 E 8th St
- **Dunkin' Donuts** • 600 S Wabash Ave
- **Starbucks** • Target • 1154 S Clark St
- **Starbucks** • 31 E Roosevelt Rd
- **Starbucks** • 555 S Dearborn St

Copy Shops

- **FedEx Kinko's** • 700 S Wabash Ave
- **The UPS Store** • 47 W Polk St

Farmers Markets

- **Printer's Row (Jun–Oct; Sat, 7 am–2 pm)** • S Dearborn St & W Polk St

Gyms

- **Bally Total Fitness** • 800 S Wells St
- **Fitness Formula** • 1151 S State Ave
- **XSport Fitness** • 819 S State St

Hardware Stores

- **South Loop Ace Hardware** • 725 S State St

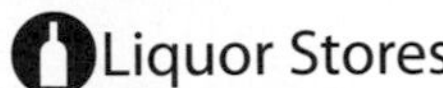

Liquor Stores

- **George's Cocktail Lounge** • 646 S Wabash Ave
- **Printers Row Wine Shop** • 719 S Dearborn St
- **Warehouse Liquors** • 634 S Wabash Ave

Nightlife

- **Buddy Guy's Legends** • 754 S Wabash Ave
- **George's Cocktail Lounge** • 646 S Wabash Ave
- **Kasey's Tavern** • 701 S Dearborn St
- **South Loop Club** • 701 S State St
- **Tantrum** • 1023 S State St

Restaurants

- **Amarit** • 600 S Dearborn St
- **Blackie's** • 755 S Clark St
- **Custom House** • 500 S Dearborn St
- **Eleven City Diner** • 1112 S Wabash Ave
- **Epic Burger** • 517 S State St
- **Hackney's** • 733 S Dearborn St
- **Mercat a la Planxa** • 638 S Michigan Ave
- **South Loop Club** • 701 S State St
- **SRO** • 610 S Dearborn St
- **Tamarind** • 614 S Wabash Ave
- **Trattoria Caterina** • 616 S Dearborn St

Shopping

- **Arts & Artisans** • 720 S Michigan Ave
- **Loopy Yarns** • 47 W Polk St
- **Printers Row Fine & Rare Books** • 715 S Dearborn St
- **Sandmeyer's Book Store** • 714 S Dearborn St

Map 9 • South Loop / South Michigan Ave

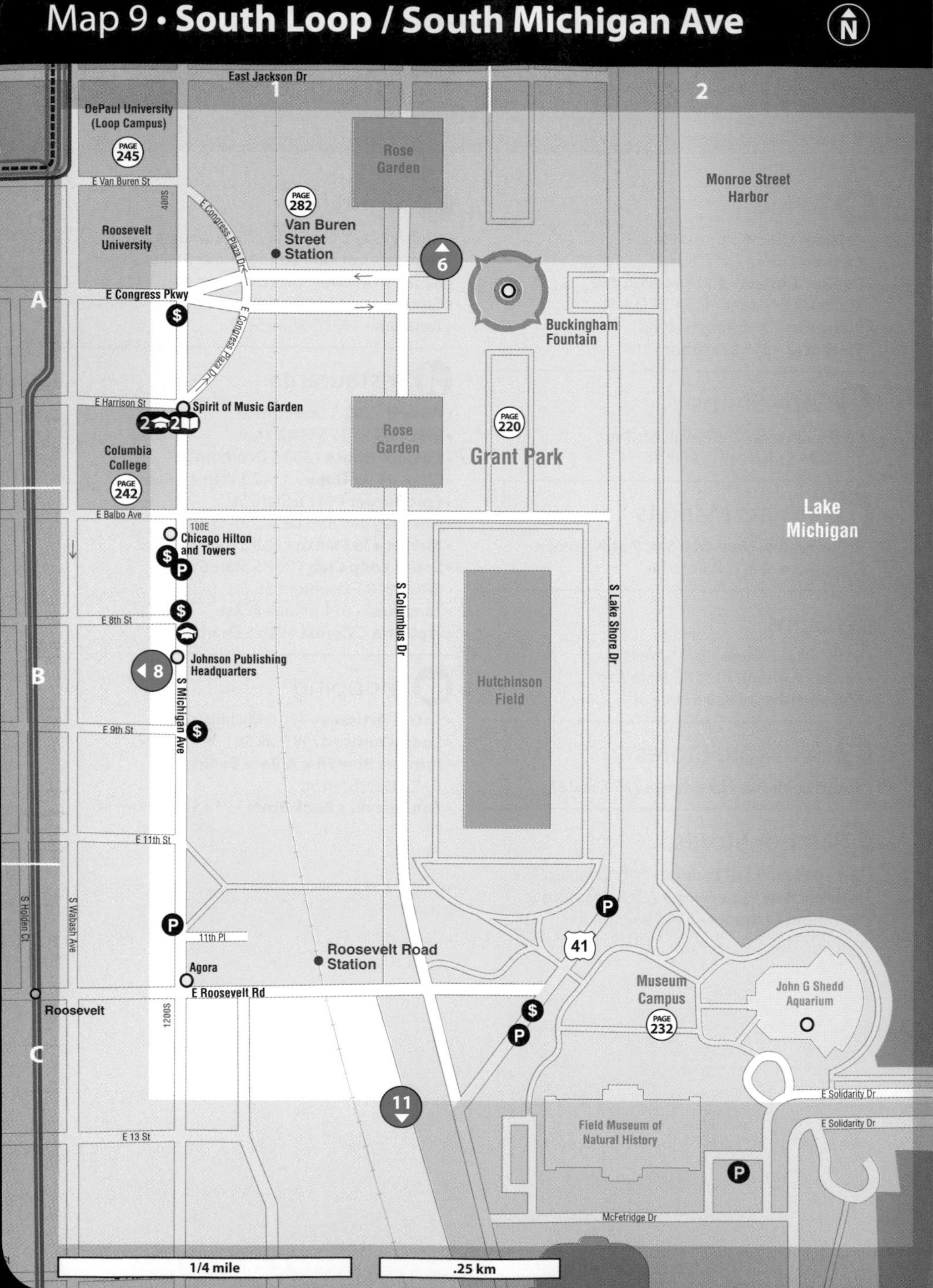

N
East Jackson Dr
1
2
DePaul University (Loop Campus)
PAGE 245
E Van Buren St
400S
E Congress Plaza Dr
Roosevelt University
PAGE 282
Van Buren Street Station
Rose Garden
Monroe Street Harbor
6
A
E Congress Pkwy
Buckingham Fountain
E Harrison St
Spirit of Music Garden
2
2
Columbia College
PAGE 242
Rose Garden
PAGE 220
Grant Park
E Balbo Ave
100E
Chicago Hilton and Towers
Lake Michigan
S Columbus Dr
S Lake Shore Dr
E 8th St
8
Johnson Publishing Headquarters
B
S Michigan Ave
Hutchinson Field
E 9th St
E 11th St
S Holden Ct
S Wabash Ave
11th Pl
Roosevelt Road Station
41
Agora
E Roosevelt Rd
Roosevelt
Museum Campus
PAGE 232
John G Shedd Aquarium
1200S
C
11
E Solidarity Dr
E Solidarity Dr
Field Museum of Natural History
E 13 St
McFetridge Dr
1/4 mile
.25 km

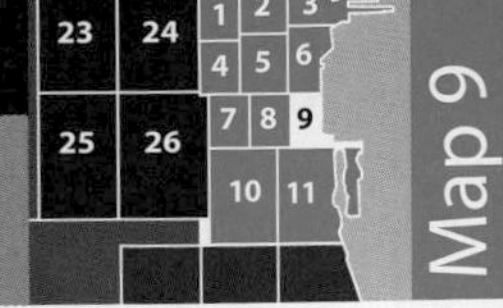

Built atop the rubble of the Great Chicago Fire of 1871, Grant Park is now affectionately known as Chicago's front yard. Spin around and you are guaranteed a view—Lake Michigan, Museum Campus, the city skyline, or the gardens of the park itself. Warm weather brings out the inline skaters, boaters and sun-worshippers while the sometimes sub-zero winter brings out the crazy joggers.

Banks

- **Citibank (ATM)** • 800 S Michigan Ave
- **First American (ATM)** • 1200 S Lake Shore Dr
- **First American (ATM)** • Congress Plaza Hotel • 520 S Michigan Ave
- **First American (ATM)** • Chicago Hilton and Towers • 727 S Michigan Ave
- **New City** • 900 S Michigan Ave

Landmarks

- **Agora** • S Michigan Ave & E Roosevelt Rd
- **Buckingham Fountain** • 500 Columbus Dr
- **Chicago Hilton and Towers** • 720 S Michigan Ave
- **John G Shedd Aquarium** • 1200 S Lake Shore Dr
- **Johnson Publishing Headquarters** • 820 S Michigan Ave
- **Spirit of Music Garden** • 601 S Michigan Ave

Libraries

- **Asher Library-Spertus Institute** • 610 S Michigan Ave
- **Library of Columbia College** • 624 S Michigan Ave

Parking

Schools

- **Columbia College** • 600 S Michigan Ave
- **East-West University** • 816 S Michigan Ave
- **Spertus College** • 610 S Michigan Ave

Map 9 • South Loop / South Michigan Ave

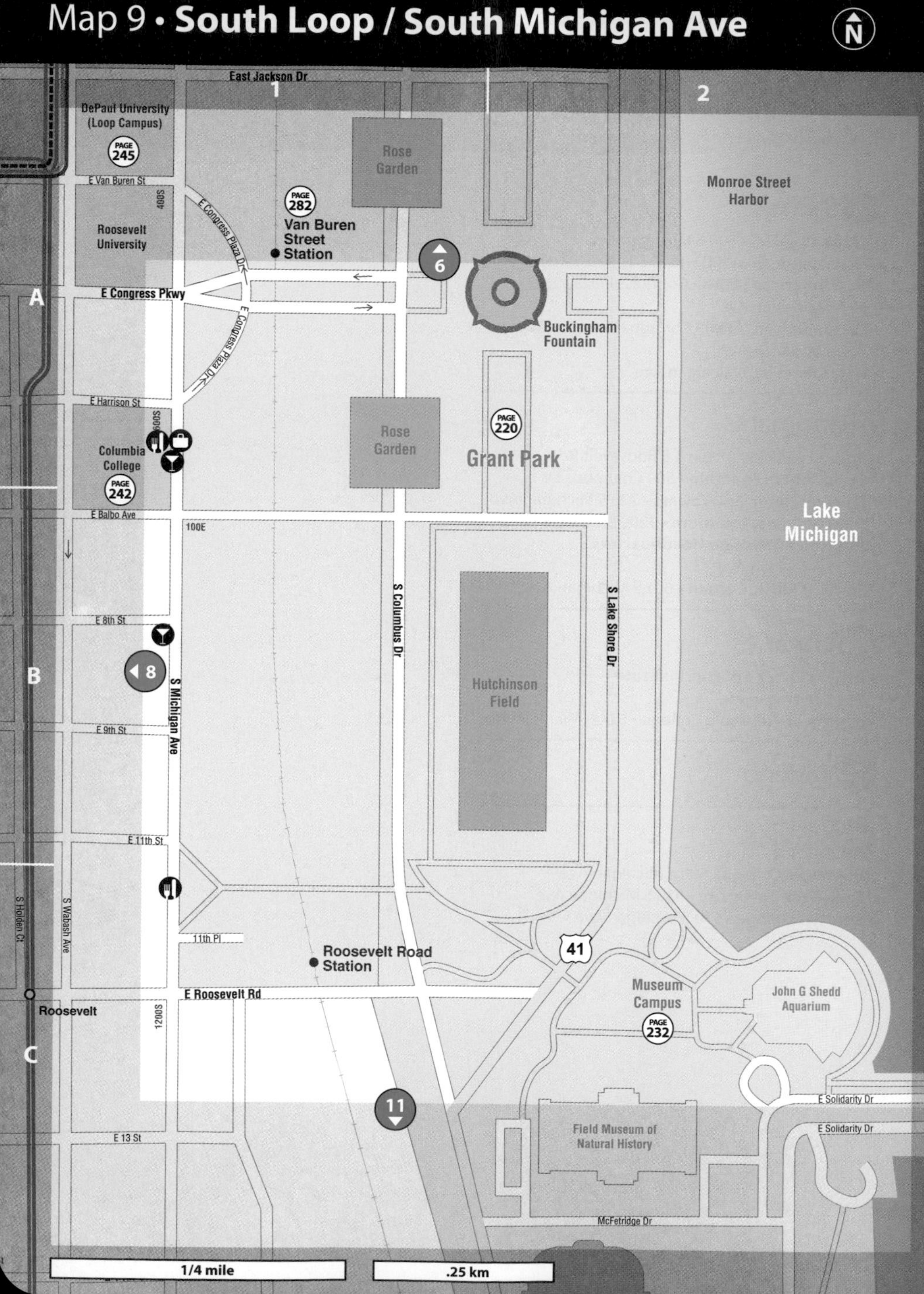

Sundries / Entertainment

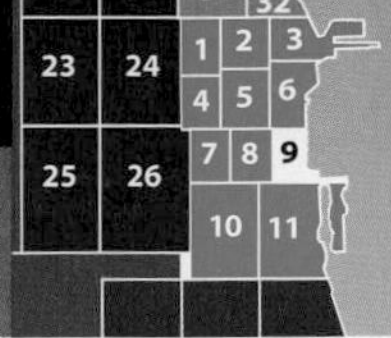

Chicago's front yard boasts gardens, recreation courts and fields, and the Shedd Aquarium. Dancers gather at the Spirit of Music Garden for the outdoor Summer Dance series, and the skyrocketing water display known as Buckingham Fountain, which, accompanied by lights and music, occurs daily and hourly for twenty minutes from dusk until 10 pm, April through October.

Nightlife

- **Savoy Bar and Grill** • 800 S Michigan Ave
- **Spertus Cafe** • 610 S Michigan Ave

Restaurants

- **Oysy** • 888 S Michigan Ave
- **Yolk** • 1120 S Michigan Ave

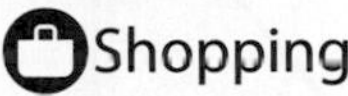

Shopping

- **Spertus Shop** • 610 S Michigan Ave

Map 10 • East Pilsen / Chinatown

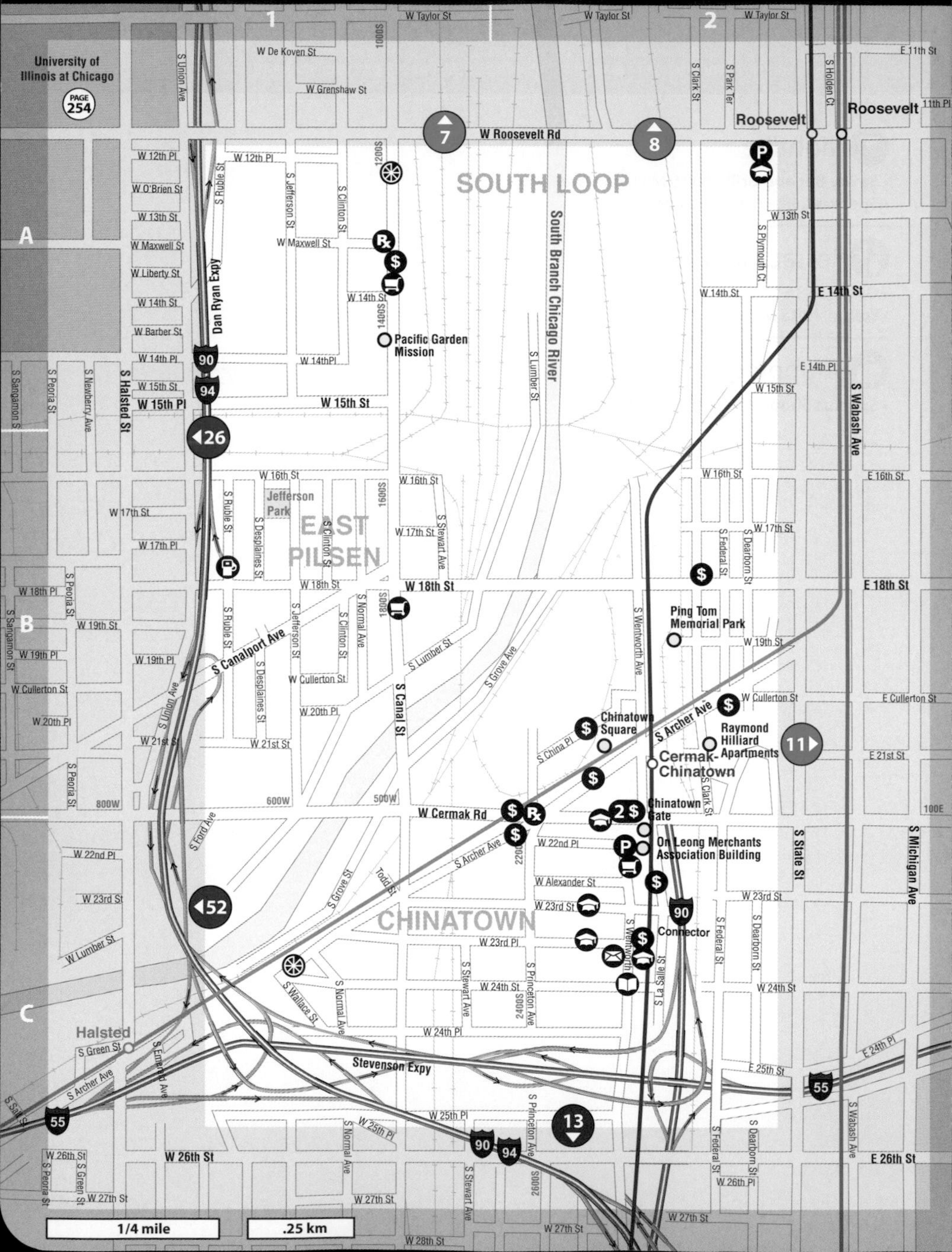

N

University of Illinois at Chicago
PAGE 254

SOUTH LOOP
EAST PILSEN
CHINATOWN

Pacific Garden Mission
Jefferson Park
Ping Tom Memorial Park
Chinatown Square
Raymond Hilliard Apartments
Cermak-Chinatown
Chinatown Gate
On Leong Merchants Association Building
Connector
Roosevelt
Halsted

Dan Ryan Expy
Stevenson Expy
South Branch Chicago River

W Taylor St
W De Koven St
W Grenshaw St
W Roosevelt Rd
W 12th Pl
W O'Brien St
W 13th St
W Maxwell St
W Liberty St
W 14th St
W Barber St
W 14th Pl
W 15th St
W 15th Pl
W 16th St
W 17th St
W 17th Pl
W 18th Pl
W 18th St
W 19th St
W 19th Pl
W Cullerton St
W 20th Pl
W 21st St
W Cermak Rd
W 22nd Pl
W Alexander St
W 23rd St
W 23rd Pl
W 24th St
W 24th Pl
W Lumber St
W 25th Pl
W 26th St
W 26th Pl
W 27th St
W 28th St
E 11th St
E 14th St
E 14th Pl
E 16th St
E 18th St
E Cullerton St
E 21st St
E 24th Pl
E 25th St
E 26th St
11th Pl

S Union Ave
S Ruble St
S Jefferson St
S Clinton St
S Desplaines St
S Normal Ave
S Canal St
S Stewart Ave
S Lumber St
S Grove St
S Canalport Ave
S Ford Ave
S Archer Ave
S China Pl
S Wentworth Ave
S Princeton Ave
S Wallace St
S Clark St
S Park Ter
S Holden Ct
S Plymouth Ct
S Federal St
S Dearborn St
S La Salle St
S State St
S Wabash Ave
S Michigan Ave
S Halsted St
S Sangamon St
S Peoria St
S Newberry Ave
S Green St
S Emerald Ave
S Union Ave
Todd St

1000S
1200S
1400S
1600S
1800S
2200S
2400S
2600S
800W
600W
500W
100E

7
8
11
13
26
52

90
94
55

1/4 mile
.25 km

Essentials

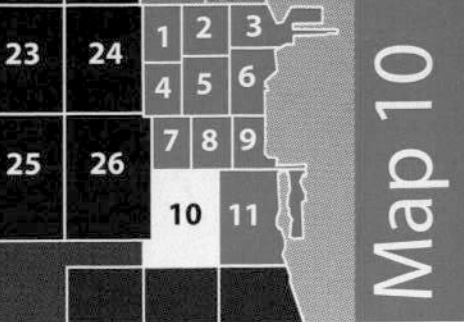

Nestled between the University of Illinois at Chicago campus and the official South Side, East Pilsen houses an interesting mix of artists, families and hipsters. The once-cheap rents are having former residents wishing they never left. Across the river in Chinatown, where rent IS still affordable, find bubble tea, bamboo plants, and baby turtles for sale all on the same street.

Banks

- **American Metro** • 2144 S Archer Ave
- **Cathay Bank** • 222 W Cermak Rd
- **Cathay Bank** • 250 W Cermak Rd
- **Charter One** • 2131 S China Pl
- **Charter One** • 2263 S Wentworth Ave
- **Chase** • 1340 S Canal St
- **Chase (ATM)** • Walgreens • 316 W Cermak Rd
- **Citibank** • 2022 S Archer Ave
- **International Bank of Chicago** • 200 W Cermak Rd
- **Lakeside** • 2200 S Archer Ave
- **National City Bank** • 1733 S Clark St
- **South Central** • 2335 S Wentworth Ave

Gas Stations

- **Shell** • 1741 S Ruble St

Landmarks

- **Chinatown Gate** • S Wentworth Ave & W Cermak Rd
- **Chinatown Square** • S Archer Ave
- **On Leong Merchants Association Building** • 2216 S Wentworth Ave
- **Pacific Garden Mission** • 1458 S Canal St
- **Ping Tom Memorial Park** • 300 W 19th St
- **Raymond Hilliard Apartments** • 2111 S Clark St

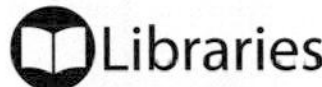

Libraries

- **Chinatown Public Library** • 2353 S Wentworth Ave

Parking

Pharmacies

- **Dominick's** • 1340 S Canal St
- **Walgreens** • 316 W Cermak Rd

Pizza

- **Connie's Pizza** • 2373 S Archer Ave
- **Domino's** • 1234 S Canal St

Post Offices

- **US Post Office** • 2345 S Wentworth Ave

Schools

- **John C Haines Elementary** • 247 W 23rd Pl
- **National Teacher's Academy** • 55 W Cermak Rd
- **Pui Tak Christian** • 2301 S Wentworth Ave
- **South Loop Elementary** • 1212 S Plymouth Ct
- **St Therese** • 247 W 23rd St

Supermarkets

- **Dominick's** • 1340 S Canal St
- **Richwell Market** • 1835 S Canal St
- **Tai Wah Grocery** • 2226 S Wentworth Ave

Map 10 • East Pilsen / Chinatown

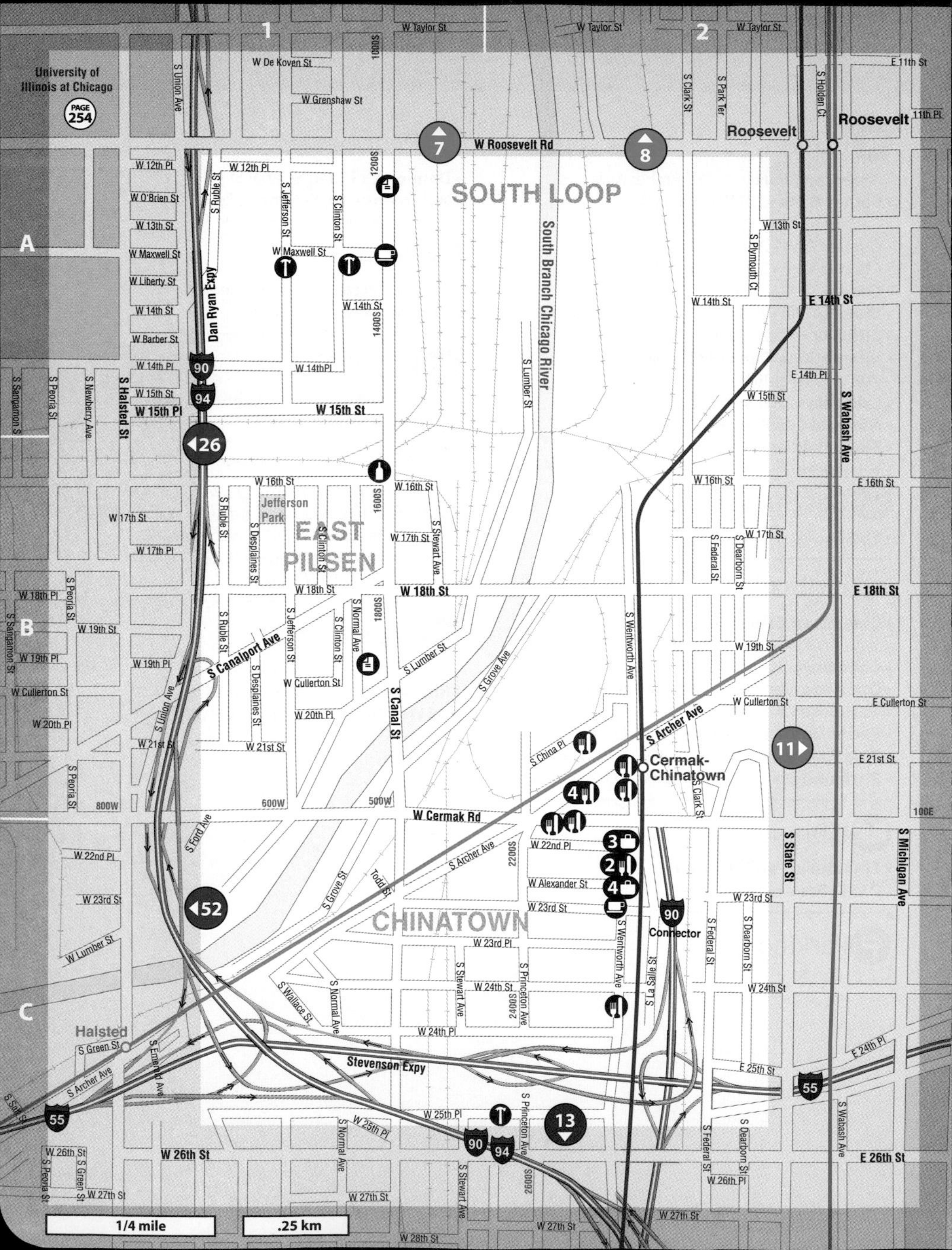

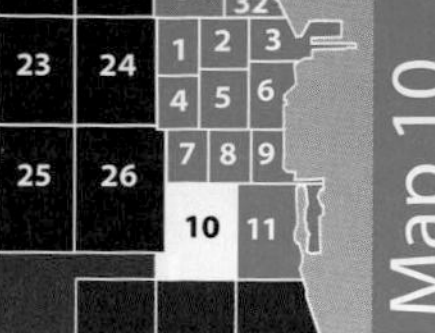

Would-be collectors make their rounds sipping wine and looking for the next Ed Paschke at the annual gallery crawl in East Pilsen; second Fridays of the month are a staple for staying current in the art scene and exploring the famous Podmajersky gardens. Find cookware, finger traps, rice candy, and bamboo back-scratchers galore while shopping Chinatown, and stop in at Joy Yee's Noodles for a tapioca freeze.

Coffee

- **Chi Cafe** • 2160 S Archer Ave
- **Starbucks** • Dominick's • 1340 S Canal St
- **Tasty Place Bakery & Cafe** • 2339 S Wentworth Ave

Copy Shops

- **Athena** • 1882 S Normal Ave
- **FedEx Kinko's** • 1242 S Canal St

Hardware Stores

- **Home Depot** • 1300 S Clinton St
- **Turek & Sons True Value** • 1333 S Jefferson St
- **Zweifel True Value Hardware** • 345 W 25th Pl

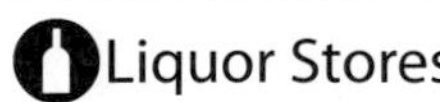

Liquor Stores

- **Vetoux Fine Wine** • 1001 S Canal St

Restaurants

- **Chi Café** • 2160 S Wentworth Ave
- **Double Li** • 228 W Cermak Rd
- **Emperor's Choice** • 2238 S Wentworth Ave
- **Evergreen** • 2411 S Wentworth Ave
- **Happy Chef Dim Sum House** • 2164 S Archer Ave
- **Joy Yee's Noodles** • 2139 S China Pl
- **Lao Sze Chuan Spicy City** • 2172 S Archer Ave
- **Phoenix** • 2131 S Archer Ave
- **Saint's Alp Teahouse** •2131 S Archer Ave
- **Shui Wah** • 2162 S Archer Ave
- **Three Happiness** • 209 W Cermak Rd
- **Won Kow** • 2237 S Wentworth Ave

Shopping

- **Chinatown Bazaar** • 2221 S Wentworth Ave
- **Feida Bakery** • 2228 S Wentworth Ave
- **Giftland** • 2212 S Wentworth Ave
- **Pacific Furniture** • 2200 S Wentworth Ave
- **Sun Sun Tong** • 2260 S Wentworth Ave
- **Ten Ren Tea** • 2247 S Wentworth Ave
- **Woks 'n' Things** • 2234 S Wentworth Ave

Map 11 • South Loop / McCormick Place

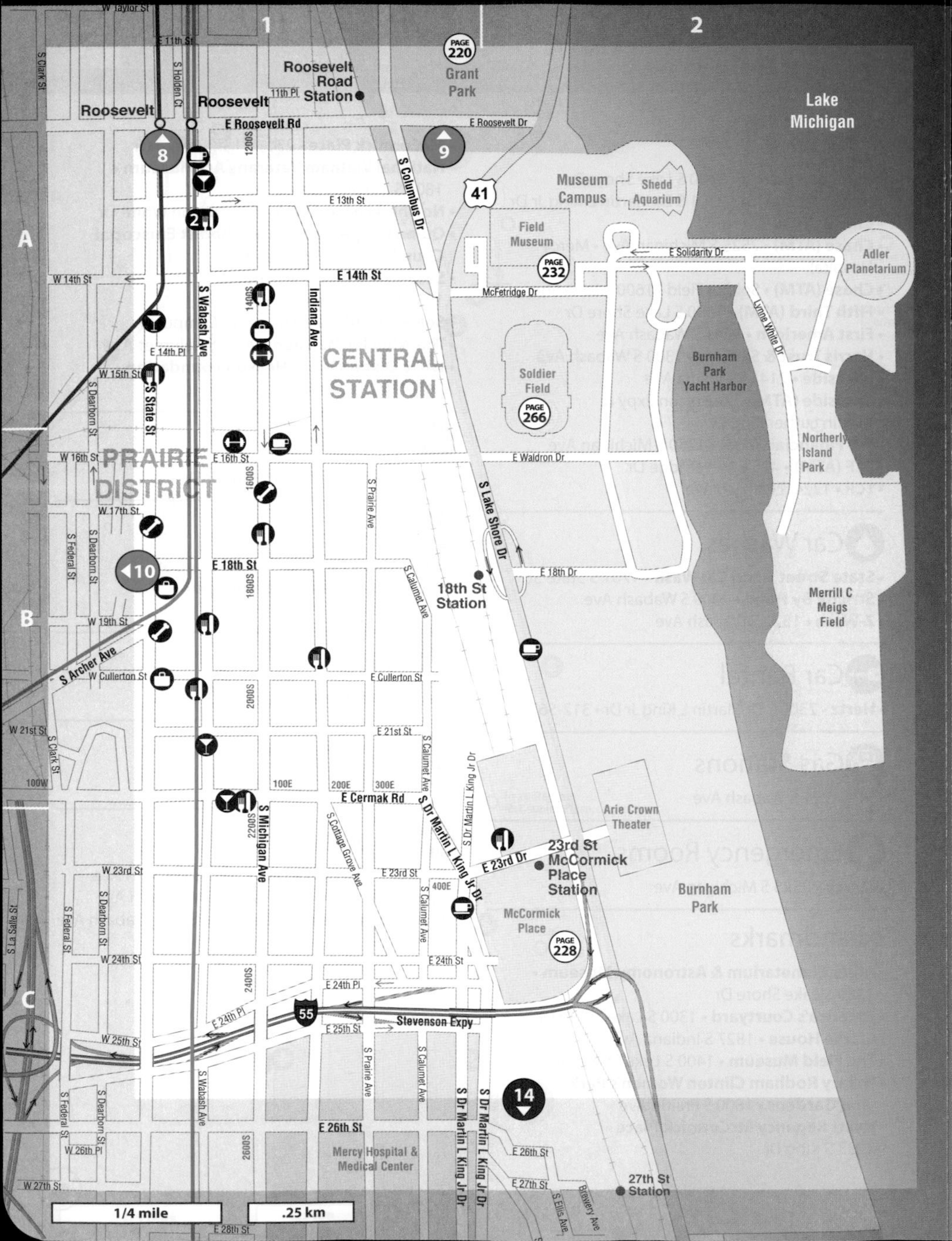

N
1
2
A
B
C
Roosevelt Road Station
Grant Park
Lake Michigan
Roosevelt
Roosevelt
E Roosevelt Rd
E Roosevelt Dr
11th Pl
W Taylor St
E 11th St
S Clark St
S Holden Ct
8
9
10
14
41
55
PAGE 220
PAGE 232
PAGE 266
PAGE 228
S Columbus Dr
Museum Campus
Shedd Aquarium
Field Museum
E 13th St
E Solidarity Dr
Adler Planetarium
E 14th St
W 14th St
McFetridge Dr
S Wabash Ave
Indiana Ave
Lynne White Dr
E 14th Pl
W 15th St
S State St
S Dearborn St
CENTRAL STATION
Soldier Field
Burnham Park Yacht Harbor
Northerly Island Park
W 16th St
E 16th St
PRAIRIE DISTRICT
E Waldron Dr
S Prairie Ave
S Lake Shore Dr
W 17th St
S Federal St
E 18th St
E 18th Dr
S Calumet Ave
18th St Station
Merrill C Meigs Field
W 19th St
S Archer Ave
W Cullerton St
E Cullerton St
W 21st St
E 21st St
100W
100E
200E
300E
E Cermak Rd
S Dr Martin L King Jr Dr
S Cottage Grove Ave
S Michigan Ave
Arie Crown Theater
23rd St McCormick Place Station
E 23rd Dr
W 23rd St
E 23rd St
400E
McCormick Place
Burnham Park
S La Salle St
W 24th St
E 24th St
E 24th Pl
E 24th Pl
Stevenson Expy
W 25th St
E 25th St
E 26th St
W 26th Pl
E 26th St
Mercy Hospital & Medical Center
W 27th St
E 27th St
S Ellis Ave
Brewery Ave
27th St Station
E 28th St
1/4 mile
.25 km
1200S
1400S
1600S
1800S
2000S
2200S
2400S
2600S

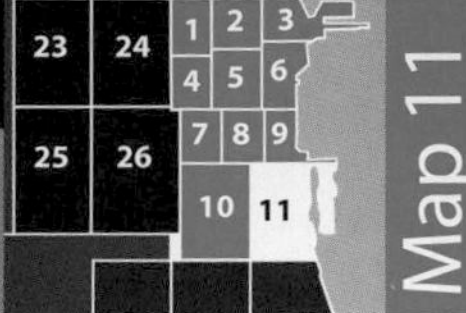

Though many Capone-related landmarks became casualties of '90s gentrification, the South Loop still boasts attractions like a burgeoning restaurant scene. The Chicago Firehouse is a fancy white-table cloth spot specializing in prime steaks and seafood, not the burgers and ribs spot conjured by its name. Trendies dine at theatrical spots like Opera while old-schoolers flock to live jazz at Velvet Lounge or toss back suds at Wabash Tap. Prestigious addresses of the Prairie Avenue Historic District attract history buffs, particularly those specializing in art and architecture.

Coffee

- **Dunkin' Donuts** • 1575 S Michigan Ave
- **Dunkin' Donuts** • 1231 S Wabash Ave
- **Starbucks** • McCormick Con Ctr—Mezzanine • 2301 S Dr Martin L King Jr Dr
- **Starbucks** • McCormick Con Center—North Food Ct • 2301 S Lake Shore Dr

Gyms

- **Curves (women only)** • 77 E 16th St
- **Phenomenal Fitness** • 1450 S Michigan Ave

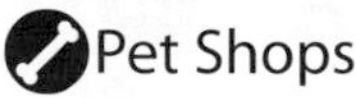

Nightlife

- **Reggie's** • 2109 S State St
- **M Lounge** • 1520 S Wabash Ave
- **Velvet Lounge** • 67 E Cermak Rd
- **Wabash Tap** • 1233 S Wabash Ave

Pet Shops

- **Dogone Fun** • 1717 S State St
- **Downtown Pets (Fish only)** • 1619 S Michigan Ave
- **Soggy Paws** • 1912 S State St

Restaurants

- **Chef Luciano** • 49 E Cermak Rd
- **Chicago Firehouse Restaurant** • 1401 S Michigan Ave
- **Cuatro** • 2030 S Wabash Ave
- **Gioco** • 1312 S Wabash Ave
- **Kroll's** • 1736 S Michigan Ave
- **La Cantina Grill** • 1911 S Michigan Ave
- **Opera** • 1301 S Wabash Ave
- **Tapas Valencia** • 1530 S State St
- **Zapatista** • 1307 S Wabash Ave

Shopping

- **Blue Star Auto Stores** • 2001 S State St
- **Cycle Bike Shop** • 1465 S Michigan Ave
- **Waterware** • 1829 S State St

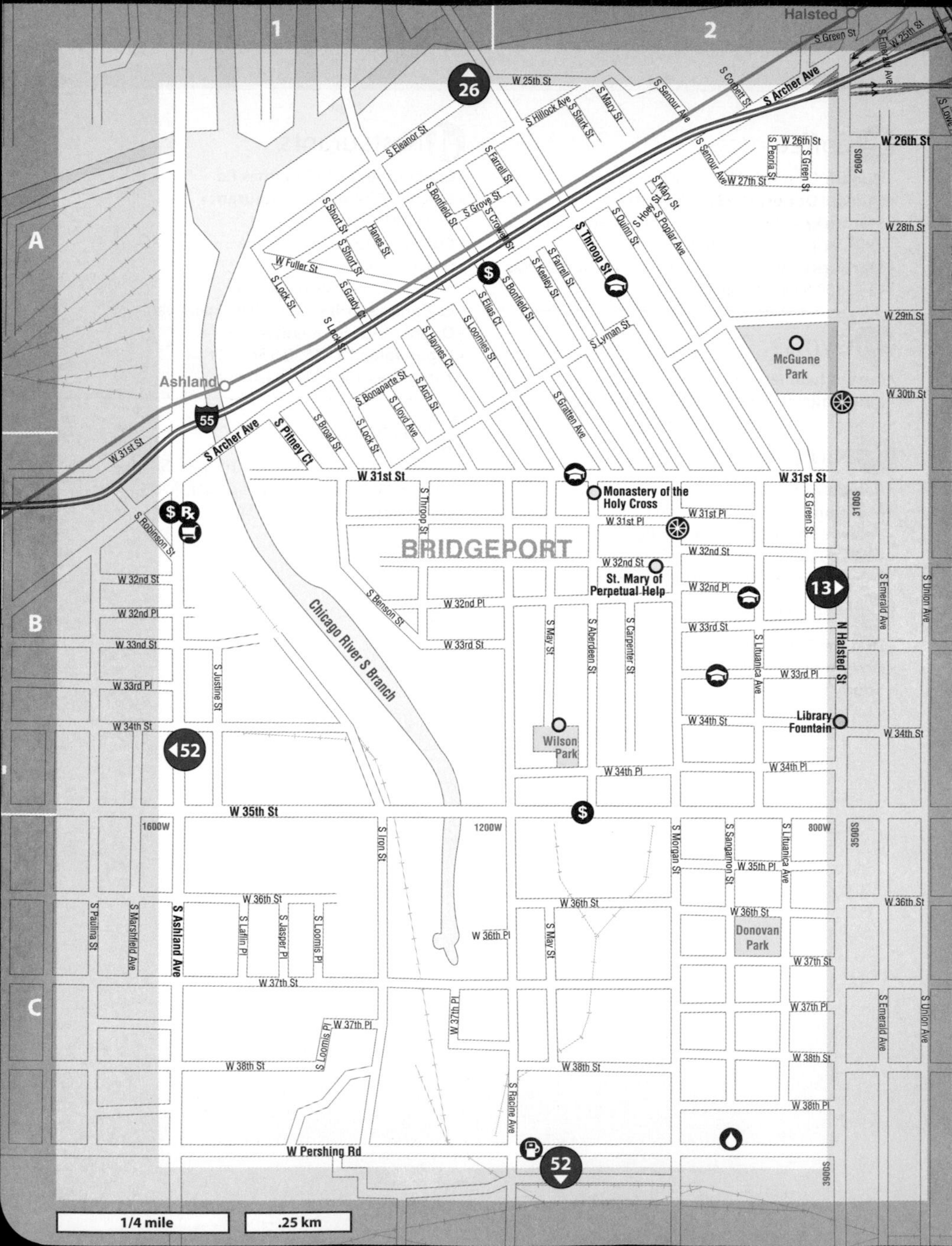

N
1
2
A
B
C
26
13
52
52
Halsted
Ashland
55
BRIDGEPORT
McGuane Park
Monastery of the Holy Cross
St. Mary of Perpetual Help
Library Fountain
Wilson Park
Donovan Park
Chicago River S Branch
S Archer Ave
W 25th St
W 26th St
W 27th St
W 28th St
W 29th St
W 30th St
W 31st St
W 31st Pl
W 32nd St
W 32nd Pl
W 33rd St
W 33rd Pl
W 34th St
W 34th Pl
W 35th St
W 35th Pl
W 36th St
W 36th Pl
W 37th St
W 37th Pl
W 38th St
W 38th Pl
W Pershing Rd
W Fuller St
S Ashland Ave
S Paulina St
S Marshfield Ave
S Laflin Pl
S Jasper Pl
S Loomis Pl
S Justine St
S Robinson St
S Iron St
S Racine Ave
S May St
S Aberdeen St
S Carpenter St
S Morgan St
S Sangamon St
S Lituanica Ave
S Green St
N Halsted St
S Emerald Ave
S Union Ave
S Lowe
S Throop St
S Benson St
S Pitney Ct
S Broad St
S Lock St
S Lloyd Ave
S Arch St
S Bonaparte St
S Haynes Ct
S Loomis St
S Elias Ct
S Bonfield St
S Keeley St
S Farrell St
S Gratten Ave
S Lyman St
S Quinn St
S Holy St
S Poplar Ave
S Mary St
S Senour Ave
S Corbett St
S Peoria St
S Hillock Ave
S Stark St
S Eleanor St
S Short St
S Hanes St
S Grove St
S Crowell St
S Grady Ct
1600W
1200W
800W
2600S
3100S
3500S
3900S
1/4 mile
.25 km

Essentials

Nestled just north of the old stockyards, this area's jumbo land parcels and warehouses ripe for conversions have spurred pockets of development. Most notable is tony Bridgeport Village, set smack-dab on a stretch of the Chicago River known as Bubbly Creek, so-named for its gaseous stew made from the animal carcasses dumped in it by the former stockyards. Its banks now boast pricey homes, but the bubbles still linger.

Banks

- **Chase** • 3145 S Ashland Ave
- **Chicago Community** • 1110 W 35th St
- **Washington Federal** • 2869 S Archer Ave

Car Washes

- **Pershing Road Car Wash** • 940 W Pershing Rd

Gas Stations

- **Citgo** • 970 W Pershing Rd

Landmarks

- **Library Fountain** • W 34th St & Halsted St
- **McGuane Park** • 2901 S Poplar Ave
- **Monastery of the Holy Cross** • 3111 S Aberdeen St
- **St Mary of Perpetual Help** • 1039 W 32nd St
- **Wilson Park** • S May St & W 34th Pl

Pharmacies

- **Dominick's** • 3145 S Ashland Ave

Pizza

- **Lina's Pizza** • 3132 S Morgan St
- **Little Caesar's Pizza** • 3010 S Halsted St

Schools

- **Armour Branch** • 911 W 32nd St
- **Charles N Holden Elementary** • 1104 W 31st St
- **Philip D Armour Elementary** • 950 W 33rd Pl
- **St Barbara Elementary** • 2867 S Throop St

Supermarkets

- **Dominick's** • 3145 S Ashland Ave

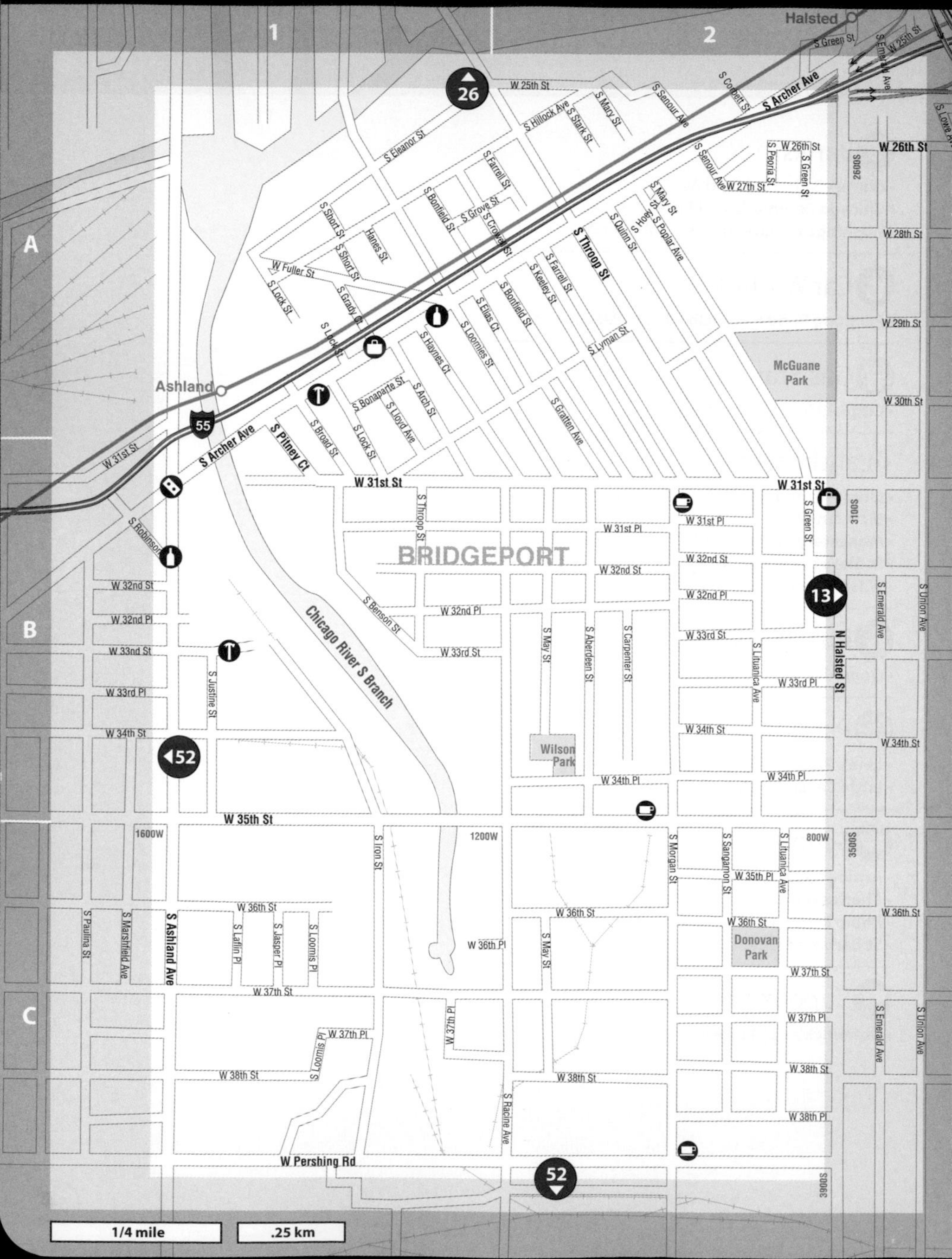

Map 12 • Bridgeport (West)

N

1
2
A
B
C

Halsted
Ashland
55
26
13
52
52

BRIDGEPORT

McGuane Park
Wilson Park
Donovan Park
Chicago River S Branch

S Archer Ave
W 25th St
S Green St
S Emerald Ave
W 25th St
S Lowe Ave
S Hillock Ave
S Stark St
S Mary St
S Senour Ave
S Corbett St
S Eleanor St
W 26th St
S Peoria St
S Green St
2600S
S Senour Ave
W 27th St
S Farrell St
S Bonfield St
S Grove St
S Crowell St
S Short St
Hanes St
S Short St
S Mary St
S Hoey St
S Poplar Ave
S Quinn St
S Throop St
W 28th St
W Fuller St
S Lock St
S Grady Ct
S Farrell St
S Keeley St
S Bonfield St
S Elias Ct
S Loomis St
S Lyman St
S Lock St
S Haynes Ct
W 29th St
S Bonaparte St
S Arch St
S Lloyd Ave
S Broad St
S Lock St
S Gratten Ave
W 30th St
W 31st St
S Pitney Ct
W 31st St
W 31st St
S Throop St
W 31st Pl
W 31st Pl
S Green St
3100S
S Robinson
W 32nd St
W 32nd St
W 32nd St
W 32nd Pl
W 32nd Pl
S Benson St
W 32nd Pl
W 33rd St
W 33rd St
W 33nd St
S Emerald Ave
S Union Ave
N Halsted St
S May St
S Aberdeen St
S Carpenter St
S Lituanica Ave
W 33rd Pl
W 33rd Pl
S Justine St
W 34th St
W 34th St
W 34th St
W 34th Pl
W 34th Pl
W 35th St
1600W
1200W
800W
3500S
S Iron St
S Morgan St
S Sangamon St
S Lituanica Ave
W 35th Pl
W 36th St
W 36th St
W 36th St
W 36th St
S Paulina St
S Marshfield Ave
S Ashland Ave
S Laflin Pl
S Jasper Pl
S Loomis Pl
W 36th Pl
S May St
W 37th St
W 37th St
W 37th Pl
W 37th Pl
W 37th Pl
S Loomis Pl
S Emerald Ave
S Union Ave
W 38th St
W 38th St
W 38th St
S Racine Ave
W 38th Pl
W Pershing Rd
3900S

1/4 mile
.25 km

Sundries / Entertainment

Hopefully, Bridgeport's residential revival will eventually spur business and entertainment in the community. (Tell your friends to invest in one of those lofts….) Right now, a big night out is watching a Sox game at a corner tavern or renting a video from Blockbuster.

Coffee

- **Bridgeport Coffeehouse** • 3101 S Morgan St
- **Dunkin' Donuts** • 970 W Pershing Rd
- **Zhou B Café** • 1029 W 35th St

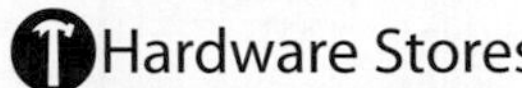

Hardware Stores

- **Cremieux Supply** • 3015 S Archer Ave
- **Elston Ace Hardware** • 1514 W 33rd St

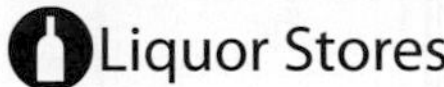

Liquor Stores

- **All Star Food & Liquors** • 2911 S Archer Ave
- **Ashland S** • 3162 S Ashland Ave

Shopping

- **Bridgeport Antique Mall** • 2963 S Archer Ave
- **Unique Thrift Store** • 3000 S Halsted St

Video Rental

- **Blockbuster** • 3145 S Ashland Ave

Map 13 • Bridgeport (East)

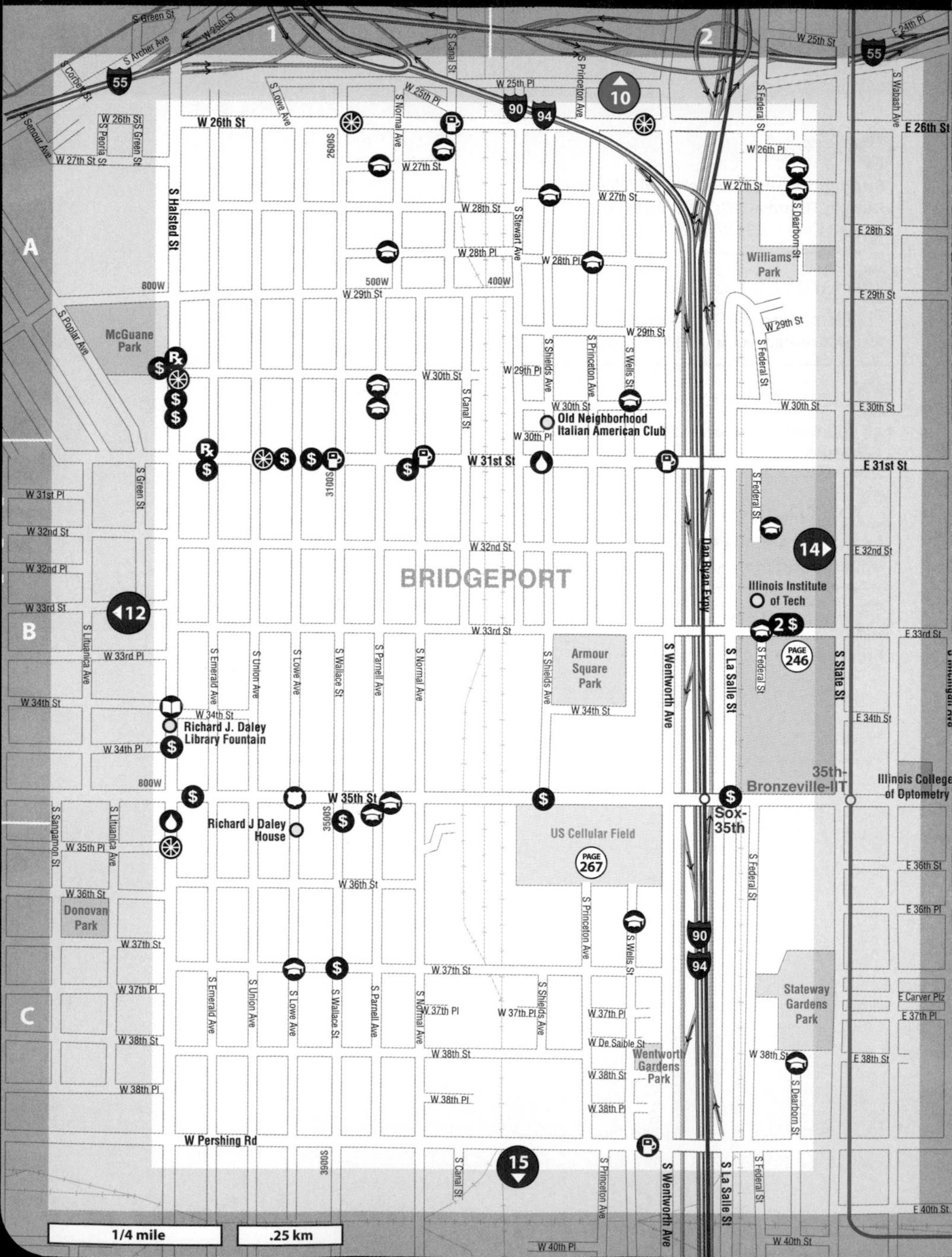
N
1
2
A
B
C
55
90
94
10
12
14
15
BRIDGEPORT
McGuane Park
Williams Park
Illinois Institute of Tech
Armour Square Park
US Cellular Field
Donovan Park
Stateway Gardens Park
Wentworth Gardens Park
Old Neighborhood Italian American Club
Richard J. Daley Library Fountain
Richard J Daley House
35th-Bronzeville-IIT
Sox-35th
Illinois College of Optometry
PAGE 246
PAGE 267
Dan Ryan Expy
S Halsted St
S Wentworth Ave
S La Salle St
S State St
S Canal St
W 26th St
W 31st St
W 35th St
W Pershing Rd
E 26th St
E 31st St
800W
500W
400W
3000S
3100S
3500S
3900S
1/4 mile
.25 km

Bridgeport exemplifies how the "City That Works" actually works. The stomping grounds of the Daley family and de facto political center of the city, Bridgeport is also the quintessential Chicago neighborhood with its close-knit residents, legions of patronage workers, and distinctive "dese, dem, and dose" vernacular.

Banks

- **Bank of America (ATM)** • 333 W 35th St
- **Charter One** • 600 W 37th St
- **Chase** • 757 W 35th St
- **Chase (ATM)** • 142 W 35th St
- **Chase (ATM)** • Walgreens • 3000 S Halsted St
- **Chase (ATM)** • 3241 S Federal St
- **Citibank** • 3430 S Halsted St
- **First American (ATM)** • 659 W 31st St
- **Marquette** • 615 W 31st St
- **Marquette (ATM)** • 501 W 31st St
- **National City Bank** • 3241 S Federal St
- **South Central** • 3032 S Halsted St
- **TCF (ATM)** • Jewel • 3033 S Halsted St
- **TCF (ATM)** • Osco • 741 W 31st St

Car Washes

- **J&J Full Service Car Wash** • 349 W 31st St
- **Looking Good Hand Car Wash** • 3540 S Halsted St

Gas Stations

- **Citgo** • 501 W 31st St
- **Clark Oil** • 444 W 26th St
- **Marathon** • 659 W 31st St
- **Mobil** • 243 W Pershing Rd
- **Shell** • 215 W 31st St

Landmarks

- **Illinois Institute of Technology** • 31st to 35th St, b/w Dan Ryan Expy & Michigan Ave
- **Old Neighborhood Italian American Club** • 3031 S Shields Ave
- **Richard J Daley House** • 3536 S Lowe Ave
- **Richard J. Daley Library Fountain** • 3400 S Halsted St

Libraries

- **Richard J. Daley Public Library** • **3400 S Halsted St**

Pharmacies

- **CVS** • 741 W 31st St
- **Walgreens** • 3000 S Halsted St

Pizza

- **Freddie's Pizza & Pasta Parlor** • 701 W 31st St
- **Little Caesars Pizza** • 3010 S Halsted St
- **Phil's Pizza** • 3551 S Halsted St
- **Punky's Pizza & Pasta** • 2600 S Wallace St
- **Ricobene's** • 252 W 26th St

Police

- **9th District (Deering)** • 3501 S Lowe Ave

Schools

- **Big Picture Company High** • 2710 S Dearborn St
- **Bridgeport Catholic Academy** • 3700 S Lowe Ave
- **Bridgeport Catholic Academy North** • 512 W 28th Pl
- **Crispus Attucks Elementary** • 3813 S Dearborn St
- **Doolittle East Primary** • 535 E 35th St
- **Doolittle Middle** • 535 E 35th St
- **George B McClellan Elementary** • 3527 S Wallace St
- **Illinois Institute of Technology** • 3300 S Federal St
- **James Ward Elementary** • 2701 S Shields Ave
- **KIPP Chicago Youth Village Academy** • 2710 S Dearborn St
- **Mark Sheridan Math & Science Academy** • 533 W 27th St
- **Robert Healy Annex** • 3040 S Parnell Ave
- **Robert Healy Elementary** • 3010 S Parnell Ave
- **Robert S Abbott Elementary** • 3630 S Wells St
- **Santa Lucia** • 3017 S Wells St
- **St Jerome** • 2805 S Princeton Ave
- **Vandercook College of Music** • 3140 S Federal St
- **Williams Elementary** • 2710 S Dearborn St
- **Williams Middle** • 2710 S Dearborn St

Map 15 • Canaryville / Fuller Park

N
1
2
A
B
C
CANARYVILLE
FULLER PARK
ROB TAYLOR HOMES
Tailor-Lauridsen Park
Fuller Park
Tailor Park
W 38th St
W 38th Pl
E 38th St
W Pershing Rd
E Pershing Rd
W 40th Pl
W 40th St
E 40th St
W 41st St
W Exchange Ave
W Root St
W 42nd St
W 42nd Pl
W 43rd St
E 43rd St
W 43rd Pl
W 44th St
W 44th Pl
W 45th St
E 45th St
W 45th Pl
W 46th St
W 46th Pl
W Swann St
W 47th St
E 47th St
47th St
W 47th Pl
W 48th St
E 48th St
W 48th Pl
W 49th St
E 49th St
W 49th Pl
W 50th St
W 50th Pl
W 51st St
E 51st St
W 51st Pl
W 52nd St
W 52nd Pl
S Emerald Ave
S Union Ave
S Lowe Ave
S Wallace St
S Canal St
S Princeton Ave
S Wentworth Ave
S La Salle St
Dan Ryan Expy
S Federal St
S Dearborn St
S Stewart Ave
S Parnell Ave
S Normal Ave
S Shields Ave
S Wells St
Portland Ave
S State St
S Wabash Ave
S Halsted St
S Michigan Ave
3900S
4300S
4700S
5100S
800W
400W
200W
90
94
13
16
52
57
2
4
1/4 mile
.25 km

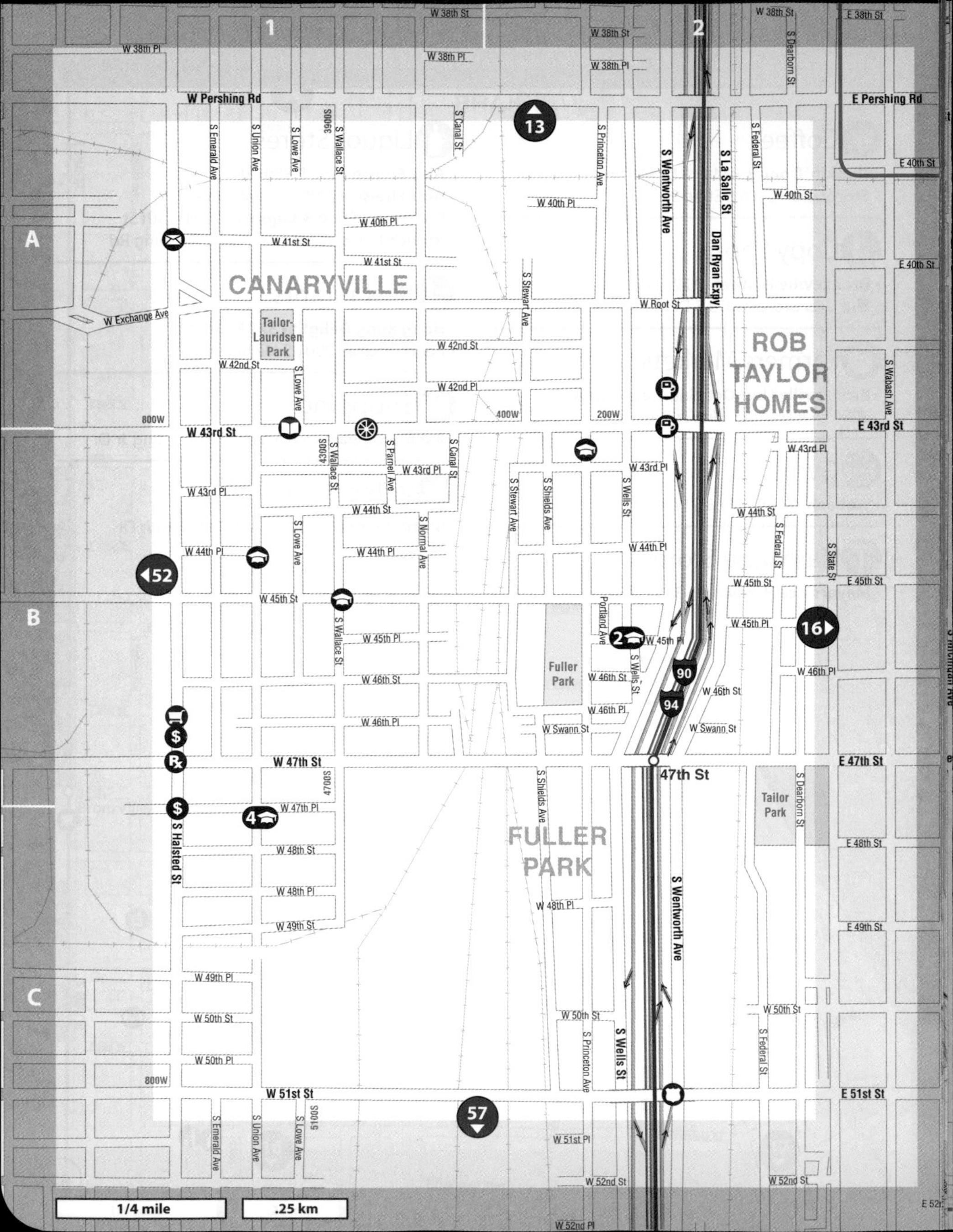

Essentials

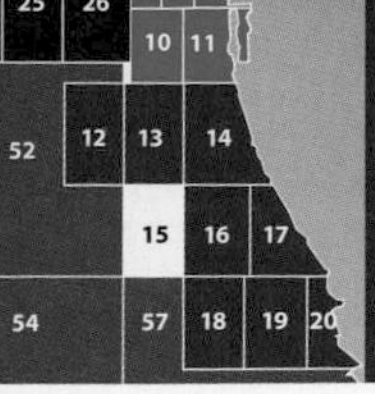

Christmas 1865 was a bad day for livestock, as the sprawling Union Stock Yards opened, sending all beasts on the lookout. All that's left now is the imposing limestone gate (moment of silence). While cattle around the country breathed a collective sigh when the Yards closed, this area headed south afterwards and is still in recovery.

Banks

- **Chase (ATM)** • Walgreens • 4701 S Halsted St
- **First American (ATM)** • 4640 S Halsted St

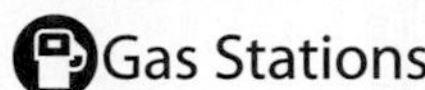

Gas Stations

- **Citgo** • 4300 S Wentworth Ave
- **Econo-Gas** • 4248 S Wentworth Ave

Libraries

- **Canaryville Public Library** • 642 W 43rd St

Pharmacies

- **Walgreens** • 4700 S Halsted St

Pizza

- **Pizza Nova** • 558 W 43rd St

Police

- **2nd District (Wentworth)** • 5101 S Wentworth Ave

Post Offices

- **US Post Office** • 4101 S Halsted St

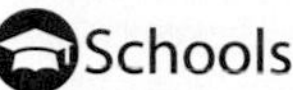

Schools

- **Alexander Graham Elementary** • 4436 S Union Ave
- **Bronzeville Academic Center** • 220 W 45th Pl
- **Francis Parkman Elementary** • 245 W 51st St
- **Garfield Alternative High** • 220 W 45th Pl
- **John H Sengstacke Achievement Academy** • 4747 S Union Ave
- **Sengstacke Academic Preparation** • 4747 S Union Ave
- **St Gabriel Elementary** • 4500 S Wallace St
- **Thomas A Hendricks Community Academy** • 4316 S Princeton Ave
- **Tilden Career Communty Academy High** • 4747 S Union Ave
- **Tilden High** • 4747 S Union Ave

Supermarkets

- **Fairplay Finer Foods** • 4640 S Halsted St

N

CANARYVILLE
FULLER PARK
ROB TAYLOR HOMES
Tailor-Lauridsen Park
Fuller Park
Tailor Park
W Pershing Rd
E Pershing Rd
W 43rd St
E 43rd St
W 47th St
E 47th St
47th St
W 51st St
E 51st St
S Halsted St
S Wentworth Ave
S La Salle St
Dan Ryan Expy
S Wells St
S Canal St
S Wallace St
S Lowe Ave
S Union Ave
S Emerald Ave
S Princeton Ave
S Stewart Ave
S Shields Ave
S Parnell Ave
S Normal Ave
S Federal St
S Dearborn St
S State St
S Wabash Ave
Portland Ave
W Exchange Ave
W Root St
W Swann St
W 38th St
W 38th Pl
W 40th Pl
W 41st St
W 42nd St
W 42nd Pl
W 43rd Pl
W 44th St
W 44th Pl
W 45th St
W 45th Pl
W 46th St
W 46th Pl
W 47th Pl
W 48th St
W 48th Pl
W 49th St
W 49th Pl
W 50th St
W 50th Pl
W 51st Pl
W 52nd St
W 52nd Pl
E 38th St
E 40th St
E 45th St
E 48th St
E 49th St
800W
400W
200W
300S
4300S
4700S
5100S
90
94

13
52
16
57

1/4 mile
.25 km

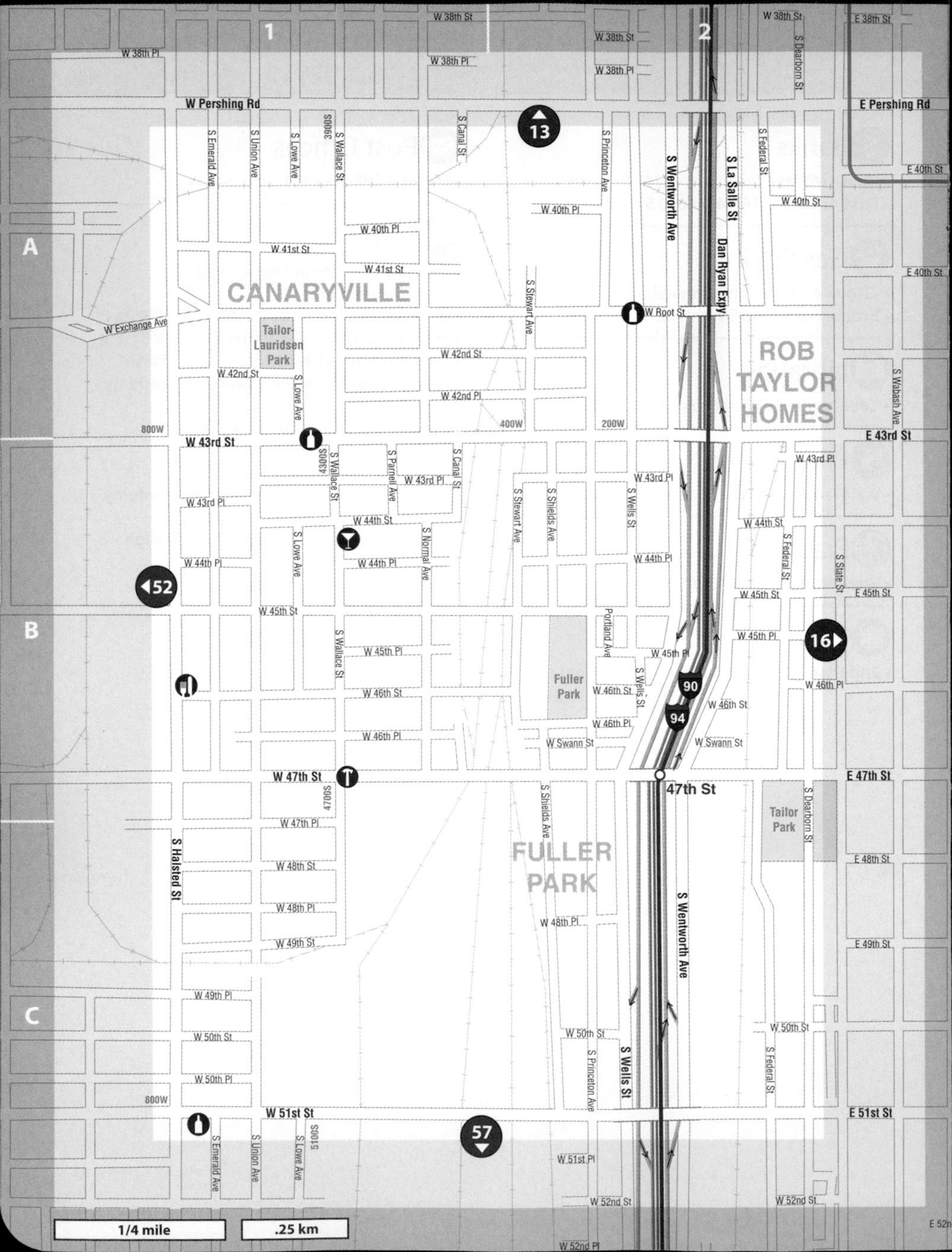

Canaryville and Fuller Park have retained scrappy and salt-of-the-earth sensibilities for years. The Union Stock Yards' closing in 1971 hit the community hard, and until recently it was a stone's throw away from the largest public housing complex in Chicago. Even urbanologists may be hard pressed to find much to do on a casual visit.

Nightlife

- **Kelley's Tavern** • 4403 S Wallace St

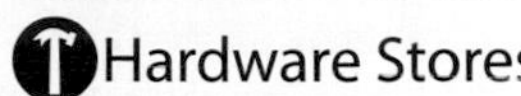

Hardware Stores

- **Discount Hardware** • 601 W 47th St

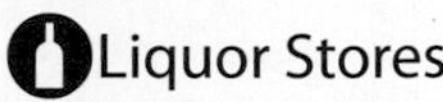

Liquor Stores

- **Dravo Liquors** • 619 W 43rd St
- **Root Inn** • 234 W Root St
- **Shamsan Food & Liquor** • 737 W 51st St

Restaurants

- **Amelia's Bar & Grill** • 4559 S Halstead St

Map 16 • Bronzeville

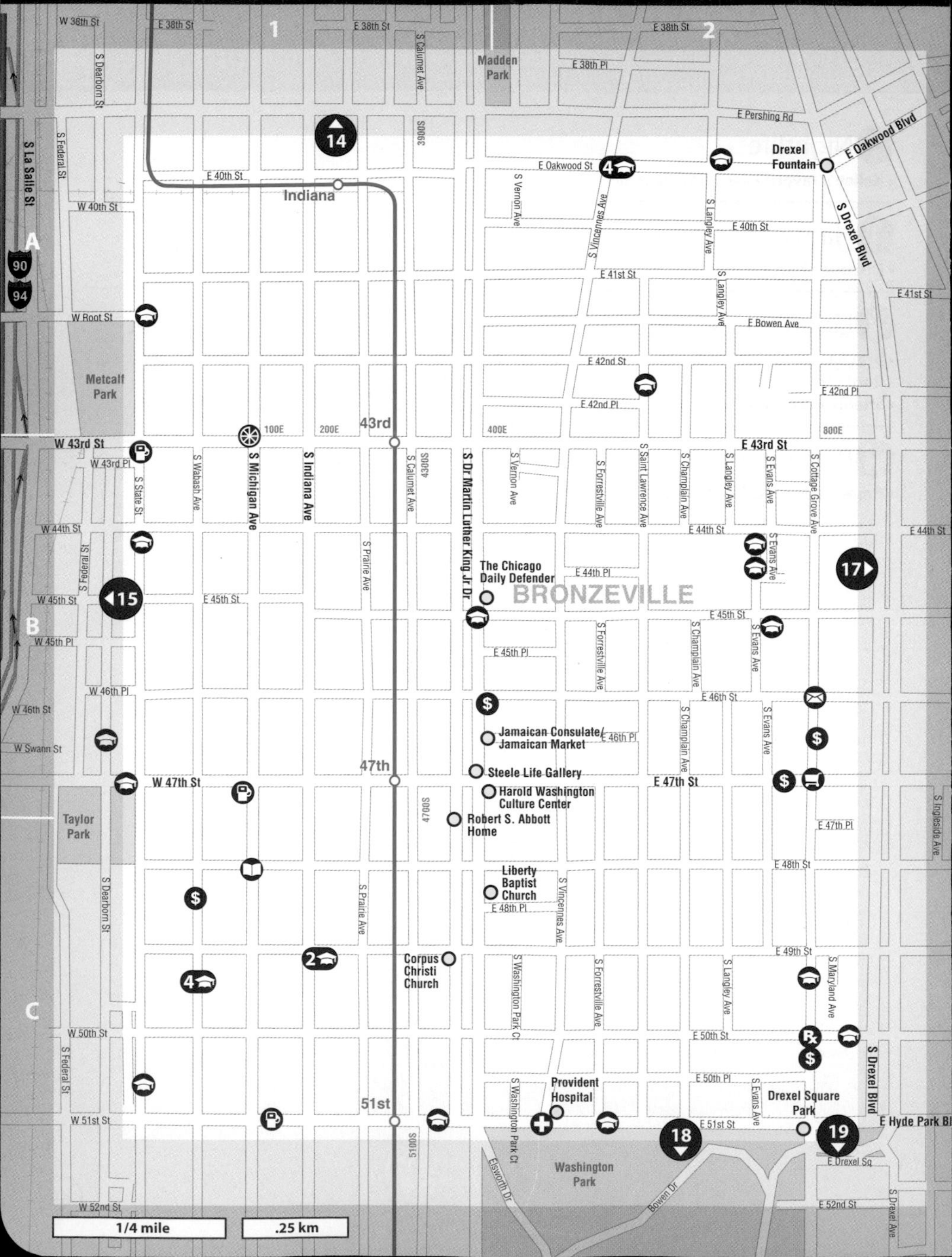

Madden Park
Indiana
43rd
47th
51st
Metcalf Park
Taylor Park
Washington Park
Drexel Square Park
Drexel Fountain
BRONZEVILLE
The Chicago Daily Defender
Jamaican Consulate/ Jamaican Market
Steele Life Gallery
Harold Washington Culture Center
Robert S. Abbott Home
Liberty Baptist Church
Corpus Christi Church
Provident Hospital
W 38th St
E 38th St
E 38th Pl
E Pershing Rd
E Oakwood Blvd
E Oakwood St
E 40th St
W 40th St
E 41st St
E Bowen Ave
W Root St
E 42nd St
E 42nd Pl
W 43rd St
E 43rd St
W 43rd Pl
W 44th St
E 44th St
E 44th Pl
W 45th St
E 45th St
W 45th Pl
E 45th Pl
W 46th Pl
W 46th St
E 46th St
E 46th Pl
W Swann St
W 47th St
E 47th St
E 47th Pl
E 48th St
E 48th Pl
E 49th St
W 50th St
E 50th St
E 50th Pl
W 51st St
E 51st St
E Hyde Park Bl
E Drexel Sq
W 52nd St
E 52nd St
S La Salle St
S Federal St
S Dearborn St
S State St
S Wabash Ave
S Michigan Ave
S Indiana Ave
S Prairie Ave
S Calumet Ave
S Dr Martin Luther King Jr Dr
S Vernon Ave
S Vincennes Ave
S Forrestville Ave
S Saint Lawrence Ave
S Champlain Ave
S Langley Ave
S Evans Ave
S Cottage Grove Ave
S Drexel Blvd
S Maryland Ave
S Ingleside Ave
S Washington Park Ct
S Drexel Ave
Ellsworth Dr
Bowen Dr
100E
200E
400E
800E
3600S
4300S
4700S
5100S
90
94
1/4 mile
.25 km

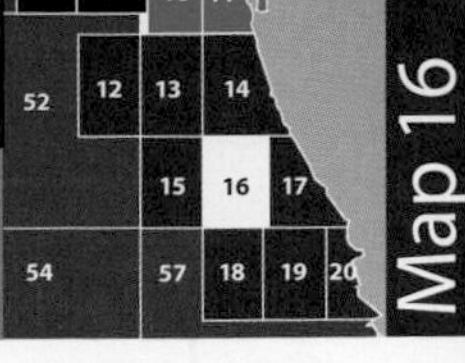

Far from its glorious roots, Bronzeville is trying to make a comeback from years of poverty, crime, empty lots, and dilapidated project housing. Today, there are many buppy implants, restored greystones, and overpriced condos. If you can wait out this slow rebirth and the recent changing of the aldermanic guard (the hat went splat after 23 years), once again, Bronzeville should become a great place to visit and an even better place to live.

Banks

- **Chase (ATM)** • Walgreens • 5036 S Cottage Grove Ave
- **Harris Trust & Savings (ATM)** • 4859 S Wabash Ave
- **Illinois Service Federal Savings** • 4619 S King Dr
- **Northern Trust (ATM)** • McDonald's • 740 E 47th St
- **Shore** • 4659 S Cottage Grove Ave

Gas Stations

- **Amoco** • 4300 S State St
- **Citgo** • 123 E 51st St
- **Marathon** • 4700 S Michigan Ave

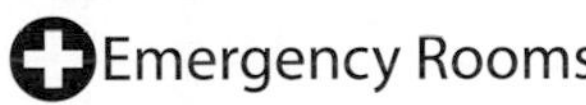

Emergency Rooms

- **Provident** • 500 E 51st St

Landmarks

- **The Chicago Daily Defender** • 4445 S King Dr
- **Corpus Christi Church** • 4900 S King Dr
- **Drexel Fountain** • S Drexel Blvd & E Oakwood Blvd
- **Drexel Square Park** • 5101 S Cottage Grove Ave
- **Harold Washington Cultural Center** • 4701 S King Dr
- **Jamaican Consulate/Jamaican Market Place** • 4655 S King Dr, Ste 201
- **Liberty Baptist Church** • 4849 S King Dr
- **Provident Hospital** • 500 E 51st St
- **Robert S Abbott Home** • 4742 S King Dr
- **Steele Life Gallery** • 4655 S King Dr

Libraries

- **Hall Public Library** • 4801 S Michigan Ave

Pharmacies

- **Walgreens** • 5036 S Cottage Grove Ave

Pizza

- **Pizza Ria** • 4300 S Michigan Ave

Post Offices

- **US Post Office** • 4601 S Cottage Grove Ave

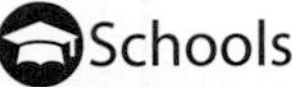

Schools

- **Anthony Overton, CPC** • 4935 S Indiana Ave
- **Anthony Overton Elementary** • 221 E 49th St
- **Bronzeville Scholastic Institute** • 4934 S Wabash Ave
- **Cain's Barber College** • 365 E 51st St
- **Carruthers Center for Inner City Studies, Northeastern Illinois University** • 700 E Oakwood Blvd
- **Colman Elementary** • 4655 S Dearborn St
- **DuSable Leadership Academy of B Shabazz** • 4934 S Wabash Ave
- **Dyett Academy Center** • 555 E 51st St
- **Hales Franciscan High** • 4930 S Cottage Grove Ave
- **Helen J McCorkle Elementary** • 4421 S State St
- **Holy Angels Elementary** • 545 E Oakwood Blvd
- **Irvin C Mollison Elementary** • 4415 S Dr Martin L King Jr Dr
- **Jean Baptiste Du Sable High** • 4934 S Wabash Ave
- **John Farren Elementary** • 5055 S State St
- **Ludwig Von Beethoven Elementary** • 25 W 47th St
- **Melville W Fuller Elementary** • 4214 S St Lawrence Ave
- **Milburn High** • 545 E Oakwood Blvd
- **St Elizabeth Elementary** • 4052 S Wabash Ave
- **William Reavis Elementary** • 834 E 50th St
- **Williams Preparatory School of Medicine** • 4934 S Wabash Ave
- **Woodson North Middle** • 4414 S Evans Ave
- **Woodson South CPC** • 4511 S Evans Ave
- **Woodson South Elementary** • 4444 S Evans Ave

Supermarkets

- **Save A Lot** • 4701 S Cottage Grove Ave

Map 16 • Bronzeville

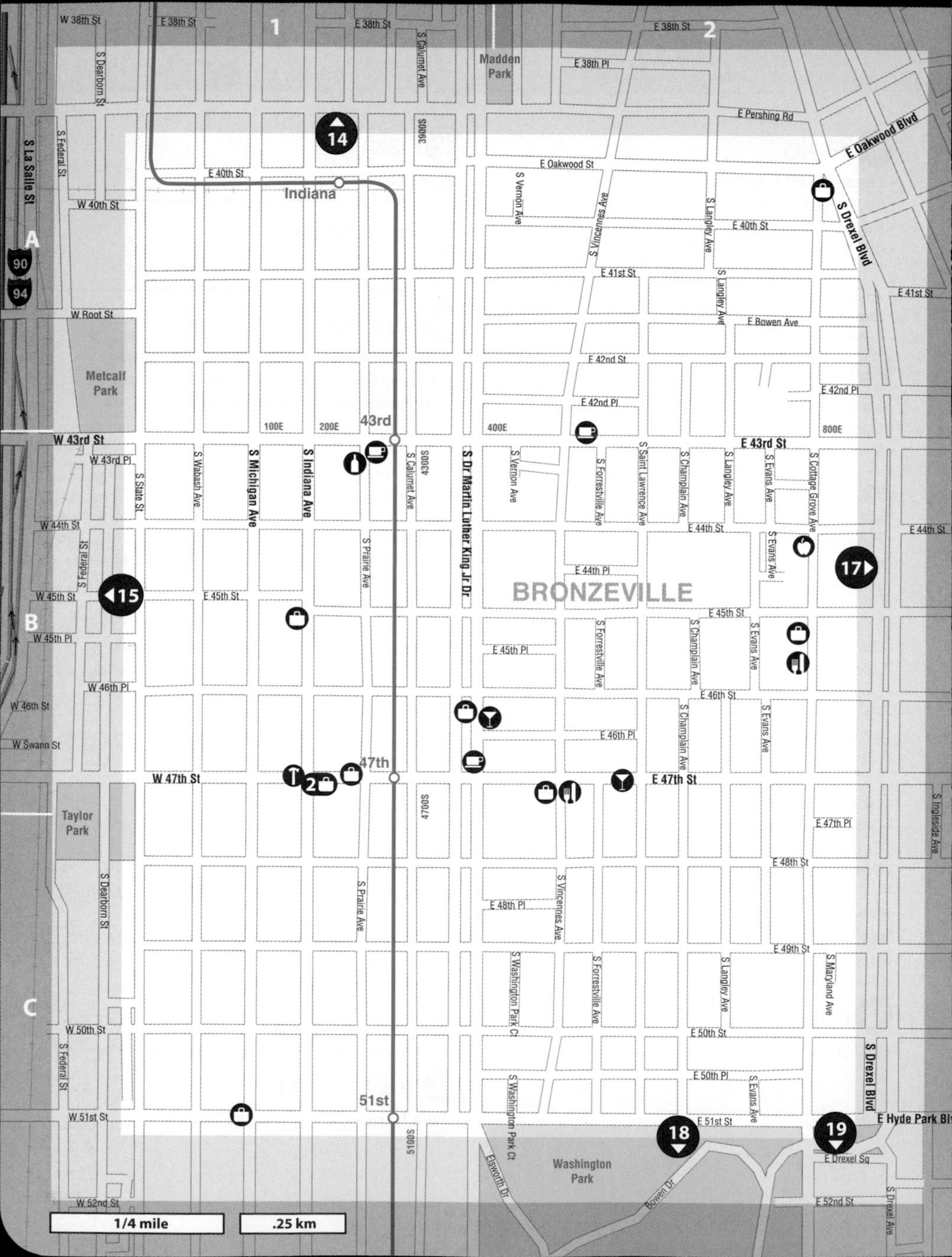

1/4 mile

.25 km

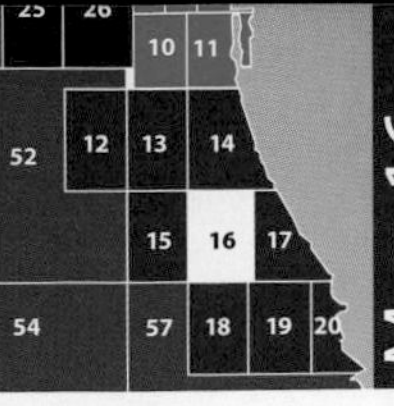

Attractions range from Jokes & Notes and the Harold Washington Cultural Center to the Afro-centric Bookstore, headquarters of the black literati, and the Steele Life Gallery, showcasing contemporary multicultural art. Sensual Steps offers sleek footwear during the day and frequent evening events. Blu 47 and Negro League Café offer upscale soul food.

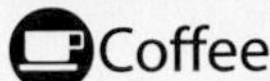

Coffee

- **Bronzeville Coffee House** • 528 E 43rd St

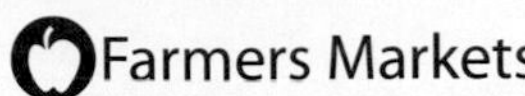

Farmers Markets

- **Bronzeville Community Market (Jun-Oct; Sat, 8 am-1 pm)** • 4400 S Cottage Grove Ave

Hardware Stores

- **Brooks Hardware** • 103 E 47th St

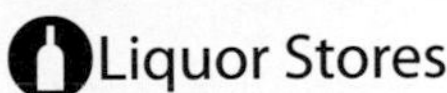

Liquor Stores

- **Calumet Food & Liquor** • 315 E 43rd St

Nightlife

- **Jokes & Notes** • 4641 S King Dr
- **New Bonanza Lounge** • 552 E 47th St
- **The Spoken Word** • 4655 S King Dr

Restaurants

- **Ain't She Sweet Café** • 4532 S Cottage Grove
- **Sweet Potatoes Café** • 501 E 47th St

Shopping

- **Afrocentric Bookstore** • 4655 S King Dr
- **Flawless** • 221 E 47th St
- **Ibiza** • 233 E 47th St
- **Issues Barber & Beauty Salon** • 3958 S Cottage Grove Ave
- **Jordan's Closet** • 106 E 51st St
- **Parker House Sausage Co** • 4605 S State St
- **Sensual Steps** • 4518 S Cottage Grove Ave
- **Stnx Galleria** • 4200 S Prairie Ave
- **Tribesmen Natural Hair Salon** • 4459 S Indiana Ave

N

1
2
A
B
C

Lake Michigan

OAKLAND
NORTH KENWOOD
KENWOOD

Burnham Park
Drexel Square Park
Little Black Pearl Art & Design Center
South Kenwood Mansions
Louis Farrakhan Home
George Blossom House
Warren McArthur House
Kenwood Park
Rainbow/PUSH Coalition Headquarters
Madison Park
Hyde Park Art Center
KAM Isaiah Israel
Barack Obama's Chicago Residence
47th

E Oakwood Blvd
S Drexel Blvd
S Oakenwald Ave
S Lake Park Ave
E 41st St
E 41st Pl
S Ellis Ave
E 42nd St
E 42nd Pl
E 43rd St
S Cottage Grove Ave
S Berkeley Ave
S Greenwood Ave
E 44th St
E 44th Pl Ext
S University Ave
E 46th St
E 47th St
E 47th Pl
S Ingleside Ave
S Woodlawn Ave
S Kimbark Ave
S Kenwood Ave
S Dorchester Ave
E 48th St
E 49th St
S Lake Shore Dr
S East End Ave
S Chicago Beach Dr
E 50th St
E 50th Pl
E Madison Park
E Hyde Park Blvd
S Blackstone Ave
S Cornell Ave
S Hyde Park Blvd
E Drexel Sq
S Drexel Ave
E 52nd St
3900S
4300S
4700S
5100S
800E
1200E
41
14
16
19
20
1/4 mile
.25 km

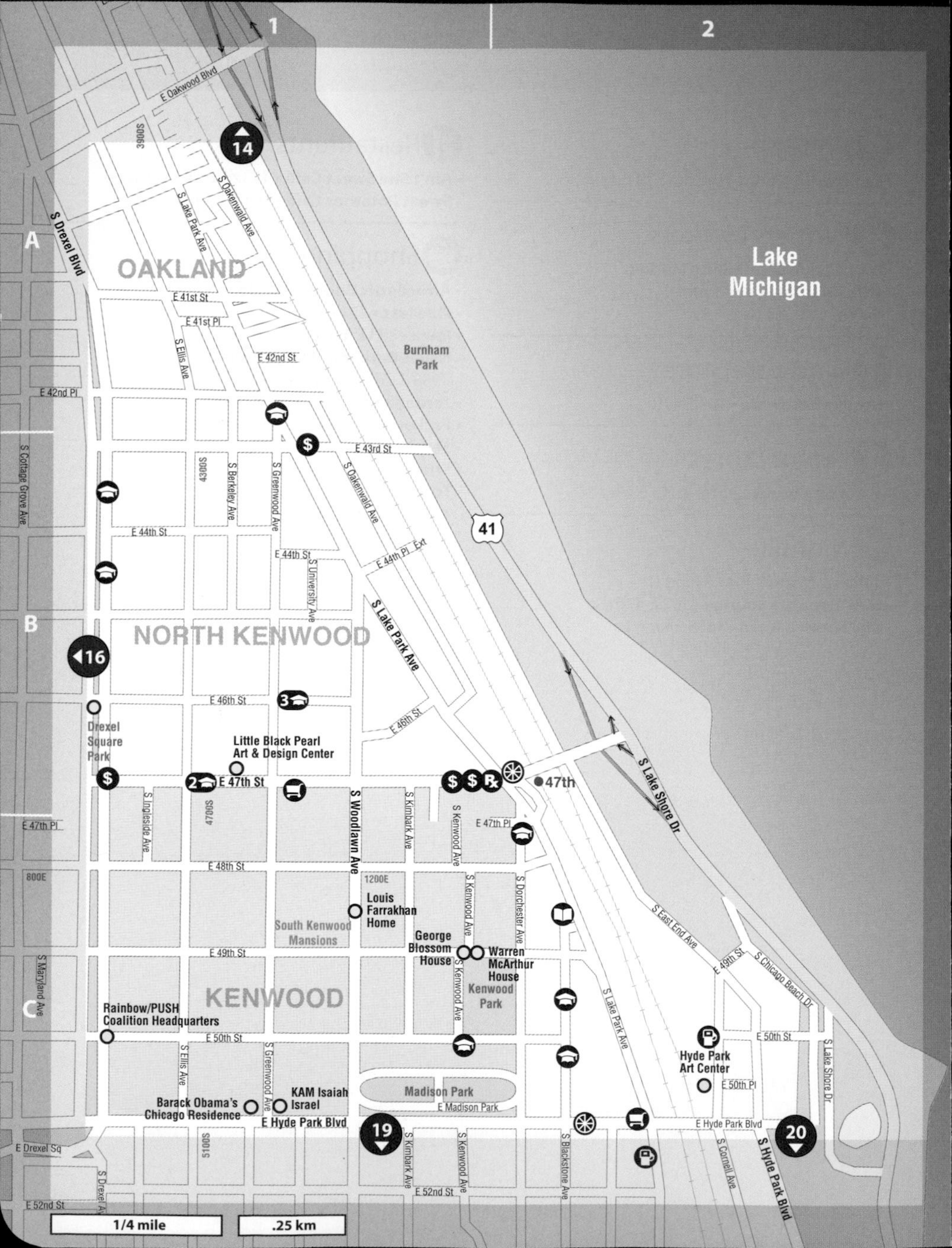

Many a 19th-century suburb prided itself on wide lawns and tranquil settings, and Kenwood was no exception. Though it was annexed to Chicago over a century ago, the suburban feeling lingers. These days, the architecturally-enriched neighborhood contains everything from the residence of Louis Farrakhan to the oldest Jewish congregation in the city, KAM Isaiah Israel.

Banks

- **Chase (ATM)** • Walgreens • 1320 E 47th St
- **Citibank** • 1310 E 47th St
- **Harris Trust & Savings** • 901 E 47th St
- **Hyde Park (ATM)** • 4301 S Lake Park Ave

Gas Stations

- **Amoco** • 5048 S Cornell Ave
- **BP** • 5130 S Lake Park Ave

Landmarks

- **Hyde Park Art Center** • 5020 S Cornell Ave
- **Barack Obama's Chicago Residence** • 5046 S Greenwood Ave
- **Drexel Square Park** • Drexel Blvd, from 51st St to 39th St
- **George Blossom House** • 4858 S Kenwood Ave
- **Hyde Park Art Center** • 5020 S Cornell Ave
- **KAM Isaiah Israel** • 1100 E Hyde Park Blvd
- **Louis Farrakhan Home** • 4855 S Woodlawn Ave
- **Little Black Pearl Art & Design Center** • 930 E 50th St
- **Rainbow/PUSH Coalition Headquarters** • 1060 E 47th S
- **Warren McArthur House** • 4852 S Kenwood Ave

Libraries

- **Blackstone Public Library** • 4904 S Lake Park Ave

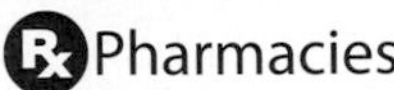

Pharmacies

- **Walgreens** • 1320 E 47th St

Pizza

- **Domino's** • 1453 E Hyde Park Blvd
- **Italian Fiesta Pizzeria** • 1400 E 47th St

Schools

- **Ancona Montessori** • 4770 S Dorchester Ave
- **Ariel Community** • 1119 E 46th St
- **Ariel Community Academy** • 1119 E 46th St
- **Creative Mansion Childrens Academy** • 4745 S Ellis Ave
- **Dr Martin Luther King Jr High** • 4445 S Drexel Blvd
- **Florence B Price Elementary** • 4351 S Drexel Ave
- **Kenwood High** • 5015 S Blackstone Ave
- **Miriam Canter Middle** • 4959 S Blackstone Ave
- **North Kenwood Oakland Charter** • 1014 E 47th St
- **North Kenwood/Oakland Elementary** • 1119 E 46th St
- **Robinson Elementary** • 4225 S Lake Park Ave
- **Shoesmith Elementary** • 1330 E 50th St

Supermarkets

- **Village Foods** • 1521 E Hyde Park Blvd
- **Zaleski & Horvath Market Cafe** • 1126 E 47th St

Map 17 • Kenwood

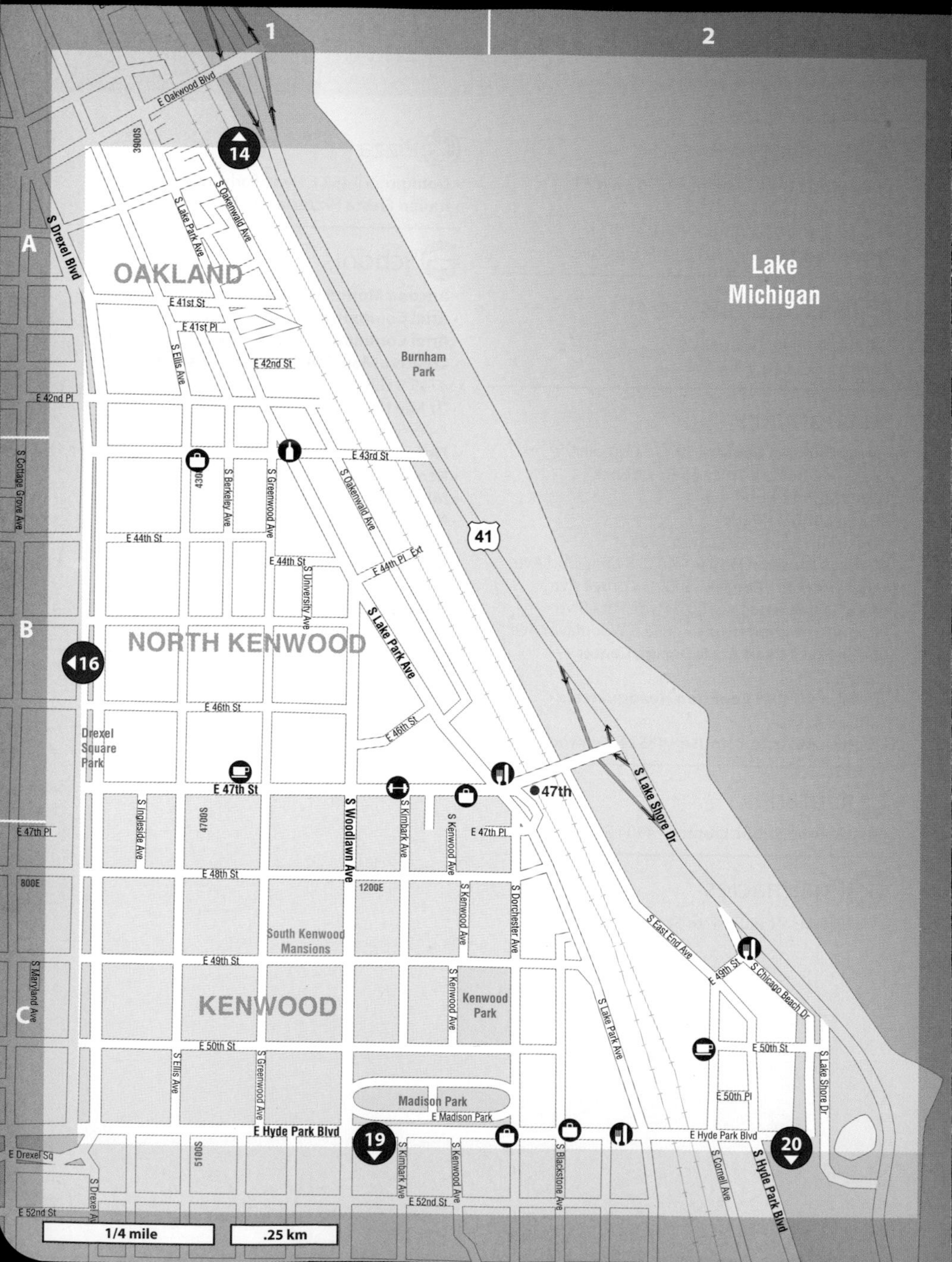

OAKLAND
NORTH KENWOOD
KENWOOD
Lake Michigan
Burnham Park
Drexel Square Park
South Kenwood Mansions
Kenwood Park
Madison Park
47th
E Oakwood Blvd
S Drexel Blvd
S Lake Park Ave
S Oakenwald Ave
E 41st St
E 41st Pl
S Ellis Ave
E 42nd St
E 42nd Pl
E 43rd St
S Cottage Grove Ave
S Berkeley Ave
S Greenwood Ave
S Oakenwald Ave
E 44th St
E 44th Pl Ext
S University Ave
E 46th St
E 47th St
E 47th Pl
S Ingleside Ave
S Woodlawn Ave
S Kimbark Ave
S Kenwood Ave
S Dorchester Ave
E 48th St
E 49th St
S Maryland Ave
E 50th St
E 50th Pl
E Madison Park
E Hyde Park Blvd
E Drexel Sq
E 52nd St
S Blackstone Ave
S Cornell Ave
S Hyde Park Blvd
S Lake Shore Dr
S East End Ave
S Chicago Beach Dr
E 49th St
3900S
4300S
4700S
5100S
800E
1200E
41
14
16
19
20
1
2
A
B
C
1/4 mile
.25 km

Sundries / Entertainment

Inquisitive urbanites will want to meander through the Little Black Pearl Art & Design Center and the Hyde Park Art Center, both of which offer classes, a swanky café, and a gallery. The old homes of President Barack Obama and retail capitalists like Julius Rosenwald and meat-packer Gustavus Swift add historical value to this community. With few close eateries, visitors may want to dine in neighboring Hyde Park.

Coffee

- **Hidden Pearl Café** • 1060 E 47th St
- **Istria Cafe** • 5030 S Cornell Ave

Gyms

- **Bally Total Fitness** • 1301 E 47th St

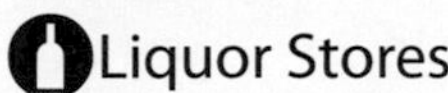

Liquor Stores

- **One Stop Food & Liquors** • 4301 S Lake Park Ave

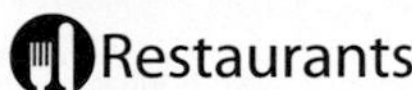

Restaurants

- **Fung's Chop Suey** • 1400 E 47th St
- **Lake Shore Café** • 4900 S Lake Shore Dr
- **Original Pancake House** • 1517 E Hyde Park Blvd

Shopping

- **Gamestop** • 1400 E 47th St
- **Max's Hair Salon** • 1453 E Hyde Park Blvd
- **Sole II Soul** • 1007 E 43rd St
- **Yehia's** • 1390 E Hyde Park Blvd

Map 18 • Washington Park

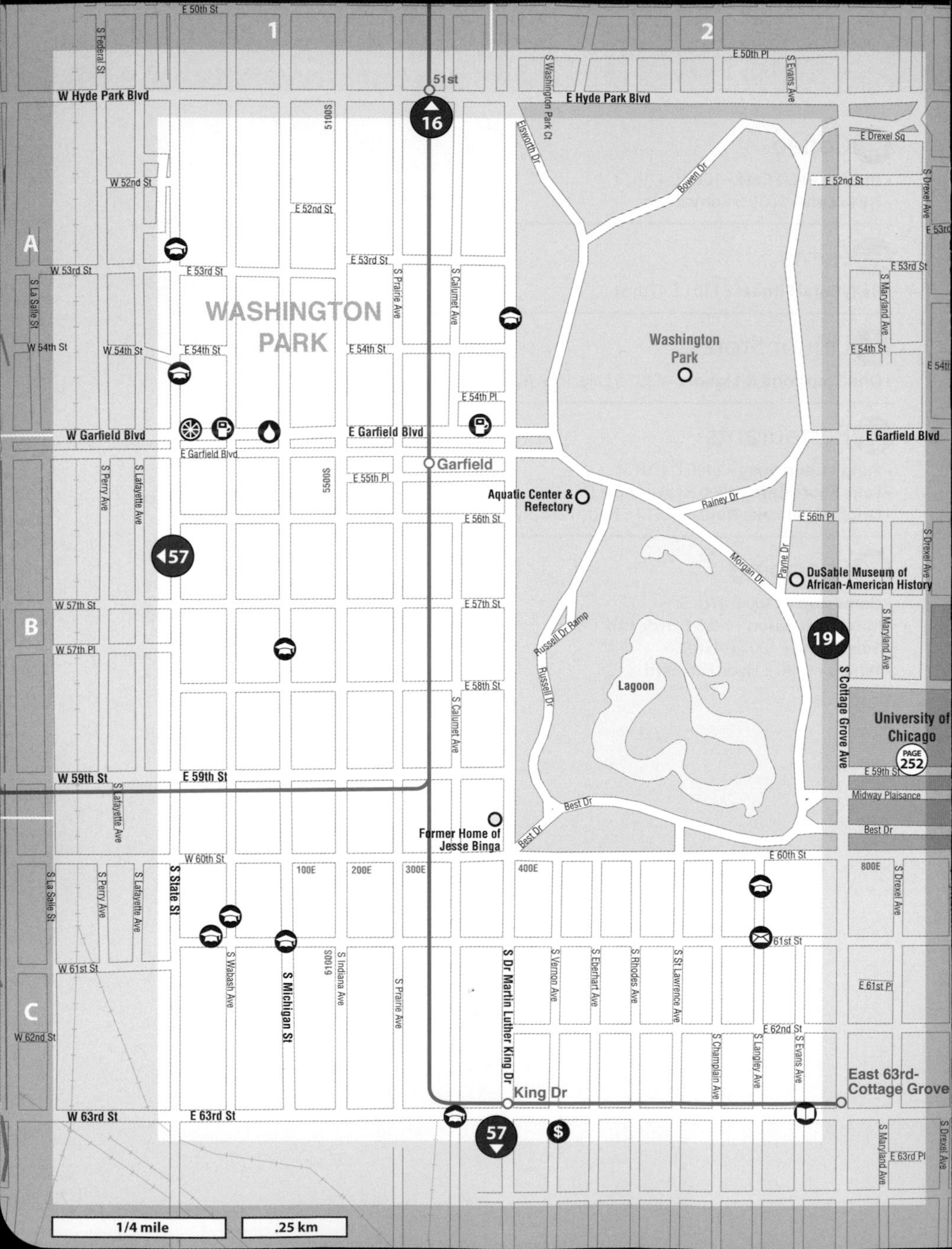

Essentials

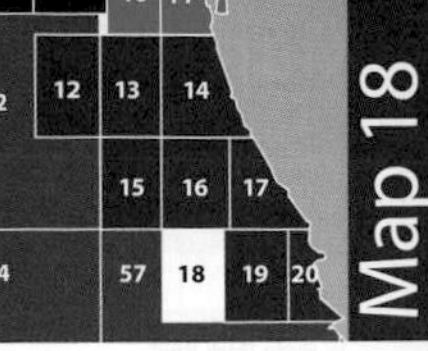

For decades, the western border of Washington Park was defined by the Robert Taylor homes. Recently, the housing projects have disappeared and the community has seen a mini-revival. The eastern half of the area is dominated by the massive park itself and its DuSable Museum of African-American History, pond, track, and swimming pool.

Banks

- **Charter One (ATM)** • 6319 S Vernon Ave

Car Washes

- **Adam's Car Wash** • 48 E Garfield Blvd

Gas Stations

- **Adam's Car Wash** • 48 E Garfield Blvd
- **Citgo** • 368 E Garfield Blvd

Landmarks

- **Aquatic Center & Refectory** • 5531 S King Dr
- **DuSable Museum of African-American History** • 740 E 56th Pl
- **Former Home of Jesse Binga** • 5922 S King Dr
- **Washington Park** • 5531 S Martin Luther King Jr Dr

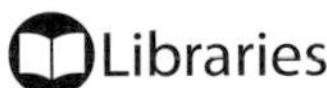

Libraries

- **Bessie Coleman Public Library** • 731 E 63rd St

Pizza

- **B&B Pizza King** • 4 W Garfield Blvd

Post Offices

- **US Post Office** • 700 E 61st St

Schools

- **ACE Technical High** • 5410 S State St
- **Austin O Sexton Elementary** • 6020 S Langley Ave
- **Beasley Academic Elementary** • 5255 S State St
- **Betsy Ross Elementary** • 6059 S Wabash Ave
- **Chicago International Elementary - Washington Park Campus** • 6105 S Michigan Ave
- **Edmund Burke Elementary** • 5356 S King Dr
- **John Foster Dulles High** • 6311 S Calumet Ave
- **Oneida Cockrell, CPC** • 30 E 61 St
- **William W Carter Elementary** • 5740 S Michigan Ave

Map 21 • Wicker Park / Ukrainian Village

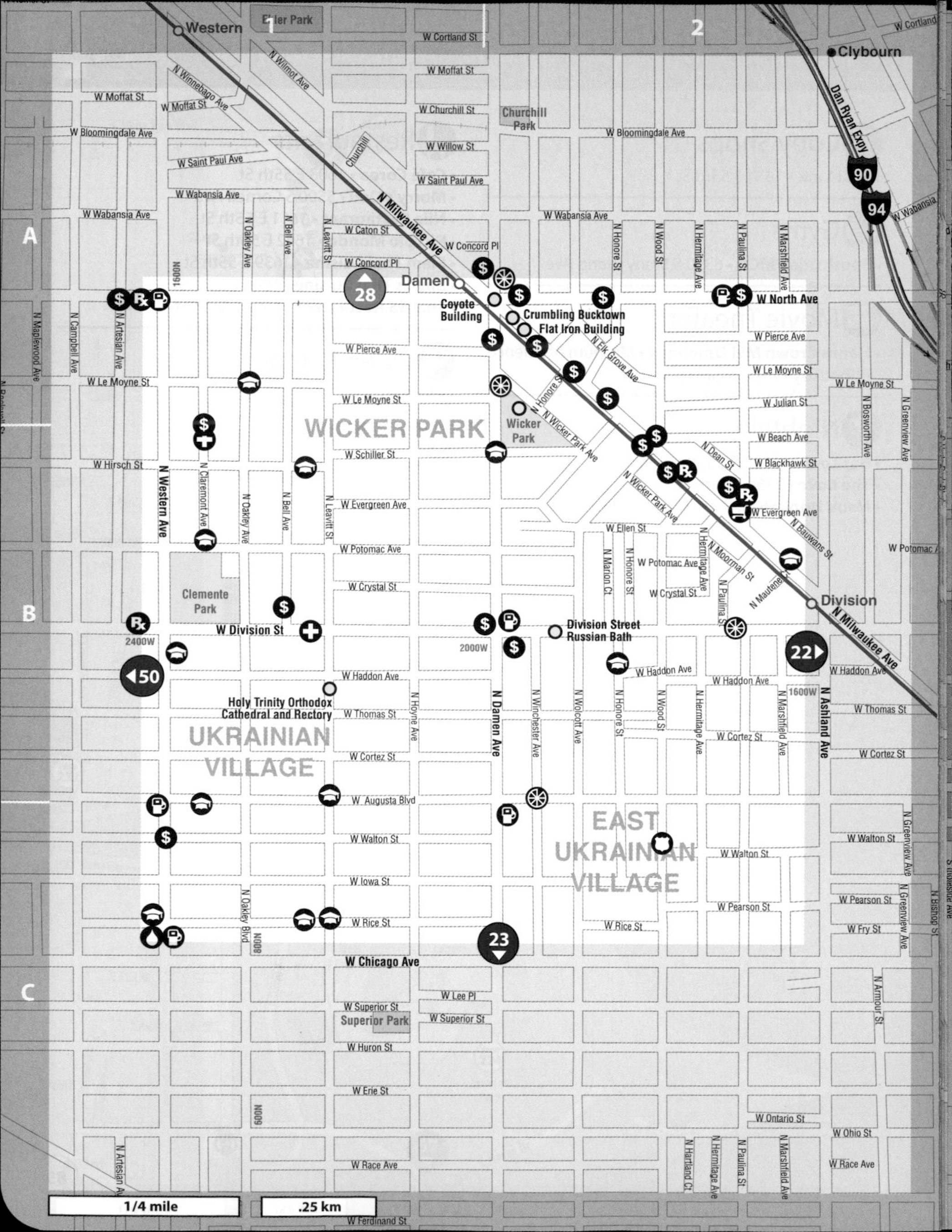

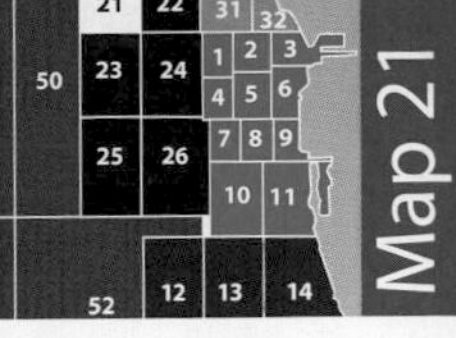

The cozy artist community in Wicker Park and Ukrainian Village is a welcome respite for those put off by yuppie attitudes and rents found city-wide. Local businesses, restaurants, and art galleries line the streets, making it the perfect place for the bespectacled, spandex-clad masses to call home.

Banks

- **Bank of America** • 1525 N Milwaukee Ave
- **Bank of America** • 2222 W Division St
- **Bank of America (ATM)** • 1145 N Western Ave
- **Bank of America (ATM)** • 1431 N Claremont Ave
- **Bank of America (ATM)** • 2233 W Division St
- **Chase** • 1849 W North Ave
- **Chase** • 1959 W Division St
- **Chase (ATM)** • Walgreens • 1372 N Milwaukee Ave
- **Chase (ATM)** • Walgreens • 2440 W North Ave
- **Citibank** • 1445 N Milwaukee Ave
- **Citibank (ATM)** • 7-Eleven • 1400 N Milwaukee Ave
- **First American (ATM)** • 1515 N Milwaukee Ave
- **First American (ATM)** • 1550 N Milwaukee Ave
- **First American (ATM)** • 1601 N Paulina St
- **MB Financial** • 936 N Western Ave
- **Midwest Bank & Trust Company** • 1601 Milwaukee Ave
- **North Community** • 1555 N Damen Ave
- **North Community** • 2000 W Division St
- **TCF** • Jewel • 1341 N Paulina St
- **TCF (ATM)** • 7-Eleven • 1400 N Milwaukee Ave

Car Washes

- **Elite Car Wash** • 823 N Western Ave

Gas Stations

- **BP** • 2405 W Augusta Blvd
- **Citgo** • 1720 W North Ave
- **Citgo** • 823 N Western Ave
- **Clark Oil** • 1949 W Augusta Blvd
- **Shell** • 1600 N Western Ave
- **Shell** • 1950 W Division St

Emergency Rooms

- **Saints Mary and Elizabeth Medical Center** • 1431 N Claremont Ave
- **Saints Mary and Elizabeth Medical Center** • 2233 W Division St

Landmarks

- **Coyote Building** • 1600 N Milwaukee Ave
- **Crumbling Bucktown** • 1579 N Milwaukee Ave
- **Division Street Russian Bath** • 1914 W Division St
- **Flat Iron Arts Building** • 1579 N Milwaukee Ave
- **Holy Trinity Orthodox Cathedral and Rectory** • 1121 N Leavitt St
- **Wicker Park** • W Schiller St & N Damen Ave

Pharmacies

- **CVS** • 2418 W Division St
- **Jewel-Osco** • 1341 N Paulina St
- **Walgreens** • 1372 N Milwaukee Ave
- **Walgreens** • 2440 W North Ave

Pizza

- **Leona's** • 1936 W Augusta Blvd
- **Lou Malnati's Pizzeria** • 1520 N Damen Ave
- **Pizza Metro** • 1707 W Division St
- **Santullo's Eatery** • 1943 W North Ave

Police

- **13th District (Wood)** • 937 N Wood St

Schools

- **A N Pritzker Elementary** • 2009 W Schiller St
- **Albert R Sabin** • 2216 W Hirsch St
- **Christopher Columbus Elementary** • 1003 N Leavitt St
- **De Diego Elementary** • 1313 N Claremont Ave
- **Frederic Chopin Elementary** • 2450 W Rice St
- **Hans Christian Andersen Elementary** • 1148 N Honore St
- **Josephinum High** • 1501 N Oakley Blvd
- **Roberto Clemente Community High** • 1147 N Western Ave
- **St Helen Elementary** • 2347 W Augusta Blvd
- **St Nicholas** • 2200 W Rice St

Supermarkets

- **Jewel-Osco** • 1341 N Paulina St

Map 21 • Wicker Park / Ukrainian Village

Sundries / Entertainment

Lincoln Park West, as it's known by some, remains one of the hippest parts of town for young artist-types, densely packed with faux-hawks, scooters, and wearable art. Fashion-forward boutiques, veggie-friendly eats, and cool cafés abound. Indie bands and avant-garde jazz wail through the night from Empty Bottle, while the hipster crowd pedi-cabs back and forth between dive bars.

Coffee

- **Alliance Bakery** • 1736 W Division St
- **Barista Coffee House** • 852 N Damen Ave
- **Café Ballou** • 939 N Western Ave
- **Caffe Gelato** • 2034 W Division St
- **Cipollina** • 1543 N Damen Ave
- **Letizia's Natural Bakery** • 2144 W Division St
- **Red Hen Bread** • 1623 N Milwaukee Ave
- **Starbucks** • 1588 N Milwaukee Ave
- **Starbucks** • 1701 W Division St

Copy Shops

- **Copymax** • 1573 N Milwaukee Ave
- **FedEx Kinko's** • 1800 W North Ave ㉔

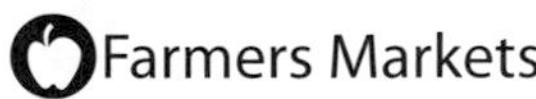

Farmers Markets

- **Wicker Park/Bucktown (Jun–Oct; Sun, 7 am–2 pm)** • W Schiller St & N Damen Ave

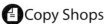

Gyms

- **Bucktown Fitness Club** • 2100 W North Ave
- **Cheetah Gym** • 1934 W North Ave

Liquor Stores

- **Carlos Food & Liquor** • 1401 N Western Ave
- **Ola's Liquor** • 947 N Damen Ave
- **Sahar Food & Liquor** • 1761 W Division St
- **Universal Food & Liquor** • 1803 W North Ave
- **Wicker Park Liquor** • 2006 W Division St

Nightlife

- **Beachwood Inn** • 1415 N Wood St
- **Between Boutique Cafe & Lounge** • 1324 N Milwaukee Ave
- **Cleo's** • 1935 W Chicago Ave
- **Club Foot** • 1824 W Augusta Blvd
- **Davenport's** • 1383 N Milwaukee Ave
- **Debonair Social Club** • 1575 N Milwaukee Ave
- **Double Door** • 1572 N Milwaukee Ave
- **Empty Bottle** • 1035 N Western Ave
- **Empire Liquors** • 1566 N Milwaukee Ave
- **Estelle's Café & Lounge** • 2013 W North Ave
- **The Flat Iron** • 1565 N Milwaukee Ave
- **Gold Star Bar** • 1755 W Division St
- **Happy Village** • 1059N Wolcott Ave
- **Inner Town Pub** • 1935 W Thomas St
- **Innjoy** • 2051 W Division St
- **Lava** • 1270 N Milwaukee Ave
- **Mana Food Bar** • 1742 W Division St
- **The Note** • 1565 N Milwaukee Ave
- **Phyllis' Musical Inn** • 1800 W Division St
- **Piece Bar** • 1927 W North Ave
- **Rainbo Club** • 1150 N Damen Ave
- **Rodan** • 1530 N Milwaukee Ave
- **Salud Tequila Lounge** • 1471 N Milwaukee Ave
- **Small Bar** • 2049 W Division St
- **Subterranean Cabaret & Lounge** • 2011 W North Ave
- **The Violet Hour** • 1520 N Damen Ave

Pet Shops

- **Doggy Style Pet Shop** • 2023 W Division St
- **Wicker Pet** • 2029 W North Ave

Restaurants

- **Big Star** • 1531 N Damen Ave
- **Bin Wine Cafe** • 1559 N Milwaukee Ave
- **Birchwood Kitchen** • 2211 W North Ave
- **Bite Cafe** • 1039 N Western Ave
- **Blue Line Club Car** • 1548 N Damen Ave
- **Bluefin** • 1952 W North Ave
- **Bob San** • 1805 W Division St
- **Cleo's** • 1935 W Chicago Ave
- **Earwax** • 1561 N Milwaukee Ave
- **Feast** • 1616 N Damen Ave
- **Fifty/50** • 2047 W Division St
- **Flash Taco** • 1570 N Damen Ave
- **Handlebar** • 2311 W North Ave
- **Jam** • 937 N Damen Ave
- **Jerry's Wicker Park** • 1938 W Division St
- **Las Palmas** • 1835 W North Ave
- **Letiza's Natural Bakery** • 2144 W Division St
- **Mana Food Bar** • 1742 W Division St
- **Milk & Honey** • 1920 W Division St
- **Mirai Sushi** • 2020 W Division St
- **People Lounge** • 1560 N Milwaukee Ave
- **Picante** • 2016 W Division St
- **Piece Bar** • 1927 W North Ave
- **Smoke Daddy** • 1804 W Division St
- **Spring** • 2039 W North Ave
- **Sultan's Market** • 2057 W North Ave
- **Taxim** • 1558 N Milwaukee Ave
- **Thai Lagoon** • 2322 W North Ave
- **Thai Vill**
- **Veggie B**

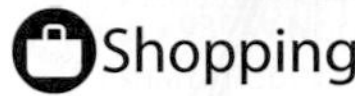

Shopping

- **Anjenu Boutique** • 1747 W Division St
- **Akira** • 1814 W North Ave
- **Art + Science Hair Salon** • 1552 N Milwaukee Ave
- **Artemio's Bakery** • 1443 N Milwaukee Ave
- **Asrai Garden** • 1935 W North Ave
- **Beadniks** • 1937 W Division St
- **Bonnie and Clyde** • 1751 W Division St
- **Broken Cherry** • 1734 W North Ave
- **Brooklyn Industries** • 1426 N Milwaukee Ave
- **Casa de Soul** • 1919 W Division St
- **Cattails** • 1935 W Division St
- **City Soles** • 1566 N Damen Ave
- **DeciBel Audio** • 1429 N Milwaukee Ave
- **G-Star** • 1525 N Milwaukee Ave
- **Greenheart** • 1911 W Division St
- **Grow** • 1943 W Division St
- **Habit** • 1951 W Division St
- **iCream** • 1537 N Milwaukee Ave
- **John Fluevog • 1539 N Milwaukee Ave**
- **Lenny & Me** • 1463 Milwaukee Ave
- **Myopic Books** • 1564 N Milwaukee Ave
- **Nina** • 1655 W Division St
- **Ouest** • 1751 W Division St
- **Paper Doll** • 2048 W Division St
- **Penelope's** • 1913 W Division St
- **Quimby's Bookstore** • 1854 W North Ave
- **Reckless Records** • 1532 N Milwaukee Ave
- **Renegade Handmade** • 1924 W Division St
- **Ruby Room** • 1743 W Division St
- **Saint Alfred** • 1531 N Milwaukee Ave
- **Silver Moon** • 1755 W North Ave
- **The Silver Room** • 1442 N Milwaukee Ave
- **Symmetry** • 1925 W Division St
- **Threadless** • 1905 W Division St
- **Untitled** • 1941 W North Ave

Video Rental

- **Blockbuster** • 1303 N Milwaukee Ave
- **Brainstorm** • 1648 W North Ave
- **Earwax** • 1561 N Milwaukee Ave
- **Mass Video** • 2014 W Division St

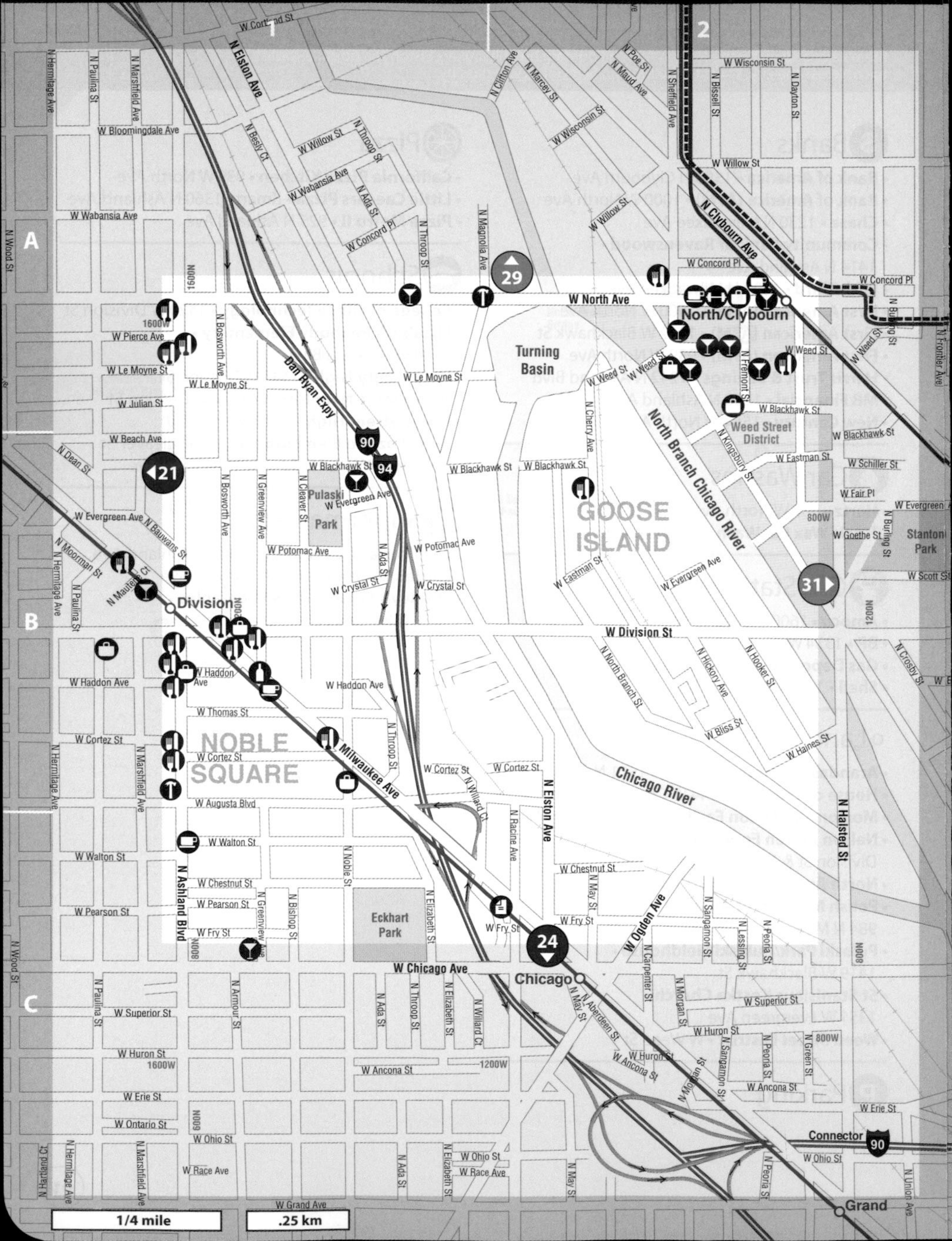

Map 22 • Noble Square / Goose Island

N

1
2
A
B
C

W Cortland St
N Elston Ave
N Clifton Ave
N Marcey St
N Poe St
N Maud Ave
N Sheffield Ave
W Wisconsin St
N Bissell St
N Dayton St
N Hermitage Ave
N Paulina St
N Marshfield Ave
W Bloomingdale Ave
N Besly Ct
W Willow St
N Throop St
W Wabansia Ave
N Ada St
W Wabansia Ave
N Wood St
W Concord Pl
N Throop St
N Magnolia Ave
N Clybourn Ave
W Concord Pl
W Concord Pl
1600W
W North Ave
North/Clybourn
N Burling St
N Frontier Ave
W Weed St
1600W
W Pierce Ave
N Bosworth Ave
W Le Moyne St
W Le Moyne St
W Le Moyne St
Dan Ryan Expy
Turning Basin
W Weed St
W Weed St
N Fremont St
W Julian St
N Cherry Ave
W Blackhawk St
North Branch Chicago River
Weed Street District
W Blackhawk St
W Beach Ave
90
N Kingsbury St
W Eastman St
W Schiller St
N Dean St
21
94
W Blackhawk St
W Blackhawk St
W Blackhawk St
N Bosworth Ave
N Greenview Ave
N Cleaver St
Pulaski Park
W Evergreen Ave
GOOSE ISLAND
W Fair Pl
W Evergreen Ave
800W
W Evergreen Ave
N Bauwans St
W Goethe St
Stanton Park
N Moorman St
W Potomac Ave
N Ada St
W Potomac Ave
W Eastman St
W Evergreen Ave
W Scott St
N Hermitage Ave
N Paulina St
N Mautene Ct
W Crystal St
W Crystal St
31
Division
1600W
W Division St
N North Branch St
N Hickory Ave
N Hooker St
N Crosby St
W Haddon Ave
W Haddon Ave
W Haddon Ave
W Thomas St
W Bliss St
W Haines St
W Cortez St
NOBLE SQUARE
N Throop St
W Cortez St
W Cortez St
W Cortez St
N Willard Ct
Chicago River
N Hermitage Ave
N Marshfield Ave
Milwaukee Ave
N Elston Ave
N Halsted St
W Augusta Blvd
N Racine Ave
W Walton St
W Walton St
N Noble St
N Ashland Blvd
W Chestnut St
W Chestnut St
W Pearson St
W Pearson St
N Greenview Ave
N Bishop St
Eckhart Park
N Elizabeth St
N May St
W Ogden Ave
N Sangamon St
N Lessing St
N Peoria St
W Fry St
W Fry St
W Fry St
24
800W
N Carpenter St
N Wood St
W Chicago Ave
Chicago
N Paulina St
N Armour St
N Ada St
N Throop St
N Elizabeth St
N Willard Ct
N May St
N Aberdeen St
N Morgan St
W Superior St
W Superior St
W Huron St
1600W
W Ancona St
1200W
W Huron St
W Ancona St
N Morgan St
N Sangamon St
N Peoria St
N Green St
800W
W Ancona St
W Erie St
W Erie St
W Ontario St
600N
W Ohio St
Connector
90
N Hartland Ct
N Hermitage Ave
N Marshfield Ave
W Race Ave
N Ada St
N Elizabeth St
W Ohio St
W Race Ave
N May St
N Peoria St
W Ohio St
N Union Ave
W Grand Ave
Grand

1/4 mile
.25 km

Funky shops and studios cluster around Milwaukee, Division, and Ashland. Savor ceviche with humorously-monikered margaritas at El Barco, or share pub-appropriate Italian fare in Corosh's courtyard patio. Clubby Weed Street district is a breeding laboratory, while at Exit, the pierced and leather-clad pretend there still is a punk scene in Chicago.

Coffee

- **Dunkin' Donuts** • 1244 N Ashland Ave
- **Lovely: A Bake Shop** • 1130 N Milwaukee Ave
- **Peet's Coffee & Tea** • 1000 W North Ave
- **Ritz Tango Café** • 933 N Ashland Ave
- **Starbucks** • 1001 W North Ave

Copy Shops

- **Carnegie Printers** • 868 N Milwaukee Ave

Gyms

- **Crunch Fitness** • 939 W North Ave

Hardware Stores

- **Ace Hardware** • 1013 N Ashland Ave
- **Home Depot** • 1232 W North Ave

Liquor Stores

- **Crater Food & Liquor** • 1144 N Milwaukee Ave

Nightlife

- **The Chipp Inn** • 832 N Greenview Ave
- **Crobar** • 1543 N Kingsbury St
- **Exit** • 1315 W North Ave
- **Joe's** • 940 W Weed St
- **Lava** • 1270 N Milwaukee Ave
- **Northland Tavern** • 1610 W North Ave
- **Republic** • 1520 N Fremont St
- **Zentra** • 923 W Weed St

Restaurants

- **Corosh** • 1072 N Milwaukee Ave
- **El Barco Mariscos Seafood** • 1035 N Ashland Ave
- **Hollywood Grill** • 1601 W North Ave
- **La Pasadita** • 1141 N Ashland Ave
- **Luc Thang** • 1524 N Ashland Ave
- **Mariscos El Veneno** • 1024 N Ashland Ave
- **NYC Bagel** • 1001 W North Ave
- **Podhalanka** • 1549 W Division St
- **Schwa** • 1466 N Ashland Ave
- **Tocco** • 1266 N Milwaukee Ave
- **Usagi Ya** • 1178 N Milwaukee Ave

Shopping

- **August Grocery** • 1500 W Division St
- **Blick Art Materials** • 1574 N Kingsbury St
- **Dusty Groove Records** • 1120 N Ashland Ave
- **Irv's Luggage Warehouse** • 820 W North Ave
- **Nina** • 1655 W Division St
- **Restoration Hardware** • 938 W North Ave
- **Roots & Culture** • 1034 N Milwaukee Ave
- **Vintage Pine** • 904 W Blackhawk St

Map 23 • West Town / Near West Side

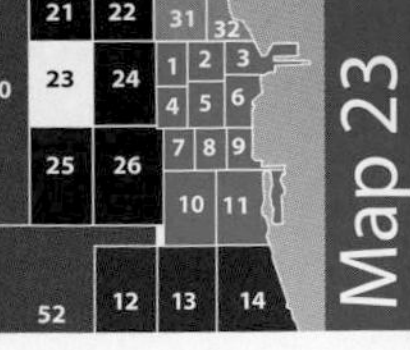

This neighborhood was once the heart of the city's produce and meat markets. United Center, a.k.a. The House That Mike Built, infused energy into the area. A few food supplier warehouses still exist, mixing in with new loft conversions. Today it's a great place to spend your money, lots of your money, on locally made and grown necessaries.

Banks

- **Bank of America (ATM)** • 1900 W Van Buren St
- **Chase (ATM)** • Rush University Medical Center • 1700 W Van Buren St
- **Chase (ATM)** • 1650 W Chicago Ave
- **Chase (ATM)** • Walgreens • 2316 W Madison St
- **Citibank (ATM)** • McDonald's • 2005 W Chicago Ave
- **Fifth Third (ATM)** • 1901 W Madison St
- **MB Financial** • 820 N Western Ave
- **National City** • 2100 W Chicago Ave
- **National City** • 2154 W Madison St
- **Self Reliance Ukrainian American Federal Credit Union** • 2332 W Chicago Ave
- **US** • 2021 W Chicago Ave
- **TCF (ATM)** • Osco • 2427 W Chicago Ave

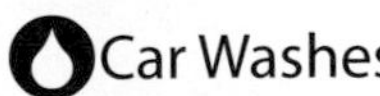

Car Washes

- **Quiroga's Detail & Hand Car Wash** • 2036 W Grand Ave

Gas Stations

- **Marathon** • 101 N Western Ave
- **Shell** • 45 N Western Ave

Landmarks

- **First Baptist Congregational Church** • 1613 W Washington Blvd
- **Metropolitan Missionary Baptist Church** • 2151 W Washington Blvd
- **Ukrainian Cultural Center** • 2247 W Chicago Ave
- **Ukrainian National Museum** • 2249 W Superior St
- **United Center** • 1901 W Madison St

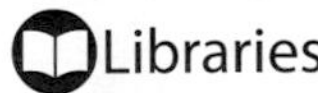

Libraries

- **Mabel Manning Public Library** • 6 S Hoyne Ave
- **Malcolm X College Library** • 1900 W Van Buren St

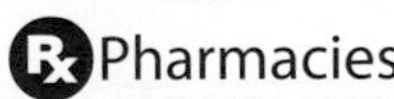

Pharmacies

- **CVS** • 2427 W Chicago Ave ㉔
- **Walgreens** • 2340 W Madison St

Pizza

- **Bacci Pizzeria** • 2343 W Chicago Ave
- **Naty's Pizza 2** • 1757 W Chicago Ave
- **Pauly's Pizza-Ria** • 1744 W Grand Ave
- **Village Pizza** • 2356 W Chicago Ave

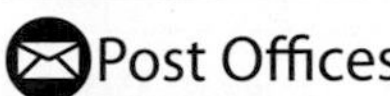

Post Offices

- **US Post Office** • 116 S Western Ave

Schools

- **Best Practice High** • 2040 W Adams St
- **Crane Achievement Academy** • 2245 W Jackson Blvd
- **Cregier Tech Prep** • 2040 W Adams St
- **Dett R Nathaniel Elementary** • 2306 W Maypole Ave
- **Ellen Mitchell Branch** • 2315 W Erie St
- **Ellen Mitchell Elementary** • 2233 W Ohio St
- **Foundations Elementary** • 2040 W Adams St
- **Healy High** • 100 N Western Ave
- **Henry Suder Elementary** • 2022 W Washington Blvd
- **Irene C Hernandez Achievement Center** • 2245 W Jackson Blvd
- **Malcolm X College** • 1900 W Van Buren St
- **Mancel Talcott Elementary** • 1840 W Ohio St
- **Nia Middle** • 2040 W Adams St
- **Phoenix Military Academy** • 145 S Campbell Ave
- **St Malachy Elementary** • 2252 W Washington Blvd
- **Victor Herbert Elementary** • 2131 W Monroe St
- **West Town High** • 2021 W Fulton St
- **William H Brown Elementary** • 54 N Hermitage Ave
- **Wilma Rudolph Learning Center** • 110 N Paulina St

Supermarkets

- **Dominick's** • 2021 W Chicago Ave

Map 23 • West Town / Near West Side

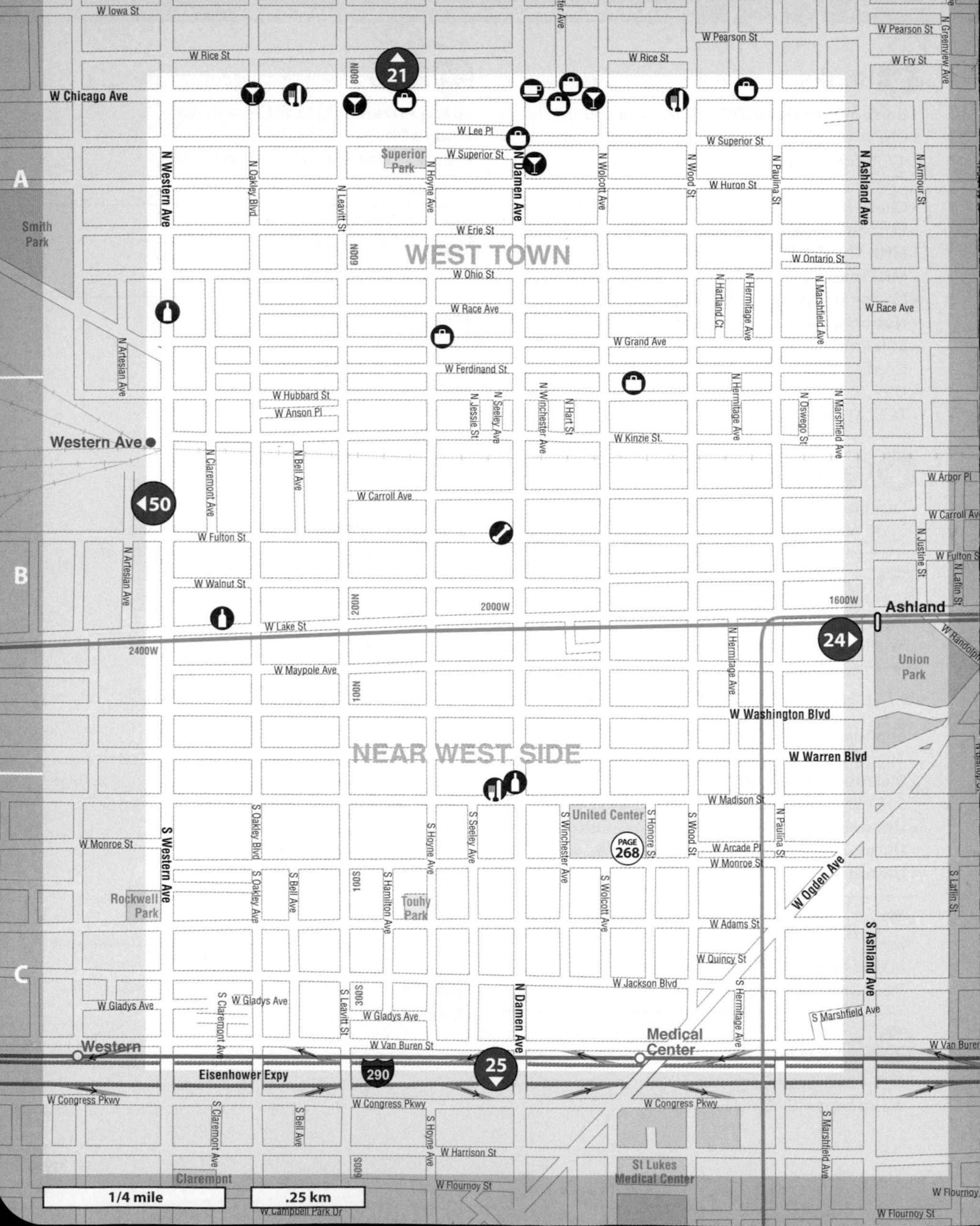

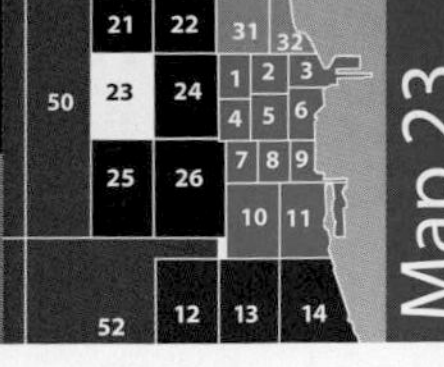

Between the architectural haven Salvage One, cowboy costumer Alcala's, designer toy store Rotofugi, and gardening boutique Sprout Home, the shopping is anything but ordinary in this neck of the woods. Get your coffee with a side of hipster at Atomix. If you've got the leggings for it, head over to Tuman's for cheap drinks and priceless people-watching.

Coffee

- **Atomix** • 1957 W Chicago Ave
- **Intelligentsia Roasting Works** • 1850 W Fulton St

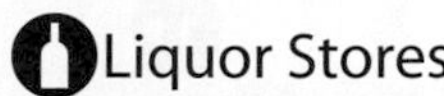

Liquor Stores

- **DiCarlo's Armanetti Liquors** • 515 N Western Ave
- **Main St Liquors** • 2000 W Madison St
- **Westlake** • 2349 W Lake St

Nightlife

- **Bar DeVille** • 1958 W Huron St
- **Cleo's** • 1935 W Chicago Ave
- **Darkroom** • 2210 W Chicago Ave
- **High Dive** • 1938 W Chicago Ave
- **Sak's Ukrainian Village Restaurant** • 2301 W Chicago Ave
- **Tuman's** • 2159 W Chicago Ave

Pet Shops

- **Windy City Parrot** • 2007 W Fulton St

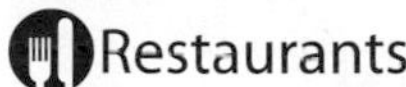

Restaurants

- **A Tavola** • 2148 W Chicago Ave
- **Chickpea** • 2018 W Chicago Ave
- **China Dragon Restaurant** • 2008 W Madison St
- **High Dive** • 1938 W Chicago Ave
- **Old Lviv** • 2228 W Chicago Ave
- **Sunrise Café** • 2012 W Chicago Ave
- **Takie Outit** • 2132 W Chicago Ave
- **Tecalitlan Restaurant** • 1814 W Chicago Ave

Shopping

- **Alcala's Western Wear** • 1733 W Chicago Ave
- **Donofrio's Double Corona Cigars** • 2058 W Chicago Ave
- **Guess Hookah** • 1829 W Chicago Ave
- **Koi 8** • 1927 W Chicago Ave
- **Modern Times** • 2100 W Grand Ave
- **Permanent Records** • 1914 W Chicago Ave
- **Rotofugi** • 1953 W Chicago Ave
- **Salvage One Architectural Elements** • 1840 W Hubbard St
- **Sprout Home** • 745 N Damen Ave
- **Tomato Tattoo** • 1855 W Chicago Ave

N

WEST TOWN

NEAR WEST SIDE

Eckhart Park

Eckhart Park/ Ida Crown Natatorium

Union Park

Skinner Park

First Baptist Congregational Church

Jackson Boulevard Historic District

Harpo Studios

Univ of Illinois at Chicago

Chicago

Grand

Ashland

Racine

UIC-Halsted

Dwight D Eisenhower Expy

90 Connector

Dan

22
23
1
4
26
PAGE 254

1/4 mile

.25 km

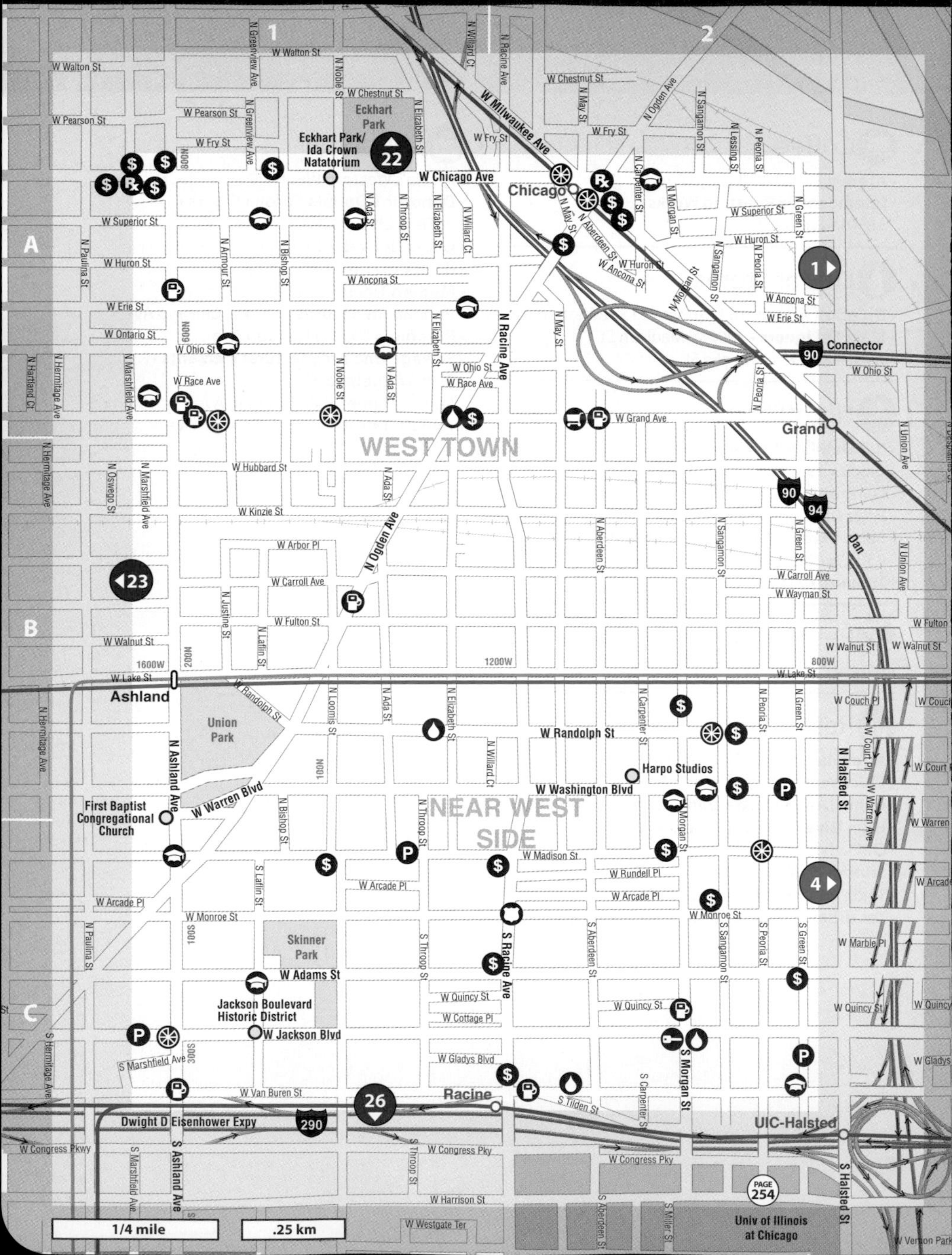

Essentials

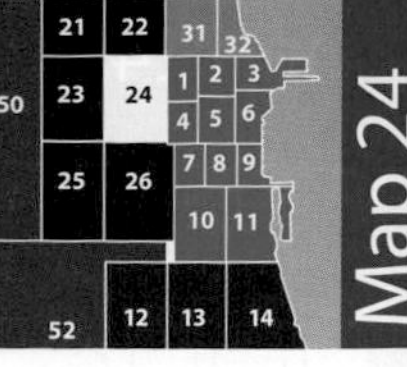

Food distribution centers and wholesalers, warehouses, and loading docks rub shoulders with an alternative gallery scene, trendy restaurants, and hot clubs in this transitional 'hood. Young Cusack-wannabes take classes at the Chicago Academy for the Arts. Break a leg.

Banks

- **American Chartered** • 932 W Randolph St
- **Banco Popular** • 1445 W Chicago Ave
- **Bank of America** • 140 S Ashland Ave
- **Bank of America** • 850 W Jackson Blvd
- **Bank of America (ATM)** • 1601 W Chicago Ave
- **Broadway** • 900 W Van Buren St
- **Charter One (ATM)** • 7-Eleven • 954 W Monroe St
- **Charter One (ATM)** • White Hen • 200 S Racine
- **Chase** • 1650 W Chicago Ave
- **Chase** • 923 W Washington Blvd
- **Citibank (ATM)** • 745 N Milwaukee Ave
- **First American (ATM)** • 1001 W Madison St
- **First American (ATM)** • 324 S Racine Ave
- **First Eagle National** • 1201 W Madison St
- **MB Financial** • 1420 W Madison St
- **North Community** • 1244 W Grand Ave
- **North Community** • 1600 W Chicago Ave
- **South Central** • 160 N Morgan St
- **TCF (ATM)** • Osco • 771 N Ogden Ave
- **US** • 745 N Milwaukee Ave

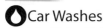

Car Washes

- **Bert's Car Wash** • 1231 W Grand Ave
- **Randolph St Auto Spa** • 1308 W Randolph St
- **Shell** • 1001 W Jackson Blvd
- **Strictly by Hand II** • 1125 W Van Buren St

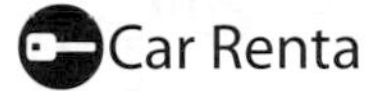

Car Rental

- **Enterprise** • 318 S Morgan St • 312-432-9780

Gas Stations

- **BP** • 1600 W Van Buren St
- **Citgo** • 1535 W Grand Ave
- **Marathon** • 1100 W Grand Ave
- **Marathon** • 335 N Ogden Ave
- **Marathon** • 649 N Ashland Ave
- **Shell** • 1001 W Jackson Blvd
- **Shell** • 1160 W Van Buren St
- **Shell** • 505 N Ashland Ave

Landmarks

- **Eckhart Park/Ida Crown Natatorium** • 1330 W Chicago Ave
- **First Baptist Congregational Church** • 1613 W Washington Blvd
- **Harpo Studios** • 1058 W Washington Blvd
- **Jackson Boulevard Historic District** • W Jackson Blvd & S Laflin St

Parking

Pharmacies

- **CVS** • 771 N Ogden Ave
- **Walgreens** • 1650 W Chicago Ave

Pizza

- **D'Agostino's Pizzeria** • 752 N Ogden Ave
- **Leona's** • 848 W Madison St
- **Moretti's** • 1645 W Jackson Blvd
- **Pie-Eyed Pizza** • 1111 W Chicago Ave
- **Ramirez Fast Food** • 1521 W Grand Ave
- **Salerno's Restaurant** • 1201 W Grand Ave
- **Tomato Head Pizza Kitchen** • 945 W Randolph St

Police

- **12th District (Monroe)** • 100 S Racine Ave

Schools

- **American Quality** • 850 W Jackson Blvd
- **Calphalon Culinary Center** • 1000 W Washington Blvd
- **Chicago Academy for the Arts** • 1010 W Chicago Ave
- **Esperanza Community Services** • 520 N Marshfield St
- **James Otis Elementary** • 525 N Armour St
- **Mark Skinner Classical** • 1443 N Ogden Ave
- **Midwest Apostolic Bible College** • 14 S Ashland Ave
- **Near North Special Ed Center** • 739 N Ada St
- **Philo Carpenter Elementary** • 1250 W Erie St
- **Santa Maria Addolorata** • 1337 W Ohio St
- **UNO Charter School Network Elementary** • 954 W Washington Blvd
- **Whitney Young High** • 211 S Laflin St

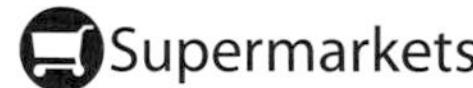

Supermarkets

- **Bari Foods** • 1120 W Grand Ave

N

Western
Medical Center
23
290
Eisenhower Expy
W Van Buren St
W Gladys Ave
W Congress Pkwy
W Harrison St
Claremont Park
W Flournoy St
W Campbell Park Dr
W Lexington St
Vietnam Survivors Memorial
Bowler Row Houses
S Bowler St
W Bowler St
W Polk St
Oakley Row Houses
W Boone St
S Ogden Ave W
S Damen Ave
St Lukes Medical Center
University of Illinois Hospital
VA Medical Center
W Arthington St
W Taylor St
W Fillmore St
W Grenshaw St
W Roosevelt Rd
2400W
2000W
1600W
ILLINOIS MEDICAL DISTRICT
W Washburne Ave
W 13th St
W Hastings St
W 14th St
W 14th Pl
26
50
W 15th St
W 15th Pl
W 16th St
W 17th St
Western Ave
W 18th St
18th
18th St L Station
W 18th Pl
Harrison Park
W 19th St
HEART OF CHICAGO
W Cullerton St
Western
Damen
W 21st St
W 21st Pl
W Cermak Rd
52
W 22nd Pl
S Western Ave
S Campbell Ave
S Claremont Ave
S Oakley Ave
S Bell Ave
S Leavitt St
S Hoyne Ave
S Seeley Ave
S Hamilton Ave
Almond St
S Winchester Ave
S Wolcott Ave
S Honore St
S Hermitage Ave
S Paulina St
S Marshfield Ave
S Wood St
S Heath Ave
S Ashland Ave
S Laflin St
Garibaldi Pl
S Bishop St
S Blue Island Ave
Polk
S Marshfield Ave
W Flournoy
W Lexington
1/4 mile
.25 km

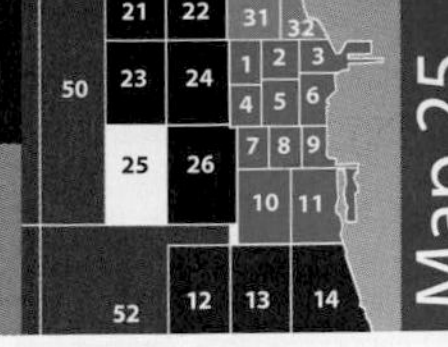

The conglomerated facilities making up the Illinois Medical District comprise the second-largest such quarter in the nation. Cook County (John H Stroger) Hospital broke ground in 1874. Its trauma center is among America's finest, if unfaithful to its "ER" rendering. Go elsewhere for non-emergency care to avoid waiting. A townhouse colony of new constructions in the area houses green MDs.

Banks

- **Bank of America** • 1705 W 18th St
- **Bank of America** • 2332 W Cermak Rd
- **Bank of America (ATM)** • 818 S Wolcott Ave
- **Bank of America (ATM)** • 1701 W Taylor St
- **Bank of America (ATM)** • 1717 W Polk St
- **Bank of America (ATM)** • 1801 W Taylor St
- **Bank of America (ATM)** • 818 S Wolcott Ave
- **Chase** • 2000 W Cermak Rd
- **Chase (ATM)** • Rush Presbyterian Hospital • 1750 W Harrison St
- **Chase (ATM)** • 1850 W Roosevelt Rd
- **Chase (ATM)** • Walgreens • 1931 W Cermak Rd
- **Chase (ATM)** • 2111 W Roosevelt Rd
- **Chase (ATM)** • Rush University Medical Center • 600 S Paulina St
- **Chase (ATM)** • Veterans Affairs Hospital • 820 S Damen Ave
- **First American (ATM)** • 2200 S Western Ave
- **Metropolitan** • 2201 W Cermak Rd
- **Metropolitan** • 2235 W Cermak Rd
- **TCF** • 818 S Wolcott Ave
- **TCF (ATM)** • UIC Sport/Fitness West • 828 S Wolcott Ave

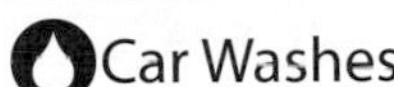

Car Washes

- **G Express Hand Car Wash** • 2323 W 18th St

Gas Stations

- **Citgo** • 2107 S Western Ave
- **Independent** • 1721 S Paulina St
- **Mobil** • 2401 W Ogden Ave
- **Shell** • 2401 W Roosevelt Rd

Emergency Rooms

- **John H Stroger Jr** • 1900 W Polk St
- **Rush-Presbyterian St Luke's** • 1650 W Harrison St
- **St Anthony's** • 2875 W 19th St
- **University of Illinois at Chicago** • 1740 W Taylor St
- **Jesse Brown VA Medical Center** • 820 S Damen Ave

Landmarks

- **18th St L station** • W 18th St & S Paulina St
- **Bowler Row Houses** • 2148 W Bowler St
- **Oakley Row Houses** • 801 S Oakley Ave
- **Vietnam Survivors Memorial** • 815 S Oakley Ave

Parking

Pharmacies

- **Walgreens** • 1931 W Cermak Rd

Pizza

- **Aurelio's Pizza** • 1545 S Western Ave
- **Bacci Pizzeria** • 2301 W Taylor St
- **Damenzo's** • 2324 W Taylor St
- **Pisa Pizza** • 2050 W Cermak Rd
- **Pizza Nova** • 1842 W 18th St

Schools

- **Chicago Hope Academy** • 2189 W Bowler St
- **Chicago Lighthouse Development** • 1850 W Roosevelt Rd
- **Children of Peace Elementary** • 1900 W Taylor St
- **Josiah L Pickard Elementary** • 2301 W 21st Pl
- **Nancy Jefferson** • 1100 S Hamilton Ave
- **Octavio Paz Middle** • 2401 W Congress Pkwy
- **Orozco Elementary** • 1940 W 18th St
- **Rush Day** • 1720 W Polk St
- **Rush University** • 600 S Paulina St
- **St Ann Grade** • 2211 W 18th Pl
- **University of Illinois at Chicago** • 840 S Wood St
- **University of Illinois College of Medicine** • 808 S Wood St
- **Washington Irving Elementary** • 749 S Oakley Blvd
- **William E Gladstone Elementary** • 1231 S Damen Ave

Supermarkets

- **Aldi** • 1739 W Cermak Rd
- **Aldi** • 2525 W Cermak Rd
- **Fairplay Finer Foods** • 2200 S Western Ave

Map 25 • Illinois Medical District

1
2
A
B
C
Western
Medical Center
23
290
Eisenhower Expy
W Van Buren St
W Gladys Ave
S Claremont Ave
S Leavitt St
S Seeley Ave
S Hermitage Ave
S Marshfield Ave
W Congress Pkwy
S Campbell Ave
S Oakley Ave
S Bell Ave
S Hoyne Ave
S Honore St
St Lukes Medical Center
W Harrison St
Claremont Park
W Flournoy St
W Campbell Park Dr
S Western Ave
W Lexington St
S Bowler St
W Bowler St
S Ogden Ave W
S Winchester Ave
S Wolcott Ave
900S
W Polk St
Polk
University of Illinois Hospital
S Paulina St
S Laflin St
Garibaldi Pl
W Boone St
W Arthington St
VA Medical Center
S Damen Ave
W Taylor St
W Fillmore St
Almond St
S Wood St
W Grenshaw St
S Hamilton Ave
W Roosevelt Rd
2400W
2000W
1200S
1600W
ILLINOIS MEDICAL DISTRICT
W Washburne Ave
W 13th St
S Heath Ave
W Hastings St
26
W 14th St
50
W 14th Pl
W 15th St
W 15th Pl
S Ashland Ave
W 16th St
1600S
W 17th St
Western Ave
W 18th St
18th
Harrison Park
W 18th Pl
W 19th St
S Bishop St
HEART OF CHICAGO
W Cullerton St
Western
Damen
W 21st St
W 21st Pl
S Blue Island Ave
W Cermak Rd
52
2200S
W 22nd Pl
1/4 mile
.25 km

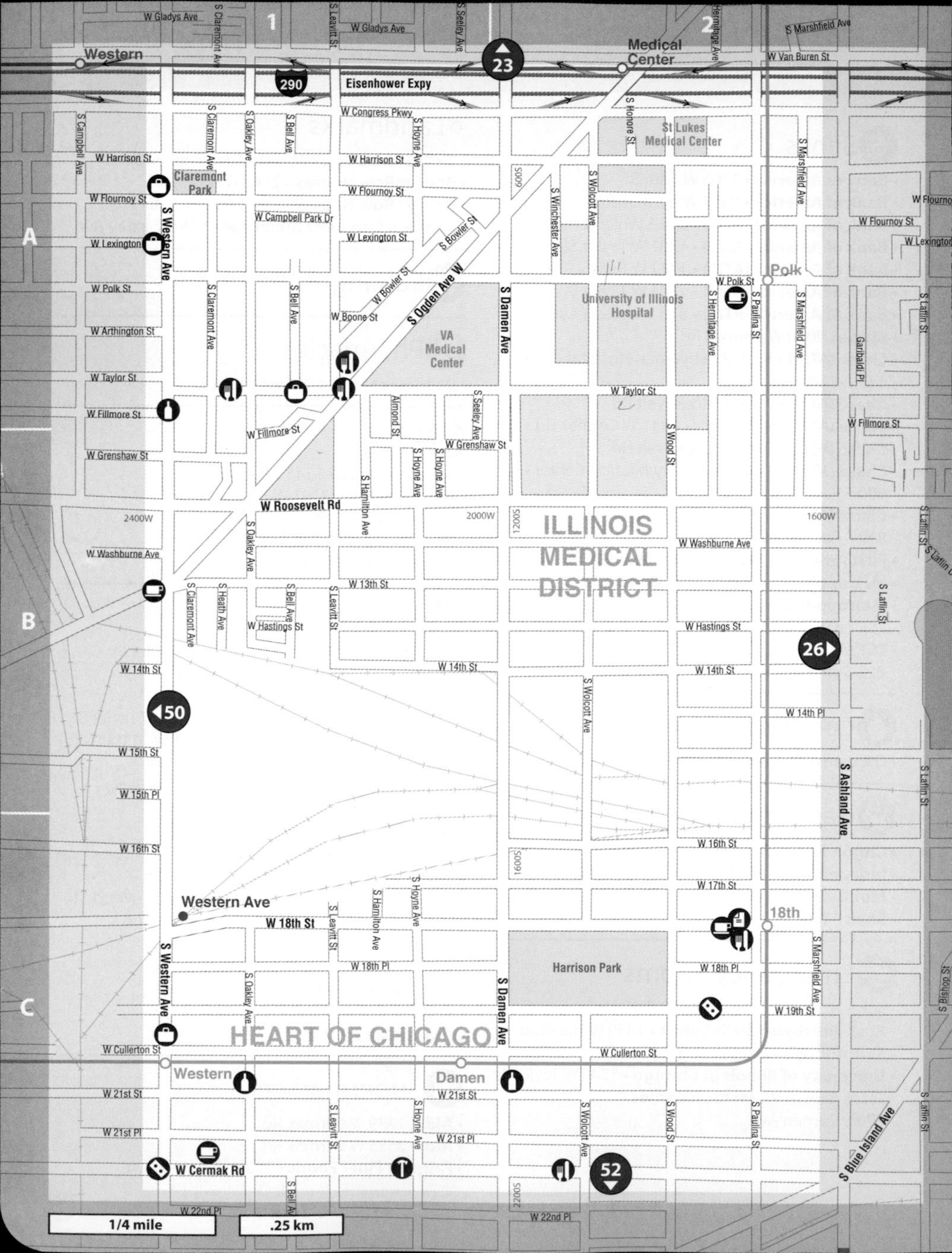

Residents of the Tri-Taylor building boom go a few blocks east to Little Italy or north to River West for nightlife and fine dining. Local options include LuLu's (for a quick lunch) and the Ferrara Bakery, with assorted treats for carry-out and a limited dine-in menu. Further south, Pilsen bleeds into the Heart of Chicago, and there's no shortage of low-priced, dependable Mexican grub (these days more and more high-end eateries are giving the Chicago Foodie scene much to chew on).

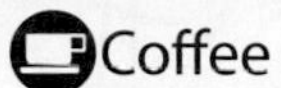

Coffee

- **Dunkin' Donuts** • 1710 W 18th St
- **Dunkin' Donuts** • 1713 W Polk St
- **Dunkin' Donuts** • 2356 W Cermak Rd
- **Dunkin' Donuts** • 2401 W Ogden Ave

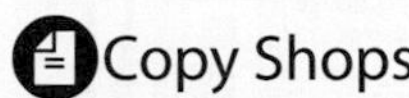

Copy Shops

- **PrintWorks Plus!** • 1720 W 18th St

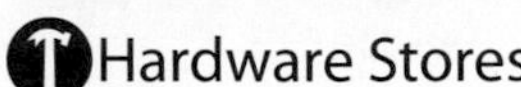

Hardware Stores

- **Mitchell Hardware & Paints** • 2141 W Cermak Rd

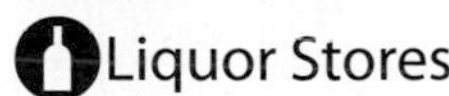

Liquor Stores

- **Helen's Grocery & Liquors** • 2300 W 21st St
- **Three Star Liquor** • 2015 S Damen Ave

Restaurants

- **Carnitas Uruapan Restaurant** • 1725 W 18th St
- **Damenzo's** • 2324 W Taylor St
- **Ferrara Bakery** • 2210 W Taylor St
- **LuLu's Hot Dogs** • 1000 S Leavitt St
- **TJ's Family Restaurant** • 1928 W Cermak Rd

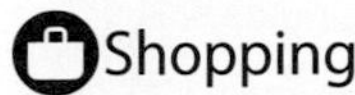

Shopping

- **Accents Flowers and Gifts** • 2246 W Taylor St
- **Salvation Army Thrift Store** • 2024 S Western Ave
- **Symmetry** • 715 S Western Ave

Video Rental

- **Blockbuster** • 2425 W Cermak Rd
- **Pedraza Video** • 1758 W 19th St

Map 26 • University Village/Little Italy/Pilsen

Essentials

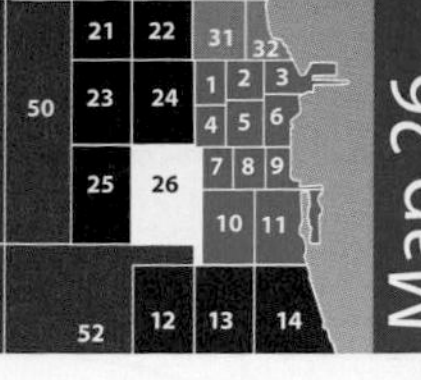

Jane Addams wouldn't recognize her old 'hood today, but it retains her feisty spirit. From the Mexican Fine Arts Museum in Pilsen to the National Italian-American Sports Hall of Fame, institutions pay homage to diverse native groups. UIC definitely holds sway around here; the area bustles with the textbook-toting set from sunup to sundown. Further south, a proud Mexican community rubs shoulders with working creatives around the 18th and Halsted artistic epicenter of Pilsen.

Banks

- **Bank of America** • 1212 S Ashland Ave
- **Bank of America (ATM)** • 700 S Halsted St
- **Bank of America (ATM)** • 750 S Halsted St
- **Bank of America (ATM)** • 1200 W Harrison St
- **Charter One (ATM)** • 1524 W Taylor St
- **Chase** • 1130 W Taylor St
- **Chicago Community** • 1800 S Halsted St
- **Citibank** • 1200 W Taylor St
- **Citibank (ATM)** • 7-Eleven • 1350 S Halsted St
- **First American (ATM)** • 1218 S Halsted St
- **First American (ATM)** • 1438 W Taylor St
- **Lakeside** • 1055 W Roosevelt Rd
- **MB Financial** • 1618 W 18th St
- **Midwest Bank & Trust Company (ATM)** • 1810 S Blue Island Ave
- **National City** • 1314 S Halsted St
- **South Central** • 1400 W 18th St
- **TCF** • 750 S Halsted St
- **TCF** • Jewel • 1220 S Ashland Ave
- **TCF (ATM)** • 7-Eleven • 1350 S Halsted St
- **Washington Federal** • 1410 W Taylor St

Car Washes

- **Speed Hand Car Wash** • 1700 S Ashland Ave
- **We Wash** • 2042 S Halsted St

Gas Stations

- **BP Amoco** • 1602 W Cermak Rd
- **Citgo** • 1491 W Roosevelt Rd
- **Marathon** • 1549 W Roosevelt Rd

Landmarks

- **National Italian American Sports Hall of Fame** • 1431 W Taylor St

Libraries

- **Lozano Public Library** • 1805 S Loomis St
- **Roosevelt Public Library** • 1101 W Taylor St
- **University of Illinois at Chicago Library** • 801 S Morgan St

Parking

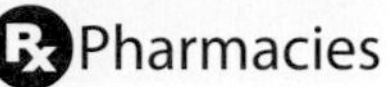

Pharmacies

- **CVS** • 1713 S Ashland Ave
- **Jewel-Osco** • 1220 S Ashland Ave

Pizza

- **Benny's Pizza II** • 1244 W 18th St
- **Caire's Pizza** • 1165 W 18th St
- **Chubby's Pizza** • 1429 W 18th St
- **Leona's** • 1419 W Taylor St
- **Pizza Tango** • 1013 W 18th St
- **Pompeii Bakery** • 1531 W Taylor St
- **Reggio's Pizza** • 1339 S Halsted St

Post Offices

- **US Post Office** • 1859 S Ashland Ave

Schools

- **Andrew Jackson Language Academy** • 1340 W Harrison St
- **Benito Juarez High** • 2150 S Laflin St
- **Bernice F Joyner CPC** • 1315 S Blue Island Ave
- **City as Classroom High** • 1814 S Union Ave
- **Galileo Scholastic Academy** • 820 S Carpenter St
- **Jane Addams High** • 1814 S Union St
- **John A Walsh Elementary** • 2015 S Peoria St
- **John M Smyth Elementary** • 1059 W 13th St
- **Joseph Jungman Elementary** • 1746 S Miller St
- **Joseph Medill Elementary** • 1301 W 14th St
- **Laurance Armour Day School RPS** • 630 S Ashland Ave
- **Manuel Perez Elementary** • 1241 W 19th St
- **McKinley Evgc** • 1326 W 14 Pl
- **Montefiore High** • 1310 S Ashland Ave
- **Moses Montefiore Middle** • 1310 S Ashland Ave
- **Perez Annex** • 2001 S Throop St
- **Peter Cooper Dual Language Academy** • 1624 W 19th St
- **Pilsen Academy** • 1420 W 17th St
- **Simpson Academy for Young Women** • 1321 S Paulina St
- **St Ignatius College Prep** • 1076 W Roosevelt Rd
- **St Pius V Elementary** • 1919 S Ashland Ave
- **St Procopius** • 1625 S Allport St
- **Thomas Jefferson Elementary** • 1522 W Fillmore St
- **Walsh Elementary** • 2015 S Peoria St

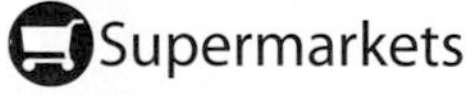

Supermarkets

- **Conte Di Savoia** • 1438 W Taylor St
- **Jewel-Osco** • 1220 S Ashland Ave

Map 26 • University Village/Little Italy/Pilsen

N

UNIVERSITY VILLAGE / LITTLE ITALY

PILSEN

University of Illinois at Chicago East Campus

PAGE 254

Arrigo Park

Sheridan Park

Addams Park

Pilgd Park

Dvorak Park

Racine

UIC-Halsted

Polk

18th

Halsted

24

4

7

25

10

12

290

90

94

1

2

A

B

C

W Gladys Blvd

W Gladys Ave

S Marshfield Ave

W Van Buren St

S Tilden St

W Congress Pkwy

W Harrison St

W Westgate Ter

W Flournoy St

W Lexington St

W Polk St

W Cabrini St

W Arthington St

W Taylor St

W Fillmore St

W Grenshaw St

W Roosevelt Rd

W Washburne Ave

W 12th Pl

W O'Brien St

W 13th St

W Maxwell St

W Hastings St

W Liberty St

W 14th St

W Barber St

W 14th Pl

W South Water Market

W 15th St

W 15th Pl

W 16th St

W 17th St

W 17th Pl

W 18th St

W 18th Pl

W 19th St

W 19th Pl

W Cullerton St

W 20th Pl

W 21st St

W 21st Pl

S Canalport Ave

W Cermak Rd

W 22nd Pl

W Vernon Park Pl

S Ashland Ave

S Racine Ave

S Morgan St

S Paulina St

S Marshfield Ave

S Laflin St

S Laflin Cir

S Bishop St

S Loomis St

S Ada St

S Lytle St

S Throop St

S May St

S Aberdeen St

S Carpenter St

S Miller St

S Sangamon St

S Peoria St

S Newbury Ave

S Halsted St

S Union Ave

S Ruble St

S Desplaines St

S Jefferson St

S Shelby Ct

S Allport St

S Blue Island Ave

S Ford Ave

Garibaldi Pl

Dan Ryan Expy

600S

1200S

1600S

2200S

1600W

1200W

800W

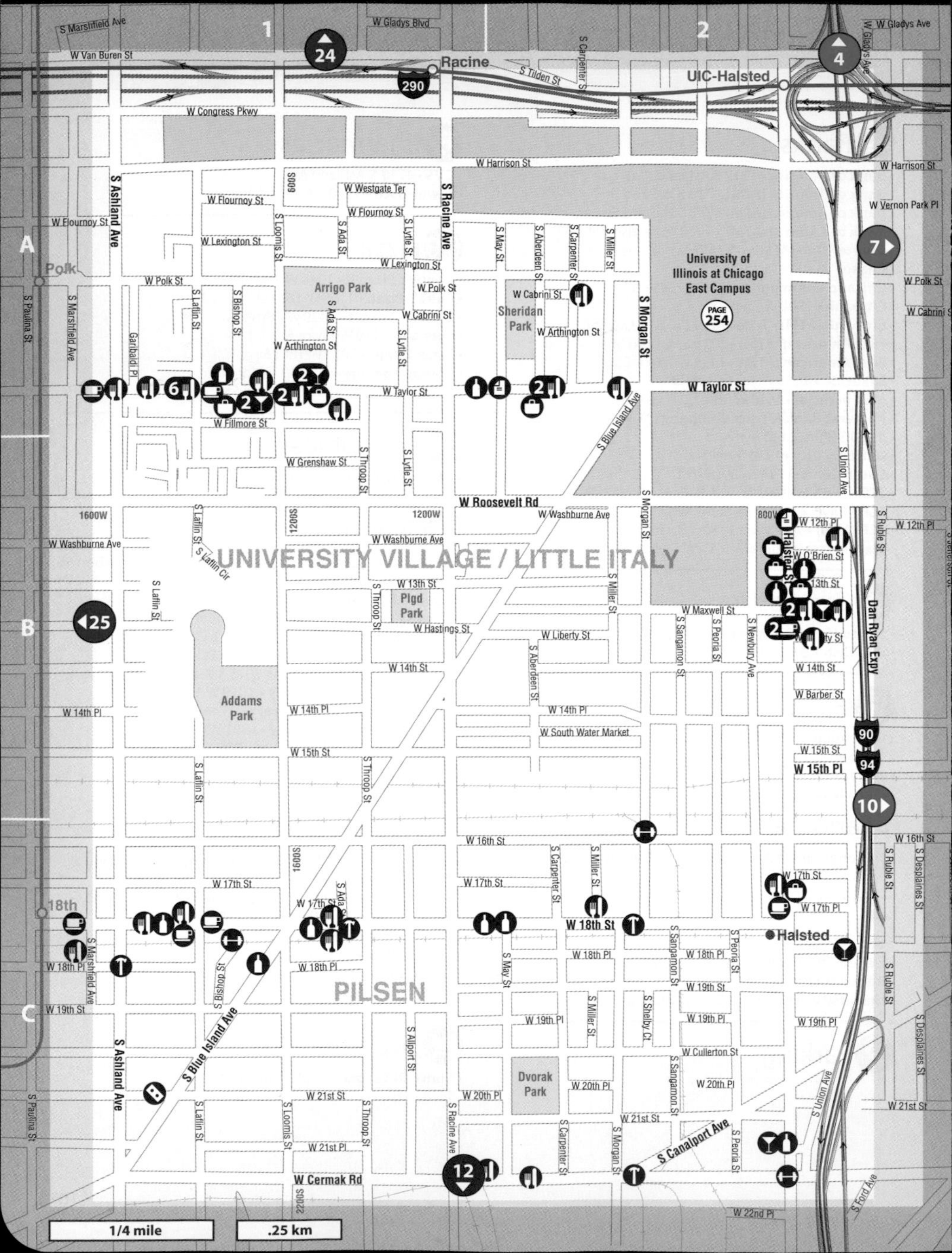

1/4 mile

.25 km

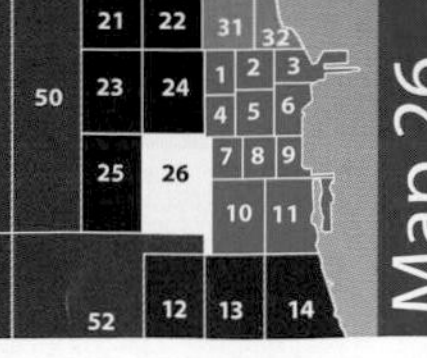

Sprawling over the city's Near West Side is the University of Illinois at Chicago. Little Italy is close at hand, and if you look closely you will note the presence of a number of thriving Italian neighborhood clubs here. Make sure and stop by Conte Di Savoia for some picnic supplies and a spare bottle of limoncello. In Pilsen, local artists frequent the Skylark, and people travel from far and wide for the authenic Mexican food on 18th Street.

Coffee

- **Café Jumping Bean** • 1439 W 18th St
- **Café Mestizo** • 1646 W 18th St
- **Caribou Coffee** • 1328 S Halsted St
- **Caribou Coffee** • 811 W Maxwell St
- **Dunkin' Donuts** • 1651 W Roosevelt Rd
- **Kristoffer's Café & Bakery** • 1733 S Halsted St
- **Mi Cafetal** • 1519 W 18th St
- **Starbucks** • 1430 W Taylor St

Copy Shops

- **Postnet** • 1258 S Halsted St
- **The UPS Store** • 1137 W Taylor St

Gyms

- **Energym** • 2201 S Halsted St
- **Go Time** • 1601 S Morgan St
- **World Gym** • 1822 S Bishop St

Hardware Stores

- **Alvarez Hardware** • 1323 W 18th St
- **La Brocha Gorda** • 974 W 18th St
- **Seigle's Lumber (lumber only)** • 977 W Cermak Rd
- **Torres Hardware** • 1836 S Ashland Ave

Liquor Stores

- **Amador Liquors** • 1167 W 18th St
- **Conte Di Savoia (wine only)** • 1438 W Taylor St
- **El Trebol Liquors** • 1135 W 18th St
- **F&R Liquor** • 2129 S Halsted St
- **Guadalajara Food & Liquors** • 1527 W 18th St
- **Harbee Liquor** • 1345 W 18th St
- **Lush Wine and Spirits** • 1257 S Halsted St
- **Taylor St Food & Liquor** • 1152 W Taylor St
- **Tito Hacienda** • 1854 S Blue Island Ave

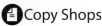

Nightlife

- **Bar Louie** • 1321 W Taylor St
- **BeviAmo Wine Bar** • 1358 W Taylor St
- **Hawkeye's Bar & Grill** • 1458 W Taylor St
- **Junior's Sports Lounge** • 724 W Maxwell St
- **Paulie's Place** • 1750 S Union Ave
- **Simone's** • 960 W 18th St
- **Skylark** • 2149 S Halsted St

Restaurants

- **Al's Beef** • 1079 W Taylor St
- **Birreria Reyes de Ocotlan** • 1322 W 18th St
- **Carm's Beef and Italian Ice** • 1057 W Polk St
- **Chez Joel** • 1119 W Taylor St
- **China Dragon Restaurant** • 1343 W 18th St
- **Couscous** • 1445 W Taylor St
- **De Pasada** • 1517 W Taylor St
- **Demitasse** • 1066 W Taylor St
- **Don Pedro Carnitas** • 1113 W 18th St
- **Express Grill** • 1260 S Union Ave
- **Francesca's** • 1400 W Taylor St
- **Franconello's Italian Restaurant** • 1301 S Halsted St
- **Golden Thai** • 1509 W Taylor St
- **Hashbrowns** • 731 W Maxwell St
- **Joy Yee's** • 1335 S Halsted St
- **Kohan Japanese Restaurant** • 730 W Maxwell St
- **La Cebollita Grill** • 1807 S Ashland Ave
- **La Vita** • 1359 W Taylor St
- **May Street Café** • 1146 W Cermak Rd
- **Mundial Cocina Mestiza** • 1640 W 18th St
- **New Rosebud Café** • 1500 W Taylor St
- **Nuevo Leon** • 1515 W 18th St
- **Pizza Tango** • 1013 W 18th St
- **Steak 'n Egger** • 1174 W Cermak Rd
- **Sweet Maple Café** • 1339 W Taylor St
- **Taj Mahal** • 1512 W Taylor St
- **Taqueria Los Comales** • 1544 W 18th St
- **Tuscany** • 1014 W Taylor St
- **WOW Café & Wingery** • 717 W Maxwell St

Shopping

- **Barbara's Bookstore** • 1218 S Halsted St
- **Conte Di Savoia** • 1438 W Taylor St
- **Cooper Used Hotel Furniture** • 1929 S Halstead St
- **Lush Wine and Spirits** • 1306 S Halsted St
- **Mario's Italian Lemonade** • 1068 W Taylor St

Map 27 • Logan Square

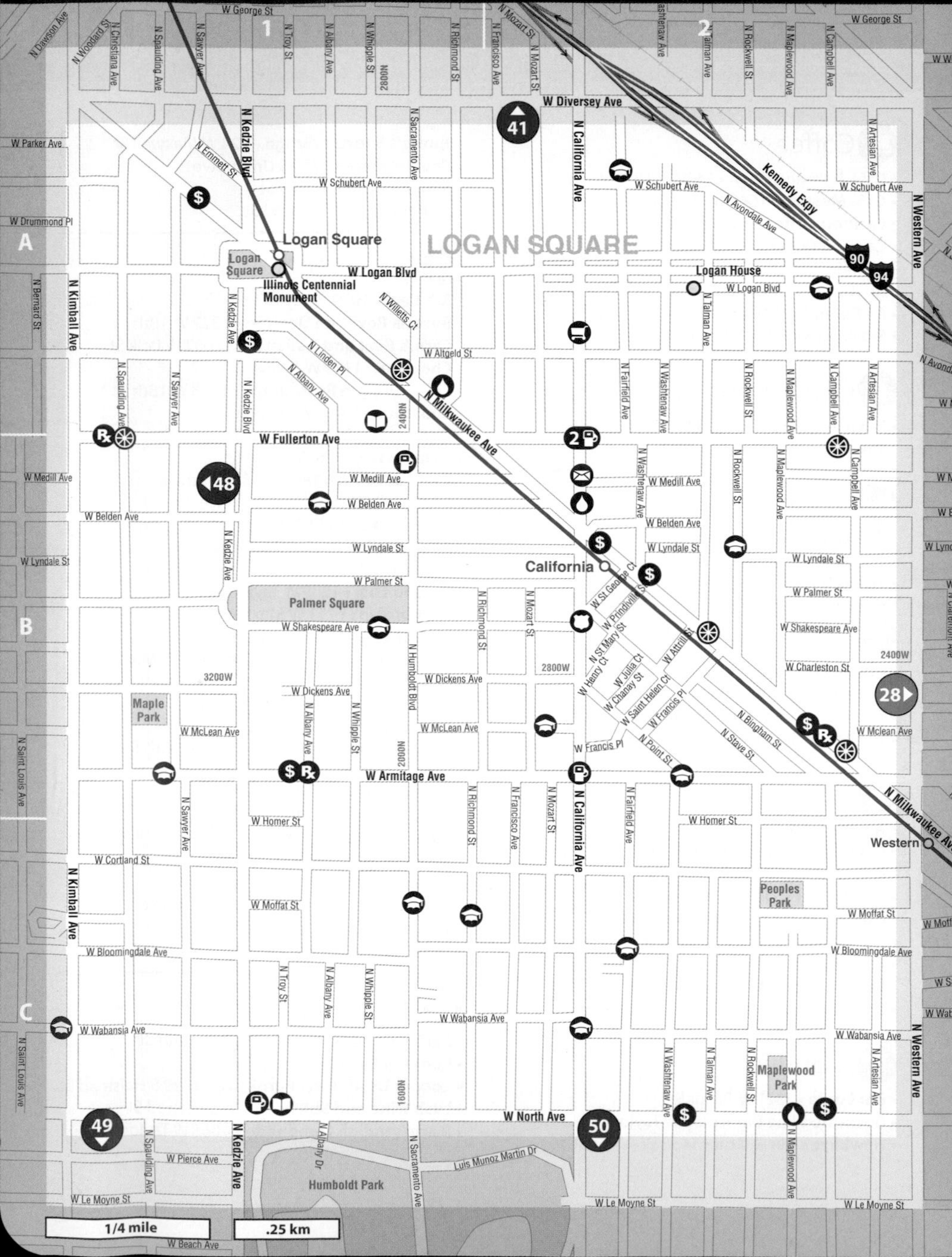

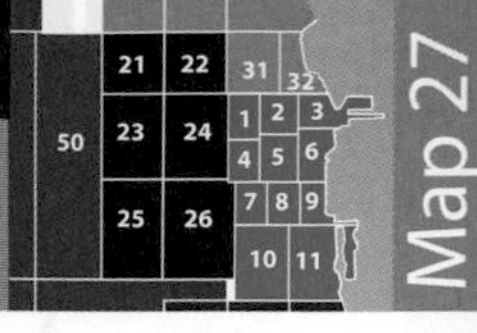

The natural redoubt for creative professionals fleeing higher rent and stroller gridlock in Wicker Park, Logan Square's leafy boulevards seem to sprout new bars and restaurants every month. Milwaukee forms the spread-out strip of commercial activity, where artsy bars mingle with auto shops and tasty 24-hour taquerias.

Banks

- **Banco Popular** • 2525 N Kedzie Blvd
- **Charter One** • 2500 W North Ave
- **Chase** • 2235 N Milwaukee Ave
- **Chase** • 2639 N Milwaukee Ave
- **Chase (ATM)** • 3110 W Armitage Ave
- **Citibank (ATM)** • 7-Eleven • 2020 N California Ave
- **Citibank (ATM)** • 2295 N Milwaukee Ave
- **Citibank (ATM)** • 7-Eleven • 2401 N Milwaukee Ave
- **First American (ATM)** • 2701 W North Ave
- **Northern Trust** • 2814 W Fullerton Ave
- **TCF (ATM)** • Osco • 2053 N Milwaukee Ave

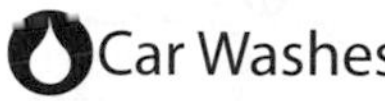

Car Washes

- **California Car Wash** • 2340 N California Ave
- **Dreamwash** • 2524 W North Ave
- **Logan Square Car Wash** • 2436 N Milwaukee Ave

Gas Stations

- **Amoco** • 2800 W Fullerton Ave
- **BP/Amoco** • 2801 W Armitage Ave
- **Citgo** • 2338 N Sacramento Ave
- **Citgo** • 3142 W North Ave
- **Shell** • 2801 W Fullerton Ave

Landmarks

- **Illinois Centennial Monument** • 3100 W Logan Blvd
- **Logan House** • 2656 W Logan Blvd

Libraries

- **Humboldt Park Public Library** • 1605 N Troy St
- **Logan Square Public Library** • 3030 W Fullerton Ave

Pharmacies

- **CVS** • 2053 N Milwaukee Ave
- **Walgreens** • 3110 W Armitage Ave
- **Walgreens** • 3320 W Fullerton Ave

Pizza

- **Big Tony's Pizza** • 3217 W Fullerton Ave
- **Congress Pizzeria** • 2033 N Milwaukee Ave
- **Domino's** • 2455 W Fullerton Ave
- **Marcello's Father & Son Restaurant** • 2475 N Milwaukee Ave
- **Lucky Vito's Pizzeria** • 2171 N Milwaukee Ave

Police

- **14th District (Shakespeare)** • 2150 N California Ave

Post Offices

- **US Post Office** • 2339 N California Ave
- **US Post Office** • 2901 W Armitage Ave

Schools

- **Bernhard Moos Elementary** • 1711 N California Ave
- **Charles R Darwin Elementary** • 3116 W Belden Ave
- **Harriet Beecher Stowe Elementary** • 3444 W Wabansia Ave
- **Humboldt Community Christian** • 1847 N Humboldt Blvd
- **J W Von Goethe Elementary** • 2236 N Rockwell St
- **Lorenz Brentano Math & Science Academy** • 2723 N Fairfield Ave
- **The Lutheran Day Nursery** • 1802 N Fairfield Ave
- **Richard Yates Elementary** • 1839 N Richmond St
- **Salem Christian** • 2845 W McLean Ave
- **Salomon P Chase Elementary** • 2021 N Point St
- **St Augustine College West** • 3255 W Armitage Ave
- **St John Berchman's** • 2511 W Logan Blvd
- **St Sylvester's** • 3027 W Palmer Blvd

Supermarkets

- **Provenance Food and Wine** • 2528 N California Ave

Map 28 • Bucktown

Separated from Lincoln Park by the freeway, Bucktown is not quite as well-situated, but its (slightly) more affordable real estate has brought in the young professionals in droves. Gentrification is gaining pace, with an ongoing influx of polished boutiques and hip baby stores. Meanwhile, the thriving art scene that once characterized Bucktown is all but a memory.

Banks

- **Charter One** • Dominick's • 2550 N Clybourn Ave
- **Chase** • 1757 W Fullerton Ave
- **Chase (ATM)** • Walgreens • 2001 N Milwaukee Ave
- **Citibank (ATM)** • McDonalds • 1951 N Western
- **Citibank (ATM)** • 7-Eleven • 2010 N Damen Ave
- **Cole Taylor** • 1965 N Milwaukee Ave
- **Fifth Third** • 2785 N Clybourn Ave
- **Harris Trust & Savings** • 2196 N Elston Ave
- **National City Bank** • 1640 W Fullerton Ave
- **National City** • 1830 W Fullerton Ave
- **National City** • 1955 N Damen Ave
- **National City** • 2300 N Western Ave
- **Northern Trust (ATM)** • 2346 N Western Ave
- **TCF (ATM)** • 7-Eleven • 2010 N Damen Ave

Car Washes

- **Bucktown Hand Car Wash** • 2036 W Armitage Ave
- **Clybourn Express & Car Wash** • 2452 N Clybourn Ave
- **Express Car Wash** • 2111 W Fullerton Ave
- **Fast Eddie's Hand Car Wash** • 1828 W Webster Ave
- **Prestige Hand Wash** • 1843 N Milwaukee Ave
- **Wash Express** • 1657 N Milwaukee Ave

Car Rental

- **Enterprise** • 1842 N Milwaukee Ave • 773-862-4700

Gas Stations

- **BP** • 2357 W Fullerton Ave
- **Citgo** • 1768 W Armitage Ave
- **Citgo** • 2501 N Western Ave
- **Citgo** • 2107 S Western Ave
- **Marathon** • 2346 N Western Ave
- **Mobil** • 1750 N Western Ave
- **Shell** • 2357 W Fullerton Ave

Landmarks

- **Margie's Candies** • 1960 N Western Ave

Libraries

- **Bucktown-Wicker Park Public Library** • 1701 N Milwaukee Ave

Pharmacies

- **Dominick's** • 2550 N Clybourn Ave
- **Target** • 2656 N Elston Ave
- **Walgreens** • 2001 N Milwaukee Ave

Pizza

- **Homemade Pizza Co** • 1953 W Wabansia Ave
- **John's Pizzeria Ristorante & Lounge** • 2104 N Western Ave
- **My Pie Pizza** • 2010 N Damen Ave
- **Plazzio's Pizza** • 1901 N Western Ave
- **Sonny's Pizza** • 2431 N Western Ave

Schools

- **Antonia Pantoja High** • 2435 N Western Ave
- **Casimir Pulaski Fine Arts Academy** • 2230 W McLean Ave
- **Chicago International Elementary - Bucktown Campus** • 2235 N Hamilton Ave
- **St Mary of the Angels** • 1810 N Hermitage Ave
- **Thomas Drummond Elementary** • 1845 W Cortland St
- **William H Prescott Elementary** • 1632 W Wrightwood Ave

Supermarkets

- **Aldi** • 1767 N Milwaukee Ave
- **Aldi** • 2600 N Clybourn Ave
- **Costco** • 2746 N Clybourn Ave
- **Dominick's** • 2550 N Clybourn Ave
- **The Goddess and Grocer** • 2200 N Elston Ave
- **The Goddess and the Grocer** • 1646 N Damen Ave
- **Olivia's Market** • 2014 W Wabansia Ave

N

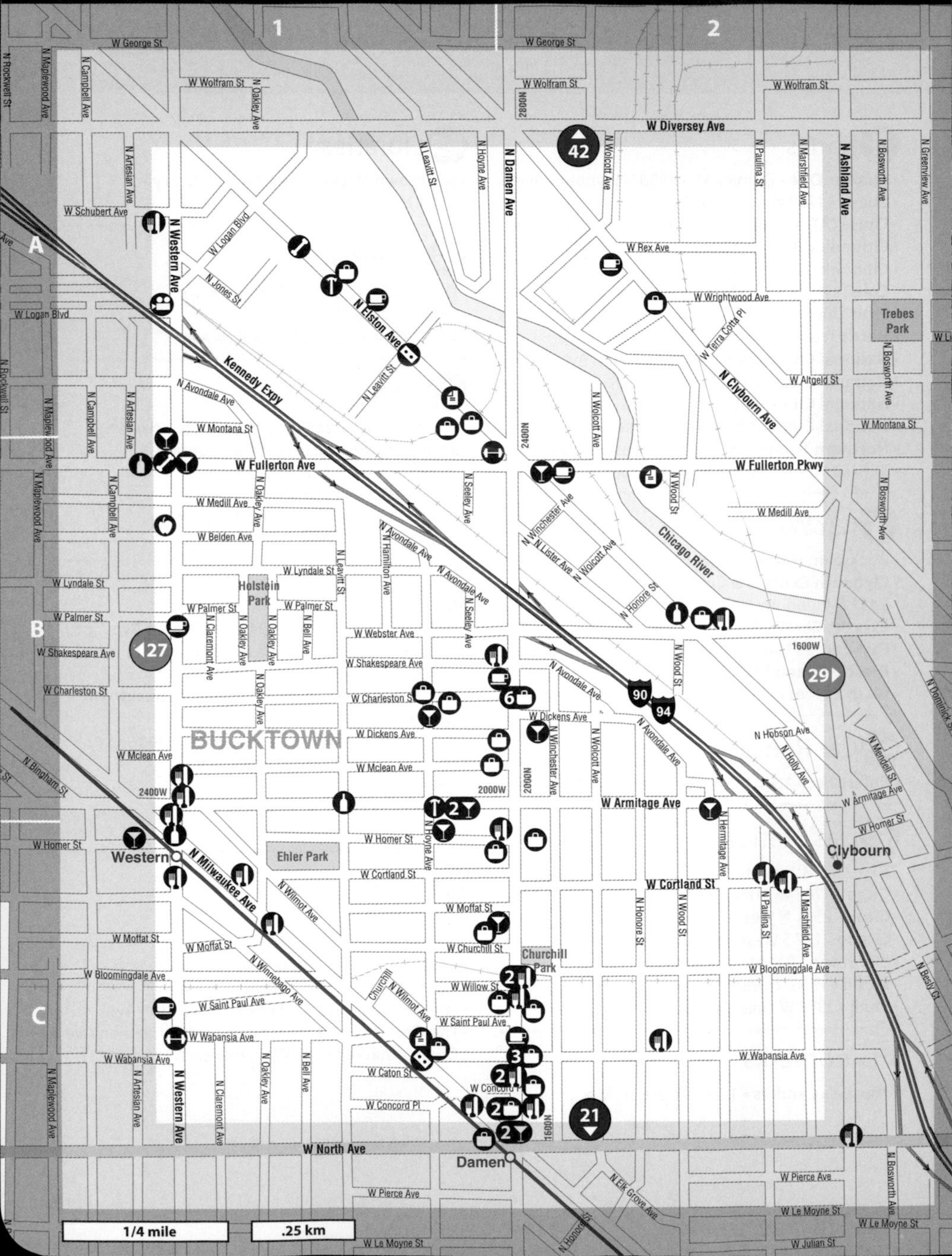

Sundries / Entertainment

You need never be hungry, thirsty, or poorly clothed in Bucktown—or have to walk more than a block or two. Budget and upscale still co-exist; take Margie's Candies and Goddess and the Grocer. Caffé De Luca is the spot for coffee, while Hot Chocolate is stroller-heaven by day, chic eatery by night. Find your niche, or better yet, do it all.

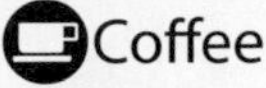

Coffee

- **Caffé De Luca** • 1721 N Damen Ave
- **Dunkin' Donuts** • 1746 N Western Ave
- **Dunkin' Donuts** • 1909 N Western Ave
- **Dunkin' Donuts** • 1927 W Fullerton Ave
- **Pura Belleza Coffee & Art** • 2161 N Western Ave
- **Red Hen Bread** • 1623 N Milwaukee Ave
- **Starbucks** • Dominick's • 2550 N Clybourn Ave
- **Starbucks** • 2577 N Elston Ave
- **Starbucks** • Target • 2656 N Elston Ave

Copy Shops

- **Office Max** • 1829 W Fullerton Ave
- **Staples Copy & Print Centers** • 2484 N Elston Ave
- **The UPS Store** • 1658 Milwaukee Ave

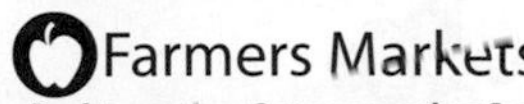

Farmers Markets

- **Bucktown (Jun-Oct; every other Sun, 7 am-2 pm)** • W Belden Ave & N Western Ave

Gyms

- **Ladies Workout Express (women only)** • 1722 N Western Ave
- **Mid-Town Athletic Club** • 2020 W Fullerton Ave

Hardware Stores

- **Home Depot** • 2570 N Elston Ave
- **Menard's** • 2601 N Clybourn Ave

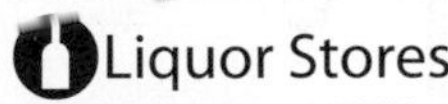

Liquor Stores

- **Bon Song Liquors** • 2000 N Leavitt St
- **Bucktown Food & Liquor** • 2422 W Fullerton Ave
- **Danny's Buy Low** • 2222 N Western Ave
- **MW Food & Liquor** • 1950 N Milwaukee Ave
- **Wine and Ciders** • 2211 N Elston Ave

Movie Theaters

- **Kerasotes City North 14** • 2600 N Western Ave

Nightlife

- **The Bluebird** • 1749 N Damen
- **Caoba Mexican Bar and Grill** • 1619 N Damen Ave
- **Cans** • 1640 N Damen Ave
- **Charleston Tavern** • 2076 N Hoyne Ave
- **Cleo's** • 2048 W Armitage Ave
- **Cortland's Garage** • 1645 W Cortland St
- **Danny's Tavern** • 1951 W Dickens Ave
- **Ed and Jean's** • 2032 W Armitage Ave
- **Gallery Cabaret** • 2020 N Oakley Ave
- **Green Eye Lounge** • 2403 W Homer St
- **Lemmings** • 1850 N Damen Ave
- **The Liar's Club** • 1665 W Fullerton Ave
- **The Map Room** • 1949 N Hoyne Ave
- **The Mutiny** • 2428 N Western Ave
- **Northside Bar & Grill** • 1635 N Damen Ave
- **Quenchers Saloon** • 2401 N Western Ave
- **WhirlyBall** • 1880 W Fullerton Ave

Pet Shops

- **... and Feathers Bird Studio** • 2406 W Fullerton Ave
- **Petsmart** • 2665 N Elston Ave

Restaurants

- **Arturo's Tacos** • 2001 N Western Ave
- **Belly Shack** • 1912 N Western Ave
- **The Bluebird** • 1749 N Damen Ave
- **Bristol** • 2152 N Damen Ave
- **Caoba Mexican Bar and Grill** • 1619 N Damen Ave
- **Café Bolero** • 2252 N Western Ave
- **Café Laguardia** • 2111 W Armitage Ave
- **Café Matou** • 1846 N Milwaukee Ave
- **Club Lucky** • 1824 W Wabansia Ave
- **Coast Sushi Bar** • 2045 N Damen Ave
- **Duchamp** • 2118 N Damen Ave
- **Fat Willy's Rib Shack** • 2416 W Schubert Ave
- **Hollywood Grill** • 1601 W North Ave ㉔
- **Honey 1 BBQ** • 2241 N Western Ave
- **Hot Chocolate** • 1747 N Damen Ave
- **Irazu** • 1865 N Milwaukee Ave
- **Jane's** • 1655 W Cortland St
- **Le Bouchon** • 1958 N Damen Ave
- **Mado** • 1647 N Milwaukee Ave
- **Margie's Candies** • 1960 N Western Ave
- **Rinconcito Sudamericano** • 2010 W Armitage Ave
- **Rio's D'Sudamerica** • 2010 W Armitage Ave
- **Riverside Deli & Café** • 1656 W Cortland St
- **Rosa de Lima** • 2013 N Western Ave
- **Silver Cloud Club & Grill** • 1700 N Damen Ave
- **Takashi** • 1952 Damen Ave
- **Vosges Haut Chocolat** • 2211 N Elston Ave

Shopping

- **Beta Boutique** • 2016 W Concord Pl
- **Clever Alice** • 1920 N Damen Ave
- **Cynthia Rowley** • 1653 N Damen Ave
- **European Imports** • 2475 N Elston Ave
- **G Boutique** • 2131 N Damen Ave
- **The Goddess and the Grocer** • 1646 N Damen Ave
- **Halo [For Men]** • 1655 N Damen Ave
- **Intermix** • 1633 N Damen Ave
- **Jean Alan** • 2134 N Damen Ave
- **Lululemon** • 1627 N Damen Ave
- **Micro Center** • 2645 N Elston Ave
- **The Needle Shop** • 2054 W Charleston St
- **p.45** • 1643 N Damen Ave
- **Pagoda Red** • 1714 N Damen Ave
- **Pavilion Antiques** • 2055 N Damen Ave
- **Psycho Baby** • 1630 N Damen Ave
- **The Red Balloon Company** • 2060 N Damen Ave
- **Robin Richman** • 2108 N Damen Ave
- **Scoop NYC** • 1702 N Milwaukee Ave
- **Soutache** • 2125 N Damen Ave
- **T-Shirt Deli** • **1739 N Damen Ave**
- **Tangerine** • 1719 N Damen Ave
- **Veruca Salt** • 1921 N Damen Ave
- **Vienna Beef Factory Store** • 2501 N Damen Ave
- **Village Discount Outlet** • 2032 N Milwaukee Ave
- **Vive La Femme** • 2048 N Damen Ave
- **Vosges Haut Chocolat** • 2211 N Elston Ave
- **White Attic** • 1842 N Damen Ave

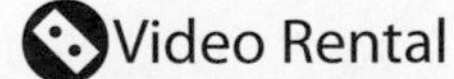

Video Rental

- **Blockbuster** • 1704 N Milwaukee Ave

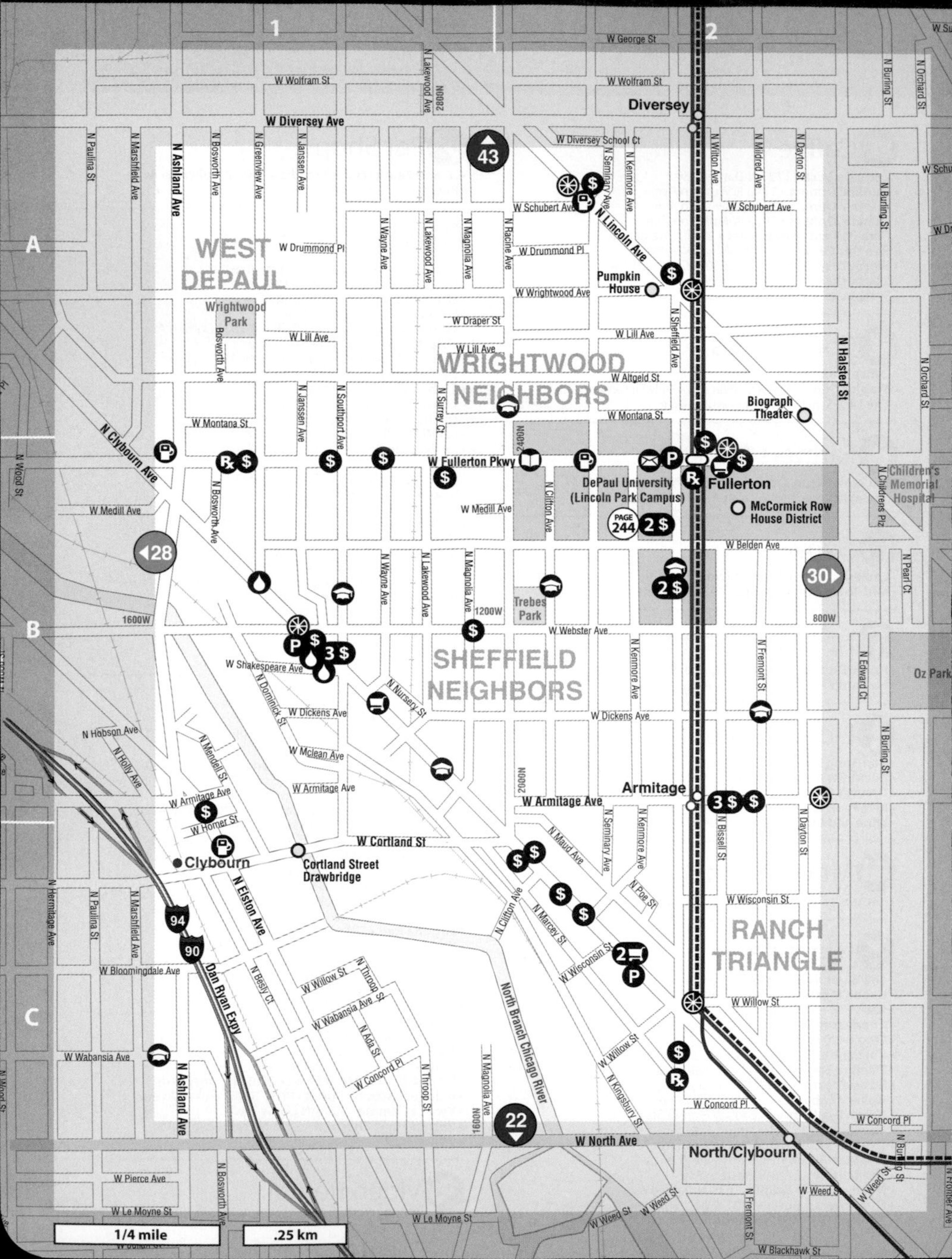

WEST DEPAUL
WRIGHTWOOD NEIGHBORS
SHEFFIELD NEIGHBORS
RANCH TRIANGLE
Diversey
Pumpkin House
Biograph Theater
DePaul University (Lincoln Park Campus)
Fullerton
McCormick Row House District
Children's Memorial Hospital
Wrightwood Park
Trebes Park
Oz Park
Armitage
Clybourn
Cortland Street Drawbridge
North/Clybourn
North Branch Chicago River
Dan Ryan Expy
W Diversey Ave
W Fullerton Pkwy
W Armitage Ave
W Cortland St
W North Ave
N Ashland Ave
N Clybourn Ave
N Elston Ave
N Lincoln Ave
N Halsted St
PAGE 244

1/4 mile
.25 km

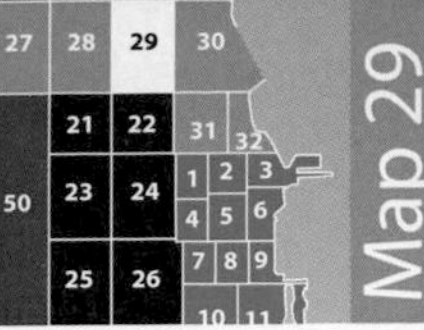

There's the good—neighborhood parks and quiet, tree-lined streets with elegant homes—the bad—an overabundance of frat boys and traffic jams—and the ugly—the occasional weekend puke puddle (DePaul University is right in the middle, you know). But it's this variety, we think, that gives this neighborhood its charm.

Banks

- **Associated (ATM)** • 1224 W Webster Ave
- **Bank of America** • 2163 N Clybourn Ave
- **Bank of America (ATM)** • 1714 N Sheffield Ave
- **Charter One (ATM)** • 7-Eleven • 2710 W Lincoln Ave
- **Chase** • 2170 N Clybourn Ave
- **Chase** • 935 W Armitage Ave
- **Chase (ATM)** • Lakeshore Athletic Club • 1340 W Fullerton Ave
- **Chase (ATM)** • Walgreens • 1520 W Fullerton Ave
- **Chase (ATM)** • Dominick's • 959 W Fullerton Ave
- **Citibank** • 1251 W Fullerton Ave
- **Citibank (ATM)** • 7-Eleven • 1942 N Elston Ave
- **Citibank (ATM)** • 1953 N Clybourn Ave
- **Citibank (ATM)** • 7-Eleven • 2181 N Clybourn Ave
- **Citibank (ATM)** • 7-Eleven • 2600 N Lincoln Ave
- **Citibank (ATM)** • 7-Eleven • 957 W Armitage Ave
- **Fifth Third** • 900 W Armitage Ave
- **First American (ATM)** • De Paul University Schmidt Academic Center • 2320 N Kenmore Ave
- **National City Bank** • 921 W Armitage Ave
- **TCF** • 1400 W Fullerton Ave
- **TCF** • 2250 N Sheffield Ave
- **TCF (ATM)** • 7-Eleven • 2181 N Clybourn Ave
- **TCF (ATM)** • DePaul University • 2235 N Sheffield Ave
- **TCF (ATM)** • DePaul University • 2320 N Kenmore Ave
- **TCF (ATM)** • 7-Eleven • 2600 N Lincoln Ave
- **TCF (ATM)** • 7-Eleven • 957 W Armitage Ave
- **US** • 1953 N Clybourn Ave

Car Washes

- **Simon's** • 1439 W Shakespeare Ave
- **We'll Clean** • 2261 N Clybourn Ave
- **White Glove Car Wash** • 1415 W Shakespeare Ave

Gas Stations

- **BP** • 1607 W Fullerton Ave
- **Mobil** • 1106 W Fullerton Ave
- **Mobil** • 1901 N Elston Ave
- **Mobil** • 2670 N Lincoln Ave

Landmarks

- **Biograph Theater** • 2433 N Lincoln Ave
- **Cortland Street Drawbridge** • 1440 W Cortland St
- **McCormick Row House District** • W Chalmers Pl
- **Pumpkin House** • 1052 W Wrightwood Ave

Libraries

- **Lincoln Park Public Library** • 1150 W Fullerton Ave

Parking

Pharmacies

- **CVS** • 1714 N Sheffield Ave
- **Dominick's** • 959 W Fullerton Ave
- **Walgreens** • 1520 W Fullerton Ave

Pizza

- **Amato's Pizza** • 953 W Willow St
- **Homemade Pizza Co** • 850 W Armitage Ave
- **Lou Malnati's Pizzeria** • 958 W Wrightwood Ave
- **Pat's Pizzeria** • 2679 N Lincoln Ave
- **Pequod's Pizzeria** • 2207 N Clybourn Ave
- **Via-Carducci's Italian Eatery** • 1419 W Fullerton Ave

Post Offices

- **US Post Office** • 2405 N Sheffield Ave

Schools

- **DePaul University (Lincoln Park Campus)** • 2250 N Sheffield Ave
- **Jefferson Center/Factory Branch** • 2032 N Clybourn Ave
- **Jonathan Burr Elementary** • 1621 W Wabansia Ave
- **Oscar F Mayer Elementary** • 2250 N Clifton Ave
- **St James Lutheran** • 2101 N Fremont St
- **St Josephat** • 2245 N Southport Ave

Supermarkets

- **Aldi** • 1836 N Clybourn Ave
- **Dominick's** • 959 W Fullerton Ave
- **Trader Joe's** • 1840 N Clybourn Ave
- **Treasure Island** • 2121 N Clybourn Ave

WEST DEPAUL
WRIGHTWOOD NEIGHBORS
SHEFFIELD NEIGHBORS
RANCH TRIANGLE

Wrightwood Park
Trebes Park
Oz Park
DePaul University (Lincoln Park Campus)
Children's Memorial Hospital

Diversey
Fullerton
Armitage
Clybourn
North/Clybourn

W George St
W Wolfram St
W Diversey Ave
W Diversey School Ct
W Schubert Ave
W Drummond Pl
W Wrightwood Ave
W Draper St
W Lill Ave
W Altgeld St
W Montana St
W Fullerton Pkwy
W Medill Ave
W Belden Ave
W Webster Ave
W Shakespeare Ave
W Dickens Ave
W Mclean Ave
W Armitage Ave
W Homer St
W Cortland St
W Wisconsin St
W Bloomingdale Ave
W Willow St
W Wabansia Ave
W Concord Pl
W North Ave
W Pierce Ave
W Le Moyne St
W Weed St
W Blackhawk St

N Paulina St
N Marshfield Ave
N Ashland Ave
N Bosworth Ave
N Greenview Ave
N Janssen Ave
N Southport Ave
N Wayne Ave
N Lakewood Ave
N Magnolia Ave
N Racine Ave
N Surrey Ct
N Clifton Ave
N Seminary Ave
N Kenmore Ave
N Sheffield Ave
N Lincoln Ave
N Wilton Ave
N Mildred Ave
N Dayton St
N Halsted St
N Burling St
N Orchard St
N Childrens Plz
N Pearl Ct
N Edward Ct
N Fremont St
N Bissell St
N Clybourn Ave
N Wood St
N Hobson Ave
N Holly Ave
N Mendell St
N Dominick St
N Nursery St
N Maud Ave
N Poe St
N Marcey St
N Elston Ave
N Besly Ct
N Throop St
N Ada St
N Kingsbury St
N Hermitage Ave
N Frontier Ave
North Branch Chicago River
Dan Ryan Expy

2800N
2400N
2000N
1600N
1600W
1200W
800W

43
28
30
22
PAGE 244

1/4 mile
.25 km

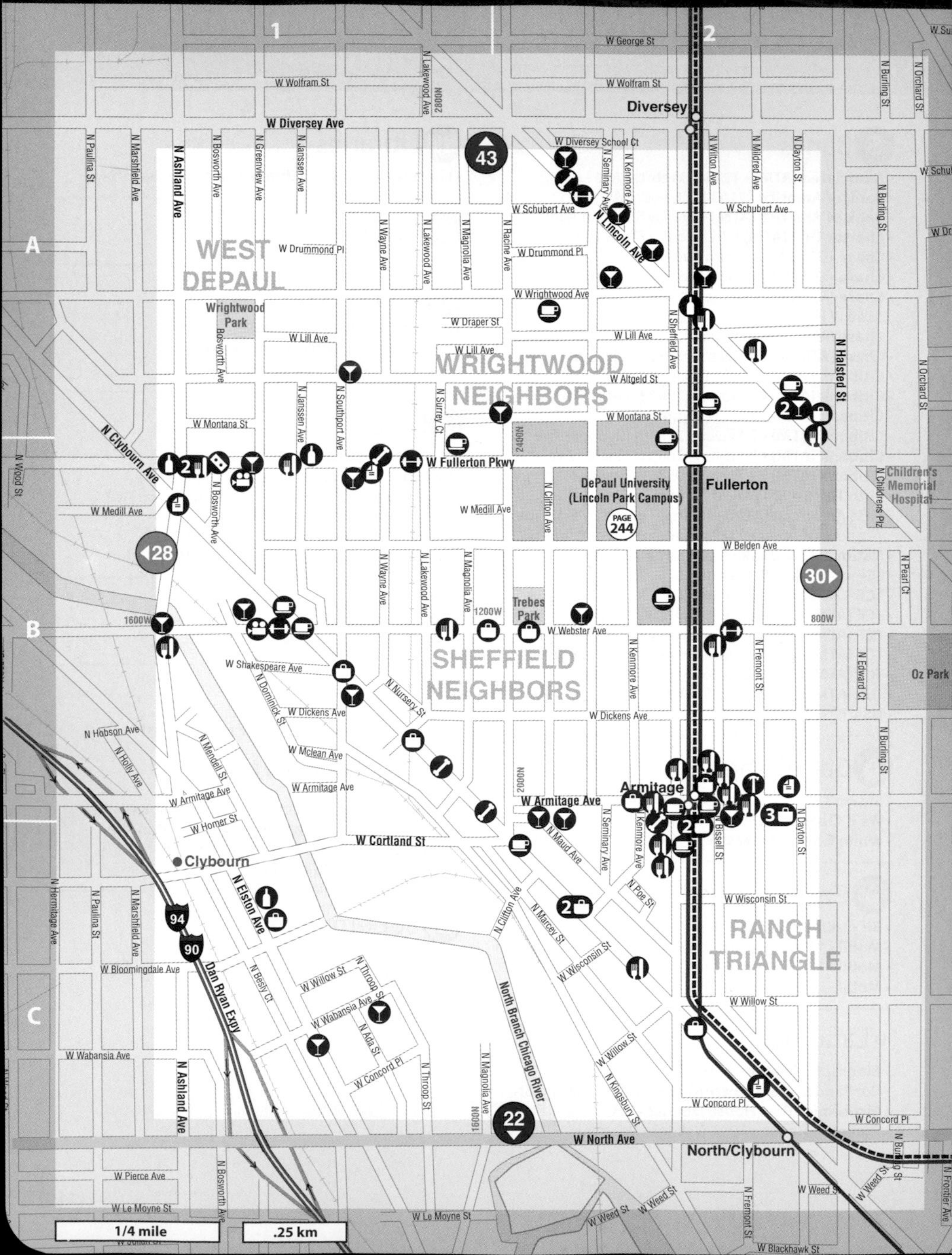

Facets runs a slate of obscure art-house films and rents DVDs as well. For music, the Hideout draws Bloodshot Records fans with its basement rec-room ambience. Aging punk rockers tipple a vast array of spirits at Delilah's. Drinks at Red Lion are a time-honored tradition for graduate students; sometimes lectures are even held upstairs.

Coffee

- **Ambrosia Café** • 1963 N Sheffield Ave
- **Argo Tea** • 958 W Armitage Ave
- **Bean Caffé** • DePaul University • 2235 N Sheffield Ave
- **Dunkin' Donuts** • 1982 N Clybourn Ave
- **Einstein Bros Bagels** • 2212 N Clybourn Ave
- **Savor the Flavor** • 2545 N Sheffield Ave
- **Starbucks** • 1001 W Armitage Ave
- **Starbucks** • 1157 W Wrightwood Ave
- **Starbucks** • 1245 W Fullerton Ave
- **Starbucks** • 2200 N Clybourn Ave
- **Starbucks** • Dominick's • 959 W Fullerton Ave

Copy Shops

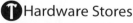

- **FedEx Kinko's** • 2300 N Clybourn Ave
- **Sir Speedy** • 1711 N Clybourn Ave
- **The UPS Store** • 1341 W Fullerton Ave
- **The UPS Store** • 858 W Armitage Ave

Gyms

- **Bally Total Fitness** • 1455 W Webster Ave
- **Crunch Fitness** • 2727 N Lincoln Ave
- **Lakeshore Athletic Club** • 1320 W Fullerton Ave
- **Webster Fitness Club** • 957 W Webster Ave

Hardware Stores

- **Armitage Hardware & Building Supply** • 925 W Armitage Ave

Liquor Stores

- **J&R Liquor & Foods** • 2401 N Ashland Ave
- **Park West Liquor & Smoke Shop** • 2581 N Lincoln Ave
- **Wine Discount Center** • 1826 N Elston Ave
- **Wine Shippers** • 1425 W Fullerton Ave

Movie Theaters

- **Facets Cinematheque** • 1517 W Fullerton Ave
- **Kerasotes Webster Place 11** • 1471 W Webster Ave

Nightlife

- **Bird's Nest Bar** • 2500 N Southport Ave
- **Cagney's** • 2142 N Clybourn Ave
- **Deja Vu** • 2624 N Lincoln Ave
- **Delilah's** • 2771 N Lincoln Ave
- **Faith & Whiskey** • 1365 W Fullerton Ave
- **Gaslight Bar & Grille** • 2426 N Racine Ave
- **The Grand Central** • 950 W Wrightwood Ave
- **Green Dolphin Street** • 2200 N Ashland Ave
- **Hideout** • 1354 W Wabansia Ave
- **Hog Head McDunna's** • 1505 W Fullerton Ave
- **Irish Eyes** • 2519 N Lincoln Ave
- **Kincade's** • 950 W Armitage Ave
- **Local Option** • 1102 W Webster Ave
- **Nic and Dino's Tripoli Tavern** • 1147 W Armitage Ave
- **The Prop House** • 1675 N Elston Ave
- **Rose's Lounge** • 2656 N Lincoln Ave
- **Webster Wine Bar** • 1480 W Webster Ave
- **Wrightwood Tap** • 1059 W Wrightwood Ave

Pet Shops

- **Barker & Meowsky** • 1003 W Armitage Ave
- **Chicago Pet Care** • 1341 W Fullerton Ave
- **Galloping Gourmutts** • 2736 N Lincoln Ave
- **Kriser's Feeding Pets For Life** • 2037 N Clybourn Ave
- **Petco** • 2000 N Clybourn Ave

Restaurants

- **Ambrosia Café** • 1963 N Sheffield Ave
- **Goose Island Brewing Company** • 1800 N Clybourn Ave
- **Green Dolphin Street** • 2200 N Ashland Ave
- **Ja' Grill** • 1008 W Armitage Ave
- **John's Place** • 1200 W Webster Ave
- **Metropolis Rotisseria & Annette's Italian Ice** • 924 W Armitage Ave
- **Ringo Sushi** • 2507 N Lincoln Ave
- **Sai Café** • 2010 N Sheffield Ave
- **Salt & Pepper Diner** • 2575 N Lincoln Ave
- **State** • 935 W Webster Ave
- **Sweet Mandy B's** • 1208 W Webster Ave
- **Sweets & Savories** • 1534 W Fullerton Ave
- **Taco & Burrito House** • 1548 W Fullerton Ave
- **Taxim** • 1558 N Milwaukee Ave
- **Tsuki** • 1441 W Fullerton Ave
- **Twisted Lizard** • 1964 N Sheffield Ave
- **Vosges Haut Chocolat** • 951 W Armitage Ave

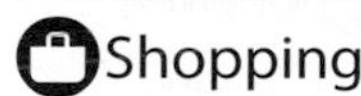

Shopping

- **Art Effect** • 934 W Armitage Ave
- **Balance Health + Wellness** • 1901 N Clybourn Ave
- **Crate & Barrel Outlet Store** • 1864 N Clybourn Ave
- **Dirk's Fish** • 2070 N Clybourn Ave
- **Eclectica** • 1006 W Armitage Ave
- **Intermix** • 841 W Armitage Ave
- **Isabella Fine Lingerie** • 840 W Armitage Ave
- **Jayson Home & Garden** • 1885 N Clybourn Ave
- **Kaveri** • 1211 W Webster Ave
- **The Left Bank** • 1155 W Webster Ave
- **Lush Cosmetics** • 859 W Armitage Ave
- **Tabula Tua** • 1015 W Armitage Ave
- **Uncle Dan's Great Outdoor Store** • 2440 N Lincoln Ave
- **Vosges Haut Chocolat** • 951 W Armitage Ave
- **Wine Discount Center** • 1826 N Elston Ave

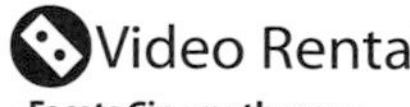

Video Rental

- **Facets Cinematheque** • 1517 W Fullerton Ave

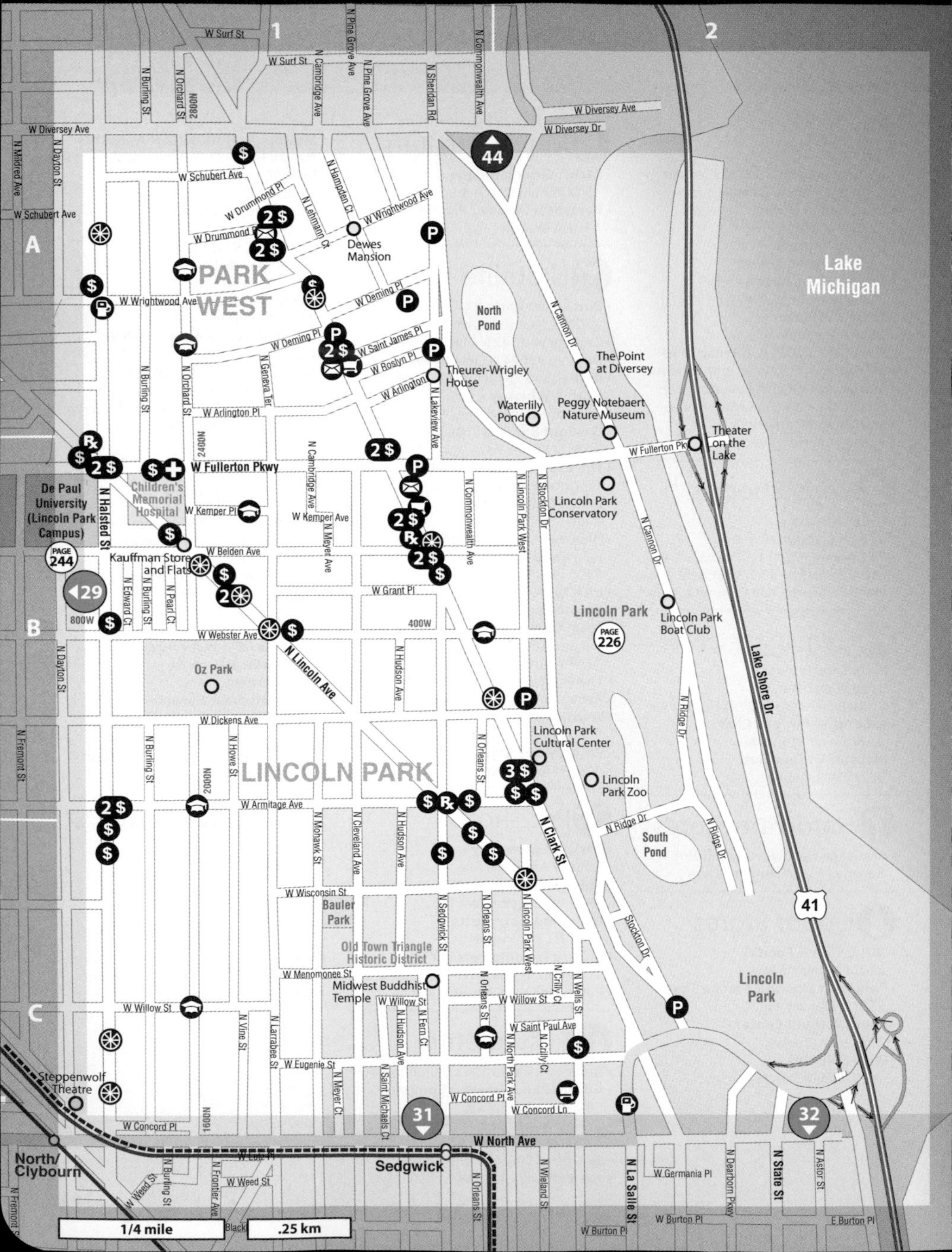

Map 30 • Lincoln Park

N

1
2
A
B
C

W Surf St
N Burling St
N Orchard St
2800N
N Cambridge Ave
N Pine Grove Ave
N Sheridan Rd
N Commonwealth Ave
W Diversey Ave
W Diversey Dr
44
N Mildred Ave
N Dayton St
W Schubert Ave
W Drummond Pl
N Lehmann Ct
N Hampden Ct
W Wrightwood Ave
Dewes Mansion
PARK WEST
W Deming Pl
W Saint James Pl
W Roslyn Pl
W Arlington Pl
Theurer-Wrigley House
N Geneva Ter
N Lakeview Ave
North Pond
N Cannon Dr
The Point at Diversey
Waterlily Pond
Peggy Notebaert Nature Museum
Theater on the Lake
Lake Michigan
2400N
W Fullerton Pkwy
W Fullerton Pky
De Paul University (Lincoln Park Campus)
N Halsted St
Children's Memorial Hospital
W Kemper Pl
W Kemper Ave
N Cambridge Ave
N Meyer Ave
N Commonwealth Ave
N Lincoln Park West
N Stockton Dr
Lincoln Park Conservatory
PAGE 244
Kauffman Store and Flats
W Belden Ave
29
N Edward Ct
N Burling St
N Pearl Ct
800W
W Grant Pl
400W
Lincoln Park
PAGE 226
Lincoln Park Boat Club
W Webster Ave
N Lincoln Ave
Oz Park
N Hudson Ave
N Ridge Dr
Lake Shore Dr
W Dickens Ave
Lincoln Park Cultural Center
N Fremont St
N Howe St
2000N
LINCOLN PARK
N Orleans St
Lincoln Park Zoo
W Armitage Ave
N Mohawk St
N Cleveland Ave
N Clark St
South Pond
W Wisconsin St
Bauler Park
N Sedgwick St
41
Old Town Triangle Historic District
Stockton Dr
W Menomonee St
Midwest Buddhist Temple
N Crilly Ct
N Wells St
Lincoln Park
W Willow St
N Vine St
N Larrabee St
N Fern Ct
W Saint Paul Ave
N North Park Ave
W Eugenie St
Steppenwolf Theatre
N Meyer Ct
N Saint Michaels Ct
W Concord Pl
W Concord Ln
31
32
1600N
W North Ave
North/Clybourn
W Weed St
N Frontier Ave
Sedgwick
N Wieland St
N La Salle St
W Germania Pl
N Dearborn Pkwy
N State St
N Astor St
W Burton Pl
E Burton Pl
Black
1/4 mile
.25 km

Essentials

Good luck finding anyone who considers Lincoln Park anything other than cushy, with its Graystone mansions and tree-lined streets. It's heaven or hell, depending on your tolerance for Trixies and Chads (the 'hood's vapid, label-conscious denizens) and traffic congestion. Parking spots are fleeting fantasies; hop on that Schwinn (or the L) to get anywhere.

Banks

- **Bank of America** • 2041 N Clark St
- **Bank of America** • 2401 N Clark St
- **Bank of America (ATM)** • 401 W Armitage Ave
- **Bank of America (ATM)** • 2240 N Lincoln Ave
- **Bank of America (ATM)** • 2621 N Clark St
- **BankFinancial** • 2424 N Clark St
- **Bridgeview** • 1970 N Halsted St
- **Charter One (ATM)** • White Hen • 2004 N Halsted St
- **Chase** • 1700 N Wells St
- **Chase** • 2501 N Clark St
- **Chase** • 2003 N Halsted St
- **Chase (ATM)** • Children's Memorial Hospital • 2300 N Childrens Plz
- **Chase (ATM)** • 2317 N Clark St
- **Citibank** • 2001 N Halsted St
- **Citibank** • 2555 N Clark St
- **Citibank (ATM)** • 7-Eleven • 2264 N Clark St
- **Citibank (ATM)** • McDonald's • 2400 N Lincoln Ave
- **Citibank (ATM)** • 7-Eleven • 2619 N Clark St
- **Citibank (ATM)** • McDonald's • 2635 N Clark St
- **Corus** • 2401 N Halsted St
- **Fifth Third (ATM)** • 2060 N Clark St
- **First American** • 356 W Armitage Ave
- **First American (ATM)** • 1925 N Lincoln Ave
- **First American (ATM)** • 1935 N Sedgwick St
- **First American (ATM)** • 1970 N Lincoln Ave
- **First American (ATM)** • Starbucks • 2521 N Clark St
- **First American (ATM)** • 2246 N Clark St
- **First American (ATM)** • 2306 N Lincoln Ave
- **First American (ATM)** • 2717 N Clark St
- **First American (ATM)** • Lincoln Park Hospital • 551 W Webster Ave
- **National City** • 2021 N Clark St
- **North Community** • 2000 N Halsted St
- **North Community** • 2201 N Halsted St
- **North Community** • 2335 N Clark St
- **North Community** • 2500 N Clark St
- **TCF (ATM)** • 7-Eleven • 2264 N Clark St
- **TCF (ATM)** • Osco • 2414 Lincoln Ave
- **TCF (ATM)** • 7-Eleven • 2619 N Clark St

Gas Stations

- **BP** • 1647 N La Salle Dr
- **Shell** • 2600 N Halsted St

Emergency Rooms

- **Children's Memorial** • 2300 Children's Plz

Landmarks

- **Dewes Mansion** • 503 N Wrightwood Ave
- **Kauffman Store and Flats** • 2312 N Lincoln Ave
- **Lincoln Park Boat Club** • 2341 N Cannon Dr
- **Lincoln Park Conservatory** • 2391 N Stockton Dr
- **Lincoln Park Cultural Center** • 2045 N Lincoln Park W
- **Lincoln Park Zoo** • 2001 N Clark St
- **Midwest Buddhist Temple** • 435 W Menomonee St
- **Oz Park** • 2021 N Burling St
- **The Peggy Notebaert Nature Museum** • 2430 N Cannon Dr
- **The Point at Diversey** • Lakefront at Diversey Harbor
- **Steppenwolf Theatre** • 1650 N Halsted St
- **Theurer-Wrigley House** • 2466 N Lakeview Ave
- **Waterlily Pond** • W Fullerton Pkwy & N Cannon Dr

Parking

Pharmacies

- **CVS** • 2414 N Lincoln Ave
- **CVS** • 401 W Armitage Ave
- **Walgreens** • 2317 N Clark St

Pizza

- **Bacino's** • 2204 N Lincoln Ave
- **Brick's Chicago** • 1909 N Lincoln Ave
- **Café Luigi** • 2548 N Clark St
- **Chicago Pizza & Oven Grinder** • 2121 N Clark St
- **Domino's** • 2231 N Lincoln Ave
- **Edwardo's Natural Pizza** • 2622 N Halsted St
- **Lincoln Park Pizza** • 2245 N Lincoln Ave
- **Pizza Capri** • 1733 N Halsted St

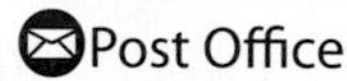

Post Offices

- **US Post Office** • 2368 N Clark St
- **US Post Office** • 2500 N Clark St
- **US Post Office** • 2643 N Clark St

Schools

- **Abraham Lincoln Elementary** • 615 W Kemper Pl
- **Francis W Parker High** • 330 W Webster Ave
- **La Salle Language Academy** • 1734 N Orleans St
- **Lincoln Park High** • 2001 N Orchard St
- **Louisa May Alcott Elementary** • 2625 N Orchard St
- **St Clement** • 2524 N Orchard St
- **Walter L Newberry Math & Science Academy** • 700 W Willow St

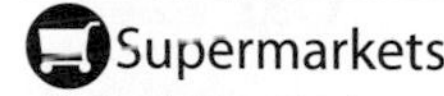

Supermarkets

- **Big Apple Finer Foods** • 2345 N Clark St
- **Lincoln Park Market** • 2500 N Clark St
- **Treasure Island** • 1639 N Wells St

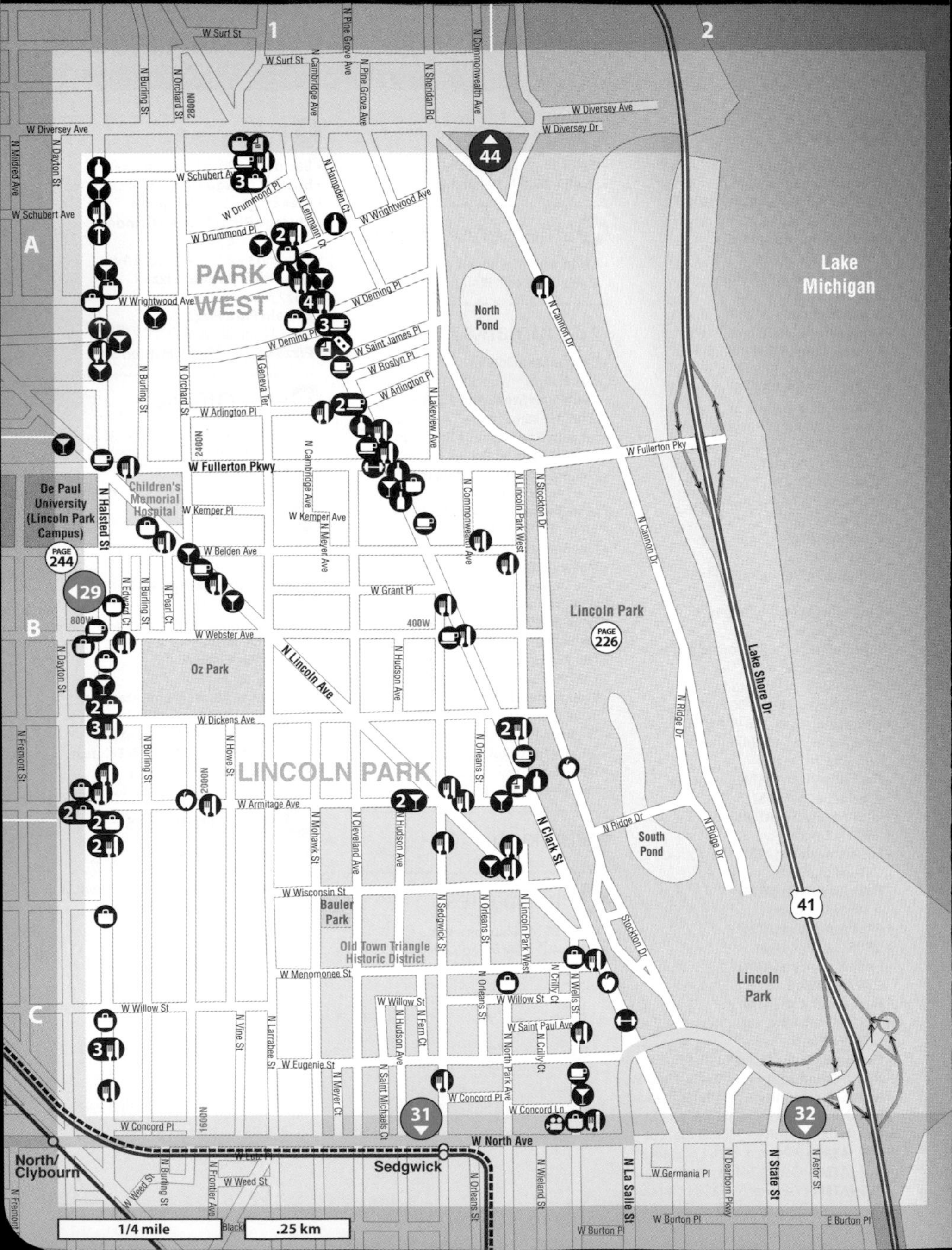

Map 30 • Lincoln Park

Posh stores like Lululemon appeal to Lincoln Park's Trixie-set. Alinea is internationally famous for its prix fixe tasting menu, while the Wieners Circle has earned notoriety for bawdy, abusive late night service. Industrial music at Neo provides a haven from collar-popped Chads, while Kingston Mines and B.L.U.E.S. are popular with blues-seeking tourists.

Coffee

- **Argo Tea** • 2485 N Clark St
- **Bourgeois Pig Café** • 738 W Fullerton Ave
- **Caribou Coffee** • 2453 N Clark St
- **Cosi** • 2200 N Clark St
- **Crepe & Coffee Palace** • 2433 N Clark St
- **Einstein Bros Bagels** • 2530 N Clark St
- **Icosium Kafe** • 2433 N Clark St
- **Noble Tree Coffee & Tea** • 2444 N Clark St
- **Savories** • 1651 N Wells St
- **Screenz** • 2717 N Clark St
- **Siena Coffee** • 2308 N Clark St
- **Starbucks** • 2063 N Clark St
- **Starbucks** • 2200 N Halsted St
- **Starbucks** • 2275 N Lincoln Ave
- **Starbucks** • 2525 1/2 N Clark St

Copy Shops

- **Screenz** • 2717 N Clark St
- **The UPS Store** • 2038 N Clark St
- **The UPS Store** • 2506 N Clark St

Farmers Markets

- **Chicago's Green City Market (May–Oct, Wed & Sat, 7 am–1:30 pm)** • 1750 N Clark St
- **Lincoln Park (Jun–Oct; Sat, 7 am–2 pm)** • W Armitage Ave & N Orchard St
- **Lincoln Park Zoo (Jun–Sept; 4th Sun of month, 9 am–4 pm)** • 2001 N Stockton Dr

Gyms

- **Equinox** • 1750 N Clark St
- **Lincoln Park Fitness Center** • 444 W Fullerton Pkwy

Hardware Stores

- **Home Depot** • 2665 N Halsted St
- **Wahler Brothers True Value** • 2551 N Halsted St

Liquor Stores

- **Chalet Wine & Cheese Shop** • 2000 N Clark St
- **Country Fresh Finer Foods** • 2583 N Clark St
- **Diamond Importers** • 528 W Wrightwood Ave
- **Dynamic Liquors** • 2132 N Halsted St
- **Miska's Liquor** • 2353 N Clark St
- **SS Food & Liquor** • 2427 N Clark St
- **Savings Unlimited** • 2353 N Clark St

Movie Theaters

- **AMC Loews Pipers Alley 4** • 1608 N Wells St

Nightlife

- **Amp Rock Lounge** • 1909 N Lincoln Ave
- **B.L.U.E.S.** • 2519 N Halsted St
- **Burwood Tap** • 724 W Wrightwood Ave
- **Crossroads Public House** • 2630 N Clark St
- **D.O.C. Wine Bar** • 2602 N Clark St
- **Duke's Bar & Grill** • 2616 N Clark St
- **Gamekeepers** • 345 W Armitage Ave
- **Glascott's** • 2158 N Halsted St
- **GoodBar** • 2512 N Halsted St
- **Hidden Shamrock** • 2723 N Halsted St
- **Kingston Mines** • 2548 N Halsted St
- **Lincoln Station** • 2432 N Lincoln Ave
- **Lion Head Pub & The Apartment** • 2251 N Lincoln Ave
- **Neo** • 2350 N Clark St
- **Park West** • 322 W Armitage Ave
- **The Second City** • 1616 N Wells St
- **Victory Liquors** • 2610 N Halsted St
- **Wise Fools Pub** • 2270 N Lincoln Ave

Restaurants

- **Alinea** • 1723 N Halsted St
- **Austrian Bakery & Deli** • 2523 N Clark St
- **Boka** • 1729 N Halsted St
- **Brick's Chicago** • 1909 N Lincoln Ave
- **Café Ba-Ba-Reeba!** • 2024 N Halsted St
- **Café Bernard** • 2100 N Halsted St
- **Charlie Trotter's** • 816 W Armitage Ave
- **Crepe & Coffee Palace** • 2433 N Clark St
- **Duke's Bar & Grill** • 2616 N Clark St
- **Dunlay's** • 2600 N Clark St
- **Fattoush** • 2652 N Halsted St
- **Frances' Deli** • 2552 N Clark St
- **Geja's Café** • 340 W Armitage Ave
- **Hai Yen** • 2723 N Clark St
- **Hema's on Clark** • 2411 N Clark St
- **Karyn's Fresh Corner** • 1901 N Halsted Ave
- **L20** • 2300 N Lincoln Park W
- **Landmark** • 1633 N Halsted St
- **Lito's Empanadas** • 2566 N Clark St
- **Mon Ami Gabi** • 2300 N Lincoln Park W
- **Molly's Cupcakes** • 2536 N Clark St
- **Nookies** • 1746 N Wells St
- **Nookies, Too** • 2114 N Halsted St
- **North Pond** • 2610 N Cannon Dr
- **Original Pancake House** • 2020 N Lincoln Park W
- **Perennial** • 1800 N Lincoln Ave
- **PS Bangkok** • 2521 N Halsted St
- **Red Rooster** • 2100 N Halsted St
- **R.J. Grunts** • 2056 N Lincoln Park W
- **Robinson's No 1 Ribs** • 655 W Armitage Ave
- **Salvatore's Ristorante** • 525 W Arlington Pl
- **Sedgwick's Bar & Grill** • 1935 N Sedgwick St
- **Sushi O Sushi** • 346 W Armitage Ave
- **Sushi Para II** • 2256 N Clark St
- **Swirlz Cupcakes** • 705 W Belden Ave
- **Tilli's** • 1952 N Halsted St
- **Toro** • 2546 N Clark St
- **Twin Anchors** • 1655 N Sedgwick St
- **Vinci** • 1732 N Halsted St
- **Wells on Wells** • 1617 N Wells St
- **Wiener's Circle** • 2622 N Clark St

Shopping

- **A New Leaf** • 1818 N Wells St
- **Art + Science Hair Salon** • 1971 N Halsted St
- **Barneys New York Co-Op** • 2209 N Halsted St
- **BCBGMAXAZRIA** • 2140 N Halsted St
- **Buy Popular Demand** • 2629 N Halsted St
- **Club Monaco** • 2206 N Halsted St
- **Crossroads Trading Co.** • 2711 N Clark St
- **Cynthia Rowley** • 810 W Armitage Ave
- **Dave's Records** • 2604 N Clark St
- **Ethan Allen** • 1700 N Halsted St
- **Fleet Feet Sports** • 1620 N Wells St
- **Francesca's Collections** • 2012 N Halsted St
- **Lori's - The Sole of Chicago** • 824 W Armitage Ave
- **Lululemon** • 2104 N Halsted St
- **McShane's** • 815 W Armitage Ave
- **Molly's Cupcakes** • 2536 N Clark St
- **Old Town Triangle** • 1763 N North Park Ave
- **Quiltology** • 2625 N Halsted St
- **Sally Beauty Supply** • 2727 N Clark St
- **Smart Optical** • 2730 N Clark St
- **Untitled** • 2707 N Clark St
- **Urban Outfitters** • 2352 N Clark St
- **White Elephant** • 2300 Childrens Plz

N
1
2
A
B
C
South Pond
Lincoln Park
PAGE 226
30
22
32
1
2
W Wisconsin St
N Bissell St
N Dayton St
N Mohawk St
N Cleveland Ave
N Hudson Ave
N Sedgwick St
N Orleans St
N Lincoln Park W
Stockton Dr
W Menomonee St
W Willow St
N Halsted St
N Burling St
N Fern Ct
N Crilly Ct
W Saint Paul Ave
W Eugenie St
N Vine St
N Meyer Ct
N Saint Michaels Ct
W Concord Pl
W Concord Ln
N State Pkwy
E North Ave
N Kingsbury St
Steppenwolf Theatre
W North Ave
North/ Clybourn
Sedgwick
W Weed St
N Fremont St
N Frontier Ave
N Ogden Ave
W Blackhawk St
N North Park Ave
N Wieland St
N Sandburg Ter
W Germania Pl
W Burton Pl
N Dearborn Pkwy
N Astor St
OLD TOWN
W Eastman St
W Schiller St
N Clybourn Ave
N Clark St
N State St
N La Salle St
N Sutton Pl
W Fair Pl
W Evergreen Ave
W Sullivan St
Chicago River
W Goethe St
Stanton Schiller Park
N Schick Pl
W Scott St
E Scott St
Clark/ Division
N Hooker St
N Orchard St
N Howe St
W Division St
N Hickory Ave
800W
200W
100W
N Crosby St
N Kingsbury St
W Elm St
E Elm St
N Cambridge Ave
N Larrabee St
N Felton Ct
W Hill St
W Maple St
W Bliss St
W Hobbie St
Seward Park
W Haines St
CABRINI GREEN
W Wendell St
N Rush St
W Oak St
N North Branch St
NEAR NORTH
W Walton St
N Franklin St
N Wells St
Washington Square Park
W Delaware Pl
W Locust St
W Iowa St
W Chestnut St
E Chestnut St
Moody Bible Institute
N Ogden Ave
N Sangamon St
N Lessing St
N Peoria St
W Pearson St
W Institute Pl
N Carpenter St
Loyola Univers (Water Tower Camp
W Chicago Ave
Chicago
N Morgan St
W Superior St
E Superior St
W Huron St
N Green St
N Orleans St
W Ancona St
W Erie St
N Wabash Ave
W Ontario St
Connector
90
W Ohio St
N Union Ave
N Desplaines St
Grand
W Grand Ave
1/4 mile
.25 km
W Illinois St

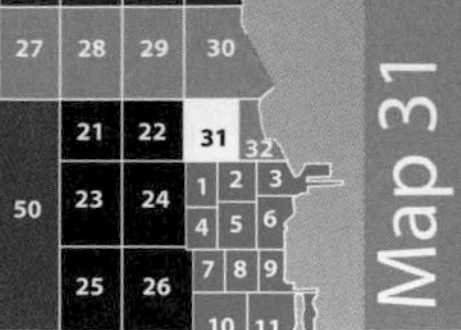

With its narrow, cobblestoned streets lined with Queen Anne-style homes and rehabbed cottages, Old Town's appropriate moniker perfectly encapsulates its nineteenth century charms. Only a few blocks to the south, the crumbling remnants of the Cabrini Green housing project still sprout amidst a string of controversial high-end developments.

Banks

- **Bank of America** • 1419 N Wells St
- **Bank of America** • 1565 N Clybourn Ave
- **Bank of America** • 1590 N Clybourn Ave
- **Bank of America** • 770 N Halsted St
- **Bank of America (ATM)** • 900 N North Branch St
- **Chase** • 1350 N Wells St
- **Chase** • 424 W Division St
- **Chase (ATM)** • 1200 N Sandburg Terrace
- **Chase (ATM)** • 1599 N Clybourn Ave
- **Chase (ATM)** • Walgreens • 1601 N Wells St
- **Chase (ATM)** • 820 N La Salle Dr
- **Citibank** • 1525 N Wells St
- **Fifth Third** • 837 W North Ave
- **First American (ATM)** • 1317 N Wells St
- **First American (ATM)** • 1500 N Wells St
- **First American (ATM)** • 1543 N Sedgwick St
- **First American (ATM)** • Amoco/BP • 1560 N Halsted St
- **First American (ATM)** • 160 W Division St
- **National City Bank** • 2021 N Clark St
- **North Community** • 1561 N Wells St

Car Washes

- **Gold Coast Car Wash** • 875 N Orleans St
- **We'll Clean** • 1520 N Halsted St

Car Rental

- **Enterprise** • 523 W North Ave

Gas Stations

- **Mobil** • 1234 N Halsted Ave

Landmarks

- **Steppenwolf Theatre** • 1650 N Halsted St

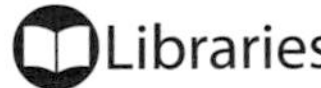

Libraries

- **Near North Public Library** • 310 W Division St

Parking

- **Central Parking** • 811 N Orleans St

Pharmacies

- **Dominick's** • 424 W Division St
- **Walgreens** • 1601 N Wells St

Pizza

- **Domino's** • 143 W Division St
- **Marcello's Father & Son Restaurant** • 645 W North Ave
- **Mangia Roma** • 1623 N Halsted St
- **Old Towne Pizza Pub** • 1339 N Wells St
- **Pizza Ria** • 1599 N Clybourn Ave

Police

- **18th District (Near North)** • 1160 N Larrabee St

Schools

- **Catherine Cook Elementary** • 226 W Schiller St
- **Catherine Ferguson CPC** • 1420 N Hudson Ave
- **Chicago Grammar** • 900 N Franklin St
- **Cornerstone Academy** • 1111 N Wells St, 4th Fl
- **Edward Jenner Academy of the Arts** • 1119 N Cleveland Ave
- **Franklin Fine Arts Center** • 225 W Evergreen Ave
- **Friedrick Von Schiller Middle** • 640 W Scott St
- **George Manierre Elementary** • 1420 N Hudson Ave
- **Immaculate Conception** • 1431 N North Park Ave
- **Lake Shore Preparatory** • 300 W Hill St
- **Mark Skinner Classical** • 1443 N Ogden Ave
- **Moody Bible Institute** • 820 N La Salle Blvd
- **Ruben Salazar Bilingual Education Center** • 160 W Wendell St
- **Walter Payton Preparatory** • 1034 N Wells St

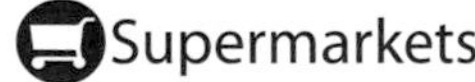

Supermarkets

- **Dominick's** • 424 W Division St

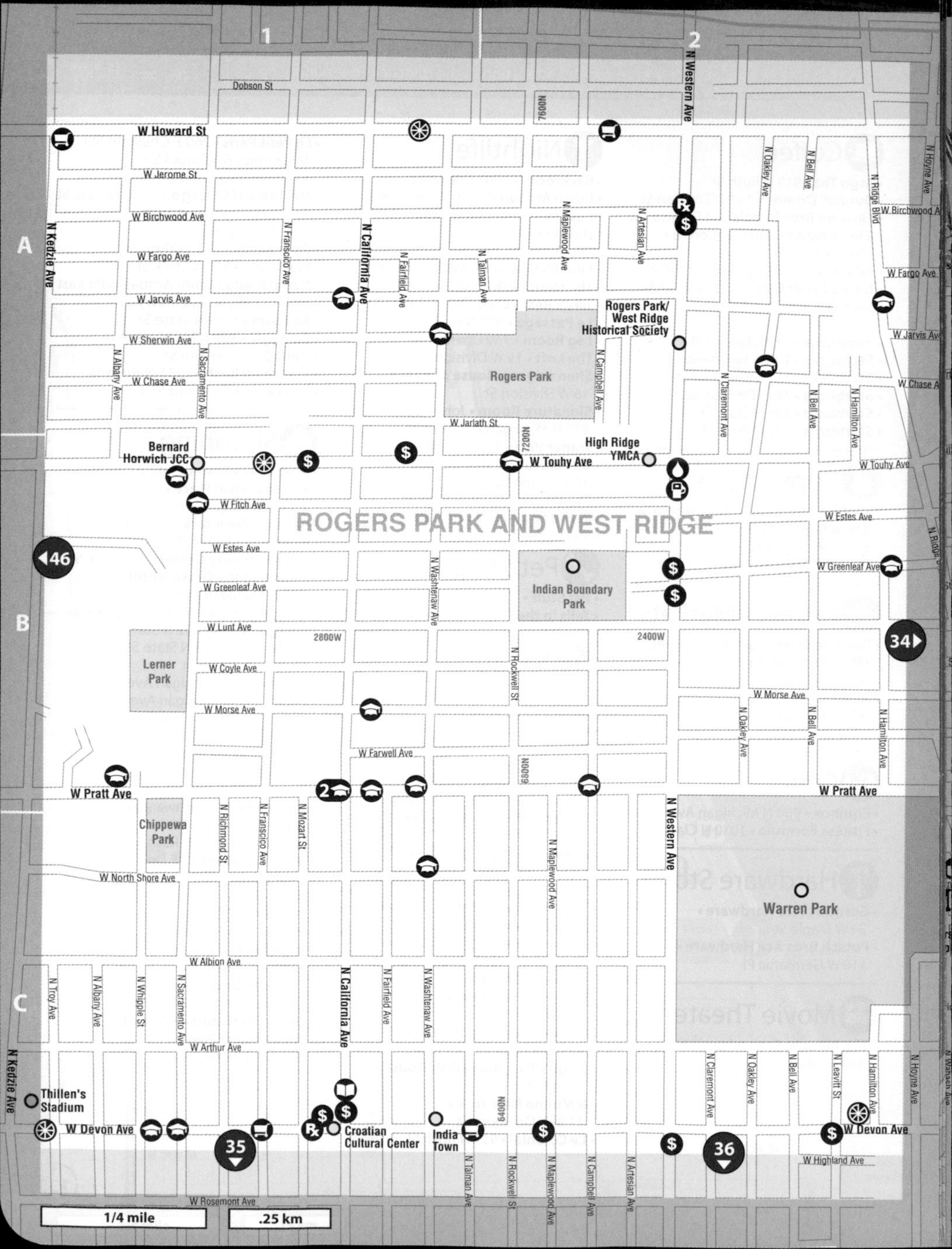
1
2
A
B
C
Dobson St
W Howard St
W Jerome St
W Birchwood Ave
W Fargo Ave
W Jarvis Ave
W Sherwin Ave
W Chase Ave
W Jarlath St
W Touhy Ave
W Fitch Ave
W Estes Ave
W Greenleaf Ave
W Lunt Ave
W Coyle Ave
W Morse Ave
W Farwell Ave
W Pratt Ave
W North Shore Ave
W Albion Ave
W Arthur Ave
W Devon Ave
W Highland Ave
W Rosemont Ave
N Kedzie Ave
N Troy Ave
N Albany Ave
N Whipple St
N Sacramento Ave
N Richmond St
N Fransicso Ave
N Mozart St
N California Ave
N Fairfield Ave
N Washtenaw Ave
N Talman Ave
N Rockwell St
N Maplewood Ave
N Campbell Ave
N Artesian Ave
N Western Ave
N Claremont Ave
N Oakley Ave
N Bell Ave
N Leavitt St
N Hamilton Ave
N Ridge Blvd
N Hoyne Ave
7600N
7200N
6800N
6400N
2800W
2400W
Rogers Park/ West Ridge Historical Society
Rogers Park
Bernard Horwich JCC
High Ridge YMCA
ROGERS PARK AND WEST RIDGE
Indian Boundary Park
Lerner Park
Chippewa Park
Warren Park
Thillen's Stadium
Croatian Cultural Center
India Town
46
34
35
36
2
1/4 mile
.25 km

West Rogers Park has an intimate, residential feel that draws many families and retirees. Cultures mix fluidly in this community. Between the Hebrew schools, the Russian shops, and the Indian markets are residential streets and five different parks with batting cages, sledding hills, baseball diamonds, tennis courts, and jogging paths. Nice.

Banks

- **Bank of America** • 2545 W Devon Ave
- **Bank of America** • 2855 W Touhy Ave
- **Chase** • 7015 N Western Ave
- **Chase (ATM)** • Walgreens • 7510 N Western Ave
- **Citibank** • 2801 W Devon Ave
- **Devon** • 6445 N Western Ave
- **First Commercial** • 2201 W Howard St
- **First Commercial** • 7050 N Western Ave
- **Shore Bank** • 7555 N California Ave
- **TCF (ATM)** • 7-Eleven • 2200 W Devon Ave
- **TCF (ATM)** • 7-Eleven • 2741 W Touhy Ave
- **TCF (ATM)** • Osco • 2825 W Devon Ave

Car Washes

- **Fast Carwash** • 7139 N Western Ave

Gas Stations

- **Marathon** • 7130 N Western Ave

Landmarks

- **Bernard Horwich JCC** • 3003 W Touhy Ave
- **Croatian Cultural Center** • 2845 W Devon Ave
- **High Ridge YMCA** • 2424 W Touhy Ave
- **India Town** • W Devon Ave & N Washtenaw Ave
- **Indian Boundary Park** • 2500 W Lunt Ave
- **Rogers Park/West Ridge Historical Society** • 7344 N Western Ave
- **Thillens Stadium** • 6404 N Kedzie Ave
- **Warren Park** • 6601 N Western Ave

Libraries

- **Northtown Public Library** • 6435 N California Ave

Pharmacies

- **CVS** • 2825 W Devon Ave
- **Walgreens** • 7510 N Western Ave

Pizza

- **Domino's** • 3144 W Devon Ave
- **Eastern Style Pizza** • 2911 W Touhy Ave
- **Gulliver's Pizzeria & Restaurant** • 2727 W Howard St
- **Villa Palermo Pizza** • 2154 W Devon Ave

Schools

- **ABC Academy Inc** • 2714 W Pratt Blvd
- **Bethesda Lutheran Elementary** • 6803 N Campbell Ave
- **Brisk Academy - Yeshivas Brisk** • 3000 W Devon Ave
- **Consolidated Hebrew High** • 2828 W Pratt Blvd
- **Daniel Boone Elementary** • 6710 N Washtenaw Ave
- **Decatur Classical** • 7030 N Sacramento Ave
- **George Armstrong Elementary** • 2110 W Greenleaf Ave
- **Hanna Sacks Girls' High** • 3021 W Devon Ave
- **Ida Crown Jewish Academy** • 2828 W Pratt Blvd
- **Jewish Children Bureau** • 3145 W Pratt Blvd
- **Lubavitch Boy's High** • 2756 W Morse Ave
- **Rogers Elementary** • 7345 N Washtenaw Ave
- **St Margaret Mary Elementary** • 7318 N Oakley Ave
- **St Scholastica High** • 7416 N Ridge Blvd
- **Virginia Frank Child Dev Center** • 3033 W Touhy Ave
- **Yeshiva Shearis Yisroel** • 2620 W Touhy Ave

Supermarkets

- **Fresh Farms International Market** • 2626 W Devon Ave
- **Jewel-Osco** • 2485 Howard St
- **New York Kosher** • 2900 W Devon Ave

N
1
2
A
B
C
Dobson St
W Howard St
W Jerome St
W Birchwood Ave
W Fargo Ave
W Jarvis Ave
W Sherwin Ave
W Chase Ave
W Jarlath St
W Touhy Ave
W Fitch Ave
W Estes Ave
W Greenleaf Ave
W Lunt Ave
W Coyle Ave
W Morse Ave
W Farwell Ave
W Pratt Ave
W North Shore Ave
W Albion Ave
W Arthur Ave
W Devon Ave
W Highland Ave
W Rosemont Ave
N Kedzie Ave
N Albany Ave
N Sacramento Ave
N Francisco Ave
N California Ave
N Fairfield Ave
N Talman Ave
N Maplewood Ave
N Artesian Ave
N Western Ave
N Oakley Ave
N Bell Ave
N Ridge Blvd
N Hoyne Ave
N Campbell Ave
N Claremont Ave
N Hamilton Ave
N Washtenaw Ave
N Rockwell St
N Richmond St
N Mozart St
N Troy Ave
N Whipple St
N Leavitt St
7600N
7200N
6800N
6400N
2800W
2400W
Rogers Park
Indian Boundary Park
Lerner Park
Chippewa Park
Warren Park
ROGERS PARK AND WEST RIDGE
46
34
35
36
7
3
3
2
1/4 mile
.25 km

Sundries / Entertainment

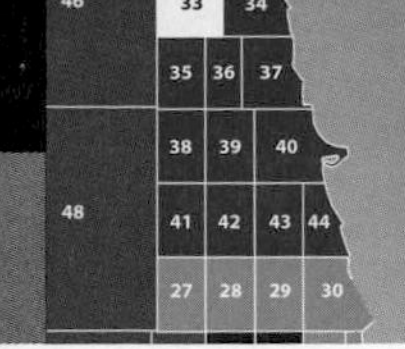

Map 33

Most of the action in West Rogers Park occurs on Devon Avenue. The international marketplace is supported by dozens of inexpensive Indian/Pakistani restaurants, Bollywood video rentals, the best saris you'll find in the States, and a slew of Islamic, Russian, and Jewish bookstores and bakeries. From the myriad dining choices, we recommend the veggie Indian fare at Uru-Swati, or the yummy Pakistani chicken at Sabri Nihari. Both are booze-free, alas.

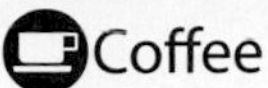

Coffee

- **Dunkin' Donuts** • 3132 W Devon Ave
- **Dunkin' Donuts** • 7578 N Western Ave

Copy Shops

- **Progress Press** • 7315 N Western Ave
- **UNIK Business Center** • 2337 W Devon Ave

Gyms

- **Curves (women only)** • 7300 N Western Ave
- **High Ridge YMCA** • 2424 W Touhy Ave

Hardware Stores

- **Basco Plumbing & True Value** • 2953 W Devon Ave
- **Chicago Coast True Value** • 6942 N Western Ave

Liquor Stores

- **Adelphi Liquors** • 2351 W Devon Ave
- **M&Y Liquor & Grocery Store** • 2252 W Devon Ave
- **Old City Liquor Limited** • 2222 W Devon Ave

Nightlife

- **Cary's Lounge** • 2251 W Devon Ave
- **Lamp Post** • 7126 N Ridge Blvd
- **McKellin's** • 2800 W Touhy Ave
- **Mullen's Sports Bar and Grill** • 7301 N Western Ave

Restaurants

- **Angin Mamiri** • 2739 W Touhy Ave
- **Annapurna** • 2608 W Devon Ave
- **Arya Bhavan** • 2508 W Devon Ave
- **Ben Tre** • 3146 W Touhy Ave
- **Candlelite** • 7452 N Western Ave
- **Chopal** • 2240 W Devon Ave
- **Good Morgan Kosher Fish Market** • 2948 W Devon Ave
- **Hashalom** • 2905 W Devon Ave
- **Hema's Kitchen** • 2439 W Devon Ave
- **Indian Garden** • 2546 W Devon Ave
- **Mysore Woodland's** • 2548 W Devon Ave
- **Sabri Nihari** • 2502 W Devon Ave
- **Siam Pasta** • 7416 N Western Ave
- **Sukhadia's** • 2559 W Devon Ave
- **Tiffin** • 2536 W Devon Ave
- **Udupi Palace** • 2543 W Devon Ave
- **Uru-Swati** • 2629 W Devon Ave
- **Viceroy of India** • 2520 W Devon Ave

Shopping

- **Argo Georgian Bakery** • 2812 W Devon Ave
- **Al Mansoor Video** • 2600 W Devon Ave
- **AutoZone** • 2555 W Touhy Ave
- **JR Dessert Bakery** • 2841 W Howard St
- **Chicago Harley Davidson** • 6868 N Western Ave
- **Levinson's Bakery** • 2856 W Devon Ave
- **Office Mart** • 2801 W Touhy Ave
- **Raj Jewels** • 2652 W Devon Ave
- **Resham's** • 2540 W Devon Ave
- **Taj Sari Palace** • 2554 W Devon Ave
- **Tel-Aviv Kosher Bakery** • 2944 W Devon Ave
- **Three Sisters Deli** • 2854 W Devon Ave

Video Rental

- **Atlantic Video Rentals (Indian)** • 2541 W Devon Ave
- **Blockbuster Videos** • 7300 N Western Ave
- **Elita Video (Russian)** • 2753 W Devon Ave
- **Golden Video** • 2761 W Devon Ave
- **New Devon Video** • 2304 W Devon Ave
- **Super Star Video (Indian and Pakistani)** • 2538 W Devon Ave
- **Sur Sangeet Video (Indian)** • 2521 W Devon Ave
- **Western Video** • 7424 N Western Ave

N

ROGERS PARK

Rogers Ave Park & Beach
Howard St Park & Beach
Fargo Ave Park & Beach
Jarvis Ave Park & Beach
Sherwin Ave Park & Beach
Chase Ave Park & Beach
Leone Park & Beach
Loyola Park
Loyola Beach
Pratt Blvd Park & Beach
Columbia Ave Park & Beach
North Shore Ave Park & Beach
Hartigan Park & Beach
Loyola University (Lake Shore Campus)
Pottawattomie Park
Touhy Park
Paschen Park
Warren Park
Robert A Black Golf Course
Bach House
Jackson/Thomas House
Rogers Park
Angel Guardian Croatian Catholic Church
Howard
Jarvis
Morse
Loyola

W Howard St
W Birchwood Ave
W Fargo Ave
W Jarvis Ave
W Sherwin Ave
W Chase Ave
W Touhy Ave
W Estes Ave
W Greenleaf Ave
W Lunt Ave
W Morse Ave
W Farwell Ave
W Pratt Blvd
W Columbia Ave
W North Shore Ave
W Wallen Ave
W Albion Ave
W Loyola Ave
W Arthur Ave
W Schreiber Ave
W Devon Ave
W Sheridan Rd
W Highland Ave
W Rosemont Ave
W Thome Ave
N Rogers Ave
N Ridge Blvd
N Clark St
N Ashland Ave
N Sheridan Rd
N Glenwood Ave
N Ravenswood Ave
N Damen Ave
N Wolcott Ave
N Paulina St
N Hermitage Ave
N Greenview Ave
N Bosworth Ave
N Newgard Ave
N Wayne Ave
N Lakewood Ave
N Magnolia Ave
N Winthrop Ave
N Broadway St
N Marshfield Ave
N Honore St
N Winchester Ave
N Seeley Ave
N Hoyne Ave
N Hamilton Ave
Elmwood Ave
Callan Ave
Clyde Ave
2000W
1600W
1200W
7600N
7200N
6800N
6400N

33
36
37
PAGE 248

1/4 mile
.25 km

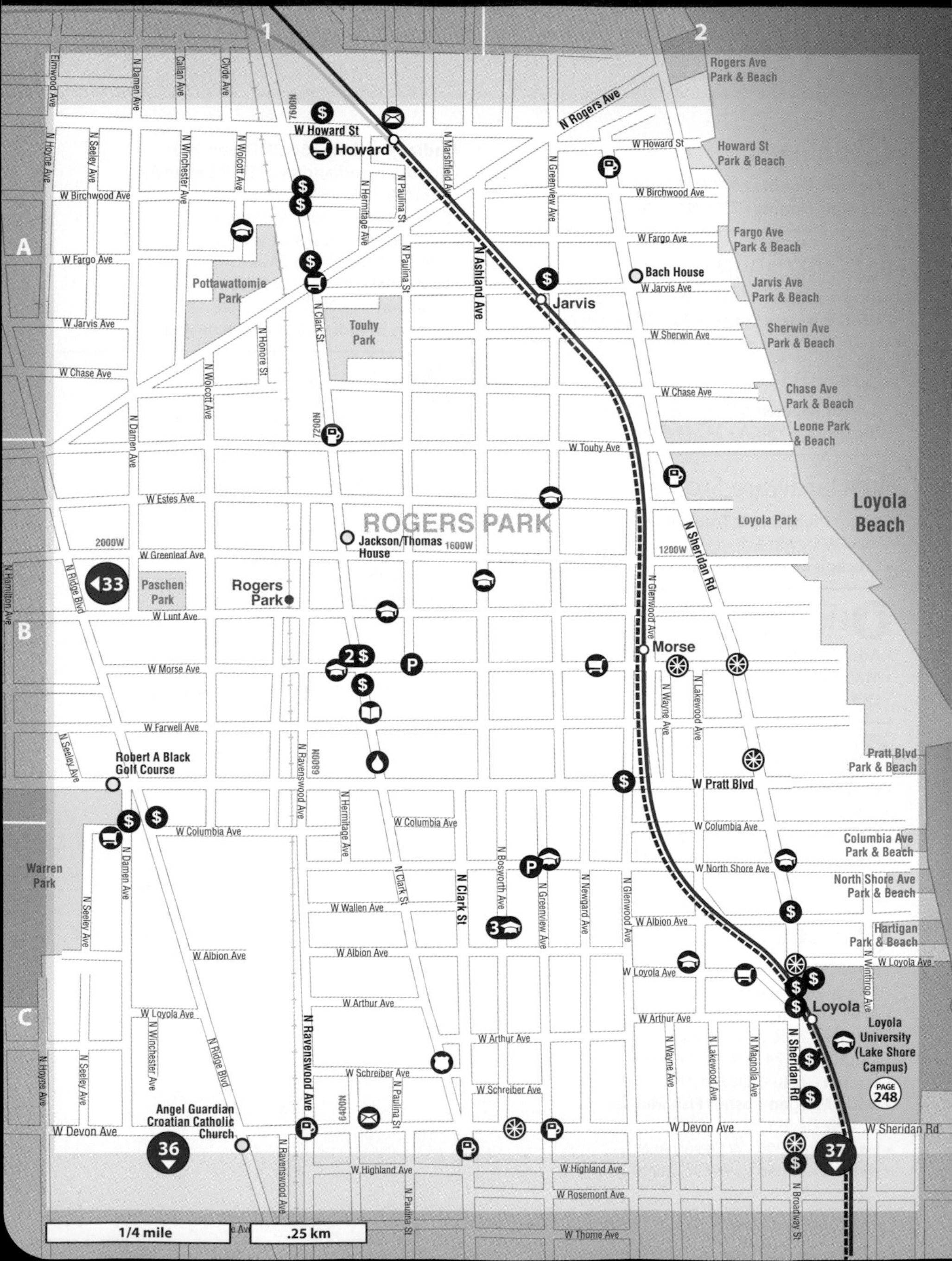

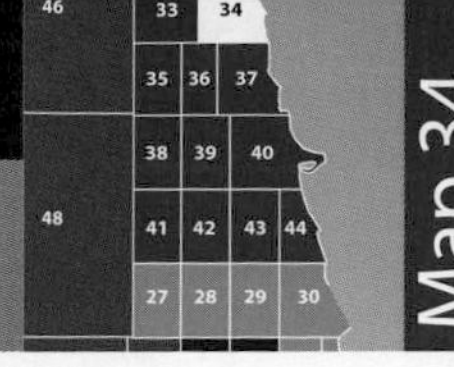

Loyola students, civic-minded young professionals, new immigrants, and old hippies populate this dense and lively 'hood. It's becoming increasingly more unaffordable to inhabit, but the middle-class residents keep fighting to keep the area mixed income. The lakefront, easy access to public transportation, cultural diversity, and Loyola Campus make it pleasant, although crime and gang activity continue to be a problem.

Banks

- **Bank of America (ATM)** • 6359 N Broadway St
- **Bank of America** • 7516 N Clark St
- **Bank of America (ATM)** • 7507 N Clark St
- **Chase** • 1763 W Howard St
- **Chase** • 6415 N Sheridan Rd
- **Chase (ATM)** • 1523 W Jarvis Ave
- **Chase (ATM)** • 6525 N Sheridan Rd
- **Chase (ATM)** • Walgreens • 7410 N Clark St
- **Citibank (ATM)** • 6401 N Sheridan Rd
- **First American (ATM)** • 6604 N Sheridan Rd
- **First American (ATM)** • 6740 N Ridge Blvd
- **First Commercial** • 6930 N Clark St
- **First Commercial** • 6945 N Clark St
- **Harris Trust & Savings** • 6538 N Sheridan Rd
- **MB Financial** • 6443 N Sheridan Rd
- **TCF (ATM)** • 7-Eleven • 1404 W Pratt Blvd
- **Washington Mutual** • 1425 W Morse Ave

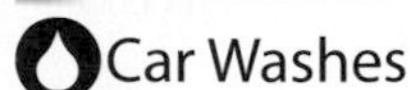

Car Washes

- **Rogers Park Auto Body Shop** • 6828 N Clark St

Gas Stations

- **Citgo** • 1500 W Devon Ave
- **Citgo** • 7138 N Sheridan Rd
- **Marathon** • 7550 N Sheridan Rd
- **Mobil** • 7201 N Clark St
- **Shell** • 6346 N Clark St
- **Shell** • 6401 N Ridge Blvd

Landmarks

- **Angel Guardian Croatian Catholic Church** • 6346 N Ridge Ave
- **Bach House** • 7415 N Sheridan Rd
- **Jackson/Thomas House** • 7053 N Ridge Ave
- **Robert A Black Golf Course** • 2045 W Pratt Blvd

Libraries

- **Rogers Park Public Library** • 6907 N Clark St

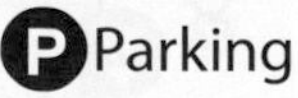

Parking

Pizza

- **Carmen's of Loyola Pizzeria** • 6568 N Sheridan Rd
- **Giordano's** • 6836 N Sheridan Rd
- **Hamilton's Pub** • 6341 N Broadway St
- **JB Alberto's** • 1326 W Morse Ave
- **Leona's** • 6935 N Sheridan Rd
- **Vince's Pizzeria** • 1527 W Devon Ave

Police

- **24th District (Rogers Park)** • 6464 N Clark St

Post Offices

- **US Post Office** • 1723 W Devon Ave
- **US Post Office** • 7617 N Paulina St

Schools

- **Chicago Math & Science Academy** • 1709 W Lunt Ave
- **Chicago Waldorf** • 1300 W Loyola Ave
- **Eugene Field Elementary** • 7019 N Ashland Blvd
- **Jordan Elementary** • 7414 N Wolcott Ave
- **Joyce Kilmer Elementary** • 6700 N Greenview Ave
- **Loyola University of Chicago** • 6525 N Sheridan Rd
- **New Field Primary** • 1707 W Morse Ave
- **North Shore Academy for Children** • 6711 N Sheridan Rd
- **Pactt Learning Center** • 7101 N Greenview Ave
- **Paideia Academy** • 6631 N Bosworth Ave
- **Peace Academy** • 6631 N Bosworth Ave
- **Roger C Sullivan High** • 6631 N Bosworth Ave

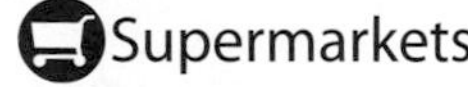

Supermarkets

- **Dominick's** • 1763 W Howard St
- **Dominick's** • 6623 N Damen Ave
- **Morse Fruit & Meat Market** • 1430 W Morse Ave
- **New Leaf Natural Grocery** • 1261 W Loyola Ave
- **Rogers Park Fruit Market** • 7401 N Clark St

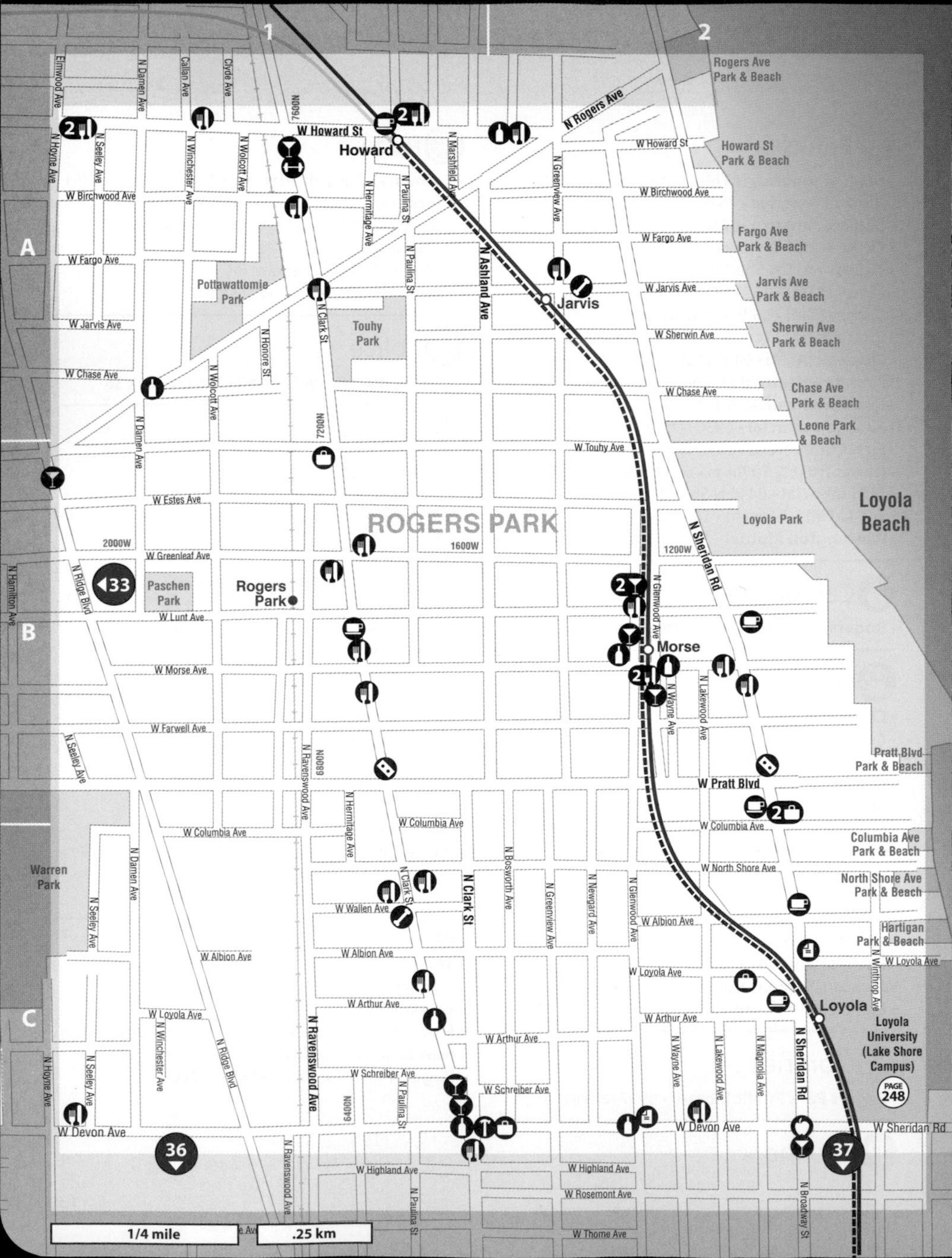

Map 34 • East Rogers Park

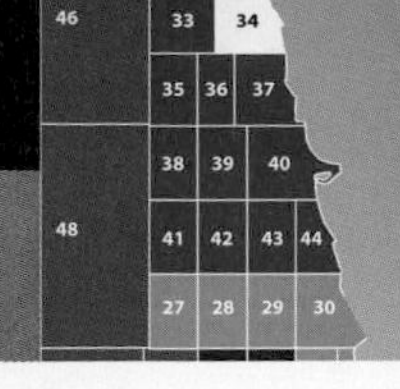

Heartland Café, featuring health-nut fare, a lefty gift shop, and live music, is the grandpapi stop. Mexican eateries offering authentic food at low prices dot Clark Street, while Howard Street's Caribbean American Bakery and Tickie's give you a sweet taste of Afro-Caribbean culture. The Jackhammer complex of gay bars offers something for everyone—a sports bar, a fern bar, and a leather bar, all-in-one.

Coffee

- **Charmers Cafe** • 1500 W Jarvis Ave
- **Dunkin' Donuts** • 1200 W Loyola Ave
- **Dunkin' Donuts** • 6970 N Clark St
- **Ennui Café** • 6981 N Sheridan Rd
- **Starbucks** • Dominick's • 1763 W Howard St
- **Starbucks** • 6738 N Sheridan Rd
- **Royal Coffee** • 6764 N Sheridan Rd

Copy Shops

- **SOS Copies** • 6604 N Sheridan Rd
- **The UPS Store** • 1400 W Devon Ave

Gyms

- **Bally Total Fitness** • 7529 N Clark St

Hardware Stores

- **Clark-Devon Hardware** • 6401 N Clark St

Liquor Stores

- **Dino's Liquors** • 6400 N Clark St
- **Golden Valley Liquors** • 1339 W Morse Ave
- **Hahn Liquors** • 1410 W Devon Ave
- **Lian's Liquor & Grocery** • 6507 N Clark St
- **Morse Liquors** • 1400 W Morse Ave
- **Sandy's Food & Meat Market** • 1534 W Howard St
- **Summit Grocery** • 7300 N Rogers Ave

Nightlife

- **Duke's Hideaway** • 6920 N Glenwood Ave
- **Hamilton's Pub** • 6341 N Broadway St
- **Hop Haus** • 7545 N Clark St
- **Jackhammer** • 6406 N Clark St
- **Lamp Post** • 7126 N Ridge Blvd
- **No Exit** • 6970 N Glenwood Ave
- **Red Line Tap** • 7006 N Glenwood Ave
- **Touche** • 6412 N Clark St

Pet Shops

- **Aquarium Gem** • 6623 N Clark St
- **Rogers Bark Pet Salon** • 1447 W Jarvis Ave

Restaurants

- **A&T Grill** • 7026 N Clark St
- **Bar-B-Que Bob's** • 2055 W Howard St
- **Buffalo Joe's** • 1841 W Howard St
- **Capt'n Nemos** • 7367 N Clark St
- **Caribbean American Bakery** • 1539 W Howard St
- **Century Public House** • 1330 W Morse Ave
- **Dagel & Beli Shop** • 7406 N Greenview Ave
- **Deluxe Diner** • 6349 N Clark St
- **El Famous Burrito** • 7047 N Clark St
- **Ethiopian Diamond** • 7537 N Clark St
- **Ghareeb Nawaz** • 2032 W Devon Ave
- **Good to Go Jamaican Jerk and Juice Bar** • 1947 W Howard St
- **Grande Noodles and Sushi Bar** • 6632 N Clark St
- **Heartland Café** • 7000 N Glenwood Ave
- **Jamaica Jerk** • 1631 W Howard St
- **La Conakry** • 2049 W Howard St
- **Masouleh** • 6653 N Clark St
- **Morseland** • 1218 W Morse Ave
- **Noon Hour Grill** • 6930 N Glenwood Ave
- **Quesadillas y Mariscos Dona Lolis** • 6924 N Clark St
- **Sahara Khabob** • 6649 N Clark St
- **Tamales lo Mejor de Guerrero** • 7024 N Clark St
- **Taste of Peru** • 6545 N Clark St
- **Thai Spice** • 1320 W Devon Ave
- **Tickie's Belizean Cuisine** • 7605 N Paulina St

Shopping

- **Armadillo's Pillow** • 6753 N Sheridan Rd
- **Flatts & Sharpe Music Company** • 6749 N Sheridan Rd
- **Mar-Jen Discount Furniture** • 1536 W Devon Ave
- **New Leaf Natural Grocery** • 1261 W Loyola Ave
- **Romanian Kosher Sausage Co** • 7200 N Clark St

Video Rental

- **Pratt Video** • 6810 N Sheridan Rd
- **Syed Video** • 6808 N Clark St

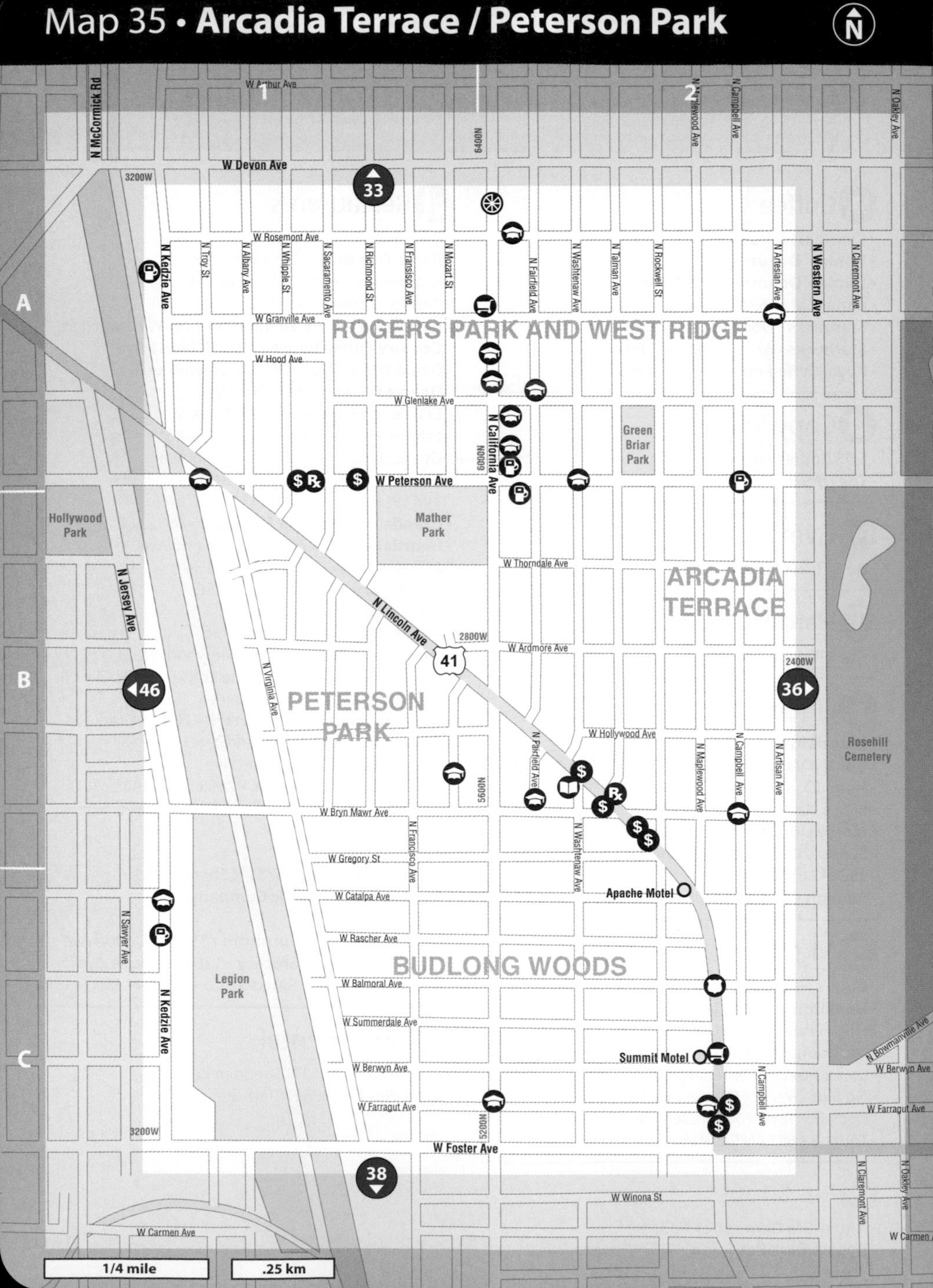

Map 35 • Arcadia Terrace / Peterson Park
N
W Arthur Ave
1
2
N McCormick Rd
6400N
N Maplewood Ave
N Campbell Ave
N Oakley Ave
W Devon Ave
3200W
33
W Rosemont Ave
N Kedzie Ave
N Troy St
N Albany Ave
N Whipple St
N Sacramento Ave
N Richmond St
N Fransisco Ave
N Mozart St
N Fairfield Ave
N Washtenaw Ave
N Talman Ave
N Rockwell St
N Artesian Ave
N Western Ave
N Claremont Ave
A
W Granville Ave
ROGERS PARK AND WEST RIDGE
W Hood Ave
W Glenlake Ave
N California Ave
6000N
Green Briar Park
W Peterson Ave
Hollywood Park
Mather Park
W Thorndale Ave
N Jersey Ave
ARCADIA TERRACE
N Lincoln Ave
2800W
W Ardmore Ave
41
2400W
B
46
36
N Virginia Ave
PETERSON PARK
W Hollywood Ave
N Fairfield Ave
N Maplewood Ave
N Campbell Ave
N Artisan Ave
Rosehill Cemetery
5600N
W Bryn Mawr Ave
N Francisco Ave
N Washtenaw Ave
W Gregory St
Apache Motel
W Catalpa Ave
N Sawyer Ave
W Rascher Ave
BUDLONG WOODS
Legion Park
W Balmoral Ave
N Kedzie Ave
W Summerdale Ave
N Bowmanville Ave
C
Summit Motel
W Berwyn Ave
N Campbell Ave
W Berwyn Ave
W Farragut Ave
5200N
W Farragut Ave
3200W
W Foster Ave
38
N Claremont Ave
N Oakley Ave
W Winona St
W Carmen Ave
W Carmen Ave
1/4 mile
.25 km

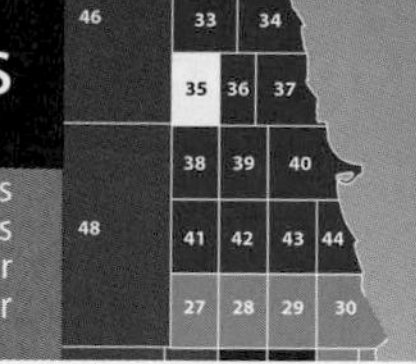

This quiet enclave snuggled between the Chicago River and Rosehill Cemetery is home to many Koreans, Middle Easterners, and Eastern Europeans. Seedy motels on Lincoln Avenue, once reputable, are being torn-down one-by-one, due to their decrepit conditions and increasingly bad reputations, making the area desirable for young families priced out of Ravenswood and Andersonville.

Banks

- **Charter One** • 5650 N Lincoln Ave
- **Chase** • 5224 N Lincoln Ave
- **Chase (ATM)** • 5233 N Lincoln Ave
- **Chase (ATM)** • Walgreens • 3019 W Peterson Ave
- **Chase (ATM)** • Walgreens • 5627 N Lincoln Ave
- **Citibank (ATM)** • 5562 N Lincoln Ave
- **First Commercial** • 2935 W Peterson Ave
- **TCF (ATM)** • 7-Eleven • 5562 N Lincoln Ave

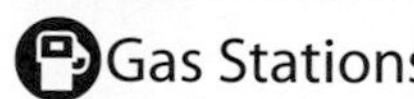

Gas Stations

- **BP** • 2751 W Peterson Ave
- **Citgo** • 5447 N Kedzie Ave
- **Citgo** • 5547 N Kedzie Ave
- **Marathon** • 2500 W Peterson Ave
- **Mobil** • 2758 W Peterson Ave

Landmarks

- **Apache Motel** • 5535 N Lincoln Ave
- **Summit Motel** • 5308 N Lincoln Ave

Libraries

- **Budlong Woods Public Library** • 5630 N Lincoln Ave

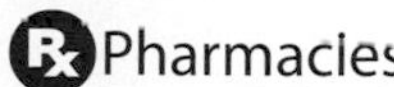

Pharmacies

- **Walgreens** • 3019 W Peterson Ave
- **Walgreens** • 5627 N Lincoln Ave

Pizza

- **Tel Aviv Kosher Pizza** • 6349 N California Ave

Police

- **20th District (Foster)** • 5400 N Lincoln Ave

Schools

- **Budlong Elementary** • 2701 W Foster Ave
- **DeWitt Clinton Elementary** • 6110 N Fairfield Ave
- **Joan Dachs Bais Yaakov Elementary** • 3200 W Peterson Ave
- **Joan Dachs Bais Yaakov Elementary** • 6110 N California Ave
- **Kiddie Kollege** • 6025 N California Ave
- **Little Harvard Academy** • 2708 W Peterson Ave
- **Lubavitch Girls High** • 2754 W Rosemont Ave
- **Minnie Mars Jamieson Elementary** • 5650 N Mozart St
- **NAES College** • 2838 W Peterson Ave
- **North Shore SDA Junior Academy** • 5220 N California Ave
- **Northside College Preparatory** • 5501 N Kedzie Ave
- **St Hilary Elementary** • 5614 N Fairfield Ave
- **St Philip Lutheran** • 2500 W Bryn Mawr Ave
- **Stuart G Ferst** • 6050 N California Ave
- **Telshe Yeshiva Chicago** • 3535 W Foster Ave
- **Victor V Neumann Alternative** • 2447 W Granville Ave
- **Yeshivas Tiferes Tzvi** • 6122 N California Ave

Supermarkets

- **Aldi** • 6220 N California Ave
- **Dominick's** • 5233 N Lincoln Ave

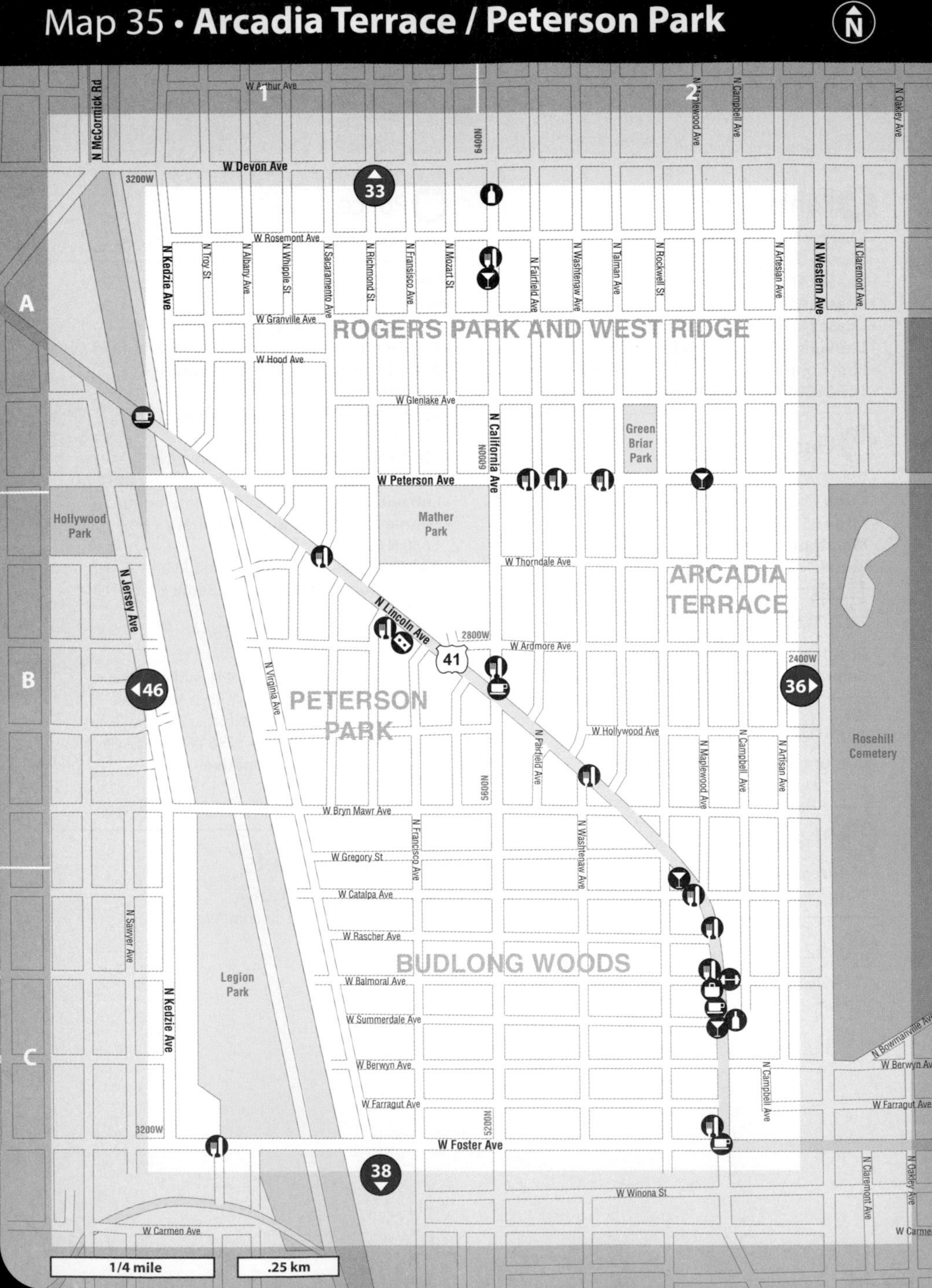

W Arthur Ave
W Devon Ave
33
W Rosemont Ave
W Granville Ave
W Hood Ave
W Glenlake Ave
W Peterson Ave
W Thorndale Ave
W Ardmore Ave
W Hollywood Ave
W Bryn Mawr Ave
W Gregory St
W Catalpa Ave
W Rascher Ave
W Balmoral Ave
W Summerdale Ave
W Berwyn Ave
W Farragut Ave
W Foster Ave
W Winona St
W Carmen Ave
N McCormick Rd
N Kedzie Ave
N Troy St
N Albany Ave
N Whipple St
N Sacramento Ave
N Richmond St
N Fransisco Ave
N Mozart St
N California Ave
N Fairfield Ave
N Washtenaw Ave
N Talman Ave
N Rockwell St
N Maplewood Ave
N Campbell Ave
N Artesian Ave
N Western Ave
N Claremont Ave
N Oakley Ave
N Jersey Ave
N Virginia Ave
N Francisco Ave
N Sawyer Ave
N Lincoln Ave
N Bowmanville Ave
ROGERS PARK AND WEST RIDGE
ARCADIA TERRACE
PETERSON PARK
BUDLONG WOODS
Green Briar Park
Mather Park
Hollywood Park
Legion Park
Rosehill Cemetery
3200W
2800W
2400W
6400N
6000N
5600N
5200N
41
46
36
38
1
2
A
B
C
1/4 mile
.25 km

Sundries / Entertainment

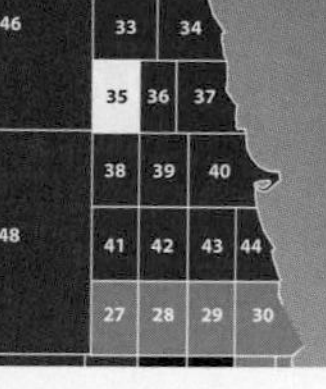

Of the bazillion tiny, unassuming Korean, Japanese, and Middle Eastern storefront restaurants peppering Peterson and Lincoln Avenues, Fondue Stube and Katsu stand out, as does Café Orange for its tentative nod at hipness—an unspeakable pretension in these parts. Local couples drink at Hidden Cove or Emerald Isle. Charcoal Delights has the best gyros this side of Greektown.

Coffee

- **Café Utjeha** • 5350 N Lincoln Ave
- **Dunkin' Donuts** • 5200 N Lincoln Ave
- **Dunkin' Donuts** • 5723 N California Ave
- **Starbucks** • 6075 N Lincoln Ave

Gyms

- **Curves (women only)** • 5360 N Lincoln Ave

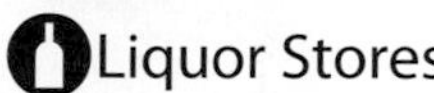

Liquor Stores

- **California Food And Liquor** • 6343 N California Ave
- **Eden Liquor Store & Foods** • 5359 N Lincoln Ave

Nightlife

- **Emerald Isle** • 2537 W Peterson Ave
- **Hidden Cove** • 5338 N Lincoln Ave
- **Karaoke Restaurant** • 6248 N California Ave
- **Lincoln Karaoke** • 5526 N Lincoln Ave

Restaurants

- **Aztecas Mexican Taqueria** • 5421 N Lincoln Ave
- **Café Orange** • 5639 N Lincoln Ave
- **Charcoal Delights** • 3139 W Foster Ave
- **Da Rae Jung** • 5220 N Lincoln Ave
- **Fondue Stube** • 2717 W Peterson Ave
- **Hai Woon Dae** • 6240 N California Ave
- **IHOP** • 5929 N Lincoln Ave
- **Katsu** • 2651 W Peterson Ave
- **Pauline's** • 1754 W Balmoral Ave
- **Pueblito Viejo** • 5429 N Lincoln Ave
- **Solga** • 5828 N Lincoln Ave
- **Sweet Collective** • 5333 N Lincoln Ave
- **Wolfy's** • 2734 W Peterson Ave
- **Woo Chon** • 5744 N California Ave

Video Rental

- **Tom Video** • 5806 N Lincoln Ave

Map 36 • Bryn Mawr / Bowmanville

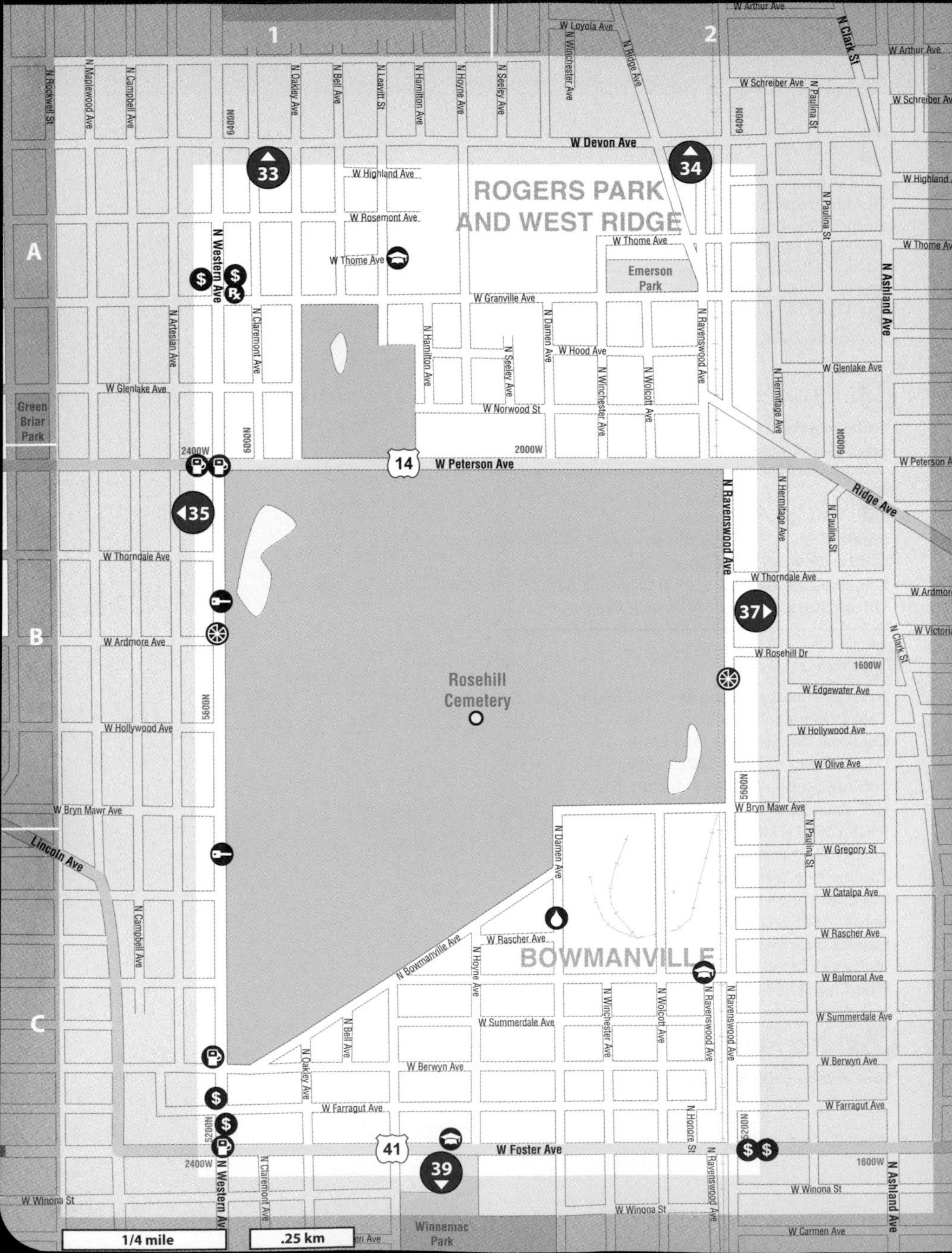

N

1
2
A
B
C

ROGERS PARK AND WEST RIDGE
BOWMANVILLE
Rosehill Cemetery
Emerson Park
Green Briar Park
Winnemac Park

W Arthur Ave
W Loyola Ave
N Clark St
W Schreiber Ave
W Devon Ave
W Highland Ave
W Rosemont Ave
W Thome Ave
W Granville Ave
W Hood Ave
W Glenlake Ave
W Norwood St
W Peterson Ave
Ridge Ave
W Thorndale Ave
W Ardmore Ave
W Victoria
W Rosehill Dr
W Edgewater Ave
W Hollywood Ave
W Olive Ave
W Bryn Mawr Ave
W Gregory St
W Catalpa Ave
W Rascher Ave
W Balmoral Ave
W Summerdale Ave
W Berwyn Ave
W Farragut Ave
W Foster Ave
W Winona St
W Carmen Ave
Lincoln Ave
N Bowmanville Ave

N Rockwell St
N Maplewood Ave
N Campbell Ave
N Oakley Ave
N Bell Ave
N Leavitt St
N Hamilton Ave
N Hoyne Ave
N Seeley Ave
N Winchester Ave
N Ridge Ave
N Paulina St
N Western Ave
N Artesian Ave
N Claremont Ave
N Damen Ave
N Wolcott Ave
N Ravenswood Ave
N Hermitage Ave
N Ashland Ave
N Honore St

6400N
6000N
5600N
5200N
2400W
2000W
1600W

14
41
33
34
35
37
39

1/4 mile
.25 km

Essentials

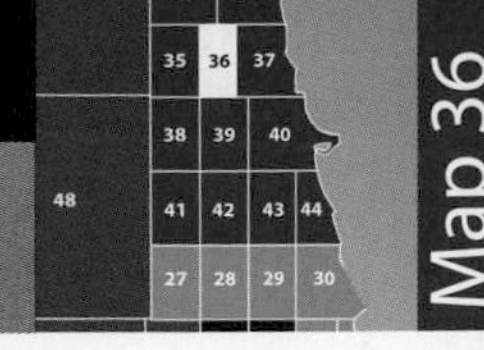

Map 36

Bowmanville, Andersonville's low-rent sibling, has had a flirtation with gentrification, but the toniest residents are still the luminaries interred at Rosehill Cemetery, including Montgomery Ward, Richard Sears, Oscar Mayer, several Chicago mayors, and one Vice President (Charles Gates Dawes). At 350 acres, Chicago's largest cemetery barely leaves room for the car dealerships along Western Avenue.

$ Banks

- **Chase** • 6210 N Western Ave
- **Chase (ATM)** • Walgreens • 6236 N Western Ave
- **Citibank (ATM)** • 7-Eleven • 1750 W Foster Ave
- **Citibank (ATM)** • 7-Eleven • 5206 N Western Ave
- **Citibank (ATM)** • 7-Eleven • 6001 N Western Ave
- **North Community** • 5241 N Western Ave
- **TCF (ATM)** • 7-Eleven • 1750 W Foster Ave
- **TCF (ATM)** • 7-Eleven • 5206 N Western Ave
- **TCF (ATM)** • 7-Eleven • 6001 N Western Ave

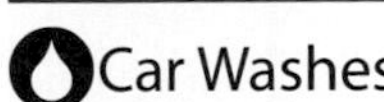

Car Washes

- **Norwood 2 Hand Carwash** • 5462 N Damen Ave

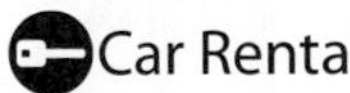

Car Rental

- **Enterprise** • 5844 N Western Ave • 773-989-3390
- **Hertz** • 5534 N Western Ave • 773-506-2125

Gas Stations

- **Citgo** • 1840 W Peterson Ave
- **Citgo** • 5300 N Western Ave
- **Shell** • 5201 N Western Ave
- **Shell** • 6000 N Western Ave

Landmarks

- **Rosehill Cemetery and Mausoleum** • 5800 N Ravenswood Ave

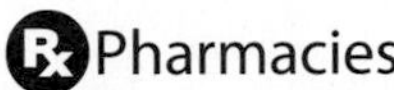

Pharmacies

- **Walgreens** • 6236 N Western Ave

Pizza

- **Delisi's Pizzeria** • 5806 N Western Ave
- **Fireside Restaurant & Lounge** • 5739 N Ravenswood Ave

Schools

- **Eliza Chappell Elementary** • 2135 W Foster Ave
- **Rogers Park Montessori** • 1800 W Balmoral Ave
- **Stone Scholastic Academy** • 6239 N Leavitt St

Map 36 • Bryn Mawr / Bowmanville

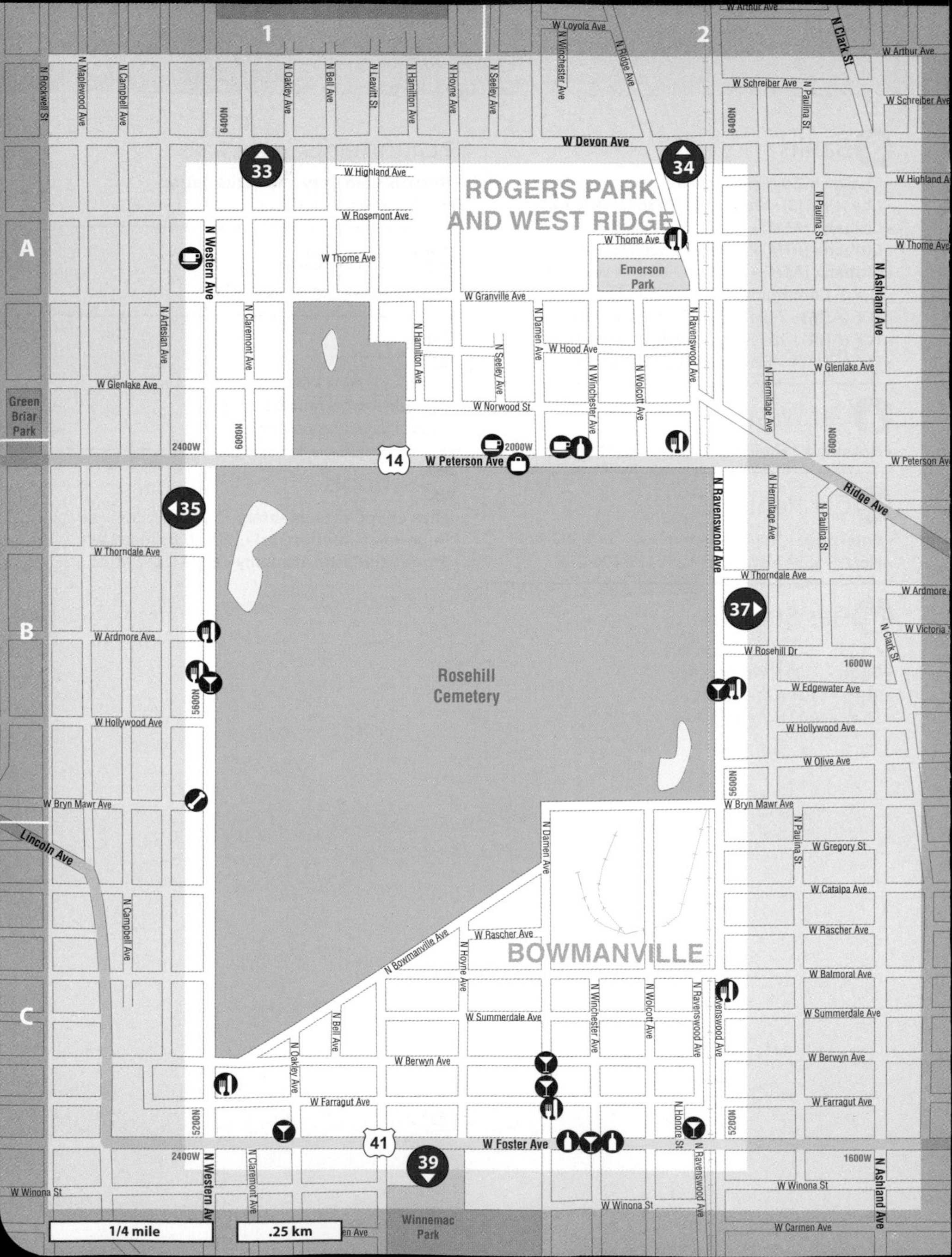

ROGERS PARK AND WEST RIDGE

Emerson Park

Rosehill Cemetery

BOWMANVILLE

Green Briar Park

Winnemac Park

1/4 mile

.25 km

Sundries / Entertainment

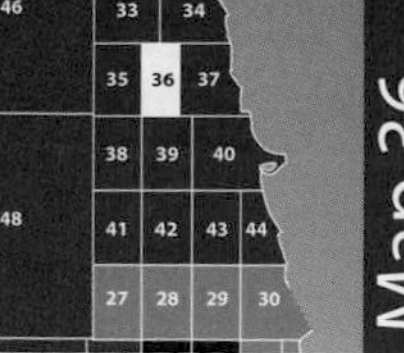

More family and Fido friendly than uber-chic, the area that circles Rosehill Cemetery is largely residential with a sprinkling of serviceable restaurants and dive bars. Dependable Fireside Restaurant & Lounge with its coveted 4 am liquor license is the place to be when the 2 am bars close. Locals swear by artsy oddball Leadway Bar & Café.

Coffee

- **Dunkin' Donuts** • 1954 W Peterson Ave
- **Dunkin' Donuts** • 6254 N Western Ave
- **Starbucks** • 2112 W Peterson Ave

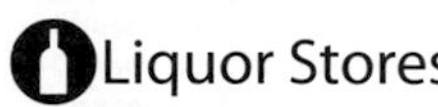

Liquor Stores

- **Diala Grocery & Liquor** • 1935 W Foster Ave
- **Foster Food & Liquor** • 1900 W Foster Ave
- **L&M Food & Liquor** • 1968 W Peterson Ave

Nightlife

- **Big Joe's 2 & 6 Pub** • 1818 W Foster Ave
- **Bobbie's Runaway** • 5305 N Damen Ave
- **Claddagh Ring** • 2306 W Foster Ave
- **Fireside Restaurant & Lounge** • 5739 N Ravenswood Ave
- **K's Dugout** • 1930 W Foster Ave
- **Leadway Bar & Café** • 5233 N Damen Ave
- **Sherry's Bar** • 5652 N Western Ave

Pet Shops

- **Four Paw Palace** • 2406 W Bryn Mawr Ave

Restaurants

- **Blue Nile** • 6118 N Ravenswood Ave
- **Delisi's Pizzeria** • 5806 N Western Ave
- **Fireside Restaurant & Lounge** • 5739 N Ravenswood Ave
- **Greenhouse Inn** • 6300 N Ridge Ave
- **Max's Italian Beef** • 5754 N Western Ave
- **San Soo Gab San** • 5247 N Western Ave
- **Yes Thai** • 5211 N Damen Ave

Shopping

- **Target** • 2112 W Peterson Ave

Map 38 • Ravenswood / Albany Park

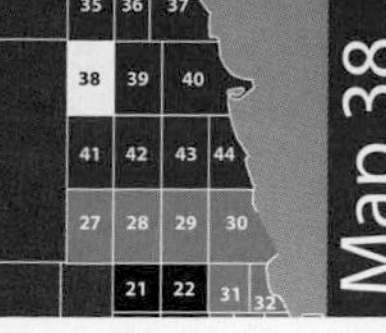

If you're hankering for halal meat or in the market to purchase a hookah, North Kedzie around Lawrence Avenue is a magnificent Middle Eastern melange of grocery stores and restaurants. If, on the other hand, you're hankering for any kind of nightlife, you'd do better to look elsewhere.

Coffee

- **Beans & Bagels** • 2601 W Leland Ave
- **Coffee Liberte** • 4807 N Spaulding Ave
- **Donut Doctor** • 3342 W Lawrence Ave
- **Dunkin' Donuts** • 3101 W Irving Park Rd
- **Dunkin' Donuts** • 4821 N Kedzie Ave
- **Jaafer Sweets** • Albany Plz Mall • 4825 N Kedzie Ave
- **Merle's Coffee Shoppe** • 4642 N Francisco Ave
- **Starbucks** • 4558 N Kedzie Ave

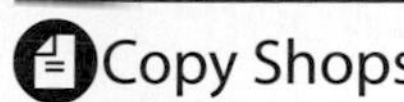

Copy Shops

- **Shree Printing Corporation** • 3011 W Irving Park Rd

Gyms

- **Galter Lifecenter** • 5157 N Francisco Ave
- **Women's Workout World (women only)** • 2540 W Lawrence Ave

Hardware Stores

- **Jay's True Value** • 4608 N Kedzie Ave
- **Lincoln Square Hardware** • 4874 N Lincoln Ave

Liquor Stores

- **Buy Low Liquor Store** • 3360 W Montrose Ave
- **Cardinal Wine & Spirits** • 4905 N Lincoln Ave
- **Charlies Supermarket** • 2941 W Montrose Ave
- **David's Food & Liquor** • 3158 W Montrose Ave
- **Food & Liquors Express** • 2752 W Lawrence Ave
- **Foremost Liquor Store** • 4616 N Kedzie Ave
- **J&A Liquors** • 3213 W Lawrence Ave
- **Jerusalem Liquors** • 3133 W Lawrence Ave
- **Peacock Liquors** • 3056 W Montrose Ave
- **Prestige Liquors** • 3210 W Montrose Ave
- **Quick Stop** • 2901 W Irving Park Rd

Nightlife

- **Brown Rice** • 4432 N Kedzie Ave
- **Lincoln Square Lanes** • 4874 N Lincoln Ave
- **Hot Shots** • 5151 N Lincoln Ave
- **Montrose Saloon** • 2933 W Montrose Ave
- **Peek Inn** • 2825 W Irving Park Rd

Pet Shops

- **Ruff Haus Pets** • 4652 N Rockwell St

Restaurants

- **Al-Amira** • 3200 W Lawrence Ave
- **Al-Khaymeih** • 4742 N Kedzie Ave
- **Arun's** • 4156 N Kedzie Ave
- **Baladna** • 4835 N Kedzie Ave
- **Brasa Roja** • 3125 W Montrose Ave
- **Cousin's IV (Incredible Vitality)** • 3038 W Irving Park Rd
- **Dawali** • 4911 N Kedzie Ave
- **Dharma Garden Thai Restaurants** • 3109 W Irving Park Rd
- **El Huarachin Huarachon** • 3320 W Lawrence Ave
- **Great Sea Chinese Restaurants** • 3254 W Lawrence Ave
- **Golden Crust Italian Pizzeria** • 4620 N Kedzie Ave
- **Kang Nam** • 4849 N Kedzie Ave
- **Kitchen Chicago** • 4664 N Manor Ave
- **Lutz Continental Café** • 2458 W Montrose Ave
- **Manzo's Ristorante** • 3210 W Irving Park Rd
- **Mi Ciudad** • 3041 W Irving Park Rd
- **Nhu Lan** • 2612 W Lawrence Ave
- **Noon O Kabab** • 4661 N Kedzie Ave
- **Old Town Tatu** • 3313 W Irving Parik Rd
- **Paradise** • 2916 W Montrose Ave
- **Pupuseria Las Delicias** • 3300 W Montrose Ave
- **Rockwell's Neighborhood Grill** • 4632 N Rockwell St
- **Salam** • 4636 N Kedzie Ave
- **Semiramis** • 4639 N Kedzie Ave
- **Thai Valley** • 4600 N Kedzie Ave

Shopping

- **Lincoln Antique Mall** • 3115 W Irving Park Rd
- **The Music Store** • 3121 W Irving Park Rd
- **Odin Tatu** • 3313 W Irving Park Rd
- **Rave Sports** • 3346 W Lawrence Ave
- **Village Discount Outlet** • 3301 W Lawrence Ave
- **Village Discount Outlet** • 4027 N Kedzie Ave

Video Rental

- **AV Video Center** • 5153 N Lincoln Ave
- **Azteca Video** • 3308 W Montrose Ave
- **Bosna Video (Primarily Serbo-Croat)** • 2501 W Lawrence Ave
- **V&K Video** • 4750 N Kedzie Ave

Map 39 • Ravenswood / North Center

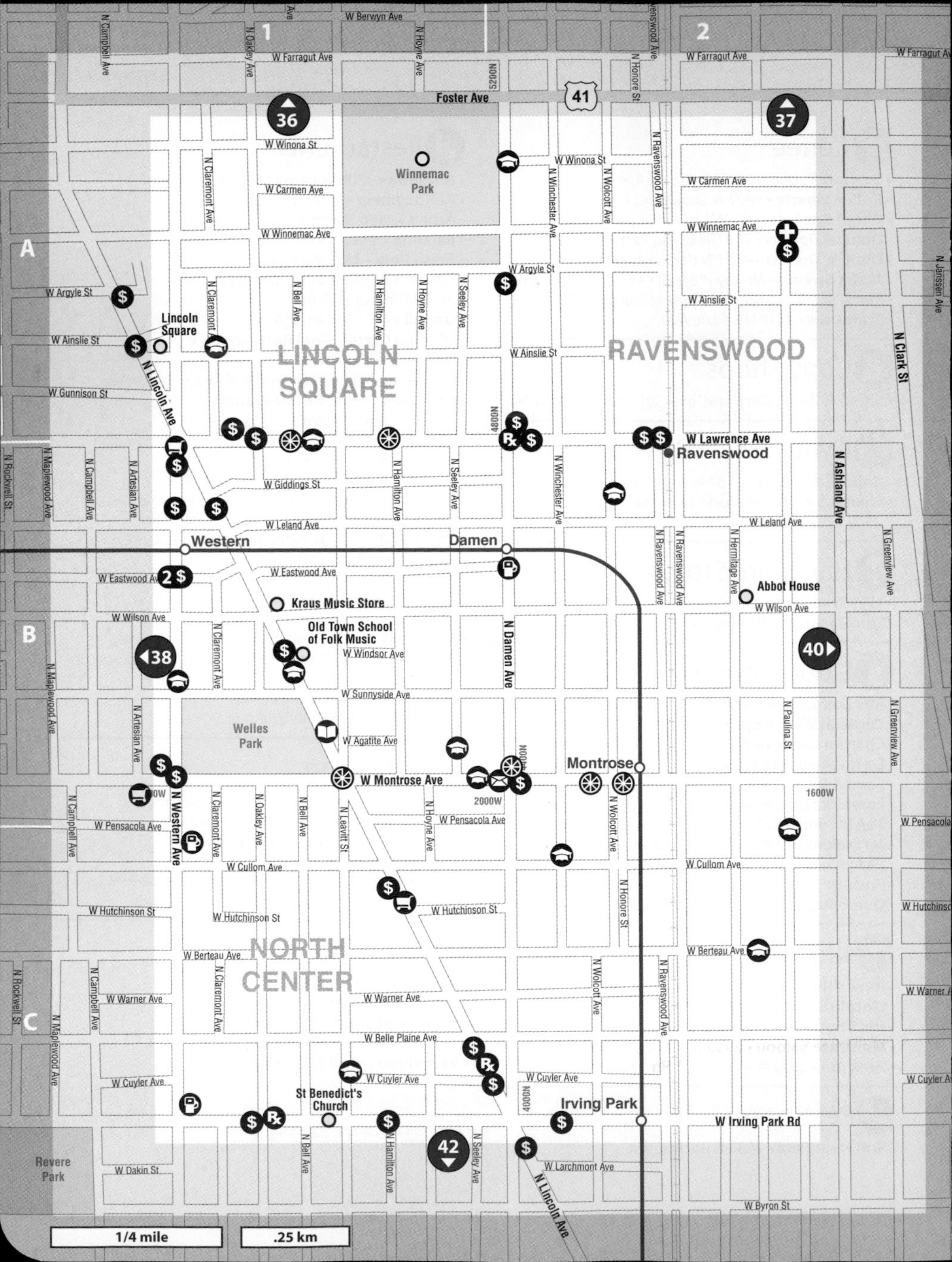
N
1
2
A
B
C
36
37
38
40
42
41
LINCOLN SQUARE
RAVENSWOOD
NORTH CENTER
Lincoln Square
Winnemac Park
Welles Park
Revere Park
Western
Damen
Ravenswood
Montrose
Irving Park
Kraus Music Store
Old Town School of Folk Music
Abbot House
St Benedict's Church
W Berwyn Ave
W Farragut Ave
Foster Ave
W Winona St
W Carmen Ave
W Winnemac Ave
W Argyle St
W Ainslie St
W Gunnison St
W Lawrence Ave
W Giddings St
W Leland Ave
W Eastwood Ave
W Wilson Ave
W Windsor Ave
W Sunnyside Ave
W Agatite Ave
W Montrose Ave
W Pensacola Ave
W Cullom Ave
W Hutchinson St
W Berteau Ave
W Warner Ave
W Belle Plaine Ave
W Cuyler Ave
W Irving Park Rd
W Larchmont Ave
W Dakin St
W Byron St
N Lincoln Ave
N Western Ave
N Damen Ave
N Ashland Ave
N Clark St
N Campbell Ave
N Oakley Ave
N Hoyne Ave
N Honore St
N Claremont Ave
N Winchester Ave
N Wolcott Ave
N Ravenswood Ave
N Bell Ave
N Hamilton Ave
N Seeley Ave
N Leavitt St
N Maplewood Ave
N Artesian Ave
N Rockwell St
N Hermitage Ave
N Paulina St
N Greenview Ave
N Janssen Ave
5200N
4800N
4400N
4000N
2000W
1600W
1/4 mile
.25 km

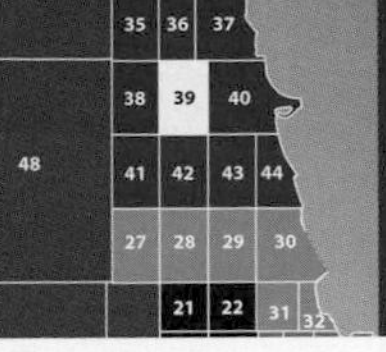

Ravenswood and North Center are by-and-large populated by clean, well-dressed white people with kids named Violet and Jack, and big, fluffy dogs called Bailey. Count these as among the Chicago neighborhoods most likely to have landscaping trucks parked in the driveways. Vestiges of old German Town exist in a social club and restaurant or two, and a twice-annual Germanfest occurring in the lot adjacent to the Western L.

Banks

- **Albany** • 4400 N Western Ave
- **Bank of America (ATM)** • 1969 W Lawrence Ave
- **Bank of America (ATM)** • 4005 N Damen Ave
- **Bank of America (ATM)** • CVS • 4800 N Damen Ave
- **Bridgeview** • 4553 N Lincoln Ave
- **Charter One** • 4037 N Lincoln Ave
- **Charter One** • 4725 N Western Ave
- **Charter One (ATM)** • 2323 W Lawrence Ave
- **Chase** • 1825 W Lawrence Ave
- **Chase** • 4711 N Lincoln Ave
- **Chase (ATM)** • Walgreens • 2301 W Irving Park Rd
- **Chase (ATM)** • Walgreens • 4801 N Lincoln Ave
- **Chase (ATM)** • Bethany Methodist Hospital • 5025 N Paulina St
- **Citibank (ATM)** • 4400 N Western Ave
- **Citibank (ATM)** • 7-Eleven • 4631 N Western Ave
- **Community Bank of Ravenswood** • 2300 W Lawrence Ave
- **Corus** • 3959 N Lincoln Ave
- **Corus** • 4800 N Western Ave
- **First American (ATM)** • 4115 N Lincoln Ave
- **Lincoln Park Savings** • 1946 W Irving Park Rd
- **Lincoln Park Savings** • 2139 W Irving Park Rd
- **North Community** • 2000 W Montrose Ave
- **TCF** • Osco • 4051 N Lincoln Ave
- **TCF** • Jewel • 4250 N Lincoln Ave
- **TCF (ATM)** • 7-Eleven • 4631 N Western Ave

Gas Stations

- **Mobil** • 4000 N Western Ave
- **Mobil** • 4638 N Damen Ave
- **Shell** • 4346 N Western Ave

Emergency Rooms

- **Methodist Hospital of Chicago** • 5025 N Paulina St

Landmarks

- **Abbott House** • 4605 N Hermitage Ave
- **Kraus Music Store** • 4611 N Lincoln Ave
- **Lincoln Square** • 4800 N Lincoln Ave
- **Old Town School of Folk Music** • 4544 N Lincoln Ave
- **St Benedict's Church** • 2215 W Irving Park Rd
- **Winnemac Park** • 5001 N Leavitt St

Libraries

- **Sulzer Public Library** • 4455 N Lincoln Ave

Pharmacies

- **CVS** • 4051 N Lincoln Ave
- **CVS** • 4800 N Damen Ave
- **Walgreens** • 2301 W Irving Park Rd

Pizza

- **Apart Pizza Company** • 2205 W Montrose Ave
- **Chicago's** • 1919 W Montrose Ave
- **Giordano's of Lincoln Square** • 2010 W Montrose Ave
- **Pizza DOC** • 2251 W Lawrence Ave
- **Stefano's** • 2124 W Lawrence Ave
- **Villa May Delicious Pizza** • 1834 W Montrose Ave

Post Offices

- **US Post Office** • 2011 W Montrose Ave

Schools

- **Adler** • 2239 W Lawrence Ave
- **James B McPherson Elementary** • 4728 N Wolcott Ave
- **John C Coonley Elementary** • 4046 N Leavitt St
- **Mary E Courtenay Language Arts Center** • 1726 W Berteau Ave
- **North Park Elementary** • 2017 W Montrose Ave
- **Old Town School of Folk Music** • 4544 N Lincoln Ave
- **Pilgrim Lutheran** • 4300 N Winchester Ave
- **Queen of Angels** • 4520 N Western Ave
- **Ravenswood Baptist Christian** • 4437 N Seeley Ave
- **Ravenswood Elementary** • 4332 N Paulina St
- **Roald Amundsen High** • 5110 N Damen Ave
- **St Matthias** • 4910 N Claremont Ave

Supermarkets

- **Aldi 2431** • W Montrose Ave
- **Dollar Tree Store** • 4738 N Western Ave
- **Jewel-Osco** • 4250 N Lincoln Ave

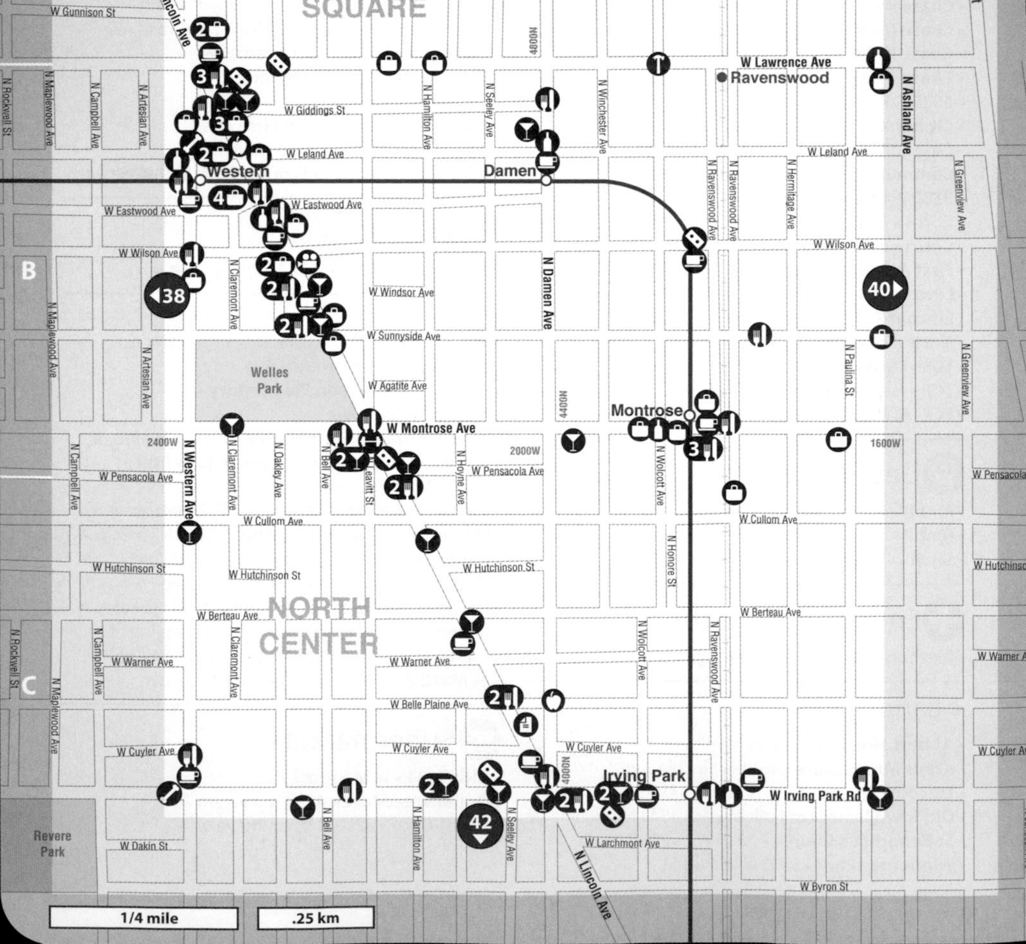

LINCOLN SQUARE
RAVENSWOOD
NORTH CENTER
Winnemac Park
Welles Park
Revere Park
Foster Ave
W Lawrence Ave
W Montrose Ave
W Irving Park Rd
N Western Ave
N Damen Ave
N Ashland Ave
N Clark St
N Lincoln Ave
Western
Damen
Ravenswood
Montrose
Irving Park
1/4 mile
.25 km

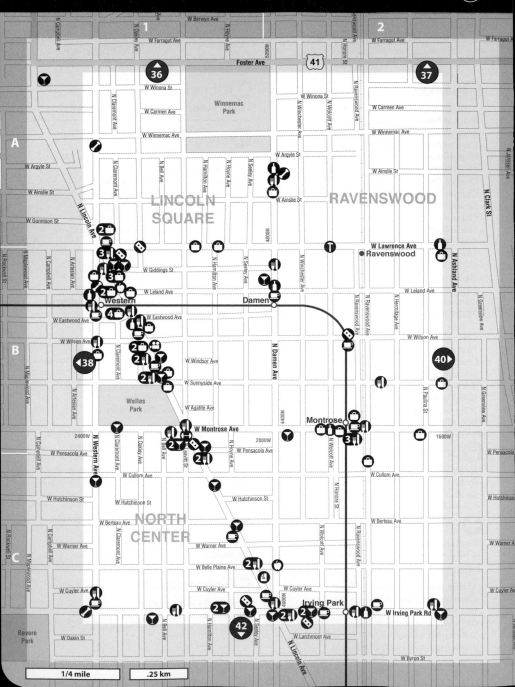

Sundries / Entertainment

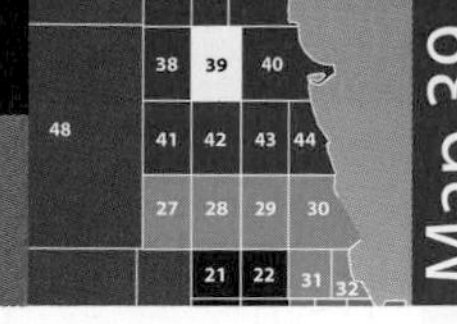

Local hippysters shop at places like the Book Celler, a cute bookshop cum wine café, browse-friendly record store, Laurie's Planet of Sound, or quirky Quake Collectables. In the evening, the stretch of Lincoln Avenue that disects this area becomes a restaurant row with neighborhood and destination dining. From old standards such as Opart and Chicago Brauhaus, to destination faves Bistro Campagne, Chalkboard, and Spacca Napoli, foodies will not go hungry.

Coffee

- **Beans & Bagels** • 1812 W Montrose Ave
- **Bourbon Cafe** • 4768 N Lincoln Ave
- **Dunkin' Donuts** • 1743 W Lawrence Ave
- **Dunkin' Donuts** • 4010 N Western Ave
- **Dunkin' Donuts** • 4645 N Western Ave
- **The Grind** • 4613 N Lincoln Ave
- **Katerina's** • 1920 W Irving Park Rd
- **Perfect Cup** • 4700 N Damen Ave
- **Red Eyes Café** • 4164 N Lincoln Ave
- **Starbucks** • 1900 W Montrose Ave
- **Starbucks** • 4015 N Lincoln Ave
- **Starbucks** • 4553 N Lincoln Ave
- **The Perfect Cup** • 4700 N Damen Ave

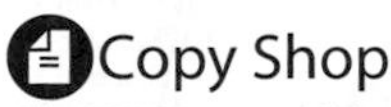

Copy Shops

- **The UPS Store** • 4064 N Lincoln Ave

Farmers Markets

- **Lincoln Square (Jun–Oct; Tues, 7 am–2 pm)** • 4700 N Lincoln Ave
- **North Center (Jun–Oct; Sat, 7 am–2 pm)** • W Belle Plaine Ave & N Damen Ave

Gyms

- **Curves (women only)** • 4351 N Lincoln Ave

Hardware Stores

- **Sears** • 1900 W Lawrence Ave

Liquor Stores

- **Best Buy Food & Liquor** • 1832 W Montrose Ave
- **Bright** • 1628 W Lawrence Ave
- **Fine Wine Brokers (wine only)** • 4621 N Lincoln Ave
- **Fox Liquors** • 4707 N Damen Ave
- **George's Liquors** • 1964 W Lawrence Ave
- **Houston Liquor & Foods** • 1829 W Irving Park Rd
- **Leland Inn** • 4662 N Western Ave
- **Windy City Liquors** • 4959 N Damen Ave

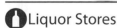

Movie Theaters

- **Davis Theater** • 4614 N Lincoln Ave

Nightlife

- **Bowman's Bar and Grill** • 4356 N Leavitt St
- **Celtic Crown Public House** • 4301 N Western Ave
- **Chicago Brauhaus** • 4732 N Lincoln Ave
- **Daily Bar & Grill** • 4560 N Lincoln Ave
- **The Globe Pub** • 1934 W Irving Park Rd
- **Grafton Pub** • 4530 N Lincoln Ave
- **Hot Shots** • 5151 N Lincoln Ave
- **Huettenbar** • 4721 N Lincoln Ave
- **Jury's Food & Drink** • 4337 N Lincoln Ave
- **Katerina's** • 1920 W Irving Park Rd
- **Laschet's Inn** • 2119 W Irving Park Rd
- **The Lincoln Lodge** • 4008 N Lincoln Ave
- **The Long Room** • 1612 W Irving Park Rd
- **Margie's Pub** • 4145 N Lincoln Ave
- **Oakwood 83** • 1959 W Montrose Ave
- **O'Donovan's** • 2100 W Irving Park Rd
- **O'Lanagan's** • 2335 W Montrose Ave
- **The Rail** • 4709 N Damen Ave
- **Resi's Bierstube** • 2034 W Irving Park Rd
- **Tiny Lounge** • 4352 N Leavitt St
- **Wild Goose** • 4265 N Lincoln Ave
- **Windy City Inn** • 2257 W Irving Park Rd

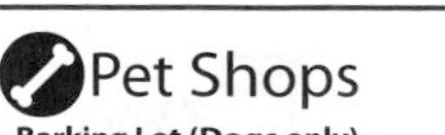

Pet Shops

- **Barking Lot (Dogs only)** • 2442 W Irving Park Rd
- **Off the Leash** • 4955 N Damen Ave
- **Paws & Claws** • 5015 N Western Ave
- **Sit!** • 2316 W Leland Ave

Restaurants

- **Bad Dog Tavern** • 4535 N Lincoln Ave
- **Bistro Campagne** • 4518 N Lincoln Ave
- **Browntrout** • 4111 N Lincoln Ave
- **Budacki's Drive-In** • 4739 N Damen Ave
- **Café 28** • 1800 W Irving Park Rd
- **Café Selmarie** • 4729 N Lincoln Ave
- **Chalkboard** • 4343 N Lincoln Ave
- **Chicago Brauhaus** • 4732 N Lincoln Ave
- **Diner Grill** • 1635 W Irving Pk Rd
- **Essence of India** • 4601 N Lincoln Ave
- **First Slice Pie Café** • 4401 N Ravenswood Ave
- **Glenn's Diner** • 1820 W Montrose Ave
- **Glunz Bavarian Haus** • 4128 N Lincoln Ave
- **Golden Angel Restaurant** • 4340 N Lincoln Ave
- **House of Wah Sun** • 4319 N Lincoln Ave
- **La Boca della Verita** • 4618 N Lincoln Ave
- **Lincoln Restaurant** • 4008 N Lincoln Ave
- **LM Le Restaurant** • 4539 N Lincoln Ave
- **Los Nopales** • 4544 N Western Ave
- **Margie's Candies** • 1813 W Montrose Ave
- **Opart Thai House** • 4658 N Western Ave
- **Orange Garden** • 1942 W Irving Park Rd
- **Over Easy Café** • 4943 N Damen Ave
- **Pannenkoeken Cafe** • 4757 N Western Ave
- **Pizza DOC** • 2251 W Lawrence Ave
- **Roong Petch Restaurant** • 1828 W Montrose Ave
- **Smokin' Woody's** • 4160 N Lincoln Ave
- **Snappy's Shrimp House** • 1901 W Irving Park Rd
- **Spacca Napoli** • 1769 W Sunnyside Ave
- **Sticky Rice** • 4018 N Western Ave
- **Tank Sushi** • 4514 N Lincoln Ave

Shopping

- **Angel Food Bakery** • 1636 W Montrose Ave
- **Arcadia Knitting** • 1613 W Lawrence Ave
- **Architectural Artifacts** • 4325 N Ravenswood Ave
- **Book Cellar** • 4736 N Lincoln Ave
- **Chicago Soccer** • 4839 N Western Ave
- **The Chopping Block** • 4747 N Lincoln Ave
- **Dark Tower Comics & Collectibles** • 4835 N Western Ave
- **Different Strummer** • 4544 N Lincoln Ave
- **East Meets West** • 2118 W Lawrence Ave
- **Eclecticity** • 4718 N Lincoln Ave
- **European Import Center** • 4752 N Lincoln Ave
- **Fleet Feet Sports** • 4555 N Lincoln Ave
- **Gallimaufry Gallery** • 4712 N Lincoln Ave
- **Glass Art & Decorative Studio** • 4507 N Lincoln Ave
- **Griffins & Gargoyles Antiques** • 2140 W Lawrence Ave
- **Happy Food Spot** • 4631 N Lincoln Ave
- **Hazel** • 1902 W Montrose Ave
- **Laurie's Planet of Sound** • 4639 N Lincoln Ave
- **Margie's Candies** • 1813 W Montrose Ave
- **Merz Apothecary** • 4716 N Lincoln Ave
- **Patina** • 4907 N Damen Ave
- **Nadeau** • 4433 N Ravenswood Ave
- **Provenance Food and Wine** • 2312 W Leland Ave
- **Quake Collectibles** • 4628 N Lincoln Ave
- **Rock N Roll Vintage Inc** • 4740 N Lincoln Ave
- **Sacred Art** • 4619 N Lincoln Ave
- **Salamander Shoes** • 4740 N Linoln Ave
- **String a Strand on Wells** • 4632 N Lincoln Ave
- **Thrifty Baby Boutique** • 4546 N Western Ave
- **Timeless Toys** • 4749 N Lincoln Ave

Video Rental

- **Blockbuster** • 1958 W Irving Park Rd
- **Blockbuster** • 2301 W Lawrence Ave
- **Darkstar Video** • 4355 N Lincoln Ave
- **Lincoln Square Video (Yugoslavian)** • 4725 N Lincoln Ave
- **Super Video** • 2055 W Irving Park Rd
- **Tom Video** • 1830 W Wilson Ave

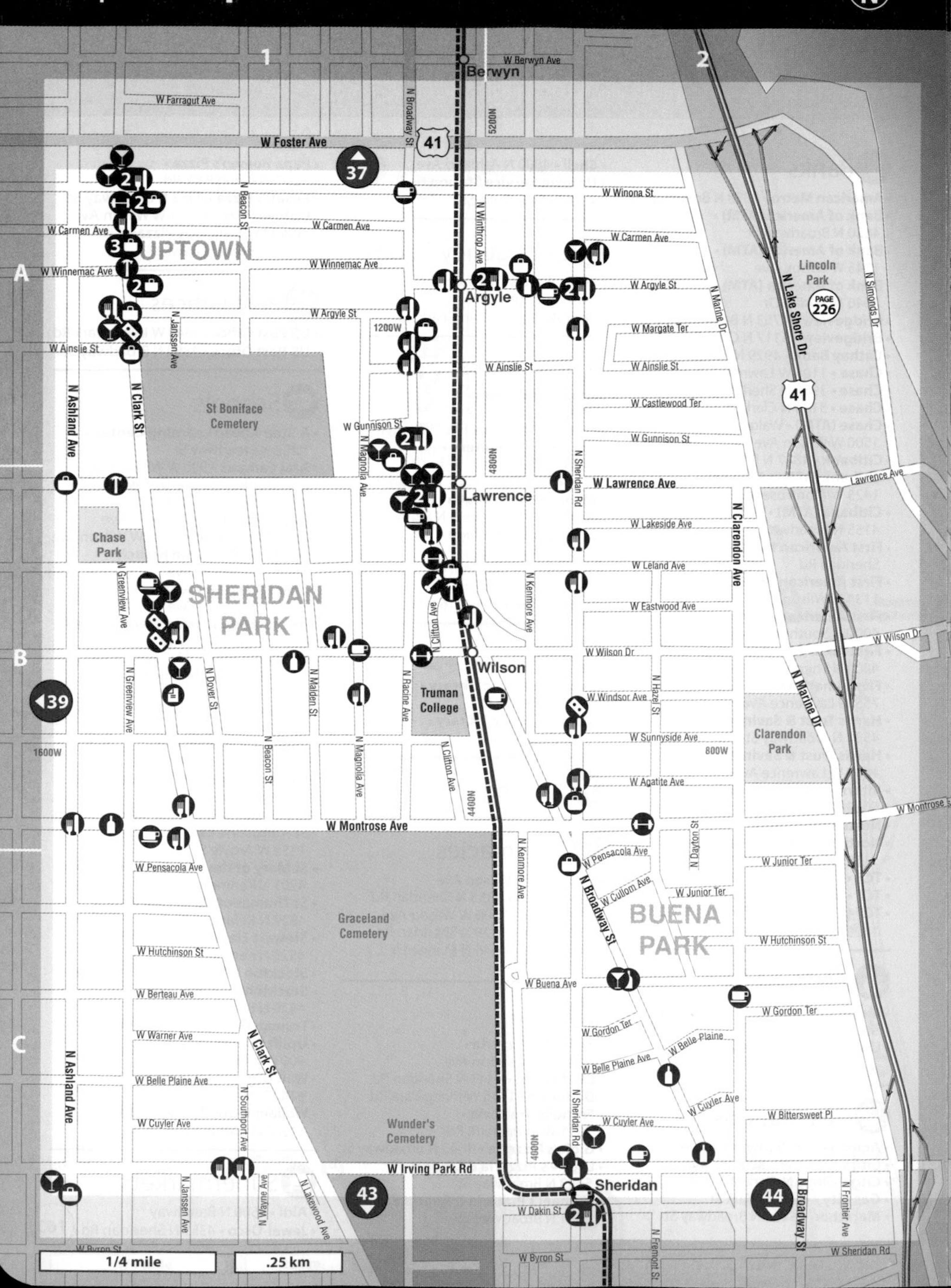

W Berwyn Ave
Berwyn
W Farragut Ave
W Foster Ave
41
37
5200N
N Broadway St
N Beacon St
W Winona St
W Carmen Ave
UPTOWN
W Winnemac Ave
N Winthrop Ave
W Argyle St
Argyle
Lincoln Park
PAGE 226
N Lake Shore Dr
N Simonds Dr
N Marine Dr
W Margate Ter
1200W
W Ainslie St
N Janssen Ave
W Castlewood Ter
N Ashland Ave
N Clark St
St Boniface Cemetery
W Gunnison St
N Magnolia Ave
4800N
N Sheridan Rd
W Lawrence Ave
Lawrence
Lawrence Ave
N Clarendon Ave
Chase Park
W Lakeside Ave
W Leland Ave
N Greenview Ave
SHERIDAN PARK
N Kenmore Ave
W Eastwood Ave
N Clifton Ave
W Wilson Dr
Wilson
Truman College
N Dover St
N Malden St
N Racine Ave
W Windsor Ave
N Hazel St
39
W Sunnyside Ave
Clarendon Park
1600W
800W
W Agatite Ave
4400N
W Montrose Ave
W Montrose
W Pensacola Ave
N Dayton St
W Junior Ter
W Cullom Ave
BUENA PARK
Graceland Cemetery
W Hutchinson St
W Buena Ave
W Berteau Ave
W Gordon Ter
W Warner Ave
W Belle Plaine
W Belle Plaine Ave
N Southport Ave
W Cuyler Ave
W Bittersweet Pl
Wunder's Cemetery
4000N
W Irving Park Rd
Sheridan
43
44
N Wayne Ave
N Lakewood Ave
N Frontier Ave
W Dakin St
N Fremont St
W Byron St
W Sheridan Rd
1/4 mile
.25 km
A
B
C
1
2

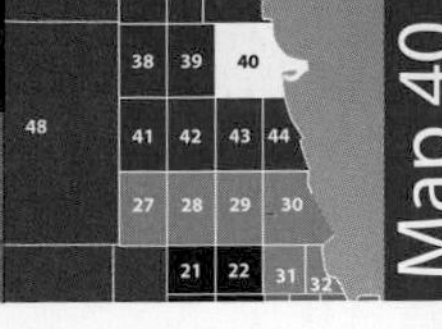

Uptown's nightlife is lively, chock full of shiny new bars as well as reliable old standbys. Green Mill (famous for live jazz and Sunday night poetry slams) and Big Chicks (a favored, gay neighborhood bar with great art) have long drawn folks to Uptown. Hopleaf is justifiably renowned for their extensive offerings of Belgian brews, and T's draws a friendly mix of local LGBTs with their great outdoor patio and budget-frienly drink and menu specials.

Coffee

- **Ch'ava Cafe** • 4656 N Clark St
- **Corona's Coffee Shop** • 909 W Irving Park Rd
- **Dollop Coffee Co** • 4181 N Clarendon Ave
- **Dunkin' Donuts** • 5130 N Broadway St
- **Dunkin' Donuts** • 1441 W Montrose Ave
- **Dunkin' Donuts** • 4547 N Broadway St
- **Emerald City Coffee** • 3938 N Sheridan Rd
- **New Chinatown Bakery & Coffee Shop** • 1019 W Argyle St
- **Starbucks** • 4600 N Magnolia Ave
- **Starbucks** • 4753 N Broadway St

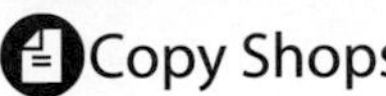

Copy Shops

- **Staples Copy & Print Centers** • 4610 N Clark St

Gyms

- **Bodyfit Athletic Club** • 4704 N Broadway St
- **Curves (women only)** • 1144 W Wilson Ave
- **Know No Limits** • 5121 N Clark St
- **World Gym** • 909 W Montrose Ave

Hardware Stores

- **Andersonville Hardware** • 5036 N Clark St
- **Crafty Beaver Home Center** • 1522 W Lawrence Ave
- **Uptown Ace Hardware** • 4654 N Broadway St

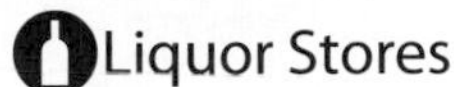

Liquor Stores

- **Foremost Liquors** • 1040 W Argyle St
- **GNS Food & Liquor** • 4092 N Broadway St
- **JJ Peppers Food Store** • 4800 N Sheridan Rd
- **Laurie's Pizzeria & Liquors** • 5153 N Broadway St
- **Manhattan Liquors** • 4200 N Broadway St
- **Rayan's Discount Liquors** • 1532 W Montrose Ave
- **Sheridan Park Food & Liquor** • 1255 W Wilson Ave
- **Sheridan-Irving Liquor** • 3944 N Sheridan Rd

Nightlife

- **Bar on Buena** • 910 W Buena Ave
- **Big Chicks** • 5024 N Sheridan Rd
- **Carol's Pub** • 4659 N Clark St
- **Crew Bar & Grill** • 4804 N Broadway St
- **Green Mill Pub** • 4802 N Broadway St
- **Holiday Club** • 4000 N Sheridan Rd
- **Hopleaf** • 5148 N Clark St
- **Konak** • 5150 N Clark St
- **The Long Room** • 1612 W Irving Park Rd
- **Max's Place** • 4621 N Clark St
- **Nick's Uptown** • 4015 N Sheridan Rd
- **Sofo Bar** • 4923 N Clark St
- **The Spot** • 4437 N Broadway St
- **T's** • 5025 N Clark St
- **The Uptown Lounge** • 1136 W Lawrence Ave
- **Wild Pug** • 4810 N Broadway

Pet Shops

- **Soggy Paws** • 1148 W Leland Ave

Restaurants

- **Agami** • 4712 N Broadway St
- **Anna Maria Pasteria** • 4400 N Clark St
- **Café Lao** • 1007 W Argyle St
- **Café Too** • 4715 N Sheridan Rd
- **Carmela's Taqueria** • 1206 W Lawrence Ave
- **Deleece** • 4004 N Southport Ave
- **Domera** • 4801 N Broadway St
- **Furama** • 4936 N Broadway St
- **Hai Yen** • 1055 W Argyle St
- **Hama Matsu** • 5143 N Clark St
- **Iyanze** • 4623 N Broadway
- **JJ Fish & Chicken** • 4515 N Sheridan Rd
- **La Amistad** • 1419 W Montrose Ave
- **La Banh Mi Hung Phat** • 4942 N Sheridan Rd
- **Le's Pho** • 4925 N Broadway St
- **Magnolia Café** • 1224 W Wilson Ave
- **Marigold** • 4832 N Broadway St
- **Mixteco Grill** •1601 W Montrose Ave
- **Palace Gate** • 4548 N. Magnolia
- **Pho 777** • 1065 W Argyle St
- **Riques** • 5004 N Sheridan Rd
- **Siam Noodle & Rice** • 4654 N Sheridan Rd
- **Silver Seafood** • 4829 N Broadway St
- **Sun Wah Bar-B-Que** • 5039 N Broadway St
- **TAC Quick** • 3930 N Sheridan Rd
- **Tapas Las Ramblas** • 5101 N Clark St
- **Taqueria los Caminos de Michoacan** • 3948 N Sheridan Rd
- **Thai Pastry** • 4925 N Broadway St
- **Titzal Cafe** • 4631 N Clark St
- **Tweet** • 5020 N Sheridan Rd
- **Winston's Cafe** • 5001 N Clark St

Shopping

- **Angel Food Bakery** • 1636 W Montrose Ave
- **Baan Home** • 5053 N Clark St
- **Eagle Leathers** • 5015 N Clark St
- **Foursided** • 5061 N Clark St
- **La Patisserie P** • 1052 W Argyle St
- **Patina Antiques** • 5137 N Clark St
- **Play It Again Sports** • 3939 N Ashland Ave
- **Salvation Army Thrift Store** • 4315 N Broadway St
- **Shake Rattle and Read Book Box** • 4812 N Broadway St
- **skinstinct** • 5135 N Clark St
- **Tai Nam Market Center** • 4925 N Broadway St
- **Tattoo Factory** • 4441 N Broadway St
- **Transistor** • 5045 N Clark St
- **Unique Thrift Store** • 4445 N Sheridan Rd
- **Uptown Bikes** • 4653 N Broadway St
- **Village Discount Outlet** • 4898 N Clark St
- **Wooden Spoon** • 5047 N Clark St

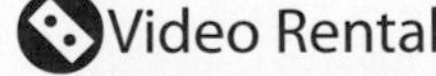

Video Rental

- **Banana Video** • 4923 N Clark St
- **Bankok Video & Grocery** • 4617 N Clark St
- **Blockbuster** • 4620 N Clark St
- **United Video** • 4519 N Sheridan Rd

Map 41 • Avondale / Old Irving

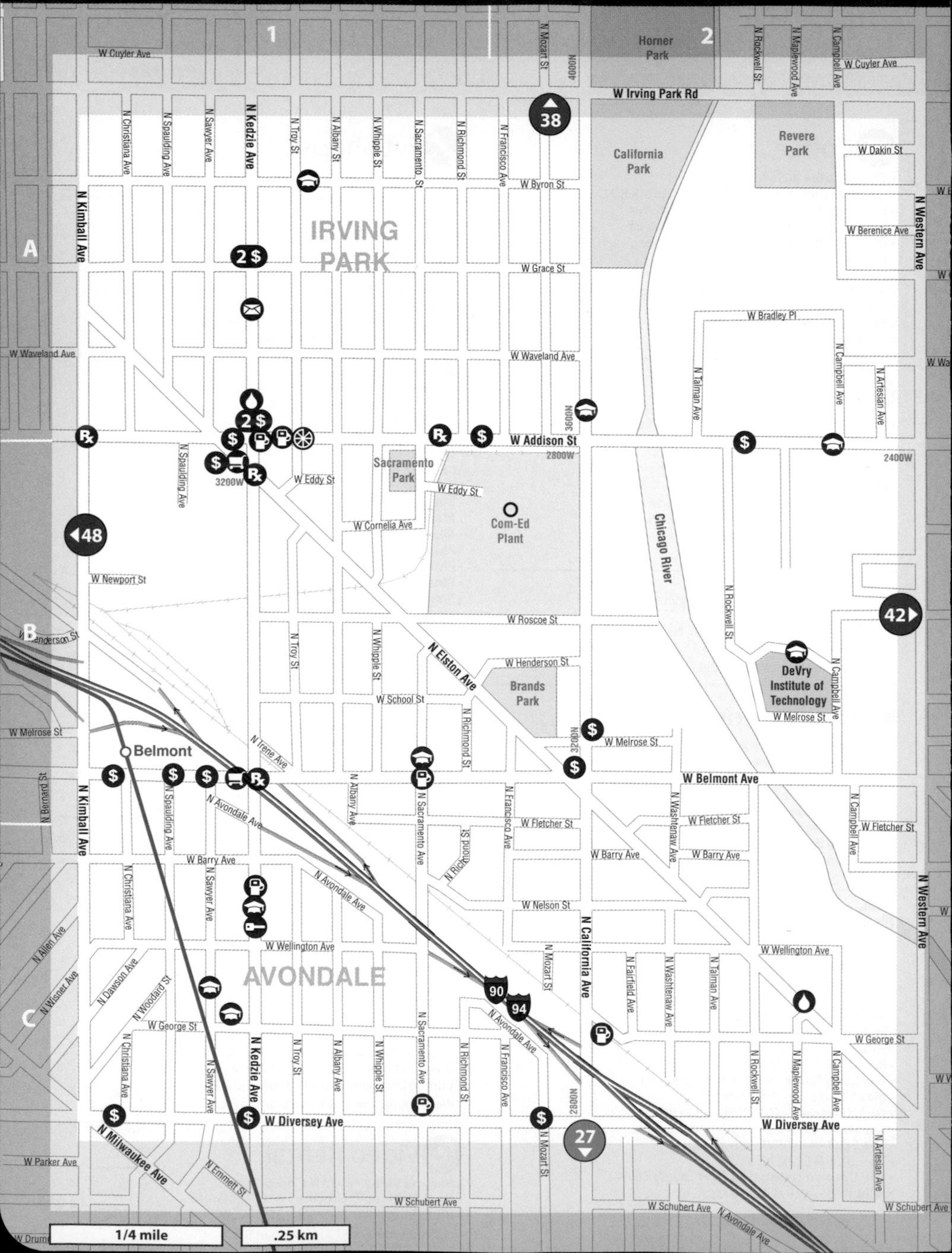

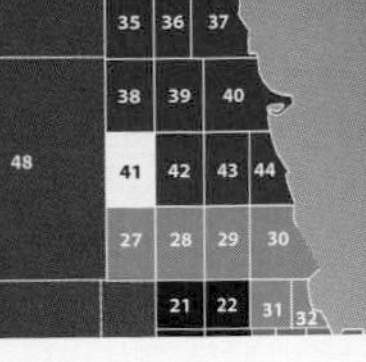

That screeching sound you hear is Avondale development, which, like much of Chicago's westward expansion, has been riding the breaks since the recession-fueled decline. Even real estate speculators are hard-pressed to gild the dandelion of frame two-flats in foreclosure. The results: bleary-eyed hipsters wandering around in confusion, wondering how the hell they ended up here.

Banks

- **Bank of America** • 3260 W Belmont Ave
- **Bank of America** • 3350 W Diversey Ave
- **Chase** • 3227 W Addison St
- **Chase (ATM)** • Walgreens 2844 W Diversey Ave
- **Chase (ATM)** • Devry University • 3300 N Campbell Ave
- **Chase (ATM)** • Walgreens 3302 W Belmont Ave
- **Citibank (ATM)** • 3611 N Kedzie Ave
- **Citibank (ATM)** • 7-Eleven • 3800 N Kedzie Ave
- **First American (ATM)** • 3201 W Diversey Ave
- **Harris Trust & Savings** • 2927 W Addison St
- **Harris Trust & Savings (ATM)** • 2550 W Addison St
- **North Community** • 2758 W Belmont Ave
- **TCF** • Jewel • 3570 N Elston Ave
- **TCF (ATM)** • 7-Eleven • 3800 N Kedzie Ave
- **US** • 3611 N Kedzie Ave

Car Washes

- **123 Hand Car Wash** • 3635 N Kedzie Ave
- **Superior Performance II** • 2933 N Elston Ave

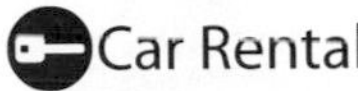

Car Rental

- **Enterprise** • 3029 N Kedzie Ave • 773-478-3310

Gas Stations

- **BP** • 3201 W Addison St
- **Citgo** • 2920 N California Ave
- **Citgo** • 3001 W Belmont Ave
- **Marathon** • 2811 N Sacramento Ave
- **Marathon** • 3057 N Kedzie Ave
- **Shell** • 3159 W Addison St

Landmarks

- **Com-Ed Plant** • N California Ave & W Roscoe St

Pharmacies

- **CVS** • 3411 W Addison St
- **Jewel-Osco** • 3572 N Elston Ave
- **Target** • 2939 W Addison St
- **Walgreens** • 3302 W Belmont Ave

Pizza

- **Little Caesars Pizza** • 3135 W Addison St

Post Offices

- **US Post Office** • 3750 N Kedzie Ave

Schools

- **A-Karrasel** • 3030 N Kedzie Ave
- **Albert G Lane Tech** • 2501 W Addison St
- **Avondale Elementary** • 2945 N Sawyer Ave
- **Carl Von Linne Elementary** • 3221 N Sacramento Ave
- **DeVry Institute of Technology** • 3300 N Campbell Ave
- **Gordon Technical High** • 3633 N California Ave
- **Grover Cleveland Elementary** • 3121 W Byron St
- **Logandale Middle** • 3212 W George St

Supermarkets

- **Jewel-Osco** • 3570 N Elston Ave

Map 41 • Avondale / Old Irving

Sundries / Entertainment

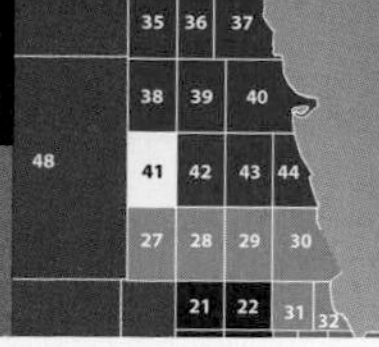

Neighborhood development may be at a standstill, but Avondale is still a destination dining hotspot. Foodies queue up for Hot Doug's gourmet hot dogs and duck fat fries and the Heavy Metal burgers at Kuma's. BYOB Urban Belly dishes up fantastic noodle bowls and dumplings, and the dreary Stadium West dive bar has transformed into the Dragon Lady Lounge, offering a vegan Korean buffet on select nights.

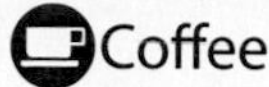

Coffee

- **Dunkin' Donuts** • 3214 N Kimball Ave
- **Dunkin' Donuts** • 3310 W Addison St
- **Dunkin' Donuts** • 3427 W Diversey Ave
- **Starbucks** • Target • 2939 W Addison St

Hardware Stores

- **Elston Ace Hardware** • 2825 W Belmont Ave
- **Home Depot** • 3500 N Kimball Ave
- **Kabbe True Value Hardware** • 2550 W Diversey Ave

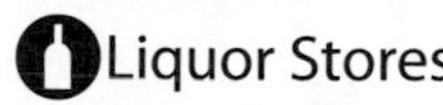

Liquor Stores

- **American Way Liquor** • 3700 N Kedzie Ave
- **Discount Store** • 3457 N Albany Ave
- **JJ Peppers** • 3201 W Diversey Ave

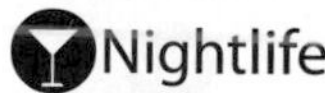

Nightlife

- **Chief O'Neill's** • 3471 N Elston Ave
- **Kuma's Corner** • 2900 W Belmont Ave
- **Ñ** • 2977 N Elston Ave
- **Nelly's Saloon** • 3256 N Elston Ave
- **Small Bar** • 2956 N Albany Ave
- **Square Bar & Grill** • 2849 W Belmont Ave

Pet Shops

- **Belmont Feed (Birds only)** • 3036 W Belmont Ave
- **Pet A Cure** • 2949 W Diversey Ave
- **Pet Supplies Plus** • 3640 N Elston Ave

Restaurants

- **The Buffet Castle** • 3326 W Belmont Ave
- **Burrito House** • 3145 W Addison St
- **Chief O'Neill's** • 3471 N Elston Ave
- **Dragon Lady Lounge** • 3188 N Elston Ave
- **Eat First Chinese Restaurant** • 3337 W Belmont Ave
- **Hot Doug's** • 3324 N California Ave
- **Kuma's Corner** • 2900 W Belmont Ave
- **La Finca** • 3361 N Elston Ave
- **Mr. Pollo** • 3000 W Belmont Ave
- **Taqueria Trespazada** • 3144 N California Ave
- **Urban Belly** • 3053 N California Ave
- **Zacatecas** • 2934 W Diversey Ave

Video Rental

- **Blockbuster** • 3951 N Kimball Ave

NORTH CENTER
ROSCOE VILLAGE
LAKEVIEW
Irving Park
Addison
Paulina
Revere Park
DeVry Institute of Technology
19th District Police Headquarters
Gross Park
Hamlin Park
Chicago River
W Irving Park Rd
W Addison St
W Belmont Ave
W Diversey Ave
N Western Ave
N Damen Ave
N Ashland Ave
N Lincoln Ave
N Clybourn Ave
W Cuyler Ave
W Belle Plaine Ave
W Dakin St
W Larchmont Ave
W Byron St
W Berenice Ave
W Grace St
W Bradley Pl
W Waveland Ave
W Patterson Ave
W Eddy St
W Cornelia Ave
W Newport Ave
W Roscoe St
W Henderson St
W School St
W Melrose St
W Fletcher St
W Barry Ave
W Nelson St
W Wellington Ave
W Oakdale Ave
W George St
W Wolfram St
W Schubert Ave
N Logan Blvd
N Campbell Ave
N Maplewood Ave
N Rockwell St
N Artesian Ave
N Claremont Ave
N Oakley Ave
N Bell Ave
N Leavitt St
N Hamilton Ave
N Hoyne Ave
N Seeley Ave
N Wolcott Ave
N Ravenswood Ave
N Hermitage Ave
N Paulina St
N Marshfield Ave
N Bosworth Ave
N Greenview Ave
N Honore St
4000N
3600N
3200N
2800N
2400W
2000W
1600W
39
41
43
28
1/4 mile
.25 km

Essentials

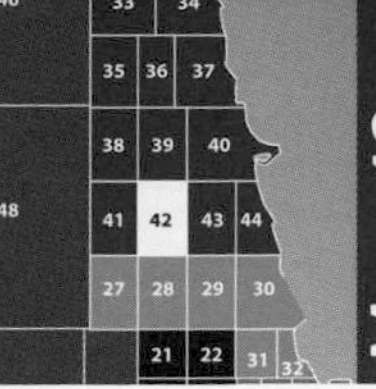

Map 42

Once a northside hipster enclave, rising prices have made Roscoe Village and West Lakeview ground-zero for the tan, fit, stroller-pushing/dog-walking set. Roscoe Avenue, which was once a trolley route leading to long defunct Revierview Amusement Park, still holds its own for neighborhood restaurants, bars, and funky boutiques.

Banks

- **Bank of America** • 3944 N Western Ave
- **Chase** • 3531 N Western Ave
- **Chase** • 3868 N Lincoln Ave
- **Chase (ATM)** • Dominicks • 3350 N Western Ave
- **Chase (ATM)** • Walgreens • 1649 W Belmont Ave
- **Chase (ATM)** • Walgreens • 3358 N Western Ave
- **Citibank (ATM)** • 7-Eleven • 3801 N Western Ave
- **First American (ATM)** • 3636 N Western Ave
- **First American (ATM)** • 1700 W Diversey Pkwy
- **First American (ATM)** • 1900 W Belmont Ave
- **First American (ATM)** • 3601 N Western Ave
- **Harris Trust & Savings (ATM)** • 3354 N Damen Ave
- **Lincoln Park Savings** • 3234 N Damen Ave
- **North Community** • 2800 N Western Ave
- **North Community** • 3401 N Western Ave
- **TCF** • Jewel • 3400 N Western Ave
- **TCF (ATM)** • 7-Eleven • 3801 N Western Ave

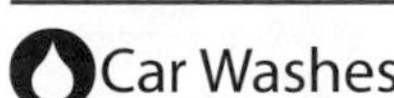

Car Washes

- **Ultra Sonic Car Wash** • 3650 N Western Ave

Car Rental

- **Enterprise** • 3844 N Western Ave • 773-539-5900

Gas Stations

- **BP/Amoco** • 3955 N Western Ave
- **Citgo** • 2401 W Diversey Ave
- **Marathon** • 3145 N Western Ave

o Landmarks

- **19th District Police Headquarters** • 2452 W Belmont Ave

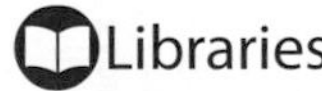

Libraries

- **Lincoln-Belmont Public Library** • 1659 W Melrose St

Pharmacies

- **CVS** • 2815 N Western Ave ⓐ
- **CVS** • 3944 N Western Ave ⓐ
- **Dominick's** • 3350 N Western Ave ⓐ
- **Jewel-Osco** • 3400 N Western Ave ⓐ
- **Walgreens** • 1649 W Belmont Ave
- **Walgreens** • 3358 N Western Ave

Pizza

- **Carreno's Pizzeria** • 1955 W Addison St
- **Pete's Pizza** • 3737 N Western Ave
- **Piazza Bella Trattoria** • 2116 W Roscoe St
- **Robey Pizza** • 1954 W Roscoe St

Police

- **19th District** • 2452 W Belmont Ave

Post Offices

- **US Post Office** • 3635 N Lincoln Ave

Schools

- **Alex Bell Elementary** • 3730 N Oakley Ave
- **Alexander Hamilton Elementary** • 1650 W Cornelia Ave
- **Cardinal Bernardin Early Child** • 1651 W Diversey Pkwy
- **Friedrich L Jahn Elementary** • 3149 N Wolcott Ave
- **George Schneider Elementary** • 2957 N Hoyne Ave
- **John L Audubon Elementary** • 3500 N Hoyne Ave
- **St Andrew Elementary** • 1710 W Addison St
- **St Benedict Elementary** • 3920 N Leavitt St
- **St Benedict High** • 3900 N Leavitt St
- **St Benedict Middle** • 3920 N Leavitt St

Supermarkets

- **Dominick's** • 3350 N Western Ave ⓐ
- **Jewel-Osco** • 3400 N Western Ave ⓐ
- **Paulina Meat Market** • 3501 N Lincoln Ave
- **Trader Joe's** • 3745 N Lincoln Ave

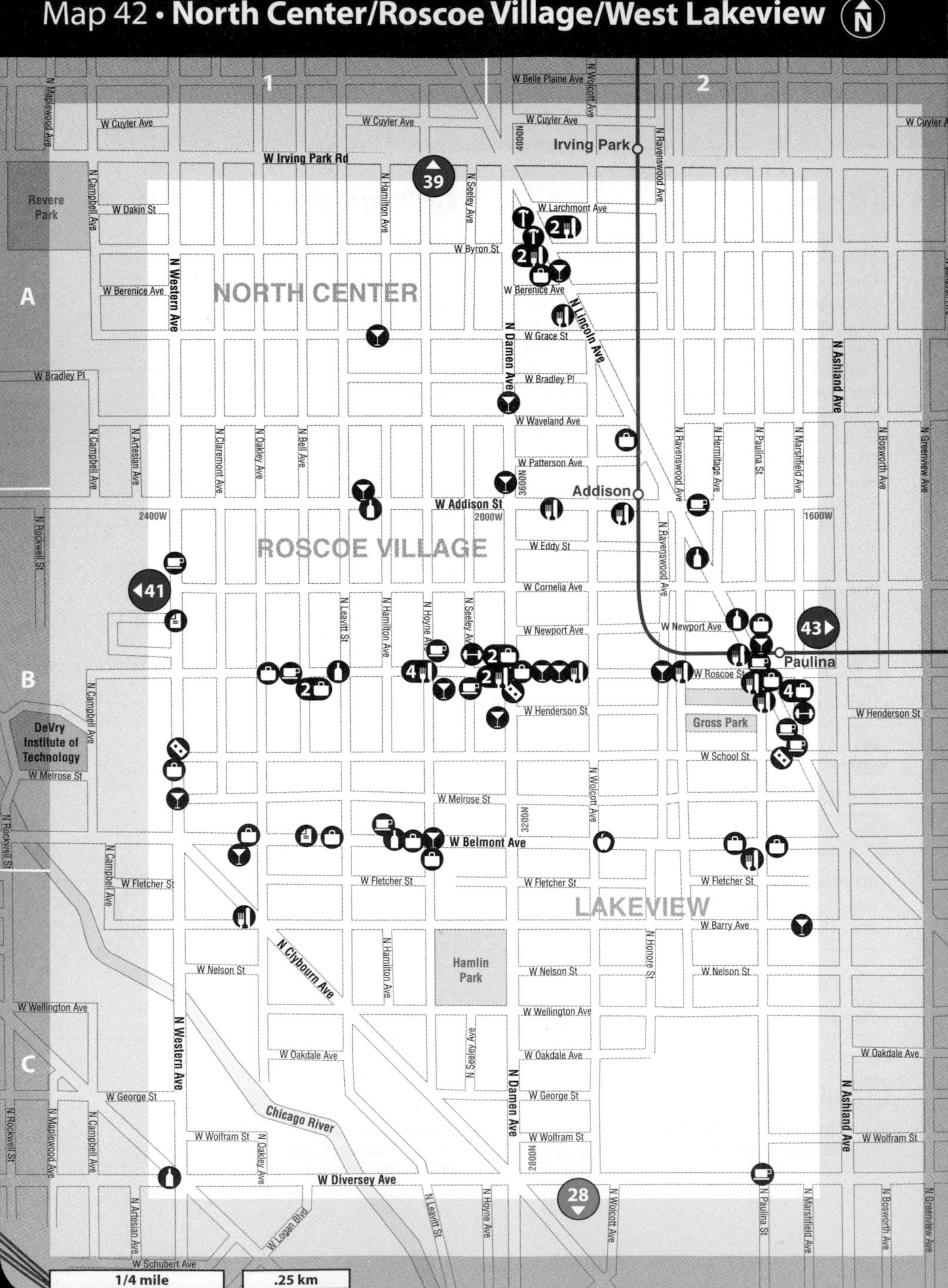

NORTH CENTER
ROSCOE VILLAGE
LAKEVIEW
Irving Park
Addison
Paulina
Revere Park
DeVry Institute of Technology
Gross Park
Hamlin Park
Chicago River
W Irving Park Rd
W Addison St
W Belmont Ave
W Diversey Ave
N Western Ave
N Damen Ave
N Ashland Ave
N Lincoln Ave
N Clybourn Ave
1/4 mile
.25 km

Sundries / Entertainment

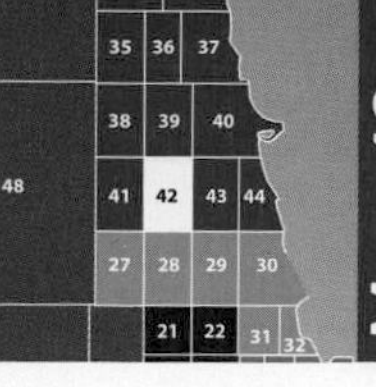

Browse the hand-picked selection at "High Fidelity" lookalike Hard Boiled Records and Video. For nightlife, sample handmade pasta and other seasonal, organic fare at Terragusto, then unwind with a pint and sing along with the jukebox at laid-back rugby bar Black Rock, or make silly faces in the photo booth of aging hipster hangout The Village Tap.

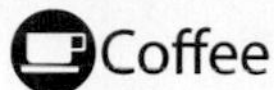

Coffee

- **Dinkel's Bakery** • 3329 N Lincoln Ave
- **Dunkin' Donuts** • 1755 W Addison St
- **Dunkin' Donuts** • 3535 N Western Ave
- **MoJoe's Café Lounge** • 2256 W Roscoe St
- **Starbucks** • 1700 W Diversey Pkwy
- **Starbucks** • 2159 W Belmont Ave
- **Starbucks** • 3356 N Lincoln Ave
- **Su Van's Café and Bake Shop** • 3351 N Lincoln Ave
- **Thai Linda Café** • 2022 W Roscoe St

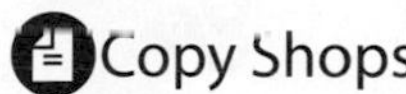

Copy Shops

- **FedEx Kinko's** • 3435 N Western Ave
- **Mail Box Plus** • 2248 W Belmont Ave

Farmers Markets

- **Roscoe Village (Jun–Oct; Sun, 7 am–2 pm)** • W Belmont Ave & N Wolcott Ave

Gyms

- **Curves (women only)** • 2037 W Roscoe St
- **Lakeview YMCA** • 3333 N Marshfield Ave

Hardware Stores

- **Community Home Supply** • 3924 N Lincoln Ave
- **Staubers Ace Hardware** • 3911 N Lincoln Ave

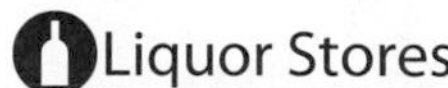

Liquor Stores

- **Armanetti Wine Shop** • 3530 N Lincoln Ave
- **Miller's Tap & Liquor Store** • 2204 W Roscoe St
- **Miska's Liquor** • 2156 W Belmont Ave
- **Pelly's Liquors** • 3444 N Lincoln Ave
- **R&S Liquor** • 2425 W Diversey Ave
- **West Lakeview Liquors** • 2156 W Addison St

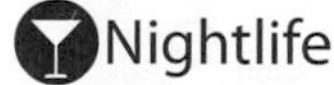

Nightlife

- **Beat Kitchen** • 2100 W Belmont Ave
- **Black Rock** • 3614 N Damen Ave
- **Cody's Public House** • 1658 W Barry Ave
- **Four Moon Tavern** • 1847 W Roscoe St
- **Four Treys** • 3333 N Damen Ave
- **G&L Fire Escape** • 2157 W Grace St
- **Hungry Brain** • 2319 W Belmont Ave
- **Martyrs'** • 3855 N Lincoln Ave
- **Mulligan's Public House** • 2000 W Roscoe St
- **Riverview Tavern & Grill** • 1958 W Roscoe St
- **Roscoe Village Pub** • 2159 W Addison St
- **Underbar** • 3243 N Western Ave
- **Waterhouse** • 3407 N Paulina Ave
- **Xippo** • 3759 N Damen Ave

Pet Shops

- **Olly's Kingdom** • 2029 W Belmont Ave
- **Sam & Willy's** • 3405 N Paulina St

Restaurants

- **90 Miles Cuban Cafe** • 3101 N Clybourn Ave
- **Delicious Cafe** • 3827 N Lincoln Ave
- **El Tinajon** • 2054 W Roscoe St
- **Fonda Del Mar** • 3908 N Lincoln Ave
- **Frasca** • 3358 N Paulina St
- **Kaze Sushi** • 2032 W Roscoe St
- **Kitsch'n on Roscoe** • 2005 W Roscoe St
- **Mrs. Murphy and Sons** • 3905 N Lincoln Ave
- **Piazza Bella Trattoria** • 2116 W Roscoe St
- **Scooter's Frozen Custard** • 1658 W Belmont Ave
- **Sola** • 3868 N Lincoln Ave
- **T-Spot Sushi** • 3925 N Lincoln Ave
- **Terragusto** • 1851 W Addison St
- **Thai Linda Café** • 2022 W Roscoe St
- **Turquoise Restaurant on Roscoe** • 2147 W Roscoe St
- **Victory's Banner** • 2100 W Roscoe St
- **The Village Tap** • 2055 W Roscoe St
- **Volo Restaurant and Wine Bar** • 2008 W Roscoe St

Shopping

- **A Cooler Planet** • 2211 W Roscoe St
- **Andy's Music** • 2300 W Belmont Ave
- **Antique Resources** • 1741 W Belmont Ave
- **Avenue** • 3322 N Western Ave
- **Bazar Apparel** • 3350 N Paulina St
- **Be Bye Baby** • 1654 W Roscoe St
- **Big Hair** • 2012 W Roscoe St
- **Caravan Beads** • 3361 N Lincoln Ave
- **Carlos and Sarah's Surplus of Options** • 3664 N Lincoln Ave
- **Father Time Antiques** • 2108 W Belmont Ave
- **Glam to Go** • 2002 W Roscoe St
- **Good Old Days Antiques** • 2138 W Belmont Ave
- **Guess Hookah** • 3357 N Lincoln Ave
- **Jazze Junque** • 3419 N Lincoln Ave
- **Lula's at the Belle Kay** • 3862 N Lincoln Ave
- **Lush Wine and Spirits** • 2232 W Roscoe St
- **Lynn's Hallmark** • 3353 N Lincoln Ave
- **Pleasure Chest** • 3436 N Lincoln Ave
- **Shangri-La Vintage** • 1952 W Roscoe St
- **Skyscraper Heels** • 2202 W Belmont Ave

Video Rental

- **Blockbuster** • 1645 W School St
- **Blockbuster** • 3322 N Western Ave
- **Hard Boiled Records and Video** • 2010 W Roscoe St

Map 43 • Wrigleyville / East Lakeview

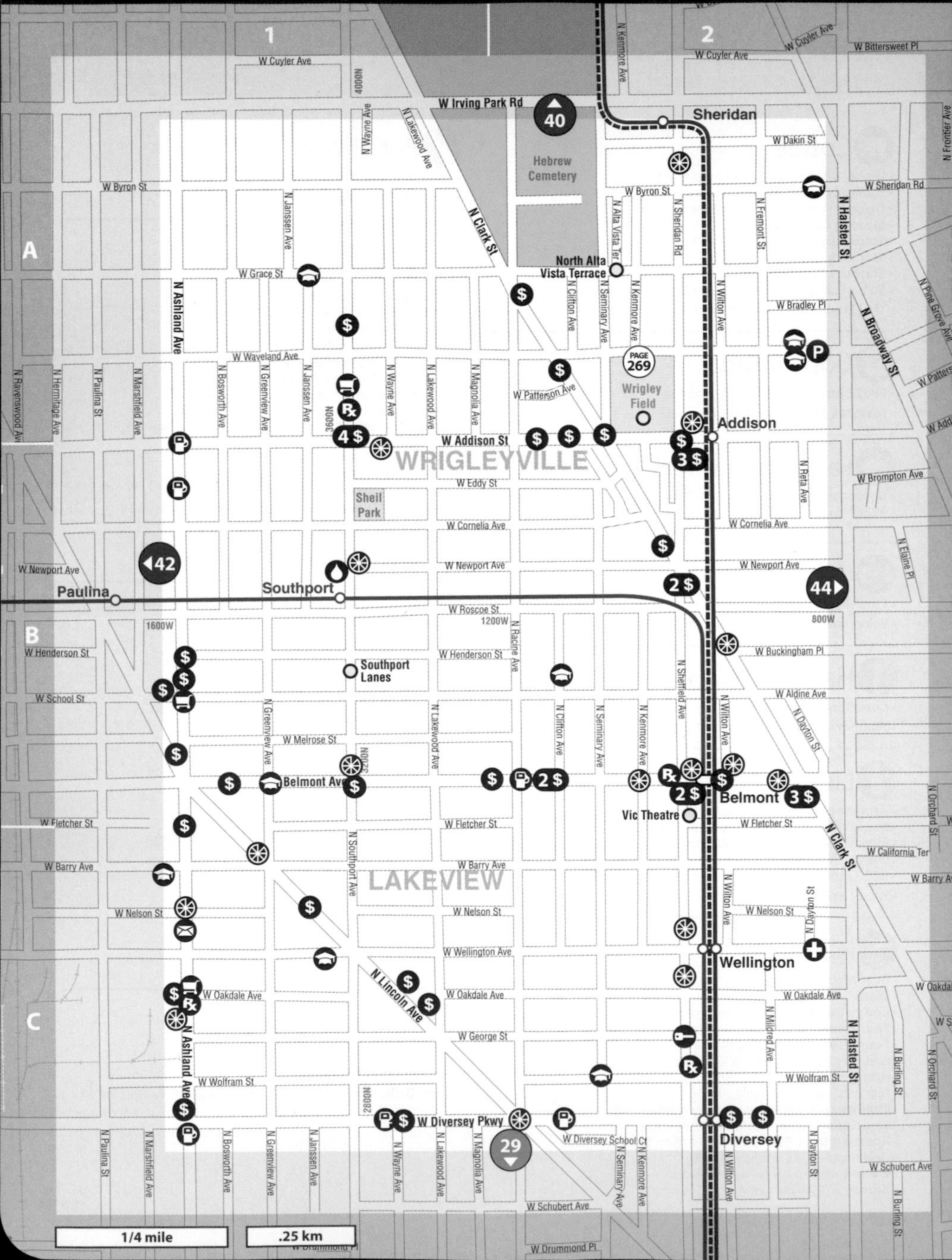

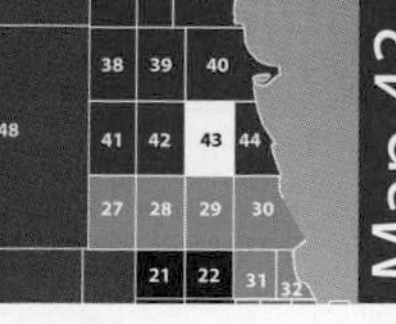

Pleasant, pretty streets belie atrocious traffic and parking, as well as the constant summertime disturbance of drunken Cubs fans roaming the streets and urinating in alleys and doorways. On the plus side, residents don't have to travel far for anything—tons of good restaurants, a variety of nightlife, the lakefront, and loads of services from groceries to video rentals cram into this youthful 'hood.

Banks

- **Bank of America** • 3201 N Ashland Ave
- **Bank of America** • 3301 N Ashland Ave
- **Bank of America** • 3215 N Lincoln Ave
- **Bank of America** • 963 W Belmont Ave
- **Bank of America (ATM)** • 948 W Addison St
- **Bank of America (ATM)** • 945 W Belmont Ave
- **Bank of America (ATM)** • 3650 N Clark St
- **Bank of America (ATM)** • 3182 N Clark St
- **Bank of America (ATM)** • 3455 N Clark St
- **Bank of America (ATM)** • 3650 N Clark St
- **Bank of America (ATM)** • 3718 N Southport Ave
- **Charter One (ATM)** • 958 W Diversey Pkwy • White Hen
- **Chase** • 1240 W Belmont Ave
- **Chase** • 2968 N Lincoln Ave
- **Chase** • 3335 N Ashland Ave
- **Chase** • 3730 N Southport Ave
- **Chase (ATM)** • 940 W Addison St
- **Citibank** • 3128 N Ashland Ave
- **Citibank (ATM)** • 7-Eleven • 1153 W Belmont Ave
- **Citibank (ATM)** • 7-Eleven • 3554 N Sheffield Ave
- **Citibank (ATM)** • 3753 N Clark St
- **Corus** • 3179 N Clark St
- **Corus** • 3604 N Southport Ave
- **First American** • 1345 W Diversey Pkwy
- **First American (ATM)** • 1001 W Belmont Ave
- **First American (ATM)** • 1153 W Addison St
- **First American (ATM)** • 1547 W Belmont Ave
- **First American (ATM)** • 2909 N Lincoln Ave
- **First American (ATM)** • 3100 N Lincoln Ave
- **First American (ATM)** • 3300 N Ashland Ave
- **First American (ATM)** • 3425 N Clark St
- **First American (ATM)** • 946 W Diversey Pkwy
- **First American** • 3166 N Clark St • Cesar's
- **Lakeside** • 2800 N Ashland Ave
- **North Community** • 1401 W Belmont Ave
- **North Community** • 3420 N Clark St
- **TCF** • Jewel • 2940 N Ashland Ave
- **TCF** • Jewel • 3630 N Southport Ave
- **TCF (ATM)** • Taco Bell • 1111 W Addison St
- **TCF (ATM)** • 7-Eleven • 1153 W Belmont Ave
- **TCF (ATM)** • 7-Eleven • 3554 N Sheffield Ave
- **TCF (ATM)** • Osco • 3637 N Southport Ave

Car Washes

- **Quiroga's Detail & Hand Car Wash** • 3448 N Southport Ave

Car Rental

- **Enterprise** • 2900 N Sheffield Ave • 773-880-5001

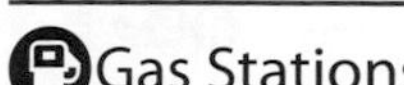

Gas Stations

- **Amoco** • 1200 W Belmont Ave
- **BP** • 1355 W Diversey Pkwy
- **Citgo** • 3600 N Ashland Ave
- **Shell** • 1160 W Diversey Pkwy
- **Shell** • 2801 N Ashland Ave
- **Shell** • 3552 N Ashland Ave

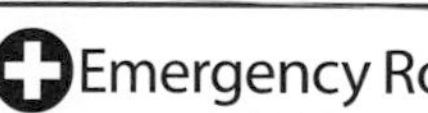

Emergency Rooms

- **Advocate Illinois Masonic Medical Center** • 836 W Wellington Ave

Landmarks

- **North Alta Vista Terrace** • 3800 N Alta Vista Terrace
- **Southport Lanes** • 3325 N Southport Ave
- **Vic Theatre** • 3145 N Sheffield Ave
- **Wrigley Field** • 1060 W Addison St

Parking

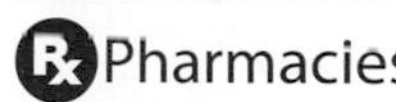

Pharmacies

- **CVS** • 3637 N Southport Ave
- **Jewel-Osco** • 2940 N Ashland Ave
- **Walgreens** • 1001 W Belmont Ave
- **Walgreens** • 2835 N Sheffield Ave, Ste 505

Pizza

- **Art of Pizza** • 3033 N Ashland Ave
- **Bacci Pizzeria** • 950 W Addison St
- **Chicago's Pizza** • 3006 N Sheffield Ave
- **Chicago's Pizza** • 3114 N Lincoln Ave
- **D'Agostino Pizzeria & Restaurant** • 1351 W Addison St
- **Gino's East** • 2801 N Lincoln Ave
- **Giordano's** • 1040 W Belmont Ave
- **Homemade Pizza Co** • 3430 N Southport Ave
- **La Gondola Pizzeria & Cucina Italiana** • 2914 N Ashland Ave
- **Leona's** • 3215 N Sheffield Ave
- **Philly's Best** • 907 W Belmont Ave
- **Pizza Capri** • 962 W Belmont Ave
- **Pizza Rustica** • 3913 N Sheridan Rd
- **Pompeii Bakery** • 2955 N Sheffield Ave
- **Sapore di Napoli** • 1406 W Belmont Ave

Post Offices

- **US Post Office** • 3024 N Ashland Ave

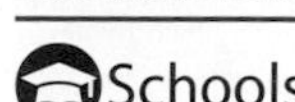

Schools

- **Augustus H Burley Elementary** • 1630 W Barry Ave
- **Hawthorne Scholastic Academy** • 3319 N Clifton Ave
- **Horace Greeley Elementary** • 832 W Sheridan Rd
- **Inter-American Elementary** • 851 W Waveland Ave
- **James G Blaine Elementary** • 1420 W Grace St
- **John V LeMoyne Elementary** • 851 W Waveland Ave
- **Louis J Agassiz Elementary** • 2851 N Seminary Ave
- **St Alphonsus Academy** • 1439 W Wellington Ave
- **St Luke Academy** • 1500 W Belmont Ave

Supermarkets

- **Jewel-Osco** • 2940 N Ashland Ave
- **Whole Foods Market** • 3300 N Ashland Ave

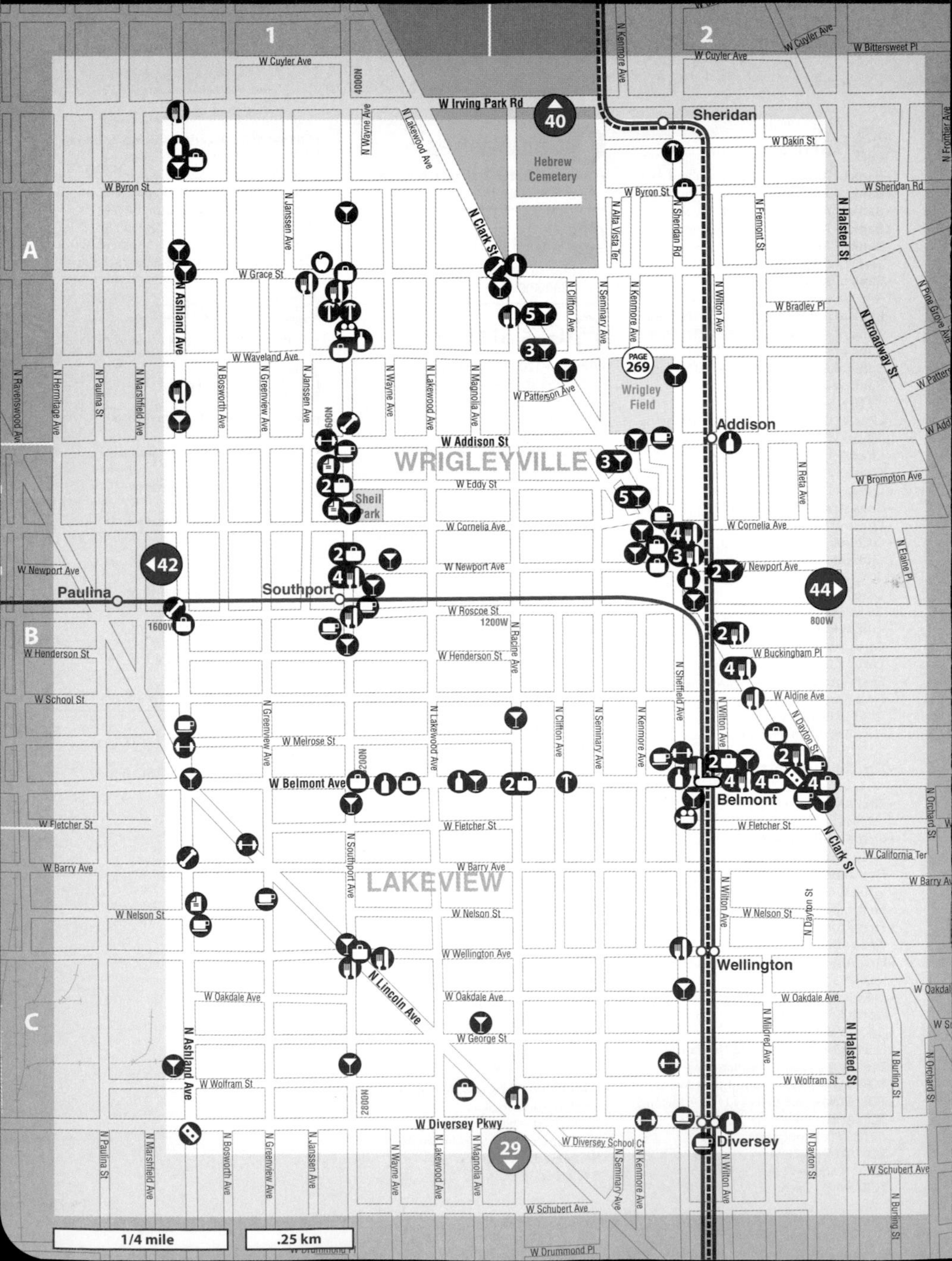

N
1
2
A
B
C
W Cuyler Ave
W Irving Park Rd
40
Hebrew Cemetery
Sheridan
W Dakin St
W Byron St
W Sheridan Rd
N Halsted St
W Grace St
N Clark St
W Bradley Pl
N Broadway St
W Waveland Ave
PAGE 269
Wrigley Field
W Patterson Ave
Addison
W Addison St
WRIGLEYVILLE
W Eddy St
Sheil Park
W Cornelia Ave
W Brompton Ave
W Newport Ave
Paulina
Southport
42
44
W Roscoe St
1600W
1200W
800W
W Henderson St
W Buckingham Pl
W School St
W Aldine Ave
W Melrose St
W Belmont Ave
Belmont
W Fletcher St
W Barry Ave
W California Ter
LAKEVIEW
W Nelson St
W Wellington Ave
Wellington
W Oakdale Ave
N Lincoln Ave
W George St
W Wolfram St
W Diversey Pkwy
W Diversey School Ct
Diversey
29
W Schubert Ave
W Drummond Pl
N Ashland Ave
N Paulina St
N Marshfield Ave
N Bosworth Ave
N Greenview Ave
N Janssen Ave
N Southport Ave
N Wayne Ave
N Lakewood Ave
N Magnolia Ave
N Racine Ave
N Clifton Ave
N Seminary Ave
N Kenmore Ave
N Sheffield Ave
N Wilton Ave
N Fremont St
N Reta Ave
N Dayton St
N Mildred Ave
N Burling St
N Orchard St
1/4 mile
.25 km

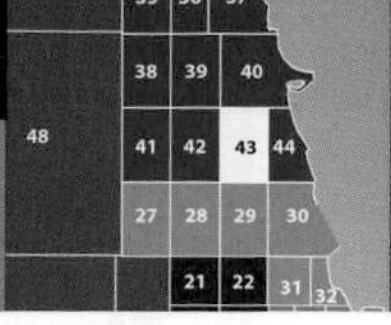

The Metro rocks this neighborhood while beautiful Music Box Theatre features art house films with a live organist on weekends. With Cubs Park dominating the 'hood it's no surprise that most local bars and restaurants cater to sports fans. S&G (aka Sam & George's) represents the very best in the Greek diner tradtition.

Coffee

- **Caribou Coffee** • 3240 N Ashland Ave
- **Dunkin' Donuts** • 3000 N Ashland Ave
- **Dunkin' Donuts** • 3200 N Clark St
- **Einstein Bros Bagels** • 3420 N Southport Ave
- **Einstein Bros Bagels** • 3455 N Clark St
- **Einstein Bros Bagels** • 933 W Diversey Pkwy
- **The Julius Meinl Café** • 3601 N Southport Ave
- **My Place for Tea** • 3210 N Sheffield Ave
- **Starbucks** • 1000 W Diversey Pkwy
- **Starbucks** • 1023 W Addison St
- **Starbucks** • 3045 N Greenview Ave
- **Starbucks** • 3184 N Clark St
- **Starbucks** • 3359 N Southport Ave

Copy Shops

- **FedEx Kinko's** • 3524 N Southport Ave ㉔
- **The UPS Store** • 3105 N Ashland Ave
- **The UPS Store** • 3540 N Southport Ave

Farmers Markets

- **Southport Green Market (Jun-Oct; Sat, 8 am-12 pm)** • 1420 W Grace St

Gyms

- **Chicago Fitness Center** • 3131 N Lincoln Ave ㉔
- **Curves (women only)** • 1409 W Addison St
- **Curves (women only)** • 2825 N Sheffield Ave
- **Lincoln Park Athletic Club** • 1019 W Diversey Pkwy
- **Number One Gym** • 3232 N Sheffield Ave
- **XSport Fitness** • 3240 N Ashland Ave ㉔

Hardware Stores

- **Ace Hardware** • 3921 N Sheridan Rd
- **Alhambra** • 3737 N Southport Ave
- **Klein True Value Hardware** • 3737 N Southport Ave
- **Tenenbaum True Value Hardware** • 1138 W Belmont Ave

Liquor Stores

- **1000 Liquors** • 1000 W Belmont Ave
- **Addison Liquors** • 932 W Addison St
- **Bel-Port Food & Liquor** • 1362 W Belmont Ave
- **East Lake View Food & Liquor** • 3814 N Clark St
- **Foremost Liquor Store** • 3014 N Ashland Ave
- **Gilday Liquors** • 946 W Diversey Pkwy
- **Gold Crown Liquors Store** • 3425 N Clark St
- **Howards Wine Cellar (wine only)** • 1244 W Belmont Ave
- **Que Syrah Fine Wines** • 3726 N Southport Ave

Movie Theaters

- **Brew & View** • 3145 N Sheffield Ave
- **Music Box Theatre** • 3733 N Southport Ave

Nightlife

- **The Ashland** • 2824 N Ashland Ave
- **Bar Celona** • 3474 N Clark St
- **Berlin** • 954 W Belmont Ave
- **Bernie's** • 3664 N Clark St
- **Cooper's** • 1232 W Belmont Ave
- **Cubby Bear** • 1059 W Addison St
- **Elbo Room** • 2871 N Lincoln Ave
- **Fizz Bar and Grill** • 3220 N Lincoln Ave
- **The Full Shilling** • 3724 N Clark St
- **Gingerman Tavern** • 3740 N Clark St
- **Ginger's Ale House** • 3801 N Ashland Ave
- **Guthrie's Tavern** • 1300 W Addison St
- **Higgins' Tavern** • 3259 N Racine Ave
- **Houndstooth Saloon** • 3438 N Clark St
- **iO** • 3541 N Clark St
- **The Irish Oak** • 3511 N Clark St
- **Jack's Bar & Grill** • 2856 N Southport Ave
- **Justin's** • 3358 N Southport Ave
- **Kirkwood** • 2934 N Sheffield Ave
- **L&L Tavern** • 3207 N Clark St
- **Lange's Lounge** • 3500 N Southport Ave
- **Lincoln Tap Room** • 3010 N Lincoln Ave
- **Merkle's Bar & Grill** • 3516 N Clark St
- **Metro** • 3730 N Clark St
- **Moxie** • 3517 N Clark St
- **Murphy's Bleachers** • 3655 N Sheffield Ave
- **Newport Bar & Grill** • 1344 W Newport Ave
- **Raw Bar** • 3720 N Clark St
- **Red Ivy** • 3525 N Clark St
- **Risque Café** • 3419 N Clark St
- **Rockit** • 3700 N Clark St
- **Schuba's** • 3159 N Southport Ave
- **Sheffield's** • 3258 N Sheffield Ave
- **Slugger's** • 3540 N Clark St
- **Smart Bar** • 3730 N Clark St
- **Sopo Lounge & Grill** • 3418 N Southport Ave
- **The Stretch Bar & Grill** • 3485 N Clark St
- **Tai's Til 4** • 3611 N Ashland Ave
- **Ten Cat Tavern** • 3931 N Ashland Ave
- **Toons Bar** • 3857 N Southport Ave
- **Uncommon Ground Café** • 3800 N Clark St
- **Underground Lounge** • 952 W Newport Ave
- **Yak-zies Wrigleyville** • **3710 N Clark St**
- **The Yard** • 3441 N Sheffield Ave

Pet Shops

- **4 Legs** • 3809 N Clark St
- **Abby's Let's Pet (Dogs only)** • 3404 N Ashland Ave
- **Dog-a-holics, Inc.** • 3608 N Southport Ave
- **Petco** • 3118 N Ashland Ave

Restaurants

- **Ann Sather Restaurant** • 909 W Belmont Ave
- **Blue Bayou** • 3734 N Southport Ave
- **Bolat** • 3346 N Clark St
- **Capt'n Nemos** • 3650 N Ashland Ave
- **Coobah** • 3423 N Southport Ave
- **Cozy Noodles n' Rice** • 3456 N Sheffield Ave
- **Duck Walk** • 919 W Belmont Ave
- **Fianco** • 3440 N Southport Ave
- **Frasca** • 3358 N Paulina St
- **Golden Apple** • 2971 N Lincoln Ave ㉔
- **Lucky's Sandwich Shop** • 3472 N Clark St
- **Matsu Yama** • 1059 W Belmont Ave
- **Matsuya** • 3469 N Clark St
- **Mia Francesca** • 3311 N Clark St
- **Mystic Celt** • 3443 N Southport Ave
- **Orange** • 3231 N Clark St
- **Panes** • 3002 N Sheffield Ave
- **Penny's Noodle Shop** • 3400 N Sheffield Ave
- **PS Bangkok** • 3345 N Clark St
- **Rise** • 3401 N Southport Ave
- **Risque Café** • 3419 N Clark St
- **S&G** • 3000 N Lincoln Ave
- **Samah** • 3330 N Clark St
- **Shiroi Hana** • 3242 N Clark St
- **Socca** • 3301 N Clark St
- **Tango Sur** • 3763 N Southport Ave
- **Twisted Spoke** • 3369 N Clark St
- **Wrigleyville Dog** • 3737 N Clark St

Shopping

- **The Alley** • 3228 N Clark St
- **Belmont Army Surplus Store** • 855 W Belmont Ave
- **Beyond the Wall** • 935 W Belmont Ave
- **Bittersweet Pastry Shop and Cafe** • 1114 W Belmont Ave
- **Bookworks** • 3444 N Clark St
- **Borrow a Dress Couture (BADC)** • 3221 N Sheffield Ave
- **Fashion Tomato** • 937 W Belmont Ave
- **Hollywood Mirror** • 812 W Belmont Ave
- **J. Toguri Mercantile Co** • 851 W Belmont Ave
- **Krista K** • 3458 N Southport Ave
- **Krista K Maternity + Baby** • 3530 N Southport Ave
- **Leahy & LaDue Consignment** • 3753 N Southport Ave
- **Midwest Stereo Pro Sounds and Lighting** • 1613 W Belmont Ave
- **Namaskar Boutique** • 3950 N Southport Ave
- **Never Mind** • 953 W Belmont Ave
- **Paper Boy** • 1351 W Belmont Ave
- **Play It Again Sports** • 3939 N Ashland Ave
- **Powell's Bookstores** • 2850 N Lincoln Ave
- **Ragstock** • 812 W Belmont Ave
- **Strange Cargo** • 3448 N Clark St
- **Thousand Waves Spa** • 1212 W Belmont Ave
- **Trousseau Lingerie** • 3543 N Southport Ave
- **Tula** • 3738 N Southport Ave
- **Uncle Dan's Great Outdoor Store** • 3551 N Southport Ave
- **Uncle Fun** • 1338 W Belmont Ave
- **Yellow Jacket** • 2959 N Lincoln Ave

Video Rental

- **Blockbuster** • 2803 N Ashland Ave
- **Nationwide Video** • 843 1/2 W Belmont Ave

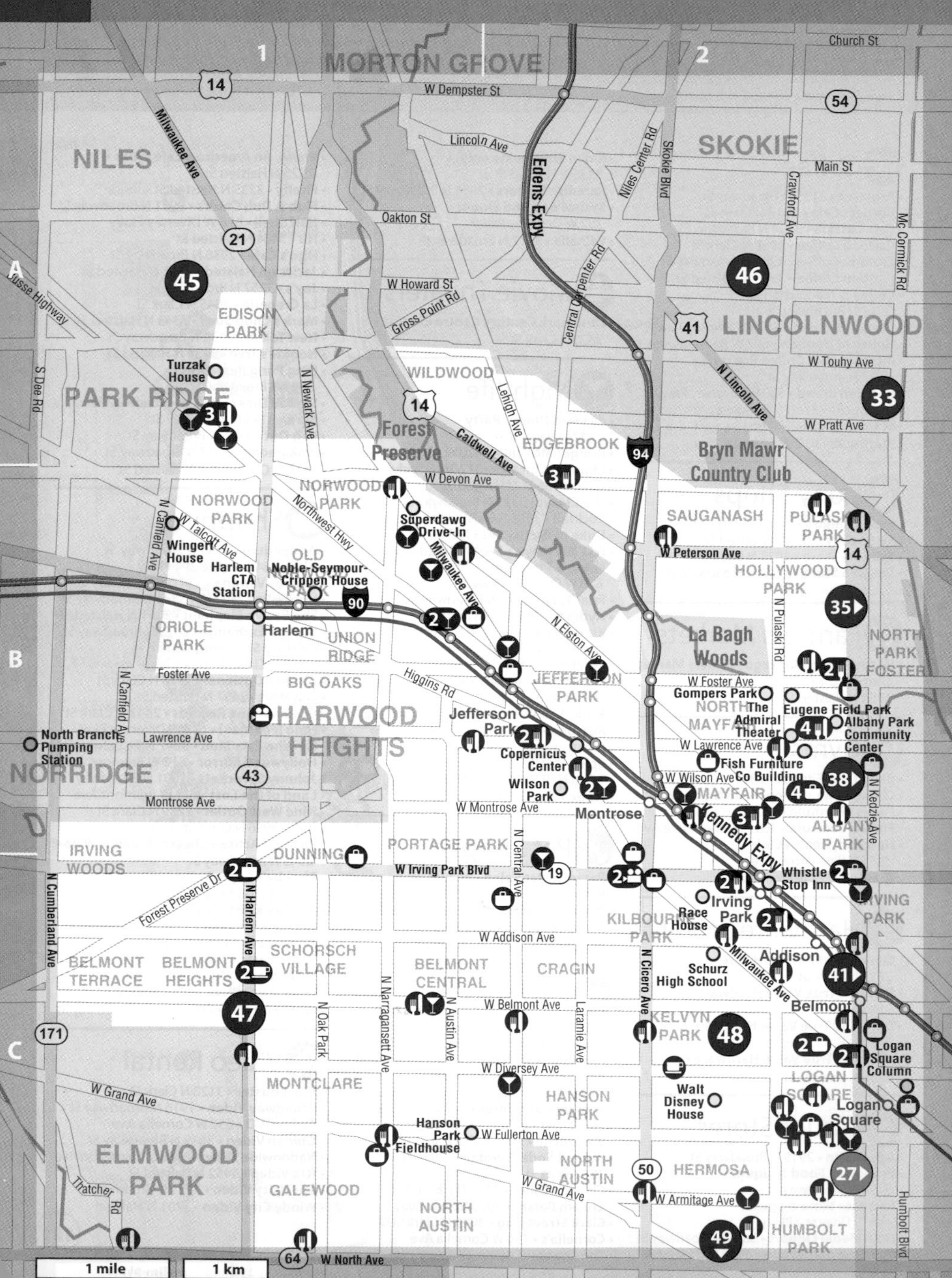
MORTON GROVE
W Dempster St
NILES
Milwaukee Ave
Lincoln Ave
Edens Expy
SKOKIE
Niles Center Rd
Skokie Blvd
Main St
Crawford Ave
Mc Cormick Rd
Oakton St
Central Carpenter Rd
Busse Highway
W Howard St
Gross Point Rd
LINCOLNWOOD
EDISON PARK
WILDWOOD
W Touhy Ave
N Lincoln Ave
Turzak House
S Dee Rd
PARK RIDGE
N Newark Ave
Lehigh Ave
W Pratt Ave
Forest Preserve
Caldwell Ave
EDGEBROOK
Bryn Mawr Country Club
W Devon Ave
NORWOOD PARK
Superdawg Drive-In
SAUGANASH
PULASKI PARK
Northwest Hwy
W Talcott Ave
N Canfield Ave
Wingert House
OLD NORWOOD PARK
Milwaukee Ave
W Peterson Ave
HOLLYWOOD PARK
Harlem CTA Station
Noble-Seymour-Crippen House
N Pulaski Rd
ORIOLE PARK
Harlem
UNION RIDGE
N Elston Ave
La Bagh Woods
NORTH PARK
FOSTER
Foster Ave
BIG OAKS
Higgins Rd
JEFFERSON PARK
W Foster Ave
Gompers Park
Eugene Field Park
N Canfield Ave
HARWOOD HEIGHTS
Jefferson Park
NORTH MAYFAIR
The Admiral Theater
Albany Park Community Center
North Branch Pumping Station
Lawrence Ave
W Lawrence Ave
Copernicus Center
Fish Furniture Co Building
NORRIDGE
Wilson Park
W Wilson Ave
MAYFAIR
N Kedzie Ave
Montrose Ave
W Montrose Ave
Montrose
Kennedy Expy
ALBANY PARK
IRVING WOODS
DUNNING
PORTAGE PARK
N Central Ave
W Irving Park Blvd
Whistle Stop Inn
IRVING PARK
N Cumberland Ave
Forest Preserve Dr
N Harlem Ave
Irving Park
Race House
KILBOURN PARK
W Addison Ave
Addison
BELMONT TERRACE
BELMONT HEIGHTS
SCHORSCH VILLAGE
BELMONT CENTRAL
CRAGIN
Schurz High School
N Cicero Ave
Milwaukee Ave
N Narragansett Ave
N Oak Park
N Austin Ave
W Belmont Ave
Laramie Ave
Belmont
KELVYN PARK
Logan Square Column
W Diversey Ave
W Grand Ave
MONTCLARE
HANSON PARK
Walt Disney House
LOGAN SQUARE
Logan Square
Hanson Park Fieldhouse
W Fullerton Ave
ELMWOOD PARK
NORTH AUSTIN
HERMOSA
W Grand Ave
Thatcher Rd
GALEWOOD
W Armitage Ave
Humbolt Blvd
NORTH AUSTIN
HUMBOLT PARK
W North Ave
Church St
1 mile
1 km

Essentials

If there's one thing you can count on in Northwest Chicago, it's that you can count on just about everything. Compared to other sections of the city, the Northwest is a bastion of stability. Most of the people and businesses have been around forever, and even typically transitory ethnic enclaves — in this case Eastern European, Middle Eastern, North African, Korean, and Italian—are fairly entrenched. That said, the slow but steady growth of the northwest side communities of Jefferson Park, Mayfair, and Edison Park is notable, as more young families discover the affordable housing and excellent school districts offered here. Additionally, Northwest Chicago is blessed with an abundance of small parks and field houses, as well as a large hunk of forest preserve, giving much of the area a bucolic, suburban feel.

Landmarks

- **The Admiral Theater** • 3940 W Lawrence Ave
- **Albany Park Community Center** • 3401 W Ainslie St
- **Copernicus Center** • 5216 W Lawrence Ave
- **Eugene Field Park** • 5100 N Ridgeway Ave
- **Gompers Park** • 4222 W Foster Ave
- **Fish Furniture Co Building** • 3322 W Lawrence Ave
- **Hanson Park Fieldhouse** • 5501 W Fullerton Ave
- **Harlem CTA Station** • 5550 N Harlem Ave
- **Logan Square Column** • 3100 W Logan Blvd
- **Noble-Seymour-Crippen House** • 5624 N Newark Ave
- **North Branch Pumping Station** • W Lawrence Ave & NE River Rd
- **Schurz High School** • 3601 Milwaukee Ave
- **Superdawg Drive-In** • 6363 N Milwaukee Ave
- **Turzak House** • 7059 N Olcott Ave
- **Walt Disney House** • 2156 N Tripp Ave
- **Whistle Stop Inn** • 4200 W Irving Park Rd
- **Wilson Park** • 4630 Milwaukee Ave
- **Wingert House** • 6231 N Canfield Ave

Sundries / Entertainment

Northwest Chicago wears its blue-collar ethnic proclivities on its sleeve. Local shops and restaurants don't go out of their way to attract clientele outside of their own, and signs, menus, and even the staff at the area's abundant Korean and Eastern European businesses make little effort to communicate in English. (The same can be said for the clientele at many of the area's numerous, ostensibly English-speaking, corner taverns.) Adventuresome diners rise to the challenge—some of the city's best unsung gems are to be found here, including Thai vegan spot Amitabul, Japanese Chiyo, and Korean So Gong Dong Tofu House (whose name is worth the trip alone). Smoque has become a destination spot for fans of quality 'cue. Toss back pints at the 5th Provence pub. Some great touring indie acts play at the Abbey Pub (The Breeders, Peaches). Rosa's Lounge is a venerable, beloved Chicago jazz and blues venue.

Movie Theaters

- **AMC Loews Norridge 10** • 4520 N Harlem Ave
- **LaSalle Bank Cinema** • 4901 W Irving Park Rd
- **Portage Theater** • 4050 N Milwaukee Ave

Nightlife

- **5th Province Pub** • Irish-American Heritage Ctr • 4626 N Knox Ave
- **Abbey Pub** • 3420 W Grace St
- **Babe's** • 4416 N Milwaukee Ave
- **The Burlington** • 3425 W Fullerton Ave
- **Edison Park Inn** • 6715 N Olmstead Ave
- **Emerald Isle** • 6686 N Northwest Hwy
- **Fantasy Lounge** • 4400 N Elston
- **Fischman Liquors** • 4780 N Milwaukee Ave
- **Flo's Algiers Lounge** • 5436 W Montrose Ave
- **Ham Tree** • 5333 N Milwaukee Ave
- **Hollywood Lounge** • 3303 W Bryn Mawr Ave
- **Jedynka Club** • 5616 W Diversey Ave
- **Jimmy Mack** • 5581 N Northwest Hwy
- **Moretti's** • 6727 N Olmsted Ave
- **New Polonia Club** • 6101 W Belmont Ave
- **Original Dugan's** • 6051 N Milwaukee Ave
- **Queen Albert Diner & Lounge** • 3506 W Irving Park Rd
- **Rabbits** • 4945 W Foster Ave
- **Rosa's Lounge** • 3420 W Armitage Ave
- **Three Counties** • 5856 N Milwaukee Ave
- **Vaughan's Pub** • 5485 N Northwest Hwy
- **Weegee's Lounge** • 3659 W Armitage Ave

Restaurants

- **Al Primo Canto** • 5414 W Devon Ave
- **Amarind's** • 6822 W North Ave
- **Amitabul** • 6207 N Milwaukee Ave
- **Big Pho** • 3737 W Lawrence Ave
- **Blue Angel** • 5310 N Milwaukee Ave ㉔
- **Brown Sack** • 3706 W Armitage Ave
- **Café con Leche** • 2714 N Milwaukee Ave
- **Carthage Café** • 3446 W Foster Ave
- **Chai's Asian Bistro** • 4748 W Peterson Ave
- **Chiyo** • 3800 W Lawrence Ave
- **Chocolate Shoppe Ice Cream** • 5337 W Devon Ave
- **Don Juan** • 6730 N Northwest Hwy
- **Eat First Chinese Restaurant** • 3337 W Belmont Ave
- **Edgebrook Coffee Shop** • 6322 N Central Ave
- **El Cubanito** • 2555 N Pulaski Rd
- **El Huarachin Huarachon** • 3320 W Lawrence Ave
- **Elliott's Seafood Grille & Chop House** • 6690 N Northwest Hwy
- **Friendship Chinese Restaurant** • 2830 N Milwaukee Ave
- **Gale Street Inn** • 4914 N Milwaukee Ave
- **Gloria's Café** • 3300 W Fullerton Ave
- **Gorditas Aguascaliente** • 2106 N Cicero Ave
- **Great Sea Chinese Restaurants** • 3254 W Lawrence Ave
- **Grota Smorgasborg** • 3112 N Central Ave
- **Halina's Polish Delights** • 5914 W Lawrence Ave
- **Hiromi's** • 3609 W Lawrence Ave
- **La Villa Restaurant** • 3638 N Pulaski Rd
- **Lawrence Fish Market** • 3914 W Lawrence Ave
- **Manee Thai** • 3558 N Pulaski Rd
- **Mayan Sol** • 3830 W Lawrence Ave
- **Mic Duck's Drive In** • 3401 W Belmont Ave
- **Mirabell** • 3454 W Addison St
- **Montasero's Ristorante** • 3935 W Devon Ave
- **Paul Zakopane's Harnas Restaurant** • 2943 N Milwaukee Ave
- **Pollo Campero** • 2730 N Narragansett Ave
- **Pupuseria Las Delicias** • 3300 W Montrose Ave
- **Red Apple** • 3121 N Milwaukee Ave
- **Ristorante Agostino** • 2817 N Harlem Ave
- **Russell's Barbecue** • 1621 N Thatcher Ave
- **Sabatino's** • 4441 W Irving Park Rd
- **Seo Hae** • 3534 W Lawrence Ave
- **Shiraz** • 4425 W Montrose
- **Shokran** • 4027 W Irving Park Rd
- **Smak-Talk** •5961 N Elston Ave
- **Smoque** • 3800 N Pulaski Rd
- **So Gong Dong Tofu House** • 3307 W Bryn Mawr Ave
- **Sol de Mexico** • 3018 N Cicero Ave
- **Super Pollo** • 3640 W Wrightwood Ave
- **Tassili Café** • 4342 N Elston Ave
- **Teresa II Polish Restaurant & Lounge** • 4751 N Milwaukee Ave
- **Trattoria Pasta D'Arte** • 6311 N Milwaukee Ave
- **Tre Kronor** • 3258 W Foster Ave
- **Via Veneto** • 6340 N Lincoln Ave
- **Zebda** • 4344 N Elston Ave
- **Zia's Trattoria** • 6699 N Northwest Hwy

Shopping

- **Albany Office Supply** • 3419 W Lawrence Ave
- **American Science & Surplus** • 5316 N Milwaukee Ave
- **Chicago Data Recovery** • 3525 W Peterson Ave
- **Discovery Clothing** • 3348 W Belmont Ave
- **Dom Itp** • 6840 W Belmont Ave
- **Fantasy Costumes** • 4065 N Milwaukee Ave
- **Fishguy** • 4423 N Elston Ave
- **Galos Caves** • 6501 W Irving Park Rd
- **H & B True Value Hardware** • 5329 Milwaukee Ave
- **Harlem Irving Plaza** • Irving Park Rd & W Forest Preserve Ave
- **Hats Plus** • 4706 W Irving Park Rd
- **Heavenly Gelato and Ice Cream** • 2654 N Sawyer Ave
- **Joong Boo Market** • 3333 N Kimball Ave
- **Kurowski Sausage Shop & Rich's Bakery** • 2976 N Milwaukee Ave
- **Maggie La Petite** • 3944 N Central Ave
- **Old Town Tatu** • 3313 W Irving Park Rd
- **Perfume Outlet** • 3608 W Lawrence Ave
- **Rave Sports** • 3346 W Lawrence Ave
- **Rolling Stone Records** • 7300 W Irving Park Rd
- **Salvation Army Thrift Store** • 3837 W Fullerton Ave
- **Srpska Tradicija** • 3615 W Lawrence Ave
- **Sweden Shop** • 3304 W Foster Ave
- **Sunrise Fresh Market** • 2722 Milwaukee Ave
- **Unique Thrift Store** • 6560 W Fullerton Ave
- **Village Discount Outlet** • 4635 N Elston Ave
- **Village Discount Outlet** • 3301 W Lawrence Ave
- **Whole Foods** • 6020 N Cicero Ave
- **WIG** • 4621 N Lawndale
- **Your Snappy Shop** • 3544 W Irving Park Rd

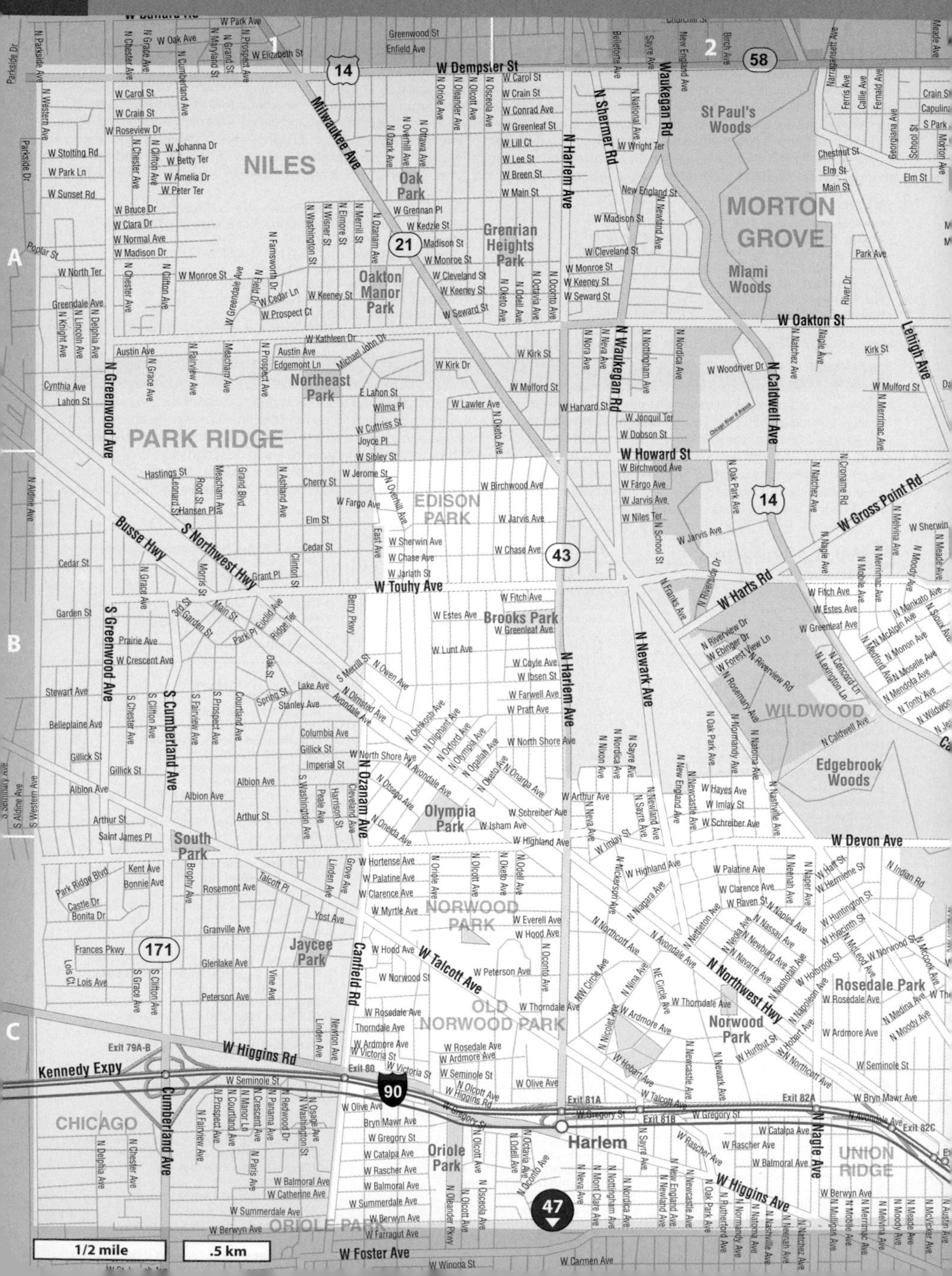
NILES
MORTON GROVE
PARK RIDGE
EDISON PARK
NORWOOD PARK
OLD NORWOOD PARK
CHICAGO
ORIOLE PARK
UNION RIDGE
WILDWOOD
Harlem
Oak Park
Grennan Heights Park
Oakton Manor Park
Northeast Park
Brooks Park
Olympia Park
South Park
Jaycee Park
Norwood Park
Oriole Park
Rosedale Park
Edgebrook Woods
St Paul's Woods
Miami Woods
Kennedy Expy
W Higgins Rd
W Dempster St
W Oakton St
W Howard St
W Touhy Ave
W Devon Ave
W Talcott Ave
W Foster Ave
N Harlem Ave
Milwaukee Ave
N Northwest Hwy
S Northwest Hwy
Busse Hwy
Canfield Rd
N Cumberland Ave
N Greenwood Ave
N Caldwell Ave
W Gross Point Rd
W Harts Rd
1/2 mile
.5 km

SKOKIE
LINCOLNWOOD
EDGEBROOK
SAUGANASH
PULASKI PARK
HOLLYWOOD PARK
Dempster St
Main St
W Oakton St
Howard St
W Touhy Ave
W Pratt Ave
Devon Ave
W Peterson Ave
W Foster Ave
Skokie Blvd
Lincoln Ave
Niles Center Rd
N Crawford Ave
McCormick Blvd
N McCormick Rd
Edens Expy
N Cicero Ave
N Central Ave
N Lehigh Ave
N Jersey Ave
N Kedzie Ave
W Gross Point Rd
Carpenter Rd
Little League Park
Oakton Park
Laramie Park
Coyle Park
Forest Glen Woods
La Bagh Woods
Peterson Park
Nature Center
Legion Park
Gompers Park
Field Park
Kiwanis
North Side Sewage Treatment Dr
Exit 37A-B
Exit 39A-B
Exit 41A-B
Exit 41C
Exit 42
Exit 83A
Exit 83B
Exit N Elston Ave
54
41
50
94
14
33
35
48
A
B
C
3
4

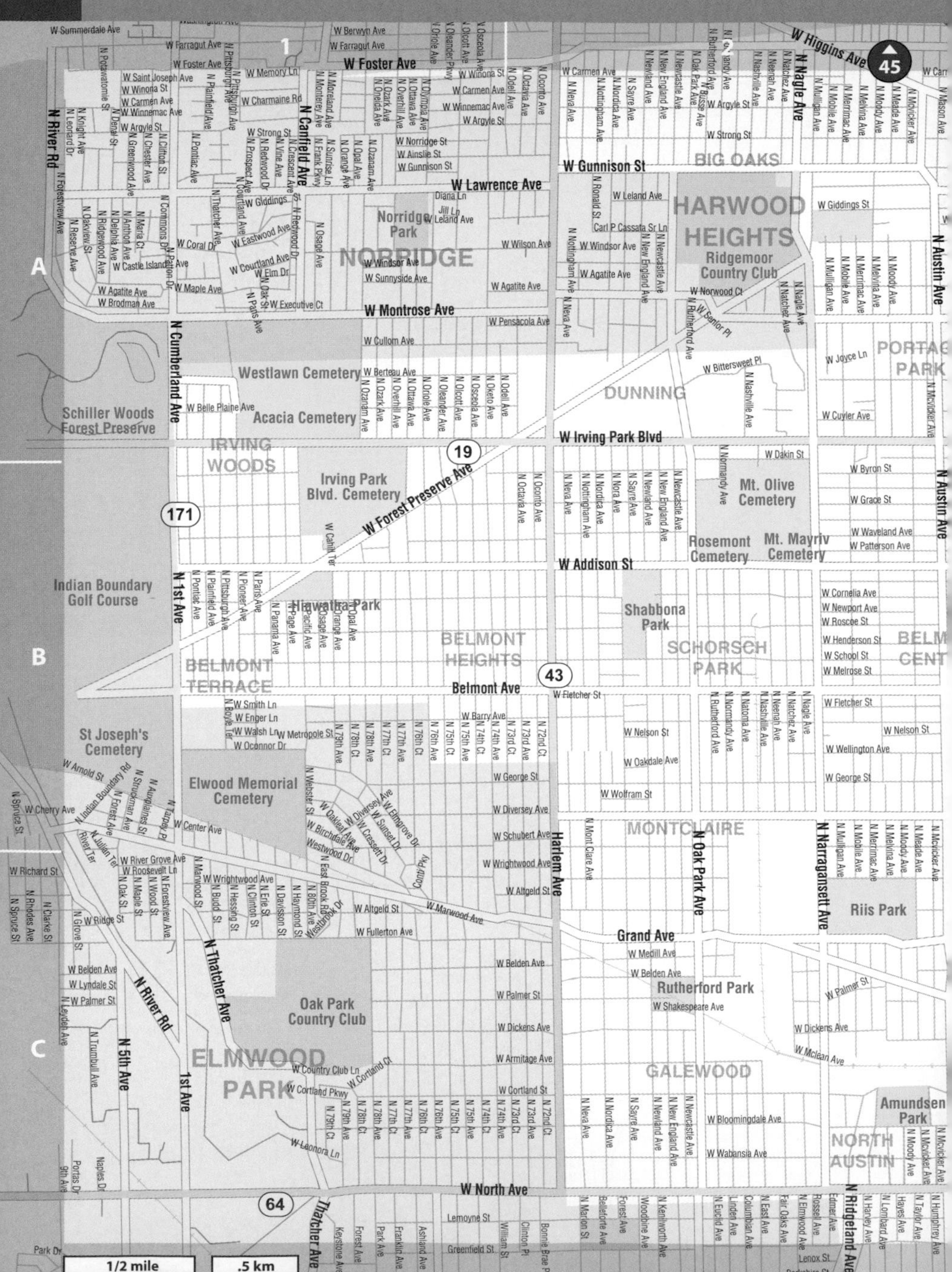

45
W Higgins Ave
W Foster Ave
W Lawrence Ave
W Gunnison St
W Montrose Ave
W Irving Park Blvd
W Forest Preserve Ave
W Addison St
Belmont Ave
Grand Ave
W North Ave
N River Rd
N Canfield Ave
N Cumberland Ave
N 1st Ave
Harlem Ave
N Oak Park Ave
N Narragansett Ave
N Nagle Ave
N Austin Ave
N Ridgeland Ave
N Thatcher Ave
Thatcher Ave
N 5th Ave
1st Ave
19
43
171
64
NORRIDGE
Norridge Park
HARWOOD HEIGHTS
Ridgemoor Country Club
BIG OAKS
DUNNING
PORTAGE PARK
Westlawn Cemetery
Acacia Cemetery
Schiller Woods Forest Preserve
IRVING WOODS
Irving Park Blvd. Cemetery
Mt. Olive Cemetery
Rosemont Cemetery
Mt. Mayriv Cemetery
Indian Boundary Golf Course
Hiawatha Park
BELMONT HEIGHTS
BELMONT TERRACE
Shabbona Park
SCHORSCH PARK
BELMONT CENTRAL
St Joseph's Cemetery
Elwood Memorial Cemetery
MONTCLAIRE
Riis Park
Rutherford Park
Oak Park Country Club
ELMWOOD PARK
GALEWOOD
Amundsen Park
NORTH AUSTIN
A
B
C
1
2
1/2 mile
.5 km

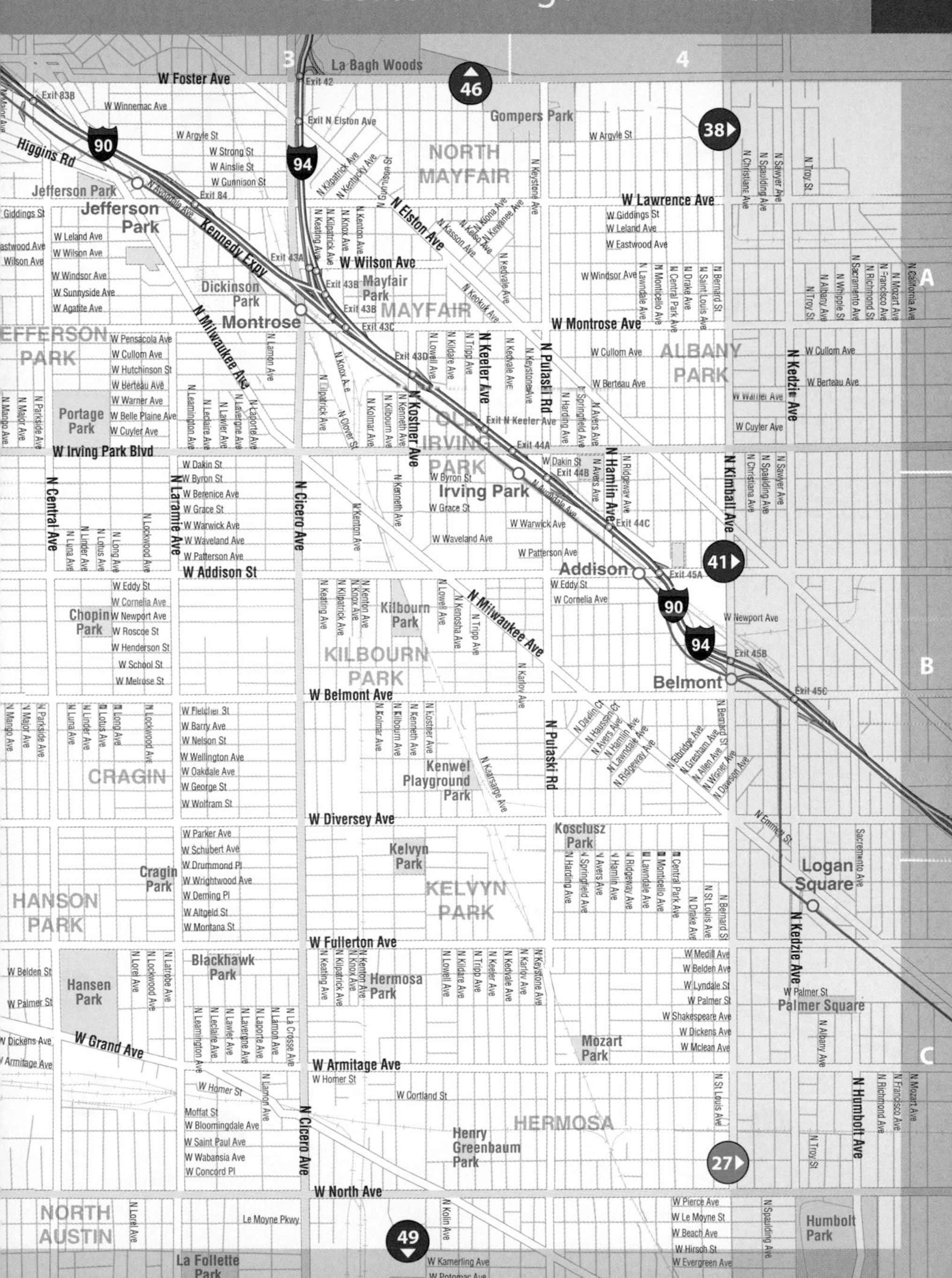
La Bagh Woods
W Foster Ave
Gompers Park
NORTH MAYFAIR
Jefferson Park
Kennedy Expy
Higgins Rd
N Elston Ave
W Lawrence Ave
Dickinson Park
Montrose
MAYFAIR
Mayfair Park
W Montrose Ave
ALBANY PARK
JEFFERSON PARK
Portage Park
N Milwaukee Ave
N Keeler Ave
N Pulaski Rd
N Kedzie Ave
OLD IRVING PARK
N Kostner Ave
W Irving Park Blvd
Irving Park
N Hamlin Ave
N Kimball Ave
N Central Ave
N Laramie Ave
N Cicero Ave
W Addison St
Addison
Chopin Park
Kilbourn Park
KILBOURN PARK
Belmont
W Belmont Ave
CRAGIN
Kenwel Playground Park
W Diversey Ave
Kosciusz Park
Logan Square
Cragin Park
Kelvyn Park
KELVYN PARK
HANSON PARK
W Fullerton Ave
Blackhawk Park
Hansen Park
Hermosa Park
Palmer Square
W Grand Ave
Mozart Park
W Armitage Ave
HERMOSA
Henry Greenbaum Park
N Humbolt Ave
W North Ave
NORTH AUSTIN
Humbolt Park
La Follette Park
46
38
41
27
49
3
4
A
B
C

Greater Chicago • West

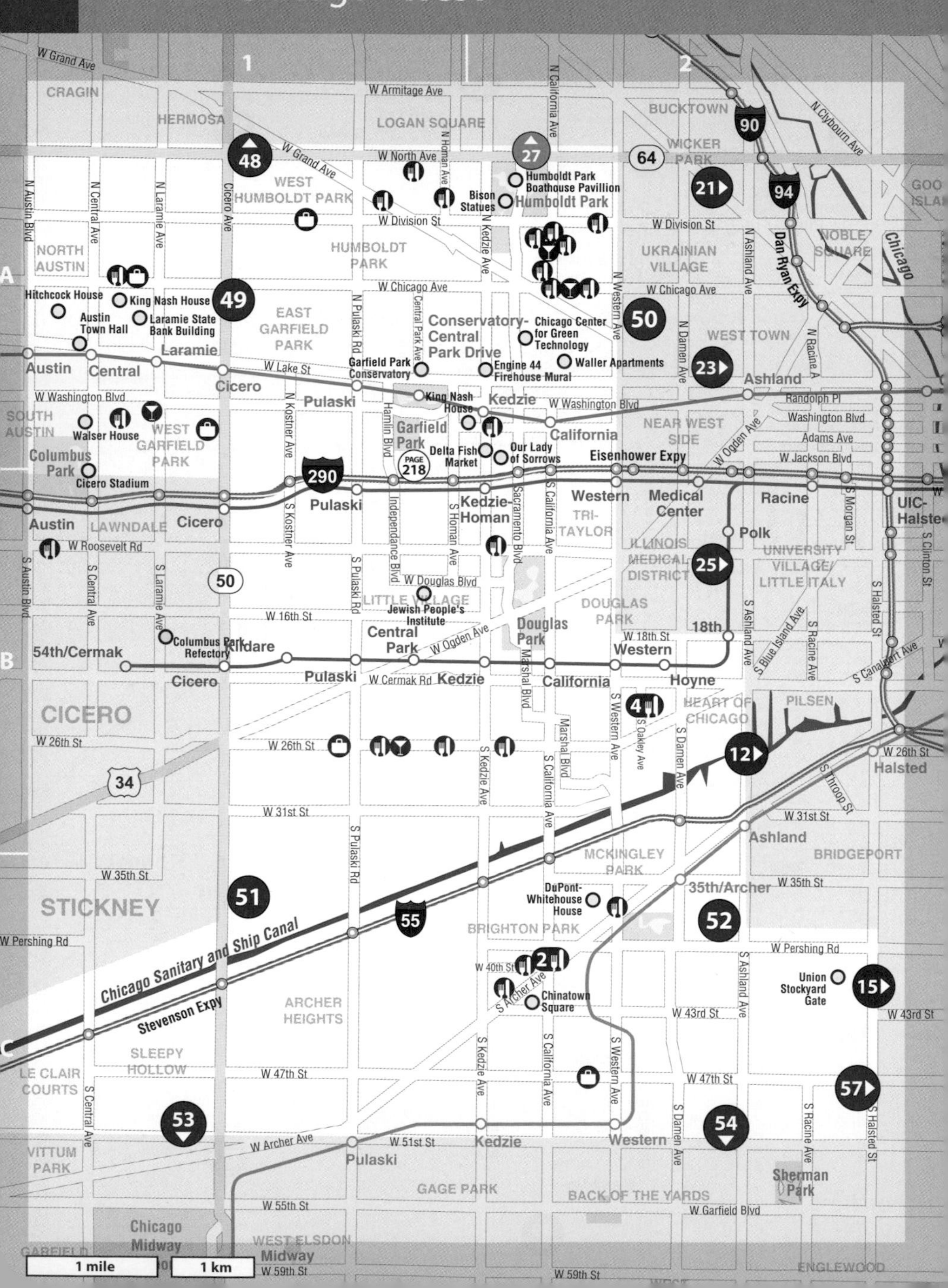

Essentials

Despite being framed by beautiful green spaces, the turf between Humboldt Park and Columbus Park continues to be some of Chicago's roughest. Garfield Park, with its historic conservatory, is a popular spot to tie the knot. 26th is the commercial artery of Little Village's thriving Mexican population. Brighton Park and Archer Heights epitomize the classic Chicago blue-collar ethic, where the labor unions rule and the Old Style flows freely.

o Landmarks

- **Austin Town Hall** • 5610 W Lake St
- **Bison Statues at Humboldt Park** • 1400 N Sacramento Ave
- **Chicago Center for Green Technology** • 445 N Sacramento Blvd
- **Chinatown Square** • S Archer Ave
- **Columbus Park Refectory** • Columbus Park, 500 S Central Ave
- **Delta Fish Market** • 228 S Kedzie Ave
- **DuPont-Whitehouse House** • 3558 S Artesian Ave
- **Engine 44 Firehouse Mural** • 412 N Kedzie Ave
- **Garfield Park Conservatory** • 300 N Central Park Ave
- **Hitchcock House** • 5704 W Ohio St
- **Humboldt Park Boathouse Pavillion** • 1301 N Humboldt Dr
- **Jewish People's Institute** • 3500 W Douglas Blvd
- **King Nash House** • 3234 W Washington Blvd
- **Laramie State Bank Building** • 5200 W Chicago Ave
- **Our Lady of Sorrows** • 3121 W Jackson Blvd
- **Union Stock Yard Gate** • Exchange Ave & Peoria St
- **Waller Apartments** • 2840 W Walnut St
- **Walser House** • 42 N Central Ave

Sundries / Entertainment

The stretch of California just east of Humboldt Park is a hipster haven of bars, restaurants and funky shops. Little Village is home to Birrieria Zaragoza, a muy authentico Mexican restaurant where the goat stew is second to none. Count on having a bawdy and bluesy good time at Linda's Lounge on West 51st. Further west, a plethora of salt-of-the-earth bars cluster in the shadow of Midway airport. Go Sox!

Nightlife

- **Archie's** • 2600 W Iowa St
- **Black Beetle** • 2532 W Chicago Ave
- **California Clipper** • 1002 N California Ave •
- **Division Street Bar & Grill** • 2525W Division St
- **Illinois Bar & Grill on 47th** • 4135 W 47th St
- **La Justicia** • 3901 W 26th St
- **Linda's Lounge** • 1044 W 51st St
- **Rooster's Place** • 4501 W Madison St
- **Rootstock Wine & Beer Bar** • 954 N California Ave

Restaurants

- **Amarind's** • 6822 W North Ave
- **Bacchanalia Ristorante** • 2413 S Oakley Ave
- **Birria Huentitan** • 4019 W North Ave
- **Birrieria Zaragoza** • 4852 S Pulaski Rd
- **Bruna's** • 2424 S Oakley Ave
- **Cemitas Puebla** • 3619 W North Ave
- **CJ's Eatery** • 3839 W Grand Ave
- **Coco** • 2723 W Division St
- **Coleman's Hickory House** • 5754 W Chicago Ave
- **Depot** • 5840 W Roosevelt Rd
- **Edna's** • 3175 W Madison St
- **El Salvador Restaurante** • 4125 S Archer Ave
- **Falco's Pizza** • 2806 W 40th St
- **Feed** • 2803 W Chicago Ave
- **Flying Saucer** • 1123 N California Ave
- **I. C. Y. Vegetarian Restaurant & Juice Bar** • 3141 W Roosevelt Rd
- **Ignotz** • 2421 S Oakley Ave
- **La Cebollita** • 4343 W 47th St
- **La Palma** • 1340 N Homan Ave
- **Lalo's** • 3515 W 26th St
- **Lindy's and Gertie's** • 3685 S Archer Ave
- **MacArthur's** • 5412 W Madison Ave
- **Maiz** • 1041 N California Ave
- **New Life Health Foods & Restaurant** • 3141 W Roosevelt Rd
- **Submarine Piers** • 4048 S Archer Ave
- **Taqueria Atotonilco** • 3916 W 26th St
- **Taqueria Los Comales** • 3141 W 26th St
- **Taqueria Los Gallos 2** • 4252 S Archer Ave
- **TipsyCake** • 1043 N California Ave
- **Tommy's Rock-n-Roll Café** • 2548 W Chicago Ave

Shopping

- **Ashland Swap-o-Rama** • 4100 S Ashland Ave
- **Ashley Stewart** • 800 N Kedzie Ave
- **Buyer's Flea Market** • 4545 W Division St
- **Dulcelandia** • 3300 W 26th St
- **Family Dollar** • 5410 W Chicago Ave
- **Family Dollar** • 1360 N Pulaski Rd
- **Hot Jams** • 4814 S Pulaski Rd
- **Moo & Oink** • 4848 W Madison St
- **Unique Thrift Store** • 3542 S Archer Ave
- **Village Discount Outlet** • 2514 W 47th St
- **Village Discount Outlet** • 4020 W 26th St
- **Watra Church Goods** • 4201 S Archer Ave

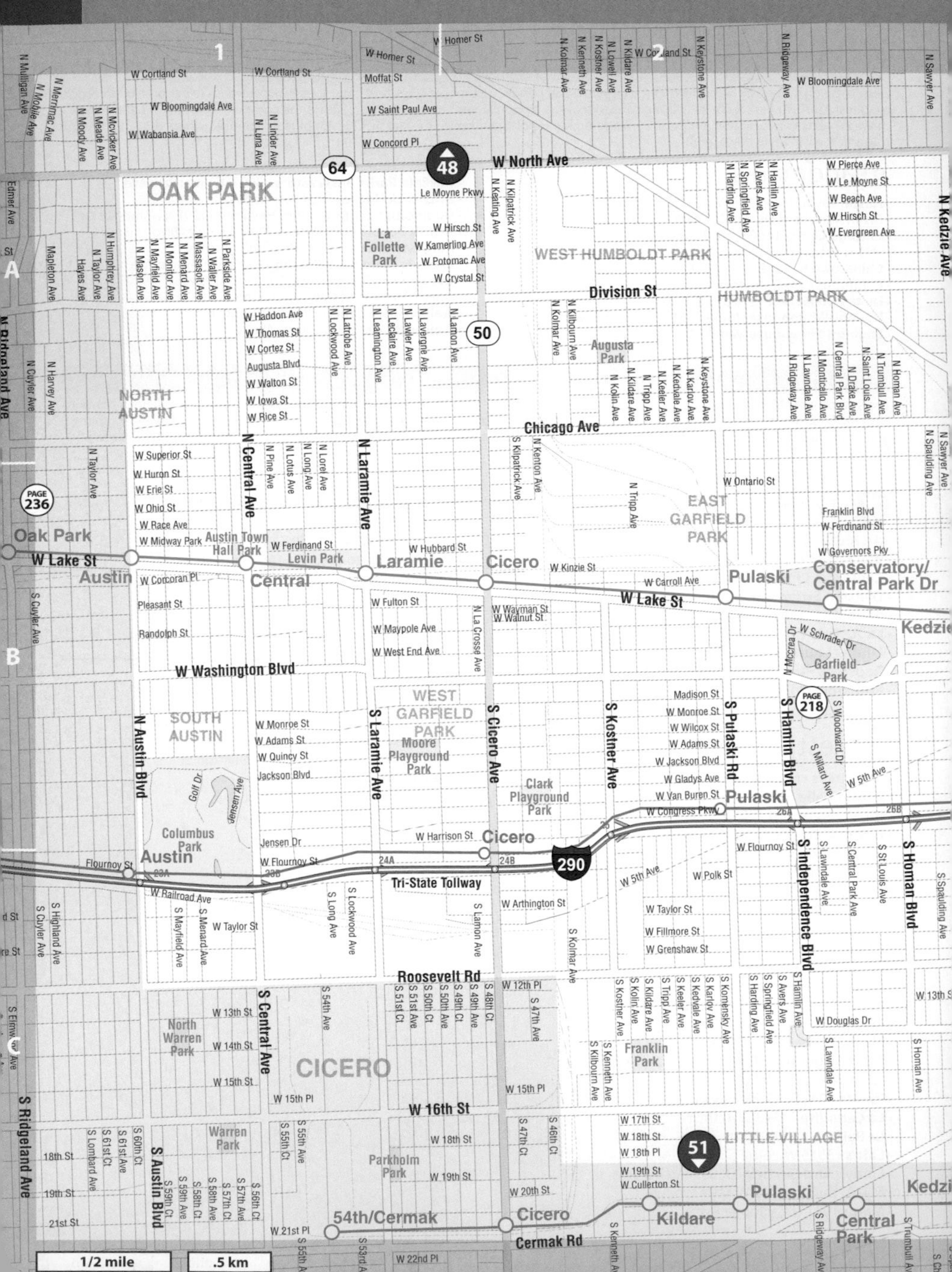
OAK PARK
NORTH AUSTIN
SOUTH AUSTIN
WEST HUMBOLDT PARK
HUMBOLDT PARK
EAST GARFIELD PARK
WEST GARFIELD PARK
CICERO
LITTLE VILLAGE
W North Ave
Division St
Chicago Ave
W Lake St
W Washington Blvd
Roosevelt Rd
W 16th St
Cermak Rd
Tri-State Tollway
N Central Ave
N Laramie Ave
S Cicero Ave
S Kostner Ave
S Pulaski Rd
S Hamlin Blvd
S Independence Blvd
S Homan Blvd
N Austin Blvd
S Austin Blvd
S Central Ave
S Laramie Ave
S Ridgeland Ave
N Ridgeland Ave
N Kedzie Ave
Oak Park
Austin
Central
Laramie
Cicero
Pulaski
Conservatory/Central Park Dr
Kedzie
54th/Cermak
Kildare
Central Park
Columbus Park
Garfield Park
Augusta Park
La Follette Park
Levin Park
Austin Town Hall Park
Moore Playground Park
Clark Playground Park
North Warren Park
Warren Park
Parkholm Park
Franklin Park
48
51
64
50
290
PAGE 236
PAGE 218
1/2 mile
.5 km

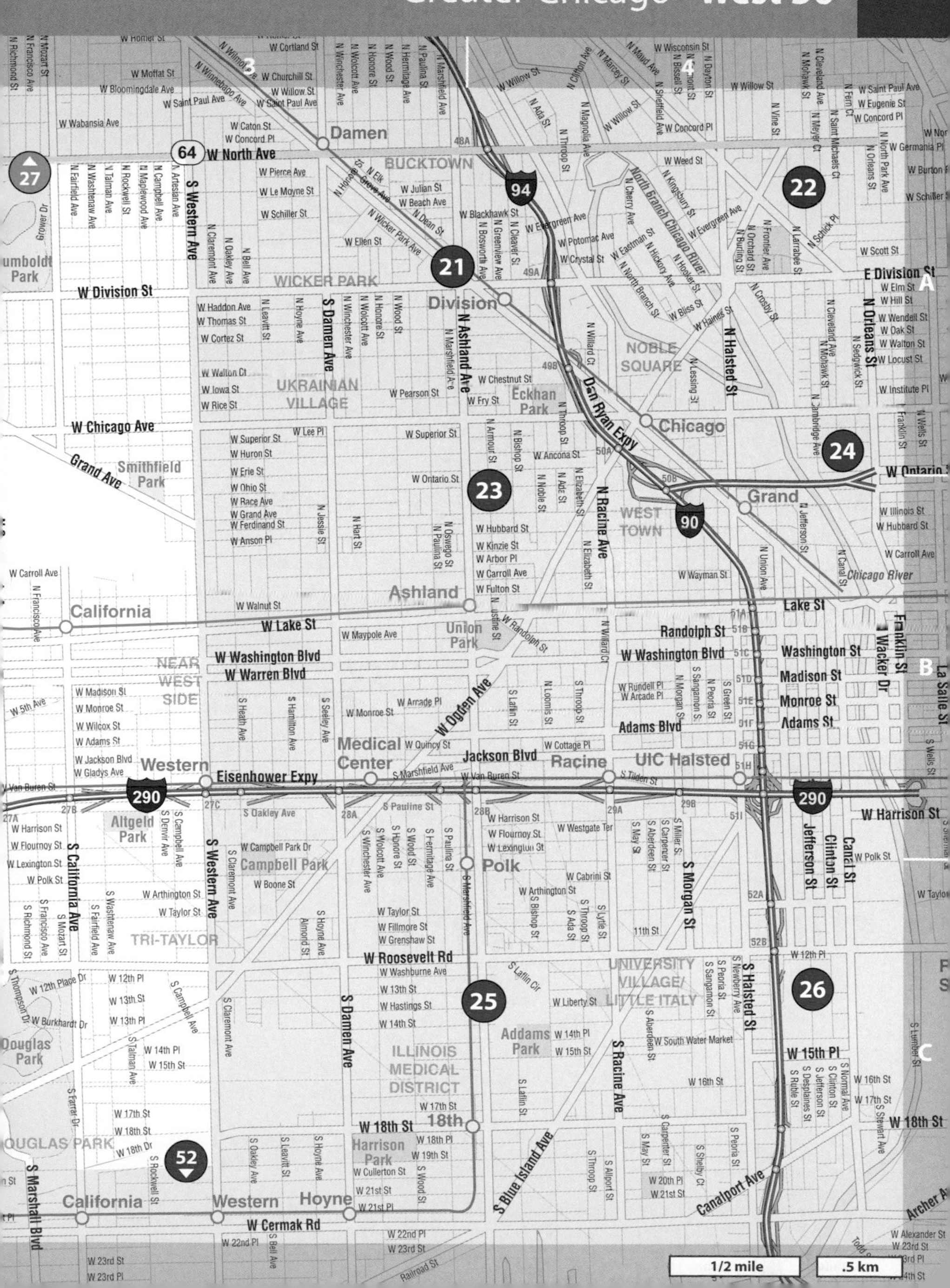

BUCKTOWN
WICKER PARK
UKRAINIAN VILLAGE
NOBLE SQUARE
WEST TOWN
Eckhart Park
Smithfield Park
Union Park
NEAR WEST SIDE
Altgeld Park
Campbell Park
TRI-TAYLOR
UNIVERSITY VILLAGE/ LITTLE ITALY
ILLINOIS MEDICAL DISTRICT
Addams Park
Harrison Park
Douglas Park
DOUGLAS PARK
Humboldt Park
Damen
Division
Chicago
Grand
Ashland
California
Western
Medical Center
Racine
UIC Halsted
Polk
18th
Hoyne
W North Ave
W Division St
W Chicago Ave
Grand Ave
W Lake St
W Washington Blvd
W Warren Blvd
Eisenhower Expy
Dan Ryan Expy
W Ogden Ave
W Roosevelt Rd
W 18th St
W Cermak Rd
S Blue Island Ave
Canalport Ave
S Western Ave
S Damen Ave
N Ashland Ave
N Racine Ave
N Halsted St
S Halsted St
S Morgan St
S Racine Ave
S California Ave
S Marshall Blvd
N Orleans St
Jefferson St
Clinton St
Canal St
Wacker Dr
Franklin St
La Salle St
W Ontario St
E Division St
Lake St
Randolph St
Washington St
Madison St
Monroe St
Adams St
Adams Blvd
Jackson Blvd
W Harrison St
W 15th Pl
W 18th St
North Branch Chicago River
Chicago River
21
22
23
24
25
26
27
52
1/2 mile
.5 km

54th/Cermak
Cicero
Kildare
Pulaski
Central Park
W Cermak Rd
W Ogden Ave
W 26th St
W 31st St
S Austin Blvd
S Laramie Ave
S Central Ave
Cicero Ave
S Pulaski Rd
W 35th St
W Pershing Rd
W 47th St
W 55th St
Archer Ave
CICERO
STICKNEY
ARCHER HEIGHTS
Piotrowski Park
Hawthorne Race Course
Chicago Sanitary and Ship Canal
LeClaire Courts
SLEEPY HOLLOW
LE CLAIR COURTS
Archer Park
Vittum Park
VITTUM PARK
Strohacker Park
WEST ELSDON
Chicago Midway Airport
Pasteur Park
Senaca Park
Midway
Airport Dr
PAGE 274
1/2 mile
.5 km

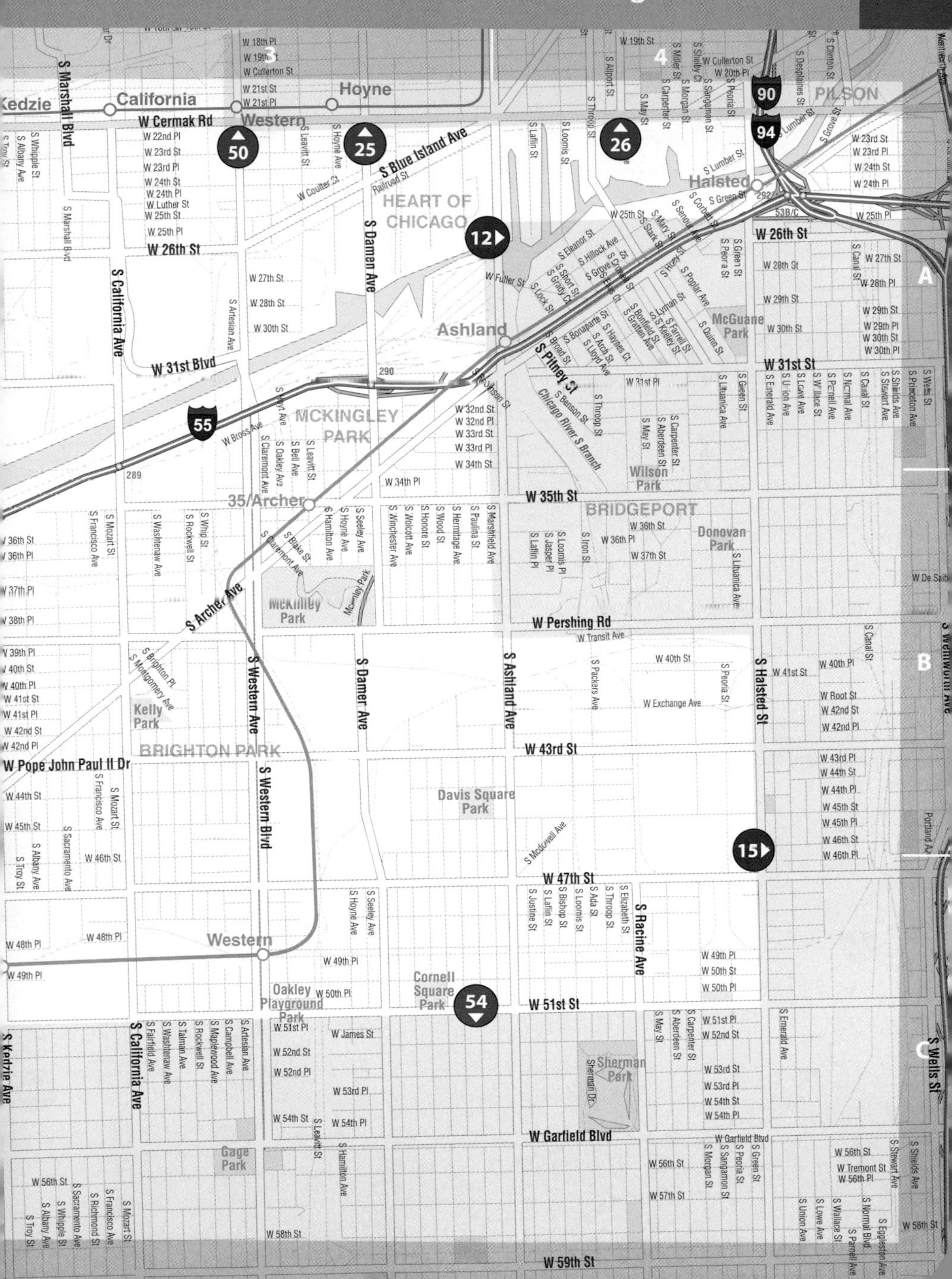

Kedzie
California
Western
Hoyne
Halsted
Ashland
35/Archer
Western
PILSON
HEART OF CHICAGO
MCKINGLEY PARK
BRIDGEPORT
BRIGHTON PARK
McKinley Park
Kelly Park
Wilson Park
Donovan Park
McGuane Park
Davis Square Park
Cornell Square Park
Oakley Playground Park
Sherman Park
Gage Park
50
25
26
12
55
15
54
90
94
A
B
C
3
4
W Cermak Rd
S Blue Island Ave
W 26th St
W 31st Blvd
W 31st St
W 35th St
W Pershing Rd
W 43rd St
W 47th St
W 51st St
W Garfield Blvd
W 59th St
W Pope John Paul II Dr
S Archer Ave
S Pitney St
Chicago River S Branch
S Marshall Blvd
S California Ave
S Damen Ave
S Western Ave
S Western Blvd
S Ashland Ave
S Halsted St
S Racine Ave
S Kedzie Ave
S Wells St
W Exchange Ave
W Transit Ave
S Packers Ave
S Mcdowell Ave
Sherman Dr
W 18th Pl
W 19th St
W Cullerton St
W 21st St
W 21st Pl
W 22nd Pl
W 23rd St
W 23rd Pl
W 24th St
W 24th Pl
W Luther St
W 25th St
W 25th Pl
W 27th St
W 28th St
W 29th St
W 30th St
W 32nd St
W 32nd Pl
W 33rd St
W 33rd Pl
W 34th St
W 34th Pl
W 36th St
W 36th Pl
W 37th St
W 37th Pl
W 38th Pl
W 39th Pl
W 40th St
W 40th Pl
W 41st St
W 41st Pl
W Root St
W 42nd St
W 42nd Pl
W 43rd Pl
W 44th St
W 44th Pl
W 45th St
W 45th Pl
W 46th St
W 46th Pl
W 48th St
W 48th Pl
W 49th Pl
W 50th St
W 50th Pl
W 51st Pl
W 52nd St
W 52nd Pl
W 53rd St
W 53rd Pl
W 54th St
W 54th Pl
W 56th St
W 56th Pl
W Tremont St
W 57th St
W 58th St
W James St
W Fuller St
W Coulter St
W Bross Ave
S Lumber St
S Green St
Railroad St
290
289
292
53B/C

Adlai E Stevenson Expy
Archer Heights
W 47th St
Back of the Yards
Garfield Ridge
Pulaski
Kedzie
Western
Gage Park
W Archer Ave
W 51st St
Sherman Park
W Garfield Blvd
W 55th St
Page 274
West Elson
Clearing
S Central Ave
Chicago Midway Airport
Midway
Midway Airport
W 59th St
S California Ave
Graffiti Mural
Englewood
Chicago Lawn
Capital Cigar Store
Ashland/ 63rd
W 63rd St
West Englewood
W 65th St
Halsted
West Lawn
Marquette Park
Marquette Rd
Bedford Park
W 71st St
S Cicero Ave
S Pulaski Rd
S Kedzie Ave
S Western Ave
S Damen Ave
S Ashland Ave
S Racine Ave
S Halsted St
Ford City
W 79st St
Burbank
Ashburn
Wrightwood
West Chatham
Scottsdale
State Ave
Gresham
Parkview
Marycrest
W 87th St
Evergreen Park
Campbell House
William MR French House
Edwin C Young House
Original Rainbow Cone
Adams House
Bronzeville Children's Museum
W 95th St
Ridge Park
Oakdale Park
Evans House
Karge House
Horton Mansion
S Walden Pkwy
Edward L Roberts House
Oak Lawn
W 99th St
Tally's Corner
Bell Tower
McDonnell House
JB Chambers House
Condos
Metra Station 103rd
Givens Irish Castle
W 103rd Rd
S Ridgeland Ave
Burhans-Ellinwood Model House
McCumber House
Ridge Historical Society
Mount Greenwood
Gately House
Blackwelder House
Frank Anderson House
Hopkinson House
Harris House
Lackmore House
Ferguson House
W 111th St
Beverly Arts Center
Metra Station 111th
Bohn Park
Arnett Chapel
Mount Greenwood Heights
Godspeed House
St.Walter Catholic Church
Holy Name of Mary Church
W 115th St
Morgan Park Apostolic Church
Tri-State Tollway
Alsip
S Vincennes St
Dan Ryan Expy
Calumet Sag Rd
W 119th St
W 127th St
1 mile
1 km

Essentials

The Southwest side comprises several communities steeped in Chicago's ethnic blue collar history, including a large Lithuanian population, Italians, Arab-Americans, African-Americans and the Irish. This cultural diversity has not arisen without conflict—Marquette Park was once a gathering spot for white-supremacy groups. Today, the park is better known for its fishing pond, golf course, and occasional outbursts of gang violence. Southernmost in the southwest side, the Beverly and Morgan Park areas are chock-a-block with historic homes and civic pride. .

o Landmarks

- **Adams House** • 9326 S Longwood Dr
- **Arnett Chapel, African Methodist Episcopal Church** • 11218 S Bishop St
- **Bell Tower Condos** • 10321 S Longwood Dr
- **Blackwelder Summerlin House** • 10910 S Prospect Ave
- **Bohn Park** • 1966 111th St
- **Bronzeville Children's Museum** • 9600 S Western Ave
- **Burhans-Ellinwood Model House** • 10410 S Hoyne Ave
- **Campbell House** • 9250 S Damen Ave
- **Capital Cigar Store** • 6258 S Pulaski Rd
- **Edward L Roberts House** • 10134 S Longwood Dr
- **Edwin C Young House** • 9215 S Pleasant Ave
- **Evans House** • 9914 S Longwood Dr
- **Ferguson House** • 10954 S Prospect Ave
- **Frank Anderson House** • 10400 S Longwood Dr
- **Gately House** • 10655 S Hoyne Ave
- **Givens Irish Castle** • 10244 S Longwood Dr
- **Goodspeed House** • 11216 S Oakley Ave
- **Graffiti Mural** • W 59th St & S Damen Ave
- **Harris House** • 10856 S Longwood Dr
- **Holy Name of Mary Church** • 11159 S Loomis St
- **Hopkinson House** • 10820 S Drew St
- **Horton Mansion** • 10200 S Longwood Dr
- **Howe House** • 10208 S Wood St
- **JB Chambers House** • 10330 S Seeley Ave
- **Karge House** • 2035 W 99th St
- **Lackore House** • 10956 S Prospect Ave
- **McCumber House** • 10305 S Seeley Ave
- **Metra 103rd/Washington Heights Rock Island District Branch Line Station** • 103rd St & Vincennes Ave
- **Metra Rock Island Main Line 111th St/Monterey Ave Station** • 111th St & Monterey Ave
- **Midway Airport** • 5700 S Cicero Ave
- **Morgan Park Apostolic Penecostal Church** • 11401 S Vincennes Ave
- **Morgan Park United Methodist Church** • 11030 S Longwood Dr
- **Oakdale Park** • 956 W 95th St
- **Original Rainbow Cone** • 9233 S Western Ave
- **Ridge Historical Society** • 10621 S Seeley Ave
- **Ridge Park** • 9625 S Longwood Dr
- **St Walter Catholic Church** • 11722 S Oakley Ave
- **William MR French House** • 9203 S Pleasant Ave

Sundries/Entertainment

Why do some jerks have to ruin the fun for everyone? After decades of notoriety as the nation's biggest, rowdiest green beer bacchanal, the Southside St. Paddy's Day parade is being reconcepted into the "Southside Irish Parade and Family Fest," guaranteeing a wholesome good time for...... zzzzzzzzzzzzzzzzzz... Huh?! What? Luckily if you're in the southwest side and you want to do something reckless and bad for you, you still have Englewood's Fat Johnnie's hot dog stand, where you can enjoy a southside institution: a tamale in a hotdog bun covered with chili and cheese. Yesssss!

Movie Theaters

- **AMC Ford City 14** • 7601 S Cicero Ave

Nightlife

- **Cookie's Cocktail Lounge** • 1024 W 79th St
- **Cork & Kerry** • 10614 S Western Ave
- **Groucho's** • 8355 S Pulaski Rd
- **Halina's Bar** • 7023 W Archer Ave
- **Jeremy Lanigan's Irish Pub** • 3119 W 111th St
- **Keegan's Pub** • 10618 S Western Ave
- **Mrs O'Leary's Dubliner** • 10910 S Western Ave
- **O'Rourke's Office** • 11064 S Western
- **Patrick's** • 6296 S Archer Ave
- **Reese's Lounge** • 1827 W 87th St
- **Sean's Rhino Bar** • 10330 S Western Ave
- **Tina's Cocktail Lounge** • 7840 S Racine Ave
- **Tom's Tap** • 6707 W Archer Ave

Restaurants

- **Beverly Woods Restaurant** • 11532 S Western Ave
- **Birrieria de la Torre** • 6724 S Pulaski Rd
- **Bobak's Sausage Company** • 5275 S Archer Ave
- **Café 103** • 1909 W 103rd St
- **Fat Johnnie's** • 7232 S Western Ave
- **Fox's Beverly Restaurant and Pizza** • 9956 S Western Ave
- **Franconello's Italian Restaurant** • 10222 S Western Ave
- **Harold's Chicken Shack** • 7274 S Racine Ave
- **Janson's Drive-In / Snyder's Red Hots** • 9900 S Western Ave
- **Koda** • 10352 S Western Ave
- **Lagniappe** • 1525 W 79th St
- **Lume's** • 11601 S Western Ave
- **New China Tea** • 4020 W 55th St
- **Nile Restaurant** • 3259 W 63rd St
- **The Original Vito and Nick's Pizzeria** • 8433 S Pulaski Rd
- **Szalas** • 5214 S Archer Ave
- **Tatra Inn** • 6040 S Pulaski Rd
- **Top Notch Beefburger** • 2116 W 95th St
- **Uncle Joe's Jerk** • 10210 S Vincennes Ave

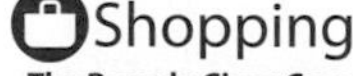

Shopping

- **The Beverly Cigar Company** • 10513 S Western Ave
- **Beverly & Novelty Costume Shop** • 11626 S Western Ave
- **Beverly Rare Records** • 11612 S Western Ave
- **Bobak's Sausage Company** • 5275 S Archer Ave
- **Calabria Imports** • 1905 W 103rd St
- **County Fair** • 10800 S Western Ave
- **Evergreen Plaza Shopping Center** • 9730 S Western Ave
- **Ford City Shopping Center** • 7601 S Cicero Ave
- **Markskis CD** • 5106 S Archer Ave
- **Mr Peabody Records** • 11832 S Western Ave
- **Ms Priss** • 9915 S Walden Pkwy
- **My Sisters' Knits** • 9907 S Walden Pkwy
- **Optimo Fine Hats** • 10215 S Western Ave
- **Southwest Ace Hardware** • 6908 W Archer Ave
- **Southwest Book & Video** • 7733 S Cicero Ave
- **Village Discount Outlet** • 6419 S Kedzie Ave
- **Village Discount Outlet** • 7443 S Racine Ave
- **World Music Company** • 1808 W 103rd St

Adlai E Stevenson Expy
S Central Ave
S Cicero Ave
S Harlem Ave
S Pulaski Rd
W 51st St
W 55th St
W 63rd St
W Archer Ave
W 47th St
79th St
W 87th St
Airport Dr
Chicago Midway Airport
Midway
Pulaski
GARFIELD RIDGE
ARCHER HEIGHTS
WEST ELSON
WEST LAWN
BEDFORD PARK
BURBANK
SCOTTSDALE
Vittum Park
Archer Park
Park Number 468
Pasteur Park
Wentworth Kinzie Park
Minuteman Park
Valley Forge Park
Nathan Hale Park
Lawler Park
West Lawn Park
Rainey Hancock Park
Scottsdale Park
Durkin Center Park
1/2 mile
.5 km

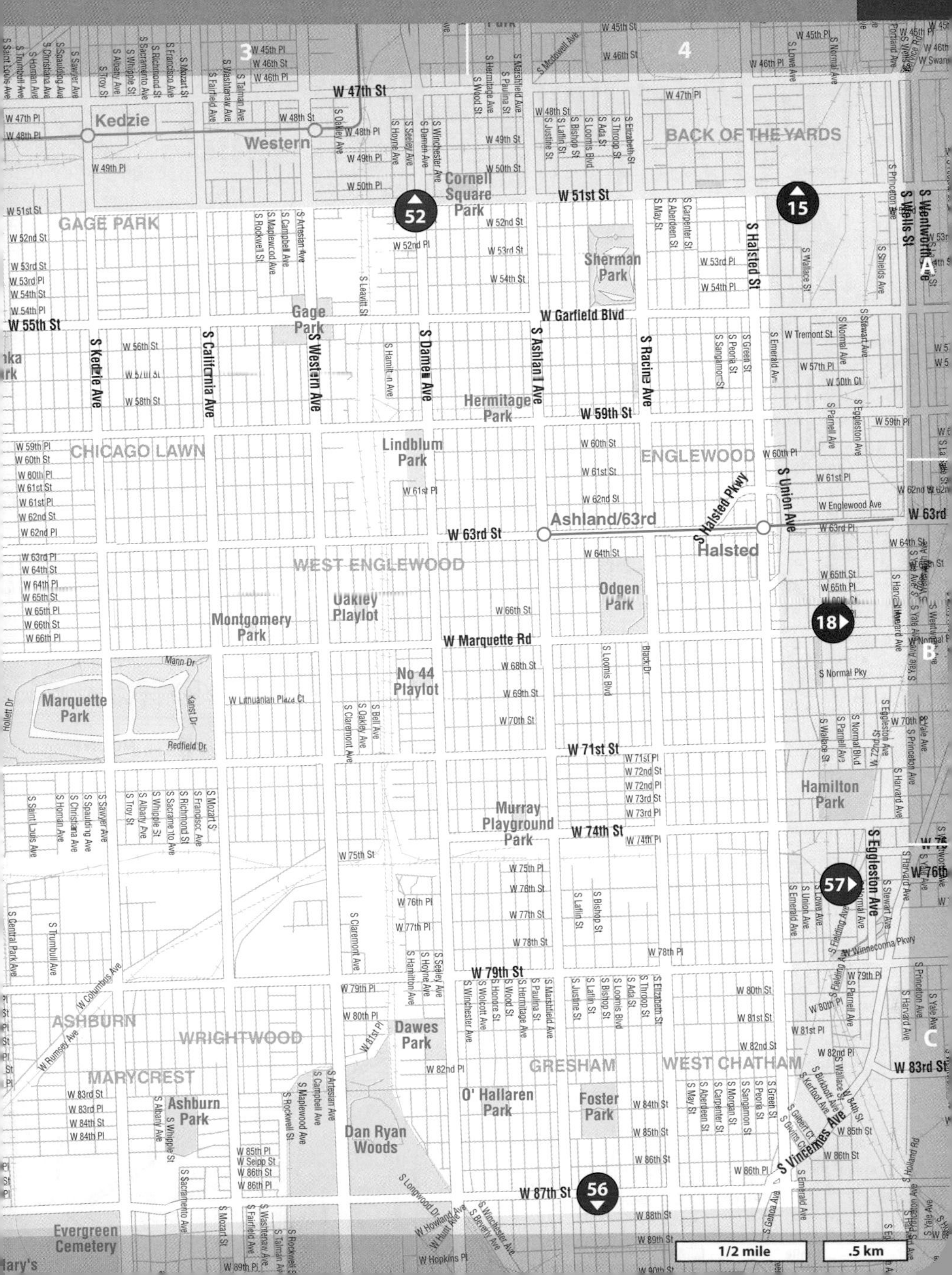
Kedzie
Western
BACK OF THE YARDS
Cornell Square Park
GAGE PARK
Sherman Park
Gage Park
W Garfield Blvd
Hermitage Park
CHICAGO LAWN
Lindblum Park
ENGLEWOOD
Ashland/63rd
Halsted
WEST ENGLEWOOD
Odgen Park
Oakley Playlot
Montgomery Park
No 44 Playlot
Marquette Park
Hamilton Park
Murray Playground Park
ASHBURN
WRIGHTWOOD
Dawes Park
MARYCREST
GRESHAM
WEST CHATHAM
Ashburn Park
O' Hallaren Park
Foster Park
Dan Ryan Woods
Evergreen Cemetery
W 47th St
W 51st St
W 55th St
W 59th St
W 63rd St
W Marquette Rd
W 71st St
W 74th St
W 79th St
W 83rd St
W 87th St
S Kedzie Ave
S California Ave
S Western Ave
S Damen Ave
S Ashland Ave
S Racine Ave
S Halsted St
S Union Ave
S Halsted Pkwy
S Eggleston Ave
S Vincennes Ave
S Wentworth Ave
S Wells St
1/2 mile
.5 km

Lake Michigan
Garfield
Garfield Blvd
Dan Ryan Expy
51st
Hyde Park Blvd
E 51st St
Washington Park
Jackson Park
W 55th St
E 59th St
East 63rd/ Cottage Grove
63rd
Halsted
E 63rd St
E Hayes Dr
WEST WOODLAWN
E Marquette Rd
69th
Oak Woods Cemetery
E 67th St
WOODLAWN
Kenna Apartments
SOUTH SHORE
South Shore Cultural Center
HAMILTON PARK
PARK MANOR
E 71st St
GRAND CROSSING
Miller House
S Jeffery Blvd
S Stony Island Ave
E 74th St
E 75th St
E 76th St
ENGLEWOOD
Auburn Park
CHATHAM
New Regal Theatre
E 79th St
79th
MARYNOOK
SOUTH CHICAGO
S Vincennes Ave
State St
S Chicago Ave
S Yates Blvd
S South Shore Dr
S Racine Ave
E 83rd St
STONY ISLAND PARK
S Commercial Ave
87th
E 87th St
Chicago Skyway
S Lafayette Ave
S Cottage Grove Ave
BURNSIDE
CALUMET HEIGHTS
Peoples Gas South Chicago
Calumet River
S Mackinaw Ave
S Ewing Ave
WEST CHESTERFIELD
PILL HILL
PRINCETON PARK
Carter G Wooden Regional Library
E 95th St
95th/Dan Ryan
Trinity United Church of Christ
Chicago State University
LONGWOOD MANOR
Robert S. Abbott Park
COTTAGE GROVE HEIGHTS
JEFFERY MANOR
S Colfax Ave
S Avenue L
E 100th St
ROSEMOOR
W 103rd St
E 103rd St
SOUTH DEERING
WASHINGTON HEIGHTS
Lilydale Progressive Missionary Baptist
S King Dr
E 106th St
S Halsted St
FERNWOOD
Pullman Clock Tower
Hyde Park
S Torrence Ave
S Avenue O
Chicago Skyway
E 111th St
ROSELAND
E 113th St
Market
Palmer Hall Park
Lilydale First Baptist Church
E 115th St
Lake Calumet
Eggers Woods
West Pullman Elementary School
W 119th St
Foster House& Stable
S State St
PULLMAN
Calumet River
S Burnham Ave
Wolf Lake Park
Indianapolis Blvd
WEST PULLMAN
West Pullman Park
Wolf Lake
Calumet Ave
Cedar Park Cemetery & Funeral Home
W 127th St
E 127th St
Ford Freeway
Vermont Ave
E 130th St
GOLDEN GATE
ALTGELD GARDENS
Forest Preserve
S Indiana Ave
S Saginaw Ave
S Brainard Ave
Little Calumet River
HEGEWISCH
ILLINOIS
INDIANA
RIVERDALE
1 mile
1 km

Essentials

As went the Chicago Steel industry, so went the southside economy, which has been struggling to recover ever since. With Olympic dreams dashed, life goes on in the southside; a geographic area that encompasses one of the most crime-riddled areas in the city between Garfield Blvd. and Englewood, as well as the comfortable middle-class enclaves of south central Chicago from South Shore to Chatham to Burnside, a bungalow-belt that defies the southside's rough-and-tumble reputation.

o Landmarks

- **Bronzeville Children's Museum** • 9301 S Stony Island Ave
- **Cedar Park Cemetary & Funeral Home** • 12540 S Halsted St
- **Chicago Skyway** • 8801 S Anthony St
- **Chicago State University** • 9501 S King Dr
- **Foster House & Stable** • 12147 S Harvard Ave
- **Kenna Apartments** • 2214 E 69th St
- **Lilydale First Baptist Church** • 649 W 113th St
- **Lilydale Progressive Missionary Baptist Church** • 10706 S Michigan Ave
- **Market Hall** • E 112th St & Champlain Ave
- **Miller House** • 7121 S Paxton Ave
- **Mosque Maryam and the Nation of Islam National Center** • 7351 S Stony Island Ave
- **New Regal Theatre** • 1641 E 79th St
- **Oak Woods Cemetery** • 1035 E 67th St
- **Palmer Park** • 201 E 111th St
- **Peoples Gas South Chicago** • 8935 S Commercial Ave
- **Pullman Clock Tower** • 11141 S Cottage Grove Ave
- **Robert S Abbott Park** • 49 E 95th St
- **South Shore Cultural Center** • 7059 South Shore Dr
- **Trinity United Church of Christ** • 400 W 95th St
- **West Pullman Elementary** • 11941 S Parnell Ave
- **West Pullman Park** • 401 W 123rd St
- **Woodson Regional Public Library** • 3525 S Halsted St

Sundries/Entertainment

75th St is a hub of southside action: legendary Army & Lou's has served soul food to every civil rights leader you can imagine. Down the street, jazz legend Von Freeman jams at the New Apartment Lounge every Tuesday night. Lee's Unleaded Blues offers a truer Chicago blues experience than anything downtown or on the northside. South Shore's Jeffrey Pub offers a friendly haven for the southside's GLBTQ folks. South Deering received its 15 minutes of fame when the smoked fish offerings of Calumet Fisheries were featured on Anthony Bourdain's No Reservations.

Movie Theaters

- **ICE Chatham 14** • 210 87th St

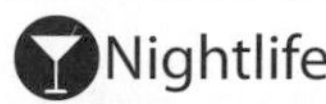

Nightlife

- **Artis Lounge** • 1249 E 87th St
- **Jeffrey Pub** • 7041 S Jeffery Blvd
- **Lee's Unleaded Blues** • 7401 S South Chicago Ave
- **New Apartment Lounge** • 504 E 75th St
- **Red Pepper's Masquerade Lounge** • 428 E 87th St
- **Reds** • 6926 S Stony Island Ave
- **Rockin' Horse** • 9942 S Torrence Ave

Restaurants

- **5 Loaves Eatery** • 405 E 75th St
- **Army & Lou's** • 422 E 75th St
- **Barbara Ann's BBQ** • 7617 S Cottage Grove Ave
- **BJ's Market & Bakery** • 8734 S Stony Island Ave
- **Café Trinidad** • 557 E 75th St
- **Cal Harbor Restaurant** • 546 E 115th St
- **Calumet Fisheries** • 3259 E 95th St
- **Capri Pizza** • 8820 S Commercial Ave
- **Captain's Hard Time** • 436 E 79th St
- **Daddy O Jerkpit** • 7518 S Cottage Grove Ave
- **Dat Old Fashioned Donut** • 8251 S Cottage Grove Ave
- **Desde Puerto Rico** • 8810 S Commercial Ave
- **Hand-Burgers** • 11322 S Halsted St
- **Heinie's Shrimp House** • 10359 S Torrence Ave
- **Helen's Restaurant** • 1732 E 79th St
- **Izola's** • 522 E 79th St
- **Jamaican Jerk Spice** • 6500 S Cottage Grove Ave
- **Lem's** • 311 E 75th St
- **Leon's Bar-B-Que** • 8249 S Cottage Grove Ave
- **Old Fashioned Donuts** • 11248 S Michigan Ave
- **The Parrot Cage** • 7059 S South Shore Dr
- **Phil's Kastle** • 3532 E 95th St
- **Pupuseria El Salvador** • 3557 E 106th St
- **Seven Seas Submarine** • 11216 S Michigan Ave
- **Soul Queen** • 9031 S Stony Island Ave
- **Soul Vegetarian East** • 205 E 75th St
- **Sunugal** • 2051 E 79th St
- **That's-A-Burger** • 2134 E 71st St
- **Three J's** • 1713 E 75th St
- **Uncle Joe's** • 8211 S Cottage Grove Ave
- **Uncle John's BBQ** • 339 E 69th St
- **Wings Around the World** • 510 E 75th St
- **Yassa African Restaurant** • 716 E 79th St

Shopping

- **A&G Fresh Market** • 5630 W Belmont Ave
- **African Hedonist** • 8501 S Cottage Grove Ave
- **Hagen's Fish Market** • 5635 W Montrose Ave
- **Halsted Indoor Mall** • 11444 S Halsted St
- **Hyman's Ace Hardware** • 8614 S Commercial Ave
- **Jordan's Beauty Supply** • 1911 E 79th St
- **K & G Fashion Superstore** • 7540 S Stony Island Ave
- **Underground Afrocentric Bookstore** • 1727 E 87th St

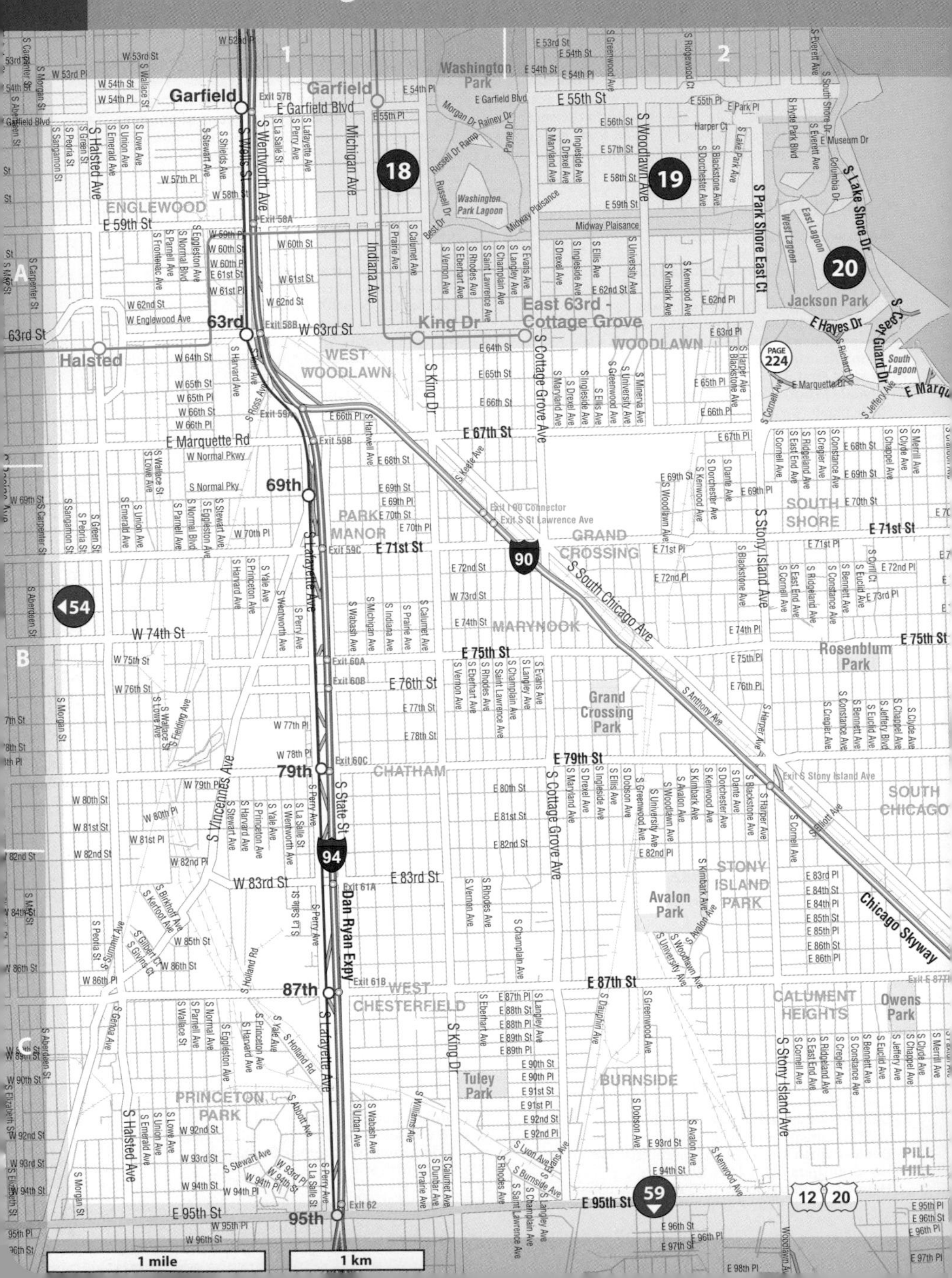
1
2
A
B
C
Garfield
Washington Park
Washington Park Lagoon
Midway Plaisance
E Garfield Blvd
E 55th St
Englewood
E 59th St
63rd
63rd St
Halsted
W 63rd St
King Dr
East 63rd - Cottage Grove
Woodlawn
West Woodlawn
Jackson Park
E Hayes Dr
S Lake Shore Dr
S Coast Guard Dr
South Lagoon
PAGE 224
18
19
20
69th
E Marquette Rd
E 67th St
Park Manor
E 71st St
Grand Crossing
South Shore
E 71st St
90
S South Chicago Ave
Marynook
W 74th St
E 75th St
Rosenblum Park
Grand Crossing Park
S Anthony Ave
79th
E 79th St
Chatham
South Chicago
S Stony Island Ave
S Cottage Grove Ave
S Vincennes Ave
S State St
94
Dan Ryan Expy
W 83rd St
E 83rd St
Avalon Park
Stony Island Park
Chicago Skyway
87th
E 87th St
West Chesterfield
Calument Heights
Owens Park
S Lafayette Ave
S King Dr
Tuley Park
Burnside
Princeton Park
S Halsted Ave
Pill Hill
E 95th St
W 95th St
95th
54
59
12
20
1 mile
1 km

3 4

A B C

Lake Michigan

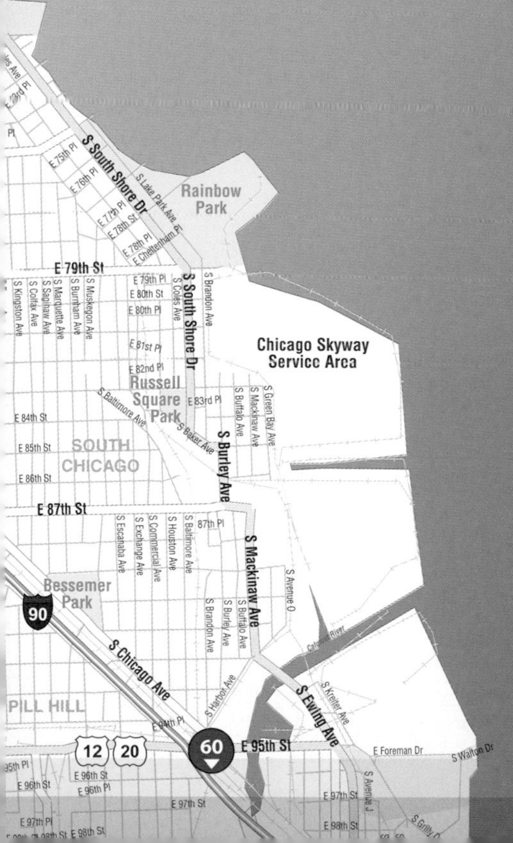

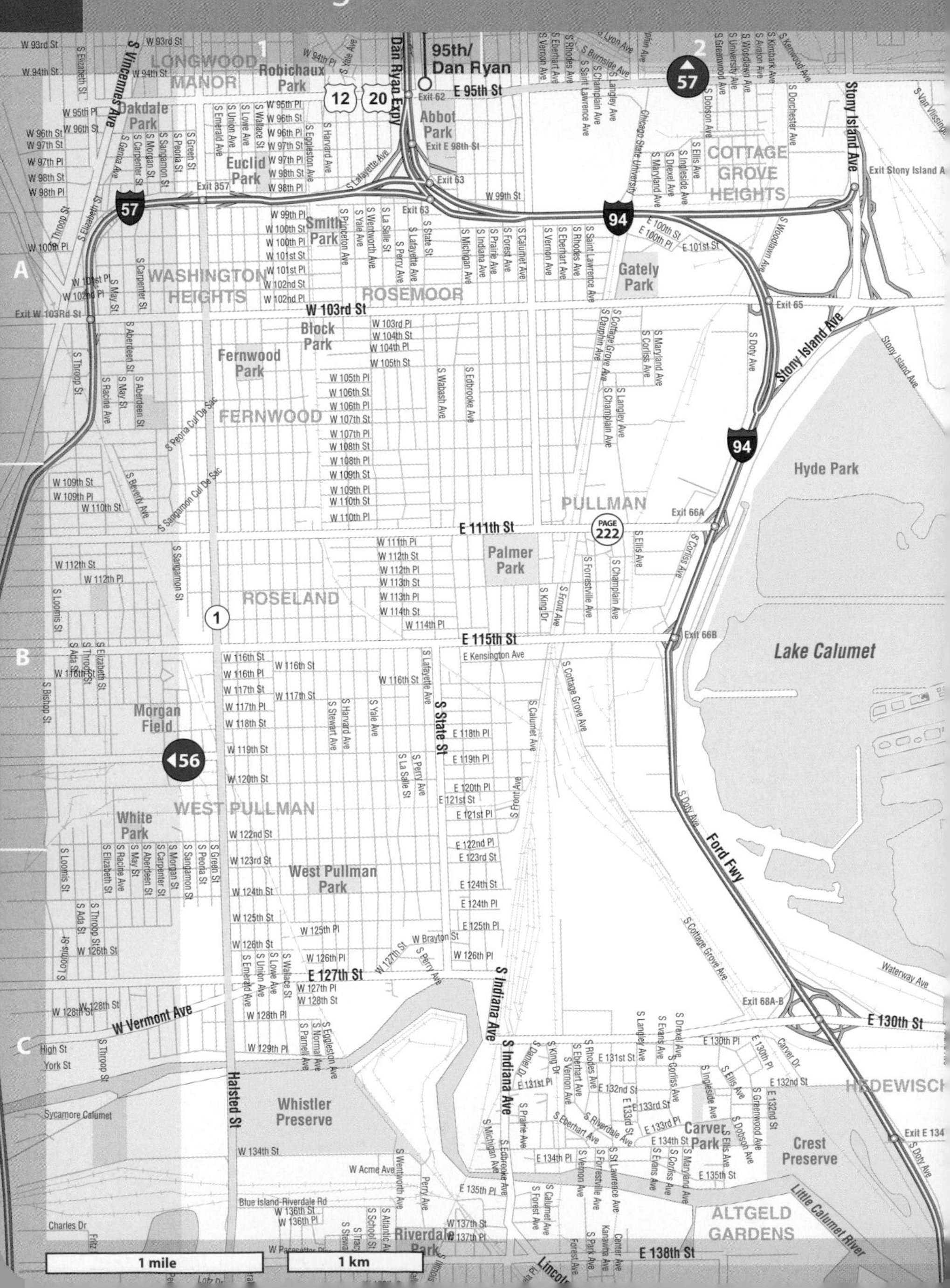
LONGWOOD MANOR
Robichaux Park
95th/ Dan Ryan
Dan Ryan Expy
E 95th St
Abbot Park
Oakdale Park
Euclid Park
COTTAGE GROVE HEIGHTS
Stony Island Ave
Smith Park
WASHINGTON HEIGHTS
ROSEMOOR
Gately Park
W 103rd St
Block Park
Fernwood Park
FERNWOOD
Hyde Park
PULLMAN
E 111th St
Palmer Park
ROSELAND
E 115th St
Lake Calumet
Morgan Field
S State St
WEST PULLMAN
White Park
West Pullman Park
Ford Fwy
E 127th St
W Vermont Ave
S Indiana Ave
E 130th St
Halsted St
Whistler Preserve
Carver Park
HEGEWISCH
Crest Preserve
ALTGELD GARDENS
Riverdale Park
E 138th St
Little Calumet River
1 mile
1 km
A
B
C
1
2

3
4
A
B
C
Lake Michigan
E 95th St
12
20
58
90
41
912
Chicago Skyway
Calumet Park
Veterans Memorial Park
Trumbull Park
JEFFERY MANOR
Wolfe Plg Park
SOUTH DEERING
Rowen Park
Eggers Woods
Calumet River
Forsyth Park
Wolf Lake Park
Wolf Lake
ILLINOIS
INDIANA
Mann Park
HEGEWISCH
Burnham Woods
Pulaski Park
S Indianapolis Ave
Calumet Ave
S Colfax Ave
S Torrence Ave
S Saginaw Ave
S Brainard Ave
S Avenue O
S Avenue L
S Ewing Ave
S Wolf Lake Blvd
E 100th St
E 103rd St
E 106th St
E 130th St
1 mile
1 km

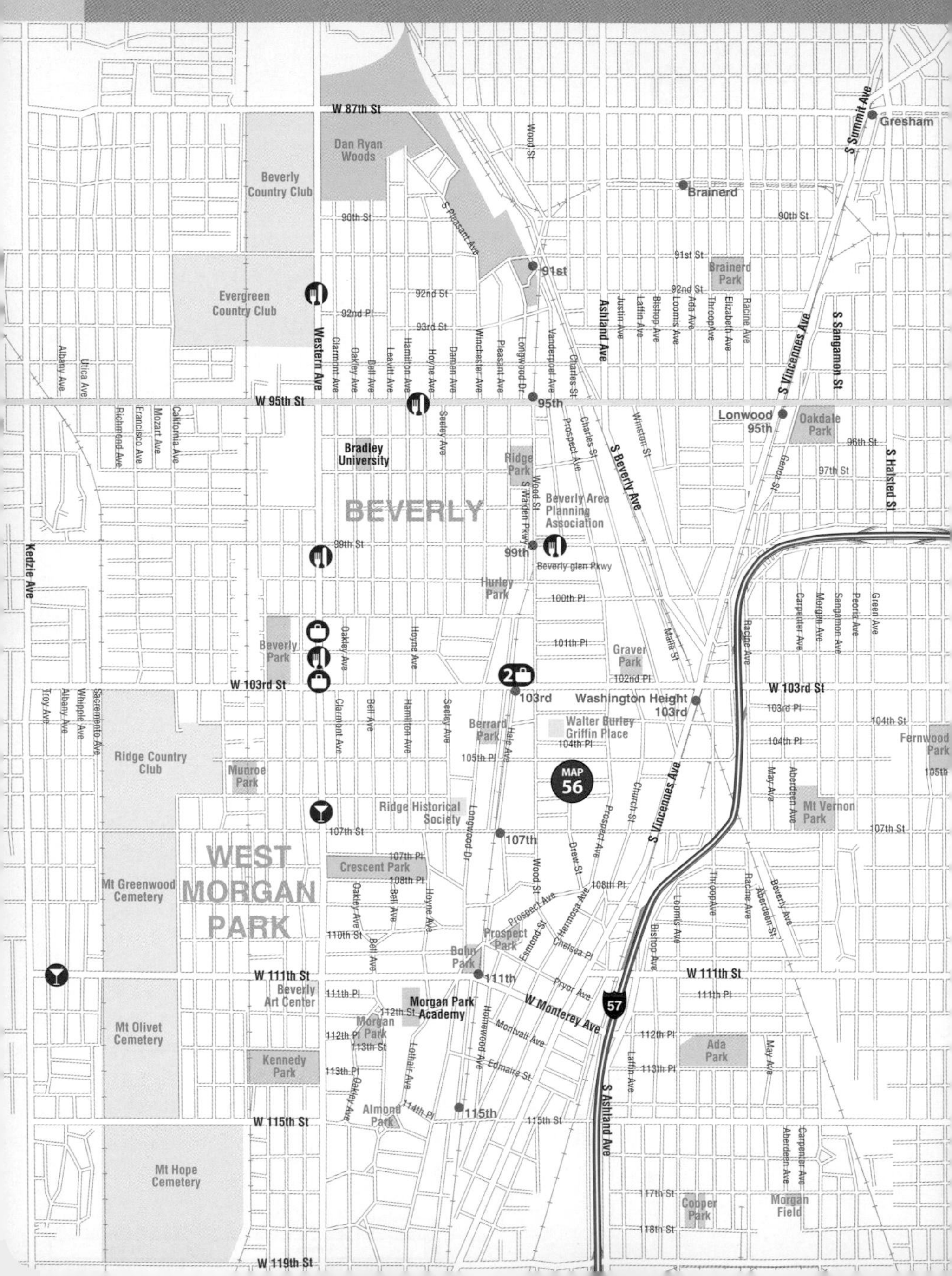

BEVERLY
WEST MORGAN PARK
Dan Ryan Woods
Beverly Country Club
Evergreen Country Club
Bradley University
Ridge Park
Beverly Area Planning Association
Hurley Park
Beverly Park
Graver Park
Washington Height 103rd
Walter Burley Griffin Place
Berrard Park
Ridge Country Club
Munroe Park
Ridge Historical Society
Crescent Park
Mt Greenwood Cemetery
Prospect Park
Bohn Park
Beverly Art Center
Morgan Park Academy
Morgan Park
Mt Olivet Cemetery
Kennedy Park
Almond Park
Mt Hope Cemetery
Brainerd
Brainerd Park
Gresham
Lonwood 95th
Oakdale Park
Fernwood Park
Mt Vernon Park
Ada Park
Cooper Park
Morgan Field
MAP 56
91st
95th
99th
103rd
107th
111th
115th
W 87th St
W 95th St
W 103rd St
W 111th St
W 115th St
W 119th St
Western Ave
Kedzie Ave
S Ashland Ave
S Vincennes Ave
S Beverly Ave
W Monterey Ave
S Halsted St
S Sangamon St
S Summit Ave
57

Overview

Beverly Hills, best known simply as Beverly, is the stronghold of Chicago's heralded "South Side Irish" community. An authentic medieval castle, baronial mansions, rolling hills, and plenty of pubs compose Chicago's Emerald Isle of 39,000 residents.

Once populated by Illinois and Potawatomi Indian tribes, Beverly became home to clans of Irish-American families after the Great Chicago Fire. Famous residents include Andrew Greeley, Brian Piccolo, George Wendt, the Schwinn Bicycle family, and decades of loyal Chicago civil servants.

Proud and protective of their turf, these close-knit South Siders call Beverly and its sister community, Morgan Park, "the Ridge." The integrated neighborhood occupies the highest ground in Chicago, 30 to 60 feet above the rest of the city atop Blue Island Ridge.

Although the Ridge is just 15 miles from the Loop, most North Siders would only trek there for the South Side Irish Parade, which attracted hundreds of thousands of people each year around St. Patrick's Day. Last year the parade committee decided the neighborhood could no longer handle the immense crowds (and drinkers) and decided to put the kibosh on 2010's parade.

But there is more than a 6-pack of reasons to visit Beverly. The Ridge Historic District is one of the country's largest urban areas on the National Register of Historic Places. Surprised, huh?

Architecture

Sadly, many Chicagoans are unaware of the rich architectural legacy on the city's far South Side. Beverly and Morgan Park encompass four landmark districts including the Ridge Historic District, three Chicago Landmark Districts, and over 30 Prairie-style structures.

Within approximately a nine-mile radius, from 87th Street to 115th Street and Prospect Avenue to Hoyne Avenue, one can view a vast collection of homes and public buildings representing American architectural styles developed between 1844 and World War II.

The 109th block of Prospect Avenue, every inch of Longwood Drive, and the Victorian train stations at 91st Street, 95th Street, 99th Street, 107th Street, 111th Street, and 115th Street are all great Chicago landmarks. Walter Burley Griffin Place on W 104th Street has Chicago's largest concentration of Prairie School houses built between 1909 and 1913 by Griffin, a student of Frank Lloyd Wright and designer of the city of Canberra in Australia.

Beverly Area Planning Association (BAPA) (11107 S Longwood Drive, 773-233-3100; www.bapa.org) provides a good architectural site map, plus events and shopping information for the district. History buffs might want to visit the Ridge Historical Society, open Tuesdays, Thursdays, and Sundays from 2 pm to 5 pm (10621 S Seeley Ave, 773-881-1675; www.ridgehistoricalsociety.org).

Culture & Events

The Beverly Arts Center is the epicenter of Ridge culture. The $8 million facility provides visual and performance art classes for all ages and hosts Chicago's only contemporary Irish film festival during the first week of March (2407 W 111th St, 773-445-3838; www.beverlyartcenter.org).

Historic Ridge homes open their doors to the public on the third Sunday of May for the annual Home Tour, Chicago's oldest such tour. Sites are chosen for their diverse architectural styles and historical significance. Tickets can be purchased through BAPA or the Beverly Arts Center for $25 in advance or $30 the day of the event. All tours depart from the Beverly Arts Center between the hours of 11 am and 5 pm; the last tour leaves at 3 pm, and homes close promptly at 5 pm. Guided trolley tours are also offered for an additional $4, departing every half hour between 11 am and 3pm. Contact BAPA at 773-233-3100 or www.bapa.org for more details.

Where to Eat

- **Café Luna**, 1742 W 99th St, 773-239-8990.
  Eclectic. Sink your teeth into their heart-healthy sandwiches and sinful desserts.
- **Franconello's**, 10222 S Western Ave, 773-881-4100.
  Italian. Perhaps the only pure Italians in Beverly making pasta dishes at this authentic Roma restaurant.
- **Janson's Drive-In**, 9900 S Western Ave, 773-238-3612.
  No indoor seating at this classic drive-thru.
- **Rainbow Cone**, 9233 S Western Ave, 773-238-7075.
  Ice cream. On summer nights more than 50 folks line up for sweet treats at this 76-year-old soda fountain.
- **Top Notch Beefburger**, 2116 W 95th St, 773-445-7218.
  Burgers really are top notch at this '50s-style grill.

Where to Drink

- **Lanigan's Irish Pub**, 3119 W 111th St, 773-233-4004.
  Anyone know where you can find a pint in Beverly? I've got quite a mean thirst.
- **Mrs. O'Leary's Dubliner**, 10910 S Western Ave, 773-238-0784. Affectionately known as the Dubliner, this is one of the many Irish pubs lining Western Avenue.

Where to Shop

- **Bev Art Brewer and Winemaker Supply**, 10033 S Western Ave, 773-233-7579.
  Everything you need to brew and bottle it yourself.
- **Calabria Imports**, 1905 W 103rd St, 773-396-5800.
  Imported Italian gourmet foodstuffs.
- **Optimo Hat Co**, 10215 S Western Ave, 773-238-2999.
  Custom made men's hats.
- **World Folk Music Company**, 1808 W 103rd St, 773-779-7059. Instruments, sheet music, and lessons for budding Guthries and Baezs.

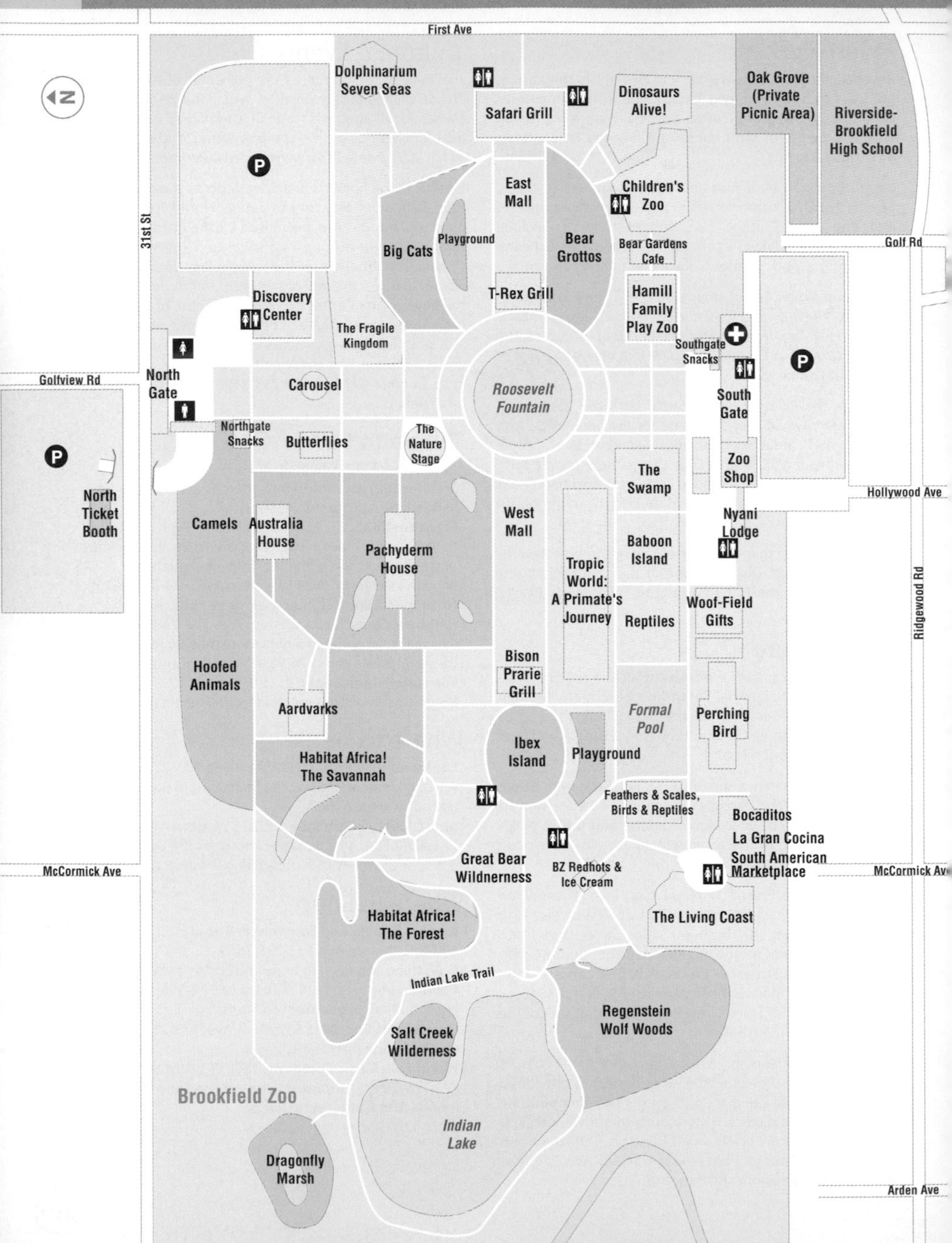

First Ave
Dolphinarium
Seven Seas
Safari Grill
Dinosaurs
Alive!
Oak Grove
(Private
Picnic Area)
Riverside-
Brookfield
High School
East
Mall
Children's
Zoo
Bear
Grottos
Bear Gardens
Cafe
Golf Rd
31st St
Big Cats
Playground
T-Rex Grill
Hamill
Family
Play Zoo
Discovery
Center
The Fragile
Kingdom
Southgate
Snacks
Golfview Rd
North
Gate
Carousel
Roosevelt
Fountain
South
Gate
Northgate
Snacks
Butterflies
The
Nature
Stage
Zoo
Shop
The
Swamp
Hollywood Ave
North
Ticket
Booth
Camels
Australia
House
Pachyderm
House
West
Mall
Nyani
Lodge
Tropic
World:
A Primate's
Journey
Baboon
Island
Reptiles
Woof-Field
Gifts
Ridgewood Rd
Hoofed
Animals
Bison
Prarie
Grill
Aardvarks
Formal
Pool
Perching
Bird
Ibex
Island
Playground
Habitat Africa!
The Savannah
Feathers & Scales,
Birds & Reptiles
Bocaditos
La Gran Cocina
South American
Marketplace
McCormick Ave
Great Bear
Wildnerness
BZ Redhots &
Ice Cream
Habitat Africa!
The Forest
The Living Coast
Indian Lake Trail
Regenstein
Wolf Woods
Salt Creek
Wilderness
Brookfield Zoo
Indian
Lake
Dragonfly
Marsh
Arden Ave

General Information

Address: 31st St & First Ave
Brookfield, IL 60513
Phone: 708-688-8000
Website: www.brookfieldzoo.org
Hours: Open daily from 10 am-5 pm, and until 6 pm daily and 7:30 on Sundays from Memorial Day to Labor Day.
Admission: $13.50 adults, $9.50 children 3-11, seniors over 65, free for children two and under

Overview

While Lincoln Park Zoo is free, Brookfield offers a far more comprehensive wild animal experience with a strong emphasis on conservation education. 216 acres of creepy critters make for a memorable day trip. We'll skip the analogy with the Joliet Riverboat Casino.

Hamill Family Play Zoo

This interactive play area is part of a program to create a huge new wing of the zoo dedicated solely to kids. Great—just what a zoo needs: more kids. Children get to interact in a variety of ways, including donning costumes to play "zoo keeper" or "ring-tailed lemur," creating and frolicking in their own simulated habitats, planting seeds in the greenhouse, or spotting creepy insects in the outdoor bug path. Think a grownup would look silly dressed like a lemur? We want to play! Admission $3.50 adults, $2.50 children 3-11, seniors over 65, free for children two and under.

Regenstein Wolf Woods

The zoo's impressive wolf exhibit allows visitors to follow the progress of a small pack of endangered male wolves as they do the wolfy things wolves do. One-way glass allows spectators to get up close and personal with the wolves without freaking them out. So far, the mirrors have been 100% unsuccessful in detecting any wolf shoplifting.

Other Exhibits

Of course the zoo is full of exhibits, some more fascinating than others. Among them are the seasonal butterfly exhibit and the dragonfly marsh. Here are some other worthwhile sights:

- **Habitat Africa**: This is broken up into two sections: The Rainforest, with its zebras and African millipedes (heebie-jeebies), and The Savannah, with our favorite, the giraffes.
- **Dolphinarium**: Dolphin shows are scheduled at regular intervals two or three times a day (sometimes more during peak seasons and on weekends).
- **Tropic World**: Visit Kamba, the baby gorilla born in front of a captivated, slightly disgusted crowd of zoo visitors (mother Koola now knows how Marie Antoinette felt when she shared the delivery of her offspring with the French peasantry) and Bakari, the newest addition to the Gorilla family, who was born to mother Binto in May '05.
- **Baboon Island**: Always a fun adventure, if for no other reason than to ogle certain colorful aspects of this animal's anatomy which we won't name (but it rhymes with "class," which we clearly don't have).
- **Bear Grottos**: Consider yourself lucky if you get a glimpse of these fascinating animals; this exhibit has unusual hours and is often unavailable.
- **Feathers and Scales: Birds and Reptiles**: We're pretty sure there are bats in there, but we've blocked the traumatic memory from our unstable minds. Enter at your own risk.

Eating at the Zoo

- **La Gran Cocina**: At the South American Marketplace. Walk-up stir-fry, chicken, pizza, and fruit.
- **Safari Grill**: Near the Seven Seas Exhibit. Burgers, pizza, sandwiches, salads, and ice cream.
- **Bison Prairie Grill**: Large restaurant on the West Mall. Grilled meat sandwiches, snacks, and sweets, plus margaritas and beer. Indoor and outdoor seating available.
- **North Gate Snack Shop and South Gate Snack Shop**: Hot dogs, subs, and ice cream located at the north and south gates.
- **Elephant Snacks**: Hot dog stand near the Pachyderm House.
- **Bear Gardens Café**: Watch bears watch you eat at this sandwich and pizza shop.
- **Nyani Lodge**: If watching monkeys throw feces at each other is your idea of a good dinnertime show, definitely check this place out.

How to Get There

By Car: From the Eisenhower or Stevens Expressway, exit at First Avenue. From there, signs will direct you the short distance to the zoo. Lot parking is $8.

By Train: From downtown Chicago, take the Burlington Northern Metra line to Zoo Stop/Hollywood Station.

By Bus: Pace buses 304 and 331 stop right at the zoo's gates.

If you're coming in from out of town, consider staying at a Holiday Inn, Doubletree Hotel, Country Inn & Suites, or Best Western all of which offer Brookfield Zoo packages, which include admission to Brookfield Zoo, admission to the Dolphin Show, admission to the Children's Zoo, 1 parking pass, and coupons for restaurants and gift shops. Details and booking information can be found on Brookfield Zoo's website, www.brookfieldzoo.org.

Marquette Rd
Hastings Ave
Main Entrance
Botanic Garden Center
Lake Cook Rd
Children's Learning Center
P
N
Chicago Botanic Garden
Bird Island
Fruit & Vegetable Garden
Gateway Visitor Center
McDonald Woods
The Crescent
Bulb Garden
Native Plant Garden
The Esplanade
Heritage Garden
Aquatic Garden
Landscape Garden
Rose Garden
Model Railroad Garden
Education Center
Dwarf Conifer
English Oak Meadow
Japanese Garden
Arbor House
Circle Garden
The Greenhouses
English Walled Garden
Waterfall Garden
Spider Land
Enabling Garden
McGinley Pavilion
Shroin House
Water Gardens
Lakeside Gardens
Skokie River
Sensory Garden
Great Basin
41
Carillon
Evening Island
Edens Expy
Edens Expy
Sun Evaluation Garden
Skokie Blvd
Marsh Island
Glencoe Golf Club
Prairie
Henrici Dr
94
Outdoor Classroom
Prairie
Children's Garden
Share Evaluation Garden
33
34

General Information

Address: 1000 Lake Cook Rd,
Glencoe, IL 60022
Phone: 847-835-5440
Website: www.chicagobotanic.org
Hours: Open 364 days, 8 am to sunset; closed Dec. 25
Admission: Free

Overview

Occupying 385 acres, the serene and lovely Chicago Botanic Garden has been the backdrop for many a chi-chi wedding since they opened the gates in 1972. Both the Ikebana Society and Macy's sponsor flower shows throughout the year; check the events schedule at www.chicagobotanic.org to see what's going on when you're visiting. The Chicago Botanic Garden also offers lifestyle/wellness classes, including yoga and tai chi. Availability and times vary, so check the website or call for more information.

Nature

Twenty-three gardens and three prairie habitats make up the Botanic Garden. Among them are a specialized Japanese garden, a rose garden, a bulb garden, a greenhouse full of tropical vegetation, a waterfall garden, and several beds solely dedicated to Indigenous plants and flowers.

Where to Eat

• **Garden Café:** Serves breakfast and café fare—salads, sandwiches, beer, and wine. Wifi enabled. Open 8 am–5 pm weekdays, 8 am–5:30 pm weekends, and open to 7 pm on Carillion Concert Mondays.

• **Garden Grille:** Grill being the operative word, serves burgers, dogs, and the like. Open from June to early September, 11am –3pm and 5pm–8 pm, featuring a barbeque buffet and beer garden.

• **Rose Terrace Café:** Enjoy a beverage overlooking the roses. Open from June to early September, 11am–5pm.

Note: Picnicking allowed in designated areas only.

How to Get There

By Car: Take I-90/94 W (The Kennedy) to I-94 (The Edens) and US 41. Exit on Lake Cook Road, then go a half-mile east to the garden. Parking costs $20 per car, $7 for seniors on Tuesdays.

By Train: Take the Union Pacific North Line to Braeside Metra station in Highland Park. Walk west about one mile along Lake Cook Road (aka County Line Road). If you ride the train to the Glencoe station, you can take a trolley directly to the garden. Round-trip tickets cost $2, free for children five and under.

By Bus: The Pace bus 213 connects at Davis Street in Evanston, and the Park Avenue Glencoe and Central Street Highland Park Metra stops. Buses don't run on Sundays and holidays.

By Bicycle: The Chicago Bikeway System winds through the forest preserves all the way up to the garden. Join it near the Billy Caldwell Golf Club at 6200 N Caldwell. A bicycle map is available on the Botanic Garden website.

Where to Stay

You can make an excursion of your visit to Ravinia and/or the Botanic Garden by booking a room at: **Renaissance Chicago North Shore** (933 Skokie Blvd, Northbrook, 847-498-6500); **Residence Inn Chicago** (530 Lake Cook Rd, Deerfield, 847-940-4644); **Hyatt Deerfield** (1750 Lake Cook Rd, 847-945-3400); **Highland Park Courtyard** (1505 Lake Cook Rd, 847-831-3338).

Ravinia Festival

Address: 200 Ravinia Park Rd,
Highland Park, IL 60035
Phone: 847-266-5100
Website: www.ravinia.org
Hours: June through mid-September,
gates open three hours before concert time

Overview

Not to be outdone, the adjoining Ravinia Festival, the nation's oldest outdoor concert venue, has been hosting classical music concerts since 1904. The summer home of the CSO, Ravinia eventually added pop and jazz to their bill, including such notables as Janis Joplin, Aretha Franklin (a Ravinia regular), k.d. lang, Tony Bennett (also a regular), as well as top names from opera and world music.

The Pavilion—Those who are serious about the music experience pay a premium for one of the 3,200 seats in this covered, open-air pavilion, affording them a view of the stage and better acoustics.

The Lawn—Although you can't see the stage, great outdoor acoustics bring the concert to you on the lawn, where blanket rights come cheap—typically $10 a pop. Just add picnic.

The Martin Theatre—The only remaining building original to the Festival, the 1904 Martin Theatre now hosts Martinis at the Martin, a cabaret series celebrating the Great American Songbook.

Eating at Ravinia

Ravinia is well known for lawn picnickers who compete to outdo each other with elaborate spreads, including roll-up tables, table linens, candelabras, champagne, and caviar. For those less ambitious, Ravinia offers take-out sandwiches and picnic fare at The Gatehouse, ice cream and other sweet treats at Carousel Ice Cream Shop, or you can make reservations to eat in at their fine-dining restaurant, Mirabelle. Ravinia Market offers eclectic food, from grilled skewers to brick-oven pizzas. The Park View and Mirabelle restaurants offer full-service dining options before the show. Wine, beer, and soft drinks are also available at concession stands throughout the park.

How to Get There

By Car: I-94 and I-294 have marked exits for Ravinia. Skip traffic back-ups on Lake Cook Road by exiting at Deerfield, Central, or Clavey Roads, and following directions to Park and Ride lots, which offer free parking and shuttle buses to Ravinia. The West Lot, Ravinia's closest parking spot, costs $15–$25 for parking and fills up early for the most popular concerts.

By Train: During festival season, the Union Pacific North Line offers the "Ravinia Special." For $7 round-trip, the train departs Madison and Canal at 5:50 pm, with stops at Clybourn, Ravenswood, Rogers Park, and Evanston, arriving at the Ravinia gates at 6:30 pm, and departing for the city 15 minutes after the concert's end.

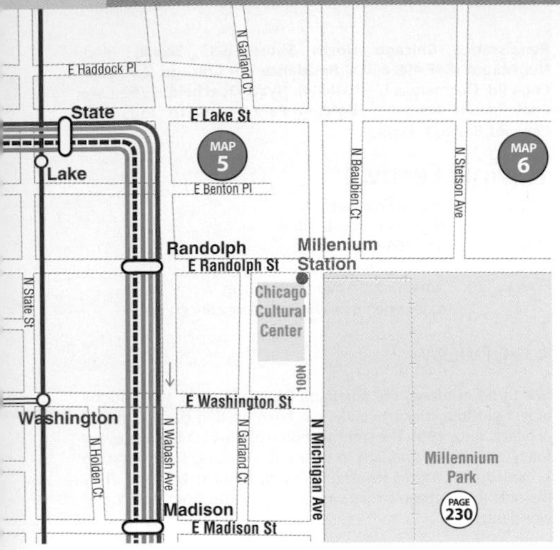

General Information

NFT Maps: 5, 6
Address: 78 E Washington St
Chicago, IL 60602
Phone: 312-744-6630
Website: www.chicagoculturalcenter.org
Hours: Mon–Thurs 8 am–7 pm, Fri 8 am–6 pm,
Sat 9 am–6 pm, Sun 10 am–6 pm,
and closed on holidays

Overview

The Chicago Cultural Center is the Loop's public arts center. Free—that's right, we said FREE—concerts, theatrical performances, films, lectures, and exhibits are offered daily. Admission to the Cultural Center and its art galleries are all free, too. Call 312-FINE ART (312-346-3278) for weekly event updates.

The building itself, constructed in 1897, is a neoclassical landmark featuring intricate glass and marble mosaics on its walls and grand stairways. Once the city's central public library, the Cultural Center boasts the world's largest Tiffany dome in Preston Bradley Hall. Free (there's that lovely word again) 45-minute architectural tours are held on Wednesdays, Fridays, and Saturdays at 1:15 pm. If you're interested in a guided group tour highlighting the building's history, call 312-744-8032 for more information. The building is also home to the Chicago Greeter Program, which allows visitors the opportunity to take a 2–3 hour walking tour with a chatty and knowledgeable guide around one of any number of neighborhoods throughout the city. Interested parties must book in advance at www.chicagogreeter.com. Surprise, surprise: it's free, as well.

Performances

The Cultural Center's free "LunchBreak" series provides downtown working stiffs with a welcome midday respite every weekday at 12:15pm.

Mondays: Classical Mondays featuring classical, chamber music and opera; in Preston Bradley Hall.

Tuesdays: Jazz, Blues and Beyond in Randolph Cafe.

Wednesdays: Dame Myra Hess Memorial Concerts featuring solo and ensemble performances of classical music showcasing young performers; in Preston Bradley Hall.

Thursdays: Daily Blend featuring acoustic pop, folk, country, and bluegrass; in Randolph Cafe.

Fridays: Music Without Borders featuring international music from around the globe; in Randolph Café.

Sunday Salon Series: Sundays, 3pm, Preston Bradley Hall. These weekly performances include long-time Chicago Cultural Center favorites, such as the Chicago chamber Orchestra, Classical Symphony Orchestra and the Protégé Philharmonic.

Call 312-FINE ART (312-346-3278) for information on frequently scheduled special programs.

Off-Loop theater productions appear regularly in the Center's Studio Theater, including the seasonal ShawChicago series featuring plays by Bernard Shaw on Saturdays, Sundays, and Mondays. Performances are free, but reservations are required (312-409-5605; www.shawchicago.org).

Art Galleries

A permanent exhibit in the Landmark Gallery, Chicago Landmarks Before the Lens is a stunning black-and-white photographic survey of Chicago architecture. Five additional galleries regularly rotate exhibits, showcasing work in many media by renowned and local artists. Tours of current exhibits are ongoing.

How to Get There

By Car: Travel down Michigan Avenue to Randolph Street. From Lake Shore Drive, exit at Randolph Street. For parking garages in the area, see Map 6.

By Train: From the Richard B. Ogilvie Transportation Center, travel east to Michigan Avenue on CTA buses 20, 56, 127, and 157. From Union Station, take CTA buses 60, 151, and 157 ($2.25, $2 with Chicago Card). From the Randolph Street station below Millennium Park, walk west across Michigan Avenue. For schedules contact the RTA Information Center (312-836-7000; www.rtachicago.com).

By L: Take the Green, Brown, Orange, Purple, or Pink Line to the Randolph stop ($2.25, $1.75 with Chicago Card). Walk east one block.

By Bus: CTA buses : 3, 145, 147, 151 stop on Michigan Avenue in front of the Cultural Center ($2.25, $2 with Chicago Card).

General Information

NFT Map: 5
Address: 400 S State St
Chicago, IL 60605
Phone: 312-747-4300
Website: www.chipublib.org

Overview

Harold Washington Library Center is the world's largest public library. Named after Chicago's first African-American mayor, the 756,640-square-foot neoclassical architectural monstrosity has over 70 miles of shelves storing more than 9 million books, microforms, serials, and government documents. Notable works of sculpture, painting, and mosaics liven up the building's ample wall space and open areas.

Harold Washington's popular library, containing current general titles and bestsellers, is easy to find on the ground floor. The library's audio-visual collection (including an impressive collection of books on tape as well as videos, DVDs, and popular music CDs) is also housed here. The second floor is home to the children's library, and the general reference library begins on the third floor where the circulation desks are located. Among the notable features of the library is the eighth floor Music Information Center housing sheet music and printed scores, 150,000 recordings, the Chicago Blues Archives, eight individual piano practice rooms, and a chamber music rehearsal room. The ninth floor Winter Garden, with its olive trees and soaring 100-foot high ceilings is a popular site for special events. If you have your sights set on getting hitched here, leave your priest or rabbi at home—the library's status as a civic building precludes religious services on its premises.

Frequent free public programs are held in the lower level's 385 seat auditorium, video theater, exhibit hall, and meeting rooms. Call 312-747-4649 for information on scheduled events. Additionally, the website houses a bbs (bulletin board system) for those participating in Chicago's "One City, One Book" reading club who want to discuss the latest selection.

Library hours are Monday through Thursday 9 am to 9 pm, Friday and Saturday 9 am to 5 pm, and Sunday 1 pm to 5 pm.

Research Services

To check the availability or location of an item, call Catalog Information at 312-747-4340 or search the library's Online Catalog on www.chipublib.org. Their Email Reference Service responds to information requests within two days. For faster answers to common research questions, check out the website's handy Virtual Library Service under Selected Internet Resources, then click on "Reference Shelf."

Computer Services

The Chicago Public Library's High Speed Wireless Internet System provides free access; all you need is a wireless enabled laptop computer, tablet PC, or PDA. The Library's network is open to all visitors free of charge and without filters. No special encryption settings, user names, or passwords are required.

The library's 96 computers with Internet access and 37 more with word processing, desktop publishing, graphic presentation, and spreadsheet applications are located on the third floor in the Computer Commons. Computer use is free and available on a first-come-first-served basis. You can reserve computers online and for up to one hour per day based on walk-in availability. For downloads, bring your own formatted disk or purchase one at the library for $2. Laser printing is also provided for 15 cents a page. Operating hours are Monday through Thursday 9 am–8:30 pm, Friday and Saturday 9 am–4:30 pm, and Sunday 1 pm–4:30 pm.

Thomas Hughes Children's Library

The 18,000-square-foot Thomas Hughes Children's Library on the second floor serves children through age 14. A British citizen and member of Parliament, Thomas Hughes was so taken by news of the tragic Chicago Fire that he started a book collection for Chicago. His collection resulted in the 8,000 titles that composed the first Chicago Public Library. In addition to more than 120,000 children's books representing 40 foreign languages, there is a reference collection on children's literature for adults. Twenty free computers, twelve with Internet connections, are also available. Children's programs are hosted weekly (312-747-4200).

Special Collections

The library's Special Collections & Preservation Division's highlights include: Harold Washington Collection, Civil War & American History Research Collection, Chicago Authors & Publishing Collection, Chicago Blues Archives, Chicago Theater Collection, World's Columbian Exposition Collection, and Neighborhood History Research Collection. The collections' reading room is closed Sunday.

How to Get There

By Car: The library is at the intersection of State Street and Congress Parkway in South Loop. Take I-290 E into the Loop. See Map 5 for area parking garages.

By L: The Brown, Purple, Orange, and Pink Lines stop at the Library Station. Exit the Red Line and O'Hare Airport Blue Line at Van Buren Station; walk one block south. Change from the Harlem/Lake Street Green Line to the northbound Orange Line at Roosevelt Road station; get off at Library Station ($2.25, $2.00 with chicago Card).

By Bus: CTA buses that stop on State Street in front of the library are the 2, 6, 29, 36, 62, 151, 145, 146, and 147.

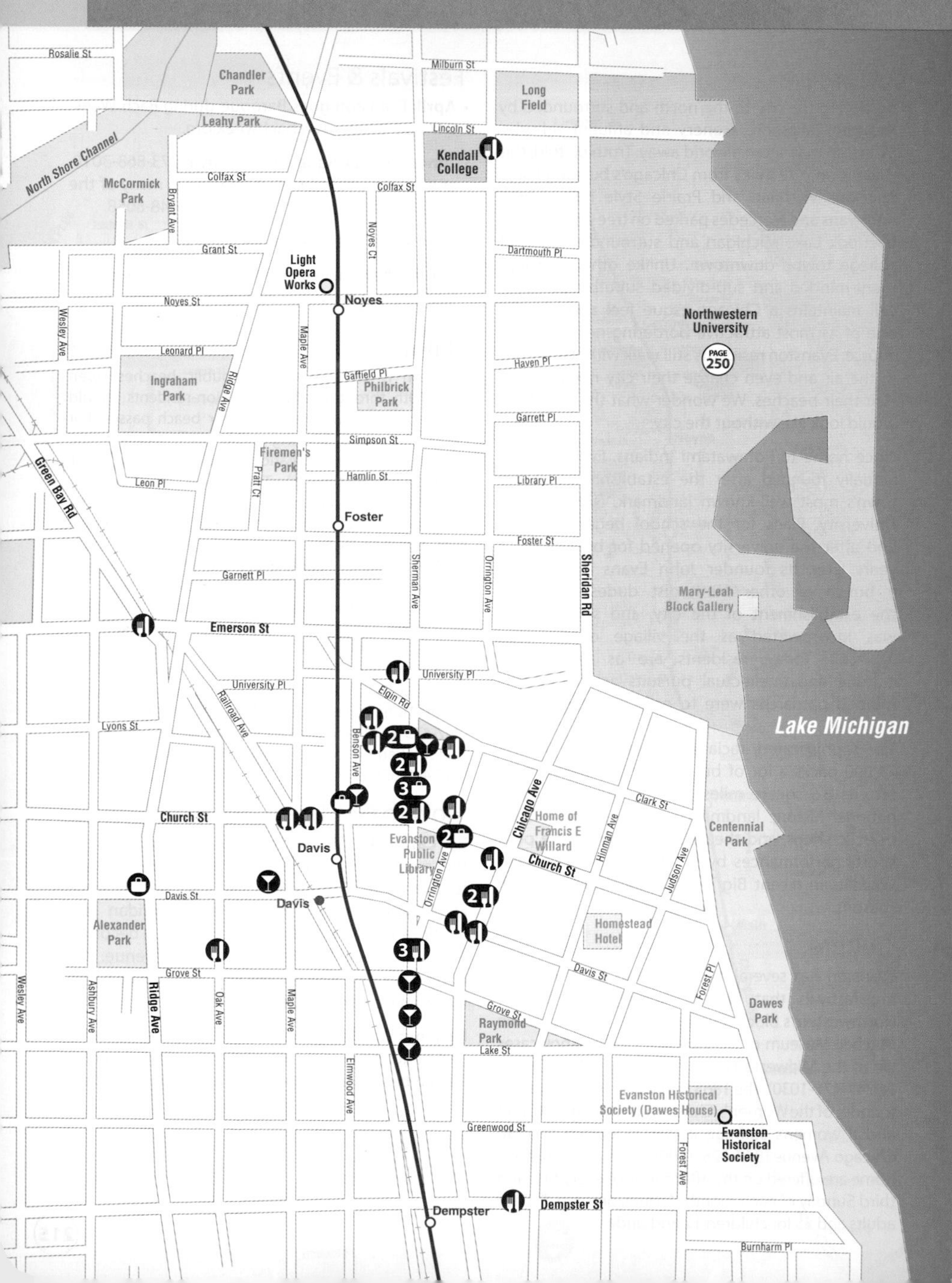

Rosalie St
Chandler Park
Milburn St
Long Field
Leahy Park
North Shore Channel
Lincoln St
Kendall College
McCormick Park
Colfax St
Colfax St
Bryant Ave
Noyes Ct
Grant St
Dartmouth Pl
Light Opera Works
Noyes St
Noyes
Northwestern University
PAGE 250
Wesley Ave
Leonard Pl
Maple Ave
Haven Pl
Ingraham Park
Ridge Ave
Garfield Pl
Philbrick Park
Garrett Pl
Simpson St
Green Bay Rd
Firemen's Park
Hamlin St
Leon Pl
Pratt Ct
Library Pl
Foster
Foster St
Sherman Ave
Orrington Ave
Sheridan Rd
Garnett Pl
Mary-Leah Block Gallery
Emerson St
University Pl
University Pl
Elgin Rd
Railroad Ave
Lyons St
Lake Michigan
Benson Ave
Chicago Ave
Clark St
Church St
Home of Francis E Willard
Hinman Ave
Centennial Park
Davis
Evanston Public Library
Church St
Orrington Ave
Judson Ave
Davis St
Davis
Alexander Park
Homestead Hotel
Davis St
Forest Pl
Grove St
Dawes Park
Wesley Ave
Ashbury Ave
Ridge Ave
Oak Ave
Maple Ave
Grove St
Raymond Park
Lake St
Elmwood Ave
Evanston Historical Society (Dawes House)
Greenwood St
Evanston Historical Society
Forest Ave
Dempster
Dempster St
Burnharm Pl

By Train: Metra's Union Pacific North Line departing from the Richard B. Ogilvie Transportation Center in West Loop stops at the downtown Davis Street CTA Center station, 25 minutes from the Loop ($3.05 one-way). This station is the town transportation hub, where Metra and L trains and buses interconnect. For all Metra, L, and CTA bus schedules, call 312-836-7000; www.rtachicago.com.

By L: The CTA Purple Line Express L train travels direct to and from the Loop during rush hours ($2.25, $2.00 with Chicago Card). Other hours, ride the Howard-Dan Ryan Red Line to Howard Street, and transfer to the Purple Line for free.

By Bus: From Chicago's Howard Street Station, CTA and Pace Suburban buses service Evanston ($2.25 via CTA, $1.75 via Pace).

Additional Information

Chicago's North Shore Convention & Visitors Bureau 866-369-0011; www.visitchicagonorthshore.com

Evanston Public Library, 1703 Orrington Ave, 847-448-8600; www.epl.org

o Landmarks

- **Evanston Historical Society** • 225 Greenwood St
- **Light Opera Works** • 927 Noyles St

Nightlife

- **1800 Club** • 1800 Sherman Ave
- **Bill's Blues Bar** • 1029 Davis St
- **Keg of Evanston** • 810 Grove St
- **Prairie Moon** • 1502 Sherman Ave
- **The Stained Glass Wine Bar** • 1735 Benson Ave
- **Tommy Nevin's Pub** • 1450 Sherman Ave

Restaurants

- **Blind Faith Café** • 525 Dempster St
- **Buffalo Joe's** • 812 Clark St
- **Café Mozart** • 600 Davis St
- **Clarke's** • 720 Clark St
- **Dave's Italian Kitchen** • 1635 Chicago Ave
- **Dixie Kitchen and Bait Shop** • 825 Church St
- **Dozika** • 601 Dempster St
- **Hecky's Barbeque** • 1902 Green Bay Rd
- **Joy Yee's Noodle Shop** • 521 Davis St
- **Kafein Café** • 1621 Chicago Ave
- **Kansaku** • 1514 Sherman Ave
- **Las Palmas** • 817 University Pl
- **Lulu's Dim Sum and Then Sum** • 804 Davis St
- **Mt Everest** • 630 Church St
- **Noodles & Company** • 930 Church St
- **Olive Mountain** • 610 Davis St
- **Pete Miller's Original Steakhouse** • 1557 Sherman Ave
- **Tapas Barcelona** • 1615 Chicago Ave
- **Trattoria Demi** • 1571 Sherman Ave
- **Unicorn Café** • 1723 Sherman Ave
- **Va Pensiero** • Margarita Inn• 1566 Oak Ave

Shopping

- **Art + Science Hair Salon** • 811 Church St
- **Asinamali Women's Boutique** • 1722 Sherman Ave
- **Bookman's Alley** • 1712 Sherman Ave
- **Campus Gear** • 1717 Sherman Ave
- **Coucou** • 1716 Sherman Ave
- **Ethical Planet** • 1110 Davis St
- **Uncle Dan's Great Outdoors** • 700 Church St
- **William's Shoes** • 710 Church St

W Kinzie St
Carroll Dr
W Carroll Ave
W Fulton St
Garfield Park Conservatory
N Avers Ave
N Central Park Ave
N St Louis Ave
N Homan Ave
W Fulton Blvd
Conservatory Dr
Pulaski
Gold Dome Building
Conservatory Central Park Drive
W Walnut St
N Pulaski Rd
N Harding Ave
W Lake St
N Hamilton Ave
W Maypole Ave
Kedzie
W Maypole Ave
W West End St
N McCrea Dr
Lagoon
W Washington Blvd
Garfield
MAP 49
W Washington Blvd
Warren Dr
W Warren Ave
Park
W Madison St
S Pulaski Rd
S Springfield Ave
S Hamilton Blvd
S Woodward Dr
S Central Park Ave
S St Louis Ave
S Homan Ave
S Spaulding Ave
W Monroe St
Cusic Ct
W Monroe St
W Wilcox Ave
W Adams Ave
Tennis Courts
W Adams St
W Jackson Blvd
W Jackson Blvd
Independence Blvd
S Christiana Ave
S Trumbull Ave
W Gladys Ave
W Van Buron St
W Fifth Ave
W Gladys Ave
S Millard Ave
Pulaski
W Congress Pkwy
290
Dwight D Eisenhower Expy
W Harrison St

Overview

For a century now, the historic West Side has been home to an equally historic botanical gem—Garfield Park Conservatory. The mid 1990s saw major restoration efforts, along with the creation of The Garfield Park Conservatory Alliance, an organization that has raised money for various programs involving the Conservatory. The rest of the vast 185-acre park boasts fishing lagoons, a swimming pool, an ice rink, baseball diamonds, and basketball and tennis courts. Garfield Park's landmark Gold Dome Building houses a fitness center, a basketball court, and the Peace Museum.

Garfield and its sister parks—Humboldt Park (1400 N Sacramento Ave, 312-742-7549) and Douglas Park (1401 S Sacramento Ave, 773-762-2842)—constitute a grand system of sprawling green spaces linked by broad boulevards designed in 1869 by William Le Baron Jenney (better known as the "father of the skyscraper"). However, Jenney's plan didn't bear fruit until almost 40 years later (after the uprooting of corrupt park officials), when Danish immigrant and former park laborer Jens Jensen became chief landscape architect. In 1908, Jensen completed the parks and consolidated their three small conservatories under the 1.8-acre Garfield Park Conservatory's curvaceous glass dome, designed to resemble a "great Midwestern haystack."

Garfield Park Conservatory

Address:	300 N Central Park Ave Chicago, IL 60624
Phone:	773-746-5100
Website:	www.garfield-conservatory.org
Hours:	9 am–5 pm daily; Wed: 9 am–8 pm
Admission:	FREE

One of the nation's largest conservatories, Garfield Park has six thematic plant houses with 1,000 species and more than 10,000 individual plants from around the world. Plants Alive!, a 5,000-square-foot children's garden, has touchable plants, a soil pool for digging, a Jurassic Park–sized bumble bee, and a two-story, twisting flower stem that doubles as a slide. School groups often book the garden for field trips, so call first to determine public access hours. Annual Conservatory events include the Spring Flower Show, Azalea/Camellia Show, Chocolate Festival, Summer Tropical Show, Chrysanthemum (Chicago's city flower) Show, and Holiday Garden Show. Call for program scheduling. Every weekend, seasonally, visitors can browse the open air Garfield Market featuring crafts, plants, and produce. There is a farmer's market at the park on Saturday mornings from June through October.

Fishing

Garfield Park's two lagoons at Washington Boulevard and Central Park Avenue and those at Douglas and Humboldt Parks are favorite West Side fishing holes. Seasonally, they are stocked with bluegill, crappie, channel catfish, and largemouth bass, along with an occasional unfortunate gang member. The fish here is perfect for those who need a little pollution with their protein. Kids can take free fishing classes at the park lagoons during the summer through the Chicago Park District (312-747-PLAY). Groups of ten kids or more fish every day of the week at a new location. You'll have to call in advance, as groups are organized by appointment only. The program runs June 20–August 12, Mon–Fri, between 10 am and 4 pm.

Nature

The Chicago Park District leads free nature walks and has created marked trails with information plaques at the city's bigger parks, Garfield, Douglas, and Humboldt Parks included. Seasonally, visitors can view as many as 100 species of colorful butterflies at the formal gardens of the three parks. The parks' lagoons are officially designated Chicago "birding parks," so take binoculars. Picnics for 50 people or more, or tent set-up, require party-throwers to obtain permits issued by the Chicago Park District.

How to Get There

By Car: Garfield Park is ten minutes from the Loop. Take I-290 W; exit on Independence Boulevard and drive north. Turn east on Washington Boulevard to Central Park Avenue. Go north on Central Park Avenue two blocks past the Golden Dome field house and Lake Street to the Conservatory. A free parking lot is on the building's south side, just after Lake Street. Street parking is available on Central Park Avenue, Madison Street, and Washington Boulevard.

By L: From the Loop, take the Green Line west ($2.25, $2.00 with Chicago Card) to the Conservatory-Central Park Drive stop, a renovated Victorian train station at Lake Street and Central Park Avenue.

By Bus: From the Loop, board CTA 20 Madison Street bus westbound ($2.25, $2 with Chicago Card). Get off at Madison Street and Central Park Avenue. Walk four blocks north to the Conservatory.

Additional Information

Chicago Park District, 312-742-PLAY; www.chicagoparkdistrict.com

Nature Chicago Program—City of Chicago and Department of the Environment, 312-744-7606; www.cityofchicago.org

Chicago Ornithological Society, 312-409-9678; www.chicagobirder.org

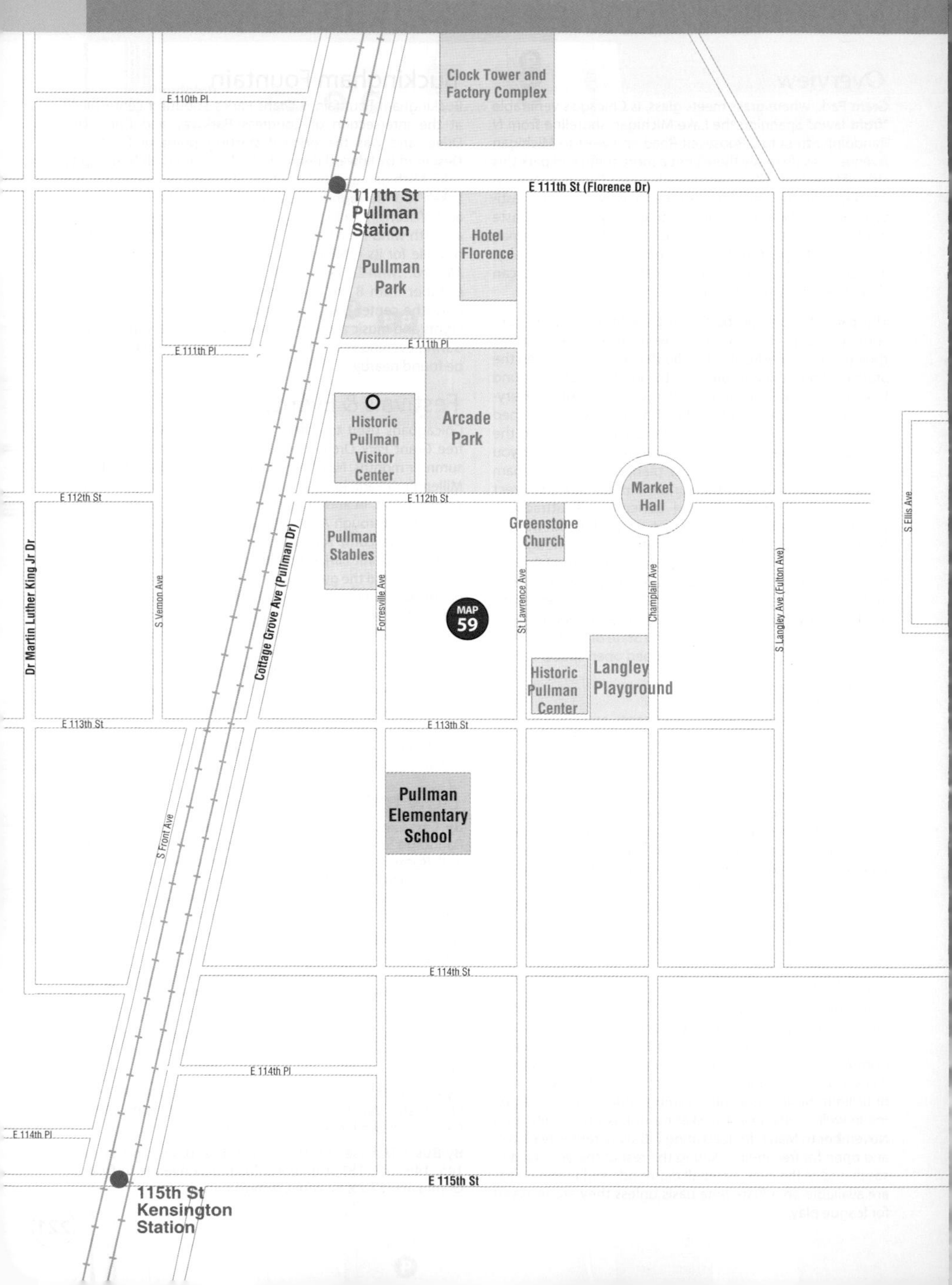

Clock Tower and Factory Complex
E 110th Pl
E 111th St (Florence Dr)
111th St Pullman Station
Hotel Florence
Pullman Park
E 111th Pl
E 111th Pl
Historic Pullman Visitor Center
Arcade Park
Market Hall
E 112th St
E 112th St
Pullman Stables
Greenstone Church
S Ellis Ave
Dr Martin Luther King Jr Dr
S Vernon Ave
Cottage Grove Ave (Pullman Dr)
Forresville Ave
MAP 59
St Lawrence Ave
Champlain Ave
S Langley Ave (Fulton Ave)
Historic Pullman Center
Langley Playground
E 113th St
E 113th St
Pullman Elementary School
S Front Ave
E 114th St
E 114th Pl
E 114th Pl
E 115th St
115th St Kensington Station

Overview

Although railroad magnate George Pullman's utopian community went belly-up, the Town of Pullman he founded 14 miles south of the Loop survives as a National Landmark Historic District. Built between 1880 and 1885, Pullman is one of America's first planned model industrial communities.

The "workers' paradise" earned Pullman humanitarian hoorahs, as well as a 6% return on his investment. Pullman believed that if laborers and their families lived in comfortable housing with gas, plumbing, and ventilation—in other words, livable conditions—their productivity would increase, as would his profits. Pullman was voted "the world's most perfect town" at the Prague International Hygienic and Pharmaceutical Exposition of 1896.

All was perfect in Pullman until a depression incited workers to strike in 1894, and the idealistic industrialist refused to negotiate with his ungrateful workers. While George Pullman's dream of a model community of indentured servitude died with him in 1897, hatred for him lived on. Pullman's tomb at Graceland Cemetery is more like a bomb shelter. To protect his corpse from irate labor leaders, Pullman was buried under a forest of railroad ties and concrete.

The grounds and buildings that make up Pullman went through most of the twentieth century stayed intact until 1998, when a man who heard voices in his head torched several of the site's primary buildings. Fortunately, die-hard Pullmanites have banded together to maintain the remaining structures, and for anyone interested in labor history or town planning, the city is worth a train or bus ride down from the Loop.

Architecture & Events

Architect Solon Beman and landscape architect Nathan Barrett based Pullman's design on French urban plans. Way back when, Pullman was made up of mostly brick rowhouses (95% still in use), several parks, shops, schools, churches, and a library, as well as various health, recreational, and cultural facilities.

Today, the compact community's borders are 111th Street (Florence Drive), 115th Street, Cottage Grove Avenue (Pullman Drive), and S Langley Avenue (Fulton Avenue). If you're interested in sightseeing within the historic district, we suggest you start at the Pullman Visitor Center (11141 S Cottage Grove Ave, 773-785-8901; www.pullmanil.org). There you can pick up free, self-guided walking tour brochures and watch an informative 20-minute film on the town's history. Call the center for additional specialty tour information and lecture details.

Along with self-guided tours, the Visitor Center offers 90 minute guided tours on the first Sunday of the month from May to October. Tours start at 1:30 and cost $7 for adults, $5 for seniors and $4 for students.

The annual House Tour on the second weekend in October is a popular Pullman event where several private residences open their doors to the public from 11 am to 5 pm on Saturday and Sunday ($17 in advance, $20 on day of event). May through October, the center also offers a ninety-minute Guided Walking Tour every first Sunday of the month at 1:30 pm ($5). Key tour sites include Hotel Florence, Greenstone Church (interior), Market Square, the stables, and the fire station.

Where to Eat

- **Seven Seas Submarine**, 11216 S Michigan Ave, 773-785-0550. Dine in or take out at this tiny sandwich shop.
- **Cal Harbor Restaurant**, 546 E 115th St, 773-264-5435. Omelettes, burgers, etc. at this family grill.

Where to Drink

- **Pullman's Pub**, 611 E 113th St, 773-568-0264. Suds in a pre-Prohibition watering hole.

How to Get There

By Car: Take I-94 S to the 111th Street exit. Go west to Cottage Grove Avenue and turn south, driving one block to 112th Street to the Visitor Center surrounded by a large, free parking lot.

By Train: Metra's Electric Main Line departs from Millennium Station (underground) at Michigan Avenue between S Water Street and Randolph Street. Ride 30 minutes to Pullman Station at 111th Street ($3.35 one-way). Walk east to Cottage Grove Avenue, and head south one block to 112th and the Visitor Center.

By L: From the Loop, take the Red Line to the 95th Street station. Board CTA 111 Pullman bus going south ($2.25, $2.00 with Chicago Card).

By Bus: CTA 4 bus from the Randolph Street Station travels south to the 95th Street and Cottage Grove stop. Transfer to 111 Pullman bus heading south ($2.50 with transfer).

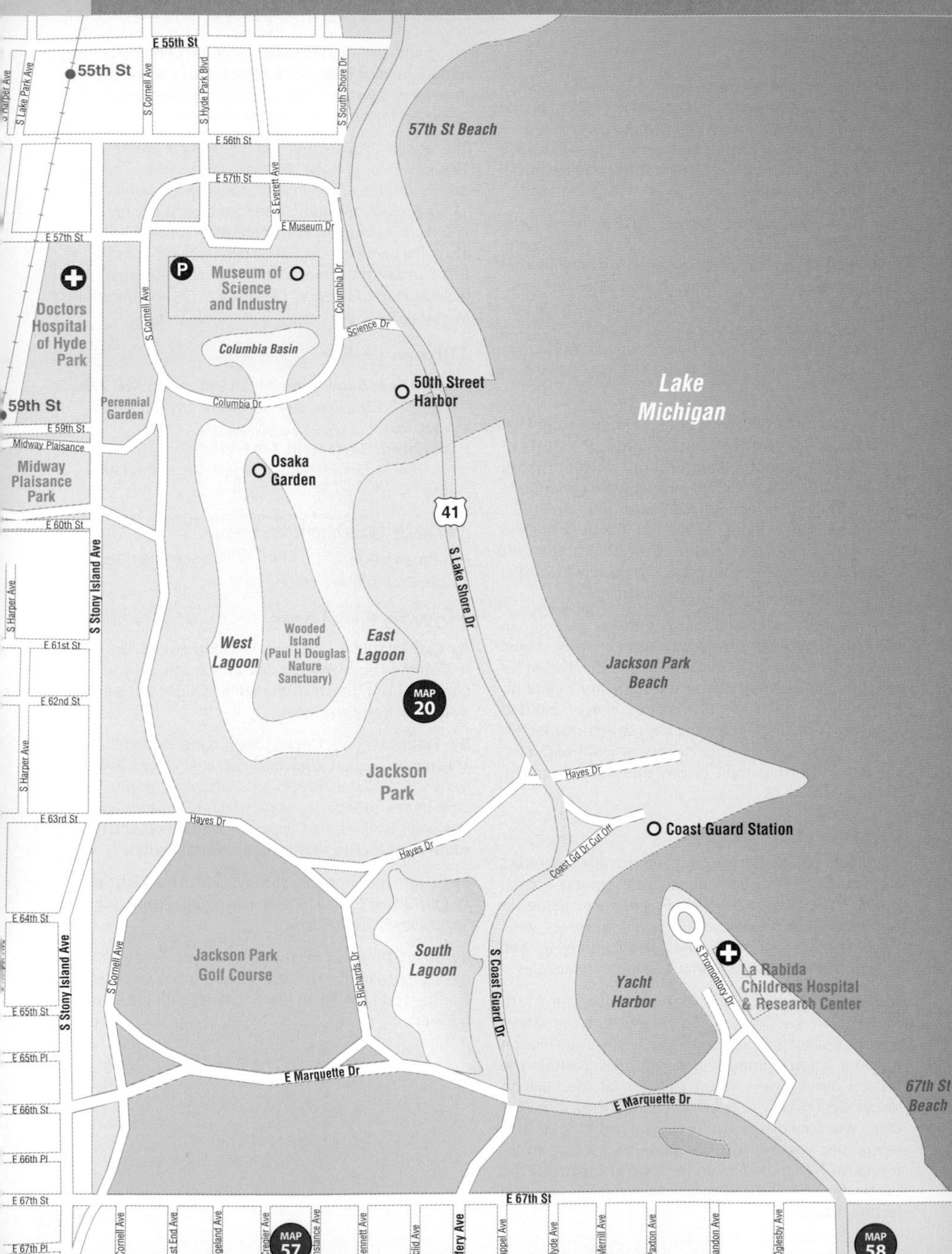

E 55th St
55th St
S Harper Ave
S Lake Park Ave
S Cornell Ave
S Hyde Park Blvd
S South Shore Dr
57th St Beach
E 56th St
E 57th St
S Everett Ave
E Museum Dr
E 57th St
Museum of Science and Industry
Doctors Hospital of Hyde Park
S Cornell Ave
Columbia Dr
Science Dr
Columbia Basin
50th Street Harbor
Lake Michigan
59th St
Perennial Garden
Columbia Dr
E 59th St
Midway Plaisance
Midway Plaisance Park
Osaka Garden
41
E 60th St
S Stony Island Ave
S Lake Shore Dr
S Harper Ave
West Lagoon
Wooded Island (Paul H Douglas Nature Sanctuary)
East Lagoon
Jackson Park Beach
E 61st St
MAP 20
E 62nd St
S Harper Ave
Jackson Park
Hayes Dr
E 63rd St
Hayes Dr
Coast Guard Station
Hayes Dr
Coast Gd Dr Cut Off
E 64th St
S Stony Island Ave
S Cornell Ave
Jackson Park Golf Course
S Richards Dr
South Lagoon
S Coast Guard Dr
S Promontory Dr
La Rabida Childrens Hospital & Research Center
Yacht Harbor
E 65th St
E 65th Pl
E Marquette Dr
E 66th St
E Marquette Dr
67th St Beach
E 66th Pl
E 67th St
E 67th St
E 67th Pl
S Cornell Ave
S East End Ave
S Ridgeland Ave
S Crandon Ave
MAP 57
S Constance Ave
S Bennett Ave
S Euclid Ave
S Jeffery Ave
S Chappel Ave
S Clyde Ave
S Merrill Ave
S Paxton Ave
S Crandon Ave
S Oglesby Ave
MAP 58

Overview

Historic Jackson Park, named for Mary Jackson, original owner of the land and cousin to president Andrew Jackson, borders Lake Michigan, Hyde Park, and Woodlawn, and was, for a long time, an unused tract of fallow land. The 500-acre parcel was eventually transformed into a real city park in the 1870s thanks to Frederick Law Olmsted of Central Park fame. The Midway Plaisance connects Jackson to Washington Park.

Jackson Park experienced its 15 minutes of worldwide fame in 1893 when it played host to the World's Fair Columbian Exposition. Today, the Museum of Science and Industry and La Rabida Children's Hospital and Research Center occupy two of the former fair structures.

Until recently Jackson Park had gone to seed, but thanks to Mayor Daley's green thumb, the government has been pumping money into park rehabilitation projects and Jackson Park is reaping the benefits. Major improvements to the area's lakefront, bike path, athletic centers, and beaches have Jackson Park shimmering again.

Museum of Science and Industry

Address:	57th St & Lake Shore Dr Chicago, IL 60637
Phone:	773-684-1414
Website:	www.msichicago.org
Hours:	Mon–Sat 9:30 am–4 pm; Sun 11 am–4 pm
Admission:	$15 for adults, ($13 for Chicagoans); $10 for children 3-11, ($9 for Chicagoans); $14 for seniors, ($12 for Chicagoans)

(Note: The Museum offers free admission on what seem to be arbitrary days, and hours vary month to month, so check the website regularly.)

The 1893 World's Fair Arts Palace is now home to the Museum of Science and Industry. The mammoth 350,000-square-foot bastion is one of the largest science museums in the world. Generations of Chicagoans and visitors have been wowed by a vast array of exhibits, including hatching baby chicks, *U-505* (the only World War II German submarine captured), and the Walk-Through Heart. The model railroad, another favorite exhibit, has been expanded to the now 3,500-square-foot *Great Train Journey*, which depicts the route from Chicago to Seattle. Other popular attractions include the coal mine, the Fairy Castle, and the Omnimax theatre showcasing scientific adventures in a five-story, domed, wrap-around theatre.

Nature

Two lagoons surround Wooded Island, a.k.a. Paul H. Douglas Nature Sanctuary. Osaka Garden, a serene Japanese garden with an authentic tea house and entrance gate, sits at the island's northern tip. The ceremonial garden, like the golden replica of Statue of the Republic on Hayes Avenue, recalls the park's 1893 Exposition origins. The Chicago Audubon Society (773-539-6793; www.chicagoaudubon.org) conducts bird walks in the park. These sites and the Perennial Garden at 59th Street and Cornell Drive are also butterfly havens.

Sports

Back in the very beginning of the 20th century, the Jackson Park Golf Course was the only public course in the Midwest. Today, the historic 18-hole course is certified by the Audubon Cooperative Sanctuary and has beautiful wilderness habitats. (Or are those scruffy fairways?) Greens fees are $23 during the week and $26 on weekends (all rates are discounted for residents). A driving range is adjacent to the course (773-667-0524).

In the past six years, the city has spent over $10 million to improve fitness facilities in its parks, and the Jackson Park field house was the happy recipient of a much-needed facelift. The swanky new weight room and gymnasium are open to adults weekdays from 9 am to 9:30 pm, and weekends from 9 am to 4:15 pm. The facilities are open to teens from 2 pm to 6 pm. Adult membership passes cost $55 for ten weeks, $25 for seniors, and teens work out for free. From Hayes Drive north along Cornell Avenue are outdoor tennis courts, baseball diamonds, and a running track. Tennis courts are on the west side of Lakeshore Drive at 63rd Street. Jackson Park's beaches are at 57th Street and 63rd Street (water playground, too). Inner and Outer Harbors allow shore fishing (6401 S Stony Island Ave, 773-256-0903). Fitness center hours are Monday-Friday 9 am-9:30 pm, Saturday 11 am-4:30 pm, Sunday 12 pm-5 pm.

Neighboring Parks

North of Jackson Park at 55th Street and Lake Shore Drive is Promontory Point, a scenic lakeside picnic spot. Harold Washington Park, 51st Street and Lake Shore Drive, has a model yacht basin and eight tennis courts on 53rd Street.

To the west, 460-acre Washington Park (5531 S Martin Luther King Dr, 773-256-1248) has an outdoor swimming pool, playing fields, and nature areas. It's also worth stopping by to see Lorado Taft's 1922 Fountain of Time sculpture and the DuSable Museum of African-American History (740 E 56th Pl, 773-947-0600; www.dusablemuseum.org).

At 71st Street and South Shore Drive are South Shore Beach, with a harbor, bird sanctuary, and South Shore Cultural Center (7059 South Shore Dr, 773-256-0149). South Shore Golf Course is a nine-hole public course. Greens fees are $14.75 weekdays and $16 on weekends (773-256-0986).

How to Get There

By Car: From the Loop, drive south on Lake Shore Drive, exit west on 57th Street. From the south, take I-94 W. Exit on Stony Island Avenue heading north to 57th Drive. The museum's parking garage entrance is on 57th Drive. The Music Court lot is behind the museum. A free parking lot is on Hayes Drive.

By Bus: From the Loop, CTA buses 6 and 10 (weekends and daily in summer) stop by the museum ($2.25, $2 with Chicago Card).

By L: (the quickest way to get to Jackson Park)**:** Take the Green Line to the Garfield Boulevard (55th Street) stop ($2.25, $2.00 with Chicago Card); transfer to the eastbound 55 bus.

By Train: Sporadic service. From the Loop's Millennium Station at Randolph Street and Van Buren Street stations, take Metra Electric service ($2.35 one-way). Trains stop at the 55th, 56th, and 57th Street Station platform (may be under construction). Walk two blocks east. From the Richard B. Ogilvie Transportation Center, walk two blocks south to Union Station on Canal Street and catch CTA bus 1.

Overview

The largest of Chicago's 552 parks, Lincoln Park stretches 1,208 acres along the lakefront from the breeder cruising scene at the North Avenue Beach to the gay cruising scene at Hollywood Beach. The park boasts one of the world's longest bike trails, but thanks to an ever-increasing abundance of stroller-pushers, leashless dogs, and earbud-wearing rollerbladers, the path proves treacherous for cyclists and pedestrians alike. Nonetheless, sporty types and summertime dawdlers still find satisfaction indoors and out at Lincoln Park. Take a break from winter inside the Lincoln Park Conservatory, a tropical paradise full o' lush green plants no matter what the thermometer reads. Public buildings, including animal houses at the Lincoln Park Zoo, Café Brauer, Peggy Notebaert Nature Museum, and vintage beach bath houses, make the park as architecturally attractive as it is naturally beautiful.

Much of southern Lincoln Park is open green space populated by football, soccer, dog play, and barbeques. Paths shaded by mature trees lead to stoic statues. Until the 1860s, Lincoln Park was nothing more than a municipal cemetery filled with the shallow graves of cholera and smallpox victims, and it was concern about a public health threat that instigated the creation of the park. Although the city attempted to relocate all the bodies in the cemetery-to-park conversion of 1869, digging doggies may unearth more than picnickers' chicken bones.

Nature

In spring, bird watchers flock to Lincoln Park's ponds and nature trails. Addison Bird Sanctuary Viewing Platform north of Belmont Harbor overlooks five fenced-in acres of wetlands and woods. Birding programs around North Pond are run by the Lincoln Park Conservancy (www.lincolnparkconservancy.org) and the Chicago Ornithological Society (312-409-9678; www.chicagobirder.org). More than 160 species of birds have been identified at the 10-acre pond. Free guided walks are held on Wednesdays starting at 7:30 am. Bring binoculars and a canteen of coffee. The Fort Dearborn Chapter of the Illinois Audubon Society hosts free park and zoo bird walks (847-675-3622; www.illinoisaudubon.org). Migratory birds gather around the revamped 1889 Alfred Caldwell Lily Pool at Fullerton Parkway and North Cannon Drive. Next to the Conservatory, Grandmother's Garden and the more formal French-style garden across the street are favorites for both wedding party photos and the homeless during the warmer months.

Sports

Baseball diamonds on the park's south end are bordered by La Salle Drive and Lake Shore Drive, next to the newly renovated field house and NorthStar Eatery. Upgrades planned for the area include a running track, soccer field, and basketball and volleyball courts. Bicyclists and runners race along Lincoln Park Lagoon to the footbridge over Lake Shore Drive to North Avenue Beach, Chicago's volleyball mecca. To reserve courts and rent equipment, go to the south end of the landmark, boat-shaped bath house (312-742-3224). Just north of the bath house is a seasonal rollerblade rink and fitness club. North of Montrose Harbor on the North Wilson Drive lakefront is a free skateboard park.

The 9-hole Sydney R. Marovitz Public Golf Course (3600 Recreation Dr, 312-742-7930) hosts hackers year-round. Snail-slow play allows plenty of time to enjoy skyline views from this lakefront cow pasture, which is always crowded. You'll never see a golf cart on this course. Greens fees are $20.50 weekdays, $23.50 on weekends, and you can rent clubs for $10. Reserve tee times by calling 312-245-0909, or show up at sunrise. The starter sits in the northeast corner of the clock tower field house. For those who want to take it even more leisurely, check out the Diversey Miniature Golf Course (312-742-7929), which offers an 18-hole course complete with waterfalls and footbridges. Diversey mini-golf rates are $7 adults, $5.50 juniors/seniors. Also nearby is the Diversey Golf Range (141 W Diversey Ave, 312-742-7929), open year-round (large bucket $13.00, small bucket $9.00).

Four clay tennis courts, the last ones left in Chicago, are open 7 am–8 pm and cost $16 per hour (the 7 am–9 am early bird special costs $24); tennis shoes are required. For reservations and further information, call 312-742-7821. Tennis courts—the free courts are on Recreation Drive at Waveland. They are free, first come, first served.

An archery range on the north end of Belmont Harbor is where the Lincoln Park Archery Club (www.lincolnparkarcheryclub.org) meets. They offer a number of clinics throughout the summer for newcomers to the sport.

Members of the Lincoln Park Boat Club row in Lincoln Park Lagoon. Rowing classes for the public are offered May through September (www.lpbc.net).

In November 2008 the South Pond next to Café Brauer closed for an $11.7 million renovation and is scheduled to reopen in early 2010 as the Nature Boardwalk. Gone will be the old swan-shaped paddleboats; they'll be replaced with boats that allow for giving nature tours. A new pavilion will house ecological learning programs and hands-on labs. Café Brauer is still open during construction. People can still fish in the lagoon and the three harbors. Belmont, Montrose, and Diversey Harbors also allow shore fishing.

Green City Market

Address:	South end of Lincoln Park between Clark and Stockton Drive
Phone:	733-880-1266
Website:	www.chicagogreencitymarket.org
Hours:	Wednesdays and Sundays, 7 am–1 pm

No Lincoln Park experience would be complete without visiting a quintessential yuppie hotspot—the farmer's market. What began in an alley next to the Chicago Theatre in 1998 has since become Chicago's only year round sustainable market, showcasing local farmers selling everything from organic produce and cheese to elk meat and microgreens (whatever those are). Free chef demonstrations take place every Saturday at 10:30 am and from June to September, a different fruit or vegetable is featured every month according to what's in season.

Lincoln Park Zoo

Address:	2200 N Cannon Dr Chicago, IL 60614
Phone:	312-742-2000
Website:	www.lpzoo.com
Hours:	April-May 10 am-5 pm; Memorial Day-Labor Day 10 am-5 pm on weekdays, 10 am-6:30 pm on weekends; September-October 10 am-5 pm; November-March 10 am-4:30 pm.
Admission:	FREE

Lions and tigers and bears and kids, oh my! We're not sure which scares us most. Established in 1868, Lincoln Park Zoo is the country's oldest free zoo, and while questions were raised in regards to nine animal deaths between 2005 and 2006, it still is a leader in wildlife conservation. National TV shows *Zoo Parade* and Ray Rayner's show *Ark in the Park* were filmed here. Look for some family (or, at least, in-law) resemblance at the cushy Regenstein Center for African Apes which opened in 2004, cost $26 million to build, and covers 29,000 square feet of living space. (Don't worry, it's supported by corporate sponsorships and private funds, not your tax dollars.) Come early and hear the white-cheek gibbons, the smallest of the ape family, mimic car alarms in their morning song to mark their territory. You may even catch one peeing off his tree before a captivated audience. Flanking the zoo's northwest side is the free Lincoln Park Conservatory, a fantastic source of oxygen renewal recommended for hangover sufferers. The new Pritzker Family Children's Zoo simulates a North American woods.

Peggy Notebaert Nature Museum

Address:	2430 N Cannon Dr Chicago, IL 60614
Phone:	773-755-5100
Website:	www.naturemuseum.org
Hours:	Mon-Sat 9:30 am-4:30 pm, Sun 12-5 pm.
Admission:	$9 adults, $7 seniors & students, $6 children ages 3–12; Thursdays free

The Peggy Notebaert Nature Museum succeeds in making Illinois' level landscape interesting. The contemporary version of the 1857 Chicago Academy of Sciences, this hands-on museum depicts the close connection between urban and natural environments and represents global environmental issues through a local lens. A flowing water lab and flitting butterfly haven invite return visits. A must-see for anyone with a passion for taxidermy and/or *Silence of the Lambs*. You can also discover how pollutive you are in your everyday life—and how to change it—in their Extreme Greenhouse exhibit. Get back to nature with a full class and summer camp schedule.

Chicago History Museum

Address:	1601 N. Clark St & North Ave Chicago, IL 60614
Phone:	312-642-4600
Website:	www.chicagohistory.org
Hours:	Mon–Wed, Fri, Sat 9:30 am–4:30 pm; Thu 9:30 am–8 pm; Sun 12–5 pm
Admission:	$14 adults, $12 seniors & students, children under 12 free; Mondays free

The Chicago History Museum holds over 20 million primary documents relating to the history of the Chicago area. Exhibits about the city's pioneer roots, architecture, music, fashion, neighborhoods, windy politics, and oral histories breathe life into an otherwise dry history. Locals can access the excellent research center (open Tuesday through Saturday, $5/day, $15/year; students through grade 12 are free) for genealogical information and housing history. North & Clark Café explores Chicago's love of food.

Performances

Lincoln Park Cultural Center (2045 N Lincoln Park W, 312-742-7726) stages plays, theater workshops, and family-friendly performances year-round. Theater on the Lake (Fullerton Ave & Lake Shore Dr, 312-742-7529) performs nine weeks of alternative drama in summer. The newly renovated theater now hosts events throughout the calendar year, thanks to much-needed climate control improvements. Lincoln Park Zoo hosts outdoor summer concerts as well. Call the events hotline at 312-742-2283.

How to Get There

By Car: Lake Shore Drive exits to Lincoln Park are Bryn Mawr Avenue, Foster Avenue, Lawrence Avenue, Wilson Drive, Montrose Drive, Irving Park Parkway, Belmont Avenue, Fullerton Avenue, and North Avenue.

Free parking lots are at Recreational Drive near Belmont Harbor and Simonds Drive near Montrose Harbor. Paid lots are at North Avenue Beach, Chicago Historical Society, Lincoln Park Zoo, and Grant Hospital Garage. Stockton Drive and Cannon Drive have free street parking. A metered lot is on Diversey Parkway, next to the golf range.

By Bus: CTA buses 151, 156, 77, 146, and 147 travel through Lincoln Park ($2.25, $2 with Chicago Card). For schedules and fares, contact the RTA Information Center (312-836-7000; www.rtachicago.com).

By L: Get off the Red Line at any stop between Fullerton and Bryn Mawr avenues ($2.25, $1.75 with Chicago Card), then head one mile east. On the Brown Line, all stops between Sedgwick and Belmont are about a mile east of the park as well.

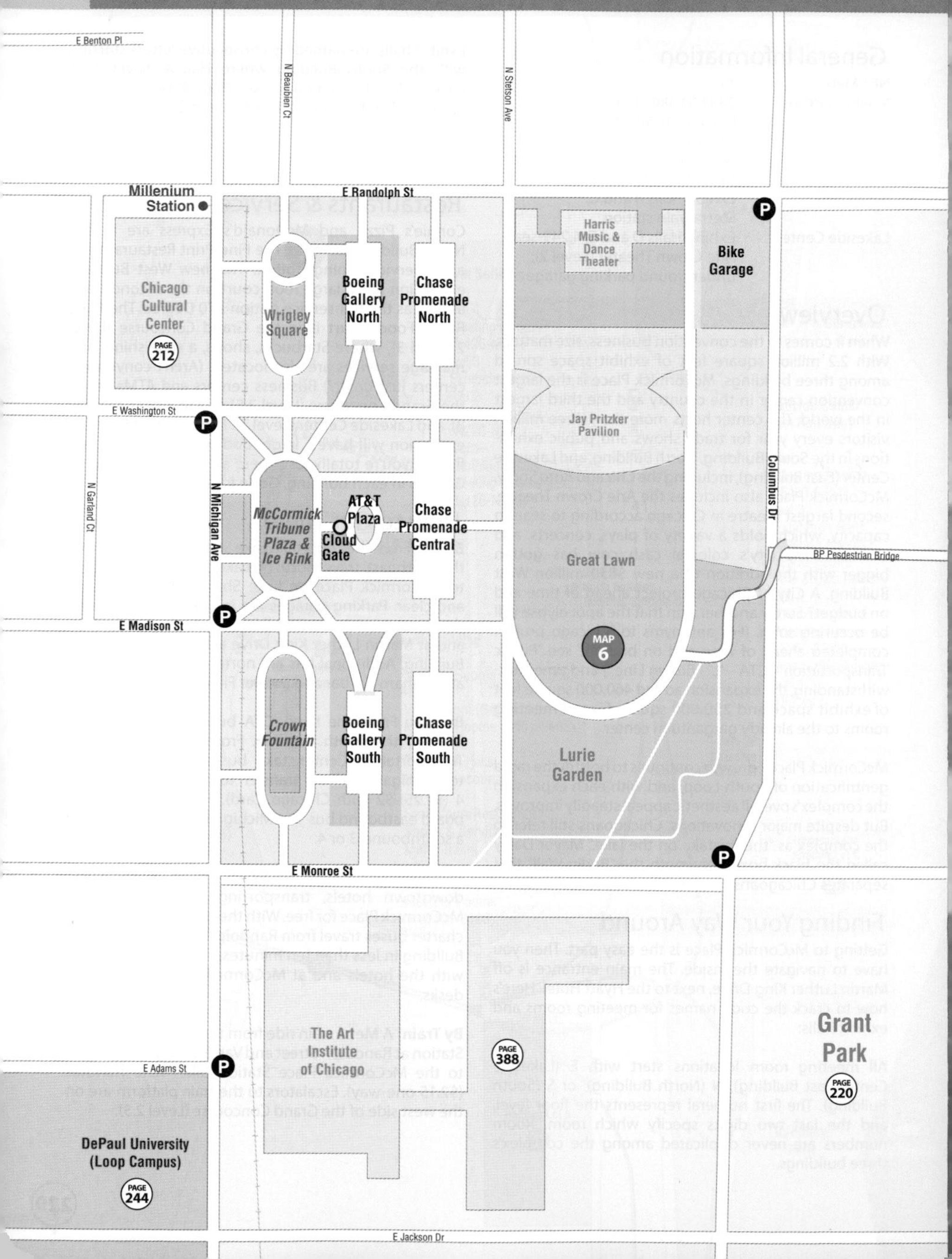

E Benton Pl
N Beaubien Ct
N Stetson Ave
Millenium Station
E Randolph St
Harris Music & Dance Theater
Bike Garage
Chicago Cultural Center
PAGE 212
Wrigley Square
Boeing Gallery North
Chase Promenade North
E Washington St
Jay Pritzker Pavilion
Columbus Dr
N Garland Ct
N Michigan Ave
McCormick Tribune Plaza & Ice Rink
AT&T Plaza
Cloud Gate
Chase Promenade Central
Great Lawn
BP Pesdestrian Bridge
E Madison St
MAP 6
Crown Fountain
Boeing Gallery South
Chase Promenade South
Lurie Garden
E Monroe St
The Art Institute of Chicago
PAGE 388
Grant Park
PAGE 220
E Adams St
DePaul University (Loop Campus)
PAGE 244
E Jackson Dr

Overview

Only four years behind schedule (who's counting?) and hundreds of millions of dollars over budget (okay, this we counted), Millennium Park finally launched itself in late 2001 as the cultural epicenter Mayor Daley promised us it would be back in 1997. Even if it did take myriad stopgap funding measures resembling yesteryear Al Capone strong-arm tactics to eternally endow us with the AT&T Plaza, McCormick Tribune Plaza & Ice Rink, and the Chase Promenade, locals and tourists alike agree it was well worth it. Even, staunch, longtime local naysayers have come to acknowledge that, when all is said and done, the end result really is an amazing addition to Grant Park's northpoint and is, without a doubt, one of downtown Chicago's crowning jewels. The last piece of the puzzle in this vision is the Art Institute's Modern Wing, designed by architect Renzo Piano. Only a couple of years behind schedule (what, you're shocked?), the wing opened with great fanfare in May 2009.

Jay Pritzker Pavilion

The cornerstone of Millennium Park, without question, is the Pritzker Pavilion. It seems the whole park may have very well been conceived to give Frank Gehry's architectural masterpiece an appropriate setting. Spectacularly innovative, the pavilion's façade features immense stainless steel ribbons unfurling 40 feet into the sky. The pavilion's stage area is as big as Orchestra Hall across the street and can accommodate a 120-person orchestra and a 150-person choir. Seating for the free concert events includes a 4,000-seat terrace and an additional 95,000-square-foot lawn area that can accommodate 7,000 picnickers. A one-of-a-kind integrated sound system offers outdoor acoustics that rival the best in the world.

Harris Music & Dance Theater

Several dance and theatrical troupes share the 1,500-seat underground space behind Gehry's behemoth bandshell, including Hubbard Street Dance Chicago (not to be missed, but good luck getting tickets!), the Chicago Children's Choir, and the Jazz Institute of Chicago. Two underground parking garages flank the theater, and as with all parking in this area, it's first come/first served and a bit of a mess on the weekends.

Tickets and schedule available at
www.harristheaterchicago.org

Nature & Sculpture

The park has several different defined spaces: Wrigley Square, with its neoclassical epistyle; the Chase Promenade, gearing up to house art fairs and ethnic festivals; and the AT&T Plaza (between the skating rink and promenade), which is home to Anish Kapoor's 100-ton stainless steel jelly-bean sculpture, *Cloud Gate* (be sure to take a picture of yourself staring into it—a dead tourist giveaway, but an awesome picture). Flanking the skating rink to the south is the modernist Crown Fountain, which features two glass brick towers, 50 feet in height, with projected video images of the faces of actual Chicago residents. The Lurie Garden, a ridiculously conceptual assemblage of seasonal foliage, offers a beautiful public gathering space as well as more contemplative environments. The BP Bridge, a 925-foot-long winding bridge—Frank Gehry's first—connects Millennium Park to Daley Bicentennial Plaza just east of the park. Clad in brushed stainless steel panels, the BP Bridge complements the Pritzker Pavilion in function as well as design by creating an acoustic barrier for traffic noise. It's well worth the walk.

Sports

The 15,910-square-foot McCormick Tribune ice skating rink opens annually in November. On Saturdays in the summer, take part in free fitness classes on the Great Lawn. The options range from tai chi to yoga, with some more danceable aerobics as well. The park also houses a state-of-the-art, heated bicycle garage, which provides parking for 300 bikes, showers, a repair facility, and a café.

Dining

The 300-seat Park Grill (voted "Top 5 Best Burger in Chicago") overlooking the skating rink offers burgers, steaks, and salads year round. In the summer, carry-away grub is available from a variety of kiosks throughout the park.

How to Get There

No matter your mode of travel, approach the area around Millennium Park with patience and allow extra time. For train, L, and bus transportation recommendations, see our Grant Park or Art Institute sections. Metra's Randolph Street train station, servicing only south-bound trains, is located under Millennium Park.

If you choose to drive, underground parking is available in several areas. Access the Grant Park North Garage from Michigan Avenue. Enter Millennium Park Garage from the lower levels of Randolph Street and mid-level of Columbus Drive.

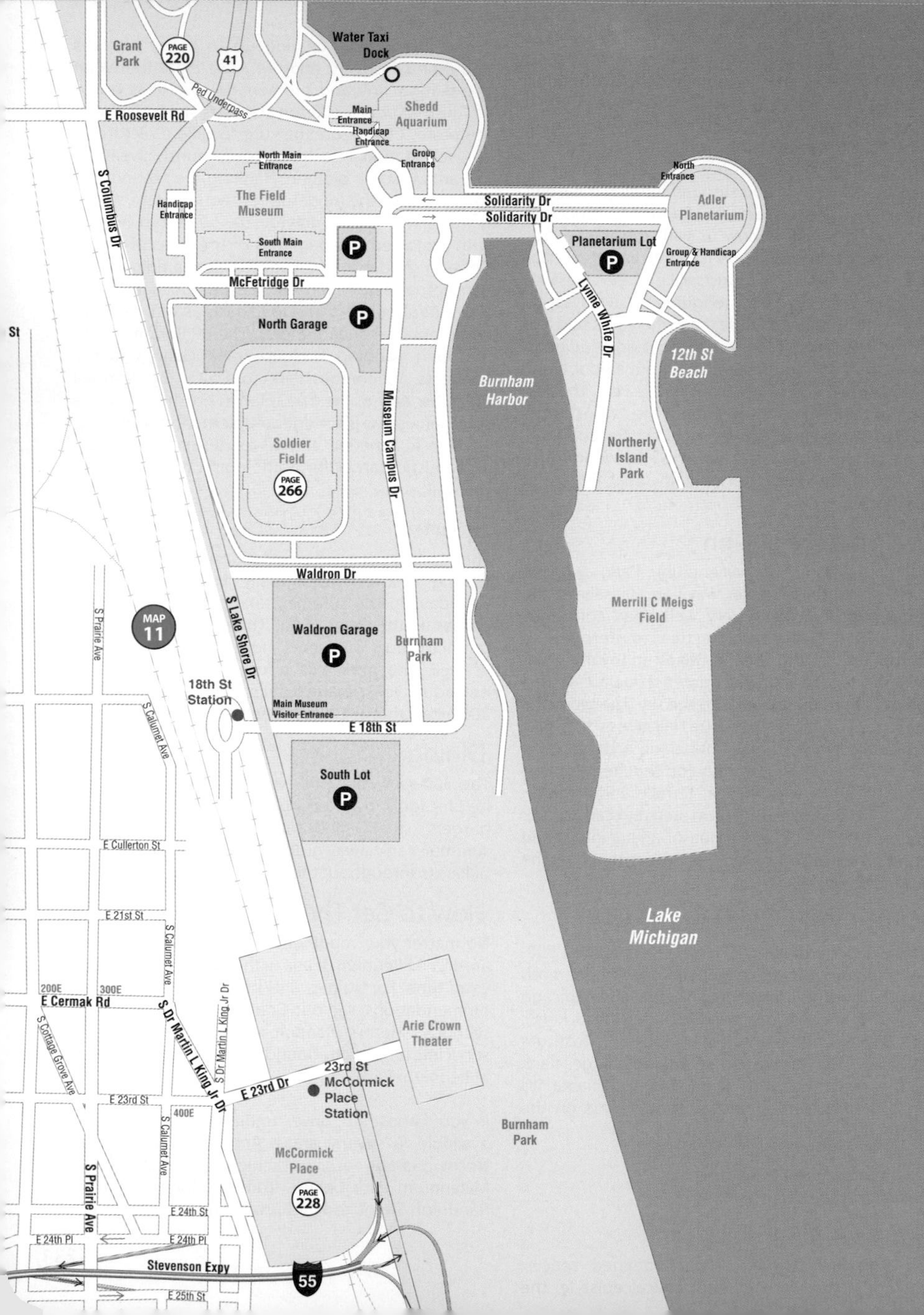

Grant Park
PAGE 220
41
Water Taxi Dock
Ped Underpass
E Roosevelt Rd
Main Entrance
Handicap Entrance
Shedd Aquarium
North Main Entrance
Group Entrance
North Entrance
Adler Planetarium
Solidarity Dr
Solidarity Dr
S Columbus Dr
Handicap Entrance
The Field Museum
South Main Entrance
Planetarium Lot
Group & Handicap Entrance
McFetridge Dr
North Garage
Lynne White Dr
St
12th St Beach
Burnham Harbor
Museum Campus Dr
Soldier Field
PAGE 266
Northerly Island Park
Waldron Dr
S Prairie Ave
MAP 11
S Lake Shore Dr
Merrill C Meigs Field
Waldron Garage
Burnham Park
18th St Station
Main Museum Visitor Entrance
S Calumet Ave
E 18th St
South Lot
E Cullerton St
E 21st St
S Calumet Ave
Lake Michigan
200E
300E
E Cermak Rd
S Dr Martin L King Jr Dr
S Dr Martin L King Jr Dr
Arie Crown Theater
S Cottage Grove Ave
23rd St McCormick Place Station
E 23rd Dr
E 23rd St
400E
Burnham Park
S Calumet Ave
McCormick Place
PAGE 228
S Prairie Ave
E 24th St
E 24th Pl
E 24th Pl
Stevenson Expy
55
E 25th St

Overview

Museum Campus is the ultimate destination for educational field trips. South of Grant Park at the intersection of Roosevelt Road and Lake Shore Drive, Museum Campus's 57 acres of uninterrupted lakefront parkland connect three world-renowned Chicago institutions: The Field Museum, Shedd Aquarium, and Adler Planetarium & Astronomy Museum. You've got Mayor Daley to thank for all of this beautiful space; it was the bossman himself who championed the rerouting of Lake Shore Drive to create the Museum Campus, which opened in 1998. Chicagoans, take note: although none of the museums that make up the museum campus are shouting from rooftops about it, all three offer reduced admission rates to locals. Be sure to ask for it.

The Field Museum

Address: 1400 S Lake Shore Dr
Chicago, IL 60605
Phone: 312-922-9410
Website: www.fieldmuseum.org
Hours: Open daily 9 am–5 pm, except Christmas
Admission: $28 Adults, $23 students & seniors, $19 children ages 4 – 11, discount for Chicagoans. Target Free Second Mondays let you in for free on the second Monday of each month.

The massive, Greek Revival-style museum constructed in 1921 houses over 20 million artifacts. From dinosaurs, diamonds, and earthworms to man-eating lions, totem poles, and mummies, there is just too much to savor in a single visit. In 2006, the museum introduced a new permanent exhibit called The Evolving Planet, featuring an interactive stroll through 4 billion years of evolution, from single-celled organisms through dinosaurs, hominids, and finally to human beings. Science: 1, Intelligent Design: 0. Another noteworthy permanent exhibit is Sue, the largest, most complete, and best preserved Tyrannosaurus Rex discovered to date. Complete with a half-smoked pack of Marlboros, since we now know that's what killed the dinosaurs. As with most museums, some temporary exhibits cost additional bucks on top of normal museum fees. Free museum tours are held weekdays at 11 am and 2 pm.

John G. Shedd Aquarium

Address: 1200 S Lake Shore Dr
Chicago, IL 60605
Phone: 312-939-2438
Website: www.shedd.org
Hours: Memorial Day–Labor Day: Daily, 9 am–6 pm (Jun–Aug open 'til 10 pm on Thurs)
Labor Day–Memorial Day: Mon–Fri: 9 am–5 pm; Sat–Sun: 9 am–6 pm. Closed Christmas
Admission: Basic admission (mini-pass) is $24.95 adults, $17.95 children ages 3-11. Discount for Chicagoans.

Opened in 1929, the Beaux Arts-style aquarium's six wings radiate from a giant, circular coral reef tank. The museum features revolving exhibits with a special focus on marine ecology and preservation. Popular favorites include Wild Reef, where you can get up close and personal with the sharks. On Thursday evenings from mid-June through August, the Shedd hosts "Jazzin at the Shedd" from 5 to 10 pm, featuring live jazz, a light sit-down dinner with cocktails overlooking the downtown skyline, and full access to the aquarium until 10 pm. The Oceanarium reopened in 2009 after a complete renovation.

Burnham Park

Burnham Park, the site of the 1933 Century of Progress exhibition, encompasses McCormick Place, Burnham Harbor, the former Merrill C. Meigs Airport (closed in a political coup by Mayor Daley in 2003), and Soldier Field. A free skateboard park is located at Lake Shore Drive and 31st Street. The 12th Street Beach, especially popular with swimmers and divers because of the deep water east of the beach, is on Northerly Island. Other beaches are at 31st Street and 49th Street. Outdoor basketball courts are east of Lake Shore Drive around 35th Street and 47th Street. Fishing is welcome along Solidarity Drive and Burnham Harbor shore,. The wilderness Nature Area at 47th Street attracts butterflies and birds.

Adler Planetarium

Address: 1300 S Lake Shore Dr
Chicago, IL 60605
Phone: 312-922-7827
Website: www.adlerplanetarium.org
Hours: 9:30 am–4:30 pm daily;
First Friday of every month: 9:30 am–10 pm;
Closed Thanksgiving and Christmas.
Admission: Monday-Friday: 10 am-4 pm, Saturday and Sunday 10 am-4:30 pm. General Admission (exhibits only): $10 adults, $6 children ages 3-14. Discounts for Chicagoans.

The Adler Planetarium & Astronomy Museum offers interactive exhibits explaining space phenomena and intergalactic events; its 2,000 historic astronomical and navigational instruments form the western hemisphere's largest collection. On the first Friday of every month, weather permitting, amateur astronomers young and old are invited to bring their own telescopes to the Planetarium lawns. Roving scientists offer tips and instructions on telescope usage and observational features. Chicago skyline views from the planetarium grounds are out of this world any day of the week, and are always worth the trip.

How to Get There

By Car: From the Loop, take Columbus Drive south; turn east on McFetridge Drive. From the south, take Lake Shore Drive to McFetridge Drive. Area parking lots are near Soldier Field, Field Museum, Adler Planetarium, and McCormick Place. All parking $16 in the lot adjacent to the Adler and $19 in the Soldier Field lot. Fees are higher on days when there's Park District-sponsored special events. Metered parking is available on Solidarity Drive.

By Bus: CTA buses 2, 6, 10, 12, 14, 127, 130, and 146 serve the area ($2.25 one-way, $2 with Chicago Card). For schedules and fares, contact the RTA Information Center at 312-913-3110; www.rtachicago.com.

By L: Ride the Orange, Red, or Green Lines to the Roosevelt Road stop ($2.25 one-way, $2.00 with Chicago Card). Walk east through the pedestrian underpass at Roosevelt Road.

By Train: From Richard B. Ogilvie Transportation Center, travel east on CTA bus 20 to State Street; transfer to the 146 ($2.25 one-way, $2 with Chicago Card). From Union Station take CTA bus 1, 126, or 151; transfer at State Street to the 10 or 146. From La Salle Street station, take the 146 ($2.25 one-way, $2 with Chicago Card). South Shore and Metra trains stop at the Roosevelt Road station.

By Trolley: Free trolleys travel to the Museum Campus from public transportation stations and some parking lots during the warmer months. See www.cityofchicago.org/transportation or call 1-877-CHICAGO for more details.

On Foot: Walk south through Grant Park past bobbing boats and the gushing Buckingham Fountain to the Museum Campus.

Water Taxis: Seasonally, water taxis operate between Navy Pier and Museum Campus (312-222-9328; www.shorelinesightseeing.com).

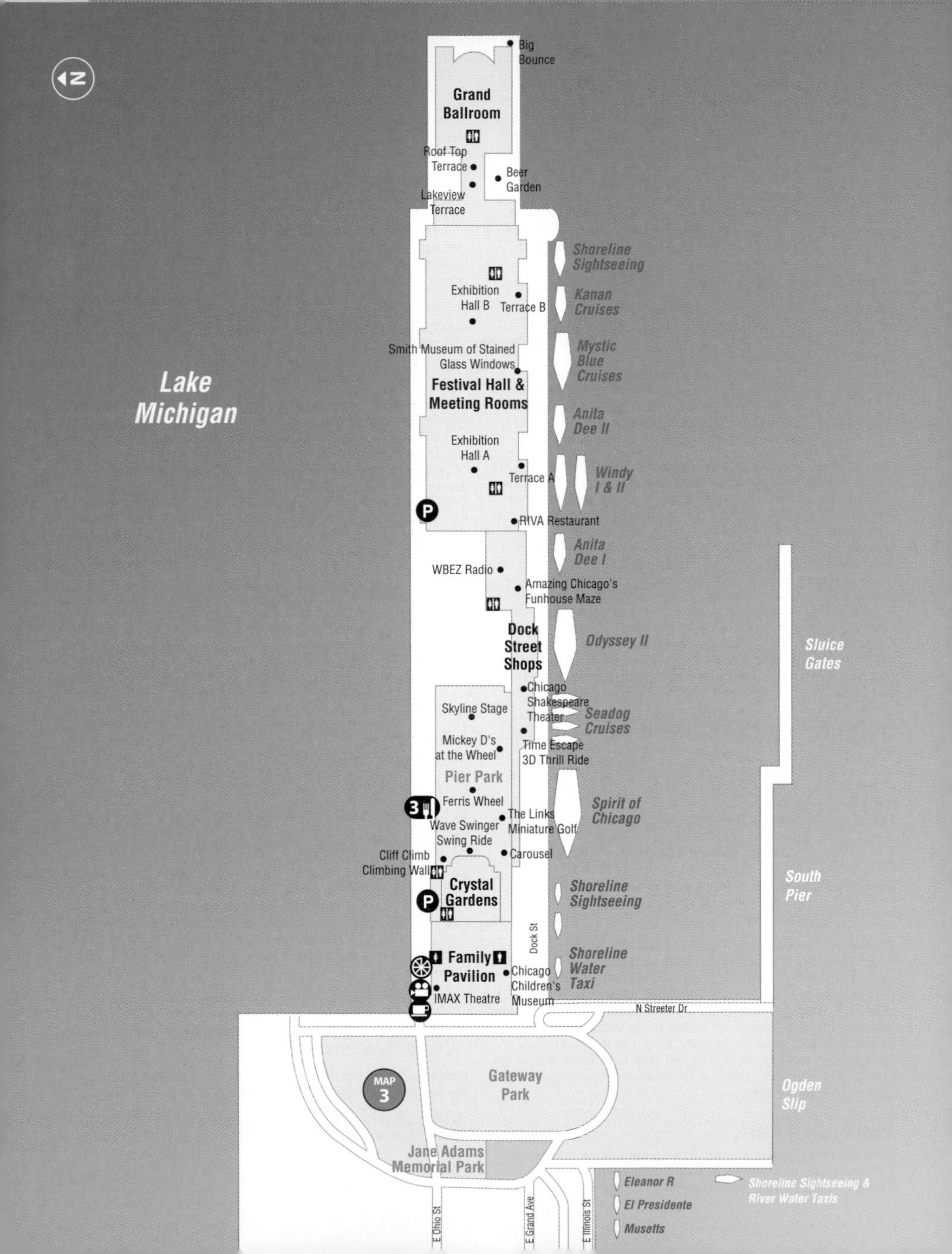

Big Bounce
Grand Ballroom
Roof Top Terrace
Beer Garden
Lakeview Terrace
Shoreline Sightseeing
Kanan Cruises
Exhibition Hall B
Terrace B
Smith Museum of Stained Glass Windows
Mystic Blue Cruises
Lake Michigan
Festival Hall & Meeting Rooms
Anita Dee II
Exhibition Hall A
Terrace A
Windy I & II
RIVA Restaurant
Anita Dee I
WBEZ Radio
Amazing Chicago's Funhouse Maze
Dock Street Shops
Odyssey II
Sluice Gates
Chicago Shakespeare Theater
Skyline Stage
Seadog Cruises
Mickey D's at the Wheel
Time Escape 3D Thrill Ride
Pier Park
Ferris Wheel
The Links Miniature Golf
Spirit of Chicago
Wave Swinger Swing Ride
Cliff Climb Climbing Wall
Carousel
Crystal Gardens
South Pier
Shoreline Sightseeing
Dock St
Family Pavilion
Shoreline Water Taxi
Chicago Children's Museum
IMAX Theatre
N Streeter Dr
MAP 3
Gateway Park
Ogden Slip
Jane Adams Memorial Park
Eleanor R
El Presidente
Musetts
Shoreline Sightseeing & River Water Taxis
E Ohio St
E Grand Ave
E Illinois St

General Information

NFT Map:	3
Address:	600 E Grand Ave Chicago, IL 60611
Phone:	312-595-7437
Website:	www.navypier.com
Pier Hours:	Opens 10 am daily. Closing times of restaurants, shops, and attractions vary by season, holiday, and public exhibitions/ events.
Skyline Stage:	1,500-seat outdoor performance pavilion in Pier Park, performances are May through September; 312-595-5022
IMAX Theatre:	312-595-5629
Free Fireworks:	Memorial Day to Labor Day, Wednesdays (9:30 pm) & Saturdays (10:15 pm). Free to the public.
WBEZ Radio:	National Public Radio's local station, 312-948-4600; www.wbez.org.
Exhibit Space:	Festival Hall, Lakeview Terrace, Ballroom Lobby, Grand Ballroom; 36 meeting rooms

Overview

A quintessential tourist trap, Navy Pier (a.k.a. the mall on the lake) is often avoided by real Chicagoans, who scoff at its self-consciously inoffensive blandness. Save for an occasional Skyline Stage concert, speed-boat ride, or high-end nosh at Riva, a trek to the pier is best reserved for those times when you have Grandma and a bevy of nieces and nephews in town, not to mention plenty of spending cash.

Opened to the public in 1916 as a municipal wharf, the pier has also done time as a) the University of Illinois at Chicago's campus, b) a hospital, c) a military training facility, d) a concert venue, and e) a white elephant. In 1989, the Metropolitan Pier and Exposition Authority invested $150 million to transform the crumbling pier into a peninsular entertainment-exhibition complex that attracts 8 million uninspired people a year. In addition to convention space, Navy Pier also houses two museums, the Shakespeare Theater, the Crystal Gardens, an outdoor concert pavilion, a vintage grand ballroom, a 15-story Ferris wheel, an IMAX Theatre, and, just for the hell of it, a radio station.

Chicago Shakespeare Theater

The Chicago Shakespeare Theater has a 510-seat, courtyard-style theater and a 180-seat studio theater that are Chicago's sole venues dedicated to performing wordsmith Willy's works. In addition to the season's plays, the theater produces Shakespeare "shorts" for younger patrons. A bookstore and teacher resource center are also on-site (312-595-5600; www.chicagoshakes.com).

Chicago Children's Museum

The Chicago Children's Museum features daily activities, a creative crafts studio, and 15 interactive exhibits ranging from dinosaur digs and waterworks to a toddler tree house, safety town, and construction zone. The museum is open Sunday–Wednesday and Friday 10 am to 5 pm, and Thursday and Saturday until 8 pm. Admission is $10 for adults and children, $9 for seniors, and Target First Free Sundays allow children 15 and under in free the first Monday of every month. Thursdays 5 pm to 8 pm are Kraft Free Family Nights, which means free admission for all. Dates vary. (312-527-1000; www.chichildrensmuseum.org).

Smith Museum of Stained Glass Windows

Smith Museum is the first stained-glass-only museum in the country. The 150 windows installed in the lower level of Festival Hall are mainly from Chicago-area buildings and the city's renowned stained glass studios. Windows representing over a century of artistic styles include works by Louis Comfort Tiffany, Frank Lloyd Wright, Louis Sullivan, and John LaFarge. The free museum is open during Pier hours (312-595-5024).

Getting There

By Car: From the north, exit Lake Shore Drive at Grand Avenue; proceed east. From the southeast, exit Lake Shore Drive at Illinois Street; go east. Three garages are on the Pier's north side, and plenty of parking lots are just west of Lake Shore Drive in Streeterville (Map 3).

By Bus: CTA buses 29, 65, 66, 120, 121, and 124 serve Navy Pier.

By L: Take the Green or Red Line to Grand Avenue ($2.25, $2.00 with Chicago Card). Board eastbound CTA Bus 29, or take the free trolley.

By Train: From Richard B. Ogilvie Transportation Center, take CTA buses 56 or 124. From Union Station, board bus 121.

By Trolley: Free, daily trolleys that typically run every 20 minutes travel between Navy Pier and State Street along Grand Avenue and Illinois Street. Pick-up points are indicated by "Navy Pier Trolley Stop" signs along the route.

By Boat: Seasonal water shuttles (one-way $3–13 adults, $3–6 kids) travel between Navy Pier and the Museum Campus and along the Chicago River to the Sears Tower (312-222-9328; www.shorelinesightseeing.com).

Pizza

• **Connie's Pizza** • 600 E Grand Ave

Coffee

• **Starbucks** • 600 E Grand Ave

Movie Theaters

• **Navy Pier IMAX Theatre** • 600 E Grand Ave

Restaurants

• **Capi's Italian Kitchen** • 700 E Grand Ave
• **Joe's Be-Bop Café & Jazz Emporium** • 700 E Grand Ave
• **Riva** • 700 E Grand Ave

North Ave
Le Moyne St
Greenfield St
Berkshire St
Division St
Thomas St
Augusta St
Iowa St
Chicago Ave
Superior St
Erie St
Ontario St
W Lake St
Common Blvd
Pleasant St
Randolph St
Washington Blvd
W Washington Blvd
Madison St
Monroe St
Adams St
Jackson Blvd
Van Muren St
Harrison St
Garfield St
Lexington St
Havard St
Filmore St
Roosevelt Rd
Hirsch St
Potomac St
Walton St
Rice St
Huron St
Ohio St
Race St
Midway St
Fulton St
West End St
N Ridgeland Ave
Harvey Ave
Lombard Ave
Hayes Ave
Taylor Ave
Humphrey Ave
Mapleton Ave
N Oak Park Ave
N Austin Blvd
Marion Ave
Bellefonte Ave
Forest Ave
Grove Ave
S Harlem Ave
S Oak Park Ave
Euclid Ave
Wesley Ave
East Ave
Scoville Ave
Elmwood Ave
S Ridgeland Ave
Cuyler Ave
Harvey Ave
Lombard Ave
Taylor Ave
Humphrey Ave
S Austin Blvd
Lyman Ave
Mason Ave
Mayfield Ave
Menard Ave
Waller Ave
Parkside Ave
Clinton Ave
Kenilworth Ave
Carpenter Ave
Grove Ave
Maple Ave
Wisconsin Ave
Wenonah Ave
Home Ave
Clinton Ave
S Austin Ave
Lindberg Park
Field Park
Taylor Park
Anderson Park
Concordia University
Frank Lloyd Wright Home & Studio
Ernest Hemingway Museum
West Suburban Hospital
Austin Gardens
Oak Park Visitor's Center
Scoville Park
Unity Temple
Harlem/Lake
Oak Park
Ridgeland
Austin
Stevenson Park
Austin Park
Historic Pleasant Home
Mills Park
Oak Park Hospital
Fox Park
Longfellow Park
Harlem
Forest Park
290
Eisenhower Expy
Oak Park Conservatory
Rehm Park
Barrie Plg Park
Columbus Park
Maple Park
Carroll Park
49
2

General Information

Oak Park Visitors Bureau:	708-524-7800; www.visitoakpark.com
Oak Park Tourist:	www.oprf.com

Overview

You can thank Oak Park for Prairie Style architecture, *A Moveable Feast*, McDonald's, and, yes, *Tarzan*. The creators of each called this charming suburb their home: Frank Lloyd Wright, Ernest Hemingway, Ray Kroc, and Edgar Rice Burroughs, respectively.

Best known for its architectural gems and strong public schools, Oak Park (pop. 52,500) is a happy hunting ground for homebuyers seeking upscale, integrated living 10 miles from the Loop. Less impressed than most with his picture-perfect hometown, Hemingway famously described Oak Park as "a village of wide lawns and narrow minds."

Village trustees must still be smarting from Hemingway's crack because they publicize an official policy on maintaining diversity. The "diversity statement" sounds like some sort of disclaimer or a zealot's vision for heaven on Earth: "Ours is a community that encourages contributions of all citizens regardless of race, gender, ethnicity, sexual orientation, disability, religion ..." —and indeed, Oak Park has quite a reputation as the place all the hip GLBT kids go when it's time to become hip GLBT parents.

Architecture

Oak Park harbors the nation's largest concentration of Frank Lloyd Wright buildings, 25 in the village and another 6 in neighboring River Forest. The village's must-see sites are located in a compact area bordered by Division Street, Lake Street, Forest Avenue, and Ridgeland Avenue. Designs by Wright, William Drummond, George W. Maher, John Van Bergen, and E. E. Roberts are represented throughout.

You can ground yourself in Prairie Style architectural principles at the brilliant Frank Lloyd Wright Home and Studio. Maintained by the Frank Lloyd Wright Preservation Trust, guided tours of the designer's personal space are offered weekdays at 11 am, 1 pm, and 3 pm and every twenty minutes on weekends between 11 am and 3:30 pm (951 Chicago Ave, 708-848-1976; www.gowright.org). Only 15 people are allowed per tour, and tickets can be purchased on the foundation's website or on-site (early arrival recommended) at a cost of $15 for adults, $12 for youth 14–17 and seniors, and free for children 3 and under. Worthwhile walking tours of the surrounding streets are also offered, and a combination tour, which includes a self-guided audio tour of the neighborhood costs $25 for adults, $20 for youth 4-17 and seniors, and free for children under 3. Worth every penny.

Completed in 1908, Unity Temple (875 Lake St, 708-383-8873; www.unitytemple-utrf.org) was Wright's first commissioned public building; today it houses Oak Park's Unitarian-Universalist congregation. Unity Temple is open daily for self-directed tours and on weekends for guided visits ($8 for adults, $6 for students and seniors). Designed by George W. Maher, Historic Pleasant Home (217 S Home Ave, 708-383-2654; www.pleasanthome.org) aptly illustrates the architectural evolution from Victorian design to early Prairie Style with tours held Thursday through Sunday at 12:30 pm, 1:30 pm, and 2:30 pm ($5 adults, $3 children; Fridays "pay what you can").

The Oak Park Visitors Center offers maps and a PDA walking tour of the Ridgeland Historic District highlighting 15 of the area's Victorian "Painted Ladies" ($10 for adults, $5 for students and seniors) 10 am–3:30 pm daily. Call 708-524-7800, or visit www.visitoakpark.com for more information.

Culture & Events

Once a year in May, the public gets to snoop inside Wright-designed private residences during the popular Wright Plus Housewalk ($95). His home-studio and Robie House in Hyde Park (shuttle provided) are also included in the tour (708-848-3559; www.gowright.org).

Get your fill of he-man author Hemingway at the Ernest Hemingway Museum (200 N Oak Park Ave, 708-848-2222; www.hemingway.org), open Sunday through Friday 1 pm–5 pm, and Saturday 10 am–5 pm ($10 adults, $8 students and seniors). His birthplace, also included with the price of admission, is located just up the street at 339 N Oak Park Avenue. For a one-stop confab with both of Oak Park's favorite sons, stroll three blocks north and two west to the 600 block of N. Kenilworth Ave, where Wright's Balch House (611) stands across the street from the Prairie Style home (600) to which Hemingway's family moved when he was 5 years old.

Summer evenings, catch Shakespeare's works performed outdoors in Austin Gardens by the Oak Park Festival Theatre company (708-445-4440; www.oakparkfestival.com). The lush Oak Park Conservatory, originally built in 1929 to provide a place for all of the exotic plants Oak Park residents collected on their travels abroad, is located at 615 Garfield Street (708-386-4700; www.oprf.com/conservatory; suggested $1 donation) and definitely worth a visit.

Landmarks

- **Frank Lloyd Wright Home and Studio** • 951 Chicago Ave

Nightlife

- **Avenue Ale House** • 825 S Oak Park Ave

Restaurants

- **Buzz Café** • 905 S Lombard Ave
- **Cucina Paradiso** • 814 North Blvd
- **Jeruselum Café** • 1030 Lake St
- **Khyber Pass** • 1031 Lake St
- **Mama Thai** • 1112 W Madison St
- **Marion Street Grill** • 189 N Marion St
- **New Rebozo** • 1116 Madison St
- **Pete's Red Hots** • 6346 W Roosevelt Rd
- **Petersen Ice Cream** • 1100 Chicago Ave
- **Poor Phil's** • 139 S Marion St

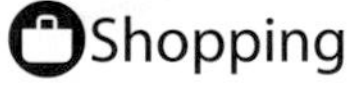

Shopping

- **Fly Bird** • 719 Lake St
- **Magic Tree Bookstore** • 141 N Oak Park Ave
- **Pumpkin Moon** • 1028 North Blvd

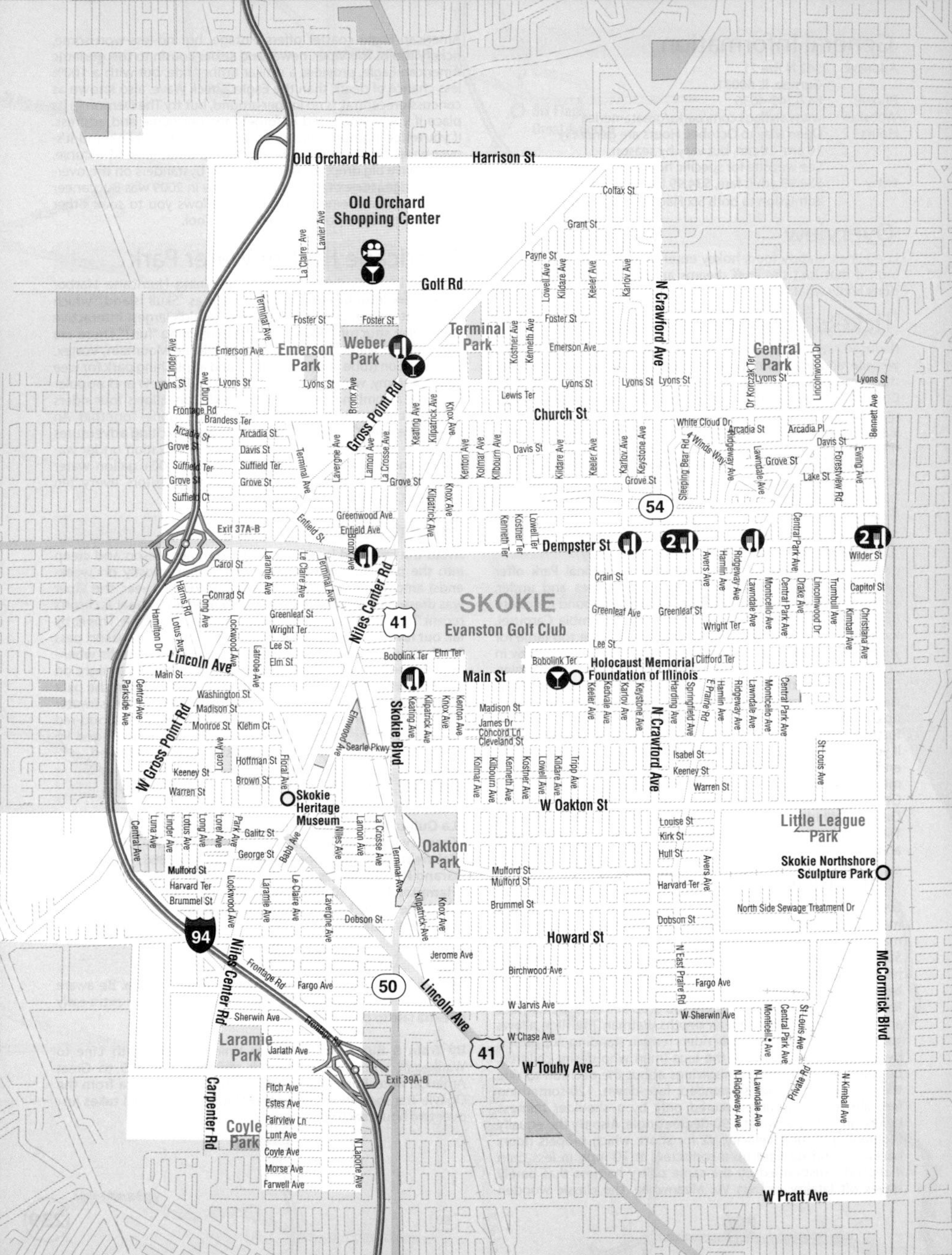
Old Orchard Rd
Harrison St
Old Orchard Shopping Center
Golf Rd
Emerson Park
Weber Park
Terminal Park
Central Park
Gross Point Rd
Church St
Dempster St
Exit 37A-B
Niles Center Rd
SKOKIE
Evanston Golf Club
Lincoln Ave
Main St
Holocaust Memorial Foundation of Illinois
W Gross Point Rd
Skokie Blvd
N Crawford Ave
Skokie Heritage Museum
W Oakton St
Oakton Park
Little League Park
Skokie Northshore Sculpture Park
Howard St
Laramie Park
Exit 39A-B
W Touhy Ave
Coyle Park
Carpenter Rd
McCormick Blvd
W Pratt Ave
94
41
50
54

General Information

www.skokie.org

Overview

When Skokie was first incorporated under the moniker Niles Centre in 1888, it was considered to be the rowdy neighbor of temperate Evanston due to the large number of taverns within its borders. By 1940, residents were clamoring for a name change and a PR facelift. In November of that year, the village was renamed Skokie after the nearby Skokie River and canals, which themselves were named after an old Native American word for "swampland." Personally, we'd be more attracted to a party town, but nonetheless, the facelift was a success. With the completion of the Edens Expressway in the 1950s, residential development in Skokie was booming.

A chunk of the growth comprised Eastern European refugees from World War II, many of whom were Jewish. It is estimated that between 1945 and 1955, 3,000 Jewish families resettled in Skokie. Synagogues and Jewish services followed, and the village soon developed a self-perpetuating reputation as a thriving Jewish enclave.

Skokie made international headlines in 1977–78 when it contested plans by the National Socialist Party of America, a branch of the American Nazi Party, to march on the village square. The NSPA was defended by the ACLU in a divisive case that brought the contest between free expression and freedom against hate speech into the international fore. As far as the NSPA was concerned, the decision to march in Skokie was an act of political manipulation. Chicago had denied the Nazis' right to march in SW Chicago's Marquette Park, which was the NSPA's home turf. The group then threatened to relocate their planned assembly to Skokie. When the Village of Skokie lost their bid to ban the march, Chicago finally conceded, allowing the Nazis to gather at Marquette Park in June 1978. A handful of Nazis showed up, countered by thousands of anti-Nazi protestors.

As if being the head of a neo-Nazi movement and threatening to march on the front lawns of concentration camp survivors doesn't already make you the world's biggest jackass/creep, NSPA leader Frank Collin secured the title in 1979 when he was arrested and incarcerated on child molestation charges.

Culture & Events

In 1988, an urban renewal project to restore the North Shore's decrepit Chicago River waterfront resulted in the two-mile Sculpture Park, an outdoor recreation area with walking paths, picnic areas, and featuring more than 72 sculptures by artists of local, national, and international renown (although, rubes that we are, we confess we haven't heard of any of 'em). The park, sandwiched between McCormick Blvd and the north branch of the Chicago River, runs the two miles from Touhy to Dempster.

Time travel through history at the Skokie Heritage Museum—an assemblage of historical photos, papers, and artifacts painstakingly gathered by the Skokie Historical Society. The museum, housed in a restored 1887 firehouse, also features the history of Skokie's firefighters. Behind the museum, an authentic 1840s log cabin relocated to this location allows kids a glimpse into the town's pioneer past.

Skokie is now home to the Illinois Holocaust Museum & Education Center (9603 Woods Dr, 847-967-4800), which opened in 2009. www.ilholocaustmuseum.org It's open to the public Tuesday, Wednesday, and Friday 10 am-5 pm, Thursday until 8 pm. Saturday and Sunday from 11 am-4 pm. Admission is $10 for adults, $6 for seniors and students aged 12-22, $5 for children 5-12.

Skokie Park District has many fairs up their sleeves, including a late-summer night's dream for kids. In the sticky heat of late-August, carnies set up for the Back-to-School Carnival. Backpack toting tots mingle with tweenies for a farewell-to-freedom bash (while parents openly celebrate with their "can't wait" grins). Running just one weekend, the summer ends with "a veritable smorgasbord" of rickety rides, corn dogs and the sickly sweet smell of elephant ears.

Every year in mid-May, the Skokie Festival of Cultures draws clog dancers, falafel hawkers, and accordion players from around the state for a weekend festival celebrating Skokie's diverse cultural heritage. The sulky loitering high-schoolers and fat ladies in track suits, on the other hand, are 100% local.

North Shore Center for the Performing Arts

Home to the Skokie Valley Symphony Orchestra, the Centre East Theater, and, most notably, the highly acclaimed Northlight Theater, the North Shore Center for the Performing Arts (9510 Skokie Blvd, 847-673-6300; www.northshorecenter.org) is a state-of-the-art performance venue. Touring artists perform here, world class theater (sometimes featuring ensemble members from Steppenwolf) is mounted here, and it's also a North Shore venue for exhibits and trade shows. Designed by architect Graham Gund in 1996, The North Shore Center for the Performing Arts has given Northeast Illinois culture seekers a reason to come to Skokie besides bagels and lox.

Where to Drink

Despite its alcohol-fueled history, Skokie is not really known as a place to imbibe socially. Young residents head to youthful watering holes in the vicinity of the Northwestern campus in formerly tee-totaling Evanston (will the ironies never end?). Meanwhile, local drunks hang out at anonymous corner taverns just like anywhere else. Retail workers, middle managers, and the secretarial set mingle and mate at the food and booze joints adjacent to Old Orchard.

Where to Eat

Old Orchard Shopping Center is filled with family-friendly chain options. Happily, Skokie still houses enough locally owned, independent restaurants to add interest and diversity to their dining scene. Folks travel from all over Chicagoland for local delis and kosher fare ever debating the superiority of Kaufman's v. New York Bagel and Bialy as THE place for a bagel and shmear.

How to Get There

By L: The Skokie Swift Yellow Line runs non-stop between the Howard Street Red Line terminus and the Skokie Dempster station at 5001 Dempster St. Trains run approximately every 10-15 minutes between 5 am and 10 pm.

By Car: Take the Edens Expressway (I-94), and exit at Dempster.

Movie Theaters

- **AMC Loews Gardens 1/6** • 4999 Old Orchard Shopping Center

Nightlife

- **Chammps** • 134 Old Orchard Ctr
- **Don's Fishmarket Tavern and Grill** • 9335 Skokie Blvd
- **Principal's Pub** • 4249 Main St

Restaurants

- **El Tipico** • 3341 Dempster St
- **Grecian Kitchen Delights** • 3938 Dempster St
- **Hub's Gyros** • 3727 Dempster St
- **Hy Life Bistro** • 4120 Dempster St
- **Kabul House** • 3320 Dempster St
- **Kaufman's Bagel & Delicatessen** • 4905 Dempster St
- **Pita Inn** • 3910 Dempster
- **Ruby of Siam** • 9420 Skokie Blvd
- **Shallots Bistro** • 4741 Main St

Columbia College Chicago

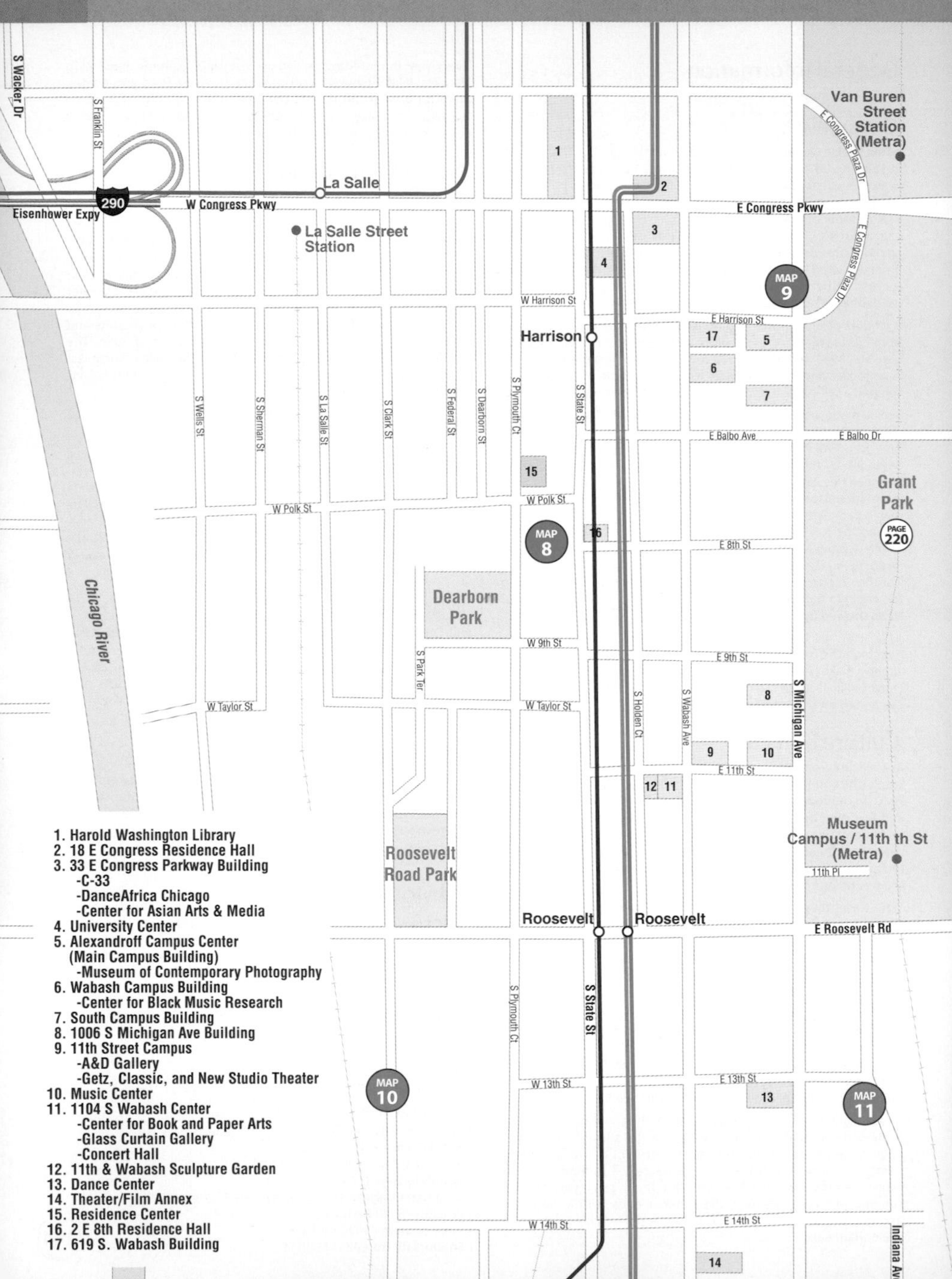

1. Harold Washington Library
2. 18 E Congress Residence Hall
3. 33 E Congress Parkway Building
   - C-33
   - DanceAfrica Chicago
   - Center for Asian Arts & Media
4. University Center
5. Alexandroff Campus Center (Main Campus Building)
   - Museum of Contemporary Photography
6. Wabash Campus Building
   - Center for Black Music Research
7. South Campus Building
8. 1006 S Michigan Ave Building
9. 11th Street Campus
   - A&D Gallery
   - Getz, Classic, and New Studio Theater
10. Music Center
11. 1104 S Wabash Center
    - Center for Book and Paper Arts
    - Glass Curtain Gallery
    - Concert Hall
12. 11th & Wabash Sculpture Garden
13. Dance Center
14. Theater/Film Annex
15. Residence Center
16. 2 E 8th Residence Hall
17. 619 S. Wabash Building

General Information

NFT Maps: 8, 9, 11
Address: 600 S Michigan Ave
Chicago, IL 60605
Phone: 312-663-1600
Website: www.colum.edu
Event Information: www.colum.edu/calendar

Overview

Named in honor of the World's Columbian Exposition, Columbia College Chicago first opened in 1890 as a women's speech academy. Over time, it has become one of America's most diverse private arts and media schools. It is best known for its film, television, and fiction departments, which turn out prominent professionals. Columbia alumni played key writing and production roles in *Barbershop*, *Real Women Have Curves*, *Analyze This*, *Schindler's List*, and *Leaving Las Vegas*. They win Emmy Awards (for art direction on *Alias*, special effects on *Star Trek: Enterprise*, animation on *Samurai Jack*, and cinematography on *Carnivale*). And they write acclaimed books (in addition to NFT); celebrated scribblers Joe Meno, Don DeGrazia, and Sam Weller all returned to Columbia's fiction writing department as faculty. Other programs include photography, dance, theater, music, art and design, journalism, fashion design, poetry, education, and management for the arts, entertainment, and media. Columbia's campus is the bustling South Loop, and its colorful student body immerse themselves in the city.

Tuition

Tuition for full-time undergrads is around $19,000. There's fees, books, art supplies, CTA passes, and obligatory museum visits, too. And have you heard about the Superdorm? There, you can live in the middle of the Loop with 1,680 of your closest friends. Hey, college is a perpetual slumber party.

Culture

Columbia College is one of Chicago's most esteemed cultural arts presenters; more than 300,000 visitors attend Columbia events each year. The college brings the DanceAfrica Chicago Festival to the city every fall and hosts a regular slate of innovative dance performances throughout the year. The Museum of Contemporary Photography is one of two fully accredited photography museums in the United States. The Chicago Jazz Ensemble, directed by trumpet virtuoso Jon Faddis, also makes its home at Columbia. The Story Week Festival of Writers, held in the spring, is among Chicago's top literary draws. The college brings in authors, editors, agents, and publishers for a week of readings, panels, and special events, such as "Read-Like-a-Rockstar" night at the Metro. Spring also brings Fashion Columbia and the Manifest Urban Arts Festival, celebrating graduate achievements. The college's galleries and theaters feature the work of students alongside notable outside artists.

- **Center for Book and Paper Arts**
  1104 S Wabash Ave, 2nd Fl
  312-344-6630
  www.colum.edu/centers/bpa
- **Museum of Contemporary Photography**
  600 S Michigan Ave
  312-663-5554
  www.mocp.org
- **A&D Gallery**
  619 S. Wabash Ave
  312-344-8687
  www.colum.edu/adgallery
- **Glass Curtain Gallery**
  1104 S Wabash Ave, 1st Fl
  312-344-6650
- **C-33**
  33 E Congress Pkwy
  312-344-7188
- **Dance Center**
  1306 S Michigan Ave
  312-344-8300
  www.dancecenter.org
- **Getz, Classic, and New Studio Theaters**
  72 E 11th St
  312-344-6126
  www.colum.edu/undergraduate/theater/calendar
- **Concert Hall**
  1014 S Michigan Ave
  312-344- 6240
- **DanceAfrica Chicago**
  33 E Congress Pkwy
  312-344-7070
  www.danceafricachicago.com
- **Center for Asian Arts & Media**
  29 E Congress Pkwy, 1st Fl
  312-344-7870
  www.asianartsandmedia.org
- **Center for Black Music Research**
  623 S Wabash Ave, Ste 600
  312-344-7559
  www.cbmr.org
- **Chicago Jazz Ensemble**
  600 S Michigan Ave
  312-344-6270
  www.chijazz.com

Department Contact Information

Undergraduate Admissions.................. 312-344-7131
Graduate Admissions.................. 312-344-7260
School of Fine and Performing Arts.................. 312-344-7298
School of Media Arts.................. 312-344-8220
School of Liberal Arts and Sciences.................. 312-344-8217

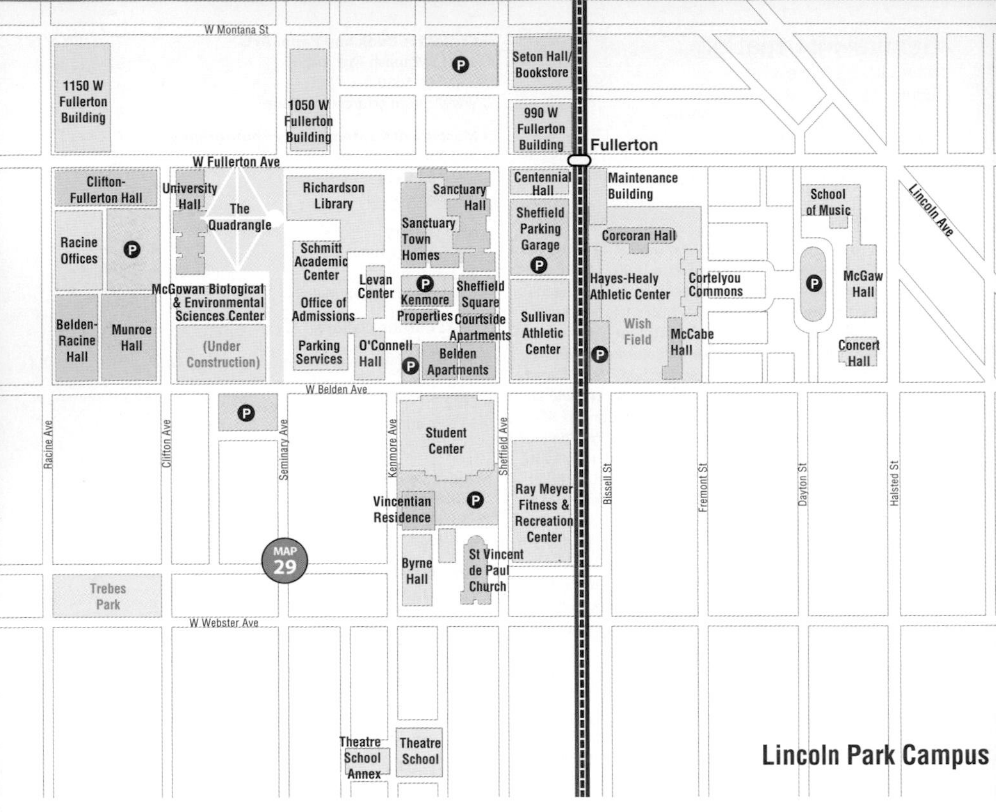

General Information

Lincoln Park Campus:	Schmitt Academic Center 2320 N Kenmore Ave Chicago, IL 60614-3298 Phone: 773-325-7000 x5700
Loop Campus:	1 E Jackson Blvd Chicago, IL 60604 Phone: 312-362-8000
Website:	www.depaul.edu
Suburban Campuses:	University Center of Lake County
(Grayslake)	847-665-4000
Naperville:	312-476-4500/630-548-9378
Oak Forest:	312-476-3000/708-633-9091
O'Hare:	312-476-3600/847-296-5348
Rolling Meadows:	312-476-4800/847-437-9522

Overview

Established in 1898 by the Vincentian Fathers as a school for immigrants, DePaul has become the country's largest Catholic university (with over 23,000 students) and the biggest private educational institution in Chicago, offering 150 undergraduate and graduate programs of study. According to The Princeton Review's recent survey of college students nationwide, DePaul students rated as some of the happiest college students in the country; it must be all the bars near campus on Halsted Street and Lincoln Avenue.

Of the university's seven campuses in the Chicago area, the Lincoln Park and Loop campuses serve as the core locations. The highly acclaimed Theatre School, College of Liberal Arts and Sciences, School of Music, and School of Education hold down the 36-acre Lincoln Park campus amidst renovated historic homes on tree-lined streets. Popular student handouts include coffee shop The Bourgeois Pig (738 W. Fullerton), where students go to *actually* study, and English pub The Red Lion (2446 N. Lincoln), where students go to blow off studying. If you venture to the upstairs level at The Red Lion, you're likely to find a graduate class drinking pints while taking in a lecture, a welcome substitute for the juvenile-feeling desk/chair combo and bright lights of a classroom. The Red Lion is rumored to be haunted, but don't ask the waitresses about it; they don't know, and it annoys them.

DePaul's Loop Campus at Jackson Boulevard and State Street is where you'll find the College of Commerce, College of Law, and School of Computer Science, Telecommunications, and Information Systems. Nationally respected Kellstadt Graduate School of Business and DePaul's thriving continuing education program, the "School of New Learning," can also be found on the Loop Campus. The heart of the

Loop campus is DePaul Center, located in the old Goldblatt Brothers Department Store, now grounded by a university-sanctioned Barnes and Noble. Most students in the Loop campus are adults, so popular hangouts include the Brown Line L, Red Line L, and Metra stations while they're all waiting for the train home. Prominent DePaul alumni include Chicago father-son mayors Richard M. Daley and his dad, the late Richard J. Daley; McDonald's Corporation's former CEO Jack Greenberg; Pulitzer Prize-winning composer George Perle; and actors Gillian Anderson and John C. Reilly.

Tuition

Full-time undergraduates paid between $26,765 (the School of Education and the Colleges of Communication, Liberal Arts and Sciences, Commerce, and Computing and Digital Media) and $29,630 (the Theatre School and the School of Music) for tuition in the 2009-2010 school year. Graduate tuition varies by department, too, but really what counts is your bar tab when you're attending school with as many bars per capita as there are in this part of town. Your beer will cost more than your books come June.

Sports

The DePaul Blue Demons might be named a bit oddly as the athletic ambassadors of the largest Catholic university in the United States, but their teams are strong despite any identity confusion. In basketball, the Blue Demons beat Kansas in a landmark battle. They made it to the National Invitation Tournament that year, but ultimately lost to Air Force in the last bracket. Lately, a few standout players have been tapped for the NBA.

For tickets, contact Ticketmaster (ticketmaster.com, 800-745-3000) or visit the ticket depot (depaulbluedemons.com, 773-325-7526, 2323 N Sheffield Ave). Look out for the twofer Tuesday deal. The Blue Demons play at McGrath Arena (women's basketball and volleyball, 2323 N Sheffield Ave), Allstate Arena (men's basketball, 6920 N Mannheim Rd, Rosemont, IL, 847-635-6601; allstatearena.com), and Wish Field and Cacciatore Stadium (men's and women's soccer and softball, respectively, both on the 900 block of Belden Ave).

DePaul's teams include men's and women's basketball, cross-country, soccer, tennis, and track and field, men's golf, and women's softball and volleyball.

Culture on Campus

DePaul's vibrant Theatre School is the oldest of its kind in the Midwest. Founded in 1925 as the Goodman School of Drama, the school stages over 200 performances during its Showcase, Chicago Playworks, New Directors Series, and School Workshop seasons. The Theatre School Showcase performs contemporary and classic plays at its 1,325-seat Merle Reskin Theatre, a French Renaissance–style theater built in 1910 and located at 60 E Balbo Drive in the South Loop. The Chicago Playworks for Families and Young Audiences and the School of Music's annual opera are also performed at the Merle Reskin Theatre. For tickets ($8–$12), directions, and parking garage locations, call 312-922-1999 or go to theatreschool.depaul.edu. Take the Red Line to the Harrison Street or Jackson Street stops just southwest of the theater. CTA buses 29, 36, 151, and 146 also stop nearby. Check the Theatre School website for New Directors Series and School Workshop productions, theater locations, and ticket prices.

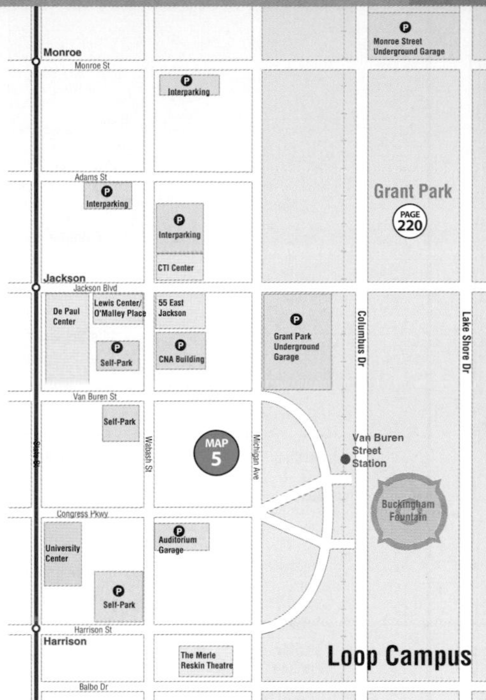

DePaul University Art Gallery is located in the John T. Richardson Library at 2350 N Kenmore Avenue (773-325-7506). Permanent collections of sculpture and oil paintings from local and international artists adorn the free gallery. A pay parking lot is located one block east of the library on N Sheffield Avenue. DePaul's John T. Richardson Library and Loop campus library in DePaul Center are open to the public year-round. Take plenty of change for the copy machines as check-out privileges are reserved for students and faculty.

Department Contact Information

Lincoln Park Campus Admissions Office............773-325-7500
Loop Campus Admissions Office..........................312-362-8300
College of Commerce 312-362-6783
College of Law..312-325-8701
Undergraduate College of Arts & Sciences...... 773-325-7310
Graduate College of Arts & Sciences...................773-325-7315
John T Richardson Library...................................... 773-325-7862
Kellstadt Graduate School of Business...............312-362-8000
Loop Campus Library 312-362-8433
School for New Learning 312-362-8001
School of Computer Science, Telecommunications
and Information Systems 312-362-8381
School of Music...773-325-7260
Theatre School...773-325-7917

Illinois Institute of Technology

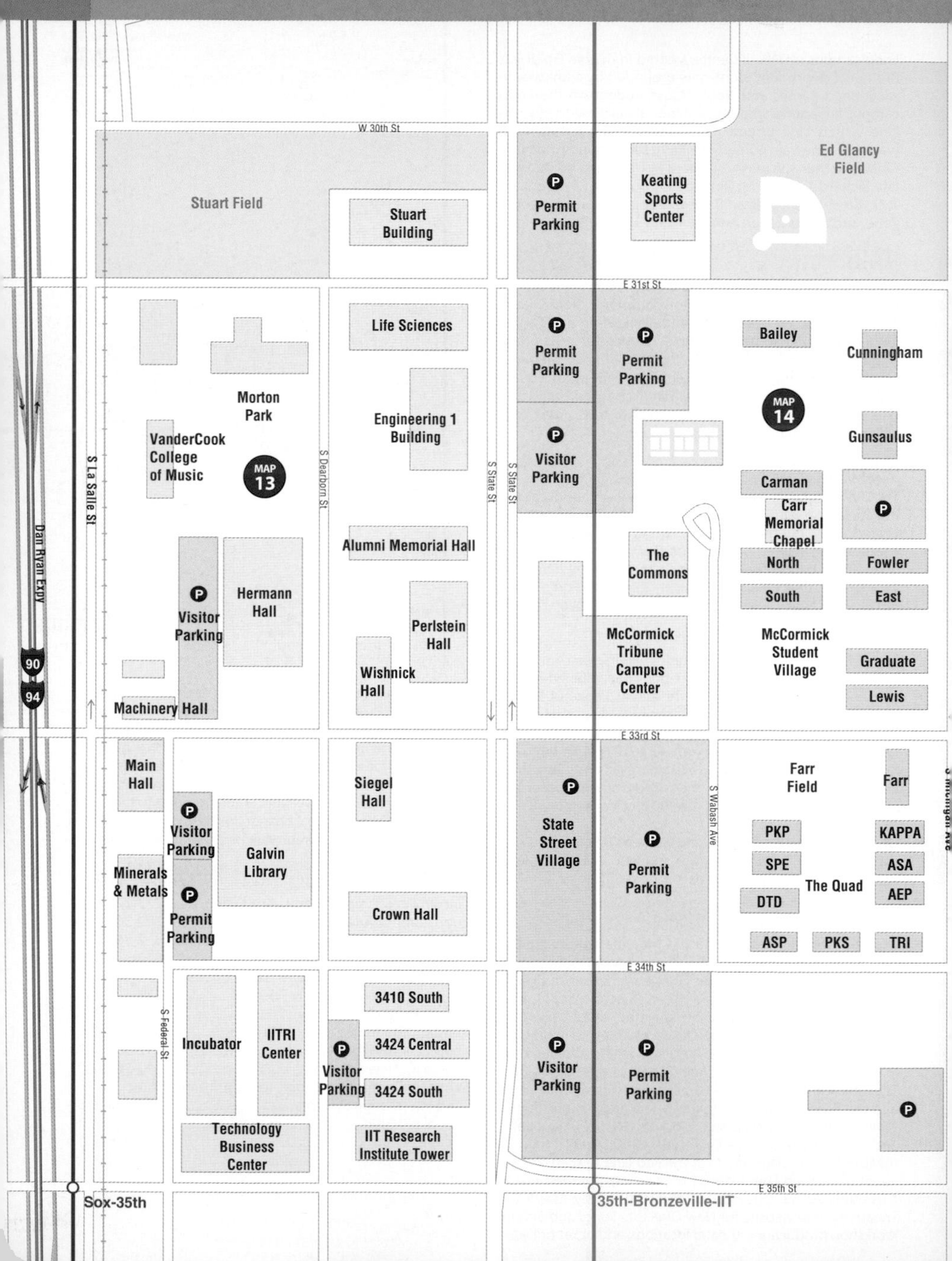

W 30th St
Stuart Field
Stuart Building
Permit Parking
Keating Sports Center
Ed Glancy Field
E 31st St
Life Sciences
Permit Parking
Permit Parking
Bailey
Cunningham
Morton Park
Engineering 1 Building
MAP 14
Gunsaulus
VanderCook College of Music
MAP 13
S Dearborn St
S State St
S State St
Visitor Parking
S La Salle St
Carman
Carr Memorial Chapel
Alumni Memorial Hall
The Commons
North
Fowler
Dan Ryan Expy
Visitor Parking
Hermann Hall
South
East
Perlstein Hall
McCormick Tribune Campus Center
McCormick Student Village
90
Graduate
94
Wishnick Hall
Lewis
Machinery Hall
E 33rd St
Main Hall
Siegel Hall
Farr Field
Farr
S Wabash Ave
Visitor Parking
State Street Village
PKP
KAPPA
SPE
ASA
Minerals & Metals
Galvin Library
Permit Parking
The Quad
AEP
DTD
Permit Parking
Crown Hall
ASP
PKS
TRI
E 34th St
3410 South
S Federal St
Incubator
IITRI Center
Visitor Parking
3424 Central
Visitor Parking
Permit Parking
3424 South
Technology Business Center
IIT Research Institute Tower
Sox-35th
35th-Bronzeville-IIT
E 35th St

General Information

NFT Map: 13, 14
Main Campus: 3300 S Federal St
Chicago, IL 60616
Phone: 312-567-3000
Website: www.iit.edu

Overview

In the 19th century, when higher education was reserved for society's upper crust, meat magnate Philip Danforth Armour put his money to good use and funded an institution dedicated to students who wished to learn a variety of industrial arts. The Armour Institute carried his name until a merger with the engineering school Lewis Institute in 1940 changed the name to Illinois Institute of Technology. Over the next 40 years, the college continued to merge with other small technical colleges, resulting in the IIT we know today. The school is as notable for its Mies Van Der Rohe–designed campus (although it is arguably not his best work) as for its groundbreaking work in aeronautics research. The new student center, designed by Dutch architect Rem Koolhaas, includes a space-aged metallic tube through which the local L train travels.

Chicago-Kent College of Law, Stuart School Graduate School of Business, and the Institute of Design are based in the Loop. The Rice campus, in west suburban Wheaton, offers undergraduate continuing education and degree programs to working professionals. The National Center for Food Safety and Technology, located in the southwest suburbs, and the IIT Research Institute, housed in IIT's tallest building on its main campus in Bronzeville, are just two of the many research organizations IIT has incorporated since 1936 to serve various needs of private industry and government. IIT grants PhDs and other professional degrees in a vast array of areas including science, mathematics, engineering, architecture, psychology, design, business, and law. The interprofessional, technology-focused curriculum is designed to prepare the 6,400 students to become groundbreakers in an increasingly complex global workplace. IIT was recently named a "College of Distinction" by a new college guide honoring some of America's top educational institutions.

In June 2004, IIT's Research Institute Life Sciences Group was awarded $28 million in research funding. The prestigious award is among the largest ever received by IITRI for drug development.

Tuition

Undergrads pay around $29,000 per academic year plus room and board, $1000 to $1,500 for books, $850 for fees including a CTA pass—not a bad deal, considering other local schools' offers....Graduate, law, and business school tuition varies by program.

Sports

IIT's Scarlet Hawks compete in the NAIA Division I Chicagoland Collegiate Athletic Conference. Sports may be a bit drab here, as IIT aborted both men's and women's basketball in 2009, but its men's and women's soccer, swimming and diving, cross-country, men's baseball, and women's volleyball are safe for now.

Developments on Campus

The newest student residency, completed in 2003, is State Street Village. Located at State and 33rd Streets, the hall was designed by well-known Chicago-based architect Helmut Jahn. The German-born designer was named one of the Ten Most Influential Living American Architects by the American Institute of Architects (AIA) in 1991. Jahn, a graduate of IIT himself, created the six-building complex across the street from Van Der Rohe's historical landmark, the S.R. Crown Hall. Jahn's new building brings student housing to a new level with poured-in-place concrete and glass-clad and corrugated stainless steel panels that reduce noise and vibrations from passing trains while simultaneously exhibiting a cutting-edge aesthetic. Currently underway is development of the $50 million University Technology Park on the main campus, to be built in phases over the next ten years.

Department Contact Information

Undergraduate Admissions.......... 312-567-3025
Graduate Admissions.......... 312-567-3020
Alumni Office.......... 312-567-5040
Armour College of Engineering 312-567-3009
Center for Law and Financial Markets.......... 312-906-6576
Center for Professional Development.......... 630-682-6040
Chicago-Kent College of Law 312-906-5000
College of Architecture 312-567-3263
College of Science & Letters.......... 312-567-3800
Keating Sports Center.......... 312-567-3000
Institute of Business and Interprofessional Studies.......... 312-567-3947
Institute of Design.......... 312-595-4900
Institute of Psychology.......... 312-567-3500
Stuart Graduate School of Business.......... 312-906-6500
University Technology Park 312-567-3900

Northwestern University (Evanston Campus)

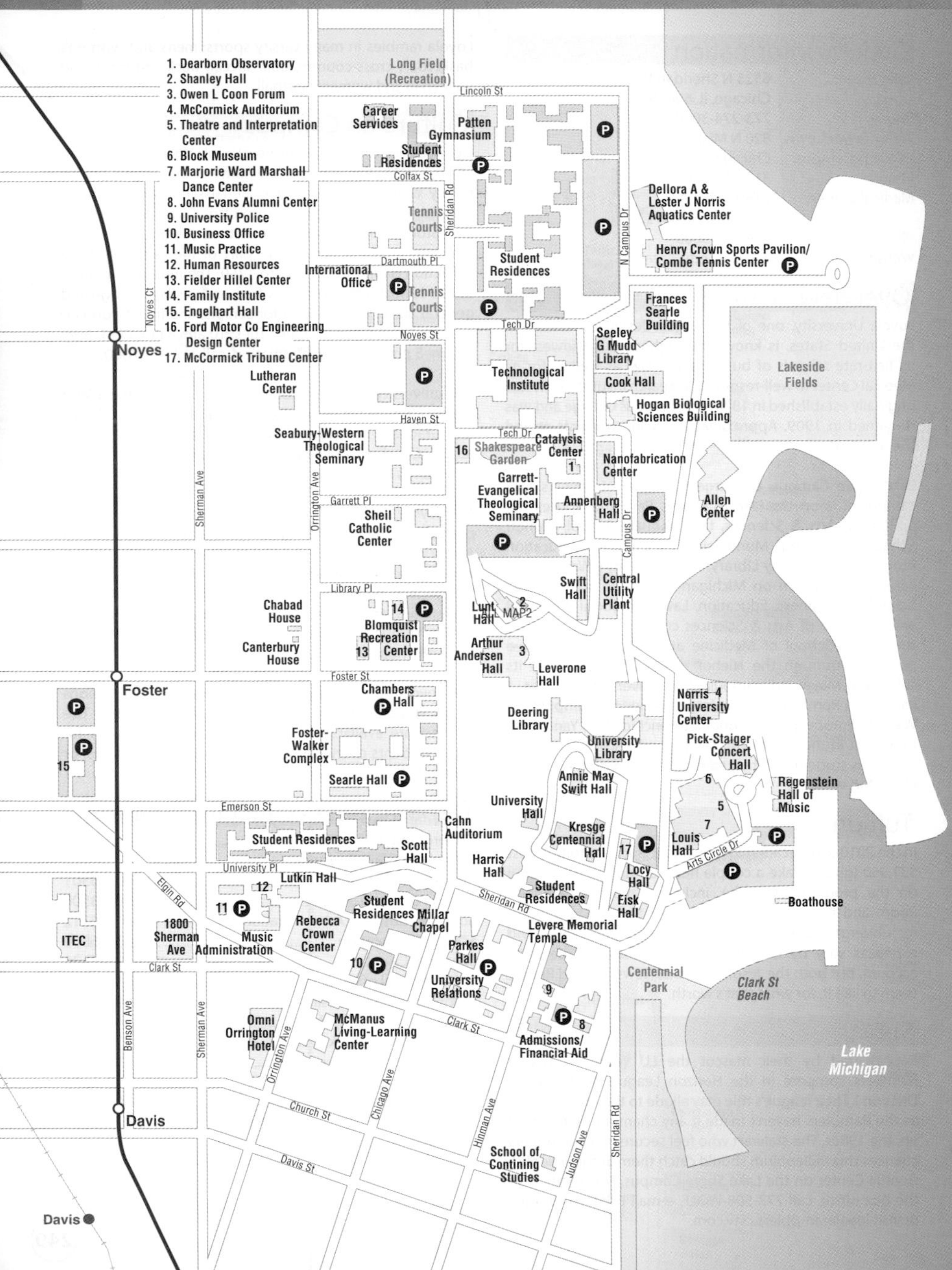

General Information

Evanston Campus:	633 Clark St Evanston, IL 60208 Phone: 847-491-3741
Chicago Campus:	Abbot Hall 710 N Lake Shore Dr Chicago, IL 60611 Phone: 312-503-8649
Website:	www.northwestern.edu

Overview

Northwestern University, along with the University of Chicago, likes to think of itself as part of the "Ivy League of the Midwest." While this might seem a lofty moniker, the University is certainly the cream of the crop in the Big Ten Conference. Almost 18,000 full- and part-time students attend Northwestern's 11 schools, located in Evanston and downtown Chicago, a far cry from the 2 original faculty members and 10 students in attendance when the school opened in 1855. The University's name was derived from its founders' desire to service the citizens of the former Northwest Territory.

Founded in 1851, Northwestern University was established in Evanston by many of the same Methodist founding fathers of the town itself, including the founder of Chicago's Board of Trade. The 240-acre lakefront campus is bordered roughly by Lincoln Street to the north and extends south to Clark Street and west to Sheridan Road. The Evanston campus houses the Weinberg College of Arts and Sciences; McCormick School of Engineering and Applied Science; the Schools of Music, Communication, Education and Social Policy; the Graduate School; Medill School of Journalism; and J.L. Kellogg School of Management.

The university did a bit of branching out when it purchased land for the Chicago campus in 1920. Located on a 25-acre lot between the lake and Michigan Avenue in the Streeterville neighborhood, the Chicago campus houses the Schools of Law, Medicine, and Continuing Studies. Graduate school and Kellogg courses are also offered at the Chicago campus. Several excellent hospitals and medical research institutions affiliated with the university dominate the northern edge of Streeterville. The Robert H. Lurie Medical Research Center at Fairbanks Court and Superior Street, completed in 2004, has expanded the university's research abilities with nine floors of laboratory space. The new Prentice Women's Hospital was completed in late 2007, offering comprehensive women's and infants' health.

Tuition

The university charges around $38,000 for combined tuition, room, and board.. Room and board rates hover around $11,294 for an undergraduate student living in a double room and on a 19-meal-per-week board plan. (Approximately 4,000 of Northwestern's 8,100 undergraduate students live in University residence halls.) Graduate school tuition and fees vary by college.

Sports

The only private school in the Big Ten conference, Northwestern trains eight men's and eleven women's intercollegiate teams along with a host of club teams. The women's lacrosse team won the NCAA national championship for each of the five years ending in 2009, a year when it also went undefeated. The Wildcats' football fortune is slowly looking up, as the purple-clad boys broke a 33-year losing streak in 2004.

The Wildcats' home is Ryan Field at 1501 Central Avenue, about three blocks west of the Central stop on the elevated Purple Line of the CTA. Basketball games are held at the Welsh-Ryan Arena behind the stadium. For tickets, call 847-491-2287. All sporting events are listed at www.nusports.com, where you can also purchase tickets online. Northwestern students can also obtain free tickets to any home game with the presentation of their Wildcard ID.

Northwestern also has men's wrestling and baseball teams, plus men's and women's basketball, golf, soccer, tennis, and swimming and diving teams. Wildcat women also complete in cross country, fencing, softball, field hockey, and volleyball.

Culture on Campus

The Mary and Leigh Block Museum of Art on the Evanston campus (40 Arts Circle Dr; 847-491-4000; www.blockmuseum.northwestern.edu) has 4,000 items in its permanent collection, including Old Masters' prints, architectural drawings, contemporary photographic images, and modern sculpture. The Block is also home to the state-of-the-art Pick-Laudati Auditorium that hosts film festivals and contemporary classics, as well as different cinema series' and lectures throughout the year. Hours: Tues: 10 am to 5 pm; Wed–Fri: 10 am to 8 pm; weekends: noon–5 pm. Admission is always free.

The Pick-Staiger Concert Hall (50 Arts Circle Dr, 847-491-5441; www.pickstaiger.com), is not only the main stage for the university's musical performances, but it is also home to several professional performance organizations such as the Chicago Chamber Musicians, Symphony of the Shores, Chicago String Ensemble, Performing Arts Chicago, and others. Each year, Pick-Staiger Concert Hall also hosts the Segovia Classical Guitar Series and the Keyboard Conversations Series. Call 847-467-4000 to purchase tickets.

For the upper echelon student interested in art or vandalism, one can visit the famed "Rock" that students began defacing in the 1940s. "Go Cats!," "Rich Kids Can Tag As Well!" and "I'm wasting my parent's money!" have all made brief appearances.

Northwestern University also runs a student newspaper, The Daily Northwestern, and a student radio station, WNUR.

Department Contact Information

Undergraduate Admissions	847-491-7271
Graduate School (Evanston)	847-491-5279
Graduate School (Chicago)	312-503-8900
Weinberg College of Arts and Sciences	847-491-7561
Feinberg School of Medicine	312-503-8649
Kellogg School of Management	847-491-3300
Medill School of Journalism	847-467-1882
School of Communication	847-491-7023
School of Continuing Studies (Evanston)	847-491-5611
School of Education and Social Policy	847-491-8193
McCormick School of Engineering and Applied Science	847-491-5220
School of Law	312-503-3100
School of Music	847-491-7575

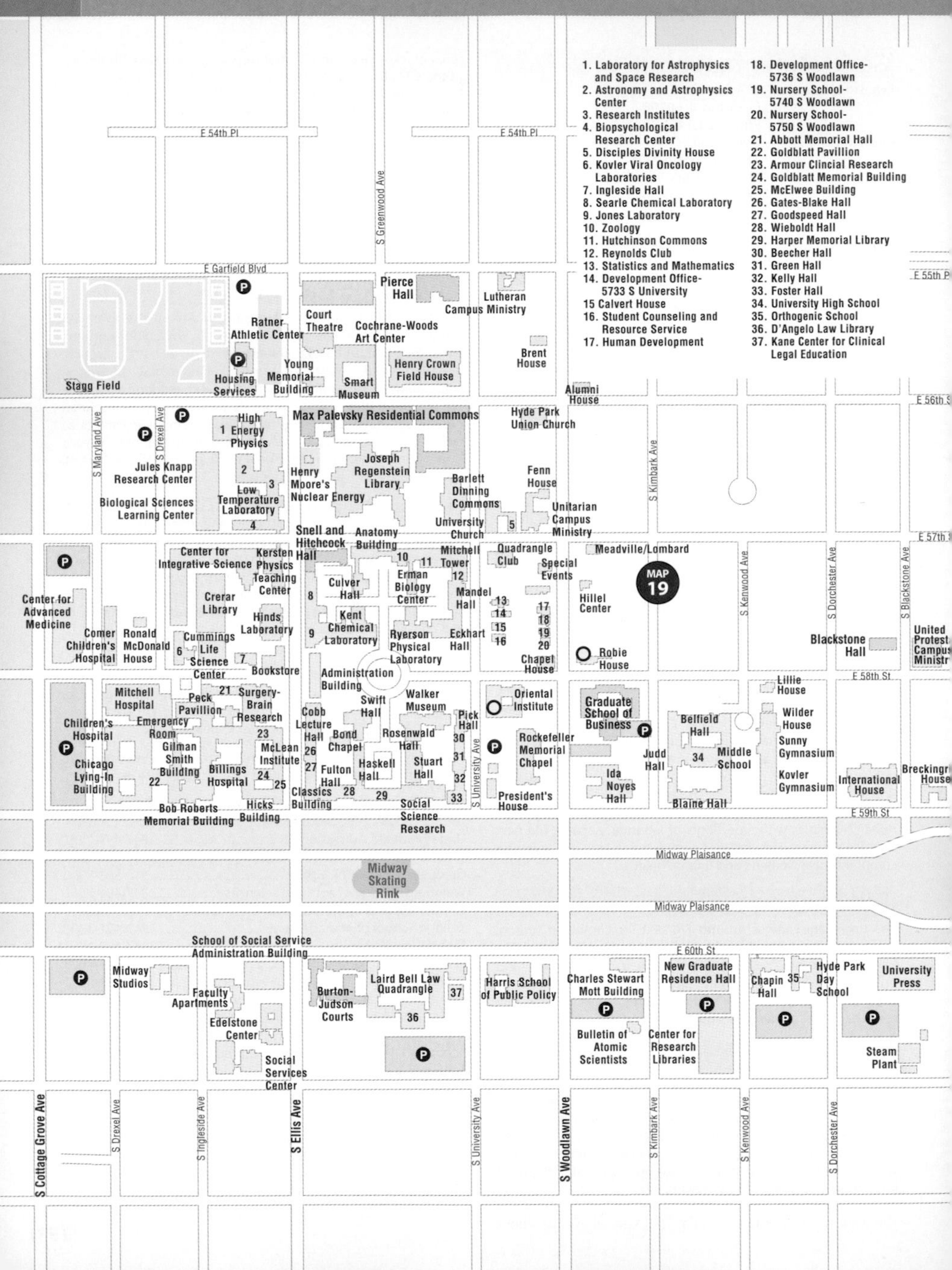
1. Laboratory for Astrophysics and Space Research
2. Astronomy and Astrophysics Center
3. Research Institutes
4. Biopsychological Research Center
5. Disciples Divinity House
6. Kovler Viral Oncology Laboratories
7. Ingleside Hall
8. Searle Chemical Laboratory
9. Jones Laboratory
10. Zoology
11. Hutchinson Commons
12. Reynolds Club
13. Statistics and Mathematics
14. Development Office-5733 S University
15 Calvert House
16. Student Counseling and Resource Service
17. Human Development
18. Development Office-5736 S Woodlawn
19. Nursery School-5740 S Woodlawn
20. Nursery School-5750 S Woodlawn
21. Abbott Memorial Hall
22. Goldblatt Pavillion
23. Armour Clincial Research
24. Goldblatt Memorial Building
25. McElwee Building
26. Gates-Blake Hall
27. Goodspeed Hall
28. Wieboldt Hall
29. Harper Memorial Library
30. Beecher Hall
31. Green Hall
32. Kelly Hall
33. Foster Hall
34. University High School
35. Orthogenic School
36. D'Angelo Law Library
37. Kane Center for Clinical Legal Education
MAP 19
E 54th Pl
E 54th Pl
S Greenwood Ave
E Garfield Blvd
E 55th Pl
E 56th St
E 57th St
E 58th St
E 59th St
Midway Plaisance
Midway Plaisance
E 60th St
S Maryland Ave
S Drexel Ave
S Kimbark Ave
S Kenwood Ave
S Dorchester Ave
S Blackstone Ave
S University Ave
S Cottage Grove Ave
S Drexel Ave
S Ingleside Ave
S Ellis Ave
S University Ave
S Woodlawn Ave
S Kimbark Ave
S Kenwood Ave
S Dorchester Ave
Stagg Field
Ratner Athletic Center
Housing Services
Young Memorial Building
Court Theatre
Pierce Hall
Cochrane-Woods Art Center
Smart Museum
Henry Crown Field House
Lutheran Campus Ministry
Brent House
Alumni House
Max Palevsky Residential Commons
Hyde Park Union Church
High Energy Physics
Jules Knapp Research Center
Biological Sciences Learning Center
Low Temperature Laboratory
Henry Moore's Nuclear Energy
Joseph Regenstein Library
Barlett Dinning Commons
Fenn House
Unitarian Campus Ministry
University Church
Snell and Hitchcock Hall
Anatomy Building
Mitchell Tower
Quadrangle Club
Meadville/Lombard
Special Events
Center for Integrative Science
Kersten Physics Teaching Center
Crerar Library
Culver Hall
Erman Biology Center
Mandel Hall
Hillel Center
Center for Advanced Medicine
Hinds Laboratory
Kent Chemical Laboratory
Comer Children's Hospital
Ronald McDonald House
Cummings Life Science Center
Bookstore
Ryerson Physical Laboratory
Eckhart Hall
Chapel House
Robie House
Blackstone Hall
United Protest. Campus Ministr
Administration Building
Mitchell Hospital
Peck Pavillion
Surgery-Brain Research
Swift Hall
Walker Museum
Oriental Institute
Graduate School of Business
Lillie House
Wilder House
Children's Hospital
Emergency Room
Gilman Smith Building
Cobb Lecture Hall
Bond Chapel
Rosenwald Hall
Pick Hall
Rockefeller Memorial Chapel
Belfield Hall
Sunny Gymnasium
Chicago Lying-In Building
Billings Hospital
McLean Institute
Fulton Hall
Haskell Hall
Stuart Hall
Judd Hall
Middle School
Kovler Gymnasium
International House
Breckingr House
Bob Roberts Memorial Building
Hicks Building
Classics Building
Social Science Research
President's House
Ida Noyes Hall
Blaine Hall
Midway Skating Rink
School of Social Service Administration Building
Midway Studios
Faculty Apartments
Edelstone Center
Social Services Center
Burton-Judson Courts
Laird Bell Law Quadrangle
Harris School of Public Policy
Charles Stewart Mott Building
Bulletin of Atomic Scientists
New Graduate Residence Hall
Center for Research Libraries
Chapin Hall
Hyde Park Day School
University Press
Steam Plant

General Information

NFT Map: 19
Mailing Address: University of Chicago
Administration Building
5801 S Ellis Ave
Chicago, IL 60637
Phone: 773-702-1234
Website: www.uchicago.edu
Visitor's Center: Ida Noyes Hall, 1st Fl
1212 E 59th St
Phone: 773-702-8650
Guest Parking: Lot located off Woodlawn Ave
b/w 58th St and 59th St Metered
parking is available north of Ida Noyes Hall.

Overview

Located amidst the pleasant tree-lined streets of Hyde Park just seven miles south of downtown Chicago, the University of Chicago is a world-renowned research institution with a winning tradition in Nobel Prizes. Eighty-five Nobel laureates have been associated with the university as faculty, students, or researchers. The university prides itself on its rigorous academic standards and top-ranked programs, while its students thrive in an environment that encourages creative exploring, taking risks, intellectual rigor, and determining the direction and focus of one's own education.

While its business, law, and medical schools are renowned for cranking out brainy gurus with assembly line efficiency, the university also has a long alumni list filled with artists, writers, politicians, film directors, and actors. To name a few: Studs Terkel, Sara Paretsky, Carol Moseley-Braun, Kurt Vonnegut, Susan Sontag, David Auburn, Ed Asner, Saul Bellow, Katharine Graham, Philip Glass, Saul Alinsky, Paul Goodman, Mike Nichols, and Second City improv theater founders Bernard Sahlins and Paul Sills.

Established in 1890, the University of Chicago was founded and funded by John D. Rockefeller. Built on 200 acres donated by Marshall Field and designed by architect Henry Ives Cobb, the university's English Gothic buildings of ivy-clad limestone ooze old money and intellectual achievements. Rockefeller described the university as "the best investment I ever made." We just hope parents footing the bill for their kids' education feel the same

Tuition

The University of Chicago operates on a trimester schedule rather than the more common two-semester academic year. An undergraduate student pays about $40,000 for tuition fees with an additional $12,000 for room and board. So if you add up all the books costs, lab fees, personal expenses…carry the one... that comes to around fifty-five grand a year. Costs for graduate students vary based on the school. Chicago has about 15,000 students, 5,000 of which are undergraduates. About 2,000 of the graduate students attend classes at the downtown riverfront campus Gleacher Center (450 N Cityfront Plaza Dr, 312-464-8787; www.gleachercenter.com), where the popular Graham School of General Studies holds most of its continuing education classes.

Sports

A long time ago, the famous nickname "Monsters of The Midway" belonged to The University of Chicago's football team (not 'da Bears'), and the institution garnered football trophies right along with Nobel Prizes. The Maroons racked up seven Big Ten Football championships between 1899 and 1924, but the gridiron glory of yore faded and losing teams became the norm. The bleachers at Stagg field, where fans once flocked to witness athletic triumphs, earned more fame as the site where Enrico Fermi and university scientists split the atom on Dec. 2, 1942. Four years later, President Robert Maynard Hutchins put in the university's walking papers from the Big Ten and abolished the football team. Perhaps this was a step towards prioritizing scholarly pursuits over athletic achievement, however the catastrophic results of the "controlled release of nuclear energy" might be to blame.

But the school hasn't totally abandoned sports. Varsity football, reinstated in 1969, is back, abeit in a different form. UChicago is a member of the NCAA Division III UAA (University Athletic Association) and hosts 19 varsity athletic sports in a conference comprised of some of the nation's leading research institutions, and since 1990 has won team championships in men's basketball, women's cross country, football, men's and women's soccer, softball, men's indoor track & field, and wrestling. The campus also boasts over 45 club sports and hundreds of intramural teams.

Culture on Campus

Located at 5757 S. Woodlawn Avenue is Frank Lloyd Wright's residential ode to all things horizontal and structurally organic: The Roble House 708-848-1976; www.gowright.org). This Prairie Style masterpiece is considered one of the most important buildings in the history of American architecture and with the exterior restoration phase recently completed on the $8-million dollar renovation, it once again appears fresh off the proverbial drafting board. (Adult tickets cost $12), children 7-18 and seniors pay $10, and if you want to adopt an art glass cabinet for restoration, its $20,000.

Two must-see but often overlooked free museums on campus are the Oriental Institute Museum (1155 E. 58th St., 773-702-9514; www.oi.uchicago.edu) and the Smart Museum of Art 5550 S. Greenwood Ave., 773-702-0200; www.smartmuseum.uchicago.edu. Showcasing ancient treasures from university digs since the 1900s (and yes, Indiana Jones did his undergraduate studies at U of C), the Oriental Institute houses permanent galleries devoted to ancient Egypt, Nubia, Persia, Mesopotamia, Syria, Anatolia, the ancient site of Megiddo, along with a rotation of special exhibits. The Smart Museum boasts a permanent collection of 10,000 fine art objects spanning five millennia of both Western and Eastern civilizations–so yes, it'll be enough to look at for that afternoon you have to kill.

To satisfy your inner cineaste, take in a picture show at Doc Films (Max Palevsky Cinema 1212 E 59th St., 773-702-8575; www.docfilms.uchicago.edu), the largest continuously running student film society in the nation. The screenings at their state-of-the-art theater range from foreign art house fare to documentaries to Hollywood classics, and feature companion lectures and Q&A with professors, actors, directors, and producers. If you're jonesing for a music fix, University of Chicago Presents is one of the city's landmark classical music presenters and features a variety of performers in the elegant, Victorian-style Mandel Hall.

The university's professional Court Theater is a nationally renowned, critically acclaimed theatre that provides fresh interpretations of classic dramas as well as more contemporary classics (5535 S Ellis Ave., 773-753-4472; www.courttheatre.org). Previous seasons have included productions of Edward Albee's *Whos' Afraid of Virginia Wolf*, Tennessee Williams' *The Glass Menagerie*, August Wilson's *Fences*, Tom Stoppard's *Arcadia*, and Tony Kushner's *Caroline, or Change*.

Department Contact Information

Log on to www.uchicago.edu/uchi/directories for a university directory and links to division and department web pages.

Undergraduate Student Admissions........773-702-8650
Biological Sciences........773-702-9000
Humanities........773-702-8512
Physical Sciences........773-702-7950
Social Sciences........773-702-8799
Divinity School........773-702-8200
Graduate School of Business........773-702-7743
Graduate Affairs........773-702-7813
Graham School of General Studies........773-702-1722
Harris Graduate School of Public Policy Studies........773-702-8401
Law School........773-702-9494
Pritzker School of Medicine........773-702-1939
School of Social Service Administration........773-702-1250

University of Illinois at Chicago

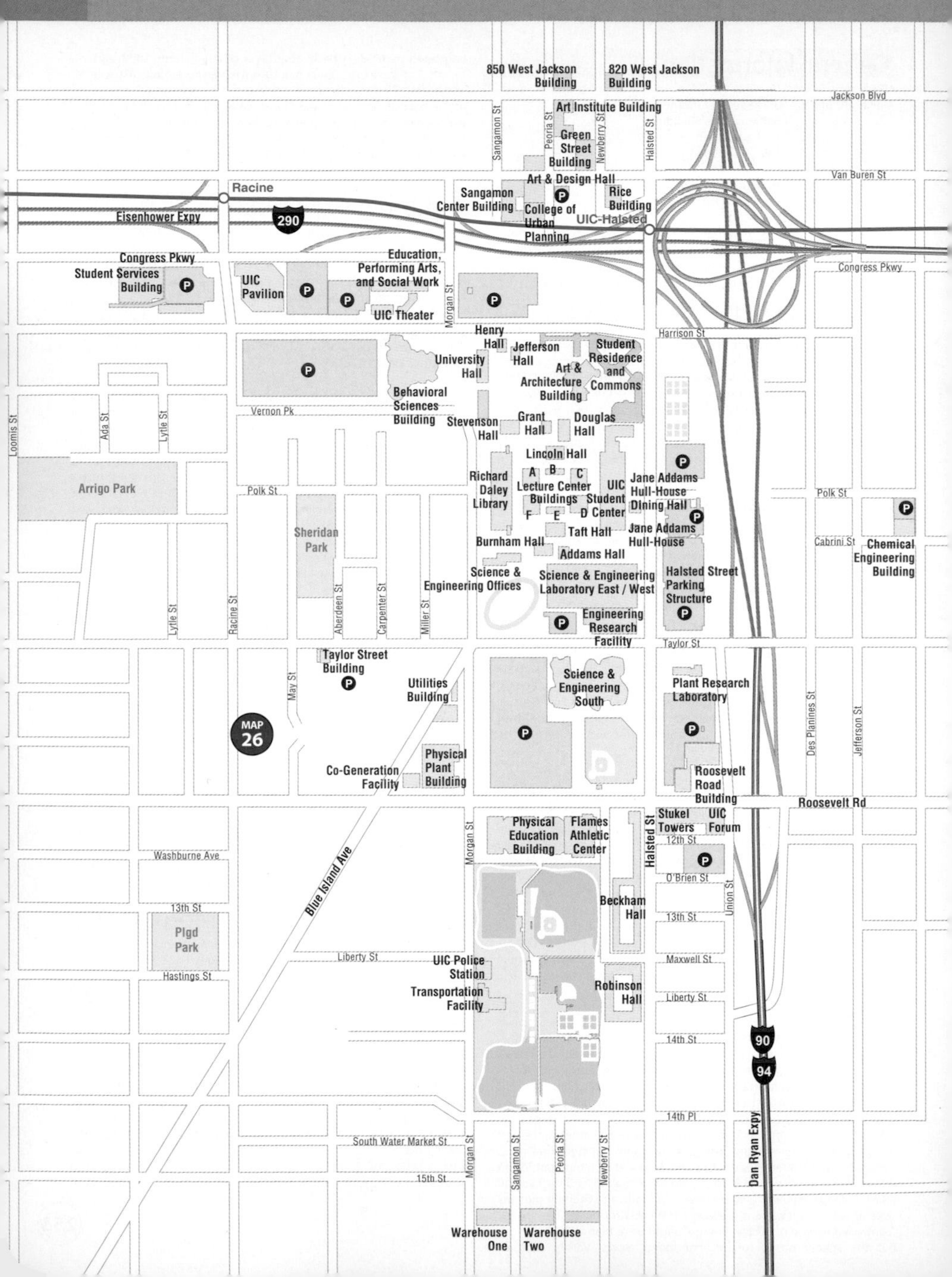

General Information

NFT Map: 26
Address: 1200 W Harrison St
Chicago, IL 60680
Phone: 312-996-7000
Website: www.uic.edu

Overview

With over 25,000 students, the University of Illinois at Chicago (UIC) is the largest university in the city. Located on the Near West Side, UIC is ethnically diverse and urban to the core. It is a leading public research university and home to the nation's largest medical school.

Its legacy as a builder in Chicago, however, is a bit spotty. In the mid-1960s, the school leveled most of what was left of a vibrant Italian-American neighborhood to build its campus next to the Eisenhower Expressway. Today, UIC continues to consume city blocks south of Roosevelt Road in further developing the South Campus. The expansions have all but erased the colorful, landmark Maxwell Street flea market area (this bustling mess of market now takes place only on Sundays along nearby S Canal Street). Of course, not eveyone is crying over the loss of the eyesore market or the decrepit, crumbling buildings and homes that comprised the area, although we question whether a community of pricey cookie-cutter townhomes really constitutes much of an improvement. One thing that everyone seems to agree on is that many of the campus's original, ugly cement slab structures are kissing the wrecking ball as well. Even with the multi-million-dollar improvements, the campus is still fairly average; unless you're going to class or the doctor, a lone trip to UIC to see the Jane Addams Hull-House Museum is sufficient.

Tuition

An Illinois resident undergraduate student's total tuition and fees ranged from approximately $12,000 (for nursing) to $16,000 (for most other programs); room and board ranged from $7,453 to $11,687 depending on the meal plan and type of housing. These figures do not include books, supplies, lab fees, or personal expenses. Primarily a commuter institution, UIC has about 48,000 undergraduates; graduate and professional enrollment varies by department.

Sports

The UIC Flames are hot these days. The men's basketball team competed in the NCAA tournament in 2004, 2002 and 1998. Additionally, the Flames women's gymnastics, tennis squad, and softball teams have all advanced to NCAA Tournament play in recent years. Other Flames men's and women's teams include swimming & diving and cross-country/track & field. UIC also has men's tennis, gymnastics, baseball, and soccer, as well as women's basketball and volleyball. Basketball games and women's volleyball matches are played at the recently renovated UIC Pavilion at the corner of S Racine Avenue and Harrison Street. For tickets, call 312-413-8421, or visit www.uicflames.com.

Too bad the NCAA doesn't have a bowling tournament because UIC would be a strong contender. The campus has its own alley located at 750 S Halsted Street (312-413-5170) where the public is welcome to sling balls and swig beers with students.

Culture on Campus

Jane Addams Hull-House (800 S Halsted St, 312-413-5353; www.uic.edu/jaddams/hull), America's first settlement house, opened in 1889. The free museum documents the pioneering organization's social welfare programs that supported the community's destitute immigrant workers. Jane Addams was cool. Way cool. Museum hours are 10 am to 4 pm Tuesday through Friday and noon to 4 pm on Sunday, closed on Mondays and Saturdays.

Department Contact Information

All area codes are 312 unless otherwise noted.

Admissions and Records	996-4350
Graduate College	413-2550
College of Architecture & the Arts	996-5611
College of Applied Health Sciences	996-6695
College of Dentistry	996-1020
College of Business Administration	996-2700
College of Education	996-5641
College of Engineering	996-2400
College of Liberal Arts and Sciences	413-2500
College of Medicine	996-3500
College of Nursing	996-7800
College of Pharmacy	996-7240
School of Public Health	996-6620
College of Social Work	996-7096
College of Urban Planning and Public Affairs	413-8088
Office of Continuing Education	996-8025
University of Illinois Medical Center	800-842-1002

Continuing Education in Chicago

Whether you want to change careers or just your waistline, learn a foreign language or learn more about the one you already know, Chicago is a great city to channel your inner student.

Get to the point of the matter with fencing classes from the Chicago Athletic Association Fencers Club. Turn off the Food Network, and learn to do it yourself at Kendall College, The French Pastry School, or The Chopping Block. Learn to put your food down with style at the Flamenco Arts Center. Find out why laughter truly is the best medicine at The Second City Training Center or Comedy Sportz. Run away and join the circus after trapeze classes from The Flying Gaonas. And discover that you really can teach an old dog new tricks at AnimalSense.

Continuing Education And Professional Development

Chicago School of Massage Therapy, www.csmt.com, 866-267-8482, 17 N State St, 5th Fl, 60602

The French Pastry School, www.frenchpastryschool.com, 312-726-2419, 226 W Jackson Blvd, 60606

Kendall College, www.kendall.edu, 866-667-3344, 900 N Branch St, 60622

Pacific College of Oriental Medicine, www.pacificcollege.edu, 888-729-4811, 3646 N Broadway, 2nd Fl, 60613

Roosevelt University, www.roosevelt.edu, 312-341-3500, 430 S Michigan Ave, 60605

School of the Art Institute of Chicago, www.saic.edu, 312-629-6100, 37 S Wabash, 7th Fl, 60603

School of Continuing Studies at Northwestern University, www.scs.northwestern.edu, 312-503-6950, 399 E Chicago Ave, 60611

A Little Bit Of Everything

AnimalSense, www.animalsense.com, 773-275-3647, various locations.

The Discovery Center, www.discoverycenter.cc, 773-348-8120, 2940 N Lincoln Ave, 60657

Gallery 37 Center for the Arts, www.g37centerforthearts.org, 312-744-8925, 66 E Randolph St, 60602

Motorcycle Riding School, www.motorcyclelearning.com, 773-968-7433, 1400 N Halsted St, 60622

Ride Chicago Motorcycle School, www.ride-chicago.com, 773-334-4998, 5215 N Ravenswood Ave

Writers The Loft, www.thewritersloft.com, 773-348-4116, 1450 W Waveland Ave, 60613

Arts And Lifestyle

Chicago Bauhaus Academy (woodworking and furniture design), www.chicagobauhaus.org, 773-761-0418, 6525 N Clark St, 60626

Comedy Sportz, www.comedysportzchicago.com, 773-549-8080, 5100 N Ravenswood Ave, 60640

Fire Arts Center of Chicago, www.firearts.org, 773-329-9908, 1907 N Mendell St, 60622

Glass Frog Studio, www.glassfrogstudio.com, 773-523-8933, 3509 S Wolcott Ave, 60609

Lillstreet Art Center, www.lillstreet.com, 773-769-4226, 4401 N Ravenswood Ave, 60640

Mudhouse Studio, www.mudhousestudio.com, 773-975-7522, 3841 N Ashland Ave, 60613

Old Town School of Folk Music, www.oldtownschool.org, 773-728-6000, 4544 N Lincoln Ave, 60625

Palette & Chisel Academy of Fine Art, www.paletteandchisel.org, 312-642-4400, 1012 N Dearborn, 60610

The Screenwriters Group, www.screenwritersgroup.com, 773-665-8500, 1803 W Byron St, 60613

The Second City Training Center, www.secondcity.com, 312-664-4032, 1616 N Wells St, 60614

WoodSmyth's (woodworking classes), www.woodsmythschicago.com, 773-477-6482, 1835 W School St, 60657

Athletics And Dance

All About Dance, www.allaboutdance.org, 773-572-8701, 2214 N Clark St, 60614

Chicago Athletic Association Fencers Club, www.caafc.com, 312-644-4880, 441 N Wabash, 60611

Chicago Sailing Club, www.chicagosailing.com, 773-871-7245, 2712 N Campbell Ave, 60647

Flamenco Arts Center, www.flamencoartscenter.com, 773-868-4130, 3755 N Western Ave, 60618

The Flying Gaonas, www.flyinggaonastrapeze.com, 773-398-9881.

JABB Gym, www.jabbboxing.com, 312-733-5222, 410 N Oakley Blvd, 2nd Flr, 60612

Latin Street Dancing, www.laboriqua.com, 312-427-2572, 540 N La Salle St, 5th Fl, 60610

The School of Ballet Chicago, www.balletchicago.org, 312-251-8838, 218 Wabash St, 3rd Fl, 60604

Together We Tri (triathalon training), www.togetherwetri.com, 866-889-3874

Food And Wine

BIN 36, www.bin36.com, 312-755-9463, 339 N Dearborn, 60610

Calphalon Culinary Center, www.calphalonculinarycenter.com, 312-529-0100, 1000 W Washington St, 60607

The Chopping Block, www.thechoppingblock.net, 773-472-6700, 4747 N Lincoln Ave; 312-644-6360, The Merchandise Mart Plaza, Ste 107, 60654.

Fox & Obel, www.fox-obel.com, 312-410-7301, 401 E Illinois St, 60611

Just Grapes, www.justgrapes.net, 312-627-9463, 560 W Washington Blvd, Ste 100, 60661

Sur La Table Culinary Center, www.surlatable.com, 312-337-0600, 52-54 E Walton St, 60611

Foreign Languages

Alliance Francaise de Chicago, www.afchicago.com, 312-337-1070, 810 N Dearborn St, 60610

Instituto Cervantes Chicago, www.chicago.cervantes.es, 312-335-1996, 31 W Ohio St, 60610

Italidea, www.italidea.org, 312-832-4053, 500 N Michigan Ave Ste 1450, 60611

General Information

Active Transportation Alliance:	9 W Hubbard St, Ste 402, www.activetrans.org; 312-427-3325
Chicago Park District:	www.chicagoparkdistrict.com; 312-742-PLAY
Chicago Cycling Club:	www.chicagocyclingclub.org; 773-509-8093 (Organized weekend rides April through October)
Chicago Transit Authority:	www.transitchicago.com
DOT Bikes Website:	www.chicagobikes.org
The Chainlink Social Network:	www.thechainlink.org

Overview

Despite the environmental, physical, and cost-saving benefits of biking, as well as ex-Mayor Daley 'efforts' to make Chicago streets more hospitable to pedallers, cyclists are still seen by many drivers as a road nuisance. Designated bike lanes on streets such as Milwaukee, Damen, King Drive and Elston are a joke, and the lack of parking enforcement, visibility, and overall awareness make these designated areas as dangerous as their unregulated side street counterparts. If the bicycle lanes are good at anything, it may be at increasing the possibility of a "dooring" by a cell-phone yammering motorist or unconcerned cabby. Furthermore, designated lakefront bike paths are anything but: a sunny Saturday morning guarantees a path that is crowded with headphone-wearing roller bladers, leashless dogs, and shoulder-to-shoulder stroller pushers—not exactly the place to practice for a Lance Armstrong-like debut. Nonetheless, every year thousands of Chicagoans choose to take their lives into their hands by taking to the street in hopes that the city will become more bike-friendly. The Active Transportation Alliance does its best to raise awareness with events like Bike the Drive in May (no cars on Lake Shore Drive for a whole morning!) and Bike to Work Week in June. Other services, like the state-of-the-art bike parking garage in Millennium Park (complete with showers!), indicate that things are improving—and locking your bike to a rack for free sure beats paying for valet parking or ever-increasing meter fees.

If you are a cyclist in Chicago, bear in mind that bicycles, like other vehicles of the roads, are subject to the same laws and rights as drivers. You might feel like you're the only biker in the city who comes to a full stop at a sign, but fastidiously sticking to the laws is a good way to make a case for drivers to accept bikers. This includes the right to take a lane and the obligation to hand signal for turns. It goes without saying that you should always ride defensively (but don't bike on sidewalks: you can be ticketed). Helmets are still optional, but you'd have to have a pretty thick head to tempt fate without one. The many white "ghost bikes" set up throughout the city serve as vigils for fallen bikers, and remind riders of the need to buy and wear a helmet. Besides, one of the many perks of cycling is that no matter how goofy you may feel in your gear, there is always someone who looks much, much stupider beside you. The same goes for an adequate assortment of chains and u-locks, as bike thievery is rampant in every neighborhood in the city. The police department now offers a bike registration service, so you'll have legal recourse if you stumble upon your stolen bike on eBay.

Bikes Onboard Mass Transit

Bicycles are permitted (free) on all L trains at all times except 7 am–9 am and 4 pm–6 pm on weekdays. Use the accessible turnstile or ask an attendant to open an access gate. Don't try to take your bike through the tall steel gates—it will get stuck! Only two bikes per carriage are allowed, so check for other bikes before you get on. The CTA has equipped all of its buses with front exterior bike racks, which are much less intimidating to use than they appear. If your bike is the first to be loaded, lower the rack and place it in position with the front wheel facing the curb. If there is already a bike on the rack, place your bike's rear wheel toward the curb. If two bikes are already loaded, wait for the next bus (whenever that may be). Bus-traveling bicyclists be warned, horror stories abound about bikes falling off racks, and there are even hit-by-bus-while-trying-to remove-bike rumors. Always tell the driver that you are going to be loading or removing your bike, and ask for help if you need it—not all bus drivers are as gruff as they appear. On Metra commuter trains, bikes are allowed to travel free of charge in off-peak hours. There is a maximum number of bikes allowed per rail car (it varies by line—check the Metra website for your planned route), so follow the conductor's instructions if he or she asks you to board a different car.

Bike Shops	*Address*	*Phone*	*Map*
Bike and Roll Chicago- Navy Pier	600 E Grand Ave	312-729-1000	03
Bike and Roll Chicago- Ohio St Beach	400 N Lake Shore Dr	312-729-1000	03
Bike and Roll Chicago	239 E Randolph St	312-729-1000	06
Bike and Roll Chicago- Adler Planetarium	1300 S Lake Shore Dr	312-729-1000	11
Cycle Bike Shop	1465 S Michigan Ave	312-987-1080	11
Blue City Cycles	3201 S Halsted St	312-225-3780	13
Bike and Roll Chicago- DuSable Museum	740 E 56th Pl	312-729-1000	18
Blackstone Bicycle Works	6100 S Blackstone Ave		19
DJ's Bike Doctor	1500 E 55th St	773-955-4400	19
Wheels and Things	1340 E 55th St	773-493-4326	19
Rapid Transit Cycle Shop	1900 W North Ave		21
Quick Release Bike Shop	1527 N Ashland Ave	773-871-3110	22
Upgrade Cycle Works	1130 W Chicago Ave	312-226-8650	24
Boulevard Bikes	2535 N Kedzie Blvd	773-235-9109	27
Smart Bike Parts	3031 W Armitage Ave	773-384-3010	27
Bike and Roll Chicago- Foster Beach	5200 N Lake Shore Dr	312-729-1000	30
Cycle Smithy	2468 N Clark St	773-281-0444	30
Dutch Bike Co.	651 W Armitage Ave	312-265-0175	30
Bike and Roll Chicago- Oak St Beach	N Lake Shore Dr & E Oak St	312-729-1000	31
Village Cycle Center	1337 N Wells St	312-751-2488	31
Bike and Roll Chicago- North Ave Beach	1603 N Lake Shore Dr	312-729-1000	32
Gary's Cycle Shop	6317 N Clark St	773-743-4201	37
Johnny Sprockets	1052 W Bryn Mawr Ave	773-293-1695	37
Iron Cycles	3136 W Montrose Ave	773-539-4766	38
Uptown Bikes	4653 N Broadway St	773-728-5212	40
Roscoe Village Bikes	2016 W. Roscoe	773-477-7550	42
Johnny Sprockets	3001 N Broadway	773-224-1079	44
Kozy's Cyclery	3712 N Halsted St	773-281-2263	44

Billiards

The city's affluent "nesters" may be more interested in big-screen TVs than pool tables these days. But you'd rather mix your pleasure with strategy, a convivial game of billiards is still a fine way of turning strangers into friends... not to mention learning the angles above the angles above the angles. Many bars, from the seedy to the swanky, have a table or four. Chicago is also home to a good number of establishments that cater specifically to pool sharks. Have a good one, and don't get hustled.

The game's popularity goes in cycles. It spiked in the '80s thanks largely to *The Color of Money*, a pool-themed film starring Paul Newman and Tom Cruise, part of which was shot at **Chris's Billiards (Map 48)**. With two-dozen tables, no booze and no nonsense, this Jefferson Park institution remains the most credible spot among Chicago's seasoned players, although it sometimes intimidates newcomers. (We wouldn't call it "sleazy," but we wouldn't eat off the floor, either.) **Uno Billiards (Map 38)** is an oasis of seediness in the otherwise upscale Albany Park area. The equipment's not in tip-top shape, but cut this place and it bleeds character. **Chicago Billiards (Map 35)** is also a hike from downtown, but it's a more family-oriented room with a full food menu. If you're looking for snooker, a billiards variation wildly popular in Britain, they've got the hook-up here.

Somewhat hipper environs can be found at **City Pool Hall Food & Spirits (Map 1)**, a well-kept room also noted for its delectable burgers, and **Pressure Billiards & Café (Map 37)**, which boasts regulation tournament tables and, on weekends, one of the city's least hack-prone standup comedy nights. If racking the balls ever gets seriously trendy again, you can bet that the folks at **G Cue Billiards (Map 24)** will be the first to know. Professional player Tom Karabatsos runs this two-level lounge, which accommodates more hangers-out than pool purists. If the massive video screens don't take your eye off the eight ball, the young, smartly dressed clientele might. The pub grub is adequate. The mixed drinks are weak. Some of our sources report nasty experiences with the staff (and not the good kind of nasty experiences, either).

For an even more gloriously inauthentic pool adventure, you can usually find a table at one of Chicago's bowling alleys. **Diversey-River Bowl (Map 42)** may be better known for its blacklights and throbbing pop soundtrack, but for those who can't shoot straight sober, it's got a game room with a full-service bar. It's open 'til 3 am on weekends. **Waveland Bowl (Map 42)** has tables all night, every night, though there's often a wait, and it's hard to focus when high school and college kids keep distracting us with their air hockey and their Dance Dance Revolution. **Southport Lanes (Map 43)** is a mite classier, with lovely Brunswick tables in a welcoming back area.

A few major music venues also have tables, where musicians can be found relieving their road-warrior angst between sound checks. Show up early at the Double Door or the Empty Bottle (See Nightlife Map 21), and you might get to hustle the people who wrote your favorite song. South Loop blues joint Buddy Guy's also offers pool, and although the cover may be a bit intimidating, there is nothing quite like shooting stick while some of Chicago's saddest songsters wail next door.

Billiards	*Address*	*Phone*	*Fee*	*Map*
City Pool Hall	640 W Hubbard St	312-491-9690	$12 per hour	01
G Cue Billiards	157 N Morgan St	312-850-3170	$14 per hour	24
Seven Ten Lounge	2747 N Lincoln Ave	773-549-2695	$12 per hour	29
Pressure Billiards & Cafe	6318 N Clark St	773-743-7665	$10 per hour	37
Uno Billiards	3112 W Lawrence Ave	773-267-8166	$10 per hour	38
Waveland Bowl	3700 N Western Ave	773-472-5900	$8-15 per hour	42
Southport Lanes	3325 N Southport Ave	773-472-6600	$20 per hour	43

Bowling

Bowling is supposed to be the most blue-collar of all sports, so in the City of Big Shoulders, you'd expect comb-overs, beer frames, unfashionable wrist guards, and visible plumber's cracks to abound. In the '90s, several local alleys jazzed it up for the teenagers with rock music and late-night fog-and-light shows, and we can live with that. Lately, however, the trend is toward atmosphere-conscious boutique spots that treat strikes and spares as an afterthought. These are nice places to take a date, but we're a little scared when so-called bowling alleys advertise "small plates."

But if you're intrigued by the idea of high-end lounges that mash-up retro kitsch with modern glam, head to **10 Pin-Strike Bar Bowl & Grille (Map 2)**, where you can sip a trend-'tini on a cushy couch with an urban professional crowd. And the upscale, Hollywood-themed chain, **Lucky Strike Lanes (Map 3)**, is a good place to kill time if you're waiting to catch a movie at the adjacent AMC River East.

If you prefer not to define your bowling experience as "sophisticated" or "cutting edge," we recommend **Lincoln Square Lanes (Map 38)**, the city's only second-floor alley, which has been open since 1918. Climb a flight of stairs above the Ace Hardware store and you'll get twelve lanes with old-school wood floors, live blues and rockabilly music on weekends, and a balcony from which to watch the action. Other good choices for an authentic Chicago bowling adventure include **Diversey-River Bowl (Map 42)**, where there's an eclectic mix of league fanatics and hipster rockers ordering bottles of Bud shaped like bowling pins, or the only-slightly-grungy **Waveland Bowl (Map 42)**, which has been open 24 hours a day, seven days a week since 1969.

For a place that successfully maintains a vibe of "real deal" authenticity while welcoming newcomers, head to the **Timber Lanes (Map 39)**, where hand scoring still reigns amidst wood-paneled walls, a pinball machine, and a well-stocked bar. Owner Bob is a ubiquitous presence during league play, bowling left-handed to maintain the pretense of fairness. Since opening 1945, they've had leagues for men, women, mixed, gay and lesbian, and the blind. They've also hosted full-contact, Mexican wrestling-style bowling and nude nights—though shoes were still required.

Bowling	*Address*	*Phone*	*Fee*	*Map*
10 Pin Bowling Lounge	330 N State St	312-644-0300		02
Lucky Strike Lanes	322 E Illinois St	312-245-8331		03
Seven Ten Lanes	1055 E 55th St	773-347-2695		19
Fireside Bowl	2648 W Fullerton Ave	773-486-2700		27
Seven Ten Lounge	2747 N Lincoln Ave	773-549-2695		29
Lincoln Square Lanes	4874 N Lincoln Ave	773-561-8191		38
Timber Lanes	1851 W Irving Park Rd	773-549-9770		39
Diversey River Bowl	2211 W Diversey Pkwy	773-227-5800		42
Waveland Bowl	3700 N Western Ave	773-472-5900		42
Southport Lanes	3325 N Southport Ave	773-472-6600		43

Weather permitting, golfers can tee up all year round in Chicago. The Chicago Park District offers six public courses open daily, dawn to dusk. At **Jackson Park's (South)** premier 18-hole facility, the scenery alone will make you forget the bustle of the city. The nine-hole **Sydney R. Marovitz (Waveland) Golf Course (43)** is usually busy, but it has great views of the lake. And **Robert A. Black's (Map 34)** nine-hole, 2,339-yard, par-33 layout was designed by the renowned Dick Nugent. In addition, the park district operates three driving ranges and three learning centers, including one for juniors at **Douglas Park**.

The Forest Preserve District of Cook County offers 10 public courses in and around the city. **Indian Boundary's (Northwest)** huge fairways and fast-moving greens make for fun play and golfers often catch glimpses of visiting deer. At **Edgebrook (Northwest)**, bordered by mature trees along the Chicago River, the signature fifth hole—a 93-yard par three with an elevated green—offers a serious test of skill. Just 10 minutes from downtown, **Bill Caldwell's (Northwest)** sharply undulating greens make it a great place to play a quick nine.

And, for a real urban golf experience, the privately owned **Harborside International**, host to some Illinois PGA events, offers two tricky 18-hole, Scottish-links courses open to the public in season. Private courses in the city include the **Beverly**, **Ridge**, and **Ridgemoor** country clubs and **Riverside Golf Club**. However, if you want to see Tiger Woods play, you'll have to head out to the suburbs; the PGA tour visits clubs like Cog Hill in southwest Lemont and the members-only Medinah Country Club in the western 'burbs.

If you prefer your golf a little smaller, in-the-know mini-golfers head to the Park Districts' exceptionally cheap miniature golf course on Diversey, or head down south to the ultimate in windmill-dodging action, supernatural-themed Haunted Trails Amusement Park. Navy Pier also has a course, but the throngs of tourists with multi-colored balls makes it hard to recommend for the putt-putt purist.

Golf Courses	*Address*	*Phone*	*Map*	*Weekdays*	*Weekends*
The Green at Grant Park	352 E Monroe St	312-987-1818	6	n/a	n/a
Robert A Black Golf Course	2045 W Pratt Blvd	312-742-7931	34	$16.25	$17.75
Sydney R Marovitz Golf Course	3600 N Recreation Dr	312-742-7930	44	$20	$23
Edgebrook Golf Course	6100 N Central Ave	773-763-8320	NW	$24	$28
Indian Boundary Golf Course	8600 W Forest Preserve Ave	773-625-9630	NW	$28	$30
Columbus Park Golf Course	5701 W Jackson Blvd	312-746-5573	W	$14.50	$15.75
Marquette Park Golf Course	6700 S Kedzie Ave	312-747-2761	SW	$15.25	$16.50
South Shore Country Club	7059 S South Shore Dr	773-256-0986	S	$14.50	$15.75
Harborside International Golf Center	11001 S Doty Ave	312-782-7837	S	$80	$92
Jackson Park Golf Course	6401 S Richards Dr	773-667-0524	S	$22.75	$25.75
Peter N Jans Community Golf Course	1031 Central St	847-475-9173	Evanston	$17	$23
Sports Park	3459 Oakton St	847-674-1500	Skokie	$16.25	$17.75

Driving Ranges	*Address*	*Phone*	*Map*	*Fees*
Diversey Driving Range	141 W Diversey Dr	312-742-7929	3	$11/100 balls, $2 clubs
Marquette Park Golf Course	6700 S Kedzie Ave	312-747-2761	SW	$7.50/60 balls
Harborside International Golf Center	11001 S Doty Ave	312-782-7837	S	$10/100 balls
Jackson Park Golf Course	6401 S Richards Dr	773-667-0524	S	Small bucket $6, large bucket $9 (no fee for clubs)

Mini Golf Courses	*Address*	*Phone*	*Map*	*Fees*
Diversey Miniature Golf	141 W. Diversey Parkway	312.742.7929		Adults $7.00, Juniors/ Seniors $5.50
Haunted Trails Amusement Park	7759 S. Harlem Ave.	708-598-8580		$5.50 before 6 p.m. $6.50 after 6 p.m.
Navy Pier Mini Golf	600 East Grand Avenue	800-595-PIER		$15

General Information

Chicago Park District: www.chicagoparkdistrict.com
312-742-PLAY (7528)
Active Transportation Alliance: www.activetrans.org
312-427-3325
Chicago Area Runner's Association: www.cararuns.org
312-666-9836

Overview

Greater Chicago offers more than 250 recreational off-road paths that allow bikers, skaters, walkers, and joggers to exercise without worrying about vehicular traffic. In addition to recreational paths in the city's parks, designated off-street trails line the Lakefront, North Shore Channel, North Branch Trail along the Chicago River, Burnham Greenway, and Major Taylor Trail.

Lakefront Trail

Chicago has one of the prettiest and most accessible shorelines of any city in the US—this is the 500-pound gorilla of recreational paths in Chicago. Use one of Lake Shore Drive's over/underpasses (generally available every half mile or so) and you'll discover 15 miles of bathing beaches and over 20 miles of bike paths—just don't anticipate being able to train for the Tour de France during summer weekends, when the sheer number of people makes it impossible to bike along the path at faster than a snail's pace. But thanks to Burnham and Bennett's 1909 "Plan for Chicago," at least we can count on the shoreline remaining non-commercial, with great cycling, jogging, blading, skating, and swimming opportunities for all.

Major Taylor Trail

If you've ever wanted to take in a slice of Chicago's southwestern-most corner (and let's face it, who hasn't?), try the six-mile bike route that begins at Dawes Park at 81st and Hamilton Streets near Western Avenue. The route incorporates an abandoned railroad right-of-way and runs to the southeast through Beverly and Morgan Park, ending up at the Cook County Forest Preserve near 130th and Halsted Streets. The trail was named in honor of cycling legend Marshall "Major" Taylor, one of the first African-American cyclists, who lived out the final years of his life in a YMCA in Chicago.

North Branch Trail

To access the northern end of the trail, take Lake Cook Road to the Chicago Botanic Garden, located east of I-94. You can also start from any of the forest preserves as the path winds southward. To access the southern end of the trail in Chicago, take Milwaukee Avenue to Devon Avenue and head a short way east to the Caldwell Woods Preserve. The North Branch winds along the Chicago River and the Skokie Lagoons, but unlike most of the other trails, this one crosses streets, so be careful and look out for cars as you approach. Still, it represents a great way to get out of the city—and if you make it all the way to the Botanic Garden, admission is free as you won't have to pay for parking!

Burnham Greenway

The 11-mile stretch of the Burnham Greenway, which extends from 104th Street on the city's south side all the way down to Lansing in the south suburbs, has undergone major work over the past few years. The trail has a bit of a checkered past (the former railroad right-of-way was once cited for major pollution), but current paving projects make it a good bet for biking, skating, and pedestrians. Expect to find all of northern Illinois' major ecosystems, from wetlands to prairies to a Ford Motor plant in close proximity to one another.

North Shore Channel Trail

This trail follows the North Shore Channel of the Chicago River from Lawrence Avenue through Lincolnwood, Skokie (where you'll find a bizarre sculpture park lining the trail), and Evanston to Green Bay Road at McCormick Boulevard. Not all of the seven miles of the trail are paved bike paths and you'll have to switch back and forth between path and street. Skokie recently paved the trail segment between Oakton and Howard Streets, but there are still many missing links in the route, much to the chagrin of Friends of the Chicago River (FOCR), who are trying to extend and improve the Channel Trail. The Green Bay Trail branches off to the north from the North Shore Channel Trail and will take you past multi-million dollar houses, cute suburban downtowns, and the Ravinia Festival.

Chicago Park District

Many of the parks under the jurisdiction of the Chicago Park District have paths dedicated to cycling, jogging, walking, rollerblading, and skating. The Chicago Area Runner's Association is so committed to lobbying for runners' rights that it successfully petitioned to have the Lincoln Park running paths plowed and salted through the winter so they could continue their running activities (though prepare to find water fountains that are shut off and bathrooms that are locked). This calls into question the sanity of such masochistic dedication, but we can only assume that the entire year is needed to prepare for the Chicago Marathon, held annually in October. Check out the chart on the facing page to determine Chicago Parks that designate jogging/walking and cycling/skating paths.

Park District—North Region	*Address*	*Phone*	*Jog/Walk*	*Bike/Skate*	*Map*
Brooks Park	7100 N Harlem Ave	773-631-4401	■		45
Emmerson Park	1820 W Granville Ave	773-761-0433	■		36
Eugene Field Park	5100 N Ridgeway Ave	773-478-9744		■	48
Oz Park	2021 N Burling St	312-742-7898	■		30
Peterson Park	5801 N Pulaski Rd	312-742-7584	■		46
Portage Park	4100 N Long Ave	773-685-7235	■		48
River Park	5100 N Francisco Ave	312-742-7516		■	38
Shabbona Park	6935 W Addison St	773-685-6205	■		47
Warren Park	6601 N Western Ave	773-262-6314	■	■	33
Frank J Wilson Park	4630 N Milwaukee Ave	773-685-6454	■		48
Winnemac Park	5100 N Leavitt St	312-742-5101	■		39

Park District—Central Region	*Address*	*Phone*	*Jog/Walk*	*Bike/Skate*	*Map*
Columbus Park	500 S Central Ave	773-287-7641	■	■	49
Douglas Park	1401 S Sacramento Ave	773-762-2842	■	■	50
Dvorak Park	1119 W Cullerton St	312-746-5083	■		26
Humboldt Park	1400 N Sacramento Ave	312-742-7549	■	■	50
Riis Park	6100 W Fullerton Ave	312-746-5363	■	■	47
Rutherford Sayre Park	6871 W Belden Ave	312-746-5368	■		47
Union Park	1501 W Randolph St	312-746-5494	■		24

Park District—Southwest Region	*Address*	*Phone*	*Jog/Walk*	*Bike/Skate*	*Map*
Bogan Park	3939 W 79th St	773-284-6456	■		53
Cornell Square Park	1809 W 50th St	312-747-6097	■		54
Hayes Park	2936 W 85th St	312-747-6177	■		54
LeClaire Courts/Hearst Community	5120 W 44th St	312-747-6438	■		53
Mt Greenwood Park	3724 W 111th St	312-747-6564	■		55
Rainey Park	4350 W 79th St	773-284-0696	■		53
Senka Park	5656 S St Louis Ave	312-747-7632	■		54
Sherman Park	1301 W 52nd St	312-747-6672	■		54
Avalon Park	1215 E 83rd St	312-747-6015	■		57
Bradley Park	9729 S Yates Ave	312-747-6022	■		60
Gately Park	810 E 103rd St	312-747-6155	■		59
Hamilton Park	513 W 72nd St	312-747-6174	■		57
Lake Meadows Park	3117 S Rhodes Ave	312-747-6287	■	■	14
Meyering Playground Park	7140 S Martin Luther King Dr	312-747-6545	■		57
Palmer Park	201 E 111th St	312-747-6576	■		59
Rosenblum Park	8050 S Chappel Ave	312-747-6649	■		60
Washington Park	5531 S Martin Luther King Dr	773-256-1248	■	■	57

Park District—Lakefront Region	*Address*	*Phone*	*Jog/Walk*	*Bike/Skate*	*Map*
Calumet Park	9801 S Ave G	312-747-6039	■		60
Jackson Park	6401 S Stony Island Ave	773-256-0903	■	■	58
Lincoln Park	2045 Lincoln Park West	312-742-7726	■	■	30
Loyola Park	1230 W Greenleaf Ave	773-262-8605	■	■	34
Rainbow Park & Beach	3111 E 77th St	312-745-1479		■	58

General Information

Chicago Park District: 312-742-PLAY (7529); www.chicagoparkdistrict.com

Overview

Due to the temperature extremes that Chicago experiences, its residents can enjoy both ice skating and inline skating at various times of the year. Ice skating can be a fun, free, winter activity if you have your own skates, and if you don't, many rinks rent them. Skateboarding is also a popular pastime and a number of parks throughout the city are equipped with skating facilities.

Inline Skating

As rollerblading continues to re-rise in popularity, especially amongst Chicago's gay community, paths and streets fill up in the summertime with these one-row rollers. Similar to bike riding, inline skating in Chicago serves dual purposes. If you plan on strapping on the blades to get from A to B, be super-careful navigating the streets. As it is, Chicago drivers tend to have difficulty seeing cyclers, and chances are they won't notice you until you've slammed into their open car door. Wear protective gear whenever possible, especially a helmet, and learn to shout loudly so that people can anticipate your approach. If recreational skating is more your speed, check out the Recreational Paths page for cool places to skate. If you'd like to join the hundreds of summer skaters out there, and you don't have your own gear, the following places offer skate rental: Londo Mondo, 1100 N Dearborn St at W Maple St, 312-751-2794; Bike Chicago at Navy Pier, 312-755-0488. Hourly rates range from $7 to $10, while daily rates are from $20 to $35.

Roller Derby

If watching skating seems far more interesting than actually lacing up, then head over to the UIC pavilion to catch the Windy City Rollers, Chicago's premiere all-female roller derby league (when in season). Featuring tattooed beauties beating the crap out of each other while skating the circular track, the WCR is unlike any other Chicago sporting event out there. Plenty of beer is served, and the atmosphere is fun and loose, while still retaining the competitive spirit that makes the Derby the Derby.

UIC Pavilion • 525 S. Racine Ave, 312-413-5740

Skate Parks

If you're more interested in adrenaline than exercise, grab your blades or board and a couple of buddies and head down to the magnificent Burnham Skate Park (east of Lake Shore Drive at 31st St, 312-747-2200). With amazing grinding walls and rails, vert walls, and banks, Burnham Park presents hours of fun and falls. Less intense but equally fun are the two skate parks with ramps, quarter pipes, and grind rails. One can be found at West Lawn Park (4233 W 65th St, 773-284-2803) the other at Oriole Park (5430 N Olcott Ave, 773-631-6197).

Ice Skating

The Park District's nine outdoor rinks offer free admission and reasonably priced skate rentals, making ice skating an excellent way to turn bitterly frozen winter lemons into recreational lemon ice. The Millennium Park ice rink (55 N Michigan Ave) is the most visible and well known downtown, but savvy skaters know to cross the BP Pedestrian Bridge for the cheaper rental and thinner crowds at the Grant Park rink (337 E Randolph St.). Rentals run $10 at Millennium Park and $6 at Grant Park. Parking for either rink is available for $14 for an hour at the Grant Park North Garage. (Enter from the Michigan Avenue median at Washington or Madison Streets.)

The Olympic-sized skating rink and warming-house complex at Midway Plaisance offer a South Side venue for dropping precise one-footed salchows on an unsuspecting public. Located at 59th and Woodlawn, the rink has free admission and $5 rental skates. During the summer, the facility is used for rollerskating and other entertainment (312-745-2470).

If you, like the rest of Chicago, have recently caught hockey fever, try your hand at one of the many adult and child leagues run year round at Johnny's Ice House, 1350 W. Madison St. Close to downtown, Johnny's offers times and skill levels for any aspiring puckster. An interior bar guarantees a good time, regardless of game results.

Other ice skating rinks are located seasonally at:

McFetridge Sports Complex (year-round) • 3843 N California Ave, 773-478-2609 (admission is $4 for kids under 12 years, $5 for adults + $3 skate rental)

Daley Bicentennial Plaza Rink • 337 E Randolph St, 312-742-7650 (free admission + $6 rental)

Johnny's Ice House • 1350 W. Madison St, 312-226-5555 (Rates vary)

McKinley Park • 2210 W Pershing Rd, 312-747-5992 (free admission + $5 rental)

Mt. Greenwood Park • 3721 W 111th St, 312-747-6564 (free admission + $5 rental)

Navy Pier Ice Rink • 600 E Grand Ave, 312-595-5100 ($12 admission + rental)

Riis Park • 6100 W Fullerton Ave, 312-746-5735 (free admission + $5 rental)

The Rink (roller skating) • 1122 E 87th St, 773-221-2600 ($1)

The Rink at Wrigley • 1060 W Addison St, 312-617-7017 ($6 admission children, $10 adults +rental)

Rowan Park • 11546 S Avenue L, 773-646-1967 (free admission + $5 rental)

Warren Park • 6601 N Western Ave, 773-761-8663 ($4 admission + $5 rental)

West Lawn Park • 4233 W 65th St, 773-284-2803 (free admission + $5 rental)

Gear

If you're after skateboard gear, check out Air Time Skate Boards at 3317 N Clark St, 773-472-6868 and Uprise Skateboard Shop at 1820 N Milwaukee Ave, 773-342-7763.

For skating equipment, Air Time; (above) also does inline skates, as does Londo Mondo which has two locations: 1100 N Dearborn Street at W Maple St, 312-751-2794; and 2148 N Halstead St, 773-327-2218.

For all your ice skating needs, try the Skater's Edge store in the McFetridge Sports Complex (3843 N California Ave, 773-463-1505). They deal in hockey skates and other equipment as well as inline skates and accessories such as sequined dresses!

General Information

General Park Info: 312-742-PLAY
Department of Beaches and Pools: 312-742-5121

The Chicago Park District offers several indoor and outdoor pools, ten of which are equipped with ramps or lifts for disability access. At the top of our list is the 500-person-capacity outdoor wonderment at **Washington Park (Map 18)**, a 50-meter pool that's connected to a large, oval, side pool where fountains spray into a zero-depth entrance. Even better—it's got a 36-foot, theme-park-style water slide. It's overrun with pool rats during open swim periods, but grown folks like the designated lap times, water aerobics classes, and adult swims.

We also like the 30-meter outdoor pool at **River Park (Map 38)**, an Albany Park spot that boasts a diving well, a spacious deck with lounge chairs and umbrella tables, and an interactive kids' water playground. And when the weather gets cold, there's great lap swimming at the Ida Crown Natatorium at **Eckhart Park (Map 24)**. What's a natatorium? It's a pool inside its own building, and this one looks like it might have been designed by Eero Saarinen, but it wasn't.

All outdoor pools are free for the summer (Memorial Day-Labor Day). During the year, all lap swim fees for indoor pools are for 10-week sessions ($20 before 9 am; $10 after 9 am), and recreational and family swims are free. Get a complete list of facilities and register for aquatic exercise, diving, lifeguard, underwater hockey, and water polo classes at http://chicagoparkdistrict.com.

Outdoor Pools	*Address*	*Phone*	*Map*
Wentworth Gardens Park	3770 S Wentworth Ave	312-747-6996	13
Taylor Park	41 W 47th St	312-747-6728	15
Washington Park	5531 S MLK Dr	773-256-1248	18
Pulaski Park	1419 W Blackhawk St	312-742-7559	22
Union Park	1501 W Randolph St	312-746-5494	24
Dvorak Park	1119 W Cullerton St	312-746-5083	26
Wrightwood Park	2534 N Greenview Ave	312-742-7816	29
River Park	5100 N Francisco Ave	312-742-7516	38
Chase Park	4701 N Ashland Ave	312-742-7518	40
McFetridge Sports Center (California Park)	3843 N California Ave	773-478-2609	41
Hamlin Park	3035 N Hoyne Ave	312-742-7785	42

Indoor Pools			
McGuane Park	2901 S Poplar Ave	312-747-6497	12
Dyett Recreational Center	513 E 51st St	312-745-1211	16
Clemente Park	2334 W Division St	312-742-7466	21
Eckhart Park/Ida Crown Natatorium	1330 W Chicago Ave	312-746-5490	24
Harrison Park	1824 S Wood St	312-746-5491	25
Sheridan Park	910 S Aberdeen St	312-746-5369	26
Stanton Park	618 W Scott St	312-742-9553	31
Mather Park	5941 N Richmond St	312-742-7501	35
Welles Park	2333 W Sunnyside Ave	312-742-7511	39
Gill Park	833 W Sheridan Rd	312-742-5807	43

While we admit we're suckers for any sport that includes the word "love" in its scoring system, we try not to think of the significance that it means "zero" in tennis talk. Find love and more at these Chicago tennis courts.

All tennis courts (except Daley Bicentennial Plaza in Grant Park, Diversey Park, Chase Park, California Park, and Waveland Park) are free and open to the public on a first-come-first-served basis. Courts are open daily—check each park for individual hours. 312-742-7529 (general info); 773-256-0949 (Lake Front Region Office).

Tennis Courts	Address	Phone	Fees	Map
Daley Bicentennial Plaza	337 E Randolph St	312-742-7648	$7/hr; reservations required	6
Grant Park	331 E Randolph St	312-742-7648		6
Roosevelt Park	62 W Roosevelt Rd	312-742-7648		8
Mandrake Park	900 E Pershing Rd	312-747-7661		12
McGuane Park	2901 S Poplar Ave	312-747-6497		12
Armour Square Park	3309 S Shields Ave	312-747-6012		13
Ellis Park	707 E 37th St	312-746-5962		14
Fuller Park	331 W 45th St	312-747-6144		15
Taylor Park	41 W 47th St	312-747-6728		15
Metcalfe Park	4134 S State St	312-747-6728		16
Kenwood Community Park	1330 E 50th St	312-747-6286		17
Washington Park	5531 S Dr Martin Luther King Jr Dr	773-256-1248		18
Nichols Park	1355 E 53rd St	312-747-2703		19
Clemente Park	2334 W Division St	312-742-7466		21
Union Park	1501 W Randolph St	312-746-5494		24
Harrison Park	1824 S Wood St	312-746-5491		25
Sheridan Park	910 S Aberdeen St	312-746-5369		26
Jonquil Park	1023 W Wrightwood Ave	N/A		29
Oz Park	2021 N Burling St	312-742-7898		30
Lake Shore Park	808 N Lake Shore Dr	312-742-7891		32
Lerner Park	7000 N Sacramento Ave	N/A		33
Rogers Park	7345 N Washtenaw Ave	773-262-1482		33
Indian Boundary Park	2500 W Lunt Ave	773-742-7887		33
Warren Park	6601 N Western Ave	773-262-6314		33
Loyola Park	1230 W Greenleaf Ave	773-262-8605		34
Pottawattomie Park	7340 N Rogers Ave	773-262-5835		34
Touhy Park	7348 N Paulina St	773-262-6737		34
Legion Park at the Chicago River	W Bryn Mawr Ave & N Virginia Ave	N/A		35
Green Briar Park	2650 W Peterson Ave	773-761-0582		35
Mather Park	5941 N Richmond St	312-742-7501		35
Emmerson Playground Park	1820 W Granville Ave	773-761-0433		36
Senn Park	1550 W Thorndale Ave	N/A		37
Horner Park	2741 W Montrose Ave	773-478-3499		38
River Park	5100 N Francisco Ave	N/A		38
Welles Park	2333 W Sunnyside Ave	312-742-7511		39
Chase Park	4701 N Ashland Ave	312-742-7518	$5/hr	40
Revere Park	2509 W Irving Park Rd	773-478-1220		41
Brands Park	3259 N Elston Ave	773-478-2414		41
McFetridge Sports Center (California Park)	3843 N California Ave	773-478-2609	$16-$24/hr	41
Hamlin Park	3035 N Hoyne Ave	312-742-7785		42
Lincoln Park-Waveland Tennis Center	W Waveland Ave & N Lake Shore Dr	312-742-7674	$7/hr; reservations required	44
Lincoln Park-Diversey Tennis Center	2800 N Lake Shore Dr	312-742-7821	$16/hr; reservations must be made in person	44

Volleyball Courts

Hoops The Gym • 312-850-4667, 1001 W Washington Blvd
State-of-the-art court rentals. 24/7.

Lincoln Park/North Avenue Beach • 312-742-7529 (reservations and price information)
101 courts—12 are always open to the public. Much league play and reserved courts.
Office hours: Mon–Fri: 1 pm–9 pm; Weekends: 8 am–5 pm.

Lincoln Park/Montrose Beach • 312-742-5121
45 courts allotted on a first-come-first-served basis. League play in the evening.

Jackson Park/63rd Street Beach • 312-742-4847
Four free courts — first-come-first-served.

Yoga	*Address*	*Phone*	*Website*	*Map*
Ab-Sutra Yoga Studio	821 W Superior St	312-235-6984	www.ab-sutra.com	1
Siddha Yoga Meditation Center	770 N Halsted St	312-738-2798	www.siddhayogachicago.org	1
Yoga Circle	401 W Ontario St	312-915-0750	www.yogacircle.com	1
Bikram Yoga	219 W Chicago Ave	312-255-9642	www.bikramcitychicago.com	2
Lakeshore Athletic Club	441 N Wabash Ave	312-644-4880	www.lsac.com	2
Yoga Now	742 N LaSalle St, Ste 201	312-280-9642	www.yoganowchicago.com	2
Lakeshore Athletic Club	333 E Ontario St	312-944-4546	www.lsac.com	3
Adia Yoga	555 W Madison St	312-902-2040	www.adiayoga.com	4
Soham Yoga	55 E Washington St	312-409-1416	www.sohamyoga.com	5
Dahn Yoga	332 N Michigan Ave	312-263-9642	www.dahnyoga.com	6
Lakeshore Athletic Club	211 N Stetson Ave	312-616-9000	www.lsac.com	6
Enso Studio	719 S State St	312-427-3676	www.ensostudio.com	8
Adia Yoga	1936 S Michigan Ave	312-326-2979	www.adiayoga.com	11
Core Studio	1505 S Michigan Ave	312-922-1680	www.corestudiochicago.com	11
Three Pillars Wellness Center	1516 E 53rd St	773-363-7607	www.3pillars.org	19
Bikram Yoga's College of India	1344 N Milwaukee Ave	773-395-9150	www.bycic.com	21
Global Yoga & Wellness Center	1823 W North Ave	773-719-6227	www.globalyogacenter.com	21
Nature Yoga Sanctuary	2021 W Division St	773-227-5720	www.natureyoga.com	21
Moksha Yoga Center	700 N Carpenter St	312-942-9642	www.mokshayoga.com	24
Nirvana Yoga	1151 W Jackson Blvd	312-829-9642	N/A	24
Sana Vita Studio	1357 W Grand Ave	312-829-8482	www.sanavitastudio.com	24
Soulistic Studio and Spa	805 N Milwaukee Ave, Ste 200	312-226-7685	www.soulisticstudiospa.com	24
Yoga Skills	310 S Racine Ave	773-908-7074	www.yogaskills.com	24
Stellaria Natural Health	2755 W Logan Blvd	773-486-3797	www.stellarianaturalhealth.com	27
Temple of Kriya Yoga	2414 N Kedzie Blvd	773-342-4600	www.yogakriya.org	27
Harmony Mind Body Fitness	1962 N Bissell St	773-296-0263	www.harmonybody.com	29
Lakeshore Athletic Club	1320 W Fullerton Ave	773-477-9888	www.lsac.com	29
Yogaview	2232 N Clybourn Ave	773-883-9642	www.yogaview.com	29
Bikram Yoga's College of India	2736A N Clark St	773-348-9642	www.bycic.com	30
Dahn Yoga	2732 N Clark St	773-755-9566	www.dahnyoga.com	30
Flow Inc Pilates + Yoga	2248 N Clark St	773-975-7540	www.flowchicago.com	30
Siddha Yoga Meditation Center	770 N Halsted St	312-738-2798	www.siddhayogachicago.org	31
Exhale Mind Body Spa	945 N State St	312-753-6500	www.exhalespa.com	32
Yoga State	850 N Lake Shore Dr	312-503-9642	www.yogastate.com	32
Blue Beryl Dharma Center	1741 W Columbia Ave	773-262-8191	www.lamalobsang.com	34
Sweet Magic Studio	6960 N Sheridan Rd	773-764-6488	www.yogakareena.com	34
Sivananda Yoga Vedanta Center	1246 W Bryn Mawr Ave	773-878-7771	www.sivananda.org/chicago	37
Yoga Now	5852 N Broadway St	773-561-9642	www.yoganowchicago.com	37
Bloom Yoga Studio	4663 N Rockwell St	773-463-9642	www.bloomyogastudio.com	38
Ki Workshop	4512 N Lincoln Ave	773-934-4216	www.kiworkshop.com	39
Om on the Range Yoga Studio	3759 N Ravenswood Ave	773-525-9642	www.omontherange.net	42
Spirit Rising Yoga	3717 N Ravenswood Ave	773-975-9754	www.spiritrisingyoga.com	42
Sweet Pea's Studio	3717 N Ravenswood Ave	773-248-9642	www.sweetpeasstudio.com	42
Chicago Yoga Center	3047 N Lincoln Ave	773-327-3650	www.yogamind.com	43
Healing Earth Resources	3111 N Ashland Ave	773-327-8459	www.healingearthresources.com	43
Moksha Yoga Center	3334 N Clark St	773-975-9642	www.mokshayoga.com	43
Namaskar Boutique	3950 N Southport Ave	773-472-0930	www.namaskarchicago.com	43
The Peace School	3121 N Lincoln Ave	773-248-7959	www.peaceschool.org	43

General Information

NFT Map:	11
Address:	1410 S Museum Campus Dr Chicago, IL 60605
Phone:	312-235-7000
Lost & Found:	312-235-7202
Website:	www.soldierfield.net
Box Office:	847-615-BEAR (2327)
Bears Website:	www.chicagobears.com
Ticketmaster:	312-559-1212; www.ticketmaster.com

Overview

Like many Bears fans, the "new" Soldier Field is big, burly, and visually abrasive, especially the pre-game tailgaters in the parking lots. Plans began for its building in 1919 as a memorial to American soldiers who died in the wars. It officially opened on October 9th, 1924 (the 53rd anniversary of the Chicago Fire) as Municipal Grant Park Stadium. Renamed and dedicated in 1925, Soldier Field eventually became a key installment in the multi-million dollar Lakefront Improvement Plan for the Chicago shoreline between Navy Pier and McCormick Place. An estimated $365 million went towards the renovation of the 63,000-seat stadium, which opened in time for the 2003-2004 NFL Season and debuted on ABC's *Monday Night Football*. Improved Solider Field amenities include 60% more seating on the sidelines, three times as many concessions stands (400), several cozy meeting nooks throughout the stadium, two 82 x 23-foot video screens, a 100,000-square-foot lounge/entertainment facility, and twice as many bathrooms (although you'd never know it judging by the lines). Critics debate whether the expanded structure resembles a giant toilet-bowl or a flying saucer. (Voters Decide: Toilet Bowl Wins in a Landslide!) With a spate of injuries dashing the high hopes of last season, the Bears will take to silvery, shiny Soldier Field this year hoping to return to the playoffs before their last Super Bowl appearance fades to a too-distant memory. Regardless of what you think it looks like.

How to Get Tickets

Contact Ticketmaster to purchase individual game tickets. Season tickets are nearly impossible to come by within the next ten years as a recent bid by a staff member has him 2,876th in line. The best way to get great seats (other than by having them left to you in a will) is to work with a licensed ticket broker. Fans marked their territory early in 2004 by purchasing a one-time Permanent Seat License (PSL), and in exchange for paying big premiums to help cover construction expenses, PSL holders are promised first choice of ticket seating each year. Of the stadium's 63,000 seats, 27,500 are PSL zones, and the remaining 33,500 are non-licensed seats in the stadium's higher altitudes. A $100 per-seat, non-refundable deposit is required to get on a season ticket waiting list. The deposit will be applied to the first year of non-PSL season tickets, and you can find an application on the Bears website.

How to Get There

By Car: From the north or south, take Lake Shore Drive; follow the signs to Soldier Field. For parking lots, exit at E McFetridge, E Waldron, E 14th Boulevard, and E 18th Drive. From the west, take I-55 E to Lake Shore Drive, turn north, and follow the signs. Travel east on I-290, then south on I-90/94 to I-55; get on I-55 E to Lake Shore Drive.

Parking lots surrounding Soldier Field cost $15 on non-event days, including the new underground North Parking Garage. Rates rise on game days. Call the Standard Parking Customer Service Hotline with questions (312-583-9153). Two parking and game-day tailgating lots are located south of Waldron Drive. There are also lots on the Museum Campus off McFetridge Drive and near McCormick Place off 31st Street and E 18th Street.

By Train: On game days, CTA Soldier Field Express bus 128 runs non-stop between the Ogilvie Transportation Center and Union Station to Soldier Field. Service starts two hours before the game, runs up to 45 minutes before kickoff, and up to 45 minutes post-game.

By L: Take the Red, Orange, or Green Lines to the Roosevelt station stop. Either board eastbound CTA bus 12 or the free Green Trolley to the Museum Campus, and then walk south to Soldier Field. Walking from Roosevelt station would take approximately 15 minutes…an alternate to waiting for the bus.

By Bus: CTA buses 12, 127, and 146 stop on McFetridge Drive near Soldier Field. Contact the RTA Information Center for routes and schedules at 312-836-7000 or online at www.rtachicago.com.

By Trolley: The Green Trolley travels along Michigan Avenue, Washington Street, Canal Street, and Adams Street to the Museum Campus. From there, you can walk south to the field. For routes and schedules, visit www.cityofchicago.org/transportation.

General Information

NFT Map: 13
Address: 333 W 35th St
Chicago, IL 60616
General Info: 312-674-1000
Ticket Sales: 866-SOX-GAME
Website: www.whitesox.com

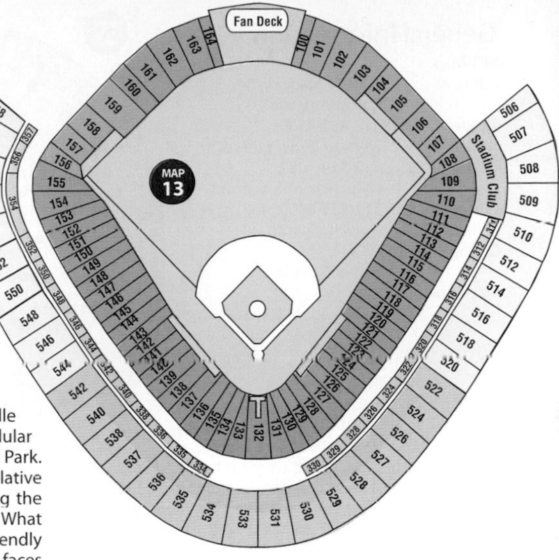

Overview

Both of Chicago's major league ballparks are named for corporations (one famous for gum, the other famous for cell phones) but the similarities end there. Any White Sox fan will tell you: tourists pay big bucks to watch ivy grow in the little place on the North Side, real baseball fans head to see the White Sox play at US Cellular Field.

Straddled by the Bridgeport and Bronzeville neighborhoods on Chicago's south side, US Cellular Field opened in 1991 to replace the old Comiskey Park. The new park was built for $167 million—a relative bargain even in 1991. Cost-cutting meant altering the original design, though, and not for the better. What the park lacks in beauty, it makes up for with its friendly staff, terrific sightlines (although the park itself faces the wrong way) and fabulous food—perennially rated among the best in Major League Baseball. Meat-eaters: follow your nose to the grilled onions and say "Polish with." Better yet, say "Polish witt." You'll get a sublimely good Polish sausage smothered in caramelized onions. And for the vegetarian, as long as you keep your voice down, you can snag a very tasty veggie dog at several of the Sox's many concession stands. Come hungry on Thursdays: Ball Park Franks are $1 and Best's kosher hot dogs are $2.50 each at select concession stands during all Thursday home games.

Look around and you'll notice that most Sox fans do enjoy their food at the ballpark—not many anorexics or bulimics in this crowd. And if you're hoping to hear about fashion, or business deals, or coffee shops, this ain't the place. Fans here talk about baseball. They love the game, and they love the team that FINALLY brought a World Series trophy to Chicago in 2005.

Nancy Faust, the hardest-working (and most creative) organist in baseball, has been the official White Sox organist since 1970 and still plays day games. And Roger Bossard—an obsessive-compulsive turf guru who consults to sports franchises around the world—maintains one of the most beautiful, truest playing real-grass surfaces in all of sports. Bill Veeck's scoreboard explodes with fireworks at each home run, and street musicians serenade fans as they head to the red line or the parking lot after games. It's all just about perfect.

How to Get Tickets

Purchase tickets through the team's website (www.whitesox.com) or at the US Cellular Field Box Office (weekdays: 10 am–6 pm, weekends: 10 am–4 pm).

Children shorter than the park's turnstile arm (approximately 36 inches) are admitted free, but must share your seat. Best Ballpark bargain: Half-Price tickets available for all regular seats (except Premium Lower Box) on Monday home games. Check the website for Value Days schedules.

How to Get There

By Car: US Cellular Field is located at the 35th Street exit off the Dan Ryan Expressway. Take I-90/94, stay in the local lanes, and exit at 35th Street. If you possess a prepaid green parking coupon or plan on paying cash for parking ($18), exit at 35th Street. Follow signs to "Sox Parking" at lots E, F, and L on the stadium's south side. Fans with red, prepaid season parking coupons exit at 31st Street, and follow signs for "Red Coupons" to lots A, B, and C just north of the stadium. If the 35th Street exit is closed due to heavy traffic, which is often the case on game days, proceed to the 39th Street exit; turn right for "Sox Parking" and left for "Red Coupons." The handicapped parking and stadium drop-off area is in Lot D, west of the field and accessible via 37th Street.

By Bus: CTA buses 24 and 35 stop closest to the park. Others stopping in the vicinity are the 29, 44, and 39. Armies of cops surround the venue on game days because the neighborhood is rough, especially at night.

By L: Ride the Red Line to the Sox-35th Street stop just west of the ballpark. Another good option, especially heading north after the game, is the Green Line. The 35th-Bronzeville-IIT (Illinois Institute of Technology) Station is a little longer walk that the Sox 35th Street stop, but always less crowded.

General Information

NFT Map: 23
Address: 1901 W Madison St
Chicago, IL 60612
Phone: 312-455-4500
Website: www.unitedcenter.com
Ticketmaster: 312-559-1212;
www.ticketmaster.com
Chicago Bulls: 312-455-4000
Bulls Website: www.bulls.com
Chicago Blackhawks:
312-455-7000
Blackhawks Website:
www.chicagoblackhawks.com

Overview

The commanding crown of Chicago's developing West Town District, the United Center is home to both the NHL's Blackhawks and the NBA's Bulls. This ultra-high-tech stadium is also a theater, convention hall, and premier concert arena. Opened in 1994, the $175 million stadium was privately funded by deep-pocketed Blackhawks owner William Wirtz and penny-pinching Bulls majority owner Jerry Reinsdorf (a privately funded and owned stadium—what a concept!) and built to replace the beloved but aging Chicago Stadium. The reinvigorated Bulls and Blackhawks franchises have pumped new energy in to the building, and the level of theatrics and delicious way-above average food, make a night at the United Center unlike anything else in the city. And just in case you forget whose "house" this is, the impressive statue of Michael Jordan located in front of the main entrance to the United Center is there to remind you.

A recent infusion of youth in both resident squads has brought a level of excitement to Chicago winter-time sports that has not been seen in years. Chicago native Derek Rose is the Bulls' cherished ingénue, sporting the blossom of youth on his cheek and the promise of future overachievements in his game. Following the recent passing of Blackhawk' owner and resident Chicago villain Bill Wirtz, the 'Hawks have seen a resurgence in talent, ticket sales, and overall interest. With one of the youngest teams in the NHL revitalizing their fan base, a new TV contract only helped spark enthusiasm, reminding everyone that Chicago, first and foremost, is a hockey town.

How to Get Tickets

Book tickets over the phone or online with Ticketmaster, by United Center mail order, or visit the United Center box office at Gate 4. Box office hours are Monday to Saturday, 11 am to 6 pm. For Bulls and Blackhawks season tickets and group bookings call the phone numbers above.

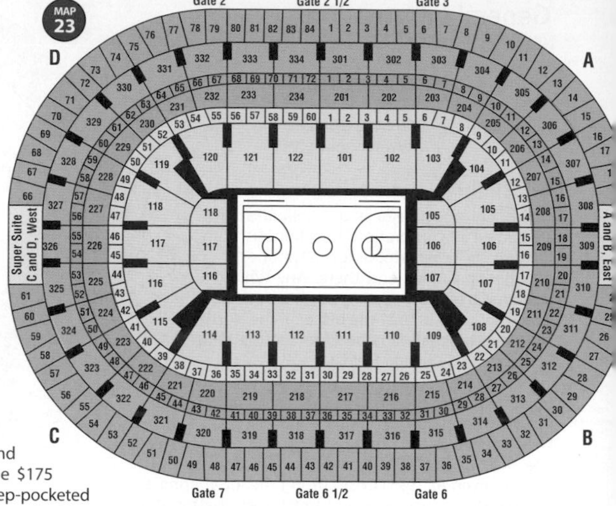

How to Get There

By Car: From the Loop, drive west on Madison Street to United Center. From the north, take I-90/94 and exit at Madison Street; head west to the stadium. From the southwest, take I-55 N to the Damen/Ashland exit; head north to Madison Street. From the west, take I-290 E to the Damen Avenue exit; go north to Madison Street.

Parking lots surround United Center, as do countless cops. General public parking is in Lot B on Warren Boulevard (cars, $15–31; limo, RV, and bus parking, $25). Lot H on Wood Street is closest to the stadium and is reserved for VIPs. Disabled parking is in Lots G and H on Damen Avenue.

By L: Take the Forest Park Branch of the Blue Line to the Medical Center-Damen Avenue Station. Walk two blocks north to United Center.

By Bus: CTA bus 19 United Center Express is the most intelligent and safest choice. In service only on event and game days, this express bus travels from Chicago Avenue south down Michigan Avenue, then west along Madison Street to the United Center. Michigan Avenue stops are at Chicago Avenue, Illinois Street, and Randolph Street. On Madison Street, stops are at State Street, Wells Street, and Clinton Street ($1.75 one-way). Service starts two hours before events and continues for 45 minutes after events. CTA bus 20 also travels Madison Street beginning at Wabash Avenue and has "owl service."

General Information

NFT Map:	43
Address:	1060 W Addison St Chicago, IL 60613
Cubs Box Office Phone:	773-404-2827
Tickets.com:	800-THE-CUBS (843-2827)
Lost & Found:	773-404-4185
Website:	www.cubs.com

Overview

In 2012, Wrigley Field will play host to the Chicago Cubs for the 97th year. Unfortunately, it has been even longer since the team has claimed a title. Built in 1914 and originally known as Weeghman Park, the stadium was renamed Wrigley Field in 1926 to honor chewing gum mogul and former Cub owner William Wrigley, Jr. It is the second-oldest ball park in Major League Baseball (Boston's Fenway Park—1912) and is a refreshing throwback to simpler times. Wrigley at it's heart, is a living, breathing, baseball museum. Ivy-strewn walls, a Merion Bluegrass and clover field, and a manual scoreboard transcend both time and technology during this age of artificial playing surfaces and high-tech But get while the getting's good, a recent team sale, and the constant threat of a name change promise that Wrigley Field probably won't be Wrigley Field much longer. The glow from night game lights warms the hearts of most North Chicago locals who aren't game attendees. On the other side of the fence, Wrigleyville activists have lobbied to limit the amount of time the lights are burning, in an attempt to limit their neighborhood's party reputation, to stop drunks peeing in alleyways, and to protect their over-inflated property values. But since the park has been there much, much longer than any of them, they really don't have much of a sober, party-pooping foot to stand on.

Wrigley Field has been the site of some of baseball's most historic moments: Ernie Banks' 500th career home run in 1970, Kerry Wood's twenty strikeouts in 1998, and Sammy Sosa's sixty home runs in 1998, 1999, and 2001. The Cubs haven't won a World Series title since their back-to-back wins over Detroit in 1907 and 1908, and haven't appeared in the Fall Classic since 1945, yet this loveable losing team has one of the most impressive attendance records in Major League Baseball. Of course, most patrons pay no attention to the game as an outing to Wrigley has become an opportunity to drink beer and "be seen." And if you're going to sit in the bleachers, you better be ready to party, because boobs of all type abound. Every year, faithful fans claim this is their year…but 2012 looks to be no better. Yet optimism remains, regardless of record, bad trades, overpaid underperforming players, and airport-style beer pricing. A day at Wrigley is like no other experience in the world, and a must-see for any self-respecting Chicagoan/baseball fan. The recent addition of the Capt. Morgan Club to the front of the park only adds to the good-time atmosphere, and there is nothing, nothing like singing "Take Me Out to The Ballpark" during the seventh inning stretch inside the friendly confines. Because no matter the score, no matter the curse, we will "root, root, root for the Cubbies.

How to Get Tickets

Individual game tickets can be purchased from the Cubs' website, by calling 800-843-2827, or in person at some Chicagoland Tickets.com outlets (if you're hanging out in Indiana or Wisconsin). You can also buy tickets at the Wrigley Field Box Office, open weekdays from 8 am to 6 pm and weekends from 9 am to 4 pm. You can usually score discount tickets to afternoon games Monday through Thursday in April, May, and September, or by waiting around the ballpark until the game starts. Especially when they are in the typical six-game losing skid. Children aged two and up require tickets.

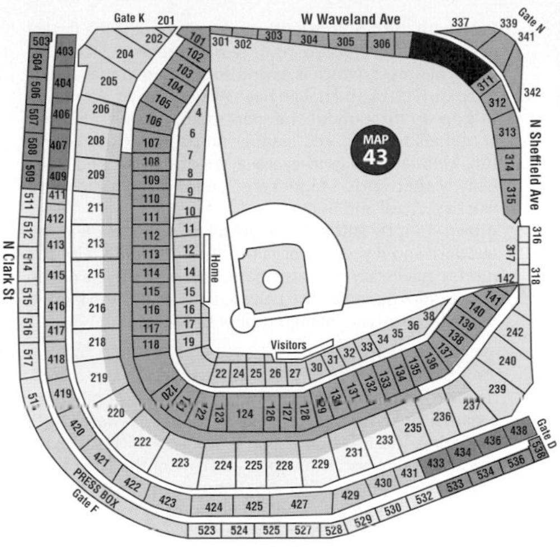

How to Get There

By Car: If you must… Remember the old days when Wrigleyville hillbillies used to let you park on their front lawns for five bucks? Well, today traffic on game days is horrendous, and parking prices are sky-high. Post-game spill-out from local bars and dozens of mindless cab drivers freeze traffic as police do their best to prevent drunken revelers from stumbling into the streets. From the Loop or south, take Lake Shore Drive north; exit at Irving Park Road, and head west to Clark Street; turn south on Clark Street to Wrigley Field. From the north, take Lake Shore Drive to Irving Park Road; head west to Clark Street, and turn south. From Chicago's West Side, take I-290 E or I-55 N to Lake Shore Drive, then follow directions above. From the northwest, take I-90 E and exit at Addison Street; travel east three miles. From the southwest side, take I-55 N to I-90/94 N. Exit at Addison Street; head east to the park.

Street parking around Wrigley Field is heavily restricted and nearly impossible. The Cubs operate a garage at 1126 W Grace Street. Purchase parking passes through the mail or at the Wrigley Field Box Office. On game nights, tow trucks cruise Wrigleyville's streets nabbing cars without a resident permit sticker. Park smart at the DeVry Institute, and catch CTA bus 154/Wrigley Express to and from the park. ($6 covers parking and roundtrip shuttle per carload.)

By L: Riding the Howard/Dan Ryan Red Line used to be the fastest and easiest way to get to Wrigley Field ($2.00 one-way). It is still easy but recent CTA overhauls, due to mismanagement, embezzlement and general misbehavior have greatly reduced service and increased wait time. Get off at the Addison Street stop one block east of the field.

By Bus: CTA buses 22, 8, and 152 stop closest to Wrigley Field ($2.00 one-way). For routes and schedules, visit www.rtachicago.com.

Even with the city constantly ranking amongst the fattest in the country, Chicagoans have had a renewed focus on physical fitness, which is saying something in the land of deep dish pizza and Italian beef. Although gyms continue to pop up throughout the metropolis, and membership continues to skyrocket, leagues and sports clubs offer a fun, alternative way to exercise, meet people, and drink heavily afterwards. Leagues aren't just limited to stalwarts like basketball and home

grown 16-inch softball; dodgeball and kickball leagues abound, and if you can organize the squad and raise the money necessary to participate, you won't even notice you're working out as you pelt some unsuspecting lame-o in the face with an inflated rubber ball.

General Tips

If you're interested in finding a specific league or group for a particular sport, a good place to start is *Chicago Athlete* magazine. This free publication is available online at www.chicagoaa.com and is on hand at many of the downtown athletic clubs and the Chicago Department of Tourism. You can look at the site to see which places carry it.

If you're a beginner, before you go spending a ton of money on your sport of choice, check out the Chicago Park District's website to see if they offer something near you on the cheap. They offer loads of clubs, training groups, and classes on a wide range of sports from archery to weightlifting to yoga. Their handy online program guide lets you search by age group, parks, program type, or zip code. The latter is particularly handy if you don't know where to find your local park district building. Check out their site for an excellent starting point for many sports teams and clubs.

Multiple Sports Leagues and Clubs

Chicago Sport and Social Club (www.chicagosportandsocialclub.com) is the mother of all of the Windy City leagues. Offering volleyball, basketball, football, floor hockey, soccer, dodge ball, dance, bowling, running, kickball, yoga, softball, rock climbing, kayaking, tennis, boot camp and boxing fitness, and even bar games (such as euchre, darts, and pool), this league has it all. Even if you're not interested in joining, you can watch the league's be-thonged hardbodies spike the ball around every summer at Oak Street Beach or vicariously take in an aerobics class while you burn your hide to a crisp.

If you're interested in something a little more (how do we put this?) *queer* in your sports experience, then join the Chicago Metropolitan Sports Association (www.chicagomsa.com). This non-profit is the largest gay and lesbian sports organization in the Midwest. Offering badminton, bowling, flag football, soccer, co-ed and women's softball, tennis, and volleyball, this league is the best place to meet other queer jocks for pick-ups (games and otherwise) and fun in the sun. Again, if you're not interested in playing, it's fun to watch. The games take place along the lakefront. Check their website for more information and game times.

Running

By far, most of the area sports groups and clubs are focused on running. We're not sure why that is, but if you're training for a running event, say, the Chicago Marathon or your first 5K, Chicago Area Runner's Association (www.cararuns.org) has you covered. This organization is for all levels of runners—from the seasoned marathoner to the amateur looking to begin running for the first time. With group runs, clinics, training programs, and a monthly newsletter, this organization has it all for anyone wanting to feel the gravel beneath their New Balances, the wind in their hair, and the lakefront gnats in their teeth.

Triathlon

Want to "tri" something a little more involved? How about a triathlon? The city offers tons of opportunities to get involved with this swim-bike-run race. These clubs run the gamut from volunteer-driven organizations to professional training for a fee. Check out Chicago Endurance Sports (www.chicagoendurancesports.com) Chicago Tri Club (www.chicagotriclub.com), Lakeview YMCA Triathlon Club (www.lakeviewymca.org/proTriathlon.html), or Together We Tri (www.togetherwetri.com). With any of these groups, you can expect to join a group that will tailor your workouts to your needs, find a supportive team environment, attend clinics on transitions and the individual sports, and get a training schedule that you can use on your non-group workout days.

Rugby

If rugby's your game, then Chicago has opportunities to join in the fun and violence. Two women's teams dominate the Chicago scene—North Shore Women's Rugby (www.northshorerugby.com) and Chicago Women's Rugby (www.cwrfc.com). For the men, Chicago offers more opportunities: Chicago Griffins Rugby Club (www.chicagogriffins.com), Chicago Lions Rugby Football Club (www.chicagolions.com), Lincoln Park Rugby Football Club (www.lprfc.com), and the South Side Irish Rugby (www.southsideirishrugby.com).

Miscellaneous

If you're interested in swimming, the Central Masters Swimming Association website has everything you're looking for. Check them out at www.chicagomasters.com. If soccer is more your thing, see the Chicago Area Soccer Association at the League Republic's website (www.leaguerepublic.com/soccer.jsp). While their site is less than user-friendly, you can click on "league search" in the upper right-hand corner of the page and type "Chicago" into the search engine. From there, you can find all of the teams you might want to join. Want to rollerblade? Get Inline… Chicagoland is the club for you! Check 'em out at www.getinlinechicagoland.com.

Whether you're an amateur or a seasoned veteran, Chicago offers many opportunities to get out there and become a jock! Check out these options, and have some fun while getting healthier.

General Information

Address:	10000 W O'Hare Chicago, IL 60666
Phone:	773-686-2200 / 800-832-6352
Website:	www.ohare.com
Ground Transportation:	773-686-8040
Lost & Found:	773-894-8760
Parking:	773-686-7530
Traveler's Aid:	773-894-2427
Police:	773-686-2385
Customs Information:	773-894-2900

Overview

O'Delay might be a more fitting name for O'Hare, although Beck might take exception to such a name change. What else can we say about one of the world's busiest airports?Still, when you think about it, it's an airport. In a major city. A major city that is sometimes covered in snow. Don't let worries of delays and frozen runways keep you grounded. While the airport is located just 17 miles northwest of the Loop, allow plenty of time to get to the airport, but don't stress to hard about security lines unless you're going to Europe. Or if it's Christmas. Or if you're going to Europe on Christmas. In the event that you do get to your gate early, take advantage of the free Wi-Fi available to download some relaxing meditation tunes. Also, keep in mind if you're taking a red-eye flight that most eateries and shops are closed at night and early morning, so bring snacks and a novel. Or maybe this book.

Expansion spells relief, according to Mayor Daley, who is pushing a controversial $6.6-billion plan designed to double O'Hare's capacity and secure its "busiest" title for the rest of the 21st century. The plan calls for building another runway, reconfiguring the other seven, building an additional entrance on the airport's west side, and spending millions soundproofing area homes and schools. Until the fated day that all improvements are complete, and probably even after that, remember that O'Hare is a large airport, in a large city. Act accordingly.

Psst. We'll tell you a secret that will make picking up guests at the airport a lot more pleasant. Sign up online for the airline to notify you of flight information and changes via your cellphone, then park your car, and head to the Hilton bar (located in the airport) to wait out the arrival. Better yet, avoid the stress of driving by taking the train in, then waiting at the Hilton bar for Aunt Sally, and load her and yourself into a cab. You probably shouldn't be driving at this point, anyway.

How to Get There

By Car: Strongly consider taking public transit to O'Hare, peek a few inches forward for information on the L. But if you absolutely must drive, pay close attention here. To be on the safe side, allow over an hour just for the drive (more during rush hours). From the Loop to O'Hare, take I-90 W. From the north suburbs, take I-294 S. From the south suburbs, take I-294 N. From the west suburbs, take I-88 E to I-294 N. Get off all of the above highways at I-190, which leads you directly to the airport. All of the major routes have clear signage, easily legible when you're moving at a snail's pace.

Parking: O'Hare Airport's parking garage reflects its hometown's passion for sports. All levels of the Main Parking Garage are "helpfully" labeled with Chicago sports teams' colors and larger-than-life logos (Wolves, Bulls, Blackhawks, White Sox, Bears, and Cubs). Annoying elevator muzak whines each team's fight song.

If this isn't enough to guide you to your car, we can't help you, because the garage's numbering-alphabetical system is more aggravating than the tinny elevator tunes.

If you're parking for less than three hours, go to Level 1. Parking costs $4 for the first 3 hours, $10 for up to 4 hours, and a deterring

How to Get There—continued

$50 per day. Overnight parking close to Terminals 1, 2, and 3 on Levels 2 through 6 of the garage or in outside lots B and C costs $30 a day. For flyers with cash to burn, valet parking is available on Level 1 of the garage for $10 per hour or $45 per day (8–24 hours). Parking in the International Terminal 5's designated Lot D costs $3 per hour for the first two hours and $2 per hour thereafter; the daily rate is $30; $50 for five days. Incoming international passengers always disembark in Terminal 5 (even if the airline departs from another terminal) because passengers must clear customs.

Long-term parking lots are Economy Lots E ($16), F ($9), and G ($13). From Lot E, walk or take the free shuttle to the free Airport Transit System (ATS) train station servicing all terminals. From Lot G, the shuttle will take you to the ATS stop in Lot E. Budget-conscious frequent flyers may want to purchase a prepaid Lot E "ExpressLane Parking" windshield tag for hassle-free, speedy departure from the airport.

By Bus: CTA buses 220 and 330 stop at the airport. If you're not near either of those bus lines, your best bet is to take your nearest bus line north or south to one of the O'Hare Blue Line train stations. The CTA also offers a special door-to-door service to and from the airport for Chicago-area residents and out-of-towners needing extra assistance. Call 312-663-4357 for additional information.

By Train: The odds of the Metra's schedule conveniently coinciding with your flight time are only slightly better than those of the Bulls winning the championship this year. The Wisconsin North Central Line departs Union Station for Antioch with a stop at the O'Hare Transfer station five times a day, starting in the afternoons on weekdays only ($3.30 one-way). Travel time is 30 minutes.

By L: We recommend the Blue Line as the best transportation method. The train runs between downtown Chicago and O'Hare 24 hours a day every 8 to 10 minutes ($2.25 one-way or $2 with Chicago Card). Travel time from the Loop is 45 minutes. The train station is on the lowest level of the airport's main parking garage. Walk through the underground pedestrian tunnels to Terminals 1, 2, and 3. If you're headed for the International Terminal 5, walk to Terminal 3 and board the free Airport Transit System (ATS) train.

By Cab: Join the cab queue at the lower level curb-front of all terminals. There are no flat rates, as all of the cabs run on meters, but you probably won't have to spend more than $40. Beware if you're traveling to certain suburbs, though. Fare rules allow cabbies to raise your fare for these routes by 50%! Ask what the fare will be when you enter the cab. Some cab companies servicing O'Hare include American United, 773-262-8633; Flash Cab, 773-878-8500; Jiffy Cab, 773-487-9000; Yellow Cab, 312-808-9130; and Dispatch, 312-829-4222.

By Kiss & Fly: The Kiss & Fly is a convenient drop-off and pick-up point for "chauffeurs" who want to avoid the inevitable chaos at the terminal curb-side. Flyers should leave enough time for the ATS transfer to their terminals. The Kiss & Fly zone is off Bessie Coleman Drive. Take I-190 to the International Terminal exit to Bessie Coleman Drive. Turn left at the light and follow Bessie Coleman Drive north to the Kiss & Fly entrance and ATS stop.

By Shuttle: Continental Airport Express (773-247-1200 or 888-2-THEVAN) provides a daily shuttle service between O'Hare and downtown Chicago from 6 am until 11:30 pm with departures approximately every 10–15 minutes. Shuttles stop at all major downtown hotels. Tickets cost $25 one-way ($46 return) for individuals, $18 per person ($34 return) for pairs going to the same destination and returning together, and $14 per person ($27 return) for three or more going to the same downtown destination and returning together. Shuttle ticket counters are located in the baggage claim areas of Terminal 1 by Door 1E and Terminal 3 at Door 3E; however, shuttles pick up passengers at Terminals 1, 2, 3, and 5. If you haven't pre-purchased a ticket at a counter, have cash ready for the driver.

Omega Airport Shuttle offers hourly service between O'Hare and

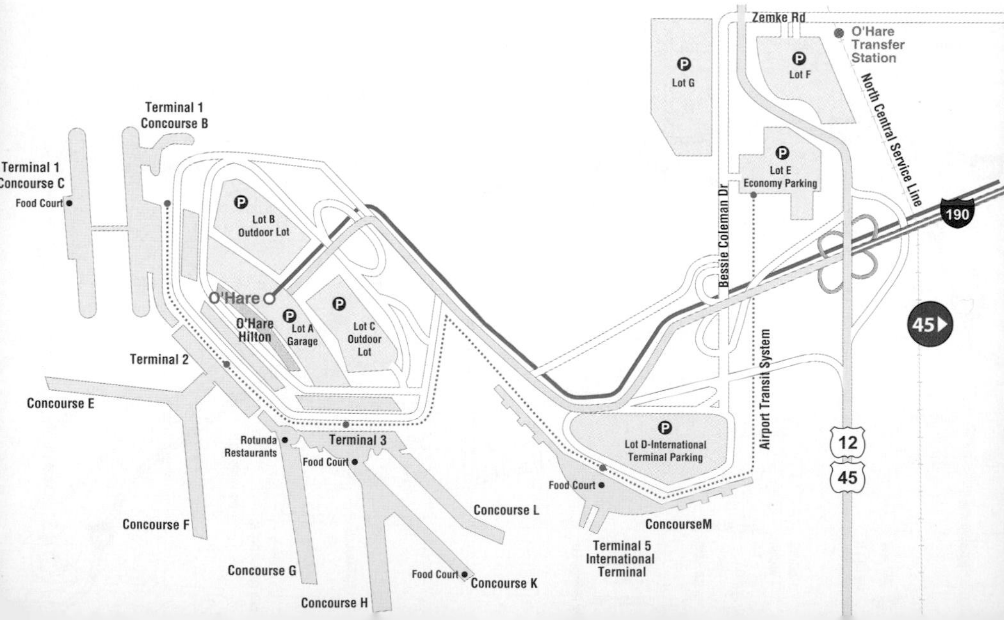

Midway beginning around 7 am each day 'til about 11:45 pm and between Hyde Park and O'Hare from 5 am to 11:45 pm. The shuttle leaves from the International Terminal's outside curb by Door 5E and from the airport's Bus Shuttle Center in front of the O'Hare Hilton Hotel by Door 4. Allow at least an hour for travel time between the airports and expect to pay $17 for a one-way fare. Omega also has over 20 pickup and drop-off locations on the South Side serving O'Hare and Midway Airports. (773-734-6688; www.omegashuttle.com).

By Limousine: Sounds pricey, but depending on where you're going and how many people you are traveling with, it may be cheaper to travel by limo than by cab or shuttle. Advance reservations recommended. Limo services include O'Hare-Midway Limousine Service, 312-558-1111 (or 800-468-8989 for airport pick-up), www.ohare-midway.com; and My Chauffeur/American Limo, 847-376-6100, www.mychauffeurchicago.com.

Airlines

Airline	*Terminal*	*Phone*
Aer Lingus	5	888-474-7424
Aero Mexico	5	800-237-6639
Air Canada	2	888-247-2262
Air Canada Jazz	2	888-247-2262
Air France	5	800-237-2747
Air India	5	800-621-8231
Air Jamaica	5	800-523-5585
Alaska Airlines	3	800-252-7522
Alitalia	5	800-223-5730
Al Nippon	1	800-235-9262
America West	2	800-843-9322
American Airlines:		800-443-7300
Domestic	3	
International	3 dep/5 arr	
American Eagle	3	800-433-7300
Asiana Airlines	5	800-227-4262
Austrian Airlines	5	800-843-0002
Aviasca	5	866-246-0961
British Airways	5	800-247-9297
BMI British Midland	5	800-788-0555
Cayman Airways	5	800-422-9626
Comair	3	800-964-2550
Continental Airlines	2	800-525-0280
Delta Airlines	3	800-221-1212
El Al	5	800-223-6700
Iberia Airlines	3 dep/5 arr	800-772-4642
Japan Airlines JAL	5	800-525-3663
JetBlue	2	800-538-2583
KLM Royal Dutch Airlines	5	800-225-2525
Korean Air	5	800-438-5000
LOT Polish Airlines	5	212-789-0970
Lufthansa	1 dep/5 arr	800-645-3880
Mexicana Airlines	5	800-531-7921
Northwest Airlines:		
Domestic	2	800-225-2525
International	2	800-447-4747
Pakistan International Airlines	5	800-221-6024
Royal Jordanian	5	800-223-0470
Scandinavian Airlines (SAS)	5	800-221-2350
South African Airways	5	800-521-4845
Spirit Airlines	3	800-772-7117
Swiss International Airlines	5	877-359-7947
TACA Airlines	5	800-400-8222
Ted Airlines	1	800-225-5833
Turkish Airlines	5	800-874-8875
United Airlines:		800-241-6522
Domestic/International dep	1, 2	
International arr	5	
United Express	1, 2	800-241-6522
US Airways	2	800-428-4322
USA 3000	5	877-872-3000
Virgin Atlantic	5	800-821-5438

Car Rental

Alamo • 560 Bessie Coleman Dr, 800-327-9633/773-694-4646
Avis • 10000 Bessie Coleman Dr, 800-331-1212/773-825-4600
Budget • 580 Bessie Coleman Dr, 800-527-0700/773-894-1900
Dollar • O'Hare Intl Arpt, 800-800-4000/866-434-2226
Enterprise • 4025 Mannheim Rd, 800-867-4595/847-928-3320
Hertz • 10000 Bessie Coleman Dr, 800-654-3131/773-686-7272
National • 560 Bessie Coleman Dr, 800-227-7368/773-694-4646
Thrifty • 3901 N Mannheim Rd, 847-928-2000

Hotels

All shuttles to airport hotels depart from the Bus Shuttle Center in front of the O'Hare Hilton Hotel in the center of the airport.

Best Western • 10300 W Higgins Rd, 847-296-4471
Clarion • 5615 N Cumberland Ave, 773-693-5800
Courtyard • 2950 S River Rd, 847-824-7000
Crown Plaza • 5440 N River Rd, 847-671-6350
Days Inn • 1920 E Higgins Rd, 847-437-1650
Comfort Inn • 2175 E Touhy Ave, 847-635-1300
DoubleTree • 5460 N River Rd, 847-292-9100
Embassy Suites • 5500 N River Rd, 847-678-4000
Four Points Sheraton • 10249 W Irving Park Rd, 847-671-6000
Hampton Inn • 3939 N Mannheim Rd, 847-671-1700
Hawthorn Suites • 1251 American Ln, 847-706-9007
Hilton • O'Hare Intl Arprt, 773-686-8000
Holiday Inn • 10233 W Higgins Rd, 847-954-8600
Hotel Sofitel • 5550 N River Rd, 847-678-4488
Hyatt Regency • 9300 W Bryn Mawr Ave, 847-696-1234
Hyatt Rosemont • 6350 N River Rd, 847-518-1234
La Quinta Inn • 1900 E Oakton St, 847-439-6767
Marriott Suites • 6155 N River Rd, 847-696-4400
Marriott Hotel • 8535 W Higgins Rd, 773-693-4444
Ramada Plaza • 5615 N Mannheim Rd, 773-693-5800
Residence Inn • 7101 Chestnut St, 847-375-9000
Sheraton Suites • 6501 N Mannheim Rd, 847-699-6300
InTown Suites • 2411 Landmeier Rd, 847-228-5500
Super 8 • 2951 Touhy Ave, 847-827-3133
Travelodge • 3003 Mannheim Rd, 847-296-5541
Westin • 6100 N River Rd, 847-698-6000
Wyndham • 6810 N Mannheim Rd, 847-297-1234

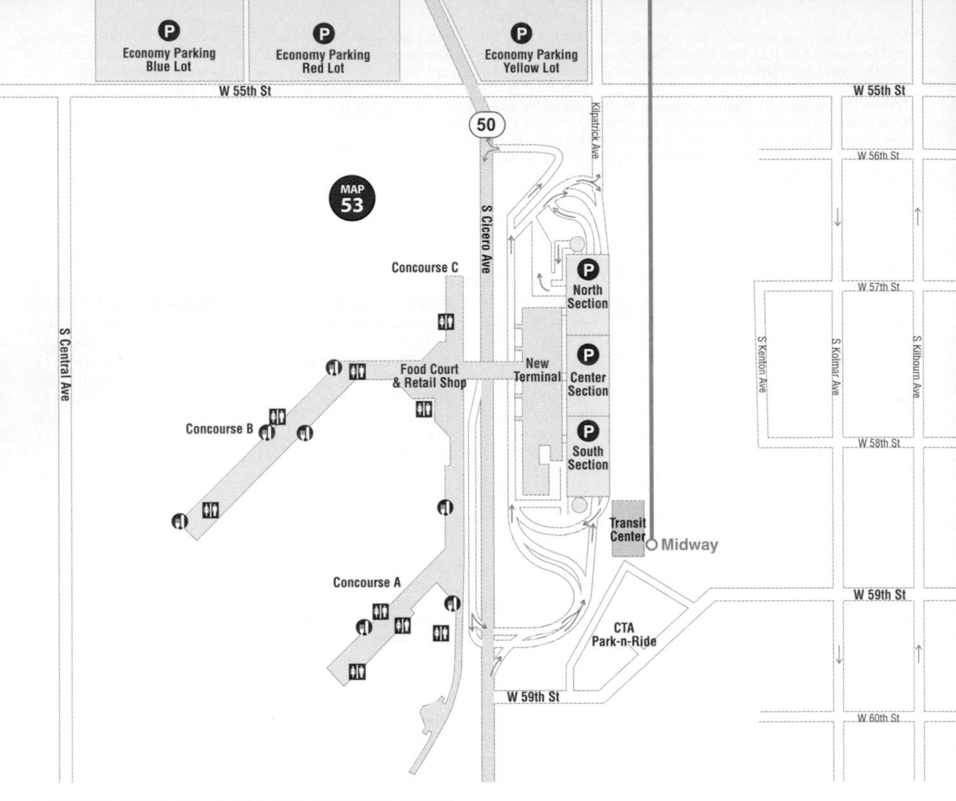

General Information

Address:	5757 S Cicero Ave Chicago, IL 60638
Phone:	773-838-0600
Website:	www.midwayairport.org
Police:	773-838-3003
Parking:	773-838-0756
Customs:	773-948-6330

Overview

Located just ten miles southwest of downtown Chicago is Midway—one of the fastest-growing airports in the country serving 47,000 passengers daily. Considered the city's outlet mall of airports, Midway primarily provides service from budget carriers like Southwest Airlines and ATA. On the positive side, it is an easy alternative to the bigger, badder O'Hare. Plus the bars for pre-flight entertainment aren't as crowded.

Expect Midway to gain altitude in national airport rankings with the recent completion of its $793 million terminal development. After ten years of planning and construction, the new features include a swank new terminal building, new concourses, a 3,000-space parking facility, food court, retail corridor, and a customs facility to facilitate international flights. In 2003, Concourses G and H were demolished to allow for the expansion of Concourse B. All the changes have upped Midway's jet gate count from 29 to 43.

Superstitious travelers beware of flying December 8th. On this date in 1972, a Boeing 737 crashed into a residential area during landing. In 2005, exactly 33 years later another Boeing slid off the runway in a landing attempt on December 8. Spooky.

How To Get There

By Car: From downtown, take I-55 S. From the northern suburbs, take I-290 S to I-55 N. From the southern suburbs, take I-294 N to I-55 N. From the western suburbs, take I-88 E to I-294 S to I-55 N. Whether you're traveling north or south along I-55, look for the Cicero Avenue/South/Midway Airport exit.

By Bus: CTA buses 55, 59, and 63 all run from points east to the airport. Take the Green Line or the Red Line to the Garfield Station and transfer to bus 55 heading west

($1.75 one-way including transfer). If you're coming from the south on the Red Line, get off at the 63rd Street stop and take bus 63 westbound ($1.80 one-way). Other buses that terminate at the airport include 54B, 379, 382, 383, 384, 385, 386, 831, and 63W.

By L: A 30-minute train ride on the Orange Line is the most convenient and cost-effective method for travel between the Loop and Midway Airport ($2.25, $2 with Chicago Card). The Orange Line's first train departs from Midway Station (last stop on the line's southern end) for the Loop at 3:55 am daily and 5:35 am on Sundays and holidays. The first train of the day from the Loop's Adams/Wabash Station at 4:29 am arrives at Midway at 4:54 am, well in advance of the airport's first early bird flight. The last train from Midway to the Loop departs at 12:56 am and arrives at 1:23 am. The final Midway-bound owl train departs from the Adams/Wabash stop around 1:29 am, arriving at Midway by 1:53 am. Trains run every five to seven minutes during rush hours, ten minutes most other times, and fifteen minutes late evenings. We recommend that wee-hours travelers stay alert at all times. A most convenient method of travel, the L drops you inside Midway airport, which while atmospherically pleasant in Winter, is also a bit of a hike. Allow about 15 minutes to cart yourself and your accoutrements to the security checkpoint.

By Cab: Cabs depart from the lower level of the main terminal and are available on a first-come-first-served basis. There are no flat rates (all cabs run on meters), but you can plan on paying around $25 to get to the Loop. Some cab companies servicing Midway include American United, 773-262-8633; Flash Cab, 773-878-8500; Flash Dispatch, 773-561-1444; Jiffy Cab, 773-487-9000; and Yellow Cab, 312-808-9130.

By Shuttle: Continental Airport Express (773-247-1200 or 888-2-THEVAN) travels between Midway and downtown and some northern suburban locations from 6 am until 10:30 pm. Shuttles depart every 15 minutes and make stops at all major downtown hotels. Tickets cost $20 one-way ($36 roundtrip) for individuals, $14 per person for pairs going to the same destination ($26 roundtrip), and $12 per person for three or more going to the same downtown destination ($22 roundtrip). The ticket counter and loading zone are in the terminal's lower level across from the baggage claim area by door LL3. To calculate a shuttle fare to north suburb locations, use the online fare calculator at www.airportexpress.com.

Omega Airport Shuttle (773-483-6634; www.omegashuttle.com) offers service leaving every 45 minutes or so between Midway and O'Hare beginning around 7 am each day with the final shuttle departing around 10 pm. Allow at least an hour for travel time between the airports and expect to pay $16 one-way. Contact Omega for information on more than 20 pickup locations on the South Side, to confirm schedules, to make reservations, and to prearrange home pickups.

By Limousine: Sounds pricey, but depending on where you're going and how many people you are traveling with, it may be cheaper to travel by limo than by cab or shuttle. Advance reservations recommended. Limo services include O'Hare-Midway Limousine Service, 312-558-1111 (or 800-468-8989 for airport pick-up), www.ohare-midway.com; and My Chauffeur/American Limo, 847-376-6100, www.americanlimousine.com.

Parking

Short-term parking is on the first floor. Parking is free for the first ten minutes, then $4 for 30 minutes to an hour. Add an additional $2 for every hour thereafter, up to $50 for 24 hours. Levels 4, 5, and 6 have the same rates for short-term parking, but the prices level off after four hours so that it only costs $36 per day. If you're planning on parking for a while, the best option is the economy lot for $14 a day on Cicero Avenue at 55th Street, a quarter-mile away. Allow extra time to take the free shuttle between the lot and the terminal.

A 6,300-space economy parking garage is now open at the corner of 55th Street and Laramie Avenue. Rates start at $2 for the first hour, $5 for the first two hours, and $12 for two to 24 hours.

Airlines

Concourse A

Air Midwest	800-637-2247
Air Tran	800-825-8538
ComAir	800-927-0927
Delta	800-221-1212
Frontier	800-432-1359
Northwest	800-225-2525
Southwest	800-435-9792
Ted/United Express	800-225-5833

Concourse B

ATA	800-225-2995
Southwest	800-435-9792

Concourse C

American	800-433-7300
Continental/ Continental Express	800-525-0280

Car Rental

Alamo	800-327-9633	Enterprise	800-566-9249
Avis	800-331-1212	Hertz	800-654-3131
Budget	800-527-7000	National	800-227-7368
Dollar	800-800-4000	Thrifty	800-527-7075

Hotels

Best Western • 8220 S Cicero Ave, 708-497-3000
Fairfield Inn • 6630 S Cicero Ave, 708-594-0090
Hampton Inn • 6540 S Cicero Ave, 708-496-1900
Hilton • 9333 S Cicero Ave, 708-425-7800
Holiday Inn Express • 6500 S Cicero Ave, 708-458-0202
Marriott Midway • 6520 S Cicero Ave, 708-594-5500
Courtyard Midway • 6610 S Cicero Ave, 708-563-0200
Sleep Inn • 6650 S Cicero Ave, 708-594-0001

General Information

Mailing address:
Chicago Transit Authority
Merchandise Mart Pl, 7th Fl
PO Box 3555
Chicago, IL 60654

Phone: 312-664-7200
CTA information: 888-YOUR CTA (968-7282)
Website: www.transitchicago.com

Overview

We may never find a system of public transit free from flaws, but if you need a quick, socially responsible way to get from A to Wrigley, CTA's your guy. Once you figure out its complicated card system, CTA service will get you relatively close to where you need to go (most of the time), and sometimes the city's trains and buses are even on schedule!

For location-to-location CTA directions and schedules, we honestly and without irony, recommend the useful CTA trip planner at tripsweb.rtachicago.com. It allows you to plan your course by either estimated departure times or desired arrival times.

Fares and Fare Cards

The city's tiered, pain-in-the-ass approach to fare payment makes it more expensive to pay with cash and easier to pay with cards. They don't call Chicago the city that works your nerves for nothing.

While busses accept cash and coin, you must use a card to ride the L. Full cash fares are $2.25. Fare card fares are $2.00 per bus ride, and $2.25 per L ride. On both bus and L, your first transfer will cost you 25 cents, and each transfer thereafter is free.

The easiest and most worry-free way to use CTA is with a pass.

- 1-Day Visitor Pass for $5.75
- 3-Day Visitor Pass for $14
- 7-Day Visitor Pass for $23
- 30-Day Visitor Pass for $86

Visitor passes give you unlimited rides on all CTA buses, L trains and PACE (suburban) buses, but CTA Visitor Passes are not valid on Metra (commuter railroad) trains. Your visitor pass activates the first time you use it—it's good for the number of consecutive days shown on the front of the card. Example: a 3-day pass is valid for 72 hours from the first time you insert it into the card reader on el turnstiles or inside the bus. At that point the expiration date and time will be printed on the back of the card.

Here's a breakdown on the benefits, limitations, and rules for fare methods..

Fare Card: You can purchase the standard paper fare card at any L station from the big blue fare card machines. Fare cards can be purchased in any amount (fare minimum is $2.25) and used on the bus or L. Fares are $2.25, plus 25 cents to transfer. Purchasing a fare card is easy—insert the amount of money you want on your card into the money-eater (whether it will actually accept your crinkly or faded dollar bills or spit them back out at you is entirely another matter), and push the "vend" button. Your card will pop out of the slot (at roughly waist level) below the money eater. Lost or stolen fare cards are not replaceable. Money can be added at any fare card machine. To use a fare card, insert it into the card reader on CTA turnstiles or inside the bus (next to the bus money-eater). No change is given from CTA fare card machines.

Chicago Card: The Chicago Card can be purchased online (allow about a week for delivery) or at participating Jewel and Dominick's grocery store locations and some currency exchanges (go to their website for addresses of participating vendors). Chicago cards can be purchased for predetermined amounts ($10, $20) or for specific amounts. Balances can be checked, and Chicago Cards can be reloaded at CTA Fare card machines. Touch the card to the Chicago Card sensor, enter your reload amount into the money eater, and retouch your card to the sensor until the readout says, "Thank you." Do not forget to retouch your card to the sensor after adding money, or the money will not be added to your card. To use the Chicago Card, simply press it against the sensor at the turnstile or on the bus. Lost or stolen Chicago Cards can be replaced, with their remaining value, for $5 if you chose the option to register the card (optional card registration is free, so why not?).

Chicago Plus Card: The Chicago Plus card is like the Chicago Card except for a few key differences. Registration of the Chicago Plus card is mandatory.

Card balances can only be checked and/or have money added (credit card only) online or by calling CTA customer service. With the Chicago Plus card, you have the option of choosing pay-as-you-go or purchasing a monthly pass. You must have an e-mail address to use a Chicago Plus card. Like the regular Chicago Card, there is a $5 fee to replace your Chicago Card Plus if it is lost or stolen.

Pass Back Option: At any time, you can share your CTA card with up to six other people traveling with you by passing the card back over the turnstile. The full fare for each rider will be deducted from your card.

Reduced Fares: Reduced fares are available for qualified passengers—people with disabilities, senior citizens, and children under 12. Regular cash fare for kid's ages 7–11 is $1. Children under age 7 ride free.

Go to the CTA website for more information about reduced fare applicability at www.transitchicago.com.

CTA Buses

CTA's buses cart about one million sweaty, crabby passengers around Chicago and its surrounding suburbs everyday; the fleet is the second-largest public transportation system in the US. CTA's 152 bus routes mirror Chicago's efficient grid system. The majority of CTA routes run north-south or east-west, and in areas where the streets are numbered, the bus route is usually the same as the street.

Recently, the entire CTA bus fleet has been overhauled to comply with ADA accessibility standards. The result is that now all buses kneel, that is, they tilt to make the first step less steep. All buses are equipped with wheelchair lifts and secure wheelchair seating. Additionally, as a boon to the visually impaired and those too busy gawking at Chicago's skyscrapers to read the signs on the front of each bus, all buses clearly and loudly announce the bus number and direction at every stop.

The newest and arguably most helpful addition to the CTA transit system is the Bus Tracker, an online resource for discovering "exactly" when your bus will arrive at its stop. Accessible via www.transitchicago.com, the Bus Tracker gives a damn good estimate of arrival times, cutting down your wait by a significant margin. You'll be grateful in December. And January. And February. And March…

Bus Stops: CTA stops are clearly marked with blue and white signs displaying the name and number of the route, as well as the final destination. Most routes operate from the early morning until 10:30 pm. Night routes, called "Night Owls," are identified on bus stop signage by an owl picture. Owl service runs approximately every half-hour through the night.

Fares: Buses accept exact fare only for individual rides. A regular one-way cash fare is $2.25. Transfers are not available with cash fares. Bus fares can also be paid with CTA fare cards or Chicago and Chicago Plus cards. In this case, the fare is $2, plus 25 cents for your first transfer, with each transfer after that *free*, for up to two hours.. The transfer fee will be charged at the next leg of your journey. You must always insert your fare card into the card machine, or press your Chicago Card on the sensor—even for the free transfer. No money will be deducted for the third leg of a journey after a transfer has been purchased (within the two hour limit).

Bicycles Onboard: Designated CTA buses are equipped with bike racks mounted on front grills to carry up to two bikes. Generally speaking, CTA bike buses are those that travel to lakefront beaches, like the 63rd Street, the #72 North Avenue buses, #77 Belmont, or the #92 Foster Avenue bus. Additional buses with bike racks are often added during summer months or for special events.

Loading your bike onto a CTA bus:

- If your bike is the first to be loaded, lower the rack and place it in position with the front wheel facing the curb.
- If there is already a bike on the rack, place your bike's rear wheel toward the curb.
- If two bikes are already loaded and the rack is full; wait for the next bus.

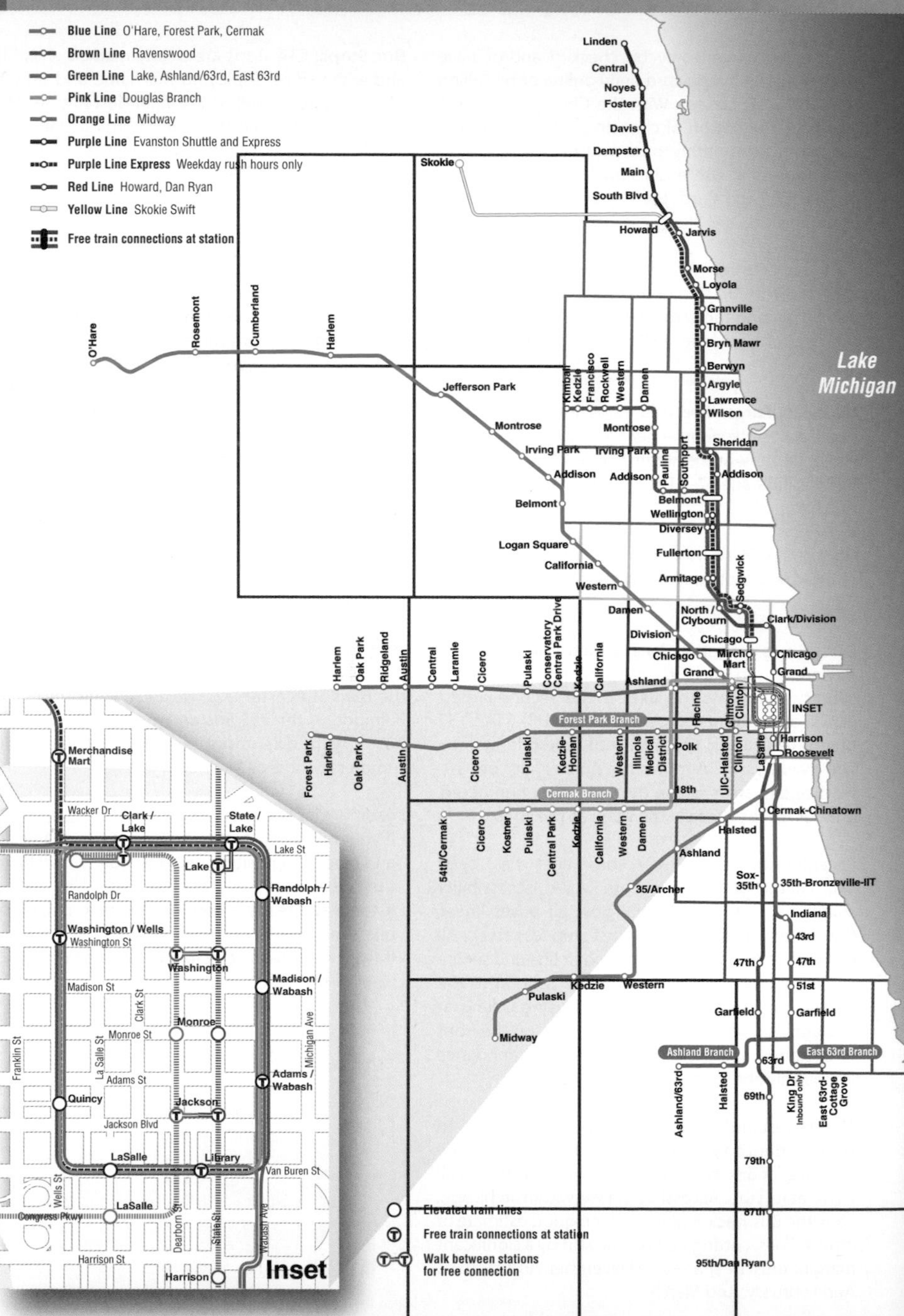
Blue Line O'Hare, Forest Park, Cermak
Brown Line Ravenswood
Green Line Lake, Ashland/63rd, East 63rd
Pink Line Douglas Branch
Orange Line Midway
Purple Line Evanston Shuttle and Express
Purple Line Express Weekday rush hours only
Red Line Howard, Dan Ryan
Yellow Line Skokie Swift
Free train connections at station
Lake Michigan
Linden
Central
Noyes
Foster
Davis
Dempster
Main
South Blvd
Skokie
Howard
Jarvis
Morse
Loyola
Granville
Thorndale
Bryn Mawr
Berwyn
Argyle
Lawrence
Wilson
Sheridan
O'Hare
Rosemont
Cumberland
Harlem
Jefferson Park
Montrose
Irving Park
Addison
Belmont
Logan Square
California
Western
Damen
Division
Chicago
Grand
Kimball
Kedzie
Francisco
Rockwell
Western
Damen
Montrose
Irving Park
Addison
Paulina
Southport
Belmont
Wellington
Diversey
Fullerton
Armitage
Sedgwick
North / Clybourn
Clark/Division
Chicago
Merch Mart
Chicago
Grand
Harlem
Oak Park
Ridgeland
Austin
Central
Laramie
Cicero
Pulaski
Conservatory Central Park Drive
Kedzie
California
Ashland
Racine
Clinton
Clinton
INSET
Forest Park Branch
Forest Park
Harlem
Oak Park
Austin
Cicero
Pulaski
Kedzie-Homan
Western
Illinois Medical District
Polk
UIC-Halsted
Clinton
LaSalle
Harrison
Roosevelt
18th
Cermak Branch
54th/Cermak
Cicero
Kostner
Pulaski
Central Park
Kedzie
California
Western
Damen
Cermak-Chinatown
Halsted
Ashland
35/Archer
Sox-35th
35th-Bronzeville-IIT
Indiana
43rd
47th
47th
51st
Kedzie
Western
Pulaski
Midway
Garfield
Garfield
Ashland Branch
East 63rd Branch
63rd
Ashland/63rd
Halsted
69th
King Dr Inbound only
East 63rd-Cottage Grove
79th
87th
95th/Dan Ryan
Elevated train lines
Free train connections at station
Walk between stations for free connection
Merchandise Mart
Wacker Dr
Clark / Lake
State / Lake
Lake St
Lake
Randolph Dr
Randolph / Wabash
Washington / Wells
Washington St
Washington
Madison St
Madison / Wabash
Clark St
Monroe
Monroe St
La Salle St
Michigan Ave
Franklin St
Adams St
Adams / Wabash
Quincy
Jackson
Jackson Blvd
LaSalle
Library
Van Buren St
Wells St
LaSalle
Congress Pkwy
Dearborn St
State St
Wabash Ave
Harrison St
Harrison
Inset

Overview

Whether traveling underground, on street level, or above the sidewalk, Chicagoans refer to their elevated rapid transit system as the "L." (Though some prefer to call it the "Smell.") No matter which one you choose, either name says Chicago as loud and clear as the high-pitched whine, guttural grumble, and steely grind of the train itself. L tracks lasso Chicago's heart, creating The Loop, where five of the seven L lines ride side-by-side above the pulsating business and financial district.

L trains make 1,452 trips each day and serve 143 stations in the Chicago Metropolitan Area. The numerous track delays and stalls in service are a burden to thousands of daily commuters. Nonetheless, due to the general directness of the L routes, easy station-to-station transfers, and the difficulties of parking (especially near popular destinations such as Grant Park and Wrigley Field), the benefits of L transportation usually outweigh the discomforts and inconveniences.

Fares

The standard full fare on CTA trains is $2.25 with or without a Chicago Card. A 25¢ transfer allows two additional rides within two hours of issuance. Transfer rates are automatically deducted from your fare card when reused within the time limit. Transferring within the rail network is free at determined, connected transfer stations.

To ride the L, you need a farecard. Read the CTA Overview for a thorough discussion on the merits of each fare card option, or go to the CTA website at www.transitchicago.com.

Frequency of Service

CTA publishes schedules that say trains run every 3 to 12 minutes during weekday rush hours and every 6 to 20 minutes all other times. Nice idea, but the truth is service can be irregular, especially during non-rush hours, after-hours, and in bad weather. While the system is relatively safe late at night, stick to stations in populated areas as much as possible. Buses with Owl Service may be better options in the wee hours.

L Lines

Blue Line: Comprising the O'Hare, Forest Park, and Cermak branches traveling west, O'Hare and Forest Park run 24-hours, while Cermak is operational only on weekdays.

Pink Line: Last year Chicago's newest rail line took over the blue line route from the loop to 54th and Cermak.

Red Line: Runs north-south from the Howard Street station down to the 95th Street/Dan Ryan station; operates 24-hours.

Brown Line: Starts from the Kimball Street station and heads south with service to the Loop and sometimes just to Belmont Avenue. On weekdays and Saturdays, the first Loop-bound train leaves Kimball Street at 4:01 am; the last train to leave the Loop is at 12:18 am. Sunday service begins at: 4 am and ends at 11:40 pm. After that, take the Red Line to Belmont Avenue, and transfer to the Brown Line where the last train leaves at 2:25 am (12:55 am on Sundays). The Brown Line also runs between Kimball Street and Belmont Avenue from 4 am to 2:04 am weekdays and Saturdays; and from 5:01 am to 2:04 am on Sundays.

Orange Line: Travels from Midway Airport to the Loop and back. Trains depart from Midway beginning at 3:55 am weekdays and Saturdays, and at 7 am on Sundays; the last train leaves the Loop for the airport at 1:29 am daily.

Green Line: Covers portions of west and south Chicago. The Harlem/Lake Street branch travels straight west. The Ashland Avenue/63rd Street and E 63rd Street/Cottage Grove branches go south and split east and west. Depending on the branch, service begins around 4 am weekdays with the last trains running around 1 am. Weekend schedules vary.

Purple Line: Shuttles north-south between Linden Place in suburban Wilmette and Howard Street, Chicago's northernmost station. Service starts at 4:35 am and ends at 12:55 am weeknights, 1:45 am on weekends, and 12:55 am Sundays. Weekdays, an express train runs between Linden Place and the Loop between 6:25 am and 10:10 am and then again between 2:55 pm and 6:15 pm. At all other times, take the **Purple Line Express** to the Howard Street station, and transfer to the Red Line to reach the Loop.

Yellow Line: Runs between the north suburban Skokie station and Chicago's Howard Street station on weekdays from 4:50 am to 10:18 pm. On weekends, take CTA bus 97 from Skokie station to Howard Street and catch the Red Line to the Loop.

Bicycles

Bicycles ride free and are permitted onboard at all times except weekdays from 7 am to 9 am and 4 pm to 6 pm. Only two bikes are allowed per car, so survey the platform for other bikes and check out the cars as they pull into the station for two-wheelers already onboard. When entering a station, either use the turnstile, or ask an attendant to open the gate. Don't try to take your bike through the tall steel gates—it WILL get stuck!

PACE Suburban – Chicago Buses

Pace buses serve over 35 million passengers in the Chicago suburbs and some parts of the city. With 240 routes covering 3,446 square miles, Pace provides a vital transportation service to commuters traveling between suburbs, within suburbs, to Metra train stations, and into the city. Buses usually run every 20–30 minutes, and service stops by mid-evening. Special express service is offered to Chicago-area entertainment and cultural venues. Contact Pace for specific bus route and schedule information (847-364-PACE; www.pacebus.com).

Park-n-Ride Stations: Pace has 11 Park-n-Ride stations located throughout Pace's six-county coverage area (check the Pace website for locations).

Fares: Pace fares cost $1.75 for both regular and local or feeder service. Transfers are $.25 for regular service. The one-way fare on express routes 355, 426, 835, and 855 costs $4. CTA Transit Cards may be used on Pace buses. Pace offers discounts for students, children, seniors, and disabled riders, as well as several bus pass package purchase options. Pass options include the Pace 30-Day Commuter Club Cards (CCC), which allows unlimited Pace rides for $50. A combined Pace/CTA 30-day unlimited pass costs $75 and can be used on all Pace buses and CTA trains and buses. The PlusBus Sticker (sold by Metra with a Metra Monthly Train Pass) costs $30 and allows unlimited Pace bus use.

Greyhound Buses

Greyhound is the rock-bottom traveler's best friend. The bus line offers dirt-cheap fares, the flexibility drifters prefer, basic station amenities (i.e. dirty toilets and vending machines that steal your money), and the gritty, butt-busting experience of traveling America's scenic blue-line highways and rural byways with some colorful characters.

Tips on riding "the Dog" out of town:

- Pack your own toilet paper and Wet Ones.
- Air freshener, deodorant, a pillow, and earplugs make being bused more bearable.
- Pack a cooler. Then padlock it.
- Charge your iPod. Seriously.
- Bring a cushion.
- Get your shots.

Stations: Greyhound's main train station is south of Union Station at 630 W Harrison St in West Loop (312-408-5800). CTA buses 60, 125, 156, and 157 make stops near the terminal. The closest L stop is on the Blue Line's Forest Park Branch at the Clinton Street Station on Congress Parkway. Additional Chicago-area Greyhound stations are located within L train stations: 14 W 95th St in the Red Line's 95th Street/Dan Ryan Station (312-408-5999), and 5800 N Cumberland Ave on the Blue Line's O'Hare Branch in the Cumberland Station (773-693-2474). The general aura of the Chicago Greyhound Station is one of seediness and squalor. Keep your belongings with you at all times.

Shipping Services: Greyhound Package Xpress offers commercial and personal shipping services and is available at all three Chicago bus stations. Packages are held at the station for pick-up. The main terminal in th South Loop also houses a UPS shipping office that provides door-to-door package delivery.

Fares: Tickets can be purchased on the phone or online with a credit card, or at a station with cash, travelers' checks, credit cards, or a voucher from the local plasma donor center (we kid!).

Regular fare pricing applies for both individual advance ticket sales and minutes-before-departure sales. Tickets can be used for travel to the designated destination on any day or at any departure time. Because Greyhound does not reserve seats, boarding occurs on a first-come-first-served basis, so get in line at the boarding zone for a choice seat. However, Greyhound's bark is bigger than its bite—if a significant number of passengers turn out for the same bus, Greyhound rolls another bus, or two, or three out on the spot. Good dog.

Children under 12 receive 40% discounts off of regular fares, seniors 62 and older receive 5% discounts, military members receive 10% discounts, and patients of Veteran's Administration Hospitals receive a 25% discount. Other discounts are available online. The cost for an individual return ticket is always deeply discounted if it is purchased at the same time as a departure ticket.

Tickets purchased three days in advance earn a half-price companion ticket (no age restrictions). Passengers accompanying someone with a disability always ride at a reduced rate.

Megabus.com

Roll over Greyhound, there's a new dog in town, and a cheaper one at that! Megabus.com is the Midwest's answer to the East Coast Chinatown buses. An import from the UK, these buses travel between most major Midwest cities, including Minneapolis, Detroit, Milwaukee, St. Louis, Cleveland, Indianapolis, and Pittsburgh! That's not a comprehensive list, and they are always adding more cities as demand increases, so check back.

Fares: And that brings us to the best part about Megabus, which is that the ticket prices are determined by how far in advance you buy your tickets, how popular the route is, and what day of the week you travel on. If your Fairy Godmother is on your side, it is possible that you could take a round-trip bus to, say, Kansas City, for TWO DOLLARS. That's right, these bus fares go as low as $1 each way. Of course, as the service becomes more popular, the fares go up. And if you're like us, you don't buy your fares months ahead of time, which adds to the cost. But even so, most fares don't go too much higher than $20 each way. Still a sweet deal, even by Greyhound standards.

Stations: Megabus doesn't have stations, per se. But you'll see the line snaking outside Union Station as you approach. Union Station in downtown Chicago is the arrival and departure stop for all buses out of Chicago. Park yourself at the east side of South Canal Street, between Jackson Blvd and Adams Street, and try to get there early. It's first come, first serve seating.

Megabus doesn't run as frequently as Greyhound, but for lapses in service, you can always check in on its umbrella company, Van Galder, which is in turned owned by the corporate bus superpower Coach USA (www.coachusa.com/vangalder or call 800-747-0994 toll free or 608-752-5407). Van Galder is a touch more expensive, but its routes are more frequent and more comprehensive.

Other important logistics: You can order your Megabus ticket online (www.megabus.com/us) or call for a reservation (877-GO-2-MEGA) up to 45 days in advance. You can only bring one piece of luggage (up to 50 pounds) to stow under the bus and one small carry-on. No bikes allowed. Megabus is more or less wheelchair accessible, just make sure you call and let them know, and they can accommodate you.

Transit • Metra Train Lines

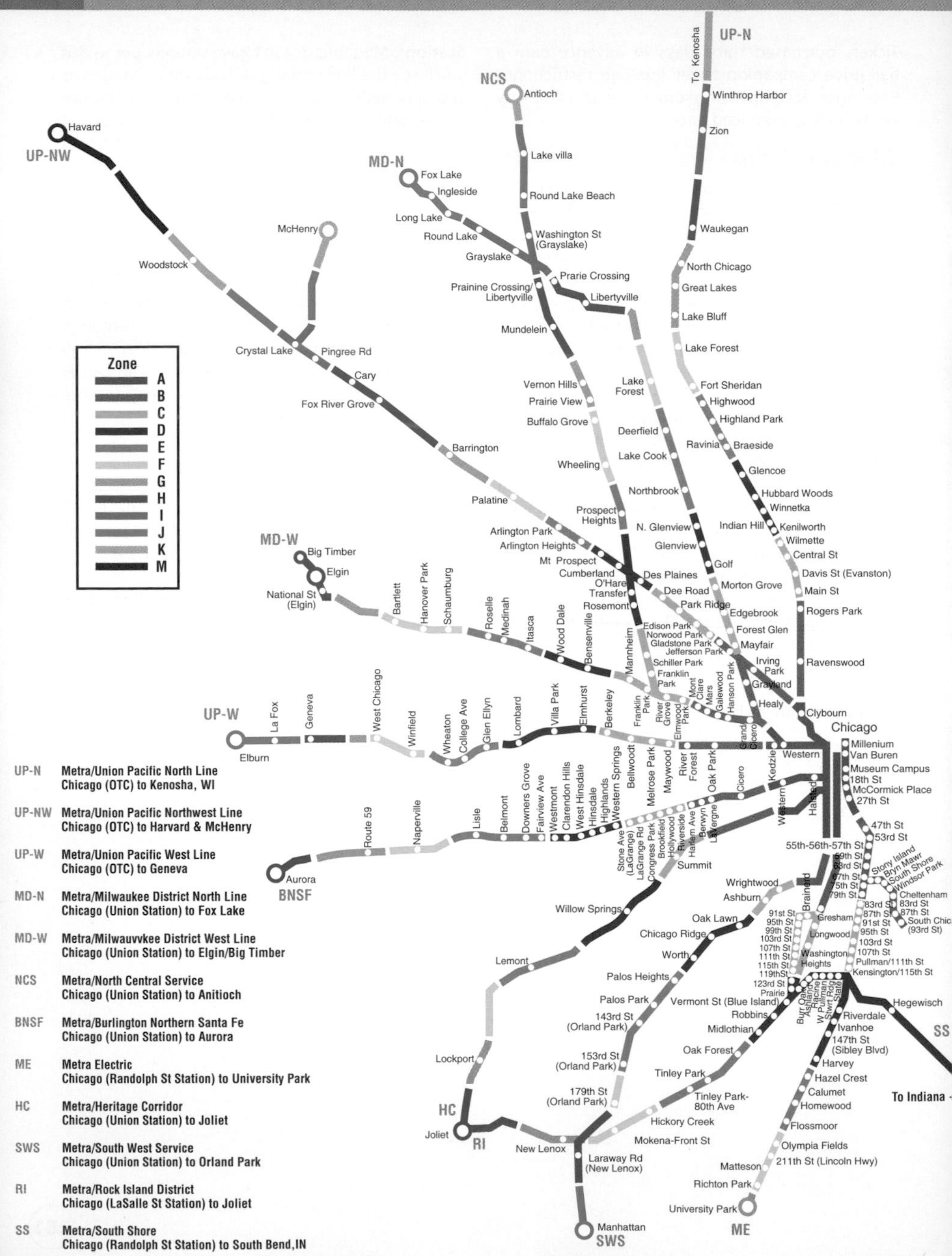

General Information

Metra Address:	Metra Passenger Services 547 W Jackson Blvd Chicago, IL 60661
Phone:	312-322-6777
Website:	www.metrarail.com
Metra Passenger Service:	312-322-6777
South Shore Metra Lines:	800-356-2079
RTA Information Center:	312-836-7000; www.rtachicago.com

Overview

With a dozen lines and roughly 495 miles of track overseen by the RTA, Metra does its best to service Cook, DuPage, Lake, Will, McHenry, and Kane counties with 230 stations scattered throughout the city and 'burbs. The rails, emanating from four major downtown stations, are lifelines for commuters traveling to and from the Loop.

The good news for Metra is that ridership is strong; the sheer multitude of folks who live in the suburbs but work in the city (and hate to deal with rush hour a-holes) means that Metra will always have a job. The bad news for riders is that parking at popular stations is difficult, if not impossible, and most people don't live close enough to Metra stations to walk. In an attempt to resolve its parking issues, Metra is purchasing land surrounding many suburban stations and constructing new parking facilities. Check out the website, www.metrarail.com, for updates on development plans.

Loop Stations

There are four major Metra train stations in the Loop from which 12 train lines emanate. Here's a chart to help clear up any possible confusion:

Station	**Line**
Richard B. Ogilvie T.C.	Union Pacific Lines
Union Station	Milwaukee District Lines North Central Service Southwest Service Burlington Northern Heritage Corridor Amtrak
LaSalle Street Station	Rock Island Line
Randolph Street Station (Millennium Station)	South Shore Railroad Metra Electric—Branches: Main Line, South Chicago, Blue Island

Fares

Depending on the number of Metra zones you traverse, one-way, full-fare tickets cost between $2.25 to $8.50. To calculate a base one-way fare, visit www.metrarail.com/Data/farechk.html. Tickets may be purchased through a ticket agent or onboard the train (with a $2 surcharge if the ticket windows were open at the time you boarded the train). There is no reserved seating.

Metra offers a number of reasonably priced ticket packages, including a Ten-Ride Ticket (which saves riders 15% off of one-way fares) and a Monthly Unlimited Ride Ticket (the most economical choice for commuters who use Metra service daily). If your commute includes CTA and/or Pace bus services, consider purchasing the Link-Up Sticker ($36) for unlimited connecting travel on CTA and Pace buses. Metra's Weekend Pass costs $7 and includes unlimited rides on Saturday and Sunday, with the exception of the South Shore route. You can buy all the aforementioned tickets in person, through the mail, or online at www.metrarail.com/TBI/index.html.

Children under age seven ride free. Children ages 7–11 ride for half-price on weekdays and for free on the weekends. Children ages 12–17 ride for half-price on weekends. Full-time grade school or high school students are eligibile to receive 50% off the cost of regular one-way fares. Senior citizens/disability fares are approximately half of the regular fare. US Military Personnel in uniform also ride Metra for half-price. Anyone wearing capri pants after Labor Day will be charged double.

Wendella RiverBuses

Spring through fall, commuters can get to North Michigan Avenue quickly on a Wendella RiverBus plying the Chicago River during rush hours, leaving from Transportation Center at the dock on the northwest corner of Madison Street. RiverBuses run daily from April 1 through November 29. The trip takes nine minutes one-way. The first boat leaves the train station dock at 7 am; the last boat departs from the dock at 400 N Michigan Avenue, at the base of the Wrigley Building at 7 pm. The fare is $2 one-way. Discounted Monthly and Ten-Ride fares are also available (312-337-1446; www.wendellariverbus.com).

Baggage & Pets

While Metra may be "the way to really fly," Metra's restrictions on baggage are more stringent than those of most airlines, though they now allow bicycles on weekday off-peak hours and on weekends (details on the "Bikes on Trains" program are divulged at metrarail.com/Special_Promotions/bikes_on_trains.html). Skis, golf clubs, non-folding carts, water buffaloes, and other large luggage items can never be transported on trains. Pets, with the exception of service animals, are also prohibited aboard trains.

General Information

Loop Station Address: Millennium Station at Randolph Street
151 E Randolph St
Underground at N Michigan Ave & E Randolph St
Chicago, IL 60601

Phone: 312-782-0676
Lost & Found: 219-874-4221 x205
Website: www.nictd.com

Overview

Although the historic South Shore train lines were built in 1903, they still get you from the Loop to Indiana's South Bend Airport in just 2.5 hours. The Northern Indiana Commuter Transportation District (NICTD) oversees the line and its modern electric trains, which serve as a vital transportation link for many northwest Indiana residents working in the Loop.

The South Shore's commuter service reflects its Indiana ridership. Outbound heading from the Loop, there are limited stops before the Hegewisch station, close to the Indiana state line. When traveling by train to Chicago's South Side, you're better off on an outbound Metra Electric Line train departing from the Randolph Street Station (see Metra page). Taking a trip on the South Shore is a rather cheap form of post-industrial voyeurism, as a complete round-trip from the Loop all the way to South Bend can be had for around $20. Along the way you will pass by dozens of antiquated factories, one of the longest stretches of sand-dunes in the Great Lakes region, and, of course, oh-so charming Gary, Indiana.

Fares

Regular one-way fares can be purchased at the stations (with cash or personal check) or on the train (cash only). Ticket prices vary with distance traveled. Tickets purchased onboard the train cost $1 more if the station's ticket windows were open at the time of departure.

Special South Shore fares and packages include commuter favorites: 10-Ride and 25-Ride tickets and the Monthly Pass which is good for unlimited travel. These can be purchased in person at stations staffed with ticket agents, station vending machines, and via the mail. Senior citizens/disability fares offer savings for persons aged 65 and older with valid identification and for disabled passengers. Students with school identification qualify for student fares, including reduced one-way tickets and discounted 25-Ride Tickets good for travel during weekdays. Youth fares include free passage for infants under two years (who must sit in a paying passenger's lap) and half off a regular fare for children aged two to 13 years. Family fares are available on weekends and holidays as well as off-peak times on weekdays. Each fare-paying adult (minimum age 21) may take up to two children (age 13 and under) with them free of charge. Additional children will be charged the reduced youth fare. There are no published fare discounts for military personnel.

Baggage & Pets

Any accompanying baggage must be placed in the overhead racks. No bicycles are permitted onboard. Apart from small animals in carry-on cages, the only pets allowed onboard are service dogs accompanied by handlers or passengers with disabilities. Animals must not occupy seats.

General Information

Amtrak Reservations: 800-USA-RAIL (872-7245)
Website: www.amtrak.com
Union Station: 225 S Canal St
Chicago, IL 60606
Phone: 312-322-6900

Overview

The best city in America for riding the rails, Chicago hubs Amtrak's 500-station national railroad network, which covers every state but Alaska, Hawaii, South Dakota, and Wyoming. Departing from Union Station, Amtrak trains head west to Los Angeles, San Francisco, Portland and Seattle; east to Washington, D.C., New York City and Boston; north to Milwaukee and Minneapolis; and south to New Orleans and San Antonio, Texas.

Fares

Amtrak offers affordable fares for regional travel, with travel times comparable to flying when you factor in today's early airport check-ins. Their prices can't compete with airfares on longer hauls, but just as airlines offer deeply discounted fares, so does Amtrak. Ask sales agents about special fares and search Amtrak's website for the best deals. (Booking in advance does present some savings.) We recommend the website, as callers risk being on hold longer than it takes to ride a train from Chicago to Los Angeles.

Amtrak offers special fares year-round for seniors, veterans, students, children under 16, and groups of two or more traveling together. The "Hot Deals" page on Amtrak's website lists sale fares. Amtrak has also hooked its cars up with plenty of travel partners to create interesting "Amtrak Vacations" packages, including air-rail deals, whereby you rail it one way and fly back the other—attractive for long-distance travel.

The prices listed below are approximate, likely to change and don't include upgrades like sleeper cars. Check with Amtrak for updates.

Service

Someday, high-speed rail may come to the Midwest. Meanwhile, only a lucky few can claim to have arrived on time when traveling the longer routes on Amtrak, so tell whoever is picking you up you'll call them on your cell phone when you get close.

Pack food for your ride, as dining-car fare is mediocre and pricey. On the upside, Amtrak's seats are comfortable and roomy; some have electric sockets for computer hookups; bathrooms are in every car; and the train is almost always clean.

And you don't have to travel light. Your ticket lets you carry on two bags and check three, each weighing up to 50 pounds. Check an additional three bags and items such as bicycles, golf bags, baby strollers, musical instruments, and skis with handling fees of $5 to $10 each. Amtrak's default liability for checked baggage tops out at $500, so if your designer duds are worth more than that you'll want to ante up for extra coverage. Weapons; large, sharp objects; corrosive or dangerous chemicals; and the like are all prohibited, just like on planes; check for current regs before you pack.

Within Illinois and to Missouri: Amtrak's Illinois Service trains travel to 28 downstate cities from Chicago daily: "The Illinois Zephyr" and "The Carl Sandburg" travel to Quincy (on the Mississippi); "Illini Service" and "The Saluki" roll between Chicago and Carbondale; "The Lincoln Service" goes through corn and soybean country to St. Louis; and "The Ann Rutledge" heads to Kansas City. Also running daily, "The Southwest Chief" stops in Kansas City five hours into its trip to Albuquerque and Los Angeles; the fare runs about $85 one way. "The City of New Orleans" makes a number of downstate stops, too.

To Milwaukee and Minneapolis: Frequent enough for commuters, "Hiawatha Service" runs seven trains daily to Sturtevant, Wisconsin (near Racine); Milwaukee's Mitchell Airport; and downtown Milwaukee, leaving Chicago about every two hours and stopping en route in suburban Glenview. The 90-minute trip costs $21 each way (a good alternative to driving on busy weekends and rush hours). "Hiawatha Service" accepts RTA Transit Checks. En route to the Northwest, "The Empire Builder" also stops in Milwaukee, as well as Minneapolis; it takes some eight and a half hours to reach the Twin Cities, with one-way fare about $92.

To Michigan: Skip scary driving through the "Snow Belt" by taking the train. Three lines offer daily service to the Winter Water Wonderland: "The Pere Marquette" heads to Grand Rapids; "The Blue Water" takes passengers to Port Huron; and "The Wolverine" goes to Ann Arbor and Detroit, among other places. The ride to the Motor City takes about six hours and costs $27 to $48 one way.

To the East Coast: "The Capitol Limited" runs daily through Cleveland and Pittsburgh to Washington, D.C., an 18-hour trip, while "The Cardinal" takes 28 hours to get to New York via Indianapolis, Cincinnati, Philadelphia, and Washington three days a week. The "Lake Shore Limited" passes through Albany, N.Y., and goes to New York City (21 hours) and Boston (24 hours). One-way tickets to the Eastern Seaboard cost between $80 and $150.

To Seattle or Portland: The "Empire Builder" takes passengers to Seattle and Portland and everywhere in between. With the journey to Seattle taking around 44 hours, we definitely recommend dropping some additional dollars on a sleeper car. One-way fare costs between $140 and $250.

To San Francisco: You'll spend two solid days and then some riding the rails during the 52-hour journey on the "California Zephyr" to San Francisco (Emeryville). The fare costs roughly $175 to $230 one-way. The "Zephyr" passes through Denver, Salt Lake City, and Sacramento, and makes a host of small-town America stops along the way.

To Los Angeles: You'll have plenty of time to study your map to the Hollywood stars on the "Southwest Chief," which departs for L.A. daily via Albuquerque, takes almost 42 hours, and costs $200 to $250 one-way.

To San Antonio: The mighty "Texas Eagle" doesn't exactly glide to the Alamo. It stops at 40 cities on its way from the Midwest to the Southwest. The 32-hour trip will cost around $117.

To New Orleans: The train Chicago's Steve Goodman made famous, "The City of New Orleans," runs from Chicago via Memphis to The Big Easy in roughly 20 hours. The fare runs about $100 to $180 one-way. Good morning, America, how are you?

Union Station

210 S Canal St at E Adams St and E Jackson Blvd • 312-655-2385 • www.chicagounionstation.com

An innovation for both design and travel, Chicago's Union Station is the "Grand Dame" of rail service in a city once considered to be the undisputed rail center of the United States. Designed by the architects Graham, Anderson, Probst, and White and built between 1913 and 1925, Union Station is a terminus for six Metra lines and a major hub for Amtrak's long-distance services. In its peak (1940s), this local transportation treasure handled as many as 300 trains and 100,000 passengers on a daily basis. While today's volume is just half that, this monumental station stands as the last remaining grand station still in use in the City of Chicago and was given landmark status in 2002. Most commuters don't take the time to gaze skyward when rushing through the Great Hall of Union Station (who really has the time to stop and assess their surroundings beyond that of their intended use?), but by not doing so, they are missing something special. Take the time to look up at the magnificent light-swathed ceiling and maybe then it will become clear why Union Station's ornate Great Hall is considered one of the United States' great interior public spaces. Union Station is also a premiere location for formal functions as it annually plays host to a multitude of private affairs and black-tie gatherings.

Both Metra's and Amtrak's train services are on the Concourse Level (ground floor) of the station. This level is then further divided into the North Concourse and South Concourse. Although not always adequately staffed, there is an information desk located between the concourses on this level. And while there is signage throughout Union Station, the many escalators, stairways, and multiple entrances/exits can make navigating the block-long building somewhat of a challenge.

Ticket Windows: The easiest way to get to Metra ticket agents is to enter Union Station at the Clinton Street entrance near East Jackson Boulevard and go down into and through the Grand Hall. Metra's ticket agents will be on your left in the North Concourse. Metra's ticket office is open weekdays 6 am–11pm, Saturday 6:30 am–11pm, and Sunday 7 am–11 pm. Metra Lines that terminate at Union Station are Milwaukee District East and West Lines, North Central Service, Burlington Northern Santa Fe, Heritage Corridor, and South West Service.

To get to the Amtrak action, enter Union Station off Canal Street, take the escalator down into the Grand Hall, and turn left. Amtrak's attractive, vintage ticket agent desk straddles the two concourses and is open daily 6 am–10 pm. Amtrak's waiting rooms and baggage claim are in the South Concourse. For more detail on Amtrak service, call 800-872-7245 or visit www.amtrak.com.

Services: On the Mezzanine/Street Level, there is a plethora of convenience stores, newsstands, and eateries. ATMs are located in both concourses on this level. One particular stop of note for contrarian travelers should be the in-house bar appropriatlely called, "The Snuggery". It's a pretty snug fit, and one can find errant Amtrak employees here, along with a revolving cast of grey-flannel suit types.

Public Transportation: The closest L stop to Union Station is Clinton Street on the Blue Line, which stops two blocks south of the station. The Orange, Brown, and Purple lines stop three blocks east of the station at the Quincy stop on Wells Street. CTA buses 1, 151, 157, and 125 all stop at Union Station. Most commuters heading to work in the Loop enter and exit the station from the Madison Street, Adams Street, and Jackson Boulevard doorways where cabs line up.

Richard B. Ogilvie Transportation Center

500 W Madison St at S Canal St • 312-496-4777

Built in 1911 and known locally as the North Western or Madison Street Station, the Metra's Union Pacific Lines originate from the Richard B. Ogilvie Transportation Center. Where Union Station is about form and function, Ogilvie focuses solely on function. Overtly stark and sterile, the tall, smoky-glass-and-green-steel-girder building replaced what was once a classic grand train station similar to the ornate, Beaux Arts-inspired Union Station. Though most of the historic fixtures have been removed, some of the original clocks remain and serve as a reminder of earlier days. Even though promised renovations of the unused historic sub-level areas have yet to come to fruition (it is hoped that the empty space under the tracks can be turned into 120,000 square feet of shops and restaurants), this highly trafficked station remains quite active. Roughly 40,000 passengers pass through the Richard B. Ogilvie Transportation Center on a daily basis.

Ticket Windows: Metra's ticket office is on the Upper Level, across from the entrance to the train platform and is open 5:30 am–12:40 am Monday–Saturday, and 7 am–12:40 am Sundays. ATMs can be found on the Upper Level at Citibank and next to the currency exchange. Public phones are also by the currency exchange in the southeast corner of the Upper Level.

Services: Loads of junk food options are available on the Street Level food court, which also serves as a make-shift waiting room for commuters. If you want healthier fare, try the Rice Market and Boudin Sourdough Bakery on the east side of the building. There is available shopping about if you're killing time or wanting to pick up a last-minute gift. An interesting and annoying amenity footnote: the only restrooms in the station are on the Street Level, which is a LONG escalator ride from the train platform. There are no plans for this to change until the proposed renovations are completed, so it's best to "go before you go."

Public Transportation: The closest L station is the Green Line's Clinton Street stop at Lake Street, several blocks north of the station. CTA buses 20, 56, and 157 board at Washington and Canal Streets and travel to North Michigan Avenue and the Loop. Coming from the Loop, take the same bus lines west across Madison Street. If you're after a cab, you'll find other like-minded commuters lining up in front of the main entrance on Madison Street between Canal and Clinton Streets.

Millennium Station

151 E Randolph St at N Michigan Ave • 312-322-7819

Nicknamed the "Triple S" (South "Start" Station), the Millennium Station serves Metra's three electric commuter rail lines in Chicago (Main Line, South Chicago Branch, Blue Island Branch) in addition to several diesel lines. The underground station, centrally located in the Loop, services up to 100,000 commuters daily. This is also the station where the South Shore Line to South Bend, Indiana originates. Schedules for all are somewhat sporadic except during weekday rush hour commutes. The Van Buren Street Station also serves both the Metra Electric and South Shore lines and is located at East Jackson Boulevard and Van Buren Street (312-322-6777). When planning train travel from the Randolph Street and Van Buren Street stations, it's best to verify schedules and stops with the RTA Information Center (312-836-7000; www.rtachicago.com) before committing to a travel plan.

Ticket Windows: Enter the Millennium Station at East Randolph Street and North Michigan Avenue. The ticket office is immediately visible upon descending the steps off Michigan Avenue or entering via the Pedway, which tunnels around the Loop and east under Michigan Avenue, ending at the station. Ticket office hours are 6 am–10:20 pm daily. The waiting room is open 5 am–12:50 am daily.

Services: Recently a few shops finally opened in this station, including an outpost of a certain very, very large coffee chain and a couple of regrettably bland retail offerings. On an upbeat note, the bathrooms are rather clean, which is a most welcome find in the Loop.

Public Transportation: Millennium Station is served by CTA buses 56, 151, 157 and on days when there are events at the United Center, express bus 19 becomes available. A little over one block west of the train station in the Loop is the Randolph Street L station, serviced by the Orange, Green, Purple, and Brown lines.

LaSalle Street Station

414 S La Salle St at E Congress Pkwy • 312-322-8957

The La Salle Street Station, located underneath the Chicago Stock Exchange, serves the Metra Rock Island District Line's passengers. This former behemoth of a station has been greatly reduced in both size and stature, handling roughly 15,000 commuters daily. The service has 11 main line stops and 10 south suburban stops on its way to Joliet.

Ticket Windows: Enter the station off LaSalle Street, take the escalator one floor up, and walk through the slim corridor to an open-air area where the tracks are. To your right you'll see the ticket office. Agents are on duty 7 am–8 pm weekdays, 10:30 am–6:30 pm on Saturday, and closed on Sunday.

Services: There are no shops to speak of at the LaSalle Street Station, but there is a waiting room is open 6 am–12 am daily.

Public Transportation: The Blue Line's La Salle Street stop at Congress Parkway and the Orange, Purple, and Brown lines' La Salle Street stop at Van Buren Street drop L riders right in front of the train station. CTA buses 6 and 146 stop near the station, as well.

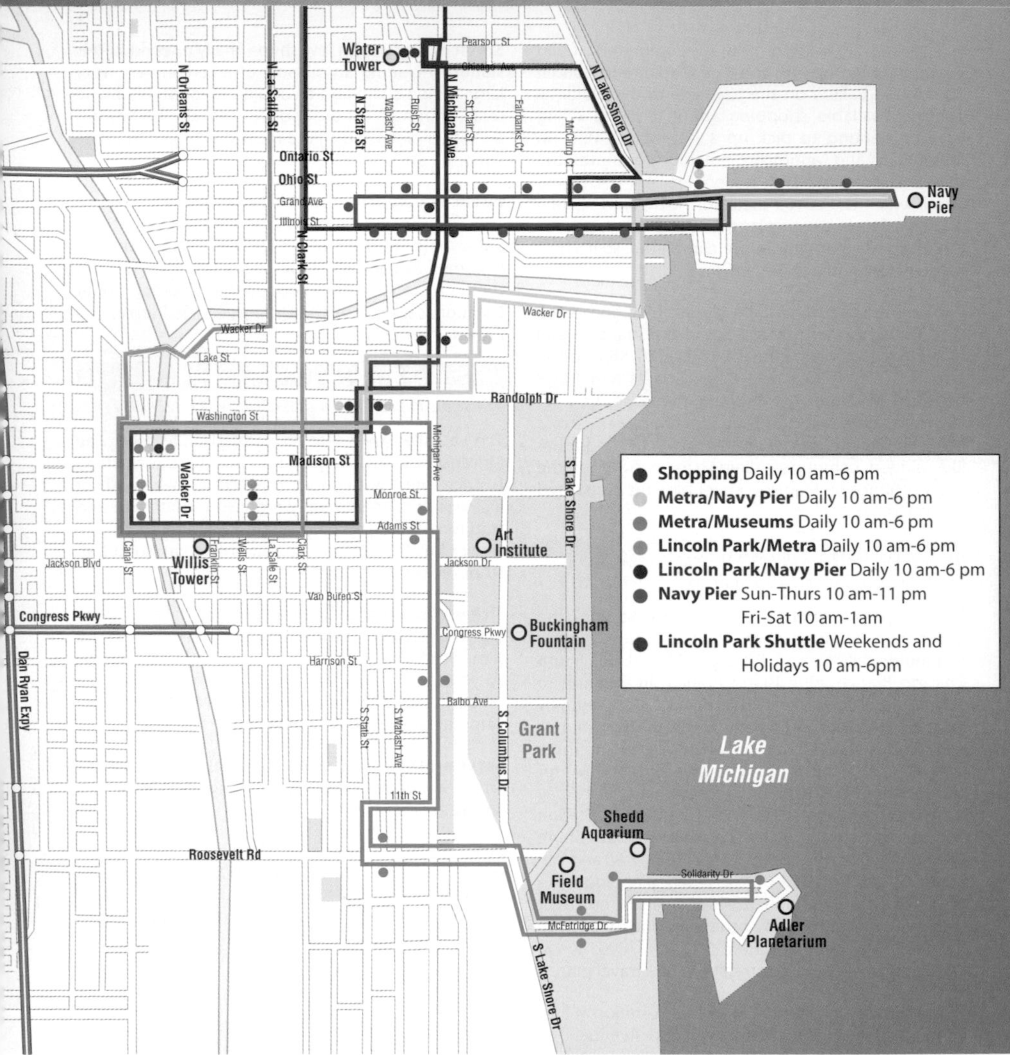

If you want to mingle with the tourists at top sightseeing and shopping destinations like Michigan Avenue, State Street, and Navy Pier, the city of Chicago makes transit easy with free "trolley" service. Most trolley-buses run every 20 minutes from 10 or 10:30 am to early evening from Memorial Day weekend through Labor Day weekend and at selected holidays. Some lines may run on weekends only (check map for specific line hours). Daily free trolley service between Navy Pier and State Street along Grand Avenue and Illinois Street runs all year round during Pier hours.

The color-coded trolley routes dovetail with CTA bus routes and make stops at major Loop L stations and Metra stations. Trolley stops are identified by graphic, color-coded signs. Because fare-based trolley companies also roam the streets, be sure to look for the "Free Trolley" sign in the front window. You don't need a ticket to ride; just hop on and off as you please. However, the lines can be long at peak times, so don't wait until the kids get cranky to head home.

For more information, contact: 877-244-2246; www.cityofchicago.org/transportation

Lake Michigan
Diversey Harbor
North Pond
Lincoln Park
Lincoln Park Lagoon
South Pond
South Pond
W Fullerton Pkwy
N Clark St
N Halsted St
W Armitage Ave
W Webster Ave
N Lincoln Ave
N La Salle St
N State Pkwy
41
MAP 29
MAP 30
MAP 31
MAP 32
MAP 22

General Information

City of Chicago Department of Transportation (DOT)
Non-Emergency/
24-Hour Road Conditions Phone: 311

Street Closings Hotline:	312-787-3387
Website:	www.cityofchicago.org

Illinois Department of Transportation (IDOT)

Phone:	217-782-7820
IDOT Traffic Hotline:	312-368-4636
Website:	www.dot.state.il.us/news.html
Chicago Skyway Bridge:	312-747-8383
Road Conditions:	800-452-4368
WBBM-AM 780:	Traffic updates every eight minutes

Orientation

Anyone who says baldness is hereditary has never found him/herself in a Chicago traffic jam, pulling out his/her hair to pass the time and calm the nerves. We highly recommend taking public transportation whenever possible, especially since Chicago has such strong bus and rail systems. But if you must drive in the city, Chicago's grid system makes it relatively easy to navigate.

The intersection of State and Madison Streets in the Loop serves as the base line for both Chicago's street and house numbering system. Running north and south is State Street—the city's east/west dividing line. Madison Street runs east and west and divides the city into north and south. Street and building numbers begin at "1" at the State and Madison Streets intersection and numerically increase going north, south, east, and west to the city limits. Street signs will let you know in what direction you're heading. The city is divided into one-mile sections, or eight square blocks, each with a consecutively higher series of "100" numbers. For example, Western Ave, sitting at 2400 W, is further west than Ashland Ave, located at 1600 W. In addition, Chicagoans numerically refer to street locations such as Irving Park Road as "40 hundred north" rather than "four thousand north." An intersting historical tidbit about the city's three primary diagonal streets: Milwaukee, Elston, and Lincoln, as that they all used to be Native American trails.

Buildings with even number addresses are on the north and west sides of streets; odd numbers sit on the south and east sides. Chicago's diagonal streets also follow the grid numbering system, most of which receive north or south addresses. East-west streets north of Madison are named, as in Fullerton or Belmont; south of Madison they are generally numbered, as in 31st or 79th, with several major streets being named. Once you get out of the city limits, good luck. Often times you will find that our suburban friends like to refer to the same road by two different names. Roads will also magically turn into something different for no apparent reason. And sometimes they don't bother putting up street signs at all.

Bridge Lift Season

While bridges spanning the Chicago River contribute to the city's architectural fame, they also serve as a major source of traffic congestion. Boating season demands that bridges lower and rise, so as to allow Chicago's elite access to Lake Michigan in their sailboats. Chicago's bridge lift season runs from early April until June. Each month has designated lift days. Lifts generally begin at 9:30 am and affect the entire downtown area between 11:30 am and 1 pm. During May, more lifts are scheduled on Saturdays between 2 pm and 4 pm. The schedule intensifies on holiday weekends to include evening rush hours. Check out the DOT's website for detailed schedules.

Snow Routes

Failure to efficiently handle city snow removal seals the re-election fate of Chicago's mayors. The Department of Streets and Sanitation manages the ice and snow removal on Chicago's streets. Over 280 salt spreaders/plows cruise 607 miles of arterial streets divided into 245 designated snow routes. Parking is automatically restricted on these routes when snow is piled at least two inches on the pavement. Unfortunately, the two-inch snow routes are a crap-shoot. Tow trucks will enforce these restrictions by their own rules, it seems. On a snow route, you will either find your car gone or buried by a passing plow. Safety dictates you keep your car off of these routes even if only an inch and a half are predicted. Priority arteries also restrict parking daily from 3 am until 7 am between December 1 and April 1, whether or not snow is present (though so far this relatively new rule has not been strictly enforced).

Major Expressways and Tollways

While the city's grid system is logical, the interstate highway system feeding into the city is confusing for those who don't travel it often. Chicago has free expressways and tollways which require paying a fee. The expressways are generally referred to by their names, such as "The Kennedy" or "The Eisenhower." When venturing to Indiana, one can experience the Chicago Skyway, a stretch of elevated road that connects I-94 and the Indiana Toll Road that soars 120 feet above the Calumet River. When using the tollways, which includes the Skyway, I-PASS speeds up the process and can be purchased through the Illinois State Toll Highway Authority by calling 800-824-7277.

DMVs

The Illinois Department of Motor Vehicles (DMV) is one of life's unavoidable hassles. But you'd be pleasantly surprised to see how many of your car-related responsibilities (like renewing your driver's license, getting vehicle registrations, etc.) can be completed online (www.dmv.org). Unless you're British and enjoy standing in line for hours. Visit the website, or call 312-793-1010 for more information.

Chicago DMVs	*Map*	*Hours*
100 W Randolph St	5	Mon–Fri: 8 am–5 pm
69 W Washington St, Concourse Level	5	Mon–Fri: 8 am–5 pm
17 N State St, Ste 1000	5	Mon–Fri: 8 am–4:30 pm
5401 N Elston Ave	46	Mon–Tues: 8:30 am–5 pm; Wed: 10 am–7 pm; Thurs–Fri: 8:30 am–5 pm
9901 S Martin Luther King Dr	59	Mon–Tues: 8:30 am–5 pm; Wed: 10 am–7 pm; Thurs–Fri: 8:30 am–5 pm
5301 W Lexington Ave	49	Tues: 9 am–7 pm; Wed–Fri: 8 am –5:30 pm; Sat: 8 am–12 pm

Zip Cars and I-Go

Eco-friendly car sharing has come to the Windy City. Two companies: Zip Car and I-Go, offer a fleet of eco-friendly vehicles (Zip Car's fleet includes Mini Coopers—cute!), at subscribers disposal for short errands or all-day rental. The cars are parked at convenient locations throughout the city. Just scan your card over the code and voila! You're in! Cars can be reserved by phone or online. For more information, including rates and vehicle locations, check out their websites.

I-Go	www.igocars.org
Zip Cars	www.zipcar.com

Overview

Parking in Chicago has never been what we would call a joyous experience. Between neighborhood permit-only parking zones, snow routes, and a contant rotation of street fairs, street cleaning, street construction, and on and on, figuring out where and how to park in the city requires an advanced degree in clusterf*ck. Some areas, like Lincoln Park, Lakeview, and Wicker Park, would test the nerves and the patience of the Dalai Lama. These areas are all easily accessible by public transit, and taxi cabs are plentiful, so don't be a jag-off and add to the problem. Just. Don't. Do. It.

In 2009, our soon-to-be-voted-out-of-office legacy mayor added to the problem by leasing all of the cities parking meters to a private firm (a 75-year lease!), causing fares to jump in some neighborhoods from .25 for a half-hour to .25 per 15 minutes, and from ending at 9, to continuing all night. Maybe the ONE positive side of the meter fiasco is the advent of Pay Boxes. These handy contraptions at least do you the courtesy of letting you pay with a credit card as they rip you off. The days of saving your quarters are over. Now just start a separate bank account for parking.

General Information

Office of the City Clerk—Parking Permits

Mailing Address:	City Hall 121 N La Salle St, Rm 107 Chicago, IL 60602
Phone:	312-744-6861
Hours:	Weekdays, 8 am–5 pm
Website:	www.chicityclerk.com

Department of Revenue (DOR)—Parking Ticket Payments

Mailing Address:	PO Box 88298 Chicago, IL 60680-1298
Phone:	312-747-4747
Website:	www.cityofchicago.org/revenue
Parking Ticket Assistance & "Boot" Inquiries:	312-744-PARK (7275)
Auto Pound Headquarters: (for towed vehicles)	312-744-4444
City Non-Emergency Phone:	311

City Stickers

Residents of Chicago who own motor vehicles (see "sadomasochist" at www.wikipedia.org) must have an annually renewed city sticker for their cars, which can be purchased from the Office of the City Clerk through the mall (by returning the renewal application you've received in the mail), in person at one of their offices, or online. Stickers may also be purchased at local currency exchanges, but you might get charged extra there. New residents are required to purchase their sticker in person with a proof of residency at one of the offices within 30 days of their move-in date. A four-passenger vehicle sticker for long-time residents costs $75, while new residents get a price cut at $37. Senior citizens are also eligible for discounts, but they check IDs, so don't pretend you're over 50; they'll find out you're lying. After March 1st of each year, half-year stickers are available at half-price for new city residents or current residents who've recently purchased a car. For more information on office locations and pricing, call 312-742-9200 or visit the City Clerk's website.

Residential Zone Permit Parking

If you're lucky enough to find a parking spot, you still need to put a permit on your car. Chicago's Residential Parking Permit program reserves street parking during peak parking hours for neighborhood residents and those who provide a service to the residents. Cars in violation of this ordinance will be ticketed. Take that, suckers. Permits cost $25 annually and are available through the Office of the City Clerk via mail, online, and in person. Applicants must have a valid Chicago City Sticker and an Illinois State license plate. One-day guest passes may also be purchased and distributed by qualified residents. Fifteen 24-hour passes cost $5 per pack at a two-pack limit, so choose your guests wisely and frugally. Check out the City Clerk website or call 312-744-5346 for more information.

Parking Tickets

The Department of Revenue (DOR) handles the payment of parking tickets. You can pay parking tickets by mail, online, or in person; scribbling curse words on it, ripping it up, and throwing it at the mailbox does not count as "paying" it, according to the stingy DOR. For the addresses and hours of payment processing and hearing facilities, see the DOR website.

Three or more unpaid tickets guarantees a metal, yellow surprise fitted to your car tire; yep, say hello to the boot. Ten or more tickets and the entire car is encased in molybdenum steel. If violations aren't paid within 24 hours of booting, your vehicle will be towed...maybe. In addition to the boot fee, towing, and storage fees must be paid to retrieve your car from a City Auto Pound. If your car is towed due to a boot, contact the City of Chicago's Ticket Help Line (312-744-7275). All payments for outstanding parking ticket debt must be made to a DOR Payment Center, not at the pound. The city has two payment plans available for motorists with large ticket fines. The General Payment Plan requires either a deposit of $500 or 25% of your parking debt (whichever is greater) in addition to all outstanding boot, towing, and storage fees. If you qualify for the Hardship Parking Payment Plan, you can make a deposit of $250 or 25% of your debt, whichever is lower. If either of these cases applies to you, we also suggest you stop parking in Chicago and find another means of travel, since you apparently can't handle the responsibility. Visit the DOR website for further requirements.

Auto Pounds

To locate your towed vehicle, contact the City of Chicago Auto Pound Headquarters (312-744-4444). There are six auto pounds in addition to the O'Hare Auto Pound (10000 W O'Hare at Remote Lot E, 773-694-0990).

For a standard vehicle, the towing fee is a hefty $150 plus a $10 per day storage fee for the first five days, $35 per day thereafter. Fees can be paid at the pound; they accept cash, cashier's checks, VISA, MasterCard, Discover, American Express, and first-born children. No arms or legs, please.

Failure to claim vehicles or request a hearing within 21 days of notification can result in your convenient mode of transportation being sold or destroyed and, even then, you still owe the city for the outstanding fines. In that case, see the rest of the Transit section for alternate ways of navigating your way through Chicago.

Important note: "Minor" street repairs and construction are common occurrences on Chicago streets, during which signs should be posted on nearby trees or parking meters stating that parking is temporarily prohibited. If you park there, you will be towed. If you parked there on purpose despite seeing the signs, well, you deserve it. If you parked there on accident, we feel for you, so read on for our tips on how to not look like a panicky idiot while trying to find your car. First of all, don't bother contacting the city pound. They will have no idea what you're talking about! Save yourself the embarrassment of reporting your car stolen, and call the number posted on the sign where your car was parked. Chances are it was kindly moved to another location so as to allow workers to continue with important road improvements, but it may not have officially been moved by the city of Chicago. Operators should be able to track it down using your license plate number since city code mandates that the kindly moving of a car must be reported within a few hours, whether it be by the city or the other parking powers that be. Otherwise, you can always walk around your neighborhood aimlessly searching for your car, but we don't recommend it. We've only been successful doing that once or twice, and, anyway, it just turned out that we forgot where we parked after a night of heavy drinking.

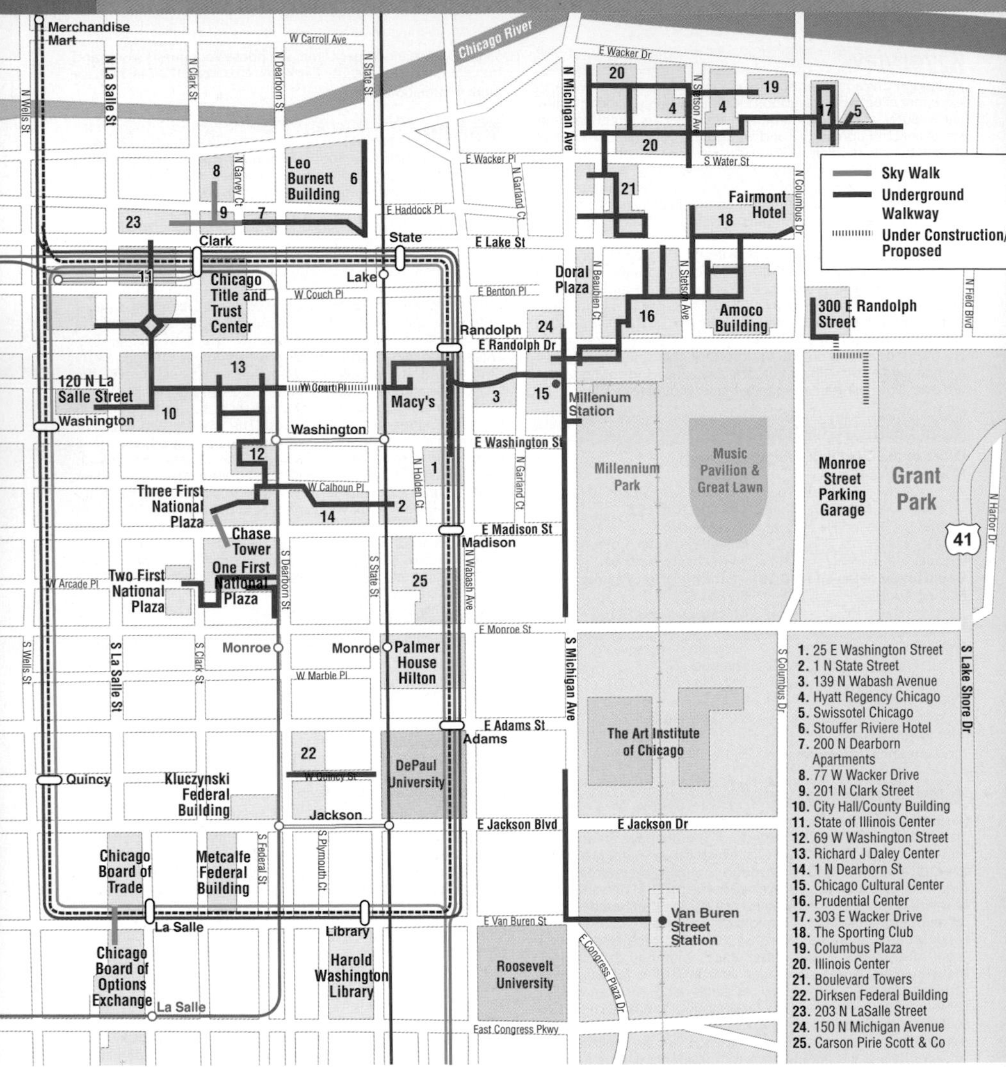

While a number of cold-weather cities are known for their above-ground walkways, Chicago is known for its Pedway, a 40-block network of tunnels and overhead bridges that connects important public, government, and private sector buildings with retail stores, major hotels, rapid transit stations, and commuter rail stations. A subterranean city with shops, restaurants, services, and public art works, the Pedway is a welcome alternative to navigating trafficked intersections on foot and walking outdoors in Chicago's frigid winters. The underground walkway system is open 24 hours; however, access to a number of the buildings is limited after standard business hours. The first Pedway links were built in 1951 to connect the State Street and Dearborn Street subways at Washington Street and Jackson Boulevard. Today, Chicago's Pedway continues to grow as city government and the private sector cooperate to expand it. Those planning on making a subterranean trip to experience the Pedway in its glory would do well to click on over to www.spiegl.org/pedway/pedway.html for a map of the whole lair.

By our minds, the designation of "landmark" can apply to buildings of architectural distinction, or the iconic Morton Salt girl, trailing sodium chloride behind her on the roof of the Elston Avenue Morton Salt facility. It could be internationally recognized Chicago iconography (Buckingham Fountain), or something only the locals are aware of ("Meet me by the Totem Pole"). Landmark status is a historical designation, but local landmarks are how you figure out where the hell you are and where you need to go.

Legacy Architecture

Early skyscrapers such as the **Monadnock Building (Map 5)** can be found in the Loop, alongside other noteworthy structures like Adler and Sullivan's historic **Auditorium Building (Map 6)**. Contrast these with Midwest native **Frank Lloyd Wright's Home and Studio (Oak Park)** in the suburb of Oak Park, whose famous Prairie style can also be seen at the **Robie House (Map 19)** on the city's south side. Jump forward a couple of decades and German Mies van der Rohe arrives on the scene, with his dictum "less is more." Trek over to the **Illinois Institute of Technology (IIT) (Map 13)** to really immerse yourself in his spare glass and steel structures. Chicago is also home to a triumvirate of quirky Bertrand Goldberg masterpieces—**Marina Towers (Map 2)**, which graces the cover of Wilco's Yankee Hotel Foxtrot, **River City (Map 7)**, and the **Raymond Hilliard Apartments (Map 10)**.

Great New Architecture

IIT is also the site of some fab new architecture, such as starchitect Rem Koolhaas's incredible **McCormick Tribune Campus Center (Map 14)**, which literally encases the L in a tube, and Helmut Jahn's **State Street Village (Map 14)**. With plans for the world's tallest and corkscrew-evoking Chicago Spire dashed due to an inability to secure financing, the city is soliciting suggestions about what to do with that giant-assed hole in the ground. Meanwhile the glittering new **Trump Tower (Map 2)** has become a new beacon on the Chicago cityscape, replacing the dismal former Sun Times building (strange how the newspaper relocated to an equally drab building only a few blocks away from the original).

Historical Houses

Built in 1836, Prairie Avenue's **Clarke House (Map 11)** claims the title of Chicago's oldest home, never mind that the original building of the northwest side's **Noble-Seymour-Crippen (Chicago Northwest)** house dates back to 1833. Although **Robie House (Map 19)** is the most famous, Frank Lloyd Wright's prairie-style homes dot Chicago's landscape, amongst them are the **Walser House (Chicago West)** and Sheridan Avenue's **Bach House (Map 34)**. Of course some homes are more renowned for their residents than their architectural or historical significance. These include the **Charlie Chaplin Home (Map 38)**, the **Ida B. Wells-Barnett Home (Map 14)**, the **Richard J. Daley House (Map 13)**, and, most famously, President **Barack Obama's Residence (Map 17)**.

Outdoor Spaces

Chicago's status as a green city got off to a good start, thanks to some forward-thinking chaps. By advocating the lakefront as a place for recreation, Daniel Burnham has left a wonderful legacy. Highlights are **Lincoln Park (Parks & Places)** with the free **Lincoln Park Zoo (Map 30))** to the north and **Jackson Park (Parks & Places)** (site of the 1893 World's Columbian Exposition) to the south. **Central Grant Park (Parks & Places)** is home to the **Buckingham Fountain (Map 9)**, and offers festivals throughout the warmer months. And don't forget the harbors. **Belmont Harbor (Map 44)** is home to the Chicago Yacht Club Sailing School, while **The Point at Diversey (Map 30)** provides a fabulous view of the city from the north. Within the downtown itself, outdoor spaces include **Daley Plaza (Map 5)** (you saw it in the movie The Lake House), which offers free lunchtime cultural events. Outside of the city limits, **Garfield Park Conservatory (Parks & Places)** is a jewel in a barren landscape.

Public Artwork

Better described as a work of art rather than simply an outdoor space, **Millennium Park (Parks & Places)** is not to be missed. Legendry architect Frank Gehry has conjured up another of his steel creations with the **Jay Pritzker Pavilion (Map 6)** (an open air venue offering complimentary concerts), while British and Spanish artists have stolen the show with **Cloud Gate (Map 6)** (otherwise known as The Bean) and **The Crown Fountain (Map 6)** (a.k.a. kiddies' pool). Another heavy concentration of public artwork is found in the Loop, with the **Joan Miro Sculpture (Map 5)** and **Alexander Calder's Flamingo (Map 5)** being amongst the high profile pieces. How often do children get the chance to slide down a Picasso?

Lowbrow Landmarks

Chicago has its share of more unassuming sights too, including the mysterious **Totem Pole (Map 44)** along the lakefront and **Agora (Map 9)**, an army of headless metal people. Also easy to miss is the amazing artwork **The Body of Lake Michigan (Southwest)**. Look up as you go through the security checkpoint at Midway airport; it's quite impressive. Out to the south west is the **Union Stockyard Gate (West)**, a reminder of the days referred to in Carl Sandburg's line "Hog Butcher for the world." You can then go sample some meat—the infamous cheezboiger—at the unpretentious **Billy Goat Tavern (Map 3)**.

Overrated Landmarks

With the nickname "The Windy City" derived from the hot air dispensed by earlier politicians, the city also has its fair share of overrated landmarks. The amazingly hideous new **Soldier Field (Map 11)** fits the bill perfectly. If there were flying saucers in classical civilization, they would look something like this. Also registering on the ugly scale is the **James R. Thompson Center (Map 5)**. Enough said. However, the prize for most over-hyped attraction must go to **Navy Pier (Parks & Places)** with its wall-to-wall tourists and mediocre eateries. Consider yourself warned.

Underrated Landmarks

On the other hand, Chicago has a lot of well-kept secrets worth exploring. Home to a large collection of art glass by Louis Comfort Tiffany, the **Chicago Cultural Center (Map 5)** and **Macy's (Map 5)** on State Street both have spectacular domes. Continuing on the glass theme, the **American Windows (Map 6)** by Marc Chagall are another treat often overshadowed by the heavy-weight impressionist collection at the **Art Institute (Map 6)**. Another find is **The Newberry Library (Map 32)**, which sits quietly on Washington Square Park, but boasts a hive of activity inside: classes, concerts, and lectures. As for the Hyde Park area, check out the **University of Chicago (Map 19)** and its **Oriental Institute Museum (Map 19)**. You'll also find the **Nuclear Energy Sculpture (Map 19)** by Henry Moore, which commemorates the first nuclear reaction which took place here. Many of the first silent pictures, starring the likes of Charlie Chaplin and Gloria Swanson (back when they had faces) were filmed at Essenay Studio, before more copacetic weather pushed the film industry out west to a little place called Hollywood.

Map 1 • River North / Fulton Market District

The Blommer Chocolate Co	600 W Kinzie St • 312-226-7700	Opened in 1939. Eventually became the largest commercial chocolate manufacturer in the US.

Map 2 • Near North / River North

Courthouse Place	54 W Hubbard St	This Romanesque-style former courthouse has witnessed many legendary trials.
Marina Towers	300 N State St	Bertrand Goldberg's riverside masterwork. Love the parking.
Merchandise Mart	222 Merchandise Mart Plz • 312-527-4141	Houses furniture showrooms and a small mall.
Rock N Roll McDonald's	600 N Clark St • 312-867-0455	Glitzy take on fast food fodder.
Sotheby's	215 W Ohio St • 312-396-9599	Renowned auction house. We bid $5.
Trump International Hotel and Tower	401 N Wabash Ave • 312-588-8000	Shiny happy 92-story skyscraper.

Map 3 • Streeterville / Mag Mile

Billy Goat Tavern	430 N Michigan Ave • 312-222-1525	Cheezborger! Cheezborger!
Chicago Spire	455 N Cityfront Plaza Dr • 312-516-4800	Proposed 2000 foot tower, due to break ground in summer 2007.
Museum of Contemporary Art	220 E Chicago • 312-280-2660	Party down on First Fridays. Get in for free on Tuesdays.
Tribune Tower	435 N Michigan Ave • 312-222-9100	Check out the stones from famous buildings around the world including a real-life rock from the moon!
Wrigley Building	400 N Michigan Ave	Monument to chewing gum.

Map 4 • West Loop Gate / Greek Town

Dugan's	128 S Halsted St • 312-421-7191	Sports bar in Greektown. Fantastic beer garden and favorite cop hangout.
Union Station	210 S Canal St • 312-322-4269	Built in 1925, the architecture is not to be missed!

Map 5 • The Loop

Chicago Board of Trade	141 W Jackson Blvd • 312-435-3590	The goddess Ceres tops this Deco monolith.
Chicago Board Options Exchange	400 S La Salle St • 312-786-5600	The world's largest options market.
Chicago Cultural Center	78 E Washington St • 312-744-6630	The spot for free lectures, exhibits, concerts, and movies.
Chicago Mercantile Exchange	20 S Wacker Dr • 312-930-8249	Economics at work in polyester jackets.
Chicago Stock Exchange	440 S La Salle St • 312-786-8803	The second-largest stock exchange in the country.
City Hall Green Roof	121 N LaSalle St	First green roof on a municipal building. Cool.
Daley Civic Plaza	50 W Washington St • 312-443-5500	Home of a Picasso sculpture, a Christmas tree ceremony, and many alfresco lunches.
Flamingo	219 S Dearborn St	Alexander Calder's fabulous red flamingo.
The Four Seasons	70 W Madison St	Mosaic by Marc Chagall—you know, the one who did all those flying people.
Harold Washington Public Library	400 S State St • 312-747-4300	The world's largest public library building; nearly 100 works of art on every floor.
James R Thompson Center	100 W Randolph St • 312-744-2400	Lots of glass combined with the colors red, silver and blue. Ghastly!
Joan Miro Sculpture	69 W Washington St	Part of the Loop's outdoor public artwork program.
Macy's	111 N State St • 312-781-1000	Folks are still mourning the passing of Marshall Fields. Luckily the clock and Tiffany dome remain.
Monadnock Building	53 W Jackson Blvd • 312-922-1890	Claim to fame: world's largest office building when completed in 1893.
Monument with Standing Beast	100 W Randolph St	Jean DuBuffet sculpture. Looks like melted snow.
Quincy L Station	220 S Wells St	Restored to its original glory.
Rookery Building	209 S La Salle St • 312-553-6150	Take a peek inside at Frank Lloyd Wright's spectacular remodelled interior.
Willis Tower (Sears Tower)	233 S Wacker Dr • 312-875-9696	Currently the tallest building in the US, with a cool skydeck.

Map 6 • The Loop / Grant Park

America Windows	111 S Michigan Ave • 312-443-3600	Spectacular stained glass by Marc Chagall.
Art Institute of Chicago	111 S Michigan Ave • 312-443-3600	World-class art museum.
Auditorium Building	430 S Michigan Ave • 312-431-2354	Designed by Louis Sullivan; on National Register of Historic Places.

Cloud Gate	201 E Randolph St • 312-742-1168	Much-photographed sculpture, affectionately known as "the bean."
The Crown Fountain	201 E Randolph St	Captivating modern take on traditional fountain, swarming with kids.
Fine Arts Building	410 S Michigan Ave • 312-566-9800	The country's first artists' colony, converted from a Studebaker carriage plant in 1898.
Jay Pritzker Pavilion	201 E Randolph St	Frank Gehry signature steel structure, offering free outdoor concerts.
Prudential Building	130 E Randolph St	Classic '50s skyscraper.
Santa Fe Building	224 S Michigan Ave	Home to the world-renowned Chicago Architecture Foundation.
Symphony Center	220 S Michigan Ave • 312-294-3000	Classical music headquarters.

Map 7 • South Loop / River City

Maxwell Street Market (Sun, 7 am–3 pm)	548 W Roosevelt Rd • 312-922-3100	Outdoor bazaar where you can shop for dish soap or bicycle parts while grazing at authentic taco stands.
Old Post Office	404 W Harrison St	This massive, vacant edifice straddling I-90/94 and I-290 is a benchmark for traffic reports.
River City	800 S Wells St	A fluid cement design experiment built by architect Bertrand Goldberg in the '80s; considered a flop, but actually brilliant.
US Postal Distribution Center	433 W Harrison St • 312-447-0979	The city's main mail routing center, employing over 6,000 people and operating 24 hours a day.

Map 8 • South Loop / Printers Row / Dearborn Park

Columbia College Center for Book & Paper Arts	1104 S Wabash Ave • 312-369-6630	Two galleries feature changing exhibits of handmade books, paper, letterpress, and other related objects.
Former Elliot Ness Building	600 S Dearborn St	If he sends one of yours to the hospital, you send one of his to the morgue…
Old Dearborn Train Station	47 W Polk St • 312-554-8100	Turn-of-the-century train station with a lighted clocktower visible for several blocks. Al Capone took a train to prison from here.
Pacific Garden Mission	646 S State St • 312-922-1462	America's oldest continuously-operating rescue mission with free showings of long running radio drama Unshackled!
River City	800 S Wells St	A fluid cement design experiment built by architect Bertrand Goldberg in the '80s; considered a flop, but actually brilliant.

Map 9 • South Loop / South Michigan Ave

Agora	S Michigan Ave & E Roosevelt Rd	If you've ever wanted to see 106 headless metal people, here's where you can.
Buckingham Fountain	500 S Columbus Dr • 312-742-7529	Built of pink marble; inspired by Versailles.
Chicago Hilton and Towers	720 S Michigan Ave • 312-922-4400	Check out the frescoes in the lobby; sneak a kiss in the palatial ballroom.
John G Shedd Aquarium	1200 S Lake Shore Dr • 312-939-2438	Marine and freshwater creatures from around the world are on view in this 1929 Classical Greek-inspired Beaux Arts structure.
Johnson Publishing Headquarters	820 S Michigan Ave • 312-322-9200	Largest African-American-owned publishing company, home of Ebony and Jet magazines.
Spirit of Music Garden	601 S Michigan Ave	Where the city struts during Chicago SummerDance.

Map 10 • East Pilsen / Chinatown

Chinatown Gate	S Wentworth Ave & W Cermak Rd	Built in 1976. The characters on the gate read "The world belongs to the people."
Chinatown Square	S Archer Ave	Restaurants, bakeries, gift stores, and herb shops.
On Leong Merchants Association Building	2216 S Wentworth Ave • 312-328-1188	1926 building inspired by architecture of the Kwangtung district of China. Now the home of the Pui Tak Center.
Pacific Garden Mission	1458 S Canal St • 312-492-9410	America's oldest continuously-operating rescue mission with free showings of long running radio drama Unshackled!
Ping Tom Memorial Park	300 W 19th St • 312-746-5962	Park with Chinese landscape elements.
Raymond Hilliard Apartments	2111 S Clark St • 312-225-3715	Another Bertrand Golberg gem going from subsidized senior housing to mixed-income residential.

Map 11 • South Loop / McCormick Place

Adler Planetarium & Astronomy Museum	1300 S Lake Shore Dr • 312-922-7827	Depression era wonder that thrilled millions at 1933 Century of Progress Exposition.
America's Courtyard	1300 S Lake Shore Dr	A spiral of stones that echoes both the Milky Way and ancient structures. Designed by Denise Milan and Ary R. Perez.
The Chicago Daily Defender	2400 S Michigan Ave • 312-225-5656	Founded in 1905, it was the country's most influential black newspaper through the '50s. Still in operation, but much-diminished.
Clarke House	1827 S Indiana Ave	Built in 1836 by an unknown architect, this Greek Revival-style home has been relocated twice and is now an official Chicago landmark.
The Field Museum	1400 S Lake Shore Dr • 312-922-9410	Go to see Sue, world's largest known T. Rex; stay for the jam-packed halls of vaguely macabre taxidermy.
Hillary Rodham Clinton Women's Park and Gardens	1800 S Prairie Ave	A garden from a former first lady.
Hyatt Regency McCormick Place	2233 S King Dr • 312-567-1234	The only hotel attached to the city's main convention center.
McCormick Place	2301 S Lake Shore Dr • 312-791-7000	Hard to miss.
National Vietnam Veterans Art Museum	1801 S Indiana Ave • 312-326-0270	Features art about the war created by Vietnam veterans from all sides of the conflict.
Northerly Island Park	1400 S Linn White Dr • 312-745-2910	Greenspace now encompassing former site of Meigs Field airport.
Quinn Chapel, African Methodist Episcopal Church	2401 S Wabash Ave • 312-791-1846	Built in 1892, this Victorian Gothic-style church houses Chicago's oldest African-American congregation.
Second Presbyterian Church	1936 S Michigan Ave • 312-225-4951	Reconstructed in 1900 by Howard Van Doren Shaw, this ponderous Gothic Revival-style church has stained glass by Tiffany.
Soldier Field	1410 Museum Campus Dr • 312-235-7000	Once on the National Register of Historic places, this renovated monster is home to Da Bears.
The Wheeler Mansion	2020 S Calumet Ave • 312-945-2020	This Second Empire-style mansion now houses a boutique hotel for high-end travelers.
Willie Dixon's Blues Heaven Foundation	2120 S Michigan Ave • 312-808-1286	Former Chess Records studio. Tours, exhibits, workshops, and performances.

Map 12 • Bridgeport (West)

Library Fountain	W 34th St & Halsted St	Pretty water.
McGuane Park	2901 S Poplar Ave • 312-747-6497	A park for playing.
Monastery of the Holy Cross	3111 S Aberdeen St • 773-927-7424	Have your breakfast served by monks in this bed and breakfast monastery.
St Mary of Perpetual Help	1039 W 32nd St • 773-927-6646	Built in the 1880s, this was the first Polish Roman Catholic Church in the US to be consecrated.
Wilson Park	S May St & W 34th Pl	A nice respite in the middle of the city.

Map 13 • Bridgeport (East)

Illinois Institute of Technology	31st to 35th St, b/w Dan Ryan Expy & Michigan Ave • 312-567-3000	Mies van der Rohe designed campus. Jewel in the crown? Crown Hall of course.
Old Neighborhood Italian American Club	3031 S Shields Ave • 312-326-6420	Founded by Angelo LaPietra, a former high-ranking Chicago mobster, after his release from Leavenworth.
Richard J Daley House	3536 S Lowe Ave	Childhood home of Mayor Richard J. Daley.
Richard J. Daley Library Fountain	3400 S Halsted St	Pretty water.

Map 14 • Prairie Shores / Lake Meadows

Black Metropolis Convention & Tourism Council	3501 S King Dr, Ste 1E • 773-373-2865	Information central for questions on everything Bronzeville.
Bronzeville 1st Bed & Breakfast	3911 S King Dr • 773-373-8081	Fine lodging in the old Goldblatt mansion.
Bronzeville Benches	S King Jr Dr b/w E 33rd St & E 35th St	13 artists created these 24 unique bench sculptures. Sit on them.
Chicago Bee Building	3647 S State St	Formerly the HQ of the *Chicago Bee* Newspaper; now offices.
Chicago Bee Public Library	3647 S State St • 312-747-6872	Originally home of black newspaper, *Chicago Bee*.
Douglas Tomb	636 E 35th St • 312-225-2620	Resting place of Lincoln's nemesis, overlooking tracks of Illinois Central railroad and the subdivision he founded. The entrance is on the east side of Lake.
Dunbar Park	300 E 31st St • 312-747-6287	Dunbar High's girl's softball team plays here.

Early Chicago Defender Building	3435 S Indiana Ave	Originally an 1899 synagogue, was home of *Chicago Defender* from 1920–1940.
Eighth Regiment Armory	3533 S Giles Ave	First armory built in US for black regiment, 1914–1918, now a Chicago public high school.
Griffin Funeral Home	3232 S King Dr • 312-842-3232	Site of Civil War era Camp Douglas, with Civil War museum, founder forefather drilled there.
Ida B Wells–Barnett Home	3624 S King Dr	Former home of the journalism and civil rights pioneer.
McCormick Tribune Campus Center	3201 S State St	Student center wrapped around the L. Wow!
Monument to the Great Northern Migration	S King Dr & E 26th St	Statue by Alison Sarr depicts a man with a briefcase atop a pile of old shoes. Represents the journey of African Americans from the south.
Olivet Baptist Church	3101 S King Dr • 312-538-0124	Church with a longstanding tradition of civil rights organizing ranging from abolitionist and feminist mass meetings to Black Panther Party programs.
Overton Hygenic Building	3619 S State St	Former headquarters of foremost producer of black cosmestics.
St James Catholic Church	2942 S Wabash Ave • 312-842-1919	Traditional community caretaking that included caring for Confederate POWs at Camp Douglas
State Street Village (IIT Student Housing)	3303 S State St • 312-808-9771	Supercool housing for this iconic institute.
Sunset Café	315 E 35th St	One of Chicago's earliest and most legendary jazz venues.
Supreme Life Insurance Company Head Office	3501 S King Dr	Built in 1921 and remodeled in 1950, this former major black insurance company enoys new life as a mixed commercial structure.
Victory Monument	S King Dr & E 35th St	Early postwar tribute to WWI's black Eighth Regiment of the Illinois National Guard that served as part of the US 370th Infantry in France.
Wabash Avenue YMCA	3763 S Wabash Ave	Since 1913 provided housing and job training for new black arrivals from the South, where the Association for the Study of Negro Life and History, the first group devoted to black studies, was founded in 1915.

Map 16 • Bronzeville

The Chicago Daily Defender	4445 S King Dr • 312-225-2400	Founded in 1905, it was the country's most influential black newspaper through the '50s. Still in operation, but much-diminished.
Corpus Christi Church	4900 S King Dr • 773-285-7720	Built in 1921 for a predominately Irish parish that rapidly evolved into a predominately black parish.
Drexel Fountain	S Drexel Blvd & E Oakwood Blvd	The city's oldest remaining fountain.
Drexel Square Park	5101 S Cottage Grove Ave	Victorian gem boasting city's oldest surviving fountain donated by prominent banking family.
Harold Washington Cultural Center	4701 S King Dr • 773-373-1900	Beautiful homage to the late mayor; it's a jaw-dropping technology & arts center.
Jamaican Consulate/ Jamaican Market Place	4655 S King Dr, Ste 201 • 773-373-8988	A bit of Kingston on the Old South Side.
Liberty Baptist Church	4849 S King Dr • 773-268-6757	An afrocentric 1958 Go-Go styled temple considered King's original Chicago workshop.
Provident Hospital	500 E 51st St • 312-527-2000	Now county controlled, this century old hospital was the first to train black doctors and nurses and the site of the first successful open heart surgery.
Robert S Abbott Home	4742 S King Dr	Former home of *Chicago Defender* founder.
Steele Life Gallery	4655 S King Dr • 773-538-4773	House of art that inspires the people.

Map 17 • Kenwood

Barack Obama's Chicago Residence	5046 S Greenwood Ave	He's been subletting lately.
Drexel Square Park	Drexel Blvd, from 51st St to 39th St	Victorian gem boasting city's oldest suriving fountain donated by prominent banking family.
George Blossom House	4858 S Kenwood Ave	Frank Lloyd Wright's early work —note the Roman influences.
Hyde Park Art Center	5020 S Cornell Ave • 773-324-5520	Has plenty of visual arts activities for the shorties and grown folk. Check out the Cocktails & Clay night!
KAM Isaiah Israel	1100 E Hyde Park Blvd	Oldest Jewish congregation in the city.
Little Black Pearl Art & Design Center	1060 E 47th St • 773-285-1211	Offers visual arts classes, a swanky art café, and a gallery.
Louis Farrakhan Home	4855 S Woodlawn Ave	Well-guarded home of the leader of the Nation of Islam.

Rainbow/PUSH Coalition Headquarters	930 E 50th St • 773-373-3366	Originally the 1924 home of KAM Isaiah Israel, Chicago's oldest Jewish congreation, with late 1940s addition.
Warren McArthur House	4852 S Kenwood Ave	More work by Frank Lloyd Wright, still tethered to Louis Sullivan.

Map 18 • Washington Park

Aquatic Center & Refectory	5531 S King Dr • 773-256-1248	Designed by Daniel Burnham's firm, the Refectory now holds locker rooms for the Aquatic Center and its 36-foot waterslide.
DuSable Museum of African-American History	740 E 56th Pl • 773-947-0600	Founded in 1961 and dedicated to preserving and honoring African-American culture. The oldest non-profit institution of its kind.
Former Home of Jesse Binga	5922 S King Dr	Home of nation's first African-American banker.
Washington Park	5531 S Martin Luther King Jr Dr • 773-256-1248	A sprawling 367-acre park with beautiful lagoons and fields. Check out the "Fountain of Time" sculpture in the southeast corner of the park.

Map 19 • Hyde Park

Drexel Fountain	5100 S Drexel Ave	The city's oldest remaining fountain.
Frederick C Robie House	5757 S Woodlawn Ave	Designed by Frank Lloyd Wright; renovations proceeding, stay tuned.
Harriet M. Harris Park	6200 S Drexel Ave	Historic Park building with Mural of Woodlawn Heroes, swimming & arts.
Midway Ice Rink	Midway Plaisance • 312-745-2470	Olympic-sized outdoor skating rink.
Nichols Park	1355 E 53rd St • 312-747-2703	Home of the Parrots of Hyde Park.
Nuclear Energy Sculpture	5600 S Ellis Ave	Birthplace of the Atomic Age.
Oriental Institute Museum	1155 E 58th St • 773-702-9514	Educate yourself.
Rockefeller Memorial Chapel	5850 S Woodlawn Ave • 773-702-2100	Built in 1928, this English Gothic styled cathedral contains one of the world's largest carillons.
University of Chicago	S University Ave & E 57th St • 773-702-1234	A pretty spot for wandering on the south side.

Map 20 • East Hyde Park / Jackson Park

Museum of Science and Industry	5700 S Lake Shore Dr • 773-684-1414	Get your geek on.
Osaka Garden/Wooded Island	Just south of the Museum of Science and Industry, b/w the West and East Lagoons	A Japanese garden in the middle of Jackson Park—why not?
Promontory Point Park	5491 S Shore Dr • 312-747-6620	Picnic with a view.

Map 21 • Wicker Park / Ukrainian Village

Coyote Building	1600 N Milwaukee Ave	This 12-story Art Deco building was constructed in 1929 and is currently a shrine to actor Peter Coyote.
Crumbling Bucktown	1579 N Milwaukee Ave	Structural icon visible from miles away; nucleus of Around the Coyote Arts Festival.
Division Street Russian Bath	1914 W Division St • 773-384-8150	Treat yourself to an old-school day at the spa, complete with Swedish massages and a granite heating room.
Flat Iron Arts Building	1579 N Milwaukee Ave • 312-335-3000	This distinct triangular-shaped building is a part of the Chicago Coalition of Community Cultural Centers and houses artist studios.
Holy Trinity Orthodox Cathedral and Rectory	1121 N Leavitt St • 773-486-6064	Designed by Louis Sullivan to look like a Russian cathedral.
Wicker Park	W Schiller St & N Damen Ave	The homes in this district reflect the style of Old Chicago.

Map 22 • Noble Square / Goose Island

Arandas Tire Repair & Rims	1511 N Ashland Ave • 773-252-6292	Glowing, plastic palm trees, metal flames on the gate, and rows of tricked-out hubcaps in the second-floor, neon-lit windows above the tire bays.
House of Crosses	1544 W Chestnut St	Eccentric owners have covered the property with hundreds of wooden crosses.
Morton Salt Elston Facility	1357 N Elston Ave • 773-235-1010	Has a painting of the famous salt girl, and, hey: acres of salt!

Nelson Algren Fountain	Division St & Ashland Blvd	Has a recent controversial addition.
North Avenue Bridge	1200 W North Ave	Wretched traffic jams; river view.
The Polish Museum of America	984 N Milwaukee Ave • 773-384-3352	Right-to-life painting on the side.
Pulaski Park/Pulaski Fieldhouse	1419 W Blackhawk St • 312-742-7559	Has an outdoor swimming pool.
St Stanislaus Kostka Church	1351 W Evergreen Ave • 773-278-2470	One of the oldest in Chicago.
Weed Street District	W Weed St	Several bars and clubs in one area. Party on.

Map 23 • West Town / Near West Side

First Baptist Congregational Church	1613 W Washington Blvd • 312-243-8047	Can seat 2000 people and houses one the largest totally enclosed organs in the country. There's a joke here somewhere.
Metropolitan Missionary Baptist Church	2151 W Washington Blvd • 312-738-0053	An attempt to find an appropriate design for the then-new Christian Science religion. Sold to Baptists in 1947.
Ukrainian Cultural Center	2247 W Chicago Ave • 773-384-6400	A gathering place to share and celebrate Ukrainian culture. Yeah!
Ukrainian National Museum	2249 W Superior St • 312-421-8020	Museum, library, and archives detail the heritage, culture, and people of Ukraine.
United Center	1901 W Madison St • 312-455-4500	Statue of His Airness still draws tourists.

Map 24 • River West / West Town

Eckhart Park/Ida Crown Natatorium	1330 W Chicago Ave • 312-746-5490	One of two swimming pools in the area.
Harpo Studios	1058 W Washington Blvd • 312-591-9222	Home of the Oprah Winfrey Show.
Jackson Boulevard Historic District	W Jackson Blvd & S Laflin St	Amazingly, this cluster of preserved late-nineteenth century mansions survives in this declining area.

Map 25 • Illinois Medical District

18th St L Station	W 18th St & S Paulina St	Gateway to Pilsen features colorful murals celebrating Mexican culture.
Bowler Row Houses	2148 W Bowler St	Historical row houses that have survived the wrecking ball.
Oakley Row Houses	801 S Oakley Ave	Italianate row houses that date back to 1870's.
Vietnam Survivors Memorial	815 S Oakley Ave	Privately funded memorial was erected by Vets.

Map 26 • University Village / Little Italy / Pilsen

National Italian American Sports Hall of Fame	1431 W Taylor St • 312-226-5566	How many Italian American sports stars do you know? DiMaggio is right out front.

Map 27 • Logan Square

Illinois Centennial Monument	3100 W Logan Blvd	Every city needs an obelisk or two…
Logan House	2656 W Logan Blvd	Renowned for over-the-top holiday décor.

Map 28 • Bucktown

Margie's Candies	1960 N Western Ave • 773-384-1035	The Beatles ate here.

Map 29 • DePaul / Wrightwood / Sheffield

Biograph Theater	2433 N Lincoln Ave • 773-871-3000	Site of gangster John Dillinger's infamous death in 1934; currently closed for renovation.
Cortland Street Drawbridge	1440 W Cortland St	Built in 1902 by John Ernst Erickson, this innovative leaf-lift bridge changed the way the world built bridges, and vice versa.
McCormick Row House District	W Chalmers Pl	Quaint example of late 19th-century urban planning and architecture.
Pumpkin House	1052 W Wrightwood Ave	A Halloween spectacle of lighted pumpkins.

Map 30 • Lincoln Park

Dewes Mansion	503 N Wrightwood Ave • 773-477-3075	Ornate historic home done in the German Baroque style and built in 1896.
Kauffman Store and Flats	2312 N Lincoln Ave	One of the oldest existing buildings designed by Adler and Sullivan. It's amazing that its characteristic features have survived.
Lincoln Park Boat Club	2341 N Cannon Dr • 866-675-2917	Paddling, rowing, and sculling since 1910.
Lincoln Park Conservatory	2391 N Stockton Dr • 312-742-7736	The place to warm up in those brutal Chicago winters.

Lincoln Park Cultural Center	2045 N Lincoln Park W • 312-742-7726	Programming in visual arts for all ages.
Lincoln Park Zoo	2001 N Clark St • 312-742-2000	Oldest free zoo in the U.S.
Midwest Buddhist Temple	435 W Menomonee St • 312-943-7801	Enter their annual haiku contest.
Oz Park	2021 N Burling St • 312-742-7898	You're not in Kansas anymore.
The Peggy Notebaert Nature Museum	2430 N Cannon Dr • 773-755-5100	An oasis for adults and kids to reconnect with nature by playing with wildflowers and butterflies.
Steppenwolf Theatre	1650 N Halsted St • 312-335-1650	The one John Malkovich, Gary Sinise, and co. started.
The Point at Diversey	Lakefront at Diversey Harbor	One of the best views of the skyline. Ever.
Theurer-Wrigley House	2466 N Lakeview Ave	Early Richard E. Schmidt (and maybe Hugh H.G. Garden) based on late-Italian Renaissance architecture.
Waterlily Pond	W Fullerton Pkwy & N Cannon Dr	You might forget you're in a city.

Map 31 • Old Town / Near North

Steppenwolf Theatre	1650 N Halsted St • 312-335-1650	The one John Malkovich, Gary Sinise, and co. started.

Map 32 • Gold Coast / Mag Mile

Charnley-Persky House	1365 N Astor St • 312-915-0105	Louis Sullivan and Frank Lloyd Wright designed this national historic landmark. Go look before it becomes a CVS.
John Hancock Building	875 N Michigan Ave • 888-875-8439	Zone out the tourists, and focus in on the prettiest view of the city.
Lake Shore Drive Apartments	860 Lake Shore Dr	Less is more—by Mies van der Rohe.
The Newberry Library	60 W Walton St • 312-943-9090	There's plenty on offer at this humanities library.
Old Playboy Mansion	1340 N State Pkwy	You have no idea what happened here.
Water Tower Place and Park	835 N Michigan Ave • 312-440-3580	Huge shopping—6 floors—Marshall Field's…er, Macy's.

Map 33 • Rogers Park / West Ridge

Bernard Horwich JCC	3003 W Touhy Ave • 773-761-9100	Community center with programming for kids/adults, pool/fitness center, senior center, and sports leagues.
Croatian Cultural Center	2845 W Devon Ave • 773-338-3839	A place where families can relax, socialize and congregate. Intended to benefit the Croatian community in Chicago (duh).
High Ridge YMCA	2424 W Touhy Ave • 773-262-8300	Community center with programming for kids/adults, summer activities, child care programs, sport teams, and a pool.
India Town	W Devon Ave & N Washtenaw Ave	Features Indian and Pakistani shops, grocery stores, restaurants, and more.
Indian Boundary Park	2500 W Lunt Ave • 773-742-7887	Petting zoo, tennis courts, chess tables, ice rink, skate park, batting cages, spray pool, with seasonal community center classes.
Rogers Park/West Ridge Historical Society	7344 N Western Ave • 773-764-4078	Photos/memorabilia/historical documents of the community's history detailing its ethnic diversity.
Thillen's Stadium	6404 N Kedzie Ave • 312-742-4870	Chicago landmark. 16 softball fields. Features little league baseball and various other games and benefits.
Warren Park	6601 N Western Ave • 773-262-6314	Seasonal free entertainment, pony rides, ethnic food festivals, amusement park rides, arts and crafts, winter sledding hill, baseball diamond, picnic pavilions, and dog play areas.

Map 34 • East Rogers Park

Angel Guardian Croatian Catholic Church	6346 N Ridge Ave • 773-262-0535	1905 red-brick Romanesque church. Turn-of-the-century German stained glass windows by Franz Mayer and F. X. Zettler.
Bach House	7415 N Sheridan Rd	One of Frank Lloyd Wright's final "small" houses, c. 1915.
Jackson/Thomas House	7053 N Ridge Ave	Lovely Italianate home dates back to 1874.
Robert A Black Golf Course	2045 W Pratt Blvd • 312-742-7931	The newest Chicago Park District course. 2,300-yard, par 33 layout for all skill levels.

Map 35 • Arcadia Terrace / Peterson Park

Apache Motel	5535 N Lincoln Ave • 773-728-9400	Another sleazy motel on Lincoln with cool vintage signs.
O-Mi Motel	5611 N Lincoln Ave • 773-561-6488	Another seedy motel on Lincoln known for vintage signs and hourly rates. Oh my!
Summit Motel	5308 N Lincoln Ave • 773-561-3762	Vintage motel vestige of former motel strip.

Map 36 • Bryn Mawr / Bowmanville

Rosehill Cemetery and Mausoleum	5800 N Ravenswood Ave 773-561-5940	Chicago's historical glitterati entombed among unsurpassed sculpture and architecture.

Map 37 • Edgewater / Andersonville

Ann Sather Restaurant	5207 N Clark St • 773-271-6677	Heavenly cinnamon rolls and swedish meatballs.
The Belle Shore Hotel Building	1062 W Bryn Mawr Ave	Former homes of roaring 1920s nightlife, now historic landmarks restored to their former glory as apartments.
Colvin House	5940 N Sheridan Rd	Designed by George Maher and built in 1909.
Edgewater Beach Apartments	5555 N Sheridan Rd	The big pink building symbolizing the end of the lakeshore bike path.
Philadelphia Church	5445 N Clark St • 773-728-5106	Complete with can't-miss neon sign.
Swedish American Museum	5211 N Clark St • 773-728-8111	Everything you want to know about Swedish culture, which is more than you thought.

Map 38 • Ravenswood / Albany Park

Albany Park Community Center	3401 W Ainslie St • 773-509-5650	Local community center at SW corner of Ainslie and Kimball.
Charlie Chaplin House	4637 N Manor Ave	Charlie Chaplin's home during his Essanay studio stint.
Fish Furniture Co Building	3322 W Lawrence Ave	Striking 1931 Art Moderne building with fish motif, currently houses Interstate Blood Bank.
North Branch Pumping Station	Lawrence Ave & the Chicago River	With its 1930s Art Deco facade, it seems like something prettier should be happening than North Side sewage pumping…
Paradise	2916 W Montrose Ave • 773-588-1989	It's a sushi restaurant. It's a beauty shop. It's a sauna ($12, unlimited time). It's Paradise. Of course, it's a neighborhood landmark.
Ravenswood Manor Park	4626 N Manor Ave	It's just a tiny triangle wedged between the non-elevated L and several streets, but it's ground zero for garden sales, neighborhood associations, dogs, kids, and community activity.
River Park	5100 N Francisco Ave	More than 30 acres of park, including one of the few city canoe launches.
Ronan Park Walking Trail	3000 W Argyle St	These boots are made for...walking!

Map 39 • Ravenswood / North Center

Abbott House	4605 N Hermitage Ave	Comely Queen Anne painted-lady built in 1891 for Abbott labs founder.
Kraus Music Store	4611 N Lincoln Ave	It's easy to overlook this Louis Sullivan beauty on a bustling commercial strip.
Lincoln Square	4800 N Lincoln Ave • 773-728-3890	A virtual tour through a European-style neighborhood.
Old Town School of Folk Music	4544 N Lincoln Ave • 773-728-6000	Northern expansion of beloved Chicago institution. Classes and concert venue.
St Benedict's Church	2215 W Irving Park Rd • 773-588-6484	The namesake of the St. Ben's neighborhood.
Winnemac Park	5001 N Leavitt St	Cute neighborhood park, replete with families and children playing.

Map 40 • Uptown

Aragon Ballroom	1106 W Lawrence Ave • 773-561-9500	One of the better smaller music venues in the city.
Essanay Studios	1333 W Argyle St	Former movie studio. Charlie Chaplin and Gloria Swanson made movies here.
Graceland Cemetery	4001 N Clark St • 773-525-1105	Chicago's famous buried in a masterpiece of landscape architecture.
Green Mill Pub	4802 N Broadway St • 773-878-5552	Chicago legend…And birthplace of the poetry slam.

Montrose Dog Beach	W Lawrence Ave & W Wilson Ave & N Simonds Dr • 312-747-2193	Fun and frolic with your pup.
St Augustine College	1333 W Argyle St • 773-878-8756	Episcopalian bilingual training school occupying original headquarters of Essanay Studios, where Chaplin, Broco Billy, and Swanson made films before moving to Southern CA.
St. Boniface Cemetery	4901 N Clark St • 773-561-2790	Historic gravestones in a scenic cemetery.
Uptown Theatre	4816 N Broadway St	An acre of seats in a magic city.

Map 41 • Avondale / Old Irving

Com-Ed Plant	N California Ave & W Roscoe St	What's that humming sound in Avondale? Must be this ginormous electrical plant.

Map 42 • North Center / Roscoe Village / West Lakeview

19th District Police	2452 W Belmont Ave • 312-744-5983	Going to "Western & Belmont" is synonymous for being in deep sh#*.

Map 43 • Wrigleyville/ East Lakeview

North Alta Vista Terrace	3800 N Alta Vista Terrace	London-style row houses with Edwardian elegance.
Southport Lanes	3325 N Southport Ave • 773-472-6600	Four hand-set lanes. Eat a Honeymooner while you wait.
Vic Theatre	3145 N Sheffield Ave • 773-472-0449	Drink, watch films, and take in an occasional band at this old theatre.
Wrigley Field	1060 W Addison St • 773-404-2827	Charm-filled and crumbling ballpark that remains indifferent to wins or losses on the field.

Map 44 • East Lakeview

Belmont Harbor	3600 Recreation Dr • 312-742-7673	Home to the Chicago Yacht Club sailing school.
Belmont Rocks	W Briar Pl at the lake	Popular lakefront hangout.
Montrose Dog Beach	Northern tip of Belmont Harbor	Fun and frolic with your pup.
The Giraffes	N Elaine Pl & W Roscoe Ave	Iconic public art.
Totem Pole	3600 N Lake Shore Dr	Where did it come from? Why is it there? Nobody knows.

Northwest

The Admiral Theater	3940 W Lawrence Ave	Built in 1928, this former vaudeville theater is now a well-known "gentlemen's club."
Copernicus Center	5216 W Lawrence Ave • 773-777-9184	Jefferson Park's cultural hub.
Eugene Field Park	5100 N Ridgeway Ave • 773-478-9744	Features a 1928 Tudor Revival fieldhouse, the Eugene Field Cultural Center (home of the Albany Park Theater Project).
Gompers Park	4222 W Foster Ave • 773-685-3270	Large riverfront park.
Hanson Park Fieldhouse	5501 W Fullerton Ave	Very old fieldhouse with WWII barracks.
Harlem CTA Station	N Harlem Ave & The Kennedy Expy	One of the more "el"egant stations.
Logan Square Column	3100 W Logan Blvd	It's just like Paris, yet different.
Superdawg Drive-In	6363 N Milwaukee Ave	Everyone knows the Superdog and his sexy girlfriend.
Walt Disney House	2156 N Tripp Ave	Where old Walt learned to ride his bike.

West

Austin Town Hall	5610 W Lake St	115-year-old former town hall; now a public recreation building.
Bison Statues at Humboldt Park	1400 N Sacramento Ave	Meet up by the Bison.
Chicago Center for Green Technology	445 N Sacramento Blvd • 312-746-9642	A green center for this self-styled green city.
Columbus Park Refectory	Columbus Park, 500 S Central Ave	Historic refectory now available for weddings and other fetes.
Delta Fish Market	228 S Kedzie Ave	Defunct fish fry-up features live blues in its parking lot.
Engine 44 Firehouse Mural	412 N Kedzie Ave	When kids do it, it's called graffiti.
Garfield Park Conservatory	300 N Central Park Ave	Tropical oasis in the midst of the urban jungle.
Our Lady of Sorrows	3121 W Jackson Blvd	Unsung treasure built in the late 19th century.
Skokie Northshore Sculpture Park	McCormick Blvd b/w Touhy Ave & Dempster St • 847-679-4265	Culture in the 'burbs. No joke.
Union Stockyard Gate	Exchange Ave & Peoria St	This limestone gate marks the place that made Chicago "hog butcher to the world."

Southwest

Adams House	9326 S Longwood Dr	A 1901 Frank Lloyd Wright gem.
Arnett Chapel, African Methodist Episcopal Church	11218 S Bishop St • 773-238-0670	One of oldest black congregations in historically black Morgan Park.
Bell Tower Condos	10321 S Longwood Dr	Built in 1916 for 13th Church of Christ Science, retains many of original architectural features including mother-of-pearl stained glass.
Blackwelder Summerling House	10910 S Prospect Ave	Built in sections from 1865 to 1873, was once Morgan Park's social center and home to Morgan Park's first village president, Isaac Blackwelder.
The Body of Lake Michigan	The ceiling near the security checkpoint at Midway Airport	Please remove your shoes. And look up.
Bohn Park	111th St & Prospect Ave	Originally known as Depot Park and sometimes called the Commons, features street lamps from 1893 World's Columbian Exposition.
Bronzeville Children's Museum	9600 S Western Ave • 708-636-9504	The romper room for learning black history for kids of all ages.
Burhans-Ellinwood Model House	10410 S Hoyne Ave	One of two 1917 models designed by Wright for a subdivision of prefabricated American-System Built Houses.
Campbell House	9250 S Damen Ave	An 1896 Tudor designed for the founder of the John H. Vanderpoel Collection.
Capital Cigar Store	6258 S Pulaski Rd	World's most conspicous cigar-store Indian.
Edward L Roberts House	10134 S Longwood Dr	An 1892 Queen Anne, now St. Barnabas's rectory, built by a lumber-milling magnate to exhibit decorative architectural details from his catalogue.
Edwin C Young House	9215 S Pleasant Ave	Robust Queen Anne with tower, front porch, and portcochiere.
Evans House	9914 S Longwood Dr	A 1908 Prairie Style gem designed by Frank Lloyd Wright.
Ferguson House	10954 S Prospect Ave	An 1873 Italianate beauty; built for the manager of Lancaster Fire Insurance.
Frank Anderson House	10400 S Pleasant Ave	Elegant Renaissance house now the residence of Chicago State University's president.
Gately House	10655 S Hoyne Ave	A 1927 neo-classical, recalling classical revival mansions of English Regency. Was home of founder of Gately's People Store based in Roseland.
Givens Irish Castle	10244 S Longwood Dr	Seminal grand dame of the mansion district in the original Beverly Hills.
Godspeed House	11216 S Oakley Ave	Farmhouse built in 1876 for the Rev. Thomas Goodspeed, pastor of Morgan Park Baptist Church and professor at Baptist Theological Seminary.
Graffiti Mural	W 59th St & S Damen Ave	An example of when it's public "art" not public "nuisance."
Harris House	10856 S Longwood Dr	A 1906 hilltop Tudor built for the founder of Rotary International.
Holy Name of Mary Church	1423 W 112th St • 773-238-6800	Opened in 1947, Morgan Park's oldest black parish.
Hopkinson House	10820 S Drew St	Italianate built for real estate dealer, landscaped by parks landscape architect Jens Jensen.
Horton Mansion	10200 S Longwood Dr	An 1890 Colonial Revival built for the founder of Chicago Bridge & Iron.
Howe House	10208 S Wood St	An 1881 Stick Style designed for one of area's oldest residents by a family friend, Daniel H. Burnham.
JB Chambers House	10330 S Seeley Ave	A 1871 blend of Gothic, Italianate, and French Empire styles.
Karge House	2035 W 99th St	A 1926 Spanish Colonial, known for distinctive stone block construction with ornate block detailing and medallions with scuplted Indian heads.
Lackmore House	10956 S Prospect Ave	Built 1801–1872 by relative of the area's first settler, DeWitt Lane.
McCumber House	10305 S Seeley Ave	A 1911 Colonial Revival once used as a Marshall Field & Co. Showcase House.
Metra 103rd/Washington Heights Rock Island District Branch Line Station	103rd St & Vincennes Ave	Refurbished handsome late Victorian gem that originally served the village of Washington Heights.
Metra Rock Island Main Line 111th St/ Monterey Ave Station	111th St & Monterey Ave	A restored at-grade Victorian gem from early 1892, built to replace 1870 station, after Rock Island railroad expanded its suburban service.

Midway Airport	5700 S Cicero Ave	World's Busiest Airport…in 1932. Today a place to fly and land cheaply, surrounded by tiny bungalows filled with various Eastern European types.
Morgan Park Apostolic Penecostal Church	11401 S Vincennes Ave • 773-239-9586	One of oldest black congregations in Morgan Park.
Morgan Park United Methodist Church	11030 S Longwood Dr • 773-238-2600	Early Prairie School treasure along the Blue Island Ridge.
Oakdale Park	956 W 95th St • 312-747-6569	A post-WWII greenspace with oak-shaded walking trails.
Original Rainbow Cone	9233 S Western Ave	People line up day and night in the summer.
Ridge Historical Society	10621 S Seeley Ave • 773-881-1675	Blue Island Ridge history is preserved in the old Walgreen mansion.
Ridge Park	9625 S Longwood Dr • 773-779-0007	Fieldhouse houses John H. Vanderpoel Art Association, comprising 600 pieces dedicated to renowed instructor at Art Institute of Chicago.
St Walter Catholic Church	11722 S Oakley Ave • 773-779-1515	Half-century-old Catholic community with modern approach to traditional values.
Walter Burley Griffin Place	W 104th Pl, Wood St to Prospect Ave	Largest concentration of Prairie Style homes in Chicago, built from 1910–1914.
William MR French House	9203 S Pleasant Ave	An 1894 Colonial Revival mansion built for the first director of the Art Institute of Chicago; sculpture by brother David Chester French.

South

Carter G Woodson Regional Library	9525 S Halsted St • 312-747-6900	Named for the "Father of Black History," houses Vivian Harsh black history collection.
Cedar Park Cemetery & Funeral Home	12540 S Halsted St • 773-785-8840	Final resting place where deer, geese, and other wildlife play in peace.
Chicago Skyway	8801 S Anthony St • 312-747-8383	Soar 125 feet over the southside on this thrilling overpass!
Chicago State University	9501 S King Dr • 773-995-2000	Metropolitan Chicago's oldest public university.
Lilydale First Baptist Church	649 W 113th St • 773-785-1976	Another cultural anchor for Roseland's historically black community.
Lilydale Progressive Missionary Baptist Church	10706 S Michigan Ave • 773-785-8623	Serving the historically black community on Roseland's northern end since the end of WWI.
Market Hall	E 112th St & Champlain Ave	George M. Pullman built colonnaded apartments surrounding a prototype shopping mall in 1893 to house friends visiting the World's Columbian Exposition.
New Regal Theatre	1645 E 79th St	80-year-old former movie-house.
Oak Woods Cemetery	1035 E 67th St	Former Mayor Washington and civil rights activist Ida B. Wells rest here.
Palmer Park	201 E 111th St • 312-747-6576	Created in 1904 to integregate social services with recreation for congested tenement districts. Features three WPA-comissioned murals by James Edward McBurney.
Pullman Clock Tower	11141 S Cottage Grove Ave • 773-785-8901	This beacon of Pullman can be seen from far and wide.
Robert S Abbott Park	49 E 95th St • 312-737-6100	Created in 1949 to serve the rapidly growing black community near 95th St & Michigan Ave; one of the first parks named after a promiment African American.
South Shore Cultural Center	7059 South Shore Dr • 773-747-2536	A glittering pearl on the south lakefront.
Trinity United Church of Christ	400 W 95th St • 773-962-5650	Where US Senator Barack Obama worships.
West Pullman Elementary	11941 S Parnell Ave • 773-535-5500	Mammoth 1894 structure featuring Romanesque stylings.
West Pullman Park	401 W 123rd St • 312-727-7090	A 1915 greenspace created to Americanize an industrializing community.

Evanston

Evanston Historical Society	225 Greenwood St • 847-475-3410	Explore Evanston's history. Closed Monday and Tuesday.
Light Opera Works	927 Noyles St • 847-869-6300	26 seasons of musical theater. Hmmmm.

Oak Park

Frank Lloyd Wright Home and Studio	951 Chicago Ave • 708-848-1976	See the drafting room where the Prairie Style was created. Inspiring.

Useful Phone Numbers

City Board of Elections	312-269-7900
State Board of Elections	217-782-4141
ComEd	800-334-7661
Peoples Gas Billing	312-240-4350
Peoples Gas Emergencies	312-240-7001
Drivers Licensing Facilities	312-793-1010
Office of Mayor Richard Daley	312-744-5000
Governor's Office	312-814-2121
General Aldermanic Information	312-744-3081

Helpful Websites and Local Blogs

Angie's List • www.angieslist.com
Membership-driven list rating local contractors and other services.
Beechwood Reporter • www.beechwoodreporter.com
Analysis of local and national politics.
Centerstage Chicago • www.centerstagechicago.com
Chicago's original online guide.
The Chicagoist • www.chicagoist.com
Local news/events blog
The Chicago Blog • http://pressblog.uchicago.edu
Publicity news from the University of Chicago Press, including book reviews, press releases, and "intelligent commentary."
Chicago City Clerk • www.chicityclerk.com
Renew your city sticker online!
Chicago Crime • www.chicagocrime.org
Chicago criminal activity and statistics.
Chicago Every Block • www.chicago.everyblock.com
Crime, news, culture & real estate block-by-block, neighborhood-by-neighborhood.
Chicago Gangs • www.chicagogangs.org
Breakdowns on Chicago gang activity, history & culture.
Chicago Hauntings • www.chicagohauntings.com
Is the price for that run-down old mansion too good to be true?
Chicago Recycling • www.chicagorecycling.org
Where to recycle anything and everything in Chicago.
City of Chicago • http://egov.cityofchicago.org
Helpful all-purpose guide to city services.
Cook County Assessor • www.cookcountyassessor.com
Research properties and tax assessments.
Cook County Tresurer • www.cookcountytreasurer.com
Pay your property tax online and download forms
Daily Candy • www.dailycandy.com/chicago
Daily dose of shopping, eating and culture.
Flavor Pill • www.chi.flavorpill.net
Lists happenings for hipsters.
Forgotten Chicago • forgottenchicago.com
Side streets and byways of the city.
Gaper's Block • www.gapersblock.com
A popular Chicago web-publication detailing local news, fun events, and cool places in the city.
Gas Prices • www.chicagogasprices.com
The scoop on the highest and lowest gas prices in the city.
Metromix • www.metromix.com
City guide put out by the Trib.
My Open Bar • http://chi.myopenbar.com
Daily updates on where to drink for free or cheap throughout the city
Not For Tourists • www.notfortourists.com
Duh.
Pitchfork Media • www.pitchforkmedia.com
Cool indie music site and sponsors of the grooviest music fest ever.
Spacefinder • www.chireader.com/spacefinder
The source for apartment rentals.
Yo Chicago • www.yochicago.com
Real estate and development news.

Taxi Cabs

Checker	312-243-2537
American United	773-248-7600
Flash Cab	773-898-8500 or 773-561-4444
Yellow Cab	800-829-4222

We're Number One!!!

World's Busiest Airport: O'Hare International
World's Largest Public Library: Harold Washington Library
World's Largest Aquarium: Shedd Aquarium
World's Largest Free Public Zoo: Lincoln Park Zoo
World's Largest Modern Art Museum:
Museum of Contemporary Art
Worlds Largest Commercial Office Building:
Merchandise Mart, 222 Merchandise Mart Plaza
World's Longest Street: Western Avenue
World's Busiest Roadway: The Dan Ryan Expressway
World's Largest Food Festival: Taste of Chicago

Chicago Timeline

1779: Jean-Baptiste Point du Sable establishes Chicago's first permanent settlement.
1803: U.S. Army constructs Fort Dearborn. It is destroyed during conflicts with Native Americans in 1812 and rebuilt in 1816.
1818: Illinois is admitted into the union.
1833: Chicago incorporates as a town of 350 people, bordered by Kinzie, Des Plaines, Madison, and the lakefront.
1837: Chicago incorporates as a city. The population is 4,170. Ogden becomes the city's first mayor.
1851: Northwestern University is founded.
1856: Fort Dearborn is demolished.
1860: Republican Party nominates Abraham Lincoln for president at Chicago's first political convention.
1865: Merry Christmas! Union Stockyards open on Christmas Day.
1869: Water tower is completed.
1871: Great Chicago Fire!
1885: World's first "skyscraper," the 9-story Home Insurance building, goes up on La Salle Street.
1886: Haymarket Riots. Eight Chicago policemen are killed.
1889: Jane Addams opens Hull House.
1892: World's first elevated trains begin operation.
1893: Columbia Exposition celebrates 400th anniversary of Columbus's discovery of America.
1907: Chicago physicist Abraham Michelson is first American to win Nobel Prize.
1910: Original Comiskey Park opens.
1914: Wrigley Field opens.
1927: $750,000 donated to city to build fountain in honor of Clarence Buckingham.
1929: John G. Shedd presents Shedd Aquarium as a "gift to the Chicago People."
1930: Adler Planetarium opens through a gift from Max Adler.
1930: Merchandise Mart built by Marshall Field.
1931: Chicagoan Jane Addams becomes first woman to win Nobel Peace Prize.
1931: Al Capone sent to prison for 11 years for evading taxes.
1934: John Dillinger shot by FBI outside Biograph Theater.
1955: O'Hare International Airport opens.
1958: End of the line: Last streetcar in Chicago stops operating.
1968: Democratic National Convention riots.
1971: Chicago Union Stock Yards are closed.
1974: Sears Tower is completed.
1983: Harold Washington elected first black mayor.
1995: A heat wave contributed to the death of over 700 Chicagoans.
1997: City Council absolves Mrs. O'Leary's cow of blame for Great Chicago Fire.
1998: Six-peat! Chicago Bulls win their sixth world championship in eight years.
2003: Four-peat! Richard M. Daley re-elected for historic fourth term!
2005: White Sox win World Series; Cubs fans heard weeping from miles away.
2007: Chicago piched as US bid for 2016 Olympics.
2008: Illinois Governor Rod Blagojevich arrested on federal corruption charges.
2011: Mayor Emanuel's election signals the end of the Daley era.

Essential Chicago Movies

Northside 777 (1948)
Man with the Golden Arm (1955)
Raisin in the Sun (1961)
Medium Cool (1969)
The Sting (1973)
Blues Brothers (1980)
Risky Business (1983)
Ferris Bueller's Day Off (1986)
Henry: Portrait of a Serial Killer (1986)
Adventures in Babysitting (1987)
Planes, Trains and Automobiles (1987)
The Untouchables (1987)
Backdraft (1991)
Candyman (1992)
Wayne's World (1992)
The Fugitive (1993)
Hoop Dreams (1994)
Mission: Impossible (1996)
My Best Friend's Wedding (1997)
High Fidelity (2000)
Save the Last Dance (2000)
What Women Want (2000)
Barbershop (2002)
Chicago (2002)
Road to Perdition (2002)
The Company (2003)
I Am Trying to Break Your Heart (2003)
Batman Begins (2005)
The Weatherman (2005)
The Break-Up (2006)
Stranger than Fiction (2006)
Public Enemies (2009)

Overview

WGN is the classic Chicago TV station. Its radio affiliate at 720 AM *is* Chicago talk radio. WGN isn't a bad place to find intelligent conversation, particularly through the long-running "Extension 720" program hosted by Milt Rosenberg. **WXRT** is the city's independent rock station—one of the few remaining stations still free from the smothering embrace of Clear Channel Communications. Their Sunday morning Beatles Brunch with host Terri Hemmert (a Chicago institution in her own right) is heaven for fans of the Fab Four. In general the station is a little heavy on the white-boy blues (think Clapton and Stevie Ray Vaughan) and crunchy rock ala Dave Matthews and Hootie—if that's your thing. Midway down the dial, alt-music station **Q101's** morning host Mancow Muller is a more immature version of Howard Stern—less sex, more body secretions. In terms of print media, we'll put it this way: the ***Tribune*** appeals to Cubs fans, while the ***Sun-Times*** is favored by White Sox fans. Chicago indie-media standard bearer (and first stop for slacker job seekers) The Chicago Reader has been weathering the effects of a media paradigm shift away from newsprint – after being bought out by Atlanta-based Creative Loafing, ongoing staff cuts have left the paper with a skeleton crew of hardworking editors. As a result, the copy has gotten increasingly fluffy, although they still manage to print hard-hitting civic stories, such as an insightful look into the Daley-orchestrated Chicago legislative swindle that led to the privatization of city parking meters.

Television

2	WBBM	(CBS)	32	WFLD	(Fox)
5	WMAQ	(NBC)	38	WCPX	ION Television
7	WLS	(ABC)	44	WSNS	(Telemundo)
9	WGN	(CW)	23	WFBT	(Brokered—ethnic)
11	WTTW	(PBS)	50	WPWR	(My 50)
20	WYCC	(PBS)	31	CLTV	(Cable)
23	WWME	(Me TV)	60	WXFT-TV	(Telefutura)
26	WCIU	(the U)	66	WGBO	(Univision)

Print

Chicago Defender	200 S Michigan Ave, Suite 1700	312-225-2400	Black community newspaper.
Chicago Free Press	3845 N Broadway St, 2nd Fl	773-868-0005	Gay community news.
Chicago Innerview Magazine	1849 S. Blue Island Avenue	312-850-3635	Free monthly music mag previewing bands coming to concert in town.
Chicago Magazine	435 N. Michigan Ave., Suite 1100	312-222-8999	Upscale glossy mag.
Chicago Reader	11 E Illinois St	312-828-0350	Free weekly with listings.
Chicago Reporter	332 S Michigan Ave	312-427-4830	Investigative reporting on issues of race, poverty, and social justice.
Chicago Sun-Times	350 N. Orleans St, 10th Fl	312-321-3000	One of the big dailies.
Chicago Tribune	435 N Michigan Ave	312-222-3232	The other big daily.
Crain's Chicago Business	360 N Michigan Ave	312-649-5411	Business news.
CS	200 W Hubbard	312-274-2500	Free monthly upscale Chicago lifestyle mag.
Daily Herald	155 E Algonquin Rd, Arlington Hts	847-427-4300	Suburban news.
Daily Southtown	6901 W 159th St, Tinley Pk	708-633-6700	News for southsiders.
Ebony	820 S Michigan Ave	312-322-9200	National glossy about African Americans.
Hoy Chicago	435 N Michigan Ave # 22	312-527-8400	Daily Spanish-language newspaper
Hyde Park Herald	1435 E. Hyde Park Boulevard	773-643-8533	Local for Hyde Parkers.
Korea Times	3720 W Devon Ave	847-626-0388	Daily Korean-language newspaper.
La Raza	6001 N Clark St	773-273-2900	Hispanic community paper.
Lerner-Booster-Skyline	7331 N Lincoln Ave, Lincolnwood	847-329-2000	Conglomeration of neighborhood papers.
N'Digo	19 N Sangamon	312-822-0202	Black community weekly.
Newcity	770 N Halsted Ave	312-243-8786	Alternative free weekly.
The Onion	47 W Division St	312-751-0503	Local listings in AV Club insert.
Red Eye	435 N Michigan Ave	312-222-4970	Commuter-targeted offshoot of the *Trib* for 20- and 30-somethings.
Time Out Chicago	247 S State St	312-924-9555	Glossy arts and entertainment weekly.
Today's Chicago Woman	150 East Huron	312-951-7600	Weekly for working women.
UR Chicago	4043 N Ravenswood	773-404-1497	Free monthly local entertainment mag.
Venuszine	2000 N. Racine, suite 3400	773-327-9790	Subscription based mag on both local and national culture and music.
Windy City Times	5443 N. Broadway	773-871-7610	Gay-targeted news weekly.

Public Radio

AM		
560	WIND	Talk
620	WTMJ	News/Talk
670	WSCR	Sports
720	WGN	Talk
780	WBBM	Talk
820	WCSN	Religious
850	WAIT	Standards
890	WLS	News/Talk
1000	WMVP	Sports
1110	WMBI	Religious
1280	WBIG	Talk
1390	WGCI	Gospel
1450	WVON	Talk (Black- oriented)
1490	WPNA	Polish
1510	WWHN	Gospel
1570	WBEE	Jazz

FM		
88.1	WCRX	Columbia College
88.5	WHPK	U of Chicago
88.7	WLUW	Loyola U
89.3	WNUR	Northwestern
90.1	WMBI	Christian
90.0	WDCB	Jazz
91.5	WBEZ	NPR
93.1	WXRT	Rock
93.9	WLIT	Adult Contemporary
94.7	WZZN	Oldies
95.1	WIIL	Rock
95.5	WNUA	Smooth jazz
95.9	WKKD	Rock
96.3	WBBM	Dance
97.9	WLUP	Rock
98.7	WFMT	Classical
99.5	WUSN	Country
92.5	WDEK	Adult hits
92.7	WKIE	Adult Hits
99.9	WRZA	Variety Hits
100.3	WNND	Adult Contemporary
101.1	WKQX	Modern Rock
101.9	WTMX	Adult Contemporary
102.7	WVAZ	Urban Contemporary
103.1	WXXY	80s
103.5	WKSC	Top 40
104.3	WJMK	Jack FM
105.1	WOJO	Spanish
105.9	WCKG	Adult Contmeporary
106.7	WYLL	Christian
107.5	WGCI	Urban Contemporary

Essential Chicago Books

Native Son, by Richard Wright.
Gripping novel about a young black man on the South Side in the '30s.

Neon Wilderness, by Nelson Algren.
Short story collection set in Ukrainian Village and Wicker Park.

One More Time, by Mike Royko.
Collection of Royko's *Tribune* columns.

The Boss: Richard M. Daley, by Mike Royko.
Biography of the former Mayor.

The Jungle, by Upton Sinclair.
Gritty look at life in the meat-packing plants.

Adventures of Augie March, by Saul Bellow.
More Chicago in the '30s.

V.I. Warshawsky, by Sara Paretsky.
Mystery series firmly rooted in Chicago landscape.

50 Years at Hull House, by Jane Addams.
Story of the Near West Side.

Secret Chicago, by Sam Weller.
Off-the-beaten path guidebook.

Ethnic Chicago, by Melvin Holli & Peter D'A. Jones.
Insider's guide to Chicago's ethnic neighborhoods.

House on Mango Street, by Sandra Cisneros.
Short story collection about a Latina childhood in Chicago.

Our America: Life and Death on the South Side of Chicago, by Lealan Jones, et al.
Life in the Chicago Projects as told by two schoolchildren.

The Coast of Chicago, by Stuart Dybek.
Short stories of Chicago denizens.

Hairstyles of the Damned, by Joe Meno.
Teen angst and punk rock in '80s Chicago.

Never a City So Real: A Walk in Chicago, by Alex Kotlowitz.
Modern reflection on the city of big shoulders.

American Pharaoh: Mayor Richard J. Daley, by Adam Cohen and Elizabeth Taylor.
Recent work that explores the life and works of Hizzoner the First.

Studs Lonigan, by James T. Farrell.
Growing up gritty and Irish in Washington Park, circa the early 20th century.

Chicago: The Second City, by A. J. Liebling.
Legendary *New Yorker* columnist and curmudgeon comes to the Windy City, gives it a new sobriquet, and tells all.

A Guide to Chicago's Murals, by Mary Lackritz Gray.
Murals, murals, and more murals.

The Pig and the Skyscraper, by Marco D'Eramo.
Wandering Italian sociologist comes to Chicago and explores the wide world of capitalism through Chicago's radical history, skyscrapers, and meat-processing plants.

The Devil in The White City by Erik Larson
Account of Chicago serial killer H.H. Holmes and the 1893 Chicago World's Fair.

Chicago Then and Now (Then & Now Thunder Bay) by Elizabeth McNulty
Explores Chicago's transformation and progression as a city.

The Lazarus Project by Alexander Hemon
A Bosnian writer investigates a historical Chicago crime.

Sin in the Second City by Karen Abbott
The colorful history of a Chicago bordello circa the 1900s.

Memory Mambo by Achy Obejas
Coming of age as a Cuban lesbian in Chicago.

The Time Traveler's Wife by Audrey Niffenegger
Break-out bestseller about time traveling love affair.

From May to September, every corner of the city is hopping with all manner of block parties, church carnivals, neighborhood festivals, and all-out hootenanny. Contact the Mayor's Office of Special Events for a complete list of the city's 100+ festivals.

Event	When & Where	Description
Chinese New Year	Sunday after the Chinese New Year (late-January or mid-February), Chinatown	2012 is the year of the Dragon. Celebrate!
Chicago Auto Show	Early February, McCormick Place	The nation's largest auto show celebrates its 101st year.
Uplift! Chicago (formerly Expo For Today's Black Woman)	Friday to Sunday, first weekend of May, McCormick Place East, 2301 S Lake Shore Dr	This faith-based event, started in 1993, is undergoing an "evolution." www.upliftchicago.com
St Patrick's Day Parade	Saturday prior to St Paddy's, Columbus Ave, Balbo to Randolph	The Chicago River turns green. On purpose.
Chicago Flower Show	Mid-March, Navy Pier	Escape from winter.
Chicago Latino Film Festival	Early April, various venues	20+-year-old festival screens the best in local and international Latino film. www.latinoculturalcenter.org/Filmfest
Great Chicago Places & Spaces	Weekend in Mid-May, various venues	An architectural love-fest with dozens of free tours around the city.
Bike Chicago	May-September, various venues	More than 100 events including "Bike the Drive" and the midnight LATE Ride.
Printers Row Book Fair	Second weekend in June, Dearborn St, b/w Harrison St & Balbo Dr	Watch for Booksellers Gone Wild, coming soon to pay-per-view.
Andersonville Midsommarfest	Second weekend in June, Clark St, b/w Foster & Balmoral Aves	Ain't it Swede?
Taste of Chicago	Last week in June, first week in July, Grant Park	Why go to a restaurant when you can eat standing up in the hot sun in a crowd?
Country Music Fest	Last weekend in June, Grant Park	Annual Lakeside hoe-down. www.cityofchicago.org/specialevents
Gay Pride Parade	Last Sunday in June, Halsted/ Broadway Sts b/w Halsted & Grace Sts	400,000 of the city's gay community and their fans take it to the streets. www.chicagopridecalendar.org
Beverly Arts Fair	Third week in June, Beverly Arts Center, 2407 W 111th St	Family fun in Beverly.
Juneteenth Celebration	Third Saturday in June, 79th & Stony Island	African-American Pride celebration includes parade, music, and lots of barbecue at Rainbow Beach.
57th Street Art Fair	First week in June, 57th & Kimbark	Oldest juried art fair in the Midwest. www.57thstreetartfair.org
Jeff Fest	Late June, Jefferson Park	Neighborhood festival of guys named Jeff. Okay, just kidding. It's Jefferson Park—get it?"
Bronzeville House Tours	Late June, 3402 S King Dr	The best way to peek into Chicago's African- American history.
Gospel Music Festival	First weekend in June, Grant Park	As much about the soul food as the music.
Chicago Blues Festival	Second weekend in June, Grant Park	Drawing the top names in blues for decades.
Old Town Art Fair	Mid-June, 1800 N Orleans St, Menominee St, Lincoln Ave	Arts and crafts.
Independence Eve Fireworks	July 3, Grant Park	Real fireworks occur when a million spectators try to leave Grant Park.
Chicago Hip-Hop Heritage Month	July 1-31, various venues	Where "New Beat" culture celebrates its past, present, and future. www.chihiphop.org.
Venetian Night	Third weekend in July, Monroe Harbor	Wow! Decked out boats!

Event	When & Where	Description
Outdoor Film Festival	Tuesdays, Mid-July to mid-August, Grant Park	Classic movies, a carafe of vino, and KFC. Life is good.
Rock Around the Block	Second weekend in July	Lots of street-festival-quality live music. Expect Bumpus and Underwater People.
Taste of Logan Square	Mid-August, Fullerton & Kedzie	It tastes cement-y.
Korean Street Festival	Mid-July, 3200–3400 W Bryn Mawr	One-stop shopping for your bibimbap, juk, and kimbap.
Fiesta Del Sol	Last weekend in July, Cermak Rd, b/w Throop & Morgan Sts	One of the most festive of the fests.
Bud Billiken Parade	Second Saturday in August, King Dr	World's biggest African-American parade. www.budbillikenparade.com
Black Harvest International Film & Video Festival	First two weeks of August, Gene Siskel Film Center, 164 N State St	Where the substance and form of black filmmaking knows no boundaries.www.siskelfilmcenter.org.
Northalsted Market Days	Second weekend in August, Halsted St b/w Belmont Ave & Addison St	See Gay Pride Parade. Add beer and live music. http://www.northalsted.com/daze.htm
Air and Water Show	Third weekend in August, lakefront	The Stealth Bombers never fail to thrill.
Viva Chicago Latin Music Fest	Last weekend in August, Grant Park	Salsa under the stars.
Taste of Polonia	Last weekend in August, 5200 W Lawrence Ave	Polka and kielbasa! Heaven! Pierogies! Paradise!
Gold Coast Art Fair	Early August, Wells St	Fine arts in a fancy neighborhood.
Summer Dance	August, Grant Park	Kick up your heels under the stars. Free lessons, and free DJs on Wednesday nights. http://egov.cityofchicago.org/SummerDance/
African Festival of the Arts	Friday to Sunday, Labor Day weekend, Washington Park, 5531 S King Dr	Last and biggest major afrocentric expo of the year. www.africainternationalhouse.org.
Celtic Fest	Second weekend in September, Grant Park	Clog dance in the bonny heath.
German-American Fest	Early September, Lincoln & Leland	Oktoberfest in Lincoln Square. Bring your own leiderhosen.
World Music Festival	Late September, Grant Park	Music acts from around the world, plus beer.
57th St Children's Book Fair	Late September, b/w Kimbark & Dorchester Aves	Lots of kids. Lots of books.
Chicago International Film Festival	October, various locations	Worthy display of the best in international cinema. www.chicagofilmfestival.org
Chicagoween	Mid to Late October, Daley Plaza	Daley Plaza becomes Pumpkin Plaza with trick-or-treating, pumpkin carving, and storytellers.
Halloween Parade	Halloween, Halsted b/w Belmont & Addison	Flamboyant Boystown costume extravaganza.
Tree Lighting	Day after Thanksgiving, Daley Plaza	Decking the halls by City Hall.
Mag Mile Lights Festival	Saturday evening before Thanksgiving, Michican Ave	Festive celebration of obligatory consumption.
Thanksgiving Parade	Thanksgiving Day morning, 8:30 am, State St	8:30 am? Yeah, as if.
Christkindlmarket	Thanksgiving Day–December, Daley Plaza	A German village appears for traditional Christmas shopping, food, and songs.

*All dates subject to change. For more up-to-date information and a schedule of neighborhood festivals, contact the Mayor's Office of Special Events at www.cityofchicago.org/specialevents.

While crime in general seems to be continuing a downward trend, in 2009, the murder level of school-aged children in Chicago was the highest in the nation, making national news headlines. The mayor says we're no worse than any other major city—it's just that our juvenile murders get properly classified. Now, doesn't that make you feel better?

Departments	*Address*	*Phone*	*Map*
1st District (Central)	1718 S State St	312-745-4290	11
9th District (Deering)	3501 S Lowe Ave	312-747-8227	13
21st District (Prairie)	300 E 29th St	312-747-8340	14
2nd District (Wentworth)	5101 S Wentworth Ave	312-747-8366	15
13th District (Wood)	937 N Wood St	312-746-8350	21
12th District (Monroe)	100 S Racine Ave	312-746-8396	24
14th District (Shakespeare)	2150 N California Ave	312-744-8290	27
18th District (Near North)	1160 N Larrabee St	312-742-5870	31
24th District (Rogers Park)	6464 N Clark St	312-744-5907	34
20th District (Foster)	5400 N Lincoln Ave	312-742-8714	35
19th District	2452 W Belmont Ave	312-744-5983	42
23rd District (Town Hall)	3600 N Halsted St	312-744-8320	44

Chicago hospitals are as varied and interesting as the citizens they serve. Although you don't have to go far to find medical facilities in this city, finding quality medical care is another story.

The Illinois Medical District on the near southwest side is one of the largest healthcare centers in the world. Here you will find the brand-new **Stroger (Map 25)** hospital (basically the infamous Cook County Hospital with a facelift), home to the nation's first and oldest trauma unit. It is by far the busiest hospital in the area and serves a large and mostly indigent population. Unless you are in danger of certain demise, avoid Stroger's emergency department since waits of up to 12 hours for a non-life-threatening reason may bore you to death. The medical campus is also home to the **University of Illinois at Chicago (Map 25)**, **Rush University Medical Center (Map 25)**, and several smaller hospitals.

On the north side, your best bet is to go to **Advocate Illinois Masonic Medical Center (Map 43)** for anything serious or **St. Joseph's Hospital** (**Map 44)** where you might get a room with a view of Lake Michigan. **Northwestern Memorial Hospital (Map 3)** is also a good choice if you are closer to downtown and/or if you have really good insurance. They also house several hospitals in the same campus, and if you break your neck craning to look up at all the pretty skyscrapers in the Streeterville 'hood, they have a first-rate spinal cord unit.

On the south side, the **University of Chicago (Map 19)** hospitals are second to none. A large and imposing set of buildings set in a somewhat dubious neighborhood, the hospital has a first-rate children's emergency department, world-renowned staff, and an excellent reputation. Park on the street at your own risk—the garage may be expensive, but so is replacing your car stereo.

Emergency Rooms	*Address*	*Phone*	*Map*
Northwestern Memorial	251 E Huron St	312-926-2000	3
Mercy	2525 S Michigan Ave	312-567-2000	11
Michael Reese	2929 S Ellis Ave	312-791-2000	14
Provident	500 E 51st St	312-572-2000	16
University of Chicago	5841 S Maryland Ave	773-702-1000	19
University of Chicago Children's	5721 S Maryland Ave	773-702-1000	19
Saints Mary and Elizabeth Medical Center	1431 N Claremont Ave	773-278-2000	21
Saints Mary and Elizabeth Medical Center	2233 W Division St	312-770-2000	21
John H Stroger Jr	1900 W Polk St	312-864-7203	25
Rush University Medical Center	1650 W Harrison St	312-942-5000	25
St Anthony's	2875 W 19th St	773-484-1000	25
University of Illinois Medical Center	1740 W Taylor St	312-355-4000	25
Jesse Brown VA Medical Center	820 S Damen Ave	312-569-8387	25
Children's Memorial	2300 Children's Plz	773-880-4000	30
Swedish Covenant	5145 N California Ave	773-878-8200	38
Methodist Hospital of Chicago	5025 N Paulina St	773-271-9040	39
Louis A Weiss Memorial	4646 N Marine Dr	773-878-8700	40
Thorek	850 W Irving Park Rd	773-525-6780	40
Advocate Illinois Masonic Medical Center	836 W Wellington Ave	773-975-1600	43
St Joseph	2900 N Lake Shore Dr	773-665-3000	44

Other Hospitals	*Address*	*Phone*	*Map*
Rehabilitation Institute of Chicago	345 E Superior St	312-238-1000	3
Kindred Chicago-Lakeshore	6130 N Sheridan Rd	773-381-1222	37
Kindred	2544 W Montrose Ave	773-267-2622	38
Chicago Lakeshore	4840 N Marine Dr	773-878-9700	40

Post Offices	*Address*	*Phone*	*Map*
US Post Office	222 Merchandise Mart Plz	312-321-0233	2
US Post Office	540 N Dearborn St	312-644-3919	2
US Post Office	227 E Ontario St	312-642-3576	3
US Post Office	168 N Clinton St	312-906-8557	4
US Post Office	100 W Randolph St	312-263-2686	5
US Post Office	211 S Clark St	312-427-0016	5
US Post Office	233 S Wacker Dr	312-876-1024	5
US Post Office	5 S Wabash Ave	312-427-0016	5
US Post Office	200 E Randolph St	312-861-0473	6
US Post Office	358 W Harrison St	312-692-6128	7
US Post Office	433 W Harrison St	312-983-7610	7
US Post Office	2345 S Wentworth Ave	312-326-6440	10
US Post Office	2035 S State St	312-225-0218	11
US Post Office	4101 S Halsted St	773-247-0731	15
US Post Office	4601 S Cottage Grove Ave	773-924-6658	16
US Post Office	700 E 61st St	773-493-4047	18
US Post Office	1526 E 55th St	773-324-0896	19
US Post Office	956 E 58th St	773-497-4047	19
US Post Office	116 S Western Ave	312-243-2560	23
US Post Office	1859 S Ashland Ave	312-733-4750	26
US Post Office	2339 N California Ave	773-489-2855	27
US Post Office	2405 N Sheffield Ave	773-929-7041	29
US Post Office	2368 N Clark St	773-549-2720	30
US Post Office	2500 N Clark St	773-477-9372	30
US Post Office	2643 N Clark St	773-525-5965	30
US Post Office	875 N Michigan Ave	312-644-0485	32
US Post Office	1723 W Devon Ave	773-743-2650	34
US Post Office	7617 N Paulina St	773-743-2830	34
US Post Office	2522 W Lawrence Ave	773-561-3330	38
US Post Office	2011 W Montrose Ave	773-472-1314	39
US Post Office	1343 W Irving Park Rd	773-327-0345	40
US Post Office	4850 N Broadway St	773-561-1720	40
US Post Office	3750 N Kedzie Ave	773-539-6210	41
US Post Office	3635 N Lincoln Ave	773-404-0980	42
US Post Office	3024 N Ashland Ave	773-248-8495	43
US Post Office	3170 N Sheridan Rd	773-244-0444	44

The Chicago Public Library System has 75 branches serving Chicago citizens. Much to the delight of many Windy City book-borrowers, the city has recently constructed several new branches and renovated over 55 existing neighborhood branches with the help of a huge capital improvement program.

With the **Harold Washington Library (Map 5)** as their anchor, two regional libraries, **Sulzer Regional Library (Map 39)** in Lincoln Square and the Southwest side's **Woodson Library (Map 59)**, serve as backup reference and research collections. It is worth noting that Harold Washington Library has a few stand-out exhibits, including one of the history of the blues in the city and, of course, one on the man himself, Chicago's first African-American mayor. Neighborhood branches are geared towards the communities they serve: **Chinatown (Map 10)** has an impressive collection of Asian studies material and literature, the **Rogers Park (Map 34**) branch features a significant Russian-language selection, and Boystown's **John Merlo (Map 44)** collection houses a considerable offering of gay literature and studies. Many of the smaller branches have a decent selection of juvenile materials as well as career guidance and adult popular literature (and Internet access). Architecturally, some of the more interesting branches include the **Chicago Bee (Map 14)** branch, the former newspaper headquarters that serves as a neighborhood landmark for Bronzeville, and the historic Pullman (Parks & Places) branch, specializing in the history of the Pullman district. Chicago's first library branch, the neo-classical **Blackstone (Map 17)** library, is named after the Stockyards magnate. Families and schools should take advantage of the Chicago Public Library System's "Great Kids Museum Passports" available only to adult Chicago residents with a valid library card. You can check out any of their free passports using your library card just like you would any other item, and the loan is good for one week. The pass entitles entry for up to 8 people to any one of the eleven participating cultural institutions in the city. If you don't have access to a library card, you can still partake in a bit of book-love by checking out one of the many free lectures or readings that take place at the Harold Washington Library and the galaxy of branch outposts throughout the year. Before visiting Chicago, visitors can also peruse some of the nice digital exhibits the Library has created at www.chipublib.org/digital/digital.html. Here they will find tributes to the late, great Mayor Harold Washington and some interesting exhibits on the history of the city's sewer system (well, interesting for us, at least). For more information, call your local library or visit the general website at www.chipublib.org.

Chicago also has many excellent research libraries and university libraries, one of which is the independent **Newberry Library (Map 32),** established in 1887. It shelves rare books, manuscripts, and maps, and hosts the raucous annual Bughouse Square debates in late July. Chicago's universities and colleges generally welcome the public to their libraries during specified hours, but it's best to call first and check.

Library	*Address*	*Phone*	*Map*
Albany Park Public Library	5150 N Kimball Ave	312-744-1933	38
Asher Library-Spertus Institute	610 S Michigan Ave	312-322-1712	9
Bessie Coleman Public Library	731 E 63rd St	312-747-7760	18
Bezazian Public Library	1226 W Ainslie St	312-744-0019	40
Blackstone Public Library	4904 S Lake Park Ave	312-747-0511	17
Bucktown–Wicker Park Public Library	1701 N Milwaukee Ave	312-744-6022	28
Budlong Woods Public Library	5630 N Lincoln Ave	312-742-9590	35
Canaryville Public Library	642 W 43rd St	312-747-0644	15
Chicago Bee Public Library	3647 S State St	312-747-6872	14
Chinatown Public Library	2353 S Wentworth Ave	312-747-8013	10
Edgewater Public Library	1210 W Elmdale Ave	312-744-0718	37
Hall Public Library	4801 S Michigan Ave	312-747-2541	16
Harold Washington Public Library	400 S State St	312-747-4300	5
Humboldt Park Public Library	1605 N Troy St	312-744-2244	27
John Merlo Public Library	644 W Belmont Ave	312-744-1139	44
King Public Library	3436 S Dr Martin Luther King Jr Dr	312-747-7543	14
Library of Columbia College	624 S Michigan Ave	312-336-7900	9
Lincoln Park Public Library	1150 W Fullerton Ave	312-744-1926	29
Lincoln-Belmont Public Library	1659 W Melrose St	312-744-0166	42
Logan Square Public Library	3030 W Fullerton Ave	312-744-5295	27
Lozano Public Library	1805 S Loomis St	312-746-4329	26
Mabel Manning Public Library	6 S Hoyne Ave	312-746-6800	23
Malcolm X College Library	1900 W Van Buren St	312-850-7000	23
Near North Public Library	310 W Division St	312-744-0991	31
The Newberry Library	60 W Walton St	312-943-9090	32
Northtown Public Library	6435 N California Ave	312-744-2292	33
Richard J. Daley Public Library	3400 S Halsted St	312-747-8990	13
Rogers Park Public Library	6907 N Clark St	312-744-0156	34
Roosevelt Public Library	1101 W Taylor St	312-746-5656	26
Sulzer Public Library	4455 N Lincoln Ave	312-744-7616	39
The Swedenborg Library	77 W Washington St, Rm 1700	312-346-7003	5
University of Chicago Harper Memorial Library	1116 E 59th St	773-702-6271	19
University of Illinois at Chicago Library	801 S Morgan St	312-996-2726	26
Uptown Public Library	929 W Buena Ave	312-744-8400	40
Woodson Regional Public Library	9525 S Halstead St	312-747-6900	49

The last FedEx drop in Chicago is at 10 pm at O'Hare Airport. Get off the Kennedy at Manheim Road South. Go to Irving Park Road and head west to the first light. Make a right on O'Hare Cargo Area Road. FedEx's address is Building 611, O'Hare Cargo Area Road (800-463-3339; www.FedEx.com).

Map 1 • River North / Fulton Market District

Self-Service	400 W Erie St	7:30 PM
Self-Service	600 W Chicago Ave	7:30 PM
Self-Service	401 W Superior St	7 PM
Self-Service	445 W Erie St	7 PM
Self-Service	770 N Halsted St	7 PM
Self-Service	430 W Erie St	6 PM

Map 2 • Near North / River North

FedEx Kinko's	444 N Wells St	9:30 PM
FedEx Kinko's	350 N Clark St	9 PM
FedEx Kinko's	222 Merchandise Mart Plz	9 PM
Self-Service	444 N Wells St	8:45 PM
Self-Service	77 W Wacker Dr	8 PM
Self-Service	205 W Wacker Dr	8 PM
Self-Service	311 W Superior St	8 PM
Self-Service	414 N Orleans St	8 PM
Self-Service	54 W Hubbard St	8 PM
Self-Service	56 W Illinois St	8 PM
Self-Service	330 N Wabash Ave	8 PM
Self-Service	420 N Wabash Ave	8 PM
Self-Service	223 W Erie St	7:45 PM
Self-Service	225 W Wacker Dr	7:30 PM
Self-Service	308 W Erie St	7:30 PM
Self-Service	343 W Erie St	7:30 PM
Self-Service	515 N State St	7:30 PM
Self-Service	730 N Franklin St	7:30 PM
Self-Service	405 N Wabash Ave	7:30 PM
Self-Service	640 N La Salle St	7:30 PM
Self-Service	1 E Wacker Dr	7:15 PM
Self-Service	35 E Wacker Dr	7 PM
Self-Service	55 W Wacker Dr	7 PM
Self-Service	211 W Wacker Dr	7 PM
Self-Service	320 W Ohio St	7 PM
Self-Service	20 W Kinzie St	7 PM
Self-Service	215 W Superior St	7 PM
Self-Service	300 N State St	7 PM
Self-Service	1 W Superior St	7 PM
Self-Service	1 E Erie St	7 PM
Self-Service	65 E Wacker Dr	6:30 PM
Self-Service	540 N Dearborn St	6:30 PM
Self-Service	325 N Wells St	6 PM

Map 3 • Streeterville / Mag Mile

Self-Service	401 N Michigan Ave	8 PM
Self-Service	211 E Chicago Ave	8 PM
Self-Service	233 E Erie St	8 PM
Self-Service	737 N Michigan Ave	8 PM
Self-Service	541 N Fairbanks Ct	8 PM
Self-Service	633 N St Clair St	8 PM
Self-Service	676 N St Clair St	8 PM
Self-Service	211 E Ontario St	7:30 PM
Self-Service	444 N Michigan Ave	7:30 PM
Self-Service	625 N Michigan Ave	7:30 PM
Self-Service	645 N Michigan Ave	7:30 PM
Self-Service	333 E Ontario St	7:30 PM
Self-Service	251 E Huron St	7:30 PM
Self-Service	150 E Huron St, #160	7:30 PM
Self-Service	400 N Michigan Ave	7:30 PM
Self-Service	505 N Lake Shore Dr	7:30 PM
Self-Service	430 N Michigan Ave	7:15 PM
Self-Service	142 E Ontario St	7 PM
Self-Service	401 E Illinois St	7 PM
Self-Service	440 N McClurg Ct	7 PM
Self-Service	455 E Illinois St	7 PM
Self-Service	676 N Michigan Ave	7 PM
Self-Service	474 N Lake Shore Dr	7 PM
Self-Service	360 N Michigan Ave	7 PM
Self-Service	512 N McClurg Ct	6:30 PM
FedEx Kinko's	540 N Michigan Ave	6 PM
Self-Service	540 N Michigan Ave	6 PM
Marcel Pack & Ship	680 N Lake Shore Dr	5 PM

Map 4 • West Loop Gate / Greek Town

Self-Service	500 W Madison St	9 PM
FedEx Kinko's	127 S Clinton St	8:45 PM
Self-Service	127 S Clinton St	8:45 PM
Self-Service	300 S Riverside Plz	8:30 PM
FedEx Kinko's	608 W Lake St	8 PM
Self-Service	550 W Washington Blvd	8 PM
Self-Service	600 W Lake St	8 PM
Self-Service	555 W Madison St	8 PM
Self-Service	10 S Riverside Plz	7:30 PM
Self-Service	222 S Riverside Plz	7:30 PM
Self-Service	833 W Jackson Blvd	7:30 PM
Self-Service	100 N Riverside Plz	7 PM
Self-Service	120 S Riverside Plz	7 PM
Self-Service	2 N Riverside Plz	7 PM
Self-Service	820 W Jackson Blvd	7 PM
Self-Service	850 W Jackson Blvd	7 PM
Self-Service	322 S Green St	7 PM
Self-Service	547 W Jackson Blvd	7 PM
Self-Service	600 W Jackson Blvd	7 PM
Self-Service	641 W Lake St	7 PM
Self-Service	550 W Jackson Blvd	7 PM
Self-Service	500 W Monroe St	6:30 PM
Self-Service	619 W Jackson Blvd	6:30 PM
Self-Service	168 N Clinton St	6 PM
Self-Service	130 S Jefferson St	6 PM
Self-Service	730 W Randolph St	6 PM
Self-Service	651 W Washington Blvd	5:30 PM
Self-Service	216 S Jefferson St	5:30 PM

Map 5 • The Loop

FedEx Kinko's	200 W Jackson Blvd	9 PM
FedEx Kinko's	227 W Monroe St	9 PM
FedEx Kinko's	111 W Washington St	9 PM
FedEx Kinko's	2 N LaSalle St	9 PM
Self-Service	333 W Wacker Dr	9 PM
Self-Service	171 N Clark St	8:30 PM
Self-Service	123 N Wacker Dr	8:30 PM
Self-Service	233 S Wacker Dr	8:30 PM
FedEx Kinko's	6 W Lake St	8 PM
FedEx Kinko's	29 S La Salle St	8 PM
FedEx Kinko's	55 E Monroe St	8 PM
Self-Service	6 W Lake St	8 PM
Self-Service	100 W Monroe St	8 PM
Self-Service	111 W Jackson Blvd	8 PM
Self-Service	175 W Jackson Blvd	8 PM
Self-Service	111 S Wacker Dr	8 PM
Self-Service	225 W Washington St	8 PM
Self-Service	30 S Wacker Dr	8 PM
Self-Service	1 N Franklin St	8 PM
Self-Service	1 S Wacker Dr	8 PM
Self-Service	10 S Wacker Dr	8 PM
Self-Service	125 S Wacker Dr	8 PM
Self-Service	150 N Wacker Dr	8 PM
Self-Service	150 S Wacker Dr	8 PM
Self-Service	20 N Wacker Dr	8 PM
Self-Service	200 S Wacker Dr	8 PM
Self-Service	200 W Madison St	8 PM
Self-Service	205 W Randolph St	8 PM
Self-Service	230 W Monroe St	8 PM

Map 5 • The Loop—*continued*

Self-Service	303 W Madison St	8 PM
Self-Service	71 S Wacker Dr	8 PM
Self-Service	210 S Clark St	8 PM
Self-Service	203 N LaSalle St	8 PM
Self-Service	200 N LaSalle St	8 PM
Self-Service	222 N LaSalle St	8 PM
Self-Service	120 N LaSalle St	8 PM
Self-Service	30 N LaSalle St	8 PM
Self-Service	134 N LaSalle St	8 PM
Self-Service	10 S LaSalle St	8 PM
Self-Service	190 S LaSalle St	8 PM
Self-Service	115 S LaSalle St	8 PM
Self-Service	208 S LaSalle St	8 PM
Self-Service	311 S Wacker Dr	7:45 PM
Self-Service	180 N Wabash Ave	7:30 PM
Self-Service	105 W Madison St	7:30 PM
Self-Service	135 S La Salle St	7:30 PM
Self-Service	407 S Dearborn St	7:30 PM
Self-Service	21 S Clark St	7:30 PM
Self-Service	36 S Wabash Ave	7:30 PM
FedEx Kinko's	101 N Wacker Dr	7 PM
FedEx Kinko's	400 S LaSalle St	7 PM
Self-Service	203 N Wabash Ave	7 PM
Self-Service	70 E Lake St	7 PM
Self-Service	100 W Randolph St	7 PM
Self-Service	1 N State St	7 PM
Self-Service	25 E Washington St	7 PM
Self-Service	33 N Dearborn St	7 PM
Self-Service	29 E Madison St	7 PM
Self-Service	55 W Monroe St	7 PM
Self-Service	30 W Monroe St	7 PM
Self-Service	29 S La Salle St	7 PM
Self-Service	11 E Adams St	7 PM
Self-Service	55 E Jackson Blvd	7 PM
Self-Service	53 W Jackson Blvd	7 PM
Self-Service	401 S State St	7 PM
Self-Service	191 N Wacker Dr	7 PM
Self-Service	200 W Adams St	7 PM
Self-Service	200 W Monroe St	7 PM
Self-Service	29 N Wacker Dr	7 PM
Self-Service	300 S Wacker Dr	7 PM
Self-Service	309 W Washington St	7 PM
Self-Service	101 N Wacker Dr	7 PM
Self-Service	10 S Dearborn St, Ste 4800	7 PM
Self-Service	20 S Clark St	7 PM
Self-Service	247 S State St	7 PM
Self-Service	100 N LaSalle St	7 PM
Self-Service	11 S LaSalle St	7 PM
Self-Service	3660 N Lake Shore Dr	7 PM
Self-Service	1 E Jackson Blvd	6:30 PM
Self-Service	55 E Monroe St	6 PM
Self-Service	209 S La Salle St	6 PM
Self-Service	131 S Dearborn St	6 PM
Self-Service	140 S Dearborn St, Ste 109	6 PM
Self-Service	230 S Dearborn St	5:45 PM
Self-Service	219 S Dearborn St	5:30 PM
Self-Service	77 W Jackson Blvd	5 PM

Map 6 • The Loop / Grant Park

FedEx Kinko's	225 N Michigan Ave	9 PM
FedEx Kinko's	34 S Michigan Ave	9 PM
FedEx Kinko's	130 E Randolph St	9 PM
Self-Service	150 N Michigan Ave	8 PM
Self-Service	200 E Randolph St	8 PM
Self-Service	300 E Randolph St	8 PM
Self-Service	333 N Michigan Ave	8 PM
Self-Service	200 S Michigan Ave	8 PM
Self-Service	224 S Michigan Ave	8 PM
Self-Service	332 S Michigan Ave	8 PM
Self-Service	30 N Michigan Ave	8 PM
Self-Service	8 S Michigan Ave	7:30 PM
FedEx Kinko's	111 E Wacker Dr	7 PM
Self-Service	111 E Wacker Dr	7 PM
Self-Service	307 N Michigan Ave	7 PM
Self-Service	155 N Michigan Ave	7 PM
Self-Service	310 S Michigan Ave	7 PM
Self-Service	430 S Michigan Ave	7 PM
Self-Service	180 N Michigan Ave	7 PM
Self-Service	20 N Michigan Ave	7 PM
Self-Service	233 N Michigan Ave	6 PM
Self-Service	200 E Randolph St	4 PM

Map 8 • South Loop / Printers Row / Dearborn Park

FedEx Kinko's	700 S Wabash Ave	8:45 PM
Self-Service	700 S Wabash Ave	8:45 PM
Self-Service	47 W Polk St	8 PM
Self-Service	536 S Clark St	7:30 PM
Self-Service	800 S Wells St	7:30 PM
Self-Service	542 S Dearborn St	7 PM
Self-Service	600 S Federal St	7 PM
Self-Service	819 S Wabash Ave	5 PM

Map 10 • East Pilsen / Chinatown

FedEx Kinko's	1242 S Canal St	8 PM
Self-Service	1242 S Canal St	8 PM
Self-Service	329 W 18th St	7:30 PM

Map 11 • South Loop / McCormick Place

Self-Service	1455 S Michigan Ave	7 PM
Self-Service	2035 S State St	5 PM

Map 12 • Bridgeport (West)

Self-Service	970 W Pershing Rd	6 PM

Map 13 • Bridgeport (East)

Self-Service	710 W 31st St	6 PM
Self-Service	3300 S Federal St	6 PM

Map 14 • Prairie Shores / Lake Meadows

Chicago Computer Club	329 E 35th St	6PM
Self-Service	10 W 35th St	6 PM

Map 19 • Hyde Park

FedEx Kinko's	1315 E 57th St	7 PM
Self-Service	1525 E 53rd St	7 PM
Self-Service	1554 E 55th St	7 PM
Self-Service	1155 E 60th St	7 PM
Self-Service	5801 S Ellis Ave	7 PM
Self-Service	1315 E 57th St	7 PM
Self-Service	E 57th St & S University Ave	7 PM
Self-Service	5841 S Maryland Ave	6:45 PM
Self-Service	1126 E 59th St	6:30 PM
Self-Service	956 E 58th St	6:30 PM
Self-Service	E 59th St & S Kimbark Ave	6:30 PM

Map 20 • East Hyde Park / Jackson Park

Post Link	1634 E 53rd St	5 PM

Map 21 • Wicker Park / Ukrainian Village

FedEx Kinko's	1800 W North Ave	8:45 PM
Self-Service	1800 W North Ave	8:45 PM
Self-Service	1520 N Damen Ave	7 PM
My Office	2136 W Division St	6 PM
Copy Max	1573 N Milwaukee Ave	6 PM

Map 22 • Noble Square / Goose Island

FedEx Kinko's	875 W Division	9:30 PM
Self-Service	935 W Chestnut St	7:30 PM
Self-Service	939 W North Ave	7 PM
Self-Service	1467 N Elston Ave	7 PM
Self-Service	1608 N Milwaukee Ave	7 PM
Self-Service	848 W Eastman St	6:45 PM

Map 23 • West Town / Near West Side

Self-Service	1700 W Van Buren St	7 PM
Self-Service	2023 W Carroll Ave	7 PM
Self-Service	265 N Western Ave	6:30 PM
Packaging & Shipping	2002 W Chicago Ave	6 PM
Self-Service	1812 W Hubbard St	5:30 PM

Map 24 • River West / West Town

Self-Service	400 N Noble St	7 PM
Self-Service	1500 W Carroll Ave	6:30 PM
Self-Service	1030 W Chicago Ave	5 PM
Pak Mail	1461 W Chicago Ave	4 PM

Map 25 • Illinois Medical District

Self-Service	1725 W Harrison St	7 PM
Self-Service	840 S Wood St	7 PM
Self-Service	820 S Damen Ave	6 PM
Self-Service	715 S Wood St	4 PM

Map 26 • University Village / Little Italy / Pilsen

Self-Service	1100 W Cermak Rd	7 PM
Self-Service	1201 W Harrison St	6:30 PM
Self-Service	851 S Morgan St	5:30 PM
Windy City Pack & Ship	1100 W Cermak Rd, Ste B423	3 PM

Map 28 • Bucktown

Self-Service	1829 W Fullerton Ave	7:30 PM
Self-Service	2349 N Elston Ave	7 PM
Self-Service	2211 N Elston Ave	6 PM

Map 29 • DePaul / Wrightwood / Sheffield

FedEx Kinko's	2300 N Clybourn Ave	8:45 PM
FedEx Kinko's	2300 N Clybourn Ave	8:45 PM
Self-Service	2300 N Clybourn Ave	8:45 PM
Self-Service	2000 N Racine Ave	7 PM
Self-Service	2323 N Seminary Ave	7 PM
Self-Service	1918 N Mendell St	6 PM
Self-Service	990 W Fullerton Ave	5:30 PM
Self-Service	1117 W Wisconsin St	4:15 PM

Map 30 • Lincoln Park

Self-Service	802 W Belden Ave	7:15 PM
Self-Service	1749 N Wells St	7 PM
Self-Service	2500 N Clark St	7 PM

Map 31 • Old Town / Near North

Self-Service	900 N Franklin St	8 PM
Self-Service	213 W Institute Pl	7:30 PM
Self-Service	820 N Orleans St	7:30 PM
Self-Service	1350 N Wells St	7 PM
Self-Service	1333 N Kingsbury St	7 PM
Cleaners Mail Comp	900 N Kingsbury St	5:30 PM

Map 32 • Gold Coast / Mag Mile

FedEx Kinko's	875 N Michigan Ave	9 PM
FedEx Kinko's	1201 N Dearborn St	8:45 PM
Self-Service	1201 N Dearborn St	8:45 PM
Self-Service	100 E Walton St	7:30 PM
Self-Service	919 N Michigan Ave	7:30 PM
Self-Service	1 E Delaware Pl	7:30 PM
Self-Service	900 N Michigan Ave	7 PM
Self-Service	980 N Michigan Ave	7 PM
Self-Service	1165 N Clark St	6:30 PM
Self-Service	875 N Michigan Ave	6:30 PM
Self-Service	844 N Rush St	6 PM
Global Postal & Shipping	1151 N State St	5 PM

Map 33 • Rogers Park / West Ridge

Self-Service	7555 N California Ave	7:15 PM
Unik Technic Corporation	2337 W Devon Ave	7 PM

Map 34 • East Rogers Park

Self-Service	1723 W Devon Ave	7 PM
Self-Service	6355 N Broadway St	6:30 PM
Self-Service	7056 N Clark St	6 PM

Map 37 • Edgewater / Andersonville

Self-Service	5419 N Sheridan Rd	7:30 PM
Bedmar Courier Express	5655 N Clark St	7 PM
Postal Mart	5250 N Broadway St	5 PM

Map 38 • Ravenswood / Albany Park

Self-Service	2522 W Lawrence Ave	7 PM

Map 39 • Ravenswood / North Center

Self-Service	1807 W Sunnyside Ave	7:30 PM
Self-Service	4619 N Ravenswood Ave	7:10 PM
Self-Service	1700 W Irving Park Rd	6:45 PM
Self-Service	4001 N Ravenswood Ave	6:30 PM
Remesas Montrose	1924 W Montrose Ave	6 PM
Self-Service	4043 N Ravenswood Ave	6 PM

Map 40 • Uptown

Self-Service	4753 N Broadway St	7 PM
Self-Service	4850 N Broadway St	6:30 PM

Map 41 • Avondale / Old Irving

Self-Service	2704 W Roscoe St	7 PM
Self-Service	3611 N Kedzie Ave	7 PM
Self-Service	3401 N California Ave	7 PM
Self-Service	2630 W Bradley Pl, #2650	6:30 PM
Self-Service	3500 N California Ave	4:30 PM

Map 42 • North Center / Roscoe Village / West Lakeview

FedEx Kinko's	3435 N Western Ave	8 PM
Self-Service	3435 N Western Ave	8 PM
Self-Service	1800 W Larchmont Ave	7:30 PM
Self-Service	3717 N Ravenswood Ave	7 PM
Mailbox Plus	2248 W Belmont Ave	6 PM

Map 43 • Wrigleyville/ East Lakeview

FedEx Kinko's	3524 N Southport Ave	8 PM
Self-Service	3524 N Southport Ave	8 PM
Self-Service	1300 W Belmont Ave	7:30 PM
Self-Service	3024 N Ashland Ave	6 PM

Map 44 • East Lakeview

FedEx Kinko's	3001 N Clark St	8 PM
Self-Service	3001 N Clark St	8 PM
Self-Service	2800 N Sheridan Rd	7 PM
Postal Place	3304 N Broadway St	6:30 PM
Steve Rozells Postal Plus	559 W Diversey Pkwy	6 PM

Chicago's LGBTQ communities are a diverse, politically-influential presence within the city. Just look to the Pride Pylon's lining North Halsted Street, designating the gay district (one of the only such official designations of a gay 'hood in the country), or the numerous politicians who vie for a prime spot in the city's enormous annual Pride Parade (which takes place in Boystown on the last Sunday in June). Boystown (a.k.a East Lakeview) and Andersonville comprise the city's two gay friendliest neighborhoods, with Clark Street, Halsted and Broadway being queer corridors of shops, restaurants and nightlife. Those two 'hoods notwithstanding, GLBTQ people and culture can be found throughout the city, from Roger's Park to Midway. Whether your interests are activism or acupuncture, draperies or drag kings, literature, liturgies, or leather bars, or any combination of the above, you will find your niche in Chicago's vibrant and diverse GLBTQ communities.

Publications/Media

Pick up a copy of the following publications, log onto a website, or tune in to find out what's happening around town, from the current political headlines to the hottest clubs. Gay rags can be found in gay-friendly book stores, cafés, bars, shops, and gay friendly transit stops.

The Field Guide to Gay and Lesbian Chicago
by Kathie Bergquist and Robert McDonald. This comprehensive guide to gay and lesbian life in Chicago is available at bookstores everywhere.

Windy City Times • www.wctimes.com
Gay and Lesbian news weekly—check this site for a calendar of events.

Identity • www.identitychicago.com
A cross-cultural GLBT monthly, focusing on race, gender, and culture published by Windy City Media Group.

OUT! Guide • Comprehensive GLBT resource guide with listings for services including therapists, carpenters, real estate brokers, accounting services, social services, restaurants, and much, much more. Indispensable!

Chicago Free Press • www.chicagofreepress.com
Weekly publication with features on political issues, arts, culture, spiritual life, entertainment, and resource lists.

Gay Chicago • www.gaychicagomag.com
One of the city's oldest gay publications, with events listings, columns, news, astrology, and reviews. Male-focused.

Chicago Gay and Lesbian Chamber of Commerce • www.glchamber.org Charged with developing gay and lesbian businesses, the chamber also hosts events for gay and lesbian professionals.

Boystown Chicago • www.boystownchicago.com
A message board, event calendar, and columnist spot for the gay and lesbian community.

Chicago Pride • www.chicagopride.com
Another site with the gay happenings across Chicago.

Boi • www.boimagazine
Heavily advertising-based guide to the club scene for circuit boys.

Windy City Radio • Tune in Sunday nights, 11 pm–midnight, on WCKG, 105.9 FM, or tune in online at www.windycityradio.com anytime.

Think Pink at WLUW Radio • www.wluw.org
Queer radio every Tuesday 6:30–8 pm.

Pink Magazine • www.pinkmag.com/chicago
Best for its listing of gay friendly businesses and restaurants.

Chicago Gay Examiner • http://www.examiner.com/x-443-Chicago-Gay-Examiner
A mostly male-focused blog about happening in the city.

Chicago Lesbian Scene Examiner
http://www.examiner.com/x-443-Chicago-Gay-Examiner
See Chicago Gay Examiner and make obvious conclusions.

Edge Chicago • http://www.edgechicago.com
Web mag with calendar and columnists.

Arts & Culture

Women & Children First Books • 5233 N Clark St
773-769-9299
Opened in 1979, Women & Children first has bragging rights as one of the nation's oldest feminist bookstores, and is almost certainly the largest. Regularly hosts events and discussions.
www.womenandchildrenfirst.com

Unabridged Books • 3251 N Broadway St
773-883-9119
Largest gay selection in the city, located in the heart of Boystown. You will find a well-annotated book selection, as well as calendars and magazines.

Gerber/Hart Gay and Lesbian Library and Archives
1127 W Granville St • 773-381-8030
This amazing library houses more than 10,000 books, magazines, newspapers, and videos. Regularly hosts both gay and lesbian book discussion groups. For special events including readings and screenings, check the website at www.gerberhart.org.

Barbara's Bookstore • 1110 N Lake St, Oak Park
708-848-9140
Gay-friendly bookstore with a large selection of gay and lesbian fiction and non-fiction titles.

Seminary Cooperative Bookstore
5757 University Ave • 773-752-4381
Located in Hyde Park, this bookstore has sections on GLBT studies.

57th Street Books • 1301 E 57th St • 773-684-1300
Another Hyde Park bookstore with a strong GLBT section.

Specialty Video • 3221 N Broadway St • 773-248-3434
5307 N Clark • 773-878-3434
Huge selection of gay and lesbian videos and DVDs. Dirty movies in the back.

Chicago Filmmakers • 5243 N Clark St • 773-293-1447
Sponsors of Reeling, the Chicago Lesbian and Gay International Film Festival.

Chicago Lesbian & Gay International Film Festival
www.chicagofilmmakers.org/reeling
Movies by and about LGBT.

Facets Multimedia • 1517 W Fullerton Ave
773-281-9075
Large selection of gay arthouse films.

About Face Theatre • 773-784-8565
Roving gay & lesbian theater company.

Theatre Building • 1225 W Belmont Ave • 773-327-5252
Many gay theatre productions are mounted here.

Aldo Castillo Gallery • 233 W Huron St • 312-327-2563
Fine arts gallery with lesbigay latino/a bent.

Woman Made Gallery • 685 N Milwaukee Ave
312-738-0400 • www.womanmade.org
Regularly features lesbian artists.

Las Manos Gallery • 5220 N Clark St • 773-728-8910
Lesbian-owned and -operated, regularly features gay and lesbian artists.

Artemis Singers • PO Box 578296 • 773-764-4465
Lesbian-feminist chorus.

Chicago Gay Men's Chorus
3540 N Southport Ave, PO Box 333 • 773-296-0541
www.cgmc.org
The name says it all. Mounts fun, campy annual Christmas concert.

Windy City Gay Chorus • 3023 N Clark St
773-404-WCGC• www.windycitysings.org
Sponsors four different gay choruses, including UNISON and The Slickers.

Lakeside Pride Freedom Band
773-381-6693 • www.lakesidepride.org
Chicago's gay & lesbian marching band. Doesn't every city have one?

Homolatte • www.homolatte.com
Bi-monthly queer spoken word and acoustic music series with writers and musicians, hosted by Out Music 2005 Artist of the Year Scott Free.

4 + 1 Productions • www.4plus1.org

Sports & Recreation

Chi-Town Squares • 5315 N Clark St • 773-339-6743
Gay and lesbian square dancing—what else?

Chicago Metropolitan Sports Association
www.chicagomsa.com • 312-409-7932
Organizes all varieties of gay and lesbian competitive athletics: bowling, softball, etc.

Chicago Smelts • 3712 N Broadway St • 312-409-4974
www.chicagosmelts.org
Gay & lesbian swim club.

Frontrunners/Frontwalkers
312-409-2790 • www.frfwchicago.org
Weekly LBG running and walking group sponsors annual "Proud to Run" race.

Windy City Rodeo • 312-409-3835 • www.ilgra.com
Rope 'em up, rough riders.

Thousand Waves Spa • 1212 W Belmont
773-549-0700 • www.thousandwavesspa.com
Women-only spa offers herb wraps and massages along with jacuzzi, steam room, and sauna.

Windy City Athletic Association • 773-327-WCAA
www.wcaa.net
Also organizes gay and lesbian competitive sports.

Social Groups/Organizations

Affinity: Advocates for African-American Lesbians
773-324-0377 • www.affinity95.org

Men of All Colors Together (MACT)
PO Box 408922, 60640 • 312-409-6916

Amigas Latinas Lesbianas/Bisexuales
312-409-5697• www.AmigasLatinas.org

Association of Latin Men for Action (ALMA)
2855 N Lincoln Ave • 773-929-7688
www.almachicago.org

Asians & Friends, Chicago • 312-409-1573
www.afchicago.org

P-FLAG • Parents & Friends of Lesbians and Gays
www.pflag.org

COLAGE Chicago
Children of Lesbians and Gays Everywhere
773-548-3349 • www.colage.org/Chicago

Chicagoland Bisexual Network
www.bisexual.org/g/chicagoland

Chicago Gender Society • PO Box 578005, 60657
708-863-7714 • www.chicagogender.com

Political Groups/Activism

Equality Illinois • 3712 N Broadway St, #125, 60613
773-477-7173 • www.equalityillinois.org

Human Rights Campaign Chicago • 800-777-4723

Oak Park Area Lesbians/Gays • 947 Garfield St
708-848-0273

Stonewall Democrats • 1830 S Michigan Ave
773-573-8838 • www.illinoisstonewall.org

Illinois Gender Advocates • 47 W Division
312-409-5489 • www.genderadvocates.org

Religious Services

AIDS Pastoral Care Network
1501 S California, 60608 • 773-257-6425

Archdiocesan Gay and Lesbian Outreach (AGLO)
711 Belmont Ave, #106, 60657 • 773-525-3872
www.aglochicago.org
Roman Catholic

Broadway United Methodist Church
3344 N Broadway St • 773-348-2679 • Reconciling

Center for Spiritual Living • 3036 N Ashland, 60657
773-248-5683 • www.chicagocsl.org • Science church

Church of the Open Door • 5954 S Albany Ave, 60629
773-778-3030 • Black LBGT church

Congregation Or Chadash • 656 W Barry Ave, 60657
773-271-2148 • www.orchadash.org • LBGT synagogue

Dignity Chicago • 312-458-9438
www.dignitychicago.org • LBGT Catholic

Good Shepherd Parish and Christ the Redeemer MCC • 7045 N Western Ave, 60645 • 773-275-7776
Non-denominational

Integrity/Chicago • PO Box 3232, Oak Park, 60303
773-348-6362
Episcopal, meets 3rd Friday for Eucharist/reception

Lake Street Church of Evanston • 607 Lake St, Evanston
847-864-2181 • www.lakestreet.org
Inside/Out GL group

Pilgrim Congregational Church • 460 Lake St, Oak Park
708-848-5860 • www.afterhours.com
Actively inclusive

Resurrection MCC • 5757 S University Ave, 60637
773-288-1535
Non-demominational

Vajrayana Buddhist Center • 3534 N Hoyne Ave, 60618
773-529-1862

Jewish Family Community Service • 5150 Golf Rd
312-357-4619

St. Paul's United Church of Christ • 2336 N Orchard St
773-348-3829

New Spirit Community Church (Oak Park)
542 S. Scoville • 708-848-5460

Health Center & Support Organizations

Haymarket Center • 932 W. Washington Street
312-226-7984

Horizons Community Services
www.horizonsonline.org
The Midwest's largest lesbian, gay, bisexual, and transgendered social service agency.

- **Lesbian and Gay Help Line** • 773-929-HELP (6 pm until 10 pm)
- **The Crisis Hotline/Anti-Violence Project** 773-871-CARE
- **Legal Services** • 773-929-HELP legal@horizonsonline.org
- **Mature Adult Program** • 773-472-6469 x245 perryw@horizonsonline.org
- **Psychotherapy Services** • 773-472-6469 x261 sarag@horizonsonline.org
- **Youth Services** • 773-472-6469 x252 premp@horizonsonline.org

Illinois State HIV/AIDS/STD Hotline
772-AID-AIDS

AIDS Foundation of Chicago
411 Wells St, Ste 300, Chicago, IL 60607
312-922-2322 • www.aidschicago.com
A charitable foundation, not a direct service provider.

AIDSCARE • 212 E Ohio, 5th Fl, Chicago, IL 60611
773-935-4663

GLAAD Chicago • PO Box 46343, Chicago, IL 60614
773-871-7633

PFLAG Chicago • PO Box 11023, Chicago, IL 60611
773-472-3079

Howard Brown Health Center • 4025 N Sheridan Rd
773-388-1600
General counseling as well as anonymous, free AIDS-testing and GLBT Domestic Violence Counseling and Prevention Program. Also provides general practitioner care for men and women, on a sliding fee scale.

Lesbian Community Care Project
Howard Brown Health Center • 773-561-4662
The lesbian health service and outreach arm of Howard Brown Health Center.

AA – New Town Alano Club
909 W Belmont Ave, 2nd Fl • 773-529-0321
Gay and lesbian AA, CA, OA, ACOA, Coda, etc.

Support Groups
Many support groups exist for men, women, and families in Chicago. Call Howard Brown or Horizons for referrals.

Center on Halstead • 3640 N Halsted, 60613
773-472-6469 • www.centeronhalsted.org
Since opening its doors to the public in 2007, The Center on Halsted, Chicago's GLBTQ community center and cultural hub, has been the meeting spot for numerous community social groups and organizations, from gay senior groups to youth programs. Groups such as the Chicago Names Project, The Chicago Gay and Lesbian Chamber of Commerce, and Amigas Latinas call the Center home. The facility houses a full-sized gymnasium, a theater, a huge outdoor deck with a vista over Halsted Street, and computer center, and shares an entry with the adjacent Whole Foods grocery store—probably the gayest Whole Foods in the nation (and that says a lot). Theatrical events, affirming liturgies, movies, recovery and support groups, co-ed volleyball and yoga for seniors are all part of the program.

Chicago House • 1925 N Clybour Ave Ste 401
773-248-5200 • www.chicagohouse.org
Homeless shelter for people living with HIV/AIDS.

Bath Houses

Steamworks • 3246 N Halsted St • 773-929-6080
If you're shy check out 'lights out' night every other Thursday.

Man's Country • 5015 N Clark St 773-878-2069
www.manscountrychicago.com
Bath house, private rooms, hot strippers.

Erotica

Banana Video • 4923 N Clark St 2nd Fl • 773-561-8322
Bijou • 1363 N Wells St • 800-932-7111
Cupid's Treasures • 3519 N Halstead St • 773-348-3884
The Ram • 3511 ½ N Halsted St • 773-525-9528

Bars & Clubs

Gay

- **3160** • 3160 N Clark St • 773-327-5969
  Piano and cabaret bar.
- **Anvil** • 1137 W Granville St • 773-973-0006
  Leather/Levis old-school joint, very local.
- **Bucks Saloon** • 3439 N Halsted St • 773-525-1125
  Typical gay watering hole.
- **Cell Block** • 3702 N Halsted St • 773-665-8064
  Leather bar.
- **Charlie's** • 3726 N Broadway St • 773-871-8887
  Country & Western, with traditional dancing after 2.
- **Chicago Eagle** • 5015 N Clark St • 773-728-0050
  Leather bar with back room.
- **Gentry on Halsted** • 3320 N Halsted St
  773-348-1053
  Cabaret shows, piano bar.
- **Hunter's** • 1932 E Higgins Rd, Elk Grove Village
  847-439-8840
  Dance/video bar in the 'burbs
- **Jackhammer**• 6406 N Clark St • (773) 753-5772
  www.jackhammer-chicago.com
  Far north, without the Boystown attitude.
- **Little Jim's** • 3501 N Halsted St • 773-871-6116
  Neighborhood bar, 4 am license.
- **Lucky Horseshoe** • 3169 N Halsted St • 773-404-3169
  Male dancers.
- **Manhandler** • 1948 N Halsted St • 773-871-3339
  Country & Western.
- **North End** • 3733 N Halsted St • 773-477-7999
  A welcoming gay sports bar.
- **Nutbush** • 7201 W Franklin St, Forest Park
  708-366-5117
  Video bar in the 'burbs.
- **Second Story Bar** • 157 E Ohio St • 312-923-9536
  Streeterville hideout.
- **Sidetrack** • 3349 N Halsted St • 773-477-9189
  Huge video bar, women welcome.
- **Touché** • 6412 N Clark St • 773-465-7400
  Far North leather bar.

Lesbian

- **Blyss Productions**
  www.myspace.com/femistryfridays
  Holds "Femistry Friday" dance parties at locations around the city.
- **The Closet** • 3325 N Broadway St • 773-477-8533
  4 am license, men welcome.
- **Chix Mix** • www.chixmixproductions.com
  Roving women's dance parties.
- **Club Intimus** • 312 W Randolph St • 312-901-1703
  Roving women's dance party. Call for info.
- **DiChano's** • 201 155th St, Calumet City • 708-891-3980
  4 am license, entertainment sometimes. Formerly known as The Patch.
- **FKA @ Big Chicks** • 5024 N. Sheridan • 773-728-5511
  First Thursday of every month. Monthly party at Big Chicks is the hippest lesbian scene in town

Spyners 4623 N. Western 773-784-8719
  www.spyners.com
  Lesbian-owned, lesbian-friendly neighborhood bar with karaoke.

- **Temptations** • 10235 W Grand Ave, Franklin Park
  847-455-0008
  Entertainment and dancing in the land of the big hair.

Both

- **Atmosphere** • 5355 N Clark St • 773-784-1100
  Neighborhood bar, dancing.
- **Berlin** • 954 W Belmont Ave • 773-348-4975
  Mixed dance clubs. Women-only nights every first and third Wednesday.
- **Big Chicks** • 5024 N Sheridan Rd • 773-728-5511
  Mostly men with free bbq/buffet every Sunday.
- **Circuit/Rehab** • 3641 N Halsted St • 773-325-2233
  Big nightclub. Women's nights on some Fridays.
- **Club Escape** • 1530 E 75th St • 773-667-6454
  Mixed dance venue, some entertainment.
- **Cocktail** • 3359 N Halsted St • 773-477-1420
  Watch male dancers, sip cocktails.
- **Escapades** • 6301 S Harlem Ave • 773-229-0886
  4 am license, dancing, videos.
- **Hydrate** • 3458 N Halsted St • 773-975-9244
  Mostly guys but girl friendly.
- **Jeffrey Pub** • 7041 S Jeffrey Blvd. • 773-363-8555
  4 am, Southside institution, dancing.
- **Pour House** • 103 155th St, Calumet City
  708-891-3980
  4 am, dancing.
- **Roscoe's** • 3356 N Halsted St • 773-281-3355
  Mostly men, cavernous, dancing, videos, café.
- **Scot's** • 1829 W Montrose Ave • 773-528-3253
  Mostly men, friendly neighborhood bar.
- **Spin Nightclub** • 800 W Belmont Ave
  773-327-7711
  Mostly men, dancing.
- **T's Bar & Restaurant** • 5025 N Clark St • 773-784-6000
  Not gay-exclusive, *very* gay-friendly. Bar food.

Serving the nation's busiest convention center, most Chicago hotels are designed for business travelers, complete with expense-account prices. Even a modest downtown room can be outrageously steep.

Livin' Large: For a special urban splurge, book a suite at one of Chicago's palace hotels, such as the **Ritz-Carlton (Map 32)**, **Four Seasons (Map 32)**, or **Peninsula (Map 2)**.

Livin' Classic: The Drake (Map 32) is the classic Chicago hotel, and a landmark for drivers heading downtown from the northside via Lake Shore Drive. **The Allerton Hotel (Map 3)** is an architecturally significant Chicago landmark circa 1934. After years of decline, it has recently been restored to its former glory. In the Loop, the **Palmer House Hilton's (Map 5)** lobby is all divans and chandeliers. More notoriously historic, the **Chicago Hilton & Towers (Map 9)** was the site of the 1969 Democratic National Convention.

Livin' Modern: Hip travelers will want to stay at one of downtown's two **W (Maps 3, 5)** Hotels, the **Sofitel (Map 32)**, **Hotel 71 (Map 2)**, or the **Hard Rock Hotel (Map 6)**, located in the vintage Union Carbide building on Michigan Avenue. **The House of Blues Hotel (Map 2)**, located next to the corn cob Marina Towers, boasts folk-art decorated rooms and a Sunday gospel brunch.

Livin' Boutique: Located in a historic landmark, the **Hotel Burnham (Map 5)** is a lovely boutique hotel near the heart of Chicago's theater district. Burnham and its Kimpton Hotel Group sisters, **Hotel Allegro (Map 5)** and **Hotel Monaco (Map 5)**, also in the theater district, feature free wine receptions every evening for hotel guests. **Hotel Blake (Map 8)** on Printer's Row offers boutique-type amenities with handsome rooms, although the views can leave a bit to the imagination.

Livin' Cheap: Steer budget-conscious out-of-town guests toward the **Travelodge Downtown (Map 8)**. It's not eye candy, but the location (just off Michigan Avenue, between Millennium Park and the Museum Campus) makes it quite a deal. Around the corner at the **Congress Plaza Hotel (Map 9)**, picketers have been toting their placards for years. The Hotel Workers Union is on strike pending serious concessions from the management, and their dispute does not seem to be cooling. The strike has hurt business, which has cut prices—let your conscience be your travel agent, and brace yourself for heckling should you book here (and remember that Upton Sinclair would not approve).

Good values can also be had away from downtown. **City Suites (Map 43)**, and its "Neighborhood Inns of Chicago" partners, **The Majestic (Map 44)**, and **Willows (Map 44)**, in Chicago's Lakeview and Lincoln Park neighborhoods, offer small hotel charm at reasonable rates. If those are still above your station, **Heart o' Chicago Motel (Map 37)** is skipping distance from the Edgewater White Castle and a short walk from the vivacious Andersonville strip. **Sheffield House (Map 43)**, once a transient hotel, offers spare, cheap rooms, appealing to backpacking European travelers and frugal Cubs fans—it's a pop fly's distance from Wrigley Field.

B&Bs: Compared to cities of similar expanse, Chicago doesn't offer much by way of B&B's. **The Wheeler Mansion (Map 11)**, near McCormick Place, is luxurious and antique-filled, with fireplaces, custom baths and bedding, and ridiculously high ceilings. The more modest **Wicker Park B&B (Map 21)** dishes up a good breakfast—the owners also own the nearby Alliance bakery, where morning sweets are baked fresh daily. **The Flemish House B&B (Map 32)** is on a quiet, tree-lined lane, a calm refuge from the Rush Street and Oak Street Beach hullabaloo. **The Old Town Bed and Breakfast (Map 4)**, run by the friendly and eccentric Serritella family, features stylish bedrooms and a common area with a grand piano, formal dining room, and deluxe gourmet kitchen available for guests to use—it's where a John Cheever character would bunk. On the Southside, the luxe **Bronzeville B&B (Map 14)** is located in the landmark Goldblatt's mansion. Nearby, the quaint **Benedictine Bed & Breakfast (Map 12)** is run by monks from the adjacent Monastery of the Holy Cross.

Livin' Real Cheap: There are also three youth hostels in Chicago open to the public with rates as low as $15 a night for card-carrying International Youth Hostel members. For deals, Hot Rooms is a Chicago-based reservation service offering low-rates on undersold rooms: www.hotrooms.com.

Livin' Flop House: Before the construction of I-90/94, Lincoln Avenue was the main access point to the city from all points north. In the 20s-40s, a bunch of motels sprouted up on north Lincoln to serve truckers and other travelers entering the city. For a while these vintage motels were popular cheap spots for touring indie bands on a budget; eventually most of them become too seedy for even traveling indie bands on a budget. Many of the motels have fallen prey to the wrecking ball; a few, including the local landmark, **The Diplomat (Map 35)** and the **Apache Motel (Map 35)** remain, frequented, we assume, by people having affairs.

As a general rule, if a Chicago hotel price seems too good to be true, it is. Chicago is chock-a-block with run-down SROs providing semi-temporary housing to the down-on-their-luck, and extremely short-term housing to the occasional unwitting and unfortunate foreign traveler, cheapskate, or hapless student.

Map 2 • Near North / River North

Hotel	Address	Phone	Pricing
Amalfi Hotel	20 W Kinzie St	312-395-9000	189
Best Western Inn	125 W Ohio St	312-467-0800	119
Comfort Inn & Suites	15 E Ohio St	312-894-0900	96
Conrad Chicago	521 N Rush St	312-645-1500	215
Courtyard Chicago River North	30 E Hubbard St	312-329-2500	149
Embassy Suites Hotel	600 N State St	312-943-3800	149
Four Points	630 N Rush St	312-981-6600	145
Hampton Inn	33 W Illinois St	312-832-0330	139
Hilton Garden Inn	10 E Grand Ave	312-595-0000	169
Holiday Inn Chicago Mark Plaza	350 West Mart Center Dr	312-836-5000	119
Holiday Inn Express Magnificent Mile	640 N Wabash Ave	312-787-4030	104
Homewood Suites	40 E Grand Ave	312-644-2222	149
Hotel 71	71 E Wacker Dr	312-346-7100	234
Hotel Sax Chicago	333 N Dearborn St	312-245-0333	189
Howard Johnson Inn	720 N La Salle St	312-664-8100	99
Inn of Chicago - Magnificent Mile	162 E Ohio St	312-787-3100	109
The James	616 N Rush St	312-337-1000	219
Ohio House Motel	600 N Lasalle Blvd	312-943-6000	95
Peninsula Chicago Hotel	108 E Superior St	312-337-2888	525
Tokyo Hotel	19 E Ohio St	312-787-4900	49
Trump International Hotel and Tower	401 N Wabash Ave	312-588-8000	345
Westin River North Chicago	320 N Dearborn St	312-744-1900	199

Map 3 • Streeterville / Mag Mile

Hotel	Address	Phone	Pricing
The Affinia Chicago	166 E Superior St	312-787-6000	149
Allerton Hotel Chicago	701 N Michigan Ave	312-440-1500	129
Courtyard Magnificent Mile	165 E Ontario St	312-573-0800	159
Crowne Plaza Avenue Hotel Chicago	160 E Huron St	877-283-5110	89
Double Tree Inn	300 E Ohio St	312-787-6100	153
Embassy Suites Lakefront	511 N Columbus Dr	312-836-5900	159
Fairfield Inn	216 E Ontario St	312-787-3777	189
InterContinental Chicago	505 N Michigan Ave	312-944-4100	152
Marriott Downtown Magnificent Mile	540 N Michigan Ave	312-836-0100	149
Omni Chicago Hotel	676 N Michigan Ave	312-944-6664	199
Park Hyatt Hotel	800 N Michigan Ave	312-335-1234	375
Red Roof Inn	162 E Ontario St	312-787-3580	80
Sheraton Hotel & Towers	301 E North Water St	312-464-1000	149
W Chicago Lakeshore	644 N Lake Shore Dr	312-943-9200	225
Wyndham Chicago	633 N St Clair St	312-573-0300	107

Map 4 • West Loop Gate / Greek Town

Hotel	Address	Phone	Pricing
Crowne Plaza Metro	733 W Madison St	312-829-5000	157
New Jackson Hotel	768 W Jackson Blvd	312-372-8856	40

Map 5 • The Loop

Hotel	Address	Phone	Pricing
Buckingham Athletic Club Hotel	440 S La Salle St	312-663-8910	155
Hampton Inn Majestic Theater District	22 W Monroe St	312-332-5052	159
Hilton Palmer House	17 E Monroe St	312-726-7500	151
Hotel Allegro	171 W Randolph St	312-236-0123	199
Hotel Burnham	1 W Washington St	312-782-1111	219
Hotel Monaco	225 N Wabash Ave	312-960-8500	219
Renaissance Chicago Hotel	1 W Wacker Dr	312-372-7200	219
Silversmith Hotel & Suites	10 S Wabash Ave	312-372-7696	239
W Chicago City Center	172 W Adams St	312-332-1200	220

Map 6 • The Loop / Grant Park

Hotel	Address	Phone	Pricing
Fairmont Hotel	200 N Columbus Dr	312-565-8000	239
Hard Rock Hotel	230 N Michigan Ave	312-345-1000	199
Hyatt Regency Chicago Hotel	151 E Wacker Dr	312-565-1234	159
Swissotel Chicago	323 E Wacker Dr	312-565-0565	219

Map 7 • South Loop / River City		*Phone*	*Pricing*
Holiday Inn	506 W Harrison St	312-957-9100	102
Map 8 • South Loop / Printers Row / Dearborn Park			
Hostelling International	24 E Congress Pkwy	312-360-0300	27
Hotel Blake	500 S Dearborn St	312-986-1234	109
Travelodge	65 E Harrison St	312-427-8000	89
Map 9 • South Loop / South Michigan Ave			
Best Western Grant Park Hotel	1100 S Michigan Ave	866-516-3164	83
Chicago Hilton and Towers	720 S Michigan Ave	312-922-4400	109
Congress Plaza Hotel	520 S Michigan Ave	312-427-3800	69
Essex Inn	800 S Michigan Ave	312-939-2800	119
Intown Suites	350 E Roosevelt Rd	630-941-9075	219
Map 11 • South Loop / McCormick Place			
Hyatt Regency McCormick Place	2233 S King Dr	312-567-1234	179
The Wheeler Mansion	2020 S Calumet Ave	312-945-2020	230
Map 12 • Bridgeport (West)			
Benedictine Bed and Breakfast	3111 S Aberdeen St	773-927-7424	145
Map 14 • Prairie Shores / Lake Meadows			
Amber Inn	3901 S Michigan Dr	773-285-1000	69
Bronzeville 1st Bed & Breakfast	3911 S King Dr	773-373-8081	175
Map 17 • Kenwood			
Ramada Inn Lake Shore	4900 S Lake Shore Dr	773-288-5800	119
Map 21 • Wicker Park / Ukrainian Village			
Wicker Park Inn B&B	1329 N Wicker Park Ave	773-486-2743	95
Map 22 • Noble Square / Goose Island			
House of Two Urns B&B	1239 N Greenview Ave	773-235-1408	165
Map 24 • River West / West Town			
Rosemoor Hotel	1622 W Jackson Blvd	312-243-2900	40
Map 26 • University Village / Little Italy / Pilsen			
Marriott	625 S Ashland Ave	312-491-1234	209
Map 27 • Logan Square			
Milshire Hotel	2525 N Milwaukee Ave	773-384-7611	46
North Hotel	1622 N California Ave	773-278-2425	80
Map 30 • Lincoln Park			
Arlington House International Hostel	616 W Arlington Pl	773-929-5380	79
Belden Stratford Hotel	2300 N Lincoln Park W	773-281-2900	119
China Doll	738 W Schubert Ave	773-525-4967	245
Parkview Hotel	1816 N Clark St	312-664-3040	169
Windy City Urban Inn	607 W Deming Pl	773-248-7091	115
Map 31 • Old Town / Near North		*Phone*	*Pricing*
Marshall Hotel	1232 N La Salle Dr	312-664-3080	50
Old Town Bed and Breakfast	1442 N Park Ave	312-440-9268	185

Map 32 • Gold Coast / Mag Mile

Ambassador East	1301 N State Pkwy	312-787-7200	109
Drake Hotel	140 E Walton St	312-787-2200	175
Flemish House of Chicago	68 E Cedar St	312-664-9981	155
Four Seasons Hotel Chicago	120 E Delaware Pl	312-280-8800	390
Gold Coast Guest House	113 W Elm St	312-337-0361	129
Hilton - The Drake	140 E Walton Pl	312-943-6678	159
Hilton Suites	198 E Delaware Pl	312-664-1100	159
Hotel Indigo	1244 N Dearborn Pkwy	312-787-4980	149
Mark Twain Hotel	111 W Division St	312-642-7150	115 weekly
Millenium Knickerbocker Hotel	163 E Walton St	312-751-8100	89
Raffaello Hotel	201 E Delaware Pl	312-943-5000	149
Residence Inn	201 E Walton St	312-943-9800	159
Ritz Carlton Hotel	160 E Pearson St	312-266-1000	390
Seneca Hotel	200 E Chestnut St	312-787-8900	99
Sofitel Water Tower	20 E Chestnut St	312-324-4000	215
Sutton Place Hotel	21 E Bellevue Pl	312-266-2100	170
Talbott Hotel	20 E Delaware Pl	312-944-4970	179
The Tremont Hotel	100 E Chestnut St	312-751-1900	89
Westin	909 N Michigan Ave	312-943-7200	169
Whitehall Hotel	105 E Delaware Pl	312-944-6300	135

Map 33 • Rogers Park / West Ridge

Baymont Inn O'Hare	2881 W Touhy Ave	847-803-9400	64

Map 34 • East Rogers Park

Super 8 Motel	7300 N Sheridan Rd	773-973-7440	89

Map 35 • Arcadia Terrace / Peterson Park

Apache Motel	5535 N Lincoln Ave	773-728-9100	50
Diplomat Motel	5230 N Lincoln Ave	773-271-5400	52
Lincoln Inn	5952 N Lincoln Ave	773-784-1118	45
Lincoln Motel	5900 N Lincoln Ave	773-561-3170	50
O-Mi Motel	5611 N Lincoln Ave	773-561-6488	25
Summit Motel	5308 N Lincoln Ave	773-561-3762	50

Map 37 • Edgewater / Andersonville

The Ardmore House	1248 W Ardmore Ave	773-728-5414	99
Heart O' Chicago Motel	5990 N Ridge Ave	773-271-9181	89

Map 40 • Uptown

Dolins Louis	4700 N Racine Ave	773-561-1741	35

Map 43 • Wrigleyville/ East Lakeview

Ambers Hotel	1632 W Belmont Ave	773-248-1740	47
Bellwood Hotel	1409 W Diversey Pkwy	773-404-6000	58
City Suites Hotel	933 W Belmont Ave	773-404-3400	109
Sheffield House	3834 N Sheffield Ave	773-248-3500	61

Map 44 • East Lakeview

Abbott Hotel	721 W Belmont Ave	773-248-2700	75
Belair Hotel	424 W Diversey Pkwy	773-248-4000	80
Best Western Hawthorne Terrace Hotel	3434 N Broadway St	773-244-3434	120
Days Inn	644 W Diversey Pkwy	773-525-7010	77
Inn at Lincoln Park	601 W Diversey Pkwy	773-348-2810	79
Majestic Hotel	528 W Brompton Ave	773-404-3499	109
The Willows Hotel	555 W Surf St	773-528-8400	109

Chicago is a kid's kind of town. From sandy beaches and leafy parks to diverse downtown museums, concerts, and suburban attractions, Chicago's options for family fun are non-stop—just like your kids.

The Best of the Best

The best part about Chicago family-style is that lots of stuff is *free*…or practically free. Great entertainment and educational venues keep cash in parents' pockets for school supplies, groceries, gas, and an occasional adult night out.

- **Top Park:** Lincoln Park (Lake Shore Dr & North Ave, 312-742-2000; www.lpzoo.com). From an expansive sandy beach, baseball diamonds, basketball courts, and bike paths to grassy meadows, fishing lagoons, museums, and the nation's oldest free zoo, Lincoln Park promises a full day of outdoor activity.
- **Generations of Amusement:** Kiddieland (8400 W North Ave, Melrose Park, 708-343-8000; www.kiddieland.com). Before Disney and Six Flags, there was Kiddieland, one of the nation's oldest family-owned and operated amusement parks. Many of the more than 30 rides and attractions are original to this wholesome, 80-year-old icon of fun including the jelly-bean-colored bumper cars, carousel, swirling tea cups, and "Little Dipper" rollercoaster. Thrill-seeking 'tweens scream on the "Log Jammer" and high-flying "Galleon." Kids need more steam? Free Pepsi served all day. Unlimited rides for $21.50 admission fee (ages six and up); $18.50 (ages 3–5, seniors); free under age two; discounted admission after 5 pm. Open April–October. Call for seasonal schedule.
- **Spellbinding Story Time:** Lincoln Park Zoo (2200 N Cannon Dr, 312-742-2000; www.lpzoo.com). Donning safari khakis and pith helmet, Professor Bonnie spins adventurous tales and sings for preschoolers at the *Farm-in-the-Zoo*. Wildly popular, this story hour is the toughest ticket in town. Arrive early to secure admission (donation suggested). At the free *Second Sunday Stories,* children's book authors read their works about life on the farm followed by activities and tours of the *Farm-in-the-Zoo*. Call for schedule.
- **Slickest Sledding Hill:** Soldier Field Lakefront Park (312-742-7529; www.chicagoparkdistrict.com). The best part of the Soldier Field's pretty 17-acre park is the free, giant sledding hill with frozen lake views. BYO ride and bundle up for frigid lakefront winds. In warmer months, check out the Children's Garden.
- **Coolest Ice Rink:** McCormick Tribune Ice Rink in Millennium Park (55 N Michigan Ave, 312-742-7529; www.chicagoparkdistrict.com). Skate hand-in-hand in the shadow of architectural landmark buildings lining the Mag Mile. Open daily, admission is free to the 16,000-square-foot rink; skate rental available and warming room on-site.
- **Best-Kept Secret:** Chicago Public Library's "Kraft Great Kids Museum Passport" (Main Branch at 400 S State St, 312-747-4300 and branches city-wide; www.chipublib.org). Families can't afford not to know about the passports—on loan for one week at a time, they provide family members with free admission to over a dozen of Chicago's premier (read: pricey) cultural institutions, including the biggies at the Museum Campus plus the Art Institute, Peggy Notebaert Museum, and Chicago History Museum (formerly the Chicago Historical Society). Available only to Chicago Public Library card-carrying adult Chicago residents. See website for participating institutions and details.
- **Railroad Shop That Rocks:** Berwyn's Toy Trains & Models (7025 Ogden Ave, Berwyn, 708-484-4384). A roundhouse of activity where engineers of all ages can play at the many display train tables and enjoy a charming, 7-by-14-foot tooting layout in the back, Keep with the transportation theme and stop by Berwyn's *Spindle*, a massive sculpture just two miles south on Cermak and Harlem—it's an enormous desk organizer, skewering eight de-commissioned cars. For real.
- **WOW Waterparks:** (312-742-7529; www.chicagoparkdistrict.com). The Chicago Park District operates over 20 free waterparks with arching jets, umbrella sprays, pipe falls, and bubble jets in Chicago's neighborhood parks and beaches. All facilities open daily in summer 11 am to 8 pm.
- **Best Beach:** North Avenue Beach (1600 North Ave, 312-742-7529; www.chicagoparkdistrict.com). From swimming, spiking volleyballs, and kickboxing to sunbathing and sipping sun-downers, this expansive beach on Lake Michigan rivals any on the California coast. The tug-boat shaped beach house has locker facilities and rents volleyball equipment, roller blades, and bikes. On the upper deck is Castaways restaurant and ice cream parlor. There's also a full outdoor fitness center with weights and spin cycles plus a roller blade rink for pick up hockey under the summer sun.
- **Sensational Soda Fountain:** Margie's Candies (1960 N Western Ave, 773-384-1035). Celebrating 85 years of scoop, this old-fashioned ice cream parlor serves yummy frozen treats like soda fountains of yesteryear. Kids who flash report cards with an A get a free ice cream cone.

- **A Child's Choice Bakery:** Sweet Mandy B's (1208 W Webster Ave, 773-244-1174). Trendy and tasty, this cheery bakery's kid confections include awesome cupcakes, chunky whoopee pies, and whimsical cut-out frosted cookies. Signature sweet: "Dirt Cups"—a cake, crushed Oreo cookie, and whipped cream combo crawling with psychedelic gummy worms.
- **Coolest Family Concerts:** Joe Segal's Jazz Showcase (59 W Grand Ave, 312-670-2473; www.jazzshowcase.com). Hipster kids and jiving parents and grandparents hang out at this swank, serious jazz club's Sunday 4 pm matinee performances where top musicians jam. Non-alcoholic beverages and snacks served. Discount adult admission; children under 12 free. All Ages Blue Chicago Show (736 N Clark St, 312-661-1003; www.bluechicago.com) on Saturday nights from 8 pm to 3 am where families rock to the Gloria Shannon Blues Band in the basement of the Blue Chicago store. Adult admission $8; kids under age 11 free. No alcohol or smoking allowed. Jammin' at the Zoo (Lincoln Park Zoo, Lake Shore Dr & North Ave, 312-742-2000; www.lpzoo.com) once a month during the summer, shows starting at 7 pm. Serving the needs of cross-generational rock aficionados, previous concerts have featured They Might Be Giants, Collective Soul and The Gin Blossoms. Adult admission $20; kids pay half that.
- **Flying High:** Mayor Daley's Kids and Kites Festival (Alternating lakefront locations, 312-744-3315; www.cityofchicago.org/specialevents). Every spring and fall, the Windy City lives up to its blow-hard reputation, lifting kids' spirits and kites to new heights along the lakefront. Kite flying professionals and instructors help enthusiasts of all ages construct kites and fly them for free. Complimentary kite kits provided or bring your own. Free family entertainment, crafts, and storytelling on-site.
- **Not So Little League:** Chicago White Sox FUN damentals Field (U.S. Cellular Field, 333 W 35th St, 312-674-1000; www.whitesox.com). Little sluggers age three and up play ball in a 15,000-square-foot field of their own within the White Sox's home park. While junior trains, parents spy the pro game going on below from the new, kid-friendly interactive baseball diamond and skills area perched above the left-field concourse. Budding all-stars hone their pitching, batting, and base-running techniques under the sharp eyes of college and pro coach-instructors from the year-round Chicago White Sox Training Academy in Lisle. Better yet, it's all free with ball-park admission.
- **Masterpiece Portraits:** Classic Kids (917 W Armitage Ave, 773-296-2607; 566 Chestnut St, Winnetka, 847-446-2064). Pricey but priceless photos from this studio capture your kid at his or her model best. Pay a $300 sitting fee plus cost for handcrafted prints and treasure your tyke forever.
- **Weirdest City Sight:** Chicago River runs green (Chicago River downtown along Wacker Dr). No, it's not algae or bile, but bio-degradable green dye. Every St. Patrick's Day, the city turns the Chicago River emerald green like the Incredible Hulk.
- **Parents' Parking Dream:** Little Parkers Program, Standard Parking Garages (888-700-7275; www.standardparking.com). Select garages downtown specially equip families for road trips home with puzzles, crayons, and coloring books. Family-friendly garage amenities include spacious bathrooms with diaper-changing stations. Some rent family videos to monthly parkers. Participating garages: Grant Park North Garage, 25 N Michigan Ave; East Monroe Garage, 350 E Monroe St; Chicago Historical Society Garage, 1730 N Stockton Dr; Huron-St. Claire Self Park near Northwestern Memorial Hospital; Erie-Ontario Self Park in Streeterville neighborhood; and 680 N Lake Shore Dr Self Park.
- **Finest Family Festival:** Tall Ships (312-744-3370; www.cityofchicago.org/specialevents). Ahoy there, matey! In early August, over 25 old-world sailing vessels drop anchor along the lakeshore at Navy Pier, DuSable Harbor, and the Chicago River filling the skyline with billowing sails. There are daily deck tours ($10 boarding fee) as well as free entertainment and fireworks.
- **Kudos Kids' Theatre:** Marriott Theatre for Young Audiences (Marriott Lincolnshire Resort, 10 Marriott Dr, Lincolnshire, 847-634-0200; www.marriotttheatre.com). Not a bad seat in the house at this intimate arena theater where actors welcome pint-sized audience participation and roam the aisles interacting with kids. Post-performance, the actors conduct Q&A answering kids' theatrical questions. Family productions run year-round. Tickets $12 per person; free parking.
- **Oscar Performances:** Children's International Film Festival (city-wide, 773-281-9075; www.cicff.org). For over two weeks each fall, Chicago's theater venues feature hundreds of witty, ingenious long- and short-form children's movies from around the world, some created by kids. Filmmakers, directors, and animators teach seminars for movie-lovers of all ages.

- **Hippest Halloween Happening:** Chicago Symphony Orchestra's Hallowed Haunts Concert (220 S Michigan Ave, 312-294-3000; www.cso.org). Skeletons rattle and ghosts boogie to classical morbid music at the Chicago Symphony Orchestra's creepy family concert featuring hair-raising Romantic-Era pieces and medieval chants. Come in costume to the concert and ghoulish pre-performance party. Tickets: $7–$45.

- **Perfect Pumpkin Patch:** Sonny Acres Farm (29 W 310 North Ave, West Chicago, 630-231-9515; www.sonnyacres.com). During October, the Feltes family homestead has it all for fall: jack-o-lanterns for carving, homemade pies, decorative Thanksgiving and Halloween displays, and a killer costume shop. Kids love the mountains of pumpkins, crunchy caramel apples, scary hay rides, youngster carnival rides, and haunted barns (one for tiny tikes and another for blood-thirsty teens). Free farm admission and parking; purchase tickets for attractions.

- **Fields of Dreams:** Of course Wrigley Field, but a family outing at the venerable ballpark amounts to a month's down payment on a mini van. For $10 or less per ticket, take the family to the 'burbs' farm league games at pristine ballparks complete with entertainment, eats, and fireworks: Kane County Cougars (34W002 Cherry Ln, Geneva, 630-232-8811; www.kccougars.com) and Shaumburg Flyers (1999 S Springinsguth Rd, Schaumburg, 847-891-2255; www.flyersbaseball.com).

- **No-Flab Family Workout:** Tri-Star Gymnastics' Family Fun Night (1401 Circle Ave, Forest Park, 708-771-7827; www.tri-stargym.org). Families bounce on trampolines, swing on bars, tumble across mats, and climb ropes together at Tri-Star's warehouse-sized gymnastic training facility. Held from 4:30 pm to 5:30 pm on Saturday nights during the school year, admission is $5 per child and parents get in free. Parental supervision (no more than two kids per adult) and signed waiver required.

- **Musical Marathon Encounter:** Chicago Symphony Orchestra's Day of Music (220 S Michigan Ave, 312-294-3333; www.cso.org). A free live music marathon lasting eight hours held each fall. In addition to the world-renowned Chicago Symphony Orchestra, hear the city's top musicians perform classical, jazz, blues, world music, plus lively family entertainment. For year-round family concert performances, check out the orchestra's Kraft Matinee Series.

- **Horse'n Around:** Arlington Park Race Track's Family Day (2200 W Euclid Ave, Arlington Heights, 847-385-7500; www.arlingtonpark.com). From mid-May through mid-September it's a sure bet you'll win big with the kids on a Sunday afternoon at the horse races. Wild West, luau, and circus-themed family activities surround the seriously fun thoroughbred racing action at this swank, clean track. Pony rides, face painters, and petting zoo on-site. From noon to 4 pm, attend the free Junior Jockey Club events (847-870-6614) including educational equine care talks and behind-the scenes track tours (children 12 and under).

- **Brightest Christmas Lights:** Cuneo Museum and Gardens' Winter Wonderland Holiday Light Festival (1350 N Milwaukee Ave, Vernon Hills, 847-362-3042; www.cuneomuseum.org). The largest drive-through Christmas display in Northern Illinois twinkles with millions of lights creating dazzling holiday scenes. Superhero and storybook light sculptures dance in the woods. Festival runs first Friday after Thanksgiving through New Year's weekend from 6 pm to 10 pm. Admission per car is $10 on weekends, $5 weekdays.

- **Winter Blahs Buster:** Fantasy Kingdom (1422 N Kingsbury St at Evergreen St, 312-642-5437; www.fantasykingdom.org). When Chicago's plunging temps prevent playground play, take tykes to this warehouse-turned-play-space magic kingdom to blow off steam. Kids clamor through a giant castle fitted with slides and tunnels (socks required) while donning Camelot costumes for dress-up fun. $12 per child.

- **Shadiest Theme Park:** Pirate's Cove (901 Leicester Rd, Elk Grove Village, 847-437-9494; www.elkgroveparks.org). On the other hand, when Chicago's soaring temps make playing outdoors as appealing as a trip down the Styx, hit this blessedly small-scale, low-tech theme park. Your (10-and-under) mateys will scramble up the Smugglers Cove, ride a rope-and-pulley griffin, and paddle around a wee lagoon, all while you actually keep cool in this heavily-shaded treasure. Great low-cost birthday party site. $6 for residents, $8 for nonresidents.

Rainy Day Activities

Art Institute of Chicago, 111 S Michigan Ave, 312-443-3600; www.artic.edu. While kids find the doll house–sized Thorne Miniature Rooms and shiny medieval armor very cool, they also discover artistic expression from around the world at the Kraft Education Center. Interactive exhibitions introduce children to art from other cultures, time periods, and world-wide geographic regions. "Edutaining" art books and masterpiece puzzles in the children's library reinforce visual learning. Free kids' programs and drawing workshops are also held throughout museum galleries. Admission is free on Tuesdays (however, donation strongly suggested); children under 5 always free.

Cernan Earth and Space Center, Triton College Campus, 2000 Fifth Ave, River Grove, 708-456-0300, ext. 3372; www.triton.edu/cernan. Named after Apollo astronaut Eugene Cernan, a native Chicagoan and the last man on the moon, this cozy planetarium's intimate dome theater features kids' star programs ($5), earth and sky shows, and laser light shows. Monthly sky watch and lectures hosted. Mini space-related museum (free admission) and great celestial gift shop.

Chicago's Museum Campus, 1200–1400 S Lake Shore Dr. The closest you'll come to an educational amusement park. Dinosaurs, live sharks, giant mechanical insects, ancient mummies, and exploding stars are just a handful of adventures your kids will encounter on the lakefront's brainy peninsula home to the Field Museum (312-922-9410; www.fieldmuseum.org), Adler Planetarium & Astronomy Museum (312-922-7827; www.adlerplanetarium.org), and John G. Shedd Aquarium (312-939-2438; www.shedd.org). Check with each institution for its free admission days and special family programs.

Diversey River Bowl, 2211 W Diversey Pkwy, 773-227-5800; www.drbowl.com. Families, couples, and serious bowlers mix it up at this upbeat city alley. Decent grilled food served and full bar on-site. Wednesday through Sunday nights at 8 pm, glow-in-the-dark bowling known as Rock 'n Bowl goes well past the little one's bedtime but is fun for teens with chaperones.

DuPage Children's Museum, 301 N Washington St, Naperville, 630-637-8000; www.dupagechildrensmuseum.org. The 45,000-square-foot museum loaded with hands-on, action-packed exhibits keeps pre-schoolers with nano-second attention spans exploring until exhaustion.

Exploritorium, 4701 Oakton St, Skokie, 847-674-1500, x2700; www.skokieparkdistrict.org. From finger paints and water games to costumes and a multi-storied jungle gym, this facility tuckers tykes out. The climbing gym outfitted with twisting ropes, tubes, and tunnels even brings out the Tarzan in parents. Miniscule admission fee; free for Skokie adult residents and kids under 3.

Federal Reserve Bank of Chicago Visitors' Center, 230 S LaSalle St, 312-322-5322; www.chicagofed.org. The buck stops here where kids learn the power of pocket change through hands-on and computerized exhibits explaining the Fed's role in managing the nation's money. Kids love the rotating, million-dollar cube of cash and $50,800 coin pit. Sneak a peak into the vault stocked with $9 million, trace our country's currency history, and learn how to identify fake bills. Free admission. Open weekdays 9 am–4 pm; free guided tours on Mondays at 1 pm.

Garfield Park Conservatory, 300 N Central Park Ave, 312-746-5100; www.garfield-conservatory.org. Kids really dig Plants Alive!, the free, landmark Conservatory's 5,000-square-foot greenhouse blooming with child-friendly vegetation. Kids climb a two-story twisting daisy stem that doubles as a slide and come nose-to-stinger with a Jurassic-sized bumble bee. Attend story-telling, plant seeds, and dig in the soil pool.

Kohl Children's Museum of Greater Chicago, 2100 Patriot Blvd, Glenview, 847-832-6600; www.kohlchildrensmuseum.org. Kids climb the rigging of a pirate ship, "ride" an L train, meander through mazes, and push mini carts through a fully stocked grocery store.

Mitchell Museum of the American Indian, 2600 Central Park Ave on Kendall College Campus, Evanston, 847-475-1030; www.mitchellmuseum.org. From real teepees and dug-out canoes to bow-and-arrows and tom-toms, this compact sensory museum's engaging hands-on exhibits and craft sessions teach kids about the rich Native American life and culture. During the school year, sessions are offered semi-monthly on Saturdays, and on Tuesdays, Wednesdays, and Thursdays in summer. All programs held from 10:30 am to noon.

Museum of Science and Industry, 57th St at S Lake Shore Dr, 773-684-1414; www.msichicago.org. The ultimate hands-on learning experience for families, this massive museum is a tsunami of scientific exploration. Favorite kid exhibits are the 3,500 square-foot The Great Train Story model railroad, the United Airlines jet, a walk-through human heart, a working Coal Mine, and the Idea Factory workshop packed with gears, cranks, and water toys. OMNIMAX Theater on-site. Call for free day schedule.

Navy Pier, 600 E Grand Ave, 312-595-7437; www.navypier.com. A mega-sized free entertainment emporium jutting into Lake Michigan, Navy Pier has an IMAX Theater and tons of carnival-like attractions. The renowned Shakespeare Theater performs kid-friendly shorts of Willy's works. The 57,000-square-foot Chicago Children's Museum has 15 permanent engaging exhibits for toddlers to pre-teens (312-527-1000; www.chichildrensmuseum.org). Museum admission free on Thursday nights from 5 pm to 8 pm.

Oak Brook Family Aquatic Center, 1450 Forest Gate Rd, Oak Brook, 630-990-4233; www.obparks.org. Wet, wild fun for the whole family at this splashy indoor aquatic facility. They've got a zero-depth pool and slide for tadpoles as well as an Olympic-sized pool for bigger fish. Special swim events include watery holiday-themed parties, arts and crafts, water sports days, and dive-in movie nights where you can watch a family flick from your inflatable raft.

Peggy Notebaert Nature Museum, 2430 N Cannon Dr, 773-755-5100; www.naturemuseum.org. Kids delight in Butterfly Haven, a soaring tropical greenhouse habitat, home to hundreds of exotic winged beauties from around the world. The Children's Gallery replicates prairie and wetland habitats. Hands-on, free scientific activities and animal feedings always scheduled. Chicago residents enjoy a $1 discount on admission fee. On Thursdays, admission is free; however donations are strongly suggested.

Pelican Harbor Indoor/Outdoor Aquatic Park, 200 S Lindsay Ln, Bolingbrook, 630-739-1700; www.bolingbrookparks.org. Chicago area's only indoor/outdoor waterpark open year-round. Kids zip down six thrilling water slides (one 75-foot tall), float on inner tubes, and plunge into the diving well. There is a large zero-depth pool for little swimmers, lap pool, sand volleyball, whirlpool, and concessions.

Shops at Northbridge, 520 N Michigan Ave, 312-327-2300; www.westfield.com/northbridge. The entire third floor is not only lined with child apparel, toy, and accessory stores, but has The LEGO Store with play stations and a spacious LEGO building zone. Best part is parents don't have to clean up those blasted colored blocks!

Spertus Museum of Judaica, 618 S Michigan Ave, 312-322-1700; www.spertus.edu/museum. The Children's ARTiFACT Center recreates an impressive archeological site where kids dig up artifacts from ancient Middle East civilizations and experiment with writing in Cuneiform. Free admission on Fridays; all-inclusive, $10 family pass sold the rest of the week.

Wonder Works, 6445 W North Ave, Oak Park, 708-383-4815; www.wonder-works.org. About half a mile west of Chicago's city limits, this modest children's museum is far more accessible for many city families than the Chicago Children's Museum at Navy Pier and boasts the triple advantages of being low-cost ($5 admission + free street parking), low-key, and packed with friendly volunteers. Usually closed on Mondays and Tuesdays, Wonder Works often makes an exception for school holidays (call to confirm, though).

Outdoor and Educational

Fresh air family fun venues that work your kids' muscles and minds pack the city and suburbs. Here are some of the best:

Brookfield Zoo, First Ave & 31st St, Brookfield, 708-485-0263; www.brookfieldzoo.org. Chicago's largest zoo, spanning 216 wooded acres, is home to over 2,500 animal residents from around the world. Hamill Family Play Zoo and the Children's Zoo offer interactive programs on animal antics and opportunities to pet kid-friendly creatures babysat by helpful docents. Several dolphin shows daily. Family and child educational classes offered, plus summer camps and special holiday events. Explore the woodsy Indian Lake district where a life-sized dinosaur "lives." Open daily. Admission is free October through March on Tuesdays and Thursdays and January through February on Saturdays and Sundays.

Cantigny Park, 1 S 151 Winfield Rd, Wheaton, 630-668-5161; www.cantignypark.com. The 15-acre complex named after a World War I battle is home to the First Division Museum showcasing the history of the famed U.S. Army's 1st Infantry Division and *Chicago Tribune* founder's Robert R. McCormick Mansion Museum. After clamoring over the cannons, kids can stop to smell the flowers blooming in the manicured gardens. Family programs and concerts scheduled year-round. Park opens Tuesday through Sunday 9 am to sunset; museum is open 9 am–4 pm. Park and museum admission free; car parking fee, $7 Monday to Friday, and $8 on the weekends. Nearby is the top-rated, public Cantigny Golf Course (630-668-3323) offering junior golf instruction and a 9-hole Youth Links Course.

Chicago Botanic Garden, 1000 Lake Cook Rd, Glencoe, 847-835-5440; www.chicagobotanic.org. Open daily, admission is free to this 385-acre living preserve with more than 1.2 million plants rooted in 23 gardens, three tropical greenhouses, three natural habitats, eight lagoons, and bike paths. Kids love the winding, willow-branch tunnel in the Children's Garden where they can dig for worms and plant seeds. On Monday nights in summer, picnickers listen to the resonating chimes of carillon bell concerts on Evening Island. Late May through October, come for the Jr. Railroad where model trains puff through a garden of America's best loved landmarks (exhibit admission charged); in early December, make sure to check out the Reindog Parade (think bassets with antlers), with or without a Fido of your own.

Cuneo Museum and Gardens, 1350 Milwaukee Ave, Vernon Hills, 847-362-3042; www.cuneomuseum.org. Kids romp through the 75-acre wooded estate's formal gardens, animal sanctuaries, and deer park surrounding a palatial Italianate mansion. Open Tuesday–Sunday 10 am–5 pm; $5 grounds admission fee; mansion tours cost $12 for adults, $7 for children.

Fermi National Accelerator Laboratory, Kirk Rd & Pine St, Batavia, 630-840-3351; www.fnal.gov. Release energy outdoors biking, hiking, and rollerblading the nature trails at the nuclear plant's 680-acre campus. Rare species of butterflies, plants, birds, and baby buffalos live on the rural grounds. Guided prairie tours offered in summer. Picnickers welcome and lake fishing available. Open daily; admission free. Kids power up their nuclear knowledge at the Leon M. Lederman Science Education Center learning about nature's secrets and how the universe began. Admission free; open weekdays. Fermilab physicists conduct behind-the-scenes lab tours and Q&A with guests the first weekend of every month.

Graceland Cemetery, Clark St & Irving Park Blvd, 312-922-3432. Eerie and educational, the famous 119-acre necropolis built in 1860 is a national architectural landmark filled with palatial mausoleums, haunting headstones, and reportedly disappearing angelic statues marking the graves of Chicago's rich, famous, and infamous. The Chicago Architecture Foundation's (www.architecture.org) spine-chilling cemetery tour is a drop-dead Halloween family favorite.

Grosse Point Lighthouse, Sheridan Rd & Central St, Evanston, 847-328-6961; www.grossepointlighthouse.net. The pretty grounds surrounding the charming, white, tapering lighthouse built in 1873 and fairy-tale stone cottage are open year-round. Tours of both structures are offered weekends June through September for children aged 8 and up. A wooded trail twists down a grassy slope to the isolated Lighthouse Landing Beach.

Tempel Lipizzans Farm, Wadsworth Rd & Hunt Club Rd, Wadsworth, 847-623-7272; www.tempelfarms.com. Trained in the centuries-old tradition of the Spanish Riding School in Vienna, dancing, white Lipizzaner stallions fly through the air performing fancy four-footed feats. Performances are Wednesdays and Sundays, June through August. Tours of the historic stables offered year-round.

Lambs Farm, 14245 W Rockland Rd, Libertyville, 847-362-4636; www.lambsfarm.org. Over 40 years old, this is Chicagoland's favorite farmyard, a non-profit residential farm for persons with developmental disabilities. Animal petting zoo, mini-golf, and vintage carousel open in season. Year-round feel-good family events include an old-fashioned Breakfast with Santa, Easter Brunch, fall festival, and more. Shops and kid-friendly country restaurant open Tuesday through Sunday.

Lincoln Park Zoo, 2200 N Cannon Dr, 312-742-2000; www.lpzoo.com. The nation's oldest free zoo hasn't rested on its laurels—come see the up-to-date Ape House, Regenstein African Journey habitat, and North American animal exhibit at the Pritzker Family Children's Zoo. Kids love the graceful giraffes, lumbering elephants, and giant hissing Madagascar cockroaches. Additional family favorites are the Farm-in-the-Zoo, lion house, sea lion pool, and old-fashioned carousel (summer). Call for information on family programs including the ever popular Night Watch where families sleep over at the zoo!

Morton Arboretum, 4100 Illinois Rte 53, Lisle, 630-968-0074; www.mortonarb.org. Forests, meadows, gardens, and wetlands cover 1,700 acres of this outdoor tree and plant museum with paved roads and 14 miles of trails for hiking and biking. Kids particularly dig the Children's Adventure Garden and Maze. Overall, a great place to tromp around and picnic. Food service on-site. Guided tours and kid/family nature classes offered year-round. Favorite family fall activities include leaf collecting and the "Scarecrow Trail." Open daily. Discounted admission on Wednesdays.

Naper Settlement, 523 S Webster St, Naperville, 630-420-6010; www.napersettlement.org. Kids experience life on the Midwestern prairie of the past at this re-creation of a 19th-century agrarian community. Working blacksmith shop, post office, and school house manned by costumed interpreters. The living history village's seasonal programs cater to kids with games, pony rides, and entertainment.

North Park Village Nature Center, 5801 N Pulaski Rd, 312-744-5472; www.cityofchicago.org/environment. You'll think you're a hundred miles west of the city at this 46-acre rolling woods and wetlands where deer roam and owls screech. Nature paths throughout. Admission free; open year-round. Popular week-long EcoExplorers summer camps for kids aged five to 14 years also offered.

Willis Tower (Sears Tower) Skydeck, 233 S Wacker Dr, 312-875-9696; www.theskydeck.com. OK, so only a pane of glass separates your baby from the sky blue. But the Knee-High Chicago kids' exhibit is worth the parental panic. Interactive displays tell tales of Chicago from a bird's eye view. A touch-and-talk computer explains city landmarks.

Classes

Many of the city's fine cultural institutions have stellar, kid-focused curricula and host popular summer camps. Chicago and suburban park districts offer solid sports instruction, dance, and crafts classes. But private specialty schools also instruct many pint-sized prodigies. Here are some of the most popular and pedigreed organizations:

Academy of Movement and Music, 605 Lake St, Oak Park, 708-848-2329. This 34-year-old school offers popular dance and movement classes. The cool, creative Boys Production class for guys ages five to nine focuses on high-energy body movement practically applied to mini-manly visual arts projects, including mazes, puzzles, murals, sculptures, and machinery.

Alliance Francaise, 810 N Dearborn St, 312-337-1070; www.afchicago.com. Cultivating everything French in Chicagoans of all ages since 1897, this institution breeds petite Francophiles through intense language classes, camps, and cultural programs.

Bubbles Academy, 1504 N Fremont St, 312-944-7677; www.bubblesacademy.com. Yoga for youngsters taught with a creative twist in an open, airy studio.

Dennehy School of Irish Dance, 2555 W 111th St, 773-881-3990; www.dennehydancers.com. A South Side Irish institution, Dennehy has churned out high-stepping Irish dancers for over forty years. Its most-famous pupil so far is egomaniac, foot-pounding Michael Flatley of stage hits *Riverdance* and *Lord of the Dance*.

Flavour Cooking School, 7401 W Madison St, Forest Park, 708-488-0808; www.flavourcookingschool.com. Kids learn to really stir it up from scrambled eggs and lasagna to stir-fry and California cuisine at this cozy cooking school and culinary cookware shop. Class content determined by chefs' ages: Kitchen Helpers (age 4–6); Young Chefs (age 7–11); Sous Chefs (age 12+). Kids' summer cooking camps are also offered.

Gallery 37, 66 E Randolph St, 312-744-8925. Spearheaded by Maggie Daley, as in Mayor Richie's wife, Gallery 37's creative curriculum provides 14- to 21-year-old Chicago residents with educational on-the-job training in the visual, literary, media, culinary, and performing arts. Under the direction of professional artists, apprentices are paid while creating art projects throughout the city such as bench-painting, sculpture, play-writing, and multicultural dance. Eight-week summer program and limited programming during school year. Applications required.

Illinois Rhythmic Gymnastics Center, 636 Ridge Rd, Highland Park, 847-831-9888; www.ilrhythmicgymnastics.com. This top flexible factory turns out more national and Olympic gymnastic team members than any other in the country.

Language Stars, locations city-wide, 866-557-8277; www.languagestars.com. Children aged one through 10 are instructed in foreign language through play-based immersion.

Lou Conte Dance Studio, 1147 W Jackson Blvd, 312-850-9766; www.hubbardstreetdance.org. The dance studio of esteemed Hubbard Street Dance Chicago offers killer classes for teens (aged 11 to 14) in hip-hop, tap, jazz, ballet, African, modern, and more. Also teaches children and teen dance classes through the new, thriving Beverly Arts Center (2407 W 111th St, 773-445-3838; www.beverlyartcenter.org).

Merit School of Music, 38 S Peoria St, 312-786-9428; www.meritmusic.org. This tuition-free conservatory provides economically disadvantaged youth with excellent instruction in playing classical and jazz instruments. An answer to the public school system's sad arts education cuts.

Music Institute of Chicago, 1490 Chicago Ave, Evanston, 847-905-1500; www.musicinst.com. Students of all ages flock to this esteemed school specializing in the Suzuki Method for many instruments. Group and private instruction in string, wind, brass, and percussion instruments offered.

Old Town School of Folk Music, 4544 N Lincoln Ave & 909 W Armitage Ave, 773-728-6000; www.oldtownschool.org. Opened in 1957, this is Chicago's premier all-American music center specializing in lessons on twangy instruments. The school is best known for its Wiggleworms music movement program catering to the under-five folk. Engaging teen curriculum in music, theater, dance, and art is also offered. Kids' concerts—actually, all concerts—rock.

Ruth Page Center for the Arts, 1016 N Dearborn St, 312-337-6543; www.ruthpage.com. Prima ballerina classes for beginners to advanced students offered at this fine school whose graduates dance for the American Ballet Theatre, the New York City Ballet, and professional companies world-wide.

Second City Training Center, 1616 N Wells St, 312-664-3959; www.secondcity.com. Sign up your bucket of laughs for famed Second City's improvisational classes. Hilarious kids ages 4–12 attend hour-long sessions on Saturdays. Teen improv program is also offered.

Sherwood Conservatory of Music, 1312 S Michigan Ave, 312-427-6267; www.sherwoodmusic.org. Over-a-century-old Sherwood Conservatory specializes in the Suzuki Method for children ages three to 12 in cello, violin, viola, flute, piano, harp, and guitar. Also teaches classes at the South Side's Beverly Arts Center (2407 W 111th St, 773-445-3838; www.beverlyartcenter.org).

The Chopping Block, 4747 N Lincoln Ave, 773-472-6700; www.thechoppingblock.net. The Lincoln Square neighborhood store and kitchen complex of this sophisticated culinary store hosts cooking classes for kids ages 7–12 two times a week. Four-day cooking camp for two hours a day held in summers.

Tri-Star Gymnastics, 1401 Circle Ave, Forest Park, 708-771-7827; www.tri-stargym.org. This women-run gym pumps out gymnastic champs ages 18 months through teens. Flexing its muscle since 1987, the not-for-profit center offers caring instruction for boys and girls in gymnastics, tumbling, and trampoline. The center is home to a GIJO Team (Junior Olympics) and USGA Teams.

Shopping Essentials

Designer duds, high-style child furniture, imaginative toys, and kids' tunes—Chicago stores have it all for newborns to teens. Here's just a sampling of the top shops:

- **Alamo Shoes** • 5321 N Clark St • 773-334-6100 6548 W Cermak Rd, Berwyn • 708-795-818 Experienced staff for toddler shoe fittings.
- **American Girl Place** • 111 E Chicago Ave 312-943-9400 • Dolls and books.
- **Bearly Used** • 401 Linden Ave, Wilmette 847-256-8700 • Fab deals on duds and furniture.
- **Building Blocks Toy Store** • 3306 N Lincoln Ave 773-525-6200 • Old-fashioned, brain-building toys.
- **Carrara Children's Shoes** • 2506 ½ N Clark St 773-529-9955 • Tot soles from Italy.
- **Children in Paradise** • 909 N Rush St • 312-951-5437 Personable kids' bookseller.
- **Cut Rate Toys** • 5409 W Devon Ave • 773-763-5740 Discounted favorites.
- **Disney Store** • 717 N Michigan Ave • 312-654-9208 Princess paraphernalia and Mouse gear.
- **Fly Bird** • 719 Lake St, Oak Park • 708-383-3330 Off-beat furnishings, fashion and toys from baby to adult
- **Forest Bootery** • 492 Central Ave, Highland Park 847-433-1911; 284 E Market Sq, Lake Forest 847-234-0201 • Great but pricey shoe store.
- **Galt Toys + Galt Baby** • 900 N Michigan Ave 312-440-9550; 2012 Northbrook Court, Northbrook 847-498-4660 • High-end toy store and baby supplies.
- **Gymboree** • 835 N Michigan Ave • 312-649-9074 Designer preemie and kids' clothes.
- **Kozy's Bike Shop** • 601 S LaSalle St • 312-360-0020 Everything for biking families.
- **LMNOP** • 2570 N Lincoln Ave • 773-975-4055 Hip, fun kids' clothes.
- **Land of Nod** • 900 W North Ave • 312-475-9903 (stores also in Oak Brook Center and Northbrook Court) • Cute kids' furniture.
- **Lazar's Juvenile Furniture** • 6557 N Lincoln Ave, Lincolnwood • 847-679-6146 Tried-and-true children's furniture store.
- **Little Strummer** • 909 W Armitage Ave 773-751-3410 • Kids' tunes.
- **Madison and Friends** • 940 N Rush St • 312-642-6403 Designer clothes.

Magic Tree Bookstore • 141 N Oak Park Ave, Oak Park 708-848-0770 • Friendly and expert independent booksellers.

- **Mini Me** • 900 N Michigan Ave • 312-988-4011 European designer clothes.
- **Oilily** • 520 N Michigan Ave • 312-527-5747 Colorful patterned kids' clothes.
- **Pottery Barn Kids** • 2111 N Clybourn Ave 773-525-8349 (stores also in Oak Brook Center, Old Orchard Center, and Deer Park Town Center) Furnishings for the completely coordinated kid's boudoir.
- **Psycho Baby** • 1630 N Damen Ave • 773-772-2815 Funky kids' clothes.
- **Pumpkin Moon** • 1028 North Blvd, Oak Park 708-524-8144 • Funky, vintage toys.
- **Red Balloon Company** • 2060 Damen Ave 773-489-9800 • Toys, clothes, furniture.
- **The Right Start** • 2121 N Clybourn Ave 773-296-4420 • Baby equipment galore.
- **Shops at Northbridge** • 520 N Michigan Ave 312-327-2300 • Entire third floor is kids' clothing, toys, and accessories, including Nordstrom.
- **The Second Child** • 954 W Armitage Ave 773-883-0880 • Gently used designer clothes.
- **Timeless Toys** • 4749 N Lincoln Ave • 773-334-4445 Old-fashioned, hand-crafted toys.
- **Toyscape** • 2911 N Broadway St • 773-665-7400 Toys galore.
- **Uncle Fun** • 1338 W Belmont Ave • 773-477-8223 Hilarious novelties and vintage tin wind-up toys.
- **U.S. Toy–Constructive Playthings** • 5314 W Lincoln Ave, Skokie • 847-675-5900 • Educational toys favored by teachers.

Where to go for more information

Chicago Parent Magazine
www.chicagoparent.com

Oaklee's Guide for Chicagoland Kids
www.oakleesguide.com

Dog Parks, Runs and Beaches

Make no bones about it, Chicago is a dog's kind of town. More than 750,000 canines live and play in the Windy City. Dogs socialize and exercise their owners daily at designated Dog-Friendly Areas (DFAs), shady parks, and sprawling beaches.

Dog-Friendly Areas

DFAs are off-leash areas reserved just for canines. Amenities vary by park but often include: doggie drinking fountains; agility equipment; wood chips, pea pebble, and asphalt surfaces; "time out" fenced-in areas for shy or overexcited dogs; trash receptacles and doggie bags for, well, not take-out; and bulletin boards and information kiosks to post animal lovers' announcements.

DFAs are managed jointly by the neighborhoods' dog owners' councils and the Chicago Park District. These spaces are essential to the happiness of Chicago dogs and their owners, as police are notorious for dealing out hefty fines and even arresting dog owners who fail to clean up after or leash their dogs. But at the DFA, canines run free and poop where they please. Just remember to clean up after your pooch, ensure that your dog is fully immunized, de-wormed, licensed, and wearing ID tags. There are limits on how many pups one person can bring at once and please no puppies under four months, dogs in heat, dogs with the name "Killer," or children under 12.

- **Challenger Park**, 1100 W Irving Park Rd (Map 40)
  Nestled next to a cemetery and under the EL tracks, this relatively new DFA has plenty of amenities and neighborhood action. Avoid at all costs during Cubs games.
- **Churchill Field Park**, 1825 N Damen Ave (Map 28)
  This triangular space next to the train tracks is covered with pea gravel and asphalt and many abandoned tennis balls (Golden Retrievers can't get enough).
- **Coliseum Park**, 1466 S Wabash Ave (Map 11)
  Long, narrow, and fenced-in park where dogs race the overhead trains. Nothing to write home about, but, hey, it's legal.
- **Hamlin Park**, 3035 N Hoyne Ave at Wellington Ave (Map 42)
  Located in the shady southwest corner, this active L-shaped park appeals to tennis-ball chasers and fetching owners.
- **Margate Park**, 4921 N Marine Dr (Map 40)
  Called "Puptown" by the Uptown canine-loving community, this beloved DFA is usually packed with doggone fun. Locals are diligent about keeping the pea gravel picked up.
- **Noethling (Grace) Park**, 2645 N Sheffield Ave (Map 29)
  Dogs and owners from the Lincoln Park area love to hang out at the "Wiggley Field" dog run—Chicago's pilot pooch park. Wiggley's got a doggy obstacle course, an asphalt surface, drinking fountain, "time out" area, and info kiosk.
- **Ohio Place Park**, N Orleans St and W Ohio St (Map 2)
  Next to the I-90/94 exit ramp, this fenced-in strip of concrete flanked by bushes isn't pretty, but a dog can play fetch here without a leash. Careful: As the lot is not a Chicago Park District facility, it is not double-gated.
- **River Park**, 5100 N Francisco Ave (Map 38)
  The city's newest DFA.
- **Walsh Playground Park**, 1722 N Ashland Ave (Map 29)
  A 4,500-square-foot park with a small off-leash area for fetching with pea gravel and shade.
- **Wicker Park**, 1425 N Damen Ave (Map 21)
  Popular pooch as well as dog owner pick-up park. Often packed with dog-walkers wrangling fleets of frisky canines.

Creating a DFA takes a serious grass-roots effort spearheaded by the neighborhood's dog owners. They must organize themselves to get the community to bow to their desires through site surveys and three community meetings and raise one-half of the funds needed to build the DFA. Most importantly, they must unleash the support of their alderman, police precinct, and park district. For information on DFAs, call the Park District at 312-742-7529. Chicago's Dog Advisory Work Group, DAWG, (312-409-2169) also assists neighborhood groups in establishing DFAs

Top Dog Parks and Beaches

Leashed dogs and well-behaved owners are welcome in most of Chicago's parks and on its beaches, except during the height of swimming season when the sands are off-limits. Here are some local canines' top picks.

- **Calumet Park and Beach (9800 South)**
  A 200-acre beach and park getaway in the city with tennis courts, baseball fields, basketball courts, water fun, and plenty of parking.
- **Dog Beach (3200 N Lake Shore Dr)**
  This crescent of sand at the north corner of Belmont Harbor is separated from the bike path by a fence, making it an unofficial dog sand box. But the water is dirty, and the police do ticket, so it's not the most ideal dog-frolicking area.
- **Horner Park (2741 W Montrose Ave)**
  Dog heaven with lots of trees, grass, squirrels to chase, and other pups to meet, particularly after work.
- **Lincoln Park (2045 Lincoln Park W)**
  Paws down, the best dog park in town for romping, fetch, and Frisbee. Unofficial "Bark Park" where pet lovers congregate is a grassy area between Lake Shore Dr and Marine Dr.
- **Montrose/Wilson Avenue Beach (MonDog) (4400 North)**
  The city's only legal off-leash beach, MonDog is perfect for pooches to practice dogpaddling. Lake water is shallow and the beachfront is wide.
- **Ohio Street Beach and Olive Park (400 N Lake Shore Dr)**
  The perfect combo for cross-training canines: Olive Park's fenced-in grassy areas for running and neighboring Ohio Street Beach's calm waters for swimming.
- **Promontory Point (5491 South Shore Dr)**
  Radical run for daring, buff dogs that dive off the scenic picnic area's rocks into the deep water below.
- **Sherman Park (1301 W 52nd St)**
  The best place in the city for a Victorian-style stroll over picturesque bridges and through lagoons.

More Doggie Information

Chicago's canine community keeps up to snuff on doggie doings through *Chicagoland Tails Magazine*, www.chicagolandtails.com and the Chicago Canine website, www.chicagocanine.com. The definitive local resource for all things dog is Margaret Littman's book *The Dog Lover's Companion to Chicago* (Avalon Travel Publishing).

Self-Storage Locations	*Address*	*Phone*	*Map*
Metro Self Storage	465 N Desplaines St	312-243-2222	1
Public Storage	362 W Chicago Ave	312-266-0170	1
Self Storage 1	360 N Union Ave	312-733-1122	1
Self Storage	1601 S Canal St	312-421-0082	10
South Loop Self Storage	1601 S Federal St	312-674-9807	10
U-haul	419 E 25th St	312-326-2860	11
Public Storage	1414 S Wabash Ave	312-427-4835	11
Safeguard Self Storage	1353 S Wabash Ave	312-431-1400	11
Public Storage	3659 S Ashland Ave	773-247-0444	12
U-Store-It	345 N Western Ave	312-421-0200	23
U-haul	2647 N Western Ave	773-227-3489	28
Storage Mart	2647 Western Ave	773-227-2195	28
Public Storage	1916 N Elston Ave	773-227-3357	29
Self Storage 1	2001 N Elston Ave	773-276-9000	29
U haul Center Lincoln Park	1200 W Fullerton Ave	773-935-0620	29
U-Store-It	1840 N Clybourn Ave	312-255-9900	29
Public Storage	1129 N Wells St	312-951-8803	31
Storage Mart	1015 N Halsted St	312-787-0001	31
Public Storage	2101 W Howard St	773-262-1161	33
Public Storage	5643 N Broadway St	773-784-2299	37
Public Storage	5733 N Broadway St	773-878-0906	37
Public Storage	4072 N Broadway St	773-404-8181	40
Public Storage	4430 N Clark St	773-989-1098	40
U-haul	4055 N Broadway St	773-871-7155	40
Public Storage	2835 N Western Ave	773-772-7535	42
Self Storage 1	3839 N Sheffield Ave	773-477-6000	43

Van and Truck Rentals		*Address*	*Phone*	*Map*
Penske	East Bank Storage	730 W Lake St	312-466-1290	4
Penske	Dumore Supplies	2525 S Wabash Ave	312-949-6260	11
U-Haul	Downtown Lock Box	1333 S Wabash Ave	312-939-2040	11
U-haul	Storage Today	419 E 25th St	312-326-2860	11
U-Haul	East Bank Storage	1200 W 35th St	773-847-2351	12
U-Haul	Car One Auto Repair	3042 S Quinn St	312-842-5022	12
U-Haul	Pro Tech Auto Repair	3700 S Ashland Ave	773-523-0444	12
Budget	Clark Accutech	444 W 26th St	312-225-1769	13
U-Haul	Value Food Center	344 E 63rd St	773-752-5749	18
U-Haul	Noah Supermarket	5539 S Michigan Ave	773-955-0938	18
U-Haul	Hyde Park Self Storage	5155 S Cottage Grove Ave	773-256-1793	19
Penske	Elite Truck Rental	265 N Western Ave	312-942-1001	23
U-Haul	Better Methods Supply	1948 W Fulton St	312-738-0225	23
U-Haul	A&C Moving Solutions	431 N Wolcott Ave	312-850-2014	23
Budget	Fleet Services	1005 W Huron St	312-226-3073	24
U-Haul	A&A Automobile Service	1352 W Lake St	312-850-3382	24
Budget	Automotriz Monterrey	2000 S Western Ave	773-847-6989	25
U-Haul	Quick Oil	2928 W Armitage Ave	773-227-6432	27
Budget	Moving Chicago	2241 N Elston Ave	773-252-0298	28
U-Haul	Sunshine Movers &Truck Rental	2323 N Damen Ave	773-772-3920	28
U-haul	Storage Today	2647 N Western Ave	773-227-3489	28
U-Haul	Branch Location	1200 W Fullerton Ave	773-935-0620	29
U-Haul	Storagemart	1015 N Halsted St	312-587-1667	31
U-Haul	Factory Muffler Complete Auto	3055 W Devon Ave	773-338-7610	33
Budget	Chicago Moves Truck Rental	5450 North Western Ave	773-539-8044	36
U-Haul	Lite Site	1610 W Highland Ave	773-465-0475	37
Budget	Chicago Moves Truck Rental	2955 W Montrose Ave	773-539-8044	38
U-haul	Center Uptown	4055 N Broadway St	773-871-7155	40
U-Haul	Volume Plastics	2631 W Barry Ave	773-583-3418	41
U-Haul	M&W Appliances Whse	3161 N Elston Ave	773-478-0616	41
U-Haul	Penas Grease & Oil	3715 N Western Ave	773-583-4658	42
U-Haul	Cubs Park Service Station	3648 N Clark St	773-935-6688	43
Budget	Branch Location	3721 N Broadway St	773-528-1770	44

Internet

		Phone	Map
Panera Bread	501 S State St	312-922-1566	8
Windy City Cyber Café	2246 W North Ave	773-384-6470	21
Efebos Internet Café	1640 S Blue Island Ave	312-633-9212	26
Panera Bread	2070 N Clybourn Ave	773-325-9035	29
Office Mart	2801 W Touhy Ave	773-262-3924	33
Panera Bread	6059 N Lincoln Ave	773-442-8210	35
Screenz	5212 N Clark St	773-334-8600	37
Ignite Center	3171 N Clybourn Ave	773-404-7033	42
Panera Bread	616 W Diversey Pkwy	773-528-4556	44
Panera Bread	6059 N Lincoln Ave	773-442-8210	NW

Wi-Fi

		Phone	Map
Caribou Coffee	600 N Kingsbury St	312-335-0576	1
Cosi	55 E Grand Ave	312-321-1990	2
Caribou Coffee	500 W Madison St	312-463-1130	4
Bean Addiction	555 W Madison St	312-474-9140	4
Caribou Coffee	10 S La Salle St	312-609-5108	5
Argo Tea	16 W Randolph St	312-553-1551	5
Lavazza	27 W Washington St	312-977-9971	5
Cosi	28 E Jackson Blvd	312-939-2674	5
Cosi	33 N Dearborn St	312-727-0290	5
Intelligentsia Coffee & Tea	53 W Jackson Blvd	312-253-0594	5
Caribou Coffee	55 W Monroe St	312-214-0852	5
Lavazza	134 N La Salle St	312-977-9701	5
Argo Tea	140 S Dearborn St	312-553-1551	5
Caribou Coffee	200 N La Salle St	312-223-1606	5
Cosi	203 N La Salle St	312-368-4400	5
Cosi	230 W Monroe St	312-782-4755	5
Cosi	230 W Washington St	312-422-1002	5
Caribou Coffee	311 W Monroe St	312-920-9746	5
Cosi	116 S Michigan Ave	312-223-1061	6
The Coffee Beanery	150 N Michigan Ave	312-781-9970	6
Caribou Coffee	41 E 8th St	312-786-9205	8
Panera Bread	501 S State St	312-922-1566	8
Caribou Coffee	800 S Wabash Ave	312-786-9205	8
Café Au Lait	1900 S State St	312-225-3940	11
Bridgeport Coffeehouse	3101 S Morgan St	773-247-9950	12
Hidden Pearl Café	1060 E 47th St	773-285-1211	17
Third World Café	1301 E 53rd St	773-288-3882	19
Istria Café	1520 E 57th St	773-955-2556	19
Einstein Bros Bagels	5706 S University Ave	773-834-1018	19
Argo Tea	5758 S Maryland Ave	773-834-0366	19
Barista Café	852 N Damen Ave	773-489-2010	21
Café Ballou	939 N Western Ave	773-342-2909	21
Filter	1585 N Milwaukee Ave	773-227-4850	21
Alliance Bakery	1736 W Division St	773-278-0366	21
Letizia's Natural Bakery	2144 W Division St	773-342-1011	21
Windy City Cyber Café	2246 W North Ave	773-384-6470	21
Coffee on Milwaukee	1046 N Milwaukee Ave	773-276-3200	22
Atomix	1957 W Chicago Ave	312-666-2649	23
Muse Café	817 N Milwaukee Ave	312-850-2233	24
West Gate Coffeehouse	924 W Madison St	312-829-9378	24
Sip Coffee House	1223 W Grand Ave	312-563-1123	24
Bialy's Café	1421 W Chicago Ave	312-733-7165	24
Swim Café	1357 W Chicago Ave	312-492-8600	24
Café Jumping Bean	1439 W 18th St	312-455-0019	26
Mi Cafetal	1519 W 18th St	312-738-2883	26
Efebos Internet Café	1640 S Blue Island Ave	312-633-9212	26
Kristoffer's Café & Bakery	1733 S Halsted St	312-829-4150	26
Coffee Beanery	2158 N Damen Ave	773-278-4200	28
Panera Bread	2070 N Clybourn Ave	773-325-9035	29
Bean Café	2235 N Sheffield Ave	773-325-4577	29
Savor the Flavor	2545 N Sheffield Ave	773-883-5287	29
Ambrosia Café	1963 N Sheffield Ave	773-404-4450	29
Bourgeois Pig Café	738 W Fullerton Ave	773-883-5282	30
Cosi	2200 N Clark St	773-472-2674	30
Caribou Coffee	2453 N Clark St	773-327-9923	30
Argo Tea	2485 N Clark St	773-733-4231	30
Argo Tea	819 N Rush St	312-951-5302	32
Ennui Café	6981 N Sheridan Rd	773-973-2233	34
Café Utjeha	5350 N Lincoln Ave	773-907-8853	35
Metropolis Coffee	1039 W Granville Ave	773-764-0400	37
Pause	1107 W Berwyn Ave	773-334-3686	37
Trivoli Café	1147 W Granville Ave	773-338-4840	37
Screenz	5212 N Clark St	773-334-8600	37
Coffee Chicago	5256 N Broadway St	773-784-1305	37
Red Eye Café	4164 N Lincoln Ave	773-327-9478	39
Perfect Cup	4700 N Damen Ave	773-989-4177	39
Café Marrakech Expresso	4747 N Damen Ave	773-271-4541	39
So Addicted	4805 N Damen Ave	773-561-3210	39
Urban Tea Lounge	838 W Montrose Ave	773-907-8726	40
Corona's Coffee Shop	909 W Irving Park Rd	773-529-1886	40
Nick's on Wilson	1140 W Wilson Ave	773-271-1155	40
Dollop Coffee	4181 N Clarendon Ave	773-755-1955	40
MoJoe's Hot House	2849 W Belmont Ave	773-596-5637	41
MoJoe's Café Lounge	2256 W Roscoe St	773-388-1236	42
Ignite Center	3171 N Clybourn Ave	773-404-7033	42
Cosi	1023 W Belmont Ave	773-868-1227	43
My Place for Tea	3210 N Sheffield Ave	773-525-8320	43
Caribou Coffee	3240 N Ashland Ave	773-281-3362	43
Mellow Grounds Coffee Lounge	3807 N Ashland Ave	773-528-2877	43
House of Hookah	607 W Belmont Ave	773-348-1550	44
Panera Bread	616 W Diversey Pkwy	773-528-4556	44
Caribou Coffee	3025 N Clark St	773-529-6366	44
Intelligentsia Coffee Roasters	3123 N Broadway St	773-348-8058	44
Argo Tea	3135 N Broadway St	773-248-3061	44
Café Latakia	3204 N Broadway St	773-929-6667	44
Caribou Coffee	3300 N Broadway St	773-477-3695	44
Caribou Coffee	3500 N Halsted St	773-248-0799	44
Panera Bread	6059 N Lincoln Ave	773-442-8210	NW
Open Hearth Coffee Shop	5207 N Kimball Ave	773-279-9686	NW
J Bean Coffee & Café	7221 W Forest Preserve Ave	708-583-2245	NW
Euro Café	3435 N Harlem Ave	773-286-8544	NW
Caffe' Italia	2625 N Harlem Ave	773-889-0455	NW
Humboldt Pie	1001 N California Ave	773-342-4743	W
Café Luna	1742 W 99th St	773-239-8990	SW
Spoon's Coffee Boutique	712 E 75th St	773-874-3847	S
Café Mozart	600 Davis St	847-492-8056	Evanston

Bowling and Billiards

Bowling and Billiards		Phone	Map
Waveland Bowl	3700 N Western Ave	773-472-5900	42

Copy Shops

Copy Shops		Phone	Map
FedEx Kinko's	444 N Wells St	312-670-4460	2
FedEx Kinko's	127 S Clinton St	312-559-1324	4
FedEx Kinko's	29 S La Salle St	312-578-8520	5
24 Seven Copies	222 N La Salle St	312-704-0247	5
FedEx Kinko's	1242 S Canal St	312-455-0920	10
FedEx Kinko's	1800 W North Ave	773-395-4639	21
FedEx Kinko's	2300 N Clybourn Ave	773-665-7500	29
FedEx Kinko's	3524 N Southport Ave	773-975-5031	43
FedEx Kinko's	3001 N Clark St	773-528-0500	44

Delivery & Messengers

Delivery & Messengers	Address	Phone	Map
Deadline Express	449 N Union Ave	312-850-1200	1
On The Fly Courier	131 N Green St	312-738-2154	4

Gyms

Gyms	Address	Phone	Map
XSport Fitness	230 W North Ave	312-932-9100	31
XSport Fitness	3240 N Ashland Ave	773-529-1461	43
Chicago Fitness Center	3131 N Lincoln Ave	773-549-8181	43

Locksmiths

Locksmiths	Phone
Safemasters	312-627-8209
Gateway Locksmith	800-964-8282
Five Star Lock & Key	773-778-2066
Always Available	773-478-1960
Aabbitt	312-719-8200
A-ABC 24-hour Locksmith	773-772-3930
A-AAround the Clock	800-281-5445

Pharmacies

Pharmacies		Phone	Map
Walgreens	641 N Clark St	312-587-1416	2
Walgreens	757 N Michigan Ave	312-664-8686	3
Walgreens	111 S Halsted St	312-[illegible]	4
Dominick's	1 N Halsted St	312-279-8861	4
Walgreens	501 W Roosevelt Rd	312-492-8559	7
Jewel-Osco	1224 S Wabash Ave	312-663-4646	8
Dominick's	1340 S Canal St	312-850-3915	10
Walgreens	316 W Cermak Rd	312-791-0392	10
Dominick's	3145 S Ashland Ave	773-247-2633	12
Walgreens	3405 S Dr MLK Jr Dr	312-326-4058	14
Walgreens	1554 E 55th St	773-667-1177	19
CVS*	2427 W Chicago Ave	773-342-6060	23
Walgreens	1931 W Cermak Rd	773-847-5781	25
Walgreens	2001 N Milwaukee Ave	773-772-2370	28
Dominick's	2550 N Clybourn Ave	773-935-5777	28
Dominick's	959 W Fullerton Ave	773-248-0049	29
Walgreens	1520 W Fullerton Ave	773-929-6968	29
CVS	1714 N Sheffield Ave	312-640-5161	29
Dominick's	424 W Division St	312-274-1299	31
Walgreens	1601 N Wells St	312-642-4008	31
Walgreens	1200 N Dearborn St	312-943-0973	32
CVS	1201 N State Pkwy	312-640-2842	32
Walgreens	7510 N Western Ave	773-764-1765	33
Walgreens	3019 W Peterson Ave	773-728-6254	35
Jewel-Osco*	5343 N Broadway St	773-334-2083	37
Jewel-Osco	5516 N Clark St	773-784-7348	37
Walgreens	5625 N Ridge Ave	773-989-7546	37
Walgreens	3153 W Irving Park Rd	773-588-9196	38
CVS*	4051 N Lincoln Ave	773-871-2611	39
Jewel-Osco	3572 N Elston Ave	773-583-9858	41
Dominick's	3350 N Western Ave	773-929-8910	42
Jewel-Osco*	3400 N Western Ave	773-327-1204	42
CVS*	3944 N Western Ave	773-279-7600	42
Jewel-Osco*	2940 N Ashland Ave	773-871-8242	43
CVS*	3033 N Broadway St	773-883-6141	44
Walgreens	3046 N Halsted St	773-325-0413	44
CVS Pharmacy	3101 N Clark St	773-477-3333	44
Walgreens	3201 N Broadway St	773-327-3591	44

** Store is open 24 hours, but the prescription counter closes at 10 pm.*

Plumbers

Plumbers	Phone
Sunrise Plumbing & Sewer	773-960-6462
Sears HomeCentral	773-737-3580
Roto-Rooter	800-438-7686
O'Bannon Plumbing & Sewer (Southside)	773-862-5112
O'Bannon Plumbing & Sewer (Northside)	773-486-5748
FPS	773-268-4604
Emergency Response	773-736-3247
Apex Plumbing & Sewer	773-477-7714
Action Plumbing & Sewer	773-376-6666
A-AAAA Plumbing & Sewer	773-282-2878
A Metro Plumbing & Sewer Service	877-872-3060
A Better Man Plumbing & Sewer	773-286-9351

Restaurants

Restaurants		Phone	
Plymouth Restaurant	327 S Plymouth Ct	312-362-1212	5
Mr Greek Gyros	234 S Halsted St	312-906-8731	4
White Palace Grill	1159 S Canal St	312-939-7167	7
Kevin's Hamburger Heaven	554 W 39th St	773-924-5771	13
Hollywood Grill	1601 W North Ave	773-395-1818	22
Express Grill	1260 S Union Ave	312-738-2112	26
Tempo	6 E Chestnut St	312-943-4373	32
Deluxe Diner	6349 N Clark St	773-743-8244	34
San Soo Gab San	5247 N Western Ave	773-334-1589	36
Al-Amira	3200 W Lawrence Ave	773-267-0333	38
Golden Apple	2971 N Lincoln Ave	773-528-1413	43
Clark Street Dog	3040 N Clark St	773-281-6690	44
Blue Angel	5310 N Milwaukee Ave	773-631-8700	NW
Izola's	522 E 79th St	773-846-1484	S
Phil's Kastle	3532 E 95th St	773-734-9591	S

Overview

Chicago is widely regarded as a world-class food destination, and rightly so, we say. Midwestern stereotypes of super sports fans inhaling Italian beef and hot links notwithstanding, Chicago is a goldmine for foodies whether they be searching for culinary nirvana at one of the city's big name, high price gastro-palaces where you have to wait weeks, or even months, to get a seat, or at one of the myriad mom-and-pop neighborhood spots where you may be the only English speaker in the place and you know the best dishes aren't always on the menu.

In the past decade, Chicago's adventuresome appetite has come to life. After an era of complacency, during which the city's top dining emporiums basically rested on their laurels, a whole new school of Chicago restaurant has come to the fore. Once fueled by students of the masters—Bayless, Trotter, Gordon Sinclair, and so on—the Chicago dining renaissance is already in its second or third generation, and now the students of the students, those who honed their skills at places like Trio and Tru, are taking the reins as they charge into Chicago's culinary future.

And anyways, you gotta problem with hot links?

What follows is a breakdown of some of our favorite spots, old and new. Of course, with every new restaurant opening, there is likely another one closing. Therefore, we offer this caveat: phone first.

That's Chicago

Some restaurants are more than just places to grab a bite. They're defining institutions of the city. The original **Billy Goat Tavern (Maps 3, 5, 24)** is known to baby boomers as the birthplace of John Belushi's "cheezeboiga" skit, but Chicagoans appreciate it as the dank watering hole where reporters from the Tribune and Sun-Times would once gather after work to talk shop. Today it's mostly frequented by wide-eyed tourists who play at slumming it. "The true originator of Chicago-style pizza" is a title claimed by nearly every pizza shack in town. Of the lot, **Pizzeria Uno's (Map 2)** claim seems the most legit—their recipe dates back to 1943. Other Chicago pizza institutions include **Lou Malnati's (Map 2)** and **Gino's East (Maps 2, 43)**. Equally important is the Chicago Dog—that is, a hot dog on a steamed bun "dragged through the garden" with a virtual salad on top—onions, relish, tomatoes, pickle spears, sport peppers, mustard (no ketchup, thank you very much), and a dash of celery salt. Post-pub dogs at **Weiner's Circle (Map 30)** are a Lincoln Park right-of-passage—the servers are infamous for their saucy attitudes. On the Northwest side, **Superdawg (West)** is a landmark. The vintage dog spot offers classic drive-in (not drive-thru) service. **Manny's Coffeeshop (Map 7)** in the South Loop is where local politicos go to make deals over meals (breakfast or lunch). For dinner they head to **Rosebud (Map 2)** for homestyle Italian. Finally, two Chicago institutions put the city on the international culinary radar. **Frontera Grill (Map 2)** packs 'em in for creative and upscale Mexican fare in a festive environment. For a more subdued experience, **Charlie Trotter's (Map 30)** pushes the culinary envelope with its own exquisite creations.

Noteworthy Newcomers

In an economic era more defined by business closings than openings, a handful of new spots succeeded in distinguishing themselves from the rest. Rick Bayless's new quick service (this is NOT fast food) restaurant, **Xoco (Map 2)** taps into a hunger for quality comfort food at affordable prices. Bucktown's **Belly Shack (Map 28)**, by the family that brought us NFT pick **Urban Belly (Map 41)**, offers affordable and well-executed comfort food with a Latin-Asian flair. With **Nightwood (Map 52)**, Logan Square pioneers Jason Hammel and Amalea Tshilds (**Lula (Map 27)**) are now gambling that Pilsen is ready to support innovative gourmet fare, and according to the accolades, they're right. In a neighborhood with no lack of moderate and upscale casual dining options, East Lakeview's **Chilam Bilam (Map 44)** offers something new to the scene with their fresh, creative Mexican BYOB. But be warned, the cramped cash-only spot only takes reservations for between 5-6 pm. Otherwise, it's first-come first-served.

Final Bow

Over the past year or so, Chicago diners have bid farewell to a number of old stalwarts, a handful of cult favorites, and more than a smattering if trendy-come-latelys. Of the first category, we mourn the loss of Bridgeport's Healthy Foods Lithuanian, where the kugala and sausages were anything but. Pricey Nick's Fishmarket seemed like it had been a part of the Loop dining scene forever. Johnny Rockets... Well, we'll probably recover just fine. Was the past years culinary focus on meat the downfall of cult vegetarian faves Alice & Friends and the Lake Side cafe? As for shuttered restaurant Fixture, we wonder at the irony. Le Lan, O Fame, Mama Desta's Red Sea, Cafe Suron, and Think Cafe will all be missed. Minnie's, which specialized in petite versions of standard bar food, maybe not so much.

Chicago's Best Dining Bets

Hey Big Spender

If you're one of the lucky suckers still feeling flush in the current economy (we'll assume you work for Goldman Sachs), or if you're just trying to max out your credit cards before filing that Chapter 7, here are some of Chicago's spendiest special-occasion options. **Charlie Trotter's (Map 30)** is the classic big bucks splurge--if you really want to go for it, reserve the kitchen table. Other classic spends include **Everest (Map 5)**, **Nomi (Map 3)**, and **Les Nomades (Map 3)**. **Tru (Map 3)** is renowned for its caviar staircase; **Spiaggia (Map 32)** for it's gorgeous lake view. Newcomer on the scene **L2O (Map 30)** defies recession trends by presenting exquisite foods at exquisite prices. For something a little more, um, unusual, Chef Homaro Canto's **Moto (Map 24)**, and James Beard-winner Grant Achatz's **Alinea (Map 30)** are known for pushing culinary frontiers with their clever, high-concept approaches to haute cuisine. On the other, neanderthal end of the spectrum, die-hard carnivores empty their wallets at Chicago classics **Morton's (Map 32)**, David Burke's **Primehouse (Map 2)**, or **Gene & Georgetti (Map 2)**.

Hey Cheapskate

Of course, you don't have to spend a fortune to eat well in Chicago. Cheap taquerias, hot dog stands, and corner grills abound. For a more unique meal, without breaking the bank, we recommend **Sticky Rice (Map 39)** Thai. This super delicious and authentic BYOB Thai spot features such exotic specialties as fried caterpillars and ant-egg omelets along with the usual curry and noodle dishes—all prepared amazingly well, and nothing on the menu tops ten bucks. For a cheap date, **La Creperie (Map 44)** is loaded with low-price charm. This 40-year-old French classic has the shabby look of Parisian authenticity, a gorgeous outdoor patio, and free live French music on Thursday evenings. **Sunshine Cafe (Map 37)** hides some of the cheapest, most delicious Japanese noodles in Chicago behind their modest, unassuming storefront.

Pizza Pizza Pizza

Chicago's a pizza city, and classic spots such as **Pizzeria Uno (Map 2)** and **Lou Malnati's (Maps 2, 21, 29)** attract tourists and suburbanites in droves. Meanwhile, **Candlelite (Map 33)** in Roger's Park has been serving fresh, hot pies to the local community for decades. Another neighborhoodie, **Pete's Pizza (Map 42)**, specializes in cracker-crisp crust and sweet sauce. **Golden Crust (Map 38)** is a family spot in Albany Park that's open (and delivers) very late. **Art of Pizza (Map 43)** has won numerous awards and acclaim for its scrumptious deep dishes. Thin-crust European-style pizzas have taken Chicago by storm. **Pizza D.O.C. (Map 39)**, Chicago's wood-fired pizza pioneer still packs 'em in for excellent, classic pies. Nearby **Spacca Napoli (Map 39)** gives the wood-fired pizza a Neapolitan twist. **Piece (Map 21)** offers precious pies to the Wicker Park crowd, and **Coalfire (Map 24)** is what the name implies—Chicago's first coal-fired pizza joint. And we'd be remiss if we didn't give props to **Great Lake Pizza (Map 37)**. There small-batch artisan pies-of-love have attracted the attention of GQ and national foodie media. Whether it's worth the 3-hour wait is for you to decide.

Vegging Out in Chicago

The phrase "vegetarian Chicago" has often seemed oxymoronic, but just as more mainstream restaurants are introducing more veggie items than the token pasta or risotto, so have more bonafide vegetarian restaurants been appearing on our beefy shores. **Chicago Diner (Map 44)** and **Heartland Café (Map 34)** (which does serve some meat) are the crunchy, old-school standard bearers. Raw foodies flock to **Cousin's Incredible Vitality (Map 38)** and **Karyn's (Map 30)** in Lincoln Park, which attracted such a following for its raw food menu that Karyn opened **Karyn's Cooked (Map 2)** in Old Town. On Devon, **Mysore Woodlands (Map 33)** serves vegetarian food from southern India, while **Arya Bhavan (Map 33)** specializes in Indian vegetarian food from the north and south. **Amitabul (Northwest)** does Vegan Thai on the Northwest side, and **Soul Vegetarian East (South)** in the Southside Chatham neighborhood. For upscale vegetarian, try the **Green Zebra (Map 24)**, or **Mana (Map 21)** in Wicker Park. In Logan Square, down-to-earth scenester spot **Lula (Map 27)** is known for being particularly vegetarian friendly. For a very special night, choose the fixed-price vegetarian tasting menus at **Arun's (Map 38)** or **Charlie Trotter's (Map 30)**. Finally, vegetarians and non-vegetarians alike line up for breakfasts served by followers of Sri Chimnoy at Roscoe Village's popular **Victory's Banner (Map 42)**.

Poor Man's Steak and Other Meaty Matters

In the past few years, **Kuma's Corner (Map 41)** has emerged as the popular and critical favorite for best burger in the city, although northside loyalists stil swear by **Moody's (Map 37)**, and southsiders hanker for **Top Notch Beefburger (Map 103)** and the hand-pressed char-drippy goodness of **That's-A-Burger (Map 104)**. Even the fast food burger has stepped up their game. The Lincoln Park outpost of the California fancy burger chain **Counter (Map 44)** offers dizzying topping options and the "only-in-California" bunless burger, while in the South Loop, **Epic Burger (Map 8)** delivers sustainable grilled ground beef on a bun.

If, on the other hand, you like your meat served on the bone with tangy sauce, head to the **Gale Street Inn (Northwest)** in Jefferson Park, street–festival mainstay **Robinson's (Maps 4, 30)**, Southside stalwart **Leon's Barbeque (South)**, hot links king **Uncle John's Barbecue (Map 104)** or **Logan Square's Calvin's BBQ (Map 27)** and **Honey 1 (Map 28)**. **Smoque (Northwest)** attracts droolers from all over the city for, arguably, Chicago's best 'cue. As for encased meats, Chicago has no lack of options--just follow the Vienna Beef signs. For something different, try encased exotic meats such as ostrich or wild boar at **Hot Doug's (Map 41)**, a destination stop for top chefs from around the world. On weekends, they feature french fries cooked in duck fat (and lines out the door).

Soul Food and Southern Cooking

We say soul food is the most American of American cuisines. On the south side, you can't go wrong with **Army & Lou's (South)**—it's a Chicago legend. **Valois (Map 19)** serves no frills, cafeteria-style soul food. **Miss Lee's Good Food (Map 18)** offers gut-busting Southern food for carry-out only, or bring your family and eat in at **Captain's Hard Time Diner (South)**. **Soul Queen (South)** cafeteria may have seen better days, but history is written in the photos on the walls. On the west side, stuff yourself silly at **Edna's** on Madison **(West)**. For Cajun food, try Chicago breakfast staple **Wishbone (Maps 24, 42)** or Jimmy Banno's famous **Heaven on Seven (Maps 3, 5)**. **Negro League Café (Map 16)** serves up soul, Cajun, and Caribbean fare. Yes, please.

Passport to Good Eating

Culinarily, you can travel the world and never leave Chicago. While some of Chicago's dining emporiums fly high on the local radar, we have a soft spot for the ramshackle storefronts where the home cooking's happening. You don't have to live in Chicago a long time to discover that Devon Street is the place to go if you crave Indian food. We love **Hema's Kitchen (Map 33)**, and the Pakistani fare at **Ghareeb Nawaz (Map 34)**. Pilsen is the destination neighborhood for Mexican muy authentico. **Nuevo Leon (Map 26)** has been serving revelatory Mexican home cooking for ages, and **Birreria**

Reyes de Ocatlan (Map 26) is a favorite of celebrity chef Rick Bayless. Off the Pilsen path, **Birrierra Zaragoza (West)** serves a traditional goat stew that really shouldn't be missed. The city's best Vietnamese can be found in the New Saigon section of Argyle Street, right under the L stop, and Albany Park is the place to go for Middle Eastern and Korean fare. Of the former, we think the classic felafel sandwiches at **Dawali (Map 38)** really are something special, stuffed with potatoes and cauliflower as well as the formed garbanzo balls. Of the latter, **Kang Nam (Map 38)** may be the best Korean BBQ in the city, but watch out because the shrewd servers will try to get you to order way more food than you want or need. The greater northwest side is bountiful with Eastern European restaurants and supper clubs. We love the insane portions, low prices and cozy vibe of **Paul Zakopane's Harnas Restaurant (Northwest)**. You'll find plenty of great African and Caribbean food behind no-frills storefronts in Roger's Park. Order the delicious Sengalese fare at **La Conakry (Map 34)** to go to avoid their gloomy dining room. **As for Good to Go Jamaican Jerk and Juice Bar (Map 34)**, the name says it all. We shouldn't have to tell you to head to Chinatown for dim sum, or Greek Town for flaming cheese. Perhaps one of the most surreal ethnic dining experiences in Chicago is the Thursday night-only all-you-can-eat Korean vegan buffet at **Dragon Lady Lounge (Map 41)**, the ultimate dive bar.

Breakfast

Okay, so you're one of those annoying people who manages to be up, dressed, and ready to go before noon. Good for friggin' you. Why don't you get out of my face and go eat at one of these popular breakfast /brunch spots: **Sweet Maple Café (Map 26)**, **Orange (Map 8, 43)**, **Ina's (Map 24)**, **Flo (Map 24)**, **Yolk (Map 9)**, **Pannenkoeken Café (Map 39)**, or **Tweet (Map 40)**.

Diners

Because sometimes you just want a cup of joe and a patty melt. We recommend: **Salt and Pepper Diner (Maps 29, 43)**, **Nookie's Tree (Map 44)**, **Ramova Grill (Map 13)**, **Salonica Grill (Map 19)**, **Lou Mitchell's (Map 4)**, **Manny's Coffee Shop (Map 7)**, **Hollywood Grill (Map 28)**, **The Golden Apple (Map 43)**, **The Golden Angel (Map 39)**, and, last but in no way least, **The S&G (Map 43)**, a.k.a. Sam and George's.

Foodies on the Web

Both professional food critics and the vox populi weigh in on the popular restaurant sites of the Chicago Reader (www.chicagoreader.com) and the Chicago Tribune's Metromix (chicago.metromix.com). Both offer search categories, so you can find places by location, price, type of cuisine, etc. If you're going somewhere off–the–beaten path, however, be sure to phone first—Metromix, in particular, often seems to be out–of–date.

Chicago Magazine's food editors will deliver the latest Chicago food gossip directly to your inbox every week or so, along with chef interviews, links, and whatever food ephemera amuses them. Subscribe to Dish for free at the Chicago Magazine website (www.chicagomag.com).

Professional chefs and passionate lay folk chat about both the latest hot spots and hidden neighborhood gems on the LTH Forum (www.lthforum.com). The foodie debates, all in the spirit of fun, can get raucous, and sometimes even local celebrity chefs enter the fore to throw down. A warning: regular posting on the LTH Forum is a tell-tale sign of your descent down the slippery slope of food geekdom.

Get it Delivered

Finally, housebound Chicagoans all hail the arrival on the scene of Grub Hub, an internet site that hooks you up with all the places that deliver to your house, and make it easy to reference past orders, save menus and order online, all from one convenient site: www.grubhub.com.

Key: $: Under $10 / $$: $10–$20 / $$$: $20–$30 / $$$$: $30–$40 / $$$$$: $40+
** : Does not accept credit cards. / † : Accepts only American Express. / † †: Accepts only Visa and Mastercard*
Time listed refers to kitchen closing time on weekend nights.

Map 1 • River North / Fulton Market District

Blue 13	416 W Ontario St	312-787-1400	$$$		Contemporary American food...on acid.
Carnivale	702 W Fulton St	312-850-5005	$$$	11:30 pm	Authentic, soulful Latin fusion cuisine.
Iguana Café	517 N Halsted St	312-432-0663	$	2 am	Internet cafe with bagels and such.
Japonais	600 W Chicago Ave	312-822-9600	$$$	11:30 pm	Elegant, way-upscale Asian.
La Scarola	721 W Grand Ave	312-243-1740	$$	11 pm	Authentic Italian in a super-close atmosphere.
Orange	730 W Grand Ave	312-942-0300	$$	3pm	Decadent brunch and hot coffee.
Piccolo Sogno	464 N Halsted St	312-421-0077	$$$$	11 pm	You wish your mama in the old country cooked this good.
Publican	837 W Fulton Market	312-733-9555	$$$	11:30 pm	Much buzzed new Kahan joint is meat and beer lover's nirvana.
Reza's	432 W Ontario St	312-664-4500	$$$	12 am	Huge portions of Persian fare.
Scoozi!	410 W Huron St	312-943-5900	$$	10 pm	Once-trendy Italian has had its day.
Steve's Deli	354 W Hubbard St	312-467-6868	$$	8pm	New York style deli, checkerboard tablecloths and all.
Zealous	419 W Superior St	312-475-9112	$$$$	10 pm	Over-the-top gourmet from Trotter protégé.

Map 2 • Near North / River North

1492 Tapas Bar	42 E Superior St	312-867-1492	$$	2 am	Tasty tapas in River North graystone.
A Mano	335 N Dearborn St	312-629-3500	$$$	11 pm	Hand-tossed thin pizzas.
Avenues	108 E Superior St	312-573-6754	$$$$$	10:30 pm	Sophisticated menu with a view.
Ben Pao	52 W Illinois St	312-222-1888	$$	11 pm	Upscale Chinese spot.
Brasserie Jo	59 W Hubbard St	312-595-0800	$$$	11 pm	Swanky French.
Brett's Kitchen	233 W Superior St	312-664-6354	$	4 pm	Charming breakfast and sandwich stop.
Café Iberico	739 N La Salle St	312-573-1510	$	1:30 am	Shoulder-to-shoulder tapas joint.
Castel Gandolfo	800 N Dearborn St	312-787-2211	$$		Less magnificent than the name implies.
Chicago Chop House	60 W Ontario St	312-787-7100	$$$$$	11:30 pm	Old-school steaks meet old-school politicos and similar characters.
Club Lago	331 W Superior St	312-951-2849	$$	11 pm	Generous servings of basic Italian.
Coco Pazzo	300 W Hubbard St	312-836-0900	$$$$$	11 pm	Hearty, high-end Italian.
Crofton on Wells	535 N Wells St	312-755-1790	$$$	11 pm	Pushing the envelope with some top regional cuisine.
Cyrano's Bistrot & Wine Bar	546 N Wells St	312-467-0546	$$	10:30 pm	Steak frites!
David Burke's Primehouse	616 N Rush St	312-660-6000	$$$$$	12 am	Aged steaks by former Smith & Wollensky VP.
English	444 N Lasalle St	312-222-6200	$$	3am	Crab burgers and other above-average pub food.
Farmerie 58	58 E Ontario St	312-440-1818	$$$$	11 pm	Sustainable if rather uninspired menu. Duck egg rolls again?
Fulton's on the River	315 N La Salle St	312-822-0100	$$$$	11 pm	Best. Oysters. In. Chicago.
Gene & Georgetti	500 N Franklin St	312-527-3718	$$$$$	12 am	Big steaks.
Gino's East	633 N Wells St	312-943-1124	$$	11 pm	Legendary deep dish pizza since 1966.
Ginza Restaurant	19 E Ohio St	312-222-0600	$$	10 pm	Unhip and unsung sushi.
Graham Elliot	217 W Huron St	312-624-9975	$$$$	10:30 pm	Over the top food gimmickry puts the irk in quirky.
Karyn's Cooked	738 N Wells St	312-587-1050	$$	10 pm	Hot vegetarian by the queen of raw food.
Keefer's	20 W Kinzie St	312-467-9525	$$$	11:30 pm	French-influenced steakhouse.
Kinzie Chophouse	400 N Wells St	312-822-0191	$$$	11 pm	Neighborhood steak house.
Klay Oven	414 N Orleans St	312-527-3999	$$	10 pm	Upscale Indian buffet.
Lawry's The Prime Rib	100 E Ontario St	312-787-5000	$$$	11 pm	Carnivore's delight.
Lou Malnati's Pizzeria	439 N Wells St	312-828-9800	$	12 am	Famous in a city famous for pizza.
Maggiano's Little Italy	516 N Clark St	312-644-7700	$$	11 pm	Gut-busting family-style Italian.
The Melting Pot	609 N Dearborn St	312-573-0011	$$$$$	2am	Cheesy indeed.
Mr Beef	666 N Orleans St	312-337-8500	$*	5 pm	Get your Italian beef fix at this tried-and-true Chicago classic.
Nacional 27	325 W Huron St	312-664-2727	$$$	11 pm	Pan-Latin supper club with dance floor. Babaloo!
Naha	500 N Clark St	312-321-6242	$$$$	10 pm	Mediterranean-inspired luxury.
Osteria Via Stato	620 N State St	312-642-8450	$$$$	11 pm	Menu-oriented Italian. Fancy, but reasonably priced.
Pizzeria Uno	29 E Ohio St	312-321-1000	$	1 am	Legendary Chicago pizza.
Quartino	626 N State St	312-698-5000	$$$	12 am	Trendy Italian small plates and house-cured salami.
Rosebud on Rush	720 N Rush St	312-266-6444	$$	12 am	A branch of Chicago's legendary, old-school Italian.
Roy's	720 N State St	312-787-7599	$$$	10 pm	Pretty Hawaiian contemporary cuisine.
Ruth's Chris Steak House	431 N Dearborn St	312-321-2725	$$$$	11:30 pm	Consistent steak chain.
Shanghai Terrace	108 E Superior St	312-573-6695	$$$$	11 pm	The city's most extravagant Chinese restaurant.
Shaw's Crab House & Blue Crab Lounge	21 E Hubbard St	312-527-2722	$$$$	11 pm	A seafood destination.
Smith & Wollensky	318 N State St	312-670-9900	$$$$	11 pm	Chicago branch of New York steak emporium.
Soupbox	50 E Chicago Ave	312-951-5900	$	11pm	12 fresh soups every day!
Sullivan's Steakhouse	415 N Dearborn St	312-527-3510	$$$$	11 pm	Another upscale steakhouse.
Sunda	110 W Illinois St	312-644-0500	$$$$	1 am	Pretentious "New Asian" for folks with more attitude than taste.
Sushi Naniwa	607 N Wells St	312-255-8555	$$	11 pm	Quality sushi. Great outdoor.
Tizi Melloul	531 N Wells St	312-670-4338	$$$	11 pm	Exotic setting for Moroccan tangines.
Topolobampo	445 N Clark St	312-661-1434	$$$$	10:30 pm	Standard bearer for upscale Mexican.
Vermillion	10 W Hubbard St	312-527-4060	$$$	11 pm	Indian-Latin fusion—what next?
Wildfire	159 W Erie St	312-787-9000	$$	11 pm	Fun, trendy American.
XOCO	449 N Clark St	312-334-3688	$$		Mexican food guru Rick Bayless's most affordable cantina.
Yolk	747 N Wells St	312-787-2277	$$	3pm	Sunny egg-fucussed breakfast and brunch.
Zocalo	358 W Ontario St	312-302-9977	$$	12am	Fresh guacamole flights, flaming cheese and tons of tequila.

Map 3 • Streeterville / Mag Mile

Atrium Wine Bar	401 E Illinois St	312-379-0132			River views for the wine and cheese crowd.
Bandera	535 N Michigan Ave	312-644-3524	$$	11 pm	Lunch above Mag Mile.
Billy Goat Tavern	430 N Michigan Ave	312-222-1525	$*	2 am	Cheezboiga; no fries, chips; pepsi, no coke.
Boston Blackies	164 E Grand Ave	312-938-8700	$$	11pm	Mag Mile burgers in a beautiful Deco setting.
Capital Grille	633 N St Clair St	312-337-9400	$$$$	11 pm	Macho steak and zin.
De La Costa	465 E Illinois St	312-464-1700	$$$$	12am	Buzz-worthy upscale pan-Latin.
D4 Irish Pub & Cafe	345 E Ohio St	312-624-8385	$$$	1 am	Upscale Irish pub with a copy of the Book of Kells.
De La Costa	465 E Illinois St	312-321-8930	$$$$	12 am	Buzz-worthy upscale pan-Latin.
Emilio's Tapas Sol y Nieve	215 E Ohio St	312-467-7177	$$$	12 am	One of the nicest branches of the local tapas chain.
Fox & Obel Café	401 E Illinois St	312-379-0112	$$	9 pm	Creative café grub with gourmet ingredients from next-door market.
Grand Lux Cafe	600 N Michigan Ave	312-276-2500	$$$	12 am	A Mag Mile vittle and view indulgence. Go ahead, be a tourist!
Heaven on Seven	600 N Michigan Ave	312-280-7774	$$	11 pm	Cajun grub and cocktails.
Indian Garden	247 E Ontario St	312-280-4910	$$	10:30 pm	Good veggie options.
Kamehachi	240 E Ontario St	312-587-0600	$$	12 am	Old school sushi spot.
Les Nomades	222 E Ontario St	312-649-9010	$$$$$	10 pm	Deluxe haute cuisine.
Nomi	800 N Michigan Ave	312-239-4030	$$$$$	10 pm	Deluxe French fusion.
Sayat Nova	157 E Ohio St	312-644-9159	$$	10 pm	Armenian.
Tru	676 N St Clair St	312-202-0001	$$$$$	11:30 pm	Dazzling contemporary cuisine.
Volare	201 E Grand Ave	312-410-9900	$$$	11 pm	Casual Italian.

Map 4 • West Loop Gate / Greek Town

9 Muses	315 S Halsted St	312-902-9922	$$$	2 am	Brick bars and backgammon.
Athena	212 S Halsted St	312-655-0000	$$$	1 am	Goddess Athena-inspired outdoor and indoor.
Avec	615 W Randolph St	312-377-2002	$$	1 am	Small plates, big flavors, chefs' hangout. 'Nuff said.
Blackbird	619 W Randolph St	312-715-0708	$$$$	11:30 pm	Chic les plus ultra.
Bombacigno's J & C Inn	558 W Van Buren St	312-663-4114	$		Traditional Italian subs.
DeCero	814 W Randolph St	312-455-8114	$$$	11pm	Made-to-order tacos, fresh fruit cocktail, Mexican heaven.
Dine	733 W Madison St	312-602-2100	$$$	11 pm	Martinis and comfort food at the Crowne Plaza.
Girl & The Goat	809 W Randolph St	312-492-6262	$$$		Small plates from *Top Chef* winner Stephanie Izard make Chicago foodies go gaga.
Gold Coast Dogs	225 S Canal St	312-258-8585	$*	10 pm	Gotta have the dogs.
Greek Islands	200 S Halsted St	312-782-9855	$$$	1 am	Noisy, fun crowd-pleasing spectacle.
J&C Inn	558 W Van Buren St	312-663-4114	$$$	2 pm	Dingy outside—best sandwiches in town inside.
Jubilee Juice	140 N Halsted St	312-491-8500	$$	10pm	A Better Smoothie.
Lou Mitchell's	565 W Jackson Blvd	312-939-3111	$*	3 pm	Rub shoulders with local pols at this legendary grill.
Meli	301 S Halsted St	312-454-0748	$	3 pm	Brunch spot makes us wanna challah.
Mr Greek Gyros	234 S Halsted St	312-906-8731	$		The best late night gyro spot in the city, hands down.
N9ne	440 W Randolph St	312-575-9900	$$$	12 am	Toast marshmallows at the table at this ultra-trendy contemporary spot.
Parthenon	314 S Halsted St	312-726-2407	$$$	12 am	Creators of flaming saganaki!
Pegasus Restaurant and Taverna	130 S Halsted St	312-226-3377	$$$	12:45 am	Rooftop garden—Chicago secret!
Perez	853 W Randolph St	312-421-2488	$$		Standard Mexican fare, outstanding pico de gallo.
Province	161 N Jefferson St	312-669-9900	$$	11:30	Ambitious organic fare strikes hits and misses.
Red Light	820 W Randolph St	312-733-8880	$$$$	12 am	Fusion of Asian dishes in a oriental atmosphere.
Robinson's No 1 Ribs	225 S Canal St	312-258-8477	$	7:30 pm	Dress down and dig in.
Rodity's	222 S Halsted St	312-454-0800	$$$	1 am	Greek lamb since 1972.
Santorini	800 W Adams St	312-829-8820	$$$	1 am	Fish, shellfish, and roasted chicken. Yum.
Sepia	123 N Jefferson St	312-441-1920	$$$$	10:30 pm	Contemp. American with flare.
Sushi Wabi	842 W Randolph St	312-563-1224	$$$	12 am	Self-consciously chic sushi.
Takumi	555 W Madison St	312-258-1010	$$		Tiny sushi spot with excellent lunch specials.
Veerasway	844 W Randolph St	312-491-0844	$$$	11 pm	Modernized, stylish Indian by Sushi Wabi and De Cero team.
Vivo	838 W Randolph St	312-733-3379	$$$$	12am	Restaurants Row's first residence of Italian dining.

Map 5 • The Loop

Atwood Café	1 W Washington St	312-368-1900	$$$	11 pm	High tea with contemporary flair.
Caffe Rom	71 S Wacker Dr	312-379-0291	$$		A slice of modern Milan in the Loop.
Everest	440 S La Salle St	312-663-8920	$$$$$	10 pm	Classic fine dining experience with a knock-out view.
Frontera Fresco	111 N State St	312-781-4884	$$	4 pm	Popular Mexican joint.
Goodwin's	175 N Franklin St	312-634-1134	$	3.30pm	Great West Loop sandwiches and wraps.
Hannah's Bretzel	180 W Washington St	312-621-1111	$	6 pm	Homemade pretzels and organic lunch fare.
Heaven on Seven	111 N Wabash Ave	312-263-6443	$$	5 pm	Cajun Chicago classic. Closed for dinner.
Jaffa Bakery	186 W Van Buren St	312-322-9007	$	3.30pm	Best fresh turkey you will ever taste.
La Cantina Enoteca	71 W Monroe St	312-332-7005	$$	12 am	Casual Italian with seafood specialty.
La Rosetta	70 W Madison St	312-332-9500	$$	9 pm	Family-style Italian.
Oasis Café	21 N Wabash Ave	312-558-1058	$$	5 pm	Middle Eastern hideout inside of a jewelry store.
Plymouth Restaurant	327 S Plymouth Ct	312-362-1212	$	24 hrs.	24-hour diner with bar and grill.
Potbelly Sandwich Works	1 N LaSalle	312-279-0436	$	7 pm	Better than Subway
Russian Tea Time	77 E Adams St	312-360-0000	$$$	12 am	Rich food. Richer interior. Copious amounts of vodka.
Salad Spinners	200 W Monroe St	312-269-5300	$	3pm	Salad chain. Lettuce 4ever.
Trattoria No 10	10 N Dearborn St	312-984-1718	$$$	10 pm	Popular pre-theater.
The Village	71 W Monroe St	312-332-7005	$$	1 am	Quaint, casual Italian looks like a village.
Vivere	71 W Monroe St	312-332-4040	$$$	11 pm	Dated Italian luxury.
Wow Bao	175 W Jackson Blvd	312-334-6395	$	6.30pm	Nice buns.

Map 6 • The Loop / Grant Park

Aria	200 N Columbus Dr	312-444-9494	$$$$	11 pm	Artistic, creative pan-global grub.
Artist's Café	412 S Michigan Ave	312-939-7855	$$	11 pm	Sit at the counter. They've got the chattiest waiters in town.
China Grill	230 N Michigan Ave	312-334-6700	$$$$$	11 pm	Les So Very Tres.
The Gage	24 S Michigan Ave	312-372-4243	$$	12 am	Classy brews, burgers and meat.
The Green at Grant Park	352 E Monroe St	312-987-1818	$$	9.30 pm	Did you make a birdie? Celebrate with a cocktail on the patio.
Park Grill	11 N Michigan Ave	312-521-7275	$$$	10:30 pm	Contemporary American cooking in Millenium Park.

Map 7 • South Loop / River City

Bake for Me	608 W Roosevelt Rd	312-957-1994	$	2 pm	Good coffee and pastries.
Manny's Coffee Shop	1141 S Jefferson St	312-939-2855	$	8 pm	Famous deli—popular with politicians.
White Palace Grill	1159 S Canal St	312-939-7167	$	24-hrs	An ode to grease, and some fine omelettes to boot.

Map 8 • South Loop / Printers Row / Dearborn Park

Amarit	600 S Dearborn St	312-939-1179	$$	11 pm	Pretty good Thai.
Blackie's	755 S Clark St	312-786-1161	$	10 pm	A famous burger, lesser-known best breakfast in South Loop on Fri, Sat, Sun.
Custom House	500 S Dearborn St	312-523-0200	$$$$	10 pm	Shaun McClain does steak house.
Eleven City Diner	1112 S Wabash Ave	312-212-1112	$$	12 am	Traditional Jewish deli.
Epic Burger	517 S State St	312-913-1373	$$	12 am	Organic fast food burger joint featuring grass-fed beef. Eye roll.
Hackney's	733 S Dearborn St	312-461-1116	$$	11:30 pm	A specialty burger and onion loaf; a north shore legend since 1939.
Mercat a La Planxa	638 S Michigan Ave	312-765-0524	$$$	11 pm	Precious Catalan tapas, or a whole suckling pig (with 48 hour notice).
South Loop Club	701 S State St	312-427-2787	$	2 am	Very casual bar/restaurant with surprisingly good kitchen.
SRO	610 S Dearborn St	312-360-1776	$$	8 pm	Boasting Chicago's #1 Turkey Burger.
Tamarind	614 S Wabash Ave	312-379-0970	$$	11 pm	Sushi and Pan-Asian; sake-based "fruitinis."
Trattoria Caterina	616 S Dearborn St	312-939-7606	$$	9 pm	A little touch of Italy, and a great value for Italian cuisine.

Map 9 • South Loop / South Michigan Ave

Oysy	888 S Michigan Ave	312-922-1127	$$$	11 pm	Chic, industrial sushi setting.
Yolk	1120 S Michigan Ave	312-789-9655	$$	3 pm	Bright, clean brunch spot with eggs o'plenty.

Map 10 • East Pilsen / Chinatown

Chi Cafe	2160 S Archer Ave	312-842-9993	$	12 am	Crowd-pleasing Pan-Asian.
Double Li	228 W Cermak Rd	312-842-7818	$$	10 pm	Authenic Schezuan in nondescript space.
Emperor's Choice	2238 S Wentworth Ave	312-225-8800	$	12 am	Start with seafood; finish with tea.
Evergreen	2411 S Wentworth Ave	312-225-8898	$$	12 am	More upscale than most Chinatown grub.
Happy Chef Dim Sum House	2164 S Archer Ave	312-808-3689	$	2 am	Entrees priced to try several dishes.
Joy Yee's Noodles	2139 S China Pl	312-328-0001	$$	10:30 pm	Huge portions of Korean and Chinese, plus bubble tea.
Lao Sze Chuan Spicy City	2172 S Archer Ave	312-326-5040	$	12 am	Authentic Chinese dishes plus great evening karaoke.
Phoenix	2131 S Archer Ave	312-328-0848	$	11 pm	The best Chinese breakfast in town.
Saint's Alp Teahouse	2131 S Archer Ave	312-842-1886	$	10.30pm	Hong Kong chain bears bubble tea.
Shui Wah	2162 S Archer Ave	312-255-8811	$	3 pm	Stand-out Chinatown dim-sum.
Three Happiness	209 W Cermak Rd	312-842-1964	$	24-hrs	Long waits for dim sum.
Won Kow	2237 S Wentworth Ave	312-842-7500	$	12 am	Cheap, tasty dim sum.

Map 11 • South Loop / McCormick Place

Chef Luciano	49 E Cermak Rd	312-326-0062	$$	7 pm	Walk-in restaurant with eclectic entrees; Italian/African/Cajun influences.
Chicago Firehouse Restaurant	1401 S Michigan Ave	312-786-1401	$$$$	10:30 pm	Transformed Chicago firehouse complete with pole and fine dining.
Cuatro	2030 S Wabash Ave	312-842-8856	$$$	11 pm	Trendy atmosphere for pan-Latin grub.
Gioco	1312 S Wabash Ave	312-939-3870	$$$	12 am	Great Italian dining.
Kroll's	1736 S Michigan Ave	312-235-1400	$$	11 pm	Chicago outpost of Green Bay grill. Packers Backers better watch their backs.
La Cantina Grill	1911 S Michigan Ave	312-842-1911	$$	11 pm	Comfy Mexican with no surprises.
Opera	1301 S Wabash Ave	312-461-0161	$$$	12 am	Theatrical Asian grub.
Tapas Valencia	1530 S State St	312-842-4444	$$	11 pm	Par for the course tapas for the South Loop.
Triad	1933 S Indiana Ave	312-225-8833	$$$	12 am	Guess what? Another sleek sushi lounge.
Zapatista	1307 S Wabash Ave	312-435-1307	$$	11 pm	Fancified Mexican food in big, loud environment.

Map 13 • Bridgeport (East)

Carbón	300 W 26th St	312-225-3200	$	11 pm	So what if they use gas? The food is still delicious.
Franco's Ristorante	300 W 31st St	312-225-9566	$$	10 pm	Family-style Italian near Sox park.
Freddie's Pizza & Pasta Parlor	701 W 31st St	312-808-0149	$	11 pm	Italian ice, beef sandwiches, and appropriate attitude.
Gio's	2724 S Lowe Ave	312-225-6368	$	9 pm	BYO Italian deli with groceries.
Kevin's Hamburger Heaven	554 W 39th St	773-924-5771	$*	24-hrs	Hamburgers and milkshakes.
Minnie Minoso's All Star Stand	333 W 35th St	312-559-1212			Multifarious food offerings between innings.
Pancho Pistola's	700 W 31st St	312-225-8808	$$	12 am	Two words: Eggs and beans.
Phil's Pizza	3551 S Halsted St	773-523-0947	$	1:30 am	Pizza-rific.
Ramova Grill	3510 S Halsted St	773-847-9058	$*	5 pm	Old-school diner.
Schaller's Pump	3714 S Halsted St	773-376-6332	$	10 pm	Try the steak sandwiches and hash browns.
Stages	657 W 31st St	312-225-0396	$	10pm	Fuel up at this diner attached to a gas station.
Wing Yip Chop Suey	537 W 26th St	312-326-2822	$*	9 pm	Nader bumper sticker on window.

Map 14 • Prairie Shores / Lake Meadows

Hong Kong Delight	327 E 35th St	312-842-2929	$$	10 pm	Not quite like being there, but close enough.
Pearl's Place	3901 S Michigan Ave	773-285-1700	$	7:45 pm	Mama's soul food at a snail's pace.

Map 15 • Canaryville / Fuller Park

Amelia's Bar & Grill	4559 S Halsted St	773-538-8200	$$	9 pm	Accomplished menu as surprising as their unlikely locale.

Map 16 • Bronzeville

Ain't She Sweet	4532 S Cottage Grove Ave	773-373-3530	$	6 pm	Fresh, hearty sandwiches, yummy treats and uncompromised service.
Blu 47	4655 S King Dr	773-536-6000	$$$	10:15 pm	Buppie hotspot, overpriced with stingy portions, but great bar.
Harold's Chicken Shack	108 E 47th St	773-285-8362	$*	4 am	It may say #7 but it is #1 around here.
Sweet Potatoes Café	501 E 47th St	773-536-5555	$	10 pm	Soul food like your auntie makes, but not better than grandma's.

Map 17 • Kenwood

Fung's Chop Suey	1400 E 47th St	773-924-2328	$*	10:30 pm	When you're thinking delivery.
Lake Shore Café	4900 S Lake Shore Dr	773-288-5800	$$	10 pm	Basic hotel food.
Original Pancake House	1517 E Hyde Park Blvd	773-288-2323	$*	5 pm	A pancake style for every person.

Map 18 • Washington Park

Miss Lee's Good Food	205 E Garfield Blvd	773-752-5253	$	11 pm	Soul food carry-out by ex-Gladys' Luncheonette.

Map 19 • Hyde Park

Backstory Cafe	6100 S Blackstone Ave	773-324-9987	$	4pm	Socially responsible, great vibe, checkers, and chess.
Bonjour Café Bakery	1550 E 55th St	773-241-5300	$	7 pm	Have a pastry and be seen.
C'Est Si Bon	5225 S Harper Ave	773-363-4123	$$	4 pm	Go for Sunday Brunch.
Calypso Café	5211 S Harper Ave	773-955-0229	$$	11 pm	Good Caribbean. Great drinks.
Cedars Mediterranean Kitchen	1206 E 53rd St	773-324-6227	$$	10 pm	Great food, horrible service.
Chant	1509 E 53rd St	773-324-1999	$$$	12 am	Upscale Asian for Hyde Parkers.
Daley's Restaurant	809 E 63rd St	773-643-0070	$$*	9 pm	The mayor ought to try this place.
Harold's Chicken	1208 E 53rd St	773-752-9260	$	11.30pm	Buckets and buckets of crispy, crumbling chicken. Best in the 'hood.
Hyde Park Gyros	1368 E 53rd St	773-947-8229	$*	10 pm	Gyros and Fried Mushrooms-yum!
Istria Cafe	1520 E 57th St	773-955-2556	$	7pm	Gelato, almost like in Italy.
Kikuya Japanese Restaurant	1601 E 55th St	773-667-3727	$$	9:30 pm	Best sushi in the neighborhood.
La Petite Folie	1504 E 55th St	773-493-1394	$$$$	10 pm	The only haute cuisine in the neighborhood. Expensive and worth it.
Maravilla's Mexican Restaurant	5211 S Harper Ave	773-643-3155	$	11 pm	Cheap, good Mexican. Stinging salsa. Open real late.
Medici on 57th	1327 E 57th St	773-667-7394	$	12 am	The essence of life at U of C.
Mellow Yellow	1508 E 53rd St	773-667-2000	$	11 pm	Comfort food for morning and night.
Nathan's	1372 E 53rd St	773-288-5353	$	10 pm	A Taste of Jamaica.
Park 52	5201 S Harper Ave	773-241-5200	$$$	11 pm	Classic American supper club comfort food in bold, Jerry Kleiner setting.
Pepe's Mexican Food	1310 E 53rd St	773-752-9300	$	10pm	Damn fine guacamole. You might want it when you're high.
Rajun Cajun	1459 E 53rd St	773-955-1145	$	9.30pm	Neon lights oversee the marriage of chicken tikka masala and cornbread.
Ribs 'N Bibs	5300 S Dorchester Ave	773-493-0400	$	1 am	Finger lickin'. Wear the bib.
Salonica	1440 E 57th St	773-752-3899	$*	9:30 pm	Where to go the morning after.
Sammy's Touch	5659 S Cottage Grove Ave	773-288-2645	$	8pm	Gyros like you once had from a street stall in New York.
The Sit Down Cafe & Sushi Bar	1312 E 53rd St	773-324-2700	$$	10.30pm	Sake with your caprese salad? Must be fusion.
Thai 55 Restaurant	1607 E 55th St	773-363-7119	$	10 pm	Good Americanized Thai.
Valois	1518 E 53rd St	773-667-0647	$*	10 pm	See Your Food.

Map 20 • East Hyde Park / Jackson Park

Café Corea	1603 E 55th St	773-288-1795	$	9 pm	Cozy Café.
Morry's Deli	5500 S Cornell Ave	773-363-3800	$*	7:45 pm	Good on the go.
Nile Restaurant	1611 E 55th St	773-324-9499	$	9 pm	Varied Middle Eastern.
Piccolo Mondo	1642 E 56th St	773-643-1106	$$	9:30 pm	Best Italian in the area.
Siam Thai Cuisine	1639 E 55th St	773-324-9296	$	10 pm	More Thai in Hyde Park.
Snail's Thai Cuisine	1649 E 55th St	773-667-5423	$	10 pm	Great Hyde Park Thai.
Thai 55 Restaurant	1607 E 55th St	773-363-7119	$	10pm	Good Americanized Thai.

Map 21 • Wicker Park / Ukrainian Village

Big Star	1531 N Damen Ave	773-235-4039	$$	2am	Pretty long wait, pretty good tacos, pretty pretty people.
Bin Wine Cafe	1559 N Milwaukee Ave	773-486-2233	$$	1 am	Casual swirl and nosh.
Birchwood Kitchen	2211 W North Ave	773-276-2100	$	8 pm	Sophisticated sandwiches for grown-ups.
Bite Cafe	1039 N Western Ave	773-395-2483	$	11:30 pm	Eat here, then Empty your Bottle next door.
Blue Line Club Car	1548 N Damen Ave	773-395-3700	$$	2 am	Mix a diner with a Martini club and here you go.
Bluefin	1952 W North Ave	773-394-7373	$$$	12 am	Upscale, trendy sushi bar.
Bob San	1805 W Division St	773-235-8888	$$$$	12:30 pm	Youthful sushi joint.
The Bongo Room	1470 N Milwaukee Ave	773-489-0690	$	2.30pm	Great breakfast spot, expect to wait on weekends.
Earwax	1561 N Milwaukee Ave	773-772-4019	$$*	12 am	Wicker Park staple and eclectic health food mecca.
Fifty/50	2047 W Division St	773-489-5050	$	1am	Great inexpensive food.
Feast	1616 N Damen Ave	773-772-7100	$$$	11 pm	Popular for Sunday brunch.
Flash Taco	1570 N Damen Ave	773-772-1997	$*	5 am	Cheap late-night tacos.
Handlebar	2311 W North Ave	773-384-9546	$$	12 am	Bicycle-themed (largely) vegetarian restaurants decorated with off-duty messengers.

Jam	937 N Damen Ave	773-489-0302	$$	-	Open for breakfast and lunch.
Jerry's Wicker Park	1938 W Division St	773-235-1006	$$	2 am	Jerry's knows good sandwiches, and isn't afraid to... make them.
Las Palmas	1835 W North Ave	773-289-4991	$	12 pm	Great al fresco Mexican goes beyond the norm.
Letiza's Natural Bakery	2144 W Division St	773-342-1011	$	11 pm	Addictive sweets and savory fare that holds its own
Mana Food Bar	1742 W Division St	773-342-1742	$$	11 pm	Gourmet vegetarian with a global influence.
Milk & Honey	1920 W Division St	773-395-9434	$	4 pm	Heaven for breakfast.
Mirai Sushi	2020 W Division St	773-862-8500	$$	11 pm	Chic dining and good sushi.
People Lounge	1560 N Milwaukee Ave	773-227-9339	$$	2 pm	Traditional tapas with international groove.
Picante	2016 W Division St	773-328-8800	$*	2:30 am	Very very very very very small taqueria.
Piece Bar	1927 W North Ave	773-772-4422	$$	-	Beer. Pizza.
Santullo's Eatery	1943 W North Ave	773-227-7960	$	3am	New York-style thin crust pizza in a deep dish town.
Smoke Daddy	1804 W Division St	773-772-6656	$	1 am	Barbecue and blues.
Spring	2039 W North Ave	773-395-7100	$$$$	10:30 pm	Vogue, overpriced Asian-inspired seafood by Shaun McClain.
Sultan's Market	2057 W North Ave	773-235-3072	$*	9 pm	Cheap Middle Eastern, groceries.
Taxim	1558 N Milwaukee Ave	773-252-1558	$$	10pm	Fancy, contemporary greek. Duck gyros, anyone?
Thai Lagoon	2322 W North Ave	773-489-5747	$$	11 pm	Great Thai, funky atmosphere.
Thai Village	2053 W Division St	773-384-5352	$	10 pm	Cheap, tasty, and great outdoor seating.
Veggie Bite	1300 N Milwaukee Ave	773-772-2483	$	11pm	Vegan fast food. Budget, belly, and bovine friendly.

Map 22 • Noble Square / Goose Island

Corosh	1072 N Milwaukee Ave	773-235-0600	$$	1 am	Italian and pub fare, great patio.
El Barco Mariscos Seafood	1035 N Ashland Blvd	773-486-6850	$$	12 am	Outdoor seating, terrific ceviche.
Hollywood Grill	1601 W North Ave	773-395-1818	$	24hts	1950s style dining 27/7.
La Pasadita	1132 N Ashland Ave	773-278-0384	$	3 am	Yummy, no-frills take-out. Order the carne asada burrito.
La Pasadita	1141 N Ashland Ave	773-278-0384	$	3am	Yummy, no-frills take-out. Order the carne asada burrito.
Mariscos El Veneno	1024 N Ashland Ave	773-252-7200	$	10 pm	Escape grimy Ashland for this tiny Mexican playa-style seafood shack.
Luc Thang	1524 N Ashland Blvd	773-395-3907	$	11 pm	Thai with Chinese and Vietnamese touches.
NYC Bagel	1001 W North Ave	312-274-1278	$	5 pm	NY-style deli, best egg salad in the city.
Podhalanka	1549 W Division St	773-486-6655	$	8 pm	Authentic Polish hole-in-the-wall with potato pancakes, buttery pierogies and more.
Schwa	1466 N Ashland Ave	773-252-1466	$$$$	10:30 pm	Innovative fine dining with a hipster vibe.
Tocco	1266 N Milwaukee Ave	773-687-8895	$$	11 pm	Come for the wood-fired pizzas. Skip everything else.
Usagi Ya	1178 N Milwaukee Ave	773-292-5885	$$	1 am	Affordable sushi.

Map 23 • West Town / Near West Side

A Tavola	2148 W Chicago Ave	773-276-7567	$$$	10:30 pm	Upscale Italian charm in an intimate setting.
Chickpea	2018 W Chicago Ave	773-384-9930	$	10 pm	It's mama's specials that keep 'em comingback at the Palestinian fave.
Old Lviv	2228 W Chicago Ave	773-772-7250	$*	8 pm	Eastern European buffet.
Pauly's Pizza-Ria	1744 W Grand Ave	312-243-4444		12am	Chicago is famous for its pizza so why no induldge in a big slice?
Sunrise Café	2012 W Chicago Ave	773-276-8290	$	3 pm	Good coffee, good breakfast puts a smile on the face.
Takie Outit	2132 W Chicago Ave	773-252-1880	$	10:30 pm	Dim sum in the tum tum.
Tecalitlan Restaurant	1814 W Chicago Ave	773-384-4285	$	2 am	Popular family-style, Mexican restaurant.

Map 24 • River West / West Town

Bella Notte	1374 W Grand Ave	312-733-5136	$$$$	11:30 pm	Romantic, Italian, and schmoozy.
Bombon Café	38 S Ashland Ave	312-733-8717	$	8 pm	Upscale tortas in a bright sunny setting!
Breakfast Club	1381 W Hubbard St	312-666-3166	$$*	3 pm	Brunch and then some.
Burger Baron	1381 W Grand Ave	312-733-3285	$	8:30 pm	Burgers and beer for the Everyman.
Butterfly Sushi Bar and Thai Cuisine	1156 W Grand Ave	312-563-5555	$$	11 pm	Cute BYOB sushi storefront in the East Village.
Café Central	1437 W Chicago Ave	312-243-6776	$$	9 pm	Tasty Puerto Rican cuisine, diner décor, and vintage neighborhood photos.

Carmichael's Chicago Steak House	1052 W Monroe St	312-433-0025	$$$$	12 am	Great steaks in a vintage style dining room.
Coalfire	1321 W Grand Ave	312-226-2625	$$	11 pm	Chicago's first coal-fired pizza.
DeCero	814 W Randolph St	312-455-8114	$$$	11 pm	Made-to-order tacos, fresh fruit cocktail, Mexican heaven.
Flo	1434 W Chicago Ave	312-243-0477	$$	11 pm	Mexican-influenced breakfast in a relaxed atmosphere.
Follia	953 W Fulton St	312-243-2888	$$$	11 pm	Swanky, upscale Italian.
Green Zebra	1460 W Chicago Ave	312-243-7100	$$$$	11 pm	Innovative and mostly vegetarian, by Spring's Shawn McClain.
Habana Libre	1440 W Chicago Ave	312-243-3303	$$††	11 pm	BYOB plantain paradise.
Ina's	1235 W Randolph St	312-226-8227	$$$	9 pm	Special occasion breakfasts. Try the scrapple—it's better than it sounds.
Jerry's West Loop	1045 W Madison St	312-563-1008	$	6 pm	Fresh and slightly gourmet concoctions.
La Sardine	111 N Carpenter St	312-421-2800	$$	10 pm	Tuesdays fixed price for $20!
Marche	833 W Randolph St	312-226-8399	$$$	12 am	Theatrical French brasserie dining.
May Street Market	1132 W Grand Ave	312-421-5547	$$$	11 pm	American / Global fusion with foam and such.
Mexique	1529 W Chicago Ave	312-850-0288	$$$	11 pm	French/Mexican pairing seems odd? Trust us, they pull it off
Moto	945 W Fulton Market	312-491-0058	$$$$	11 pm	Conceptual laboratory food creations.
Oggi Trattoria Café	1378 W Grand Ave	312-733-0442	$$	9pm	One of the godfathers of the neighborhood.
one sixtyblue	1400 W Randolph St	312-850-0303	$$$	10.30pm	Upscale, less-stuffy-than-Tru New American.
Otom	951 W Fulton Market	312-491-5804	$$$	12 am	Moto's cheaper, less scientific neighbor.
The Red Canary	695 N Milwaukee Ave	312-846-1475	$$	2am	River West's highly anticipated new "gastro-lounge"!
Salerno's Pizza and Pasta	1201 W Grand Ave	312-666-3444	$	11 pm	Tony Soprano would be proud, and full.
Silver Palm	768 N Milwaukee Ave	312-666-9322	$$$	2 am	Dine in a 1940s train car on upscale American food.
Sushi X	1136 W Chicago Ave	312-491-9232	$$	12 am	Speakeasy sushi bar with fish so fresh they swim to your plate. BYOB.
Swim Café	1357 W Chicago Ave	312-492-8600	$	6 pm	Fresh, homemade breakfast and lunch fair with aquatic theme.
Twisted Spoke	501 N Ogden Ave	312-666-1500	$	3 am	Famous for serving smut movies and eggs simultaneously.
Vinnie's Sub Shop	1204 W Grand Ave	312-738-2985	$	5 pm	No frills, handy for construction workers.
Vivo	838 W Randolph St	312-733-3379	$$$$	12 am	Restaurants Row's first residence of Italian dining.
West Town Tavern	1329 W Chicago Ave	312-666-6175	$$$	10 pm	Upscale comfort food.
Windy City Café	1062 W Chicago Ave	312-492-8010	$	4 pm	Small town diner feel and menu, grab a booth.
Wishbone	1001 W Washington Blvd	312-850-2663	$$	10 pm	Comfort food, comfort folks.

Map 25 • Illinois Medical District

Carnitas Uruapan Restaurant	1725 W 18th St	312-226-2654	$*	5 pm	Carnitas muy necesitas.
Damenzo's	2324 W Taylor St	312-421-1142	$	1 am	Pizza, pizza puffs, small bar.
Ferrara Bakery	2210 W Taylor St	312-666-2200	$	6 pm	Serving Italian pastries since 1908.
Los Alamos	2157 S Damen Ave	773-254-8095	$*	10 pm	Great Taqueria
LuLu's Hot Dogs	1000 S Leavitt St	312-243-3444	$*	1 am	Dog's popular with local med students.
TJ's Family Restaurant	1928 W Cermak Rd	773-927-3349	$*	10 pm	Neighborhood diner.

Map 26 • University Village / Little Italy / Pilsen

Al's Beef	1079 W Taylor St	312-226-4017	$*	1 am	Where's the beef? Right here.
Birreria Reyes de Ocotlan	1322 W 18th St	312-733-2613	$$	9pm	Local no-frills Mexican favored by Rick Bayless.
Carm's Beef and Italian Ice	1057 W Polk St	312-738-1046	$*	11 pm	Italian subs and sausages.
Chez Joel	1119 W Taylor St	312-226-6479	$$$	11 pm	Delicious French cuisine in Little Italy.
Couscous	1445 W Taylor St	312-226-2408	$$	9:30 pm	Middle Eastern and Maghrebin Cuisine. Unique falafel.
De Pasada	1517 W Taylor St	312-243-6441	$	12 pm	Inexpensive, good quality Mexican—friendly staff.
Don Pedro Carnitas	1113 W 18th St	312-829-4757	$*	3 pm	Mexican fast food muy authentico.
Demitasse	1066 W Taylor St	312-226-7669	$	3 pm	Delightful breakfast spot.
Express Grill	1260 S Union Ave	312 738-2112	$		A 24/7 greasy spoon with noteworthy hot dogs.
Francesca's	1400 W Taylor St	312-829-2828	$$	11 pm	Loud, bustling dining room.
Franconello's Italian Restaurant	1301 S Halsted St	312-421-1301	$	10:30 pm	UIC outpost of Beverly Italian.
Golden Thai	1509 W Taylor St	312-733-0760	$	10 pm	Always busy, but there's better Thai out there.
Hashbrowns	731 W Maxwell St	312-226-8000	$$	3pm	Sweet potato hashbrowns - enough said.
Joy Yee's	1335 S Halsted St	312-997-2128	$$	12am	Good Asian food, better bubble tea.
Kohan Japanese Restaurant	730 W Maxwell St	312-421-6254	$$	10 pm	Sushi for UIC students.

La Cebollita Grill	1807 S Ashland Ave	312-492-8443	$*	10 pm	Gorditas, sopas, to dine-in or carry out.
La Vita	1359 W Taylor St	312-491-1414	$$$	11 pm	Date-spot for northern Italian.
May Street Café	1146 W Cermak Rd	312-421-4442	$	10:30 pm	Inexpensive, super casual pan-Latin.
Mundial Cocina Mestiza	1640 W 18th St	312-491-9908	$$	10 pm	Lovingly-prepared, family-owned Mexican.
New Rosebud Café	1500 W Taylor St	312-942-1117	$	11:30 pm	Popular with the United Center crowd.
Nuevo Leon	1515 W 18th St	312-421-1517	$*	4 am	Real-deal Mexican grub in Pilsen.
Pizza Tango	1013 W 18th St	312-421-2111	$	10 pm	Argentinean-style thin crust pizza.
Steak 'n Egger	1174 W Cermak Rd	312-226-5444	$	24-hrs	24-hour comfort food.
Sweet Maple Cafe	1339 W Taylor St	312-243-8908	$	2 pm	Super-homey breakfast, homemade biscuits.
Taj Mahal	1512 W Taylor St	312-226-6546	$$	10 pm	Affordable Indian.
Taqueria Los Comales	1544 W 18th St	312-666-2251	$*	1 am	Mexican fast food in cheerful environment.
Tuscany	1014 W Taylor St	312-829-1990	$$	11 pm	Elegant Taylor Street Italian.
WOW Café & Wingery	717 W Maxwell St	312-997-9969	$	12 am	N'awlins wing joint with a plethora of sauces.

Map 27 • Logan Square

Anong Thai	2532 N California Ave	773-292-5007	$		Much closer than Charley Thai, if you live near it.
Azucar	2647 N Kedzie Ave	773-486-6464	$$	2 am	Clubby tapas spot.
Bonsoiree Café and Delicacies	2728 W Armitage Ave	773-486-7511	$$	10 pm	This new spot is all about cozy seating and creative catering.
Borinquen Restaurant	1720 N California Ave	773-227-6038	$	12 am	Order a jibarito—a steak sandwich between two plantain slices.
Buona Terra Ristorante	2535 N California Ave	773-289-3800	$$	11 pm	Logan Square shmoozy Italian.
Café Bolero	2252 N Western Ave	773-227-9000	$$	12 am	Tasty Cuban fare.
Caliente	2556 W Fullerton Ave	773-772-4355	$$	11 pm	Heat up the night, or morning, with Pan-Latin eats and a BYOB policy.
Charley Thai Place	3209 W Armitage Ave	773-278-3200	$		Good old BYOB Thai.
Choi's Chinese Restaurant	2638 N Milwaukee Ave	773-486-8496	$$	9 pm	Good, fresh Chinese food.
Cozy Corner Diner & Pancake House	2294 N Milwaukee Ave	773-276-2215	$	-	Perfect if your brunch doesn't need salmon or capers.
Dunlay's on the Square	3137 W Logan Blvd	773-227-2400	$$	11 pm	American food and sports viewing.
El Charro	2410 N Milwaukee Ave	773-278-2514	$		24/7 taqueria. Conveniently adjacent to Two Way Lounge.
El Cid	2115 N Milwaukee Ave	773-252-4747	$	1 am	Authentic Mexican for the masses.
El Nandu	2731 N Fullerton Ave	773-278-0900	$$	12 am	Argentinian delicacies mixed with music.
Fat Willy's Rib Shack	2416 W Schubert Ave	773-782-1800	$$	11 pm	Finger-lickin' ribs and brisket.
Hachi's Kitchen	2521 N California Ave	773-276-8080	$$	12 am	Locals rave over this Logan Square sushi spot.
Johnny's Grill	2545 N Kedzie Blvd	773-278-2215	$	10 pm	Diner food for the grunge crowd.
Longman & Eagle	2657 N Kedzie Ave	773-276-7110	$$		Bourbon like nobody's business; also a restaurant and six-room inn.
Lula Café	2537 N Kedzie Blvd	773-489-9554	$$	10 pm	Pan-ethnic nouveau for hipsters.
Philly's Best	2436 N Milwaukee Ave	773-772-6152	$	11pm	Gigantic steak sandwiches, et al.
Real Tenochtitlan	2451 N Milwaukee Ave	773-227-1050	$$$	11 pm	Come for Chef Geno Bahena's amazing moles. BYOB.
Taqueria Moran	2226 N California Ave	773-235-2663	$	10 pm	Stand apart marinated pork tacos.
Treat	1616 N Kedzie Ave	773-772-1201	$$	10pm	BYOB Indian-inspired hideaway.

Map 28 • Bucktown

Arturo's Tacos	2001 N Western Ave	773-772-4944	$	10 pm	24-hour taqueria boasts cheap eats and a boisterous crowd.
Belly Shack	1912 N Western Ave	773-252-1414	$$	10pm	Latin/Asian/Incredible. BYOB and please don't skip dessert.
The Bluebird	1749 N Damen Ave	773-486-2473	$$$	2 am	American tapas and wine bar.
Bristol	2152 N Damen Ave	773-862-5555	$$	12 am	Fancy meat and beer in noisy atmosphere a.k.a classic gastropub.
Café Bolero	2252 N Western Ave	773-227-9000	$$	12am	Tasty Cuban fare.
Café Laguardia	2111 W Armitage Ave	773-862-5996	$$	11 pm	Cuban food like you wouldn't believe.
Café Matou	1846 N Milwaukee Ave	773-384-8911	$$$	11 pm	Fantastic French food, dodgy locale.
Caoba Mexican Bar and Grill	1619 N Damen Ave	773-342-2622	$$	12am	Best on Sunday afternoon when appetizers are half-priced.
Club Lucky	1824 W Wabansia Ave	773-227-2300	$$	12 am	Italian retro-styled joint.
Coast Sushi Bar	2045 N Damen Ave	773-235-5775	$$	12 am	BYOB sushi.
Duchamp	2118 N Damen Ave	773-235-6434	$$	11 pm	The communal table craze spreads to this worthy Bucktown spot.
Fat Willy's Rib Shack	2416 W Schubert Ave	773-782-1800	$$	11pm	Finger-lickin' ribs and brisket.
Hollywood Grill	1601 W North Ave	773-395-1818	$	24-hrs	24-hour Wicker Park dive.
Honey 1 BBQ	2241 N Western Ave	773-227-5130	$$	12 am	BBQ cooked in a big ole smoker. Yum.
Hot Chocolate	1747 N Damen Ave	773-489-1747	$$	12 am	Much more than just hot chocolate.
Irazu	1865 N Milwaukee Ave	773-252-5687	$*	9:30 pm	Hipsters and bikers gather 'round for Central American staples.
Jane's	1655 W Cortland St	773-862-5263	$$$	11 pm	Good-for-you gourmet.
Le Bouchon	1958 N Damen Ave	773-862-6600	$$	12 am	Affordable, crowded French.

Mado	1647 N Milwaukee Ave	773-342-2340	$$$	11 pm	Simple but trendy place.
Margie's Candies	1960 N Western Ave	773-384-1035	$	11 pm	Immense ice cream concoctions.
Rinconcito Sudamericano	2010 W Armitage Ave	773-489-3126	$$	10 pm	Yummy South American food.
Rio's D'Sudamerica	2010 W Armitage Ave	773-276-0170	$$$$	12 am	Swanky South American for date nights.
Riverside Deli & Café	1656 W Cortland St	773-278-3354	$$*	5 pm	Great deli, with awesome Sunday brunch.
Rosa de Lima	2013 N Western Ave	773-342-4557	$$	10 pm	You don't know Peruvian food until you eat at Rosa de Lima.
Silver Cloud Club & Grill	1700 N Damen Ave	773-489-6212	$$	12 am	A mac & cheese and meat-loaf kind of place.
Takashi	1952 N Damen Ave	773-772-6170	$$$	10:30 pm	Japanese fusion by James Beard Award winning chef.
Vosges Haut Chocolat	2211 N Elston Ave	773-388-5560	$	8pm	Gourmet chocolates.

Map 29 • DePaul / Wrightwood / Sheffield

Ambrosia Café	1963 N Sheffield Ave	773-404-4450	$	3 am	Smoothies and hookahs? Huh.
Goose Island Brewing Co	1800 N Clybourn Ave	312-915-0071	$	1 pm	Pub grub at its best.
Green Dolphin Street	2200 N Ashland Ave	773-395-0066	$$$$	11 pm	Live jazz club and contemporary American.
Ja' Grill	1008 W Armitage Ave	773-929-5375	$$	11 pm	Fun, authentic Jamaican in Lincoln park? Go figure.
John's Place	1200 W Webster Ave	773-525-6670	$$	11 pm	Healthy comfort food.
Metropolis Rotisseria & Annette's Italian Ice	924 W Armitage Ave	773-868-9000	$*	9:30 pm	Nice combo: Chicken shack & frozen treats.
Ringo Sushi	2507 N Lincoln Ave	773-248-5788		11 pm	All-u-can-eat & BYOB. Nice.
Sai Café	2010 N Sheffield Ave	773-472-8080	$$$	12 am	Traditional sushi place.
Salt & Pepper Diner	2575 N Lincoln Ave	773-525-8788	$*	4 pm	Cheap breakfasts in an area with few such options.
State	935 W Webster Ave	773-975-8030	$$$	12 am	Flashy service-oriented spot with concierge service.
Sweet Mandy B's	1208 W Webster Ave	773-244-1174	$	10 pm	Picture-perfect sweet shoppe.
Sweets & Savories	1534 W Fullerton Ave	773-281-6778	$$$	11pm	Exquisite Sunday brunch.
Taco & Burrito House	1548 W Fullerton Ave	773-665-8389	$*	5 am	Super-cheap burrito shack, open very late
Taxim	1558 N Milwaukee Ave	773-252-1558	$$	10 pm	Fancy, contemporary greek. Duck gyros, anyone?
Tsuki	1441 W Fullerton Ave	773-883-8722	$$	12 am	It was bound to happen: tapas + sushi.
Twisted Lizard	1964 N Sheffield Ave	773-929-1414	$$	12 am	Yuppie Mexican.

Map 30 • Lincoln Park

Alinea	1723 N Halsted St	312-867-0110	$$$$$	10 pm	Conceptual experiments in fine dining.
Austrian Bakery & Deli	2523 N Clark St	773-244-9922	$	8:30 pm	Low-carb diets are so over. Celebrate here.
Boka	1729 N Halsted St	312-337-6070	$$$	12 am	Ambitious menu, swank décor.
Bourgeois Pig Cafe	738 W Fullerton Ave	773-883-5282	$		Let them eat cake. (and drink coffee)
Brick's Chicago	1909 N Lincoln Ave	312-255-0851	$$	9 pm	Thin-crust pizza and Trappist ales hold sway here.
Café Ba-Ba-Reeba!	2024 N Halsted St	773-935-5000	$$$	12 am	Noisy, bustling tapas joint.
Café Bernard	2100 N Halsted St	773-871-2100	$$	11:30 pm	Charming French.
Charlie Trotter's	816 W Armitage Ave	773-248-6228	$$$$$	10:30 pm	World-famous nouvelle cuisine.
Crepe & Coffee Palace	2433 N Clark St	773-404-1300	$	10 pm	Serious crepe lovers.
Dunlay's	2600 N Clark St	773-883-6000	$$$	11 pm	Casual traditional american dinner spot.
Duke's Bar & Grill	2616 N Clark St	773-248-0250	$$	2am	If a bar were a log cabin with tasty burgers.
Fattoush	2652 N Halsted St	773-327-2652	$$	11 pm	Nicely priced Middle-East nosh.
Frances' Deli	2552 N Clark St	773-248-4580	$	8 pm	Inventive deli.
Geja's Café	340 W Armitage Ave	773-281-9101	$$$	12:30 am	Romantic fondue with live flamenco.
Hai Yen	2723 N Clark St	773-868-4888	$$	10 pm	Little Vietnam favorite swanked up for Lincoln Park.
Hema's on Clark	2411 N Clark St	773-529-1705	$$	11 pm	Almost as good as original on Devon.
Karyn's Fresh Corner	1901 N Halsted Ave	312-255-1590	$$	10 pm	The queen of raw food.
L20	2300 N Lincoln Park W	773-868-0002	$$$$	10pm	Spendy seafood joint specializing in strange name pronunciations and tasty sea creatures.
Landmark	1633 N Halsted St	312-587-1600	$$$$	2 am	Cavernous club restaurant for Lincoln Parkers and the Steppenwolf crowd.
Lito's Empanadas	2566 N Clark St	773-857-1337	$	9 pm	He don't make no burritos.
Mon Ami Gabi	2300 N Lincoln Park W	773-348-8886	$$$	11 pm	French bistro.
Nookies	1746 N Wells St	312-337-2454	$*	9:45 pm	Inventive omelettes with some strong coffee.
Nookies, Too	2114 N Halsted St	773-327-1400	$	12 am	Inventive omelettes with some strong coffee.
North Pond	2610 N Cannon Dr	773-477-5845	$$$$	10 pm	Earthy contemporary American.
Original Pancake House	2020 N Lincoln Park W	773-929-8130	$$*	4 pm	Breakfast-y grill.

Perennial	1800 N Lincoln Ave	312-981-7070	$$$$	10pm	Instant gratification for foodies across from the Green City Market.
PS Bangkok	2521 N Halsted St	773-348-0072	$	11 pm	Popular Thai with delivery.
R.J. Grunts	2056 N Lincoln Park W	773-929-5363	$$	10:30 pm	Comfy, psychedelic salad bar and burger joint.
Red Rooster	2100 N Halsted St	773-929-7660	$$$	11:30 pm	Inauspicious entrance, with authentic France beyond.
Robinson's No 1 Ribs	655 W Armitage Ave	312-337-1399	$*	10 pm	Down home ribs in Lincoln Park.
Salvatore's Ristorante	525 W Arlington Pl	773-528-1200	$$$	10 pm	Cute neighborhood Italian.
Sedgwick's Bar & Grill	1935 N Sedgwick St	312-337-7900	$	12 am	Home-style breakfast buffet.
Sushi O Sushi	346 W Armitage Ave	773-871-4777	$$	11 pm	Newly remodeled fresh seafood.
Sushi Para II	2256 N Clark St	773-477-3219	$$	10:30 pm	A.Y.C.E. sushi that's good. No, really.
Swirlz Cupcakes	705 W Belden Ave	773-404-2253	$	7 pm	Gourmet cupcakes, including gluten-free options.
Tilli's	1952 N Halsted St	773-325-0044	$$	11 pm	Cute staff and good food.
Toro	2546 N Clark St	773-348-4877	$$	11 pm	Worth the wait for raw fish lovers
Treats Frozen Desserts	2224 N Clark St	773-472-6666	$	12am	Guilt-free ice cream.
Twin Anchors	1655 N Sedgwick St	312-266-1616	$$	12 am	Sinatra came for the ribs and stayed for the drinks and atmosphere.
Vinci	1732 N Halsted St	312-266-1199	$$$	11:30 pm	Homemade pasta raises the bar.
Wells on Wells	1617 N Wells St	312-944-1617	$$	2am	Two words: pretzel buns.
Wiener's Circle	2622 N Clark St	773-477-7444	$*	5:30 am	Classic dogs served with a generous helping of sass.

Map 31 • Old Town / Near North

Big & Little's	939 N Orleans St	312-943-0000	$		Fish-and-chips shack run by Hell's Kitchen contestant.
Bistrot Margot	1437 N Wells St	312-587-3660	$$$$	11 pm	Great date place.
Chic Café	361 W Chestnut St	312-944-0882	$$	8 pm	Gourmet prix fixe by culinary students.
The Dining Room at Kendall College	900 N North Branch St	312-752-2328	$$	8pm	When students cook: Gourmet food, layman price!
Dinotto Ristorante	215 W North Ave	312-202-0302	$$	12 am	Everyone's a regular at this neighborhood Italian joint.
Eve	840 N Wabash Ave	312-266-3383	$$$$	10 pm	They make a sausage out of lobster.
Fireplace Inn	1448 N Wells St	312-664-5264	$$$	1:30 am	Popular spot to watch sports.
Fresh Choice	1534 N Wells St	312-664-7065	$*	10 pm	Sandwich and smoothie king.
Garlic and Chili	1232 N La Salle Dr	312-255-1717	$	9:30 pm	Off the beaten track and located next to the transient motel, it's a hidden gem.
Kamehachi	1400 N Wells St	312-664-3663	$$$	1:30 am	Sushi favorite with upstairs lounge.
Kiki's Bistro	900 N Franklin St	312-335-5454	$$$$	10 pm	Stylish French.
Las Pinatas	1552 N Wells St	312-664-8277	$$	12 am	Festive atmosphere, fantastic food.
Mangia Roma	1623 N Halsted St	312-475-9801	$$	10:30 pm	Casual Roman spot with pizza.
Mizu	315 W North Ave	312-951-8880	$$	10:30 pm	Sushi and skewered meats with dipping sauces.
MK	868 N Franklin St	312-482-9179	$$$$	10 pm	Very stylish.
O'Brien's	1528 N Wells St	312-787-3131	$$$	12:30 pm	Best outdoor in Old Town.
Old Jerusalem	1411 N Wells St	312-944-0459	$$	11 pm	Cheap, good food.
Old Town Brasserie	1209 N Wells St	312-943-3000	$$$	1:30 am	Classic French comfort food in cozy room.
Perennial	1800 N Lincoln Ave	312-981-7070	$$$$	10 pm	Instant gratification for foodies across from the Green City Market.
Sammy's Red Hots	238 W Division St	312-266-7290	$		The seediness only makes it better.
Salpicon	1252 N Wells St	312-988-7811	$$	11 pm	Colorful Mexican with tequila tastings.
Topo Gigio Ristorante	1516 N Wells St	312-266-9355	$$$	11 pm	Crowded reliable Italian. Big outdoor.
Wells on Wells	1617 N Wells St	312-944-1617	$$	2 am	Two words: pretzel buns.

Map 32 • Gold Coast / Mag Mile

Ashkenaz	12 E Cedar St	312-944-5006	$	7 pm	Chicago's true Jewish deli.
Balsan	11 E Walton St	312-646-1400	$$$	12am	The high-end Elysian Hotel's "casual" option.
Bistro 110	110 E Pearson St	312-266-3110	$$$	11 pm	Popular Sunday jazz brunch.
Bistrot Zinc	1131 N State St	312-337-1131	$$	11 pm	Quiet elegance.
Bombon Café	1000 N Clark St	312-787-7717	$	8pm	Upscale tortas.
Cafe des Architectes	20 E Chestnut St	312-324-4063	$$$	10 pm	French Mediterranean with late kitchen.
Cape Cod Room	140 E Walton Pl	312-787-2200	$$$$	11 pm	Over-the-top nautical décor.
Carmine's	1043 N Rush St	312-988-7676	$$$	12:30 am	Crowded and pricey Italian.
Chestnut Street Cafe	200 E Chestnut St	312-943-0034	$		Relatively cheap breakfast and lunch just off the Mag Mile.
The Drawing Room	937 N Rush St	312-255-0022	$$		Le Passage's foray into swank cocktails and sit-down dining.
Freshii	835 N Michigan Ave	312-202-9009	$	4.30pm	Tasty wraps, hold the guilt.
Eve	840 N Wabash Ave	312-266-3383	$$$$	10pm	They make a sausage out of lobster.
Fornetto Mei	107 E Delaware Pl	312-573-6301	$$$	10 pm	Authentic pizza. Deep dish lovers stay away.
Gaylord Chicago	100 E Walton St	312-664-1700	$		Improbably named Indian spot.
Gibson's Steakhouse	1028 N Rush St	312-266-8999	$$$$$	12 am	If you love steak, get a reservation.

The Goddess and Grocer	25 E Delaware Pl	312-896-2600	$		Specialty groceries and ready-made gourmet sandwiches.
Hugo's Frog Bar & Fish House	1024 N Rush St	312-640-0999	$$$	12 am	Hearty seafood.
Il Mulino New York	1150 N Dearborn St	312-440-8888	$$$$$	11 pm	Top NYC Italian with top NYC prices.
Le Colonial	937 N Rush St	312-255-0088	$$$	12 am	Indochine comes to the Second City. Very nice.
Le Petit Paris	260 E Chestnut St	312-787-8260	$$$$	10 pm	Shhh! Don't tell anyone about this Gallic hideaway!
McCormick & Schmick's	41 E Chestnut St	312-397-9500	$$$$	12 am	Seafood chain that outdoes itself on portions and taste.
Morton's of Chicago	1050 N State St	312-266-4820	$$$$$	11 pm	The steakhouse standard.
Mr J's Dawg & Burger	822 N State St	312-943-4679	$*	12 am	Mom & pop burger joint.
Original Pancake House	22 E Bellevue Pl	312-642-7917	$$*	5 pm	The apple waffle/pancake is right!
Pane Caldo	72 E Walton St	312-649-0055	$$$$	11 pm	Tucked-away genius Italian trattoria.
Paris Cafe	810 N Clark St	312-255-0811	$$		French resto and bar heavy on ambiance.
Pump Room	1301 N State Pkwy	312-266-0360	$$$$$	12 am	Chicago old-school tradition. Dress code.
Ra Sushi	1139 N State St	312-274-0011	$$$	1am	Rock-n-roll sushi bar.
Sarah's Pastries & Candies	70 E Oak St	312-664-6223	$	10 pm	Decadent cakes and other goodies.
Signature Room	875 N Michigan Ave	312-787-9596	$$$$	11pm	It's the view, not the food. Proposal hot spot.
Spiaggia	980 N Michigan Ave	312-280-2750	$$$$$	10:30 pm	One of Chicago's best—gorgeous lake view and Italian cuisine.
Table 52	52 W Elm St	312-573-4000	$$$	10pm	Oprah-sanctioned New American.
Table Fifty-Two	52 W Elm St	312-573-4000	$$$	10 pm	Upscale southern food by Oprah's ex-chef.
Tavern on Rush	1031 N Rush St	312-664-9600	$$$$	1 am	Summer mainstay, American menu.
Tempo	6 E Chestnut St	312-943-4373	$$*	24-hrs	24/7 patio seating and huge menu.

Map 33 • Rogers Park / West Ridge

Angin Mamiri	2739 W Touhy Ave	773-262-6646	$$	9.30pm	Chicago's first Indonesian spot.
Annapurna	2608 W Devon Ave	773-764-1858	$	11 pm	Vegetarian fast food.
Arya Bhavan	2508 W Devon Ave	773-274-5800	$$	11 pm	Northern Indian all-vegetarian.
Ben Tre	3146 W Touhy Ave	773-465-3011	$	9 pm	Comfy Vietnamese comfort food.
Candlelite	7452 N Western Ave	773-465-0087	$	2 am	Rogers Park pizza institution, with cocktails.
Chopal	2240 W Devon Ave	773-338-4080	$*	11pm	When you need a kebob—late.
Good Morgan Kosher Fish Market	2948 W Devon Ave	773-764-8115	$$*	2 am	Fish market/restaurant in the Devon kosher strip.
Hashalom	2905 W Devon Ave	773-465-5675	$*	9 pm	Israeli/Moroccan, kosher, BYOB, closed Sat/Sun.
Hema's Kitchen	2439 W Devon Ave	773-338-1627	$$	11pm	Like naan other.
Indian Garden	2546 W Devon Ave	773-338-2929	$$	10:15 pm	Get your tandoori here.
Mysore Woodland's	2548 W Devon Ave	773-338-8160	$$	10 pm	One of the better Indian spots in this strip.
Sabri Nihari	2502 W Devon Ave	773-465-0899	$$	10 pm	No booze here but super way delicious Pakistani food. Let's go!
Siam Pasta	7416 N Western Ave	773-274-0579	$	11 pm	Bangkok home cookin'.
Sukhadia's	2559 W Devon Ave	773-338-5400	$	9:30 pm	Indian sweet maker and caterer.
Tiffin	2536 W Devon Ave	773-338-2143	$$	10:30 pm	Most upscale Indian restaurant on Devon, yet moderately priced.
Udupi Palace	2543 W Devon Ave	773-338-2152	$	9:30 pm	Pure vegetarian Indian food, low-fat, not too spicy.
Uru-Swati	2629 W Devon Ave	773-262-5280	$*	10pm	Vegetarian fast food and snacks.
Viceroy of India	2520 W Devon Ave	773-743-4100	$$	10:30 pm	Popular Indian restaurant, vegetarian options.

Map 34 • East Rogers Park

A&T Grill	7026 N Clark St	773-274-0036	$	9 pm	Classic diner-grill.
Bar-B-Que Bob's	2055 W Howard St	773-761-1260	$$	11pm	Best ribs on the far North Side.
Buffalo Joe's	1841 W Howard St	773-764-7300	$*	11 pm	Wings and fast food carryout spot, with a soul food flava.
Capt'n Nemos	7367 N Clark St	773-973-0570	$	7 pm	Free soup sample while you wait at this always jovial local sandwich chain.
Caribbean American Bakery	1539 W Howard St	773-761-0700	$	8 pm	Jamaican bakery featuring meat pies, pastries, and jerk chicken for carryout.
Century Public House	1330 W Morse Ave	773-654-5100	$$$	12 am	RoPa organic gastropub only open during shows at adjacent Morse theater.
Dagel & Beli Shop	7406 N Greenview Ave	773-743-2354	$	10 pm	Dyslexic sandiwches.
Deluxe Diner	6349 N Clark St	773-743-8244	$*	24-hrs	Retro-styled greasy spoon.
El Famous Burrito	7047 N Clark St	773-465-0377	$*	1 am	Best greasy burrito in Chicago.
Ethiopian Diamond	7537 N Clark St	773-764-2200			Roger's Park outpost of beloved Uptown Ethiopian.
Ghareeb Nawaz	2032 W Devon Ave	773-761-5300	$*	12 am	Indo-Pakistani lunch counter on the east side of the strip.

Good to Go Jamaican Jerk and Juice Bar	1947 W Howard St	773-381-7777	$$	11 pm	Jamaican cuisine.
Grande Noodles and Sushi Bar	6632 N Clark St	773-761-6666	$$	10 pm	Damn fine pot stickers.
Heartland Cafe	7000 N Glenwood Ave	773-465-8005	$$	11 pm	Brown rice, socialist newspapers, and vegetarian tidbits reign here.
Jamaica Jerk	1631 W Howard St	773-764-1546			Jamaican comfort food best for carry-out.
La Conakry	2049 W Howard St	773-262-6955	$$	10 pm	Order the flavorful Senegales food to go and avoid the drab dining room.
Masouleh	6653 N Clark St	773-262-2227	$*	10 pm	Within this unassuming storefront lies the best Iranian food in the city.
Morseland	1218 W Morse Ave	773-764-8900	$$$	2 am	Rogers Park café with ambitious fare.
Noon Hour Grill	6930 N Glenwood Ave	773-338-9494	$	4 pm	Korean diner and grill is neighborhood favorite.
Quesadillas y Mariscos Dona Lolis	6924 N Clark St	773-761-5677	$*	10 pm	Authentic quesadillas and gorditas with interesting ingredients.
Sahara Khabob	6649 N Clark St	773-262-6000			Local fave for fresh & tasty Middle eastern.
Tamales lo Mejor de Guerrero	7024 N Clark St	773-338-6350	$*	8 pm	Carry out tamales so good, that may ruin "the tamale guy" for you.
Taste of Peru	6545 N Clark St	773-381-4540	$	12 am	Barebones spot for cheap. authentic Peruvian food.
Thai Spice	1320 W Devon Ave	773-973-0504	$	11 pm	Look beyond the grim exterior for freshly prepared Thai.
Tickie's Belizean Cuisine	7605 N Paulina St	773-973-3919	$	8 pm	Authentic Caribbean food in cheerful storefront across from the Howard L.

Map 35 • Arcadia Terrace / Peterson Park

Aztecas Mexican Taqueria	5421 N Lincoln Ave	773-506-2052	$	12 am	Standard Mexican fare.
Café Orange	5639 N Lincoln Ave	773-275-5040	$$	2 am	Korean and Japanese fare with a hip vibe and occasional karaoke.
Charcoal Delights	3139 W Foster Ave	773-583-0056	$	11 pm	Great gyros to go.
Da Rae Jung	5220 N Lincoln Ave	773-907-9155			Mom and Pop Seoul food storefront.
Fondue Stube	2717 W Peterson Ave	773-784-2200	$$	12 am	Fun fondue!
Hai Woon Dae	6240 N California Ave	773-764-8018	$$	10 pm	Fish heads and pork shoulders above competing late-night Korean bbq joints.
IHOP	5929 N Lincoln Ave	773-769-1550	$	12 am	It's an IHOP for pete's sake. What else do you need to know?
Katsu	2651 W Peterson Ave	773-784-3383	$$$	10 pm	Familiar, family sushi place.
Pueblito Viejo	5429 N Lincoln Ave	773-784-9135	$$	2:20 am	Adorable Columbian village-theme with live music on weekends.
Solga	5828 N Lincoln Ave	773-728-0802	$$$	11 pm	Korean BBQ with charcoal grill.
Sweet Collective	5333 N Lincoln Ave	773-293-0888	$	6 pm	It's the homemade ice cream, stupid.
Wolfy's	2734 W Peterson Ave	773-743-0207	$	9 pm	Dine in and carry out dogs, burgers, and such.
Woo Chon	5744 N California Ave	773-728-8001	$	12 am	Authentic Korean BBQ. Brusque but oddly fun service.

Map 36 • Bryn Mawr / Bowmanville

Blue Nile	6118 N Ravenswood Ave	773-465-6710	$	10 pm	Hefty portions of Ethiopian stews to be sopped up with inerja.
Delisi's Pizzeria	5806 N Western Ave	773-784-6320	$	10:30 pm	Chicago memorabilia, great pizza and complimentary Tootsie Rolls.
Fireside Restaurant & Lounge	5739 N Ravenswood Ave	773-561-7433	$$	3 am	Cajun-tinged barfood and late kitchen.
Greenhouse Inn	6300 N Ridge Ave	773-273-4182	$	2:30 pm	Church and bridge groups meet for homemade soups.
Max's Italian Beef	5754 N Western Ave	773-989-8200	$$*	7 pm	Chicago institution; home of the pepper-and-egg sandwich.
Pauline's	1754 W Balmoral Ave	773-561-8573	$	3pm	Weekend breakfast hotspot; try the famous five-egg omelet, if you must.
San Soo Gab San	5247 N Western Ave	773-334-1589	$$	24-hrs	Do-it-yourself Korean barbeque at 4 am.
Yes Thai	5211 N Damen Ave	773-878-3487	$	10:30 pm	Noodles and curries in a cozy atmosphere

Map 37 • Edgewater / Andersonville

Andie's	5253 N Clark St	773-784-8616	$$	11:30 pm	Fresh Middle Eastern in airy atmosphere.
Ann Sather Restaurant	5207 N Clark St	773-271-6677	$	2 pm	Heavenly cinnamon rolls and swedish meatballs.
Anteprima	5316 N Clark St	773-506-9990	$$$	11 pm	This cozy A-Ville Italian just feels right.
Antica Pizzeria	5663 N Clark St	773-944-1492	$	10 pm	Brick oven goodness.
Bananas Foster Cafe	1147 W Granville Ave	773-262-9855	$$	11 pm	Shephard's Pie and Fish and Chips adjacent to the Red Line stop.
Big Jones	5347 N Clark St	773-275-5725	$$$	10 pm	High falutin' southern chow.

Edgewater Beach Cafe	5545 N Sheridan Rd	773-275-4141			Neighborhood Frenchie in the pink building.
En'thai'ce	5701 N Clark St	773-275-3555	$$	10pm	Good neighborhood Thai, moderately priced.
Ethiopian Diamond	6120 N Broadway St	773-338-6100	$$$	11 pm	Visit for jazz on Fridays.
Flourish Bakery Café	1138 W Bryn Mawr	773-271-2253	$	9 pm	Three words—red velvet cake.
Francesca's Bryn Mawr	1039 W Bryn Mawr Ave	773-506-9261	$$	11 pm	Dined in an SRO before?
George's Ice Cream and Sweets	5306 N Clark St	773-271-7600	$		Ice cream of every flavor. Fat Elvis tastes the best.
Great Lake	1477 W Balmoral Ave	773-334-9270	$$$	9PM	Excellent pizza. With cheese from Wisconsin!
Hamburger Mary's	5400 N Clark St	773-784-6969	$$	11 pm	Flamboyant burger joint popular with families and The Gays.
Huey's Hot Dogs	1507 W Balmoral Ave	773-293-4800	$*	8 pm	Fast, friendly dogs and burgers.
Icosium Kafe	5200 N Clark St	773-271-5233	$*	11 pm	It's crepe-tastic!
Indie Café	5951 N Broadway St	773-561-5577	$$	10:30 pm	Thai and sushi. Yummy and cheap.
Jin Ju	5203 N Clark St	773-334-6377	$$$	11 pm	Upscale Korean.
Kitchen Sink Cafe	1107 W Berwyn Ave	773-944-0592	$	8.30pm	Serves savory specialty mochas. Has a nice skylight.
La Cocina de Frida	5403 N Clark St	773-271-1907	$$	11pm	Doubles as a Kahlo art gallery. Eat and observe!
La Fonda Latino	5350 N Broadway St	773-271-3935	$$	9:30 pm	Real tasty pan-Latin.
Loving Hut	5812 N Broadway	773-275-8797	$		Vegan diner with new owners. Bright decor, cheap and crunchy.
M Henry	5707 N Clark St	773-561-1600	$$	2:30 pm	Stylish brunch option in Andersonville.
Moody's Pub	5910 N Broadway St	773-275-2696	$	2 am	Burgers only, but the best.
Piatto Pronto	5624 N Clark St	773-334-5688	$	9pm	Tasty sandwiches for not a lot of dough.
Pasticceria Natalina	5406 N Clark St	773-989-0662	$	8 pm	Friggin' amazing sicilian pastries and sweets.
RAS Dashen Ethiopian Restaurant	5846 N Broadway St	773-506-9601	$$	11 pm	Traditional Ethiopian comfort food; vegan-friendly.
Reza's	5255 N Clark St	773-561-1898	$$	12 am	Many Persian options, leftovers for lunch the next day.
Sabaidee	5359 N Broadway St	773-506-0880	$*	8:30 pm	Homemade sausages and other Laotian specialties.
Sunshine Cafe	5449 N Clark St	773-334-6214			Wait on weekends for excellent & cheap Japanese noodles.
Svea	5236 N Clark St	773-275-7738	$*	3:30 pm	Adorable, tiny Swedish diner.
Tanoshii	5547 N Clark St	773-878-6886	$$	12 am	Order from the chef for innovative sushi.
Taste of Lebanon	1509 W Foster Ave	773-334-1600	$*	7:30 pm	Dongy room, rock-bottom prices, above-average Mid-east fare.

Map 38 • Ravenswood / Albany Park

Al-Amira	3200 W Lawrence Ave	773-267-0333	$*	24 hrs	Standard Mid-East grub in a 'hood full of better options, but open 24 hours.
Al-Khaymeih	4742 N Kedzie Ave	773-583-0999	$	11 pm	Lebanese eatery with better-than-average vegetarian appetizers.
Arun's	4156 N Kedzie Ave	773-539-1909	$$$$$	10:30 pm	Worldwide rep for four-star prix fixe Thai.
Baladna	4835 N Kedzie Ave	773-583-6695	$	11 pm	One of many choices for Middle-Eastern carry-out on this strip.
Brasa Roja	3125 W Montrose Ave	773-866-2252	$$	10 pm	Friendly Columbian place specializing in flame-roasted chicken.
Cousin's IV	3038 W Irving Park Rd	773-478-6868	$$	11:30 pm	Overcooking not a prob at this raw restaurant.
Dawali	4911 N Kedzie Ave	773-267-4200			Try the "classic felafel" sandwich with potato and cauliflower.
Dharma Garden Thai Restaurants	3109 W Irving Park Rd	773-588-9140	$	10 pm	Thai vegetarian and seafood dishes. Karaoke some evenings.
El Huarachin Huarachon	3320 W Lawrence Ave	773-267-3926	$*	10 pm	Crazy good homestyle Mexican.
Golden Crust Italian Pizzeria	4620 N Kedzie Ave	773-539-5860	$	2 am	Honkin' portions of the Italian-American comfort food of yore.
Great Sea Chinese Restaurants	3254 W Lawrence Ave	773-478-9129	$$	10:30 pm	Otherwise basic Chinese locally famous for its hot wings.
Kang Nam	4849 N Kedzie Ave	773-539-2524	$$	10:30 pm	Could be the best Korean BBQ in town. Crazy excellent.
Kitchen Chicago	4664 N Manor Ave	773-463-0863	$	2 pm	Café food: soup, sandwiches, sweets.
Lutz Continental Café	2458 W Montrose Ave	773-478-7785	$$	10 pm	If Grandma was German, she would serve these pastries.
Manzo's Ristorante	3210 W Irving Park Rd	773-478-3070	$$	1:30 am	Do not miss the Sunday buffet. Tasty, plentiful and cheap Italian.
Mi Ciudad	3041 W Irving Park Rd	773-866-2066	$$	11.30pm	Simple Ecuadorean: corn cakes, empanadas, fruit shakes.
Nhu Lan	2612 W Lawrence Ave	773-878-9898	$	8 pm	Vietnamese sandwich shop.
Noon O Kabab	4661 N Kedzie Ave	773-279-9309	$	11 pm	Bring a doggie bag for day-after lunch.
Paradise	2916 W Montrose Ave	773-588-1989	$$*	10:30 pm	Competent sushi connected to a Korean spa.
Pupuseria Las Delicias	3300 W Montrose Ave	773-267-5346	$	10 pm	Corn meal fritters stuffed with joy.

Rockwell's Neighborhood Grill	4632 N Rockwell St	773-509-1871	$	11 pm	Familiar bar food and brunchtime favorites in a friendly atmosphere.
Salam	4636 N Kedzie Ave	773-583-0776	$*	10 pm	Home of the 19-cent falafel.
Semiramis	4639 N Kedzie Ave	773-279-8900	$$	10 pm	Lebanese with great value to quality ratio. Try the sumac fries.
Thai Valley	4600 N Kedzie Ave	773-588-2020	$*	10 pm	BYOB Thai restaurant with lunch specials.

Map 39 • Ravenswood / North Center

Bad Dog Tavern	4535 N Lincoln Ave	773-334-4040	$$	12 am	Food, fireplace, and folk music.
Bistro Campagne	4518 N Lincoln Ave	773-271-6100	$$	10:30 pm	Organic French fare in a cozy room.
Budacki's Drive-In	4739 N Damen Ave	773-561-1322	$	8 pm	Artery clogging late-night eats.
Browntrout	4111 N Lincoln Ave	773-472-4111			Sustainable hoodie with a fish proclivity.
Café 28	1800 W Irving Park Rd	773-528-2883	$$	10:30 pm	Trendy Cuban.
Café Selmarie	4729 N Lincoln Ave	773-989-5595	$$	11 pm	Bright clean, bakery/cafe with wine and beer.
Chalkboard	4343 N Lincoln Ave	773-477-7144	$$$	10 pm	Inventive spin on comfort classics.
Chicago Brauhaus	4732 N Lincoln Ave	773-784-4444	$$	12 am	Live German music in beerhouse atmosphere.
Diner Grill	1635 W Irving Pk Rd	773-248-2030	$*	24-hrs	Home to the infamous "Slinger." Motto: eat it here, leave it somewhere else.
Essence of India	4601 N Lincoln Ave	773-506-0002	$$	10:30 pm	Traditional northern Indian food, fancier than Devon St.
First Slice Pie Café	4401 N Ravenswood Ave	773-506-1719	$$*	6 pm	Upscale café benefiting the hungry in more ways than one.
Glenn's Diner	1820 W Montrose Ave	773-506-1720	$$	9 pm	Fish-focused American fare.
Glunz Bavarian Haus	4128 N Lincoln Ave	773-472-4287	$$	11 pm	Weiner schnitzel and beer.
Golden Angel Restaurant	4340 N Lincoln Ave	773-583-6969	$*	24-hrs	24-hour diner.
House of Wah Sun	4319 N Lincoln Ave	773-477-0800	$	11:30 pm	Chinese/Cantonese/Mandarin eatery.
La Boca della Verita	4618 N Lincoln Ave	773-784-6222	$$	11 pm	Cozy Italian café.
Lincoln Restaurant	4008 N Lincoln Ave	773-248-1820	$$	11 pm	Old-school family joint. Been there forever.
LM Le Restaurant	4539 N Lincoln Ave	773-942-7585	$$$		Ready for Bistro Campagne oveflow.
Los Nopales	4544 N Western Ave	773-334-3149	$$	10 pm	Creative, cheap Mexican BYOB.
Margie's Candies	1813 W Montrose Ave	773-348-0400	$	11 pm	Ridiculously decadent sundaes and homemade confections.
Opart Thai House	4658 N Western Ave	773-989-8517	$	10:45 pm	Local favorite for fresh Thai. BYOB.
Orange Garden	1942 W Irving Park Rd	773-525-7479	$$	10 pm	Over seventy years of Cantonese cooking.
Over Easy Café	4943 N Damen Ave	773-506-2605	$	3 pm	Bright breakfast spot.
Pannenkoeken Cafe	4757 N Western Ave	773-769-8800	$	3 pm	It's like having dessert for breakfast!
Pizza DOC	2251 W Lawrence Ave	773-784-8777	$$	11 pm	Popular spot for wood-fired pizzas. Early for families, later for dates.
Roong Petch Restaurant	1828 W Montrose Ave	773-989-0818	$	10 pm	Vegetarians get their own special menu.
Smokin' Woody's	4160 N Lincoln Ave	773-880-1100	$$	11 pm	Ribs 'n' wings 'n' other sticky eats.
Snappy's Shrimp House	1901 W Irving Park Rd	773-244-1008	$	10pm	Frozen or friend shrimp to go.
Spacca Napoli	1769 W Sunnyside Ave	773-878-2420	$$	10 pm	Neapolitan styles pizza in Ravenswood.
Sticky Rice	4018 N Western Ave	773-588-0133	$	12 am	No frills storefront serves amazing Thai for cheap!
Tank Sushi	4514 N Lincoln Ave	773-769-2600	$$	11:30 pm	Fresh sushi with Latin flair.

Map 40 • Uptown

Agami	4712 N Broadway St	773-506-1845	$$$	2 am	Swanky sushi.
Anna Maria Pasteria	4400 N Clark St	773-506-2662	$$	11 pm	Cute, neighborhood Italian, casual date spot.
Cafe Lao	1007 W Argyle St	773-275-5092	$*	11pm	Straighforward, well-executed Laotian.
Café Too	4715 N Sheridan Rd	773-275-0626	$	9 pm	Uptown café provides job training for the homeless.
Carmela's Taqueria	1206 W Lawrence Ave	773-275-5321			Above average al pastor (for the northside).
Deleece	4004 N Southport Ave	773-325-1710	$$	11 pm	Ambitious global fare in cute storefront.
Demera	4801 N Broadway St	773-334-8787	$$	4 pm	Neighborhood Ethiopian.
Furama	4936 N Broadway St	773-271-1161	$$	10 pm	Dim sum with karaoke.
Hai Yen	1055 W Argyle St	773-561-4077	$$	10:30 pm	Chinese and veggie pho.
Hama Matsu	5143 N Clark St	773-506-2978	$$$	10:30 pm	Japanese and Korean fare.
Iyanze	4623 N Broadway St	773-944-1417	$$	10 pm	Spacious pan-African from folks who brought us Lakeview's Bolat.
JJ Fish & Chicken	4515 N Sheridan Rd	773-275-3474	$*	9 pm	Fried catfish, perch and okra…a heart attack waiting to happen.
La Amistad	1419 W Montrose Ave	773-878-5800	$	9pm	No fusion here, just reliable Mexican.
La Banh Mi Hung Phat	4942 N Sheridan Rd	773-878-6688	$*	6pm	Savory Vietnamese sandwiches.
Le's Pho	4925 N Broadway St	773-784-8723	$	11pm	Vietnamese soup for beginners and veterans alike.
Magnolia Café	1224 W Wilson Ave	773-728-8785	$$	11:30 pm	American bistro.
Marigold	4832 N Broadway St	773-293-4653	$$$	11 pm	Tasty, but is it that much better than take-out?

Mixteco Grill	1601 W Montrose Ave	773-868-1601	$$	11 pm	BYO at this tasty, stand out Mexican Grill by a Frontera alum.
Palace Gate	4548 N. Magnolia	773-769-1793	$$	10pm	True blue Ghanaian grub.
Pho 777	1065 W Argyle St	773-561-9909	$	10pm	Try the tripe.
Riques	5004 N Sheridan Rd	773-728-6200	$	11 pm	Inexpensive and creative Mexican BYOB.
Siam Noodle & Rice	4654 N Sheridan Rd	773-769-6694	$	9:30 pm	Damn fine Thai food.
Silver Seafood	4829 N Broadway St	773-784-0668	$	1 am	Asian delights from the sea.
Sun Wah BBQ	5039 N Broadway St	773-769-1254	$$	10 pm	Notable for the barbequed ducks hanging in the window.
TAC Quick	3930 N Sheridan Rd	773-327-5253	$$	11 pm	Cheap and delicious. Thai-language menu available for the adventurous.
Tapas Las Ramblas	5101 N Clark St	773-769-9700	$$	12am	Let's try traditinal tapas in this high turnover locale. Why not?
Taqueria los Caminos de Michoacan	3948 N Sheridan Rd	773-296-9709	$	5 am	No ambiance, bad Mexican soap operas, incredibly delicious regional Mexican food.
Thai Pastry	4925 N Broadway St	773-784-5399	$	11 pm	Free pastry with every order!
Titzal Cafe	4631 N Clark St	773-271-4631			Chilaquiles and oatmeal shakes.
Tweet	5020 N Sheridan Rd	773-728-5576	$$	10:30 pm	Gourmet food without pretension.
Winston's Cafe	5001 N Clark St	773-728-0050	$		New-agey music, kaleidoscopic bar, leather-bar-turned-cafe. Interesting.

Map 41 • Avondale / Old Irving

The Buffet Castle	3326 W Belmont Ave	773-267-6688	$	10:30 pm	Smorgasbord, Chinese-style. MSG a plenty.
Burrito House	3145 W Addison St	773-279-9111	$	2 am	At least they're open late.
Chief O'Neill's	3471 N Elston Ave	773-583-3066	$	10 pm	Excellent traditional pub fare.
Dragon Lady Lounge	3188 N Elston Ave	773-597-5617			Korean dive bar with GREAT vegan buffet.
Eat First Chinese Restaurant	3337 W Belmont Ave	773-588-7071		11 pm	No dining room to speak of, but super-fast delivery of standard Chinese.
Hot Doug's	3324 N California Ave	773-279-9550	$*	4 pm	Super popular gourmet hot dogs and duck fat fries.
Kuma's Corner	2900 W Belmont Ave	773-604-8769	$$	2 am	Heavy metal bar and grill with famous burgers and lots of ink.
La Finca	3361 N Elston Ave	773-478-4006	$	10 pm	Friendly, family run servicable Mexican and margaritas.
Mr. Pollo	3000 W Belmont Ave	773-509-1208	$	9 pm	South American chicken joint. Get a guanabana shake.
Taqueria Trespazada	3144 N California Ave	773-539-4533	$*	2 am	Tasty, cheap tacos and salsas—no atmosphere.
Urban Belly	3053 N California Ave	773-583-0500	$$	11 pm	Incredibly good dumplings and noodle bowls, quick turn around BYOB.
Zacatecas	2934 W Diversey Ave	773-278-4828	$	3 am	Taqueria. Typical.

Map 42 • North Center / Roscoe Village / West Lakeview

90 Miles Cuban Cafe	3101 N Clybourn Ave	773-248-2822			Casual Cuban, counter-seating only.
Delicious Cafe	3827 N Lincoln Ave	773-477-9840			Vegan cafe fare.
El Tinajon	2054 W Roscoe St	773-525-8455	$$	10 pm	Good, cheap Guatemalan. Great mango margaritas.
Fonda Del Mar	3908 N Lincoln Ave	773-489-3748	$$		Stylish Mexican food minus the price tag.
Frasca	3358 N Paulina St	773-248-5222	$$	11pm	European-style pizza with a cozy wine bar and outdoor seating.
Kaze Sushi	2032 W Roscoe St	773-327-4860	$$	11:30 pm	Innovative, gourmet sushi.
Kitsch'n on Roscoe	2005 W Roscoe St	773-248-7372	$$	10 pm	Clever retro food and tiki bar. Friendly staff.
Lucky's Sandwich Shop	3472 N Clark St	773-549-0665	$	2am	They put fries IN the sandwich. Genius.
Mrs. Murphy and Sons	3905 N Lincoln Ave	773-248-3905	$$$	11 pm	Fancy Irish food: An oxymoron, or reality? Decide for yourself here.
Piazza Bella Trattoria	2116 W Roscoe St	773-477-7330	$$$	11 pm	Neighborhood Italian.
Scooter's Frozen Custard	1658 W Belmont Ave	773-244-6415	$	10pm	The tastiest custard this side of St. Louis.
Sola	3868 N Lincoln Ave	773-327-3868	$$$	10:30 pm	Contemporary American with Polynesian flair.
T-Spot Sushi	3925 N Lincoln Ave	773-549-4500	$$	11 pm	Good sushi and tea in small Euro-fancy room. BYOB.
Terragusto	1851 W Addison St	773-248-2777	$$	9:30 pm	Italian market with café.
Thai Linda Café	2022 W Roscoe St	773-868-0075	$$	9:45 pm	Standard-issue neighborhood Thai.
Turquoise Restaurant on Roscoe	2147 W Roscoe St	773-549-3523	$$	12 am	Fresh and creative Middle-Eastern fare.
Victory's Banner	2100 W Roscoe St	773-665-0227	$	3 pm	Vegetarian brunch served by toga-clad Sri Chimnoy followers.
Volo Restaurant and Wine Bar	2008 W Roscoe St	773-348-4600	$$$	12 am	New American small plates with swirl.

Map 43 • Wrigleyville / East Lakeview

Ann Sather Restaurant	909 W Belmont Ave	773-348-2378	$	3 pm	Warm, family friendly ambience, Swedish comfort food.
Blue Bayou	3734 N Southport Ave	773-871-3300	$$	11 pm	New Orleans-themed, in case you couldn't guess.
Bolat	3346 N Clark St	773-665-1100	$$	11 pm	West African cuisine—try the okra with rice.
Capt'n Nemos	3650 N Ashland Ave	773-929-7687	$	9 pm	Great sandwiches and yummy soup.
Coobah	3423 N Southport Ave	773-528-2220	$$	2 am	Trendy Latin spot near Music Box.
Cozy Noodles n' Rice	3456 N Sheffield Ave	773-327-0100	$$	10.30pm	Yep, it's cozy.
Duck Walk	919 W Belmont Ave	773-665-0455	$	11 pm	Your basic Thai, cheap but good.
Fianco	3440 N Southport Ave	773-327-6400			Neighborhood Italian.
Frasca	3358 N Paulina St	773-248-5222	$$	11 pm	European-style pizza with a cozy wine bar and outdoor seating.
Golden Apple	2971 N Lincoln Ave	773-528-1413	$	24-hrs	24-hour greasy hangover food. Once featured on This American Life.
Lucky's	3472 N Clark St	773-549-0665	$	3 am	They put fries IN the sandwich. Genius.
Matsu Yama	1059 W Belmont Ave	773-327-8838	$$	12 am	Lovely, fresh sushi.
Matsuya	3469 N Clark St	773-248-2677	$$	11:30 pm	One of the best on Sushi Row.
Mia Francesca	3311 N Clark St	773-281-3310	$$	11 pm	Contemporary Italian date place.
Mystic Celt	3443 N Southport Ave	773-529-8550	$$	2 am	Irish pub-style restaurant. Awesome Irish eggrolls.
Orange	3231 N Clark St	773-549-4400	$$	2 pm	Super stylish brunches.
Panes	3002 N Sheffield Ave	773-665-0972	$	10 pm	Homemade sandwiches, muffins, cookies, and brownies.
Penny's Noodle Shop	3400 N Sheffield Ave	773-281-8222	$$	10:30 pm	Pad thai, pad see ew, popular place for a lite lunch.
PS Bangkok	3345 N Clark St	773-871-7777	$	11:30 pm	Popular neighborhood Thai that delivers.
Rise	3401 N Southport Ave	773-525-3535	$$	11:30 pm	Sushi nightspot.
Risque Cafe	3419 N Clark St	773-525-7711	$$$*	2 am	Tangy barbecue and over 300 craft beers.
S&G	3000 N Lincoln Ave	773-935-4025	$	24-hrs	Cop hangout with chintzy decorating and fake plants. In other words, we love it.
Samah	3330 N Clark St	773-248-4606	$$	3am	Hookahs and food. Earthy and Mediterranean.
Shiroi Hana	3242 N Clark St	773-477-1652	$$	10:30 pm	Standard sushi spot.
Socca	3301 N Clark St	773-248-1155	$$	11 pm	Tasty, satisfying Mediterannean.
Tango Sur	3763 N Southport Ave	773-477-5466	$$	11:30 pm	Vegetarian's vision of hell: big juicy Argentine steaks.
Twisted Spoke	3369 N Clark St	773-525-5300	$	1 am	Plays porn and serves eggs late night on weekends, slow service.
Wrigleyville Dog	3737 N Clark St	773-296-1500	$*	4 am	Post Metro stop for chili-cheese fries.

Map 44 • East Lakeview

Adesso	3332 N Broadway St	773-868-1516	$$	11:30 pm	Italian comfort food.
Aladdin's Eatery	614 W Diversey Pkwy	773-327-6300	$	11pm	Fresh Middle-Eastern.
Angelina Ristorante	3561 N Broadway St	773-935-5933	$$$	11 pm	Casual, romantic Italian.
Ann Sather Broadway Cafe	3411 N Broadway St	773-305-0024	$	3 pm	Airy branch of local comfort food chain.
Arco de Cuchilleros	3445 N Halsted St	773-296-6046	$$$	12 am	Intimate tapas; great sangria.
The Bagel	3107 N Broadway St	773-477-0300	$	11 pm	Great deli fare.
Baladoche	2905 N Clark St	773-880-5090	$	11 pm	Don't call them waffles.
Bobtail Soda Fountain	2951 N Broadway St	773-880-7372	$	11 pm	Norman Rockwell would be proud.
Chicago Diner	3411 N Halsted St	773-935-6696	$$	11 pm	A vegetarian institution.
Chilam Balam	3023 N Broadway	773-296-6901			Yummy organic, small plate Mexican.
Clark Street Dog	3040 N Clark St	773-281-6690	$*	3 am	24-hour hot dogs and cheese fries.
Cornelia's	750 W Cornelia Ave	773-248-8333	$$	11 pm	Tres Gay Boystown ski lodge / cabaret lounge.
The Counter	666 W Diversey Pkwy	773-935-1995	$$	11 pm	Great burgers and shakes. The heart attack is worth it.
Erwin, An American Café & Bar	2925 N Halsted St	773-528-7200	$$$$	10 pm	Elegant.
Firefly	3335 N Halsted St	773-525-2505	$$	1 am	Upscale neighborhood joint.
Flub A Dub Chub's	3021 N Broadway St	773-857-6500	$	11pm	Hot dogs Chicago-style. No ketchup.
Half Shell	676 W Diversey Pkwy	773-549-1773	$$$*	11:30 pm	Casual raw bar.
HB	3404 N Halsted St	773-661-0299	$$$	10:30 pm	Nice date spot for upscale comfort food.
Hiro's Café	2936 N Broadway St	773-477-8510	$$	11pm	Enjoy a side of Beyonce with your sushi.
Jack's on Halsted	3201 N Halsted St	773-244-9191	$$$$	11:30 pm	Great wine list.
Joy's	3257 N Broadway St	773-327-8330	$$	11 pm	Standard noodles, soup, or fried rice; impressively simple.
La Creperie	2845 N Clark St	773-528-9050	$$	11 pm	Live French music. Shabby, but cute.
Mark's Chop Suey	3343 N Halsted St	773-281-9090	$	11 pm	The BEST eggrolls.
New Tokyo	3139 N Broadway St	773-248-1193	$$	10:45 pm	Reasonably priced sushi and BYOB at this cozy Japanese spot.
Nookie's Tree	3334 N Halsted St	773-248-9888	$	n/a	24-hour diner.

Ping Pong Restaurant	3322 N Broadway St	773-281-7575	$$$	12 am	Always busy BYO, hit or miss Asian fusion.
Stella's Diner	3042 N Broadway St	773-472-9040	$	10 pm	Can you say diner?
Sura	3124 N Broadway St	773-248-7872	$$	2 am	Classy Thai bistro with funky swinging chairs in the bar.
Veg Out	3176 N Broadway St	773-880-6452	$*	9 pm	Melange of pimped-out greens.
Wakamono	3317 N Broadway St	773-296-6800	$$	11:30 pm	Sushi and Japanese small plates.
Yoshi's Café	3257 N Halsted St	773-248-6160	$$$	11 pm	Franco-Japanese fusion.

Northwest

Al Primo Canto	5414 W Devon Ave	773-631-0100	$$$$	10 pm	"Endless feast" of terrific Brazillian food.
Amitabul	6207 N Milwaukee Ave	773-774-0276	$$	10 pm	Buddha-inspired Korean Vegan.
Balanced Kitchen	6263 N McCormick Blvd	773-463-1085	$$	7 pm	No meat, dairy, or wheat. Why live?
Big Pho	3821 W Lawrence Ave	773-866-2015	$*	10pm	Vietnamese comfort food in a bowl.
Birria Huentitan	4019 W North Ave	773-276-0768	$*	24-hrs	Cheap late night eats and huge burritos.
Blue Angel	5310 N Milwaukee Ave	773-631-8700	$	24-hrs	Chicago's only stunt-flier-themed 24-hour diner.
Borincuba	3424 W Irving Park Rd	773-866-2822	$$	8 pm	Home-cooking from Cuba and Puerto Rico.
Brown Sack	3706 W Armitage Ave	773-661-0675	$*	7 pm	Pick up gourmet sandwiches and amazing malts or milkshakes.
Café con Leche	2714 N Milwaukee Ave	773-289-4274	$*	8 pm	Huevos con chorizo and a quick cup of joe start the morning right.
Carthage Café	3446 W Foster Ave	773-539-9004	$$	3 am	Hook up with a hookah and taste exotic Tunisian specialtes.
Chai Asian Bistro	4748 W Peterson Ave	773-481-0008	$	10 pm	Good by any standard. Great for the Northwest side.
Chiyo	3800 W Lawrence Ave	773-267-1555	$$$	12 am	Order their 7-course kaiseki menu a few days in advance. Otherwise, opt for the sukiyaki.
Chocolate Shoppe Ice Cream	5337 W Devon Ave	773-763-9778	$*	11 pm	Ice cream shop on acid.
Don Juan	6730 N Northwest Hwy	773-775-6438	$$	11 pm	Popular Mexican spot.
Edgebrook Coffee Shop	6322 N Central Ave	773-792-1433	$*	2 pm	Old-school homemade diner grub
El Cubanito	2555 N Pulaski Rd	773-235-2555	$*	5 pm	Yummy Cuban sammiches.
Elliott's Seafood Grille & Chop House	6690 N Northwest Hwy	773-775-5277	$$$	11pm	Grilling steaks and seafood for 70 years.
Fonda Del Mar	3749 W Fullerton Ave	773-489-3748	$$	11 pm	Stylish Mexican food minus the price tag.
Friendship Chinese Restaurant	2830 N Milwaukee Ave	773-227-0970	$$	10:30 pm	Classy Chinese.
Gale Street Inn	4914 N Milwaukee Ave	773-725-1300	$$$	10:30 pm	Classy ribs 'n' jazz joint.
Gloria's Café	3300 W Fullerton Ave	773-342-1050	$$	9 pm	Columbian comfort food and cafe fare.
Grota Smorgasborg	3112 N Central Ave	773-622-4677	$$	10 pm	All-you-can-eat chow in medieval-feeling banquet hall.
Halina's Polish Delights	5914 W Lawrence Ave	773-205-0256	$*	9 pm	Tiny authentic Polish diner.
Hiromi's	3609 W Lawrence Ave	773-588-6764	$	2 am	Phillipino and Japanese food. Tagalong karaoke (English on request).
Joy Ribs	6320 N Lincoln Ave	773-509-0211	$$	12 pm	Korean BBQ done one better with a zingy marinade.
La Villa Restaurant	3638 N Pulaski Rd	773-283-7980	$$	1:30 am	Neighborhood family-friendly eatery.
Mario's Café	5241 N Harlem Ave	773-594-9742	$	2:30 am	Need a quick Bulgarian fix? Mario's is the place.
Mayan Sol	3830 W Lawrence Ave	773-539-4398	$$*	10 pm	Upscale Central American and South American cuisine.
Mirabell	3454 W Addison St	773-463-1962	$$	11 pm	Adorable German tavern.
Montasero's Ristorante	3935 W Devon Ave	773-588-2515	$$	10 pm	Don't be surprised to find an envelope full of unmarked bills in the toilet tank.
Pollo Campero	2730 N Narragansett Ave	773-622-6657	$	10 pm	Guatemalan fried-chicken chain.
Red Apple	3121 N Milwaukee Ave	773-588-5781	$	9:30 pm	Polish comfort food. Is there any other kind?
Ristorante Agostino	2817 N Harlem Ave	773-745-6464	$$	11 pm	Elegant date place for impeccable Italian.
Sabatino's	4441 W Irving Park Rd	773-283-8331	$$	12:30 am	Romantic date place.
Seo Hae	3534 W Lawrence Ave	773-539-2444	$$	10 pm	No frills family-owned Korean place.
Shiraz	4425 W Montrose Ave	773-777-7275	$$	11 pm	Try a Koobideh at this Persian spot.
Smak-Tak	5961 N Elston Ave	773-763-1123	$	9 pm	Great pierogis on a penny budget.
Smoque	3800 N Pulaski Rd	773-545-7427	$$	10 pm	BYOBBBQ!
So Gong Dong Tofu House	3307 W Bryn Mawr Ave	773-539-8377	$$	10 pm	Yummy Korean tofu soup spot.
Sol de Mexico	3018 N Cicero Ave	773-282-4119	$$$	10 pm	Creative, upscale Mexican food in a dressed-up taqueria.
Super Pollo	3640 W Wrightwood Ave	773-278-9227	$	9:30 pm	Cheap, delicious Puerto Rican.
Teresa II Polish Restaurants & Lounge	4751 N Milwaukee Ave	773-283-0184	$$*	11 pm	Clean your plate or Teresa will scold you.
Trattoria Pasta D'Arte	6311 N Milwaukee Ave	773-763-1181	$$	11 pm	Upscale, creative Italian.
Tre Kronor	3258 W Foster Ave	773-267-9888	$$	10 pm	Swedish institution.
Via Veneto	6340 N Lincoln Ave	773-267-0888	$$$	11 pm	Trattoria food in a banquet hall body.
Zia's Trattoria	6699 N Northwest Hwy	773-775-0808	$$$	11pm	Edison Park's version of swanky.

West

Amarind's	6822 W North Ave	773-889-9999	$$	10 pm	People drive from all over for awesome Thai food.
Bacchanalia Ristorante	2413 S Oakley Ave	773-254-6555	$$*	11 pm	Cozy Italian spot.
Bruna's	2424 S Oakley Ave	773-254-5550	$$	11 pm	Cozy old-school Italian.
CJ's Eatery	3839 W Grand Ave	773-292-0990	$$	9 pm	Diner meets soul food meets south of the border.
Coco	2723 W Division St	773-384-4811	$$$	1 am	Upscale contemporary and classic Puerto Rican.
Coleman's Hickory House	5754 W Chicago Ave	773-287-0363	$	3 am	Killer chicken and ribs at dirt cheap prices.
Depot	5840 W Roosevelt Rd	773-261-8422	$	10 pm	Lovingly homemade diner classics
Edna's Restaurant	3175 W Madison St	773-638-7079	$	7 pm	Best soul food on the west side.
El Salvador Restaurante	4125 S Archer Ave	773-579-0405	$$*	9 pm	Pupusas and more.
Falco's Pizza	2806 W 40th St	773-523-7996	$	1:30 am	Popular casual Italian spot.
Feed	2803 W Chicago Ave	773-489-4600	$$*	10 pm	Tasty grilled chicken.
Flying Saucer	1123 N California Ave	773-342-9076	$$	10 pm	Creative diner fare at hipster hangout.
Haro	2436 S Oakley Ave	773-847-2400	$$	1 am	The small plate madness is spreading!!!
Humboldt Pie	1001 N California Ave	773-342-4743	$	10 pm	Spacious, eccentric coffeehouse and pizza place.
I.C.Y. Vegetarian Restaurant & Juice Bar	3141 W Roosevelt Rd	773-762-1090	$	11pm	Veggie diner fare.
Ignotz	2421 S Oakley Ave	773-579-0300	$$*	11 pm	Northern Italian in cozy setting.
La Palma	1340 N Homan Ave	773-862-0886	$	8 pm	Authentic Puerto Rican grub at no-frills cafeteria.
Lalo's	3515 W 26th St	773-522-0345	$$	10 pm	Local chain popular for their margaritas.
Lindy's and Gertie's	3685 S Archer Ave	773-927-7807	$	12 am	Local chili and ice-cream chain.Try the chili-ice-cream sundae.
MacArthur's	5412 W Madison Ave	773-261-2316	$*	9 pm	Sweet potatoes, collard greens, and grits, cafeteria style.
Maiz	1041 N California Ave	773-276-3149	$*	10 pm	Homemade corn masa antojito heaven.
New Submarine Pier	4048 S Archer Ave	773-890-4733	$*	10 pm	Best subs on this side of town.
Taqueria Atotonilco	3916 W 26th St	773-762-3380	$*	11 pm	Quick, friendly eat-in or take-out hangover cure-all.
Taqueria Los Comales	3141 W 26th St	773-247-0977	$*	5 am	Stop for excellent tacos on your way home from jail.
Taqueria Los Gallos 2	4252 S Archer Ave	773-254-2081	$*	12am	Homestyle food from Jalisco.
Taqueria Puebla Mexico	3625 W North Ave	773-772-8435	$*	9 pm	Authentic Mexican from the Puebla region.
TipsyCake	1043 N California Ave	773-384-4418	$$$	6 pm	Sumptious cakes.
Tommy's Rock-n-Roll Café	2548 W Chicago Ave	773-486-6768	$	4 pm	Homemade donuts, sandwiches, and guitars.

Southwest

Beverly Woods Restaurant	11532 S Western Ave	773-233-7700	$$$	8 pm	Banqueting traditional in original Beverly Hills.
Birrieria de la Torre	6724 S Pulaski Rd	773-767-6075	$*	10pm	Soup, soup, oh Mexican soup...
Bobak's	5275 S Archer Ave	773-735-5334	$	9 pm	A melange of Polish buffet and supermarket, Chicago style.
Café 103	1909 W 103rd St	773-238-5115	$$$	10 pm	Finally, fine-dining in Beverly.
Fox's Beverly Restaurant and Pizza	9956 S Western Ave	773-239-3212	$$	10 pm	Sweet sauce + crispy thin crust = the southside's best pizza.
Franconello's Italian Restaurant	10222 S Western Ave	773-881-4100	$$	11 pm	Peek-a-boo with the chefs in the exhibition kitchen as they crank out old-world class.
Harold's Chicken Shack	7247 S Racine Ave	773-783-9499	$*	2 am	Stand out branch of local chicken chain.
Hoe China Tea	4020 W 55th St	773-284-2463	$	9:30 pm	Come for the fruity cocktails.
Janson's Drive-In / Snyder's Red Hots	9900 S Western Ave	773-238-3612	$*	10 pm	No indoor seating at this classic drive-thru.
Koda	10352 S Western Ave	773-445-5632	$$$	11 pm	No surprises in this servicable Beverly Bistrot.
Lagniappe	1525 W 79th St	773-994-6375	$$	8 pm	Like a trip to N'Awlins but with better food.
Lume's	11601 S Western Ave	773-233-2323	$	3:45 pm	Where the beautiful people breakfast and lunch 'til evening.
Nile	3259 W 63rd St	773-434-7218	$	11pm	Possibly the best Middle Eastern grub in Chicago.
The Original Vito and Nick's Pizzeria	8433 S Pulaski Rd	773-735-2050	$$*	11 pm	Da pizza's all dat matters here, kay?
Rhythm & Spice	2501 W 79th St	773-476-5600	$	10pm	Order the jerk chicken, duh.
Sunugal	2051 E 79th St	773-721-5600	S	10:30 pm	Friendly Sengalese for cheap.
Szalas	5214 S Archer Ave	773-582-0300	$$$	11 pm	Outrageously campy decor!
Tatra Inn	6040 S Pulaski Rd	773-582-8313	$	8 pm	Eastern European smorgasbord.
Top Notch Beefburger	2116 W 95th St	773-445-7218	$*	8:30 pm	Burgers and fries in 50's environment—very Happy Days.

Uncle Joe's Jerk	10210 S Vincennes Ave	773-779-9966	$	8 pm	Beverly Plaza location, where jerk salad is to slay for.
Veggie Bite	3031 W 111th St	773-239-4367	$	10 pm	Vegan fast food. Budget, belly, and bovine friendly.

South

Army & Lou's	422 E 75th St	773-483-3100	$$	10 pm	Southside soul food.
Atomic Sub	6353 S Cottage Grove Ave	773-684-2602	$*	3 pm	Watch out, the bomb has hit!
Barbara Ann's BBQ	7617 S Cottage Grove Ave	773-651-5300	S*	12 am	Better than average 'cue and links.
BJ's Market & Bakery	8734 S Stony Island Ave	773-374-4700	$	9 pm	Popular sunday soul food buffet.
Café Trinidad	557 E 75th St	773-846-8081	$$	9 pm	Great seafood options like curry crab and red snapper.
Cal Harbor Restaurant	546 E 115th St	773-264-5435	$*	6 pm	Omelettes, burgers, etc. at family grill.
Captain Hard Times	436 E 79th St	773-487-2900	$$$	12 am	Southside date destination.
Chatham Pancake House	700 E 87th St	773-874-0010	$	3 pm	Cheap, hearty breakfast.
Dat Old Fashioned Donut	8251 S Cottage Grove Ave	773-723-1002	$*	10 pm	Krispy Kreme, eat your heart out.
Helen's Restaurant	1732 E 79th St	773-933-9871	$*	7 pm	Southern cafeteria with downhome cooking.
Izola's	522 E 79th St	773-846-1484	$$	24-hrs	Homey southern food in 24-hour diner.
Lem's	311 E 75th St	773-994-2428	$*	2 am	The gold standard of BBQ joints.
Leon's Bar-B-Que	8249 S Cottage Grove Ave	773-488-4556	$*	3 am	Southside BBQ fixture.
Old Fashioned Donuts	11248 S Michigan Ave	773-995-7420	$	6 pm	Donuts as an art form.
The Parrot Cage	7059 S South Shore Dr	773-602-5333	$$$	10 pm	Fine dining brought to you by Washburne College culinary students.
Phil's Kastle	3532 E 95th St	773-734-9591	$*	24-hrs	50s soda shop with prices to match.
Pupuseria El Salvador	3557 E 106th St	773-374-0490	$	7 pm	Addictive Central American stuffed griddle patties.
The Rib Joint	432 W 87th St	773-651-4108	$	12:45 am	What else? Ribs, of course!
Seven Seas Submarine	11216 S Michigan Ave	773-785-0550	$*	8 pm	Dine in or take out at this tiny sandwich shop.
Soul Queen	9031 S Stony Island Ave	773-731-3366	$	12 am	Inexpensive comfort food.
Soul Vegetarian East	205 E 75th St	773-224-0104	$$	11 pm	Vegetarian soul food? SVE pleases even the skeptics.
Tropic Island Jerk Chicken	1922 E 79th St	773-978-5375	$	11 pm	Caribbean carry-out.
Uncle John's Barbecue	337 E 69th Pl	773-892-1233	$*	10 pm	Heavenly bbq for takeout only.
Vegetarian Fun Foods Supreme	1702 E 87th	773-734-6321	$*	10pm	Veggie fast food dive
Yassa African Caribbean	716 E 79th St	773-488-5599	$$	10 pm	Lots of vegetarian options at this Sengalese spot.

Evanston

Blind Faith Café	525 Dempster St	847-328-6875	$$	10 pm	Vegetarian. Healthy, fiber-filled fare for the Birkenstock set. Food so earthy, you'll need to floss the dirt from your teeth.
Buffalo Joe's	812 Clark St	847-328-5525	$*	12 am	Kick-ass wings and more!
Café Mozart	600 Davis St	847-492-8056	$	11 pm	Wireless Internet, leopard couch, snarky staff.
Clarke's	720 Clark St	847-864-1610	$	2 am	Inexpensive sandwiches and omelettes.
Dave's Italian Kitchen	1635 Chicago Ave	847-864-6000	$$	10:45 pm	Family pasta joint with a killer wine list.
Dixie Kitchen and Bait Shop	825 Church St	847-733-9030	$$	11 pm	Hot cornmeal johnnycakes, fried green tomatoes, corn fritters, North Carolina pulled pork and black eyed peas. Lawd!
Dozika	601 Dempster St	847-869-9740	$$	10 pm	Pan-Asian cuisine. Expensive, but nice variety.
Hecky's Barbeque	1902 Green Bay Rd	847-492-1182	$$	10 pm	It's the sauce that's the boss.
Joy Yee's Noodle Shop	521 Davis St	847-733-1900	$$	10:30 pm	Pricey, trendy "bubble tea" specialists.
Kafein Café	1621 Chicago Ave	847-491-1621	$	2 am	Open 'til 2 am on weeknights and 3 am on weekends, perfect for those late-night cram sessions.
Kansaku	1514 Sherman Ave	847-864-4386	$$$	10pm	Chic but approachable sushi.
Las Palmas	817 University Pl	847-328-2555	$$	11 pm	High-priced margaritas; fresh Mexican fare.
The Lucky Platter	514 Main St	847-869-4064	$$	10 pm	Unique comfort food complimented by David Lynch-esque folk art décor.
Lulu's Dim Sum and Then Sum	804 Davis St	847-869-4343	$$	11 pm	Best Pad Thai in Evanston. Huge portions, reasonably priced.
Mt Everest	630 Church St	847-491-1069	$$$	10 pm	Nepalese and Indian food with lunch buffet.
Mustard's Last Stand	1613 Central St	847-864-2700	$*	10:30 pm	Legendary hot dog institution.
Narra	1710 Orrington Ave	847-866-8700	$$$$	10 pm	Unpretentious fine dining in the Hotel Orrington.
Noodles & Company	930 Church St	847-733-1200	$$	10 pm	Thai noodles, pasta, even mac and cheese!

Olive Mountain	610 Davis St	847-475-0380	$$	10:30 pm	Middle Eastern specialties.
Pete Miller's Original Steakhouse	1557 Sherman Ave	847-328-0399	$$$$$	1:30 am	American. Beef bubbas stake out this joint.
Tapas Barcelona	1615 Chicago Ave	847-866-9900	$$$	11 pm	Spanish. Lick your fingers with friends over tasty tapas and sangria.
Trattoria Demi	1571 Sherman Ave	847-332-2330	$$	10 pm	Good Italian food in a cozy setting.
Unicorn Café	1723 Sherman Ave	847-332-2312	$*	12 am	Quaint and reasonably priced.
Va Pensiero	1566 Oak Ave	847-475-7779	$$$$$	10 pm	Italian. Classy, romantic supper club offering over 250 Italian wines. A "pop the question" kind of place.
Vive la Crepe	1565 Sherman Ave	847-570-0600	$$	10pm	Cute psuedo-French place for a cheap date.

Oak Park

Buzz Café	905 S Lombard Ave	708-524-2899	$	9 pm	Neighborhood-centric, good food, quirky art, live story-telling, and music. Nuff said!
Café Le Coq	734 Lake St	708-848-2233	$$$$	10 pm	French Bistro wows Oak Park foodies, just down the street from many of Oak Park's sites.
Cucina Paradiso	814 North Blvd	708-848-3434	$$$	10:30 pm	Italian. Fork-twirling Oak Parkers come a-datin' at this friendly pasta place and bar.
Jeruselum Café	1030 Lake St	708-848-7734	$$	11 pm	Terrific Middle Eastern food, with an extensive juice bar.
Khyber Pass	1031 Lake St	708-445-9032	$$	10 pm	Indian. Taxi drivers and curry-loving locals fill up on lunch and dinner buffets.
Mama Thai	1112 W Madison St	708-386-0100	$$	10 pm	Inexpensive, charming, and delicious.
Marion Street Grill	189 N Marion St	708-383-1551	$$$	10 pm	Inviting, upscale restaurant featuring fresh seafood, steaks, and chops. Impressive wine list.
New Rebozo	1116 Madison St	708-445-0370	$$$	10:30 pm	Best Mexican in town with a delicious upscale tweak to the specials.
Oak Park Abbey	728 Lake St	708-358-8840	$$	11 pm	Small plates have struck Oak Park and continue to spread!
Pete's Red Hots	6346 W Roosevelt Rd	708-383-6122	$*	12 am	Fast food at its finest. Best fries ever.
Petersen Ice Cream	1100 Chicago Ave	708-386-6131	$$	10 pm	American. Comfort food and silky ice cream make this diner a popular destination.
Philander's Oak Park	1120 Pleasant St	708-848-4250	$$$$	11:30 pm	Seafood. Marine cuisine served in handsome atmosphere; nightly, fishtail to live jazz.
Poor Phil's	139 S Marion St	708-848-0871	$$	1 am	Popcorn is free; popcorn shrimp isn't.

Navy Pier

Bubba Gump Shrimp Co	700 E Grand Ave	312-252-4867	$$	12 am	Navy Pier tourist trap.
Capi's Italian Kitchen	700 E Grand Ave	312-276-0641	$$	10 pm	Hand-tossed brick oven pizza.
Joe's Be-Bop Café & Jazz Emporium	700 E Grand Ave	312-595-5299	$$$	10 pm	Live jazz and Southern food from the owners of Jazz Showcase.
Riva	700 E Grand Ave	312-644-7482	$$$	11 am	Touristic fine dining on the Pier.

Skokie

Barnum and Bagel	4700 Dempster St	847-676-4466	$	9 pm	Eat-in deli popular with families.
Don's Fishmarket	9335 Skokie Blvd	847-677-3424	$$$	11 pm	Popular seafood restaurant features "Shrimp Extravaganza", "Crabfest", and "Lobsterfest."
El Tipico	3341 Dempster St	847-676-4070	$$	11:30 pm	Skokie's favorite margarita and burrito joint.
Grecian Kitchen Delights	3938 Dempster St	847-677-5507	$	9 pm	Mostly carryout with good value Greek Chicken.
Hub's Ribs	3727 Dempster St	847-673-9409	$	12 am	Nothing kosher or vegetarian-friendly about this local bbq favorite.
Hy Life Bistro	4120 Dempster St	847-674-2021	$$$*	9 pm	Kosher restaurant that is vegetarian-friendly.
Kabul House	3320 Dempster St	847-763-9930	$$	10 pm	One of Chicagoland's few Afghani restaurants.
Kaufman's Deli	4905 Dempster St	847-677-9880	$	8 pm	This is THE deli that people return to. Best bagels in the Midwest.
Papillon	5111 Brown St	847-763-1322	$$$	10 pm	French fine dining in downtown Skokie.
Pita Inn	3910 Dempster	847-677-0211	$	12 am	Local favorite for cheap, speedy falafel and shawerma.
Ruby of Siam	9420 Skokie Blvd	847-675-7008	$$	11 pm	Authentic and appealing Thai food.
Shallots Bistro	4741 Main St	847-677-3463	$$$$	10 pm	Kosher fine dining—closed Fridays and Saturdays

Chicago is a city of neighborhoods, and as such, we are a city of great little neighborhood taverns. These are the places where the beer you drink is on tap, the bartender throws a basket of pretzels in front of you when you grab your stool, and on any given weekday between 5 and 7 you're likely to see the same sad sacks you see every night, stealing precious time between the bossman and the kids. And then there's the jukebox. The best ones feature all your favorite bar songs, from Hank Williams to The Cars, Blondie to Sly and the Family Stone, and "My Way" sung in Polish or Korean just for the hell of it.

Although you'll find a low-key feel at many bars, there's always something going on in the city. To help you keep on top of it all, check out listings in The Reader, Time Out Chicago, and New City. Websites like Gapers Block (http://www.gapersblock.com) and My Open Bar (http://chi.myopenbar.com) list events and specials. Weekly e-mails from Flavorpill (http://flavorpill.com/chicago) and The A.V. Club (http://www.avclub.com/chicago) will keep your inbox full of things to do.

Dive Bars

Rub shoulders with the characters from a Nelson Algren story at any of the following joints: **Cal's (Map 5)** in the South Loop attracts local winos along with shaggy looking roadies and local slummers from the nearby University Center. In Old Town, the **Old Town Ale House (Map 31)** was once voted best dive bar in the country by someone-mumblemumble-we-forget-who. In Rogers Park, **The Lamp Post (Map 34)** has long drawn a friendly crowd of boozy locals. Other dives such as **Ola's Liquor (Map 21)** can be identified by the mere presence of the "Old Style" bar sign out front.

Arty Crowd

Young urban arty types have carved out their kitsch-embracing niches at Ukrainian Village and Wicker Park spots such as **Club Foot (Map 21)**, **The Gold Star Bar (Map 21)**, **The Inner Town Pub (Map 21)**, **Lava (Map 22)**, **Rainbo Club (Map 21)**, and **Small Bar (Map 21)**, while their Pilsen and River West brethren drink their PBR at **Skylark (Map 26)** and **The Fulton Lounge (Map 24)**, respectively. On the west side, **The California Clipper (West Chicago)** appeals to today's rat pack wannabes, and on the north side, get drunk with happy hipsters and local punters at **The Village Tap (Map 42)**, **The Long Room (Map 39)**, and **the Edgewater Lounge (Map 37)**.

Live Music

Some of Chicago's best live music venues are also neighborhood spots. The legendary Checkerboard Lounge is making a comeback in Hyde Park as **The New Checkerboard Lounge for Blues & Jazz (Map 19)**. **The Velvet Lounge (Map 11)**, on the Near South Side, is a legendary avant-garde jazz dive of the old school tradition. **Katerina's (Map 39)**, on an unassuming stretch of Irving Park in North Center, features regular live gypsy music along with local acts. In the West Village, the **Empty Bottle (Map 21)** is the place to catch touring indie bands. Further west, **Rosa's Lounge (Northwest Chicago)** is a friendly venue for live blues. Catch jazz legend Von Freeman jamming at Chatham's **New Apartment Lounge (South Chicago)** every Wednesday night, or live jazz any night of the week at Uptown's **Green Mill Lounge (Map 40)**. On the northwest side, **The Abbey Pub (Northwest)** features everything from alternative rock acts like The Breeders and Peaches, to singer-songwriter showcases and burlesque. If you want to put some twang in your thang, alt-country acts from the Bloodshot Records label regularly perform at Bucktown's **Hideout (Map 29)**.

Shake a Tailfeather

In Chicago, even the best place to get your groove on is often the one right around the corner. Despite the concentration of huge, dazzling and super expensive high-concept nightclubs in River North and River West, (which are typically the domains of tourists and suburbanites), many local folk prefer smaller, friendlier, and cheaper local options to catch Saturday (or Monday, or Thursday) night fever. In Lincoln Park, **Neo (Map 30)** attracts children of the Eighties and their wannabes with retro dance tunes ranging from goth to new wave. Legendary gay bar **Berlin (Map 43)**, in Lakeview, draws a pansexual crowd for their ever-rotating array of theme nights. **Smart Bar (Map 43)**, in the basement of the rock club **Metro (Map 43)**, spins dance music with an edge. **Funky Buddha (Map 1)** draws a diverse crowd united by a desire to get funky.

What's Your Poison?

Whether you are a wino, a beer swiller, a whiskey sipper or a tequila shooter, have we got a bar for you. If you're a brewhead, then you surely know that Chicago's home to some of the best beer bars in the country, including microbrew afficionados **The Map Room (Map 28)**, **Sheffield's (Map 43)**, **Risque Café (Map 43)**. At all of those locations, be prepared to read before you order because they have full-on booklets listing all their brews. At **Quenchers (Map 28)** you can drink your way around the world. If it's Belgians you crave, try getting a seat at Andersonville's **Hopleaf (Map 40)**. If it's something stronger that you crave, **Deliliah's (Map 29)** serves a world-class collection of whiskey to an amiable crowd of aging hipsters and once-were punks, while fans of the cactus tipple at **Salud Tequila Lounge (Map 21)**. **Marty's (Map 37)** and **Martini Ranch (Map 2)** are fine places to be shaken and not stirred. Vinticultural thrill-seekers need look no further than **The Tasting Room (Map 24)** where the wine selection is as fine as the view.

In the last couple of years, the cocktail has become king in Chicago, with many noted mixologists shaking up fresh ingredients to make some of the best stuff you've ever tasted. Adam Seger at **Nacional 27 (Map 2)** grows his own herbs at the bar for use in innovative mojitos and caipirinhas. Charles Joly holds court at **The Drawing Room at Le Passage (Map 32)** with his takes on classic cocktails. **The Violet Hour (Map 21)** is designed as a speakeasy (look for the yellow light outside) with some of the best mixes in the city. You can also find the speakeasy theme at 1914 at the back of **Red Ivy (Map 43)**. For those who appreciate a good cocktail but are on a budget, check out **The Whistler (Map 27)**, whose short list of classic cocktails won't sap your wallet.

Irish Pubs

Yes, Chicago is full of Irish—and "Irish"—pubs. Some are pretty damn authentic though, so if you're on the north side and it's a good Shepherd's Pie or football match you're craving along with your pint, seek out **Johnny O'Hagan's (Map 43)**, **The Irish Oak (Map 43)**, **Chief O'Neill's (Map 41)**, or **The Globe Pub (Map 39)**. On the southside, well, you can't even contemplate Irish drinking culture in the city without a tip o' the hat to the strip of Western Avenue in Beverly that is home to the annual Southside St. Patrick's Day Parade. **Keegan's Pub (Southwest)**, **Cork & Kerry (Southwest)**, and **Mrs. O'Leary's Dubliner (Southwest)** are all loaded with craic. Every Friday and Saturday Night, the **Irish-American Heritage Center (Northwest)** hosts the **Fifth Province Pub (Northwest)**, an authentic Irish Pub, featuring Irish beer, Irish food, and Irish entertainment

Smoker-Friendly

Since the smoking ban hit, it's harder than ever to enjoy two vices at once. However, some places are more enjoyable than others, including the stoop at **Club Foot (Map 21)**, the beer garden at **Happy Village (Map 21)**, the back porch at **Simon's (Map 37)**, and **Fizz Bar & Grill (Map 43)** that's tented during the winter.

Map 1 • River North / Fulton Market District

Emmit's Irish Pub & Eatery	495 N Milwaukee Ave	312-563-9631	An old-school Chicago establishment.
Funky Buddha Lounge	728 W Grand Ave	312-666-1695	See and be seen at this trendy live music lounge.
Lumen	839 W Fulton St	312-733-2222	Cool, expensive decor and cool, expensive drinks.
The Motel Bar	600 W Chicago Ave	312-822-2900	Hotel bar without the hourly rates!
Rednofive & Fifth Floor	440 N Halsted St	312-733-6699	Two levels of existence: downstairs=dancing, upstairs=posing.
Richard's Bar	491 N Milwaukee Ave	312-733-2251	Old man bar good for starter drinks.

Map 2 • Near North / River North

Andy's	11 E Hubbard St	312-642-6805	Old-school jazz…a Chicago legend.
Bin 36	339 N Dearborn St	312-755-9463	Wineology 101.
Blue Frog Bar & Grill	676 N La Salle Dr	312-943-8900	Chutes and Ladders, Howdy Doody, and Karaoke.
Brehon Pub	731 N Wells St	312-642-1071	Irish pub, lots of TVs for Masterpiece Theater…uh, sports.
Bull and Bear	431 N Wells St	312-527-5973	Got cash? Reserve a table with its own beer tap.
Celtic Crossings	751 N Clark St	312-337-1005	No food, all alcohol - a true Irish pub.
Clark Street Ale House	742 N Clark St	312-642-9253	No pretense, just beer - and lots of it.
Enclave	220 W Chicago Ave	312-654-0234	So big they have a floorplan on the website.
English	444 N Lasalle St	312-222-6200	Pimm's Cups and Earl Grey Mint Martinis. Adequately priced.
Green Door Tavern	678 N Orleans St	312-664-5496	A Chicago landmark; old-school classic.
Howl at the Moon	26 W Hubbard St	312-863-7427	Late-night dinner and pianists who encourage patrons to sing.
The Lucky Lady	440 N State St	312-670-0335	River North's version of a dive bar.
Martini Park	151 W Erie St	312-640-0577	Trendy, cavernous spot with a long martini list.
Martini Ranch	311 W Chicago Ave	312-335-9500	Martinis and after-work mingling.
Ontourage	157 W. Ontario	312-573-1470	Fat chance getting near any of the celebrities who come here.
Pippin's Tavern	806 N Rush St	312-787-5435	Old union haunt = lots of beer.
Pops for Champagne	601 N State St	312-266-7677	Jazz and champers.
Redhead Piano Bar	16 W Ontario St	312-640-1000	Snug piano bar favorite of the area.
Rossi's Liquors	412 N State St	312-644-5775	A dive in the best sense of the word.
Social Twenty-Five	25 W Hubbard St	312-925-7634	High-class sports bar with live music on the weekends.
Sound Bar	226 W. Ontario	312-787-4480	High-end bells and whistles dance club with tough door.
Spy Bar	646 N Franklin St	312-337-2191	Basement club, house music, fashionable crowd, pricey drinks.
Stay	111 W Erie St	312-475-0816	Exclusive after-hours bar, if you can find it.
Streeter's Tavern	50 E Chicago Ave	312-944-5206	Ritzy dive bar for students and tourists.
Swirl Wine Bar	111 W Hubbard St	312-828-9000	Nibble upstairs on Pan-Asian food, and recline downstairs to lounge.
Vision	632 N Dearborn St	312-266-1944	Attached to Excalibur; a modern alternative to the oxygen bar.

Map 3 • Streeterville / Mag Mile

Billy Goat Tavern	430 N Michigan Ave	312-222-1525	Cheezboiga; no fries, chips; pepsi, no coke.
Reagle Beagle	160 E Grand Ave	312-755-9645	Relive the 80s at this cozy bar & grill.
Timothy O'Toole's Pub	622 N Fairbanks Ct	312-642-0700	Irish sports bar with tons of TV space.

Map 4 • West Loop Gate / Greek Town

Dylan's	118 S Clinton St	312-876-2008	Unpretentious West Looper with grub.
Nara	623 W Randolph St	312-887-9999	Hip and laid-back Korean bar.
Spectrum Bar & Griull	233 S Halsted St	312-715-0770	Sports bar with Mediterranean flair.
Snuggery Saloon & Dining Room	225 S Canal St	312-441-9334	Commuter bar inside Union Station.

Map 5 • The Loop

Base Bar	230 N Michigan Ave	312-345-1000	Pricey drinks in the lobby of the Hard Rock Hotel.
Brando's Speakeasy	343 S Dearborn St	773-216-3213	Karaoke to "Free Bird" drunk on fancy martinis or cheap beer.
Cal's	400 S Wells St	312-922-6392	Dictionary definition of "dump" that draws grungy rockers and neighborhood drunks.
Ceres Cafe	141 W Jackson Blvd	312-427-3443	Chicago Board of Trade.
Close Up 2	416 S Clark St	312-385-1111	Sophisticated smooth jazz in the heart of the financial district.
Dugan's	128 S Halsted St	312-421-7191	Lively Irish pub. Free popcorn to help soak up the booze.
Exchequer Pub	226 S Wabash Ave	312-939-5633	Loop location for the working class.
Manhattans	415 S Dearborn St	312-957-0460	Tired of martini bars? Try small but fun Manhattans.
Miller's Pub	134 S Wabash Ave	312-263-4988	A Loop tradition.
Monk's Pub	205 W Lake St	312-357-6665	Wall of books. And beer.
Petterino's	150 N Dearborn St	312-422-0150	Go to church on Sunday, then cabaret here on Monday.
Potter's Lounge	17 E Monroe St	312-917-4933	Posh cocktails in the Palmer House Hilton.

Map 6 • The Loop / Grant Park

Houlihan's	111 E Wacker Dr	312-616-3663	Trendy, semi-obnoxious sports bar.
Tango Chicago	408 S Michigan Ave	312-850-1078	Come for the dance lessons; stay for the cheese spread.

Map 8 • South Loop / Printers Row / Dearborn Park

Buddy Guy's Legends	754 S Wabash Ave	312-427-1190	One of the oldest blues clubs in Chicago, and the hardest to get a drink in.
George's Cocktail Lounge	646 S Wabash Ave	312-427-3964	Columbia students and faculty quaff in this dive between classes.
Kasey's Tavern	701 S Dearborn St	312-427-7992	108-year-old neighborhood oasis.
South Loop Club	701 S State St	312-427-2787	There's something creepy about this place.
Tantrum	1023 S State St	312-939-9160	Tucked-away, nicely appointed bar that attracts a lively South Loop following.

Map 9 • South Loop / South Michigan Ave

Savoy Bar and Grill	800 S Michigan Ave	312-939-1464	Serious drinking in a kooky '50s hotel; early morning breakfast.

Map 11 • South Loop / McCormick Place

M Lounge	1520 S Wabash Ave	312-447-0201	Chic lounge with live jazz.
Reggie's	2109 S State St	312-949-0121	Record store, all-age live music venue, and sports bar & grill all in one place.
Velvet Lounge	67 E Cermak Rd	312-791-9050	Raw, gritty jazz haven.
Wabash Tap	1233 S Wabash Ave	312-360-9488	South Loop, no ties, relax-after-work joint.

Map 13 • Bridgeport (East)

Cobblestone's Bar and Grill	514 W Pershing Rd	773-624-3630	Keep it down during a Sox game.
Ethyl's Party	2600 S Wentworth Ave	312-326-3811	Funeral home turned neighborhood bar-with free snacks on weekends.
Schaller's Pump	3714 S Halsted St	773-376-6332	Neighborhood Sox bar with grub.

Map 16 • Bronzeville

Jokes & Notes	4641 S King Dr	773-373-3390	Upscale comedy/jazz club on fire, with stainless steel bar.
Jimbo's Lounge	3258 S Princeton Ave	312-326-3253	In your face blues and jazz.
The Spoken Word	4655 S King Dr	773-373-2233	Poetry n' jazz.

Map 18 • Washington Park

Odyssey II Cocktail Lounge	211 E Garfield Blvd	773-947-0956	So laid back, they don't even have set hours.

Map 19 • Hyde Park

The Falcon Inn	1601 E 53rd St		Cheap dive of regulars where you can hide out.
New Checkerboard Lounge for Blues and Jazz	5201 S Harper Ave	773-684-1472	This legendary blues and jazz club is back!
The Pub	1212 E 59th St	773-702-9737	A basement student bar redeemed by the people-watching and wood panels.
Seven Ten Lanes	1055 E 55th St	773-347-2695	1920s décor in Hyde Park haven.
Woodlawn Tap & Liquor Store	1172 E 55th St	773-643-5516	U of Chicago legend.

Map 20 • East Hyde Park / Jackson Park

Bar Louie	5500 S South Shore Dr	773-363-5300	Corporate chain martini bar.
The Cove	1750 E 55th St	773-684-1013	Down-and-outers meet life-of-the-minders.
Noon Hookah Lounge	1617 E 55th St	773-643-1670	Wire up by day, relax with a smoke by night.

Map 21 • Wicker Park / Ukrainian Village

Beachwood Inn	1415 N Wood St	773-486-9806	Atari, potato chips and basement-price beers.
Between Boutique Café & Lounge	1324 N Milwaukee Ave	773-292-0585	Home of the beer martini.
Club Foot	1824 W Augusta Blvd	773-489-0379	Cool rock bar, cheap drinks, and DJs every night.
Davenport's	1383 N Milwaukee Ave	773-278-1830	Once legendary skanker bar, now yuppy fern bar. Whattya gonna do?
Debonair Social Club	1575 N Milwaukee	773-227-7990	Friendly and glam go hand in hand in this hipster club.
Double Door	1572 N Milwaukee Ave	773-489-3160	Top local and national alt-rock acts.
Empire Liquors	1566 N Milwaukee Ave	773-278-1600	Eclectic DJs and overflow crowds.
Empty Bottle	1035 N Western Ave	773-276-3600	Avant-garde jazz and indie rock. Smells like cat.
Estelle's Café & Lounge	2013 W North Ave	773-782-0450	Lat time we were here a girl puked on my shoes and no one cared.
The Flat Iron	1565 N Milwaukee Ave	773-365-9000	Average and open late.
Gold Star Bar	1755 W Division St	773-227-8700	Hear the Cars and Cash in under an hour.
Happy Village	1059 N Wolcott Ave	773-486-1512	Ping pong inside, lush beer garden outside—a divey gem.
Inner Town Pub	1935 W Thomas St	773-235-9795	Wicker Park art dorks.
Innjoy	2051 W Division St	773-394-2066	WP Scene-ster place for drinking and local acts.
Lava	1270 N Milwaukee Ave	773-342-5282	Former dive bar has reopened as a swank club.
Mana Food Bar	1742 W Division St	773-342-1742	Gourmet vegetarian with a global influence.
The Note	1565 N Milwaukee Ave	773-489-0011	Eclectic jazz-type fare.
Phyllis' Musical Inn	1800 W Division St	773-486-9862	Divey hot-spot for local music acts.
Piece Bar	1927 W North Ave	773-772-4422	Beer. Pizza.
Rainbo Club	1150 N Damen Ave	773-489-5999	Cool-kid mecca and favorite hang of local celeb John Cusack. Enough said.
Rodan	1530 N Milwaukee Ave	773-276-7036	Ultra modern lounge—video mirrors in the bathrooms.
Salud Tequila Lounge	1471 N Milwaukee Ave	773-235-5577	Tequila lounge…Salud!
Small Bar	2049 W Division St	773-772-2727	Small is the new big at this hipster-cool, cozy hang.
Subterranean Cabaret & Lounge	2011 W North Ave	773-278-6600	Semi-cool music spot.
The Violet Hour	1520 N Damen Ave	773-252-1500	Speakeasy that makes perfect drinks. Get there early.

Map 22 • Noble Square / Goose Island

The Chipp Inn	832 N Greenview Ave	312-421-9052	Swig a Schlitz with hipsters at this vintage storefront tavern.
Crobar	1543 N Kingsbury St	312-266-1900	Club creatures come for the music, tourists come for the creatures.
Exit	1315 W North Ave	773-395-2700	Ooohhh. Dark and scary. Eighties punk/goth throwback.
Joe's	940 W Weed St	312-337-3486	Huge sports bar and music venue for national bands and drunk people.
Lava	1270 N Milwaukee Ave	773-342-5282	Former dive bar has reopened as a swank club.
Northland Tavern	1610 W North Ave	773-342-8181	No-frills dive full of characters.
Republic	1520 N Fremont St	312-731-6200	Meet Trixie and Chad at this enormous club.
Zentra	923 W Weed St	312-787-8899	Image is everything. National DJ acts, fashionable crowd, and hookahs.

Map 23 • West Town / Near West Side

Bar Deville	1958 W Huron St	312-929-2349	A local scene for those who love a proper drink and a respectable atmosphere.
Cleo's	1935 W Chicago Ave	312-243-5600	Hooray for Wing Night Mondays.
Darkroom	2210 W Chicago Ave	773-276-1411	No flash is necessary; artsy crowd, electro music, and industry parties.
High Dive	1938 W Chicago Ave	773-235-3483	Beating the pants off everyday bar food. Make this your reliable favorite.
Sak's Ukrainian Village Restaurant	2301 W Chicago Ave	773-278-4445	One of the few bastions of the old country remaining in the Village.
Tuman's	2159 W Chicago Ave	773-782-1400	Revived local legend. Cheap beer and comfort food.

Map 24 • River West / West Town

Betty's Blue Star Lounge	1600 W Grand Ave	312-243-1699	Where hipsters get drunk and f*ck.
Cobra Lounge	235 N Ashland Ave	312-226-6300	Live bands, DJ, and no TVs.
Five Star Bar & Grill	1424 W Chicago Ave	312-850-2555	Thirty bourbons, upscale bar menu, pool and a stripper pole.
Fulton Lounge	955 W Fulton Market	312-942-9500	Hip but laid back, cool music, outside seating.
J Patricks	1367 W Erie St	312-243-0990	Irish flags, beers, and accents.
Jak's Tap	901 W Jackson Blvd	312-666-1700	From the good folks who brought us the Village Tap.
Juicy Wine Company	694 N Milwaukee Ave	312-492-6620	Find hard-to-find wines, meats and cheeses at this wine bar.
Mahoney's Pub & Grille	551 N Odgen Ave	312-733-2121	Hard-core sports bar.
Matchbox	770 N Milwaukee Ave	312-666-9292	Chicago's smallest bar…bar none.
Relax Lounge	1450 W Chicago Ave	312-666-6006	This classic fifties-style lounge offers spiked milkshakes.
Sonotheque	1444 W Chicago Ave	312-226-7600	Super sleek: the design, the crowd, the music.
Stanley's Kitchen & Tap on Racine	324 S Racine Ave	312-433-0007	Sunday brunch here includes a bloody mary bar and Southern fare.
Tasting Room	1415 W Randolph St	312-942-1313	Swank, low-key wine bar.
Twisted Spoke	501 N Ogden Ave	312-666-1500	$2 Jim Beams served by suicide girls and free porn on Saturday nights.
Victor Hotel	311 N Sangamon St	312-773-6900	Vintage lounge with dramatic decor.

Map 26 • University Village / Little Italy / Pilsen

Bar Louie	1321 W Taylor St	312-633-9393	Generally good music and decent entrees.
BeviAmo Wine Bar	1358 W Taylor St	312-455-8255	Good selection, if a bit pricey.
Hawkeye's Bar & Grill	1458 W Taylor St	312-226-3951	Quality bar food (including the healthy side).
Junior's Sports Lounge	724 W Maxwell St	312-421-2277	Sports bar with upscale pretensions.
Paulie's Place	1750 S Union Ave	312-829-7724	A real dive bar with no hipsters in sight.
Simone's	960 W 18th St	312-666-8601	Hipster bar made from funky recycled materials.
Skylark	2149 S Halsted St	312-948-5275	Hip hangout for Pilsen arty crowd.

Map 27 • Logan Square

Fireside Bowl	2648 W Fullerton Ave	773-486-2700	No longer a punk rock venue, it's just bowling now.
Longman & Eagle	2657 N Kedzie Ave	773-276-7110	Bourbon like nobody's business; also a restaurant and six-room inn.
The Rocking Horse	2535 N Milwaukee Ave	773-486-0011	Generically hip bar and brunch spot to bookend your debauchery.
Ronny's	2101 N California Ave	n/a	Garage rock lounge with a microwave.
Streetside Cafe	3201 W Armitage Ave	773-252-9700	Micro-brews, DJs spin smooth house, ample ambiance
Tini Martini	2169 N Milwaukee	312-269-2900	Velvet ropes in this stretch of Milwaukee? Give me a break.
Two Way Lounge	2928 W Fullerton Ave	773-227-5070	This downright rugged bar offers cheap Old Style.
Whirlaway	3224 W Fullerton Ave	773-276-6809	Old Style, old couches, and a truly eclectic jukebox.
The Whistler	2421 N milwaukee Ave	773-227-3530	Classic cocktails, live music, and art gallery all in one!

Map 28 • Bucktown

The Bluebird	1749 N Damen	773-486-2473	American tapas and wine bar.
Caoba Mexican Bar and Grill	1619 N Damen Ave	773-342-2622	Cheesy, overpriced chest hair-and gold chain bar.
Cans	1640 N Damen Ave	773-227-2277	Canned beers galore! Loud crowd, loud music, great hot wings!
Charleston Tavern	2076 N Hoyne Ave	773-489-4757	Yuppie dive.
Cleo's	2048 W Armitage Ave	773-227-6700	Cruisy neighborhood spot.
Cortland's Garage	1645 W Cortland St	773-862-7877	Garage-themed bar for wanna-be grease monkeys.
Danny's Tavern	1951 W Dickens Ave	773-489-6457	Hipster house bar with candlelit alcoves.
Ed and Jean's	2032 W Armitage Ave	773-395-3475	Your dive bar home away from home.
Gallery Cabaret	2020 N Oakley Ave	773-489-5471	Hip dive bar with local acts, attracts plenty of wannabe barflies.
Green Eye Lounge	2403 W Homer St	773-227-8851	Microbrews within crawling distance of the Blue Line Western stop.
Lemmings	1850 N Damen Ave	773-862-1688	Lite Brite works of art.
The Liar's Club	1665 W Fullerton Ave	773-665-1110	Only sometimes overly hipster, otherwise rad music and good times.
The Map Room	1949 N Hoyne Ave	773-252-7636	Global theme mixed with the occasional free buffet.
The Mutiny	2428 N Western Ave	773-486-7774	All bands start somewhere…unfortunately it's here.
Northside Bar & Grill	1635 N Damen Ave	773-384-3555	Popular Wicker Park pick-up bar.
Quenchers Saloon	2401 N Western Ave	773-276-9730	Crowded on the weekends, but ultra comfy couches and free popcorn.
WhirlyBall	1880 W Fullerton Ave	800-8-WHIRLY	Drinking while driving bumper cars. Safety is nothing to me.

Map 29 • DePaul / Wrightwood / Sheffield

Bird's Nest Bar	2500 N Southport Ave	773-472-1582	Cheap wings, live music, and plenty of bros.
Cagney's	2142 N Clybourn Ave	773-857-1111	Old-timey meets high-tech at this sports bar.
Deja Vu	2624 N Lincoln Ave	773-871-0205	Rock-themed 4 am bar for the messy college crowd.
Delilah's	2771 N Lincoln Ave	773-472-2771	Punk rock dive specializing in whisky.
Faith & Whiskey	1365 W Fullerton Ave	773-248-9119	Rockin' Lincoln Park with over 100 whiskeys.
Gaslight Bar & Grille	2426 N Racine Ave	773-929-7759	Like you never left OSU.
Gin Mill	2462 N Lincoln Ave	773-549-3232	Ever see a college kid drink gin?
The Grand Central	950 W Wrightwood Ave	773-832-4000	Hip but not hipster.
Green Dolphin Street	2200 N Ashland Ave	773-395-0066	Big band and jazz venue that serves late-night dinner and vibrations.
Hideout	1354 W Wabansia Ave	773-227-4433	Haven for alt-country and other quirky live tune-age.
Hog Head McDunna's	1505 W Fullerton Ave	773-929-0944	Lincoln Parksy music spot…for the not-so-musically inclined.
Irish Eyes	2519 N Lincoln Ave	773-348-9548	…are often crying.
Kincade's	950 W Armitage Ave	773-348-0010	Happy-hour sports bar.
Local Option	1102 W Webster Ave	773-348-2008	Neighborhood hole-in-the-wall and proud of it.
Nic and Dino's Tripoli Tavern	1147 W Armitage Ave	773-477-4400	Quality bar food.
The Prop House	1675 N Elston Ave	773-486-4000	In the middle of an industrial area; house beats resonate.
Rose's Lounge	2656 N Lincoln Ave	773-327-4000	DePaul dive chock full of tchotchkes and cheap beer.
Webster Wine Bar	1480 W Webster Ave	773-868-0608	Perfect place for "getting to know you" while enjoying flights and pairings.
Wrightwood Tap	1059 W Wrightwood Ave	773-549-4949	Neighborhood feel-good spot.

Map 30 • Lincoln Park

Amp Rock	1909 N Lincoln Ave	312-376-1860	Rock out in this basement lounge that features loaded iPods.
B.L.U.E.S.	2519 N Halsted St	773-528-1012	Smaller but notorious blues bar with an older African-American crowd.
Burwood Tap	724 W Wrightwood Ave	773-525-2593	Chug-a-lug.
Crossroads Public House	2630 N Lincoln Ave	773-248-3900	Cavernous "Irish" bar without the Irish flair.
D.O.C. Wine Bar	2602 N Clark St	773-883-5101	Unwind with a glass of Pinot by the fireplace. (Choose from Noir or Gregio!)
Duke's Bar & Grill	2616 N Clark St	773-248-0250	If a bar were a log cabin with tasty burgers.
Gamekeepers	345 W Armitage Ave	773-549-0400	Where young singles mingle.
Glascott's	2158 N Halsted St	773-281-1205	Wannabe Irish joint with frat-boy written all over it.
GoodBar	2512 N Halsted St	773-296-9700	Candles, DJ, wine bar.
Hidden Shamrock	2723 N Halsted St	773-883-0304	We played darts with Joe Walsh here one night. Righteous.
Kingston Mines	2548 N Halsted St	773-477-4646	Chicago blues bar in a neighborhood safe for tourists.
Lincoln Station	2432 N Lincoln Ave	773-472-8100	Back room is good for events.
Lion Head Pub & The Apartment	2251 N Lincoln Ave	773-348-5100	DePaul nightspot.
Neo	2350 N Clark St	773-528-2622	Popular eighties retro night. Gag me with a spoon.
Park West	322 W Armitage Ave	773-929-1322	Costs extra to reserve a table.
The Second City	1616 N Wells St	312-337-3992	Drama and food in front of you.
Victory Liquors	2610 N Halsted St	773-348-5600	Hope you like Notre Dame.
Wise Fools Pub	2270 N Lincoln Ave	773-929-1300	Vibes are high for live local legends and jam sessions.

Map 31 • Old Town / Near North

boutique	809 W Evergreen Ave	312-751-2900	Hip-hop club with Asian vibe.
Burton Place	1447 N Wells St	312-664-4699	Great late night; good bar food.
McGinny's Tap	313 W North Ave	312-943-5228	Laid-back crowd.
Old Town Ale House	219 W North Ave	312-944-7020	Crusty old-timers meet performing arts crowd.
Spoon	1240 N Wells St	312-642-5522	Trendy young crowd.
Weeds	1555 N Dayton St	312-943-7815	Pinball, bras, shoes, poetry, and tequila.
Zanies Comedy Club	1548 N Wells St	312-337-4027	After a few drinks, everything is funny. Well, almost.

Map 32 • Gold Coast / Mag Mile

Backroom	1007 N Rush St	312-751-2433	Old jazz club w/ lots of baby boomers.
Butch McGuire's	20 W Division St	312-337-9080	Wet T-shirt contests anyone?
Coq d'Or	140 E Walton St	312-932-4622	A sophisticate's lodge: red leather, dark wood, torch singers and pub food. Inside the Drake Hotel.
Dublin's	1050 N State St	312-266-6340	Gold Coast pub.
The Drawing Room	937 N Rush St	312-255-0022	Le Passage's foray into swank cocktails and sit-down dining.
Finn McCool's	15 W Division St	312-337-4349	McNot.
The Hunt Club	1100 N State St	312-988-7887	The ultimate yuppy sports bar.
Jilly's Retro Club	1007 N Rush St	312-664-1001	Gold digger's haven. Jerry Springer's old hangout.
Le Passage	937 N Rush St	312-255-0022	Jeremy Piven tried to pick up one of our friends here one time.
Leg Room	7 W Division St	312-337-2583	Huge singles scene.
The Loft	15 W Division St	312-337-4349	Dance clubs with poles above Finn McCools. Cringing as we type.
Shenanigans House of Beer	16 W Division St	312-642-2344	Another Rush vicinity hellhole.
Signature Lounge	875 N Michigan Ave	312-787-9596	Unbelievable view from the women's room.
Trader Vic's	1030 N State St	312-642-6500	Tiki time has never been better.
Underground Wonder Bar	10 E Walton St	312-266-7761	Mostly jazz.
The Whisky	1015 N Rush St	312-475-0300	Great summer place where hip and trendy folks abound.
Zebra Lounge	1220 N State St	312-642-5140	Garish, cramped piano bar—in other words, it's a hit.

Map 33 • Rogers Park / West Ridge

Cary's Lounge	2251 W Devon Ave	773-743-5737	Locals' place to go for a nightcap.
Lamp Post	7126 N Ridge Blvd	773-465-9571	Friendly place to catch a game or toss darts.
McKellin's	2800 W Touhy Ave	773-973-2428	Cozy neighborhood Irish bar.
Mullen's Sports Bar and Grill	7301 N Western Ave	773-465-2113	Food until 1 am (10 pm on Sundays).

Map 34 • East Rogers Park

Duke's Hideaway	6920 N Glenwood Ave	773-764-2826	Start boozin' at 7 am.
Hamilton's Pub	6341 N Broadway St	773-764-8133	Watering hole popular with Loyola students.
Hop Haus	7545 N Clark St	773-262-3783	Burgers n' beer.
Jackhammer	6406 N Clark St	773-743-5772	Gay bar with a welcoming neighborhood vibe.
No Exit	6970 N Glenwood Ave	773-743-3355	Standard coffee house.
Poitin Stil	1502 W Jarvis Ave	773-338-3285	What's in a name? Cozy little neighborhood Irish joint.
Red Line Tap	7006 N Glenwood Ave	773-274-5463	Brews and bands on the Red Line.
Touche	6412 N Clark St	773-465-7400	Drunken gay leather bar.

Map 35 • Arcadia Terrace / Peterson Park

Emerald Isle	2537 W Peterson Ave	773-561-6674	Ahh, the Emerald Isle!
Hidden Cove	5338 N Lincoln Ave	773-275-6711	Sports bar with trivia, darts, and karaoke.

Karaoke Restaurant	6248 N California Ave	773-274-1166	Korean food and private karaoke rooms.
Lincoln Karaoke	5526 N Lincoln Ave	773-895-2299	Korean karaoke parlor with bar and private party rooms.

Map 36 • Bryn Mawr / Bowmanville

Big Joe's 2 & 6 Pub	1818 W Foster Ave	773-784-8755	Corner bar endorsed by the Windy City Darters.
Bobbie's Runaway	5305 N Damen Ave	773-271-6488	Mr. Winkie holds court here.
Claddagh Ring	2306 W Foster Ave	773-271-4794	Traditional Irish-American bar.
Fireside Restaurant & Lounge	5739 N Ravenswood Ave	773-561-7433	Good late-night bar with above average grub.
K's Dugout	1930 W Foster Ave	773-561-2227	Drink and watch sports, drink and watch sports, drink and…
Leadway Bar & Café	5233 N Damen Ave	773-728-2663	Artsy bar with free picture-painting and pool-playing.
Sherry's Bar	5652 N Western Ave	773-784-2143	The perfect local spot for the aging hipsters who've been moving into this 'hood.

Map 37 • Edgewater / Andersonville

@tmosphere	5355 N Clark St	773-784-1100	Trendy gay bar with dance floor and DJs.
Charlie's Ale House	5308 N Clark St	773-751-0140	Family-friendly spot with reliable grub.
Edgewater Lounge	5600 N Ashland Ave	773-878-3343	Alehouse with open-mike on Tuesdays for singers.
Farragut's Tavern	5240 N Clark St	773-728-4903	Neighborhood dive, less yuppy than Simon's.
Granville Anvil	1137 W Granville Ave	773-973-0006	Gay old-timers drink here.
Hamilton's Pub	6341 N Broadway St	773-764-8133	Watering hole popular with Loyola students.
In Fine Spirits Wine Lounge	5420 N Clark St	773-334-9463	Lounge companion to conterminous store. Impressive cocktails.
Joie de Vine	1744 W Balmoral Ave	773-989-6846	Casual wine bar popular with local lesbians.
Marty's Wine and Martini Bar	1511 W Balmoral Ave	773-561-6425	Compact and classy.
Moody's Pub	5910 N Broadway St	773-275-2696	Best beer garden in the city. Long wait times.
Ole St Andrew's Inn	5938 N Broadway St	773-784-5540	Food and spirits…of the haunted sort.
Ollie's	1064 W Berwyn Ave	773-784-5712	A rare quiet neighborhood joint.
Pumping Company	6157 N Broadway St	773-465-9500	Cozy neighborhood dive with a fireplace and beergarden.
Simon's	5210 N Clark St	773-878-0894	Thrift-store-attired hipsters and Swedish nautical theme.
Sovereign	6202 N Broadway St	773-274-0057	Cheap, laidback neighborhood joint frozen in time.
StarGaze	5419 N Clark St	773-561-7363	Lesbian bar with salsa on Friday nights.

Map 38 • Ravenswood / Albany Park

Brown Rice	4432 N Kedzie Ave	312-543-7027	Tiny venue for tiny jazz acts.
Hot Shots	5151 N Lincoln Ave	773-334-5338	Romanian music.
Lincoln Square Lanes	4874 N Lincoln Ave	773-561-8191	Brews and bowling above a hardware store. Cheap date.
Montrose Saloon	2933 W Montrose Ave	773-463-7663	Classic Chicago "Old Style." No cell phones, please.
Peek Inn	2825 W Irving Park Rd	773-267-5197	Cool little dive worth a peek.

Map 39 • Ravenswood / North Center

Bowman's Bar and Grill	4356 N Leavitt St	773-478-9999	Cozy, upscale bar with obligatory exposed brick.
Celtic Crown Public House	4301 N Western Ave	773-588-1110	Great specials without over-Irishing it!
Chicago Brauhaus	4732 N Lincoln Ave	773-784-4444	More German than Germany…even in Oktober.
Daily Bar & Grill	4560 N Lincoln Ave	773-561-6198	Bar food in retro ambiance.
The Globe Pub	1934 W Irving Park Rd	773-871-3757	Great music venue gone sportsbar.
Grafton Pub	4530 N Lincoln Ave	773-271-9000	Outstanding bar food and friendly atmosphere.
Hot Shots	5151 N Lincoln Ave	773-334-5338	Romanian music.
Huettenbar	4721 N Lincoln Ave	773-561-2507	German-town favorite with great beer selection.
Jury's Food & Drink	4337 N Lincoln Ave	773-935-2255	Local spot with bar food.
Katerina's	1920 W Irving Park Rd	773-348-7592	Live jazz, gypsy music, and local rock at this European lounge.
Laschet's Inn	2119 W Irving Park Rd	773-478-7915	Pull on the Lederhosen!
The Lincoln Lodge	4008 N Lincoln Ave	773-251-1539	A funny night on the town.
The Long Room	1612 W Irving Park Rd	773-665-4500	Yes, it's long, but not as long as you might think.
Margie's Pub	4145 N Lincoln Ave	773-477-1644	Bikers and burnouts and boozers…oh my!
Oakwood 83	1959 W Montrose Ave	773-327-2785	Glorified version of your uncle Frank's basement.
O'Donovan's	2100 W Irving Park Rd	773-478-2100	It's a neighborhood bar. You can watch sports.
O'Lanagan's	2335 W Montrose Ave	773-583-2252	Not an Irishman in sight!
The Rail	4709 N Damen Ave	773-878-9400	One-time dive, the rail rocks in Ravenswood.
Resi's Bierstube	2034 W Irving Park Rd	773-472-1749	Wear your leiderhosen.
Tiny Lounge	4352 N Leavitt St	773-463-0396	Tiny name, but big on flavorful cocktails.
Wild Goose	4265 N Lincoln Ave	773-281-7112	Guy's bar. Cheap eats, TVs and games.
Windy City Inn	2257 W Irving Park Rd	773-588-7088	Nice family feel…if you're from Kentucky.

Map 40 • Uptown

Bar on Buena	910 W Buena Ave	773-525-8665	Microbrews and tasty burgers in this plush neighborhood café. All-you-can-eat pasta on Wednesdays!
Big Chicks	5024 N Sheridan Rd	773-728-5511	Friendly gay bar with fabulous art collection.
Carol's Pub	4659 N Clark St	773-334-2402	Hillbillies gone yuppie…thanks to a little press.
Crew Bar & Grill	4804 N Broadway St	773-784-4811	Gay sports bar with 50 beers and several televisions, or vice versa.
Green Mill Pub	4802 N Broadway St	773-878-5552	Chicago legend… And birthplace of the poetry slam.
Holiday Club	4000 N Sheridan Rd	773-348-9600	The Rat Pack is back! With food.

Hopleaf	5148 N Clark St	773-334-9851	Tons of imports if you can get a seat.
Konak	5150 N Clark St	773-271-6688	Overflow option for when Hopleaf is too packed, which means always.
The Long Room	1612 W Irving Park Rd	773-665-4500	Yes, it's long, but not as long as you might think.
Max's Place	4621 N Clark St	773-784-3864	At $1.25 per draft, who wouldn't pass out?
Nick's Uptown	4015 N Sheridan Rd	773-975-1155	Open late with a great beer selection.
Sofo Bar	4923 N Clark St	773-784-7636	Friendly boy's bar by owner of T's.
The Spot	4437 N Broadway St	773-728-8934	Three floors and constant special events.
T's	5025 N Clark St	773-784-6000	Popular with local gays and lesbians.
The Uptown Lounge	1136 W Lawrence Ave	773-878-1136	Former dump becomes trendy lounge in up-and-coming neighborhood.
Wild Pug	4810 N Broadway St	773-784-4811	The local gay pub, with dancing on the weekend.

Map 41 • Avondale / Old Irving

Chief O'Neill's	3471 N Elston Ave	773-583-3066	Celtic music and top-of-the-line pub food.
Kuma's Corner	2900 W Belmont Ave	773-604-8769	Heavy metal bar with great microbrew selection and kobe beef sliders.
Ñ	2977 N Elston Ave	773-866-9898	Argentine flair with electro grooves.
Nelly's Saloon	3256 N Elston Ave	773-588-4494	Romanian hangout with occasional live music.
Small Bar	2956 N Albany Ave	773-509-9888	This Logan Square watering hole offers great domestic and imported booze and a chill vibe.
Square Bar & Grill	2849 W Belmont Ave	773-267-0123	A burger showdown in Avondale.

Map 42 • North Center / Roscoe Village / West Lakeview

Beat Kitchen	2100 W Belmont Ave	773-281-4444	Hip music spot in a not so hip hood.
Black Rock	3614 N Damen Ave	773-348-4044	Not sure what this place is.
Cody's Public House	1658 W Barry Ave	773-528-4050	Named after the owner's dog.
Four Moon Tavern	1847 W Roscoe St	773-929-6666	Neighborhood tavern. Cozy back room. Thespian crowd.
Four Treys	1952 W Henderson St	773-549-8845	One of 5,000 drinking options in this area.
G&L Fire Escape	2157 W Grace St	773-472-1138	Attention ladies! It's a fireman's hangout!
Guess Hookah	3357 N Lincoln Ave	773-868-4837	Weekend Dj's, BYO but buy your tabacco in the shop.
Hungry Brain	2319 W Belmont Ave	773-935-2118	Mellow, friendly artist hangout. Experimental jazz on Sundays.
Martyrs'	3855 N Lincoln Ave	773-404-9494	Great stage for live acts.
Mulligan's Public House	2000 W Roscoe St	773-549-4225	Villagers do not go thirsty.
Riverview Tavern & Grill	1958 W Roscoe St	773-248-9523	Another Roscoe Village watering hole.
Roscoe Village Pub	2159 W Addison St	773-472-6160	Karaoke in a dive bar... doesn't get much better than that.
The Village Tap	2055 W Roscoe St	773-883-0817	Neighborhood icon with a touch of class.
Underbar	3243 N Western Ave	773-404-9363	There are more depressing 4 am bars.
Waterhouse	3407 N Paulina Ave	773-871-1200	Local lounge aiming for a classy feel.
Xippo	3759 N Damen Ave	773-529-9135	Martini lounge in unlikely 'hood.

Map 43 • Wrigleyville / East Lakeview

The Ashland	2824 N Ashland Ave	773-883-7297	Daily specials and greasy food.
Bar Celona	3474 N Clark St	773-244-8000	Two bars, one in the basement, DJ spins upstairs.
Berlin	954 W Belmont Ave	773-348-4975	Tiny classic "pansexual" dance club.
Bernie's	3664 N Clark St	773-525-1898	Favored Wrigleyville spot.
Cooper's	1232 W Belmont Ave	773-929-2667	Beer and stylish/casual bar food.
Cubby Bear	1059 W Addison St	773-327-1662	Drunk cubs fans and bar bands.
Elbo Room	2871 N Lincoln Ave	773-549-5549	Didn't RATT play here?
Fizz Bar and Grill	3220 N Lincoln Ave	773-348-6000	Good specialty drinks. Tiki nights and more.
The Full Shilling	3724 N Clark St	773-248-3330	Best Wrigleyville bar.
Gingerman Tavern	3740 N Clark St	773-549-2050	Plays classical music to ward off Cubs fans.
Ginger's Ale House	3801 N Ashland Ave	773-348-2767	European Futbol. Goal!
Guthrie's Tavern	1300 W Addison St	773-477-2900	Comfortable atmosphere, good drinks, a range of board games to play with.
Higgins' Tavern	3259 N Racine Ave	773-281-7637	Yuppies and drunks.
Houndstooth Saloon	3438 N Clark St	773-244-1166	Southern hospitality and Crimson Tide alumni and fans.
iO	3541 N Clark St	773-880-0199	Get laughs and get drunk.
The Irish Oak	3511 N Clark St	773-935-6669	Seriously authentic Irish pub.
Jack's Bar & Grill	2856 N Southport Ave	773-404-8400	Classy wine bar.
Justin's	3358 N Southport Ave	773-929-4844	Great bar for Sunday football.
Kirkwood	2934 N Sheffield Ave	773-770-0700	Drink like a fish or out of a fish bowl.
L&L Tavern	3207 N Clark St	773-528-1303	Overfriendly dive bar with decent jukebox.
Lange's Lounge	3500 N Southport Ave	773-472-6030	Total dive, but not disgusting.
Lincoln Tap Room	3010 N Lincoln Ave	773-868-0060	Great mix of people, comfortable couches.
Merkle's Bar & Grill	3516 N Clark St	773-244-1025	Cubs + Iowa Hawkeyes = sports year-round.
Metro	3730 N Clark St	773-549-0203	Internationally renowned venue for top local and touring rock music.
Moxie	3517 N Clark St	773-935-6694	Trendy, narrow bar with expensive fancy drinks.
Murphy's Bleachers	3655 N Sheffield Ave	773-281-5356	Outdoor Cubbie haven with drunks galore.
Newport Bar & Grill	1344 W Newport Ave	773-325-9111	For an ass-whooping in Pictionary, meet us here tomorrow night.
Raw Bar	3720 N Clark St	773-348-7291	Post-Metro rock star hangout.
Red Ivy	3525 N Clark St	773-472-0900	Part sports bar, part pizzeria, part speakeasy.

Risque Cafe	3419 N Clark St	773-525-7711	Tangy BBQ and over 300 craft beers
Rockit	3700 N Clark St	773-645-4400	River North hotspot's new location now sporting drunken Cubs fans.
Schuba's	3159 N Southport Ave	773-525-2508	Top live music staple with attached restaurant.
Sheffield's	3258 N Sheffield Ave	773-281-4989	Outdoor area attracts afternoon revelers. Great beer selection.
Slugger's	3540 N Clark St	773-248-0055	Batting cages—some people's heaven, others' hell.
Smart Bar	3730 N Clark St	773-549-0203	Club kids unite!
Sopo Lounge & Grill	3418 N Southport Ave	773-348-0100	Really popular with the local yuppie crowd, but great specials.
The Stretch Bar & Grill	3485 N Clark St	773-755-3980	Wrigleyville's upscale choice for watching sports and eating good grub.
Tai's Til 4	3611 N Ashland Ave	773-348-8923	Well, they're open till 4 am, so you can probably guess what it's like. Hookup central.
Ten Cat Tavern	3931 N Ashland Ave	773-935-5377	Artsy type relaxing spot.
Toons Bar	3857 N Southport Ave	773-935-1919	Buncha characters in that joint (groan). But seriously, folks, check out the black-light mural by the bathrooms.
Uncommon Ground Café	3800 N Clark St	773-929-3680	Local acts play while sipping a latte.
Underground Lounge	952 W Newport Ave	773-327-2739	Cool music spot tucked away below the street.
Yak-zies Wrigleyville	3710 N Clark St	773-525-9200	Loud post Cubs hangout.
The Yard	3441 N Sheffield Ave	773-477-9273	Features cozy beer garden amongst old horse stables.

Map 44 • East Lakeview

44th Ward Dinner Party	3542 N Halsted St	773-857-2911	Build your own grilled cheese and get your groove on.
Bridget McNeill's	420 W Belmont Ave	773-248-6654	A fun hangout and godsend for those living along the lake.
Charlie's Chicago	3726 N Broadway St	773-871-8887	Gay country and western bar. That's right.
Circuit	3641 N Halsted St	773-325-2233	Huge Boys Town dance club—recently remodeled.
The Closet	3325 N Broadway St	773-477-8533	Boy-friendly lesbian bar, 4 am license.
Cocktail	3359 N Halsted St	773-477-1420	Small dance floor, occasional male strippers.
Duke of Perth	2913 N Clark St	773-477-1741	Shades of Edinburgh, along with requisite whiskies and haddock.
F. O'Mahony's	3701 N Broadway St	773-549-0226	Food when you need it (late!) and a seasonal menu.
Firkin & Pheasant	670 W Diversey Pkwy	773-327-7040	British pub feel with loads of TV's.
Friar Tuck	3010 N Broadway St	773-327-5101	Enter through a barrel. Yup, a barrel.
Hydrate	3458 N Halsted St	773-975-9244	Just what Boystown needs—a gay-friendly fern bar!
Kit Kat Lounge	3700 N Halsted St	773-525-1111	Live drag queen shows.
Little Jim's	3501 N Halsted St	773-871-6116	Halsted Street Gay Dive.
minibar	3341 N Halsted St	773-871-6227	Fancy cocktails in a smoke-free lounge.
Monsignor Murphy's	3019 N Broadway St	773-348-7285	Irish Pub with plenty of board games.
Rocks Lakeview	3463 N Broadway St	773-472-0493	Microbrews, good whisky list, and excellent bar food.
Roscoe's	3356 N Halsted St	773-281-3355	Cavernous mingling for the gay sweater set.
Sidetrack	3349 N Halsted St	773-477-9189	Popular showtune sing-a-longs!
Spin	800 W Belmont Ave	773-327-7711	Lots of theme days throughout the week.
Town Hall Pub	3340 N Halsted St	773-472-4405	Unassuming, mixed clientele, live music.
Wilde	3130 N Broadway St	773-244-0404	Classy bar for bookish set.

Northwest

5th Province Pub	4626 N Knox Ave	773-282-7035	Authentic pub located in the Heritage Center.
Abbey Pub	3420 W Grace St	773-478-4408	Reputable live music venue.
Babe's	4416 N Milwaukee Ave	773-545-3137	Warm, pleasant Jeff Park local option.
The Burlington	3425 W Fullerton Ave	773-384-3243	Low-key candlelit drinks
Edison Park Inn	6715 N Olmsted Ave	773-755-1404	All in one bowling, pizza parlor & sports bar.
Emerald Isle	6686 N Northwest Hwy	773-775-2848	The brothers and sisters of Kerry gather here.
Fantasy Lounge	4400 N Elston Ave	773-685-8083	Neighborhood place with eclectic live music offerings.
Fischman Liquors	4776 N Milwaukee Ave	773-545-0123	We call beer "piwo" 'round here.
Flo's Algiers Lounge	5436 W Montrose Ave	773-736-1111	The name evokes Casablanca, the environment, Kiev.
Ham Tree	5333 N Milwaukee Ave	773-792-2072	Neigborhood place with beer garden.
Hollywood Lounge	3301 W Bryn Mawr Ave	773-588-9707	Friendly neighborhood bar with extensive beer selection.
Jimmy Mack	5581 N Northwest Hwy	773-631-1466	After 9 pm, lots of Bikers but no Bears.
Moretti's	6727 N Olmsted Ave	773-631-1223	Sports-guy type of hangout.
New Polonia Club	6101 W Belmont Ave	773-237-0571	A polish bar on the NW side? Go figure.
Original Dugan's	6051 N Milwaukee Ave	773-467-5555	The perfect neighborhood dive.
Rosa's Lounge	3420 W Armitage Ave	773-342-0452	Revered Chicago Blues staple.
Three Counties	5856 N Milwaukee Ave	773-631-3351	Popular afterwork neighborhood bar.
Vaughan's Pub	5485 N Northwest Hwy	773-631-9206	Cozy neighborhood joint with nice beer selection and Irish food.
Weegee's Lounge	3659 W Armitage Ave	773-384-0707	Swank pub with craft beers and a '50s cocktail menu.

West

Black Beetle	2532 W Chicago Ave	773-384-0701	Displaced suburbanites in the heart of Humbolt Park.
California Clipper	1002 N California Ave	773-384-2547	An art-dork and hipster haven.
La Justicia	3901 W 26th St	773-522-0041	Live rock-en-español on Friday nights only!
Rootstock Wine & Beer Bar	954 N California Ave	773-292-1616	Drink and nosh with lots of choices.

Southwest

Cork & Kerry	10614 S Western Ave	773-445-2675	We think we've actually seen a Leprechaun here.
Groucho's	8355 S Pulaski Rd	773-767-4838	Mainstream and big-hair live rock venue.
Jeremy Lanigan's Irish Pub	3119 W 111th St	773-233-4004	Live celtic music from time-to-time.
Keegan's Pub	10618 S Western Ave	773-233-6829	Another Irish joint on the South Side. Go figure.
Mrs O'Leary's Dubliner	10910 S Western Ave	773-238-0784	Quaint, with locals and expats and hand-carved booths. Sing along to old Irish jukebox tunes.
Patrick's	6296 S Archer Ave	773-581-4036	A classic neighborhood spot.
Sean's Rhino Bar	10330 S Western Ave	773-238-2060	The new kid on the block (1999) offers darts, pool, drink specials and decent pub grub.

South

Jeffrey Pub	7041 S Jeffery Blvd	773-363-8555	Gay men and lesbians mingle at this southside dance club.
New Apartment Lounge	504 E 75th St	773-483-7728	Where Von Freeman jams every Tuesday night.
Red Pepper's Masquerade Lounge	428 E 87th St	773-873-5700	Sports bar and grill with live entertainment.
Reds	6926 S Stony Island Ave	773-643-5100	Popular place to mack on the opposite sex.

Evanston

1800 Club	1800 Sherman Ave	847-733-7900	Always busy, thanks to cheap drinks and trivia night.
Bill's Blues Bar	1029 Davis St	847-424-9800	Chicago transplant Bill Gilmore invades Evanston.
Keg of Evanston	810 Grove St	847-869-9987	DJ on the weekends. Dollar drafts on Wednesdays!
Prairie Moon	1502 Sherman Ave	847-864-8328	Weekly drink specials.
The Stained Glass Wine Bar	1735 Benson Ave	847-864-8600	240 varieties of wine, braised rabbit, and frog legs.
Tommy Nevin's Pub	1450 Sherman Ave	847-869-0450	Evanston's answer to live music joints.

Oak Park

Avenue Ale House	825 S Oak Park Ave	708-848-2801	Really great place to grab a beer (or frozen margarita or sangria) and watch a game. Tasty grub. Great patio.

Skokie

Chammps	134 Old Orchard Ctr	847-673-4778	Sports bar chain. Just about perfect.
Don's Fishmarket Tavern and Grill	9335 Skokie Blvd	847-677-3424	Yuppy watering hole connected to Don's Fishmarket.
Principal's Pub	4249 Main St	847-675-7773	Local beer and shot option.

Mag Mile and Oak Street: Bring Your Bars of Gold

The Mag Mile has long replaced State Street as downtown Chicago's premier (and tourist-friendly) shopping strip. This stretch of prime real estate, spanning from the Chicago River to Oak Street features Chicago outposts of many destination shopping spots, including **Niketown (Map 3)**, **The Apple Store (Map 3)**, **Needless-Markup** (a.k.a. **Neiman-Marcus (Map 3)**, **American Girl Place (Map 2)**, and the high-end boutiques and department stores, (think **Tiffany (Map 3)**, **Gucci (Map 32)**, and **Hermes (Map 32)**) connected to **Water Tower Place (Map 32)** and the **900 North Michigan Mall (Map 32)**.

Around the corner on Oak Street lay tonier boutiques. While Mag Mall attracts goggle-eyed Midwestern families, who'll likely stop for lunch at the Cheesecake Factory or Bubba Gump, Oak Street appeals more to the Gold Coast and North Shore set: **Prada (Map 32)**, **Ultimo (Map 32)**, **Barney's (Maps 30, 32)** and **BCBG MAXAZRIA (Map 32)** are all located on this tiny strip.

Not far away on Rush Street, **Ikram (Map 32)** is a favorite of First Lady Michelle Obama.

Boutique Shopping

You don't have to go down to Oak Street to find funky designer boutiques selling everything from original fashions by local designers to housewares and hostess gifts. Lincoln Park and Wicker Park in particular are heavy on cool women's fashion boutiques. In Lincoln Park, check out Armitage, Clark, and Halsted for shops such as **Lori's Designer Shoes (Map 30)**, **Cynthia Rowley (Map 30),** and **Kaveri (Map 29)**. In Wicker Park, the highest concentration of cool little shops, like the fashion boutiques **Habit (Map 21)** and **Penelope (Map 21)**, line Division street, but if you love to shop, you'll want to work the whole Bermuda triangle of Division, Milwaukee and North Avenue. Southport Avenue in Wrigleyville boasts a string of women's boutiques, including **Krista K (Map 43)**, **Leahy & LaDue Consignment (Map 43)**, and **Trousseau (Map 43)**.

Best of the 'Hoods

In many cases, Chicago's neighborhood shopping destinations say something unique about the character of the 'hood. Funky little punk-rock indie shops in Logan Square for example, or gay-friendly places like **GayMart (Map 44)**, **Unabridged Bookstore (Map 44)**, and **He Who Eats Mud (Map 44)** in Boystown. Lincoln Square caters to the NPR-lovin' micro-brew swillers who call that 'hood home, and Andersonville has something for everyone: feminist books (**Women & Children First (Map 37)**), chic home furnishings, men's and women's fashions, Swedish souvenirs, and, count them, two clean, friendly and non-oogly-feeling sex-toy stores (**Early to Bed (Map 37)** and **Tulip (Maps 37, 44)**).

Ethnic enclaves also make for great shopping. Try gifts and cookware in Chinatown, gorgeous saris and Bollywood flicks on West Devon, hookahs and Moroccan teas sets on north Kedzie in Albany Park, and Irish arts and crafts in Beverly.

One Man's Trash...

Is another man's treasure. Whether you wants are driven by the desire to save the planet or you just want to save a buck, Chicago offers a plentitude of places to buy other people's old crap. Vintage wear boutiques thrive in arty 'hoods like Wicker Park, East Lakeview, and Roscoe Village. Some faves: **Una Mae's Freak Boutique (Map 21)**, **Silver Moon (Map 21)** and the **Hollywood Mirror (Map 43)**. **Ragstock (Maps 43, 21)** used-and-off sale clothing chain has two Chicago outposts—one near Clark and Belmont, the other on Milwaukee Avenue.

For one-stop antique shopping, check out one of Chicago's many antique malls—huge enclosed spaces that lease space to small dealers. Not to be missed are the **Broadway Antique Mall (Map 37)**, the **Edgewater Antique Market (Map 37)**, and the **Lincoln Antique Mall (Map 38)**.

In terms of thrift stores, there's either a **Salvation Army (Maps 25, 29, 40, NW)**, a **Unique Thrift (Map 40)** or a **Village Discount (Maps 28, 38, 40, 42, NW, W, SW)** in nearly every neighborhood in the city. Meanwhile, the **Brown Elephant (Maps 37, 44)** thrift stores benefit Howard Brown Health Center's HIV research, whereas the **White Elephant (Map 30)** benefits the Children's Memorial Hospital.

Audiophilia

Although two huge chain record stores (Tower Records and the Virgin Superstore) have folded in the past few years, Chicago loves our independent record stores. Among our faves, **Reckless Records (Maps 21, 44)** serves the indie rock crowd. **Borderline (Maps 21, 44)** spins Euro dance hits. **Gramaphone (Map 44)** is where Chicago's DJs pick-up the hottest wax. Speaking of wax, **Dr. Wax (Map 19)** and **Hyde Park Records (Map 19)** supplies Hyde Parkers with all its old-school vinyl needs, while **Dusty Groove (Map 22)**, which specializes in old R&B and soul, provides the same service to West Towners. **Laurie's Planet of Sound (Map 39)**, in Lincoln Square, offers an eclectic array of mostly-indie music without the attitude that is often associated with record store clerks.

For stereo equipment and electronics, DJ's shop at **Midwest Stereo (Map 43)**. **DeciBel (Map 21)** serves the Wicker Park and Bucktown crew. Saturday **Audio Exchange (Map 43)**, only open on Thursdays, Saturdays, and Sundays, sells high-end stereo brands for cheap, (well, relatively cheap, anyways) as well as used and refurbished woofers, tweeters, receivers, and all that other audio-geek stuff.

Get Foodie

The gourmet and specialty food trade has exploded in the past few years, as have the high-end houseware stores that are supplying upscale home cooks with their Le Creuset pans and Wüstof knives. Today, if you find yourself hard-up for locally-produced caviar, lavender extract, stinky artisinal cheese, curry leaves, or whatever other weird ingredient they don't stock at the Jewel, all you have to do is follow your nose. Of Chicago's many, many gourmet or specialty food shops, there are a few that are particularly dear to our hearts. **Pastoral Artisan (Map 44)**, a specialty cheese and wine shop, is a great stop on your way to a dinner party to pick up cheese, wine, olives, or other tasty treats. We also love **Goddess and the Grocer (Maps 28, 32)**, **Provenance Food and Wine (Map 27)**, and, perhaps, the best-smelling shop in town, Old Town's **The Spice House (Map 31)**. Ethnic markets are great places to track down hard-to-find ingredients. **Middle East Bakery (Map 37)** in Andersonville sells amazing homemade hummus and felafel, as well as olive oil, pine nuts, and dried fruit at prices significantly lower than Whole Paycheck. Oh, and that local caviar? Look no further than **The Fishguy Market (Northwest)**.

Mall Rats

Normally we'd scoff, but look, it's Chicago, and it gets damn cold. So, if occasionally you want to do your shopping without having to venture too far into the great outdoors, we're not going to point any fingers.

On the Mag Mile, **Water Tower Place (Map 32)** offers pretty typical mall fare—there's a Gamer's Paradise, Godiva, and Victoria's Secret—but their food court has more in common with a Las Vegas buffet than anywhere you'd be able to grab an Orange Julius or a Mrs. Fields cookie. A block north, the shops at **900 N Michigan (Map 32)**, offer higher-end fare, (no surprise, as it's attached to the super-luxe Four Seasons hotel). Shops here include Coach, Diesel, MaxMara, and Williams-Sonoma. In East Lakeview, the **Century Shopping Mall (Map 44)** is kept in business by its fine art house cinema and Bally's outpost, certainly not by the mundane shops contained within (Limited, Express, or Bath & Body Works, anyone?). Housed in a building where bombers were built during WWII, today the huge **Ford City Mall (Southwest)** is a popular hang-out for local kids without much else to do, but otherwise boasts nothing very exceptional—a few low-end department stores, a movie theater, and all of the shops and fast food joints you'd expect to find in a mall. Anchored by a Target and a Kohl's, **Harlem Irving Plaza (Northwest)**, like the Ford City Mall, is a popular stomping ground for high school students but offers little beyond the same old shops despite that location-specific nom de mall.

Oddities

Some of our favorite Chicago shops defy easy definition. Among them, **American Science and Surplus (Northwest)** offers one-stop shopping for professional-quality laboratory beakers, school supplies, crime-scene tape, pirate flags, and life-sized anatomy models. At **Uncle Fun (Map 43)** you can find all the coolest vintage and wind-up toys, as well as oodles of strange and playful things for under $5, making it the gag gift headquarters of Chi-town. Recent acquisitions: a bacon-scented air-freshener, a week's worth of fake moustaches, and a "Mr. T in Your Pocket" keychain. Ah, youth. Relive it again at again at **Izzy Rizzy's House of Tricks (Southwest)**, where you can stock up on plastic vomit, hand-buzzers, and stink bombs. Finally, to cast a curse or to break one, stop by **Athenian Candle Company (Map 4)**, where, in addition to 12-foot, gold-detailed, church-quality candles, you can also pick up a bottle of "Law Be Gone" floor wash or "Love Come Back" air spray.

State Street: Student Mecca

The student population in the Loop has soared, thanks to new student housing for Columbia and School of the Art Institute Students. State Street has made a comeback by filling up with cheap, hip chic catering to this crowd. **Loehmann's (Map 5)**, **H&M, (Map 5)**, and **Urban Outfitters (Map 5)** all have outposts on this strip. **Blick Art Materials (Map 5)** and **Central Camera (Map 5)** cater to the art student within all of us.

Map 1 • River North / Fulton Market District

Doolin's	511 N Halsted St	312-243-9424	Party decorations galore, closed Sundays.
L. Isaacson & Stein's Fish Market	800 W. Fulton	312-421-2444	Fish gutters! Quick and fresh!
Veruca Salt	521 N Kingsbury St	773-276-3888	Flirty ladies fashions.

Map 2 • Near North / River North

American Girl Place	111 E Chicago Ave	877-247-5223	Stepford dolls for your tween.
Drinks Over Dearborn	650 N Dearborn St	312-337-9463	Chic boutique liquor store.
Jazz Record Mart	27 E Illinois St	312-222-1467	Jazz lover's emporium.
Jonathan Adler	676 N Wabash Ave	312-274-9920	Hip and happy home furnishings.
Montauk	401 N Wells St	312-951-5688	The most comfortable sofas.
Paper Source	232 W Chicago Ave	312-337-0798	Great paper and invitations.
P.O.S.H.	613 N State St	312-280-1602	An Aladdin's cave featuring old hotel silverware and other finds.

Map 3 • Streeterville / Mag Mile

Apple Store	679 N Michigan Ave	312-981-4104	All of their newest and shiniest offerings, plus classes and seminars.
Chicago Place	700 N Michigan Ave	312-266-7710	Upscale mall.
Disney Store	717 N Michigan Ave	312-654-9208	M-i-c-k-e-Why?
Neiman-Marcus	737 N Michigan Ave	312-642-5900	Affectionately known as "Needless Mark-up" by those who can afford it anyway.
Niketown	669 N Michigan Ave	312-642-6363	Nike label sports clothing.
Ralph Lauren	750 N Michigan Ave	312-280-1655	If you love those little polo horses...
Tiffany & Co	730 N Michigan Ave	312-944-7500	Lack's appropriate breakfast options.

Map 4 • West Loop Gate / Greek Town

Athenian Candle Co	300 S Halsted St	312-332-6988	Candles, curse-breakers, Greek trinkets, and much more.
Athens Grocery	324 S Halsted St	312-332-6737	THE destination for feta, olives, or a whole lamb.
Greek Town Music	330 S Halsted St	312-263-6342	Music, T-shirts, hats—everything Greek!
Northwestern Cutlery	810 W Lake St	312-421-3666	The self-described "candy store for cooks."
Pan Hellenic Pastry Shop	322 S Halsted St	312-454-1886	Greek sweets in Greektown.

Map 5 • The Loop

American Music World	111 N State St	312-781-4050	The place to go if you're looking to buy an instrument.
Arts & Artisans	35 E Wacker Dr	312-578-0126	Art Gallery.
Ashley Stewart	7 W Madison St	312-920-0646	Clothes for your curves.
Avenue	231 S State St	312-697-1219	Modern plus-size clothes.
Borders	150 N State St	312-606-0750	State Street books.
Carson Pirie Scott	1 S State St	312-641-7000	Department store.
Central Camera Company	230 S Wabash Ave	312-427-5580	Family owned camera shop.
Florodora	330 S Dearborn St	312-212-8860	Vintage-inspired, wildly-priced.
Gallery 37 Store	66 E Randolph St	312-744-7274	Speciality gifts.
Garrett Popcorn Shop	26 W Randolph St	312-201-0511	The caramel cheddar mix is their classic.
Kramer's Health Food Center	230 S Wabash Ave	312-922-0077	Healthy hippie haven.
Lush Cosmetics	111 N State St Macy's Building	312-795-0863	Handmade soaps and natural cosmetics—too bad they aren't edible!
Macy's	111 N State St	312-335-7700	The former home of Chicago establishment Marshall Field's.
A New Leaf	312 S Dearborn St	312-427-9097	Florists of paradise. Minus the price.
Pastoral Artisan Cheese, Bread & Wine	53 E Lake St	312-658-1250	One of Chicago's favorite cheese shops. Start your picnic here.
Rock Records	175 W Washington St	312-346-3489	Good CD store.
Sears	2 N State St	312-373-6000	Blue-collar stalwart.
Urban Outfitters	20 S State St	312-269-9919	Retro fun clothing, nifty gifts and silly t-shirts.

Map 6 • The Loop / Grant Park

Arts & Artisans	108 S Michigan Ave	312-641-0088	Art gallery.
Chicago Architecture Foundation	224 S Michigan Ave	312-922-3432	All things architectural: tours, exhibits, shopping.
Museum Shop of the Art Institute	111 S Michigan Ave	800-518-4214	Art Institute gift shop.
Poster Plus	200 S Michigan Ave	312-461-9277	Vintage posters and custom framing.
Precious Possessions	28 N Michigan Ave	312-726-8118	Mineral shop.

Map 7 • South Loop / River City

Fishman's Fabrics	1101 S Des Plaines St	312-922-7250	Huge fabric wholesaler.
Lee's Foreign Car Service	727 S Jefferson St	312-663-0823	Import parts and service.
Morris & Sons	557 W Polk St	312-243-5635	Mostly men, off-price Italian designers.
Vogue Fabrics	623 W Roosevelt Rd	312-829-2505	An iconic craft store in East Pilsen for over 60 years.

Map 8 • South Loop / Printers Row / Dearborn Park

Arts & Artisans	720 S Michigan Ave	312-786-6224	Art Gallery.
Loopy Yarns	47 W Polk St	312-583-9276	For all your knitting needs. Classes, too.
Printers Row Fine & Rare Books	715 S Dearborn St	312-583-1800	Fine and rare books.
Sandmeyer's Book Store	714 S Dearborn St	312-922-2104	Dream come true if you love books and atmosphere.

Map 9 • South Loop / South Michigan Ave

Spertus Shop	610 S Michigan Ave	312-322-1740	Unique Hanukkah gifts include yiddishwear and the Moses action figure.

Map 10 • East Pilsen / Chinatown

Chinatown Bazaar	2221 S Wentworth Ave	312-225-1088	Part clothing store, part knick-knack shop.
Feida Bakery	2228 S Wentworth Ave	312-808-1113	Tasty Chinese baked goods.
Giftland	2212 S Wentworth Ave	312-225-0088	With a premium on Hello Kitty and other sorts of "Asian adorableness."
Pacific Furniture	2200 S Wentworth Ave	312-808-0456	Mostly home furnishings.
Sun Sun Tong	2260 S Wentworth Ave	312-842-6398	Stock up on Chinese herbs and teas.
Ten Ren Tea	2247 S Wentworth Ave	312-842-1171	The only place to buy ginseng.
Woks 'n' Things	2234 S Wentworth Ave	312-842-0701	Stir-fry utensils and cookware.

Map 11 • South Loop / McCormick Place

Blue Star Auto Stores	2001 S State St	312-225-0717	All your auto needs.
Cycle Bicycle Shop	1465 S Michigan Ave	312-987-1080	Bike shop, obviously.
Waterware	1829 S State St	312-225-4549	Designer plumbing fixtures.

Map 12 • Bridgeport (West)

Best's Kosher Outlet Store	1000 W Pershing Rd	773-650-6338	Packaged deli meats and made-to-order sandwiches.
Bridgeport Antiques	2963 S Archer Ave	773-927-9070	Old stuff.
Unique Thrift Store	3000 S Halsted St	312-842-0942	Half-off Mondays and Early-Bird Thursdays!

Map 13 • Bridgeport (East)

Ace Bakery	3241 S Halsted St	312-225-4973	Excellent breads and pastries.
Augustine's Spiritual Goods	3327 S Halsted St	773-843-1933	Mystical and religious knick-knacks.
Bridgeport News Travel & Tours	3252 S Halsted St	312-842-5883	Travel store.
Health King Enterprise & Balanceuticals Group	238 W 31st St	312-567-9978	Natural remedies.
Henry's Sports & Bait Shop	3130 S Canal St	312-225-8538	Fishing mecca.
Let's Boogie Records & Tapes	3321 S Halsted St	773-254-0139	Music.

Map 14 • Prairie Shores / Lake Meadows

Ashley Stewart	3455 S Dr Martin L King Jr Dr	312-567-0405	Women's clothing.

Map 16 • Bronzeville

Afrocentric Bookstore	4655 S King Dr	773-924-3966	The authority on Afrocentic literature.
Flawless	221 E 47th St	773-268-1870	Busy, neighborhood barbershop with loads of cute boys.
Ibiza	233 E 47th St	773-924-5199	High-fashion hip-hop rock star gear & denim.
Issues Barber & Beauty Salon	3958 S Cottage Grove Ave	773-924-4247	Beauty salon.
Jordan's Closets	106 E 51st St	773-624-4104	Adorable resale shop for sassy little girls and fashionista mommies.
Leaders 1354	4351 S Cottage Grove Ave	773-285-1067	The place for hip-hop fit and skateboards and spray-pained murals of Harold Washington, Marley, Che, and Malcolm.
Sensual Steps	4518 S Cottage Grove Ave	773-548-FEET	A sanctuary for fancy kicks, handbags, camisoles, jewelry, and shawls by black designers.
Synx Galleria	4700 S Prairie Ave	773-548-4110	Fashionable & upscale athletic shoe shop.
Tribesmen Natural Hair Salon	4459 S Indiana Ave	773-268-6900	Spot looks like a throw back from the Black Panther Party days.

Map 17 • Kenwood

Gamestop	1400 E 47th St	773-285-3215	Teen boy's hang-out.
Max's Hair Salon	1453 E Hyde Park Blvd	773-288-2255	The place to go if you need to straighten every kink on your nappy little head.
Sole II Soul	1007 E 43rd St	773-336-8614	Sexy chick heels & boots, birkenstock babes beware.
South Shore Decor	1328 E 47th St	773-373-3116	Wall coverings, paint, blinds, and window treatments galore.
Yehia's	1390 E Hyde Park Blvd	773-548-5848	Infamous for their blow dry and cuts on Afro hair.

Map 18 • Washington Park

The Cat's Meow A "Pamper Me" Boutique	6107 S King Dr	773-684-3220	Sexy lingerie, games, toys, and other classy mut to keep his attention.

Map 19 • Hyde Park

57th Street Books	1301 E 57th St	773-684-1300	Brainy, independent bookstore.
The Baby PhD Store	5225 S Harper Ave	773-684-8920	For the smart kid.
Borders	1539 E 53rd St	773-752-8663	Check out the outside Patio.
Dr Wax Records and Tapes	5226 S Harper Ave	773-493-8696	Old-style vinyl.
Freehling Pot and Pan Company	1365 E 53rd St	773-643-8080	All sorts of kitchen gadgets, plus bulk coffee and tea.
Futons N More	1370 E 53rd St	773-324-7083	Futons 'n' more.
House of Africa	1510 E 63rd St	773-324-6858	Afrocentric everything.
Hyde Park Produce	1226 E 53rd St	773-324-7100	A grocery store full of cheap produce and ethnic ingredients.
Hyde Park Records	1377 E 53rd St	773-288-6588	Buy/sell vintage LPs.
O'Gara & Wilson	1448 E 57th St	773-363-0993	Rare and out-of-print books.
Powell's Bookstores	1501 E 57th St	773-955-7780	Famous bookstore.
Toys Et Cetera	1502 E 55th St	773-324-6039	Just for fun.
Wesley's Shoe Corral	1506 E 55th St	773-667-7463	Shoes.
Wheels and Things	5210 S Harper Ave	773-493-4326	Bike sales and repairs.

Map 20 • East Hyde Park / Jackson Park

Art's Cycle Sales & Service	1652 E 53rd St	773-363-7524	Bike sales and repairs.

Map 21 • Wicker Park / Ukrainian Village

Akira	1814 W North Ave	773-489-0818	High fashion for wanna-be Eurotrash.
Anjenu Boutique	1747 W Division St	773-469-2212	Excellent paper store offering a bevy of local and letterpressed cards.
Art + Science Hair Salon	1552 N Milwaukee Ave	773-227-4247	Beakers bring you back to science class. Student discounts available.
Artemio's Bakery	1443 N Milwaukee Ave	773-342-0757	Mexican sweetstuffs.
Asrai Garden	1935 W North Ave	773-782-0680	Unique home accents and garden doo dads.
Beadniks	1937 W Division St	773-276-2323	DIY activity of the 00s.
Black Walut Gallery	2135 W Division St	773-772-8870	Handcrafted hardwood furniture along with modern art and accessories.
Bonnie and Clyde	1751 W Division St	773-235-2680	Trashy, trendy esoterica.
Broken Cherry	1734 W North Ave	773-278-4000	Rockin' boutique with custom apparel options.
Brooklyn Industries	1426 N Milwaukee Ave	773-360-8182	Sustainable yet industrial designs.
The Brown Elephant	1459 N Milwaukee Ave	773-252-8801	Resale boutique benefits Howard Brown Health Center.
Casa de Soul	1919 W Division St	773-252-2520	Asian/African-inspired global lifestyle boutique for men and women.
Cattails	1935 W Division St	773-486-1621	A unique flower market.
City Soles	1566 N Damen Ave	773-489-2001	You could wear your paycheck, one on each foot. But beautifully handcrafted European soles.
DeciBel Audio	1429 N Milwaukee Ave	773-862-6700	New and used stereo equipment.
G-Star	1525 N Milwaukee Ave	773-342-2623	More denim than your little heart could desire.
Greenheart	1911 W Division St	312-264-1625	Fair-trade items galore!
Grow	1943 W Division St	773-489-0009	Stylish, organic wares for your tots.
Habit	1951 W Division St	773-342-0093	Indie/local designer's collective.
iCream	1537 N Milwaukee Ave	773-342-2834	Techno ice cream: hydrogen robo-machine operated.
Jade	1557 N Milwaukee Ave	773-342-5233	Hip women's boutique.
John Fluevog	1539 N Milwaukee Ave	773-772-1983	Funky, eco-friendly shoes.
Language	1537 N Milwaukee Ave	773-777-2574	Hip yet sophisticated wares hang in this small women's boutique.
Lenny & Me	1463 Milwaukee Ave	773-489-5576	Vintage furniture and clothing haven. In with the old.
Lille	1923 W North Ave	773-342-0563	Great little things for the home.

Myopic Books	1564 N Milwaukee Ave	773-862-4882	A Wicker Park brainy-hipster institution.
Paper Doll	2048 W Division St	773-227-6950	Paper, cards, and great gifts.
Penelope's	1913 W Division St	773-395-2351	Pad your wardrobe with adorable at remarkably reasonable prices..
Plein Aire	2036 W Division St	773-227-3722	Cute, affordable boutique.
Porte Rouge	1911 W Division St	773-269-2800	Fancy French housewares and free tea.
Quimby's Bookstore	1854 W North Ave	773-342-0910	Books and music.
Reckless Records	1532 N Milwaukee Ave	773-235-3727	Mostly indie music-new and used.
Renegade Handmade	1924 W Division St	773-227-2707	Purchase wares by hipster crafters all year round.
Ruby Room	1743 W Division St	773-235-2323	A "spa for the spirit" of the chic.
Silver Moon	1755 W North Ave	773-235-5797	Amazing vintage.
The Silver Room	1442 N Milwaukee Ave	773-278-7130	Clothing and accessories.
Threadless	1905 W Division St	773-698-7042	Get your snarky t-shirt on.
Tatine	1742 W Division St	773-342-1890	Fancy candle/soap store.
Untitled	1941 W North Ave	773-342-0500	Uber-hipster clothing.

Map 22 • Noble Square / Goose Island

Arandas Tire Repair & Rims	1511 N Ashland Ave	773-252-6292	Hubcaps galore, from cheapie basics to bangin' bling.
August Grocery	1500 W Division St	773-252-9560	This mini grocery offers gourmet-to-go and plenty of fresh fish.
Blick Art Materials	1574 N Kingsbury St	312-573-0110	Get creative here.
Dusty Groove Records	1120 N Ashland Ave	773-342-5800	Vinyl and CDs. Specializes in funk, soul, rare groove, now sound, and world music.
Irv's Luggage Warehouse	820 W North Ave	312-787-4787	Carries some discounted luggage and briefcases.
Lovely: A Bake Shop	1130 N Milwaukee Ave	773-572-4766	Bread pudding for real.
Nina	1655 W Division St	773-486-8996	Yarn shop includes delicate, frayed thread from old saris.
Restoration Hardware	938 W North Ave	312-475-9116	Fancy housewares.
Roots & Culture	1034 N Milwaukee Ave	773-580-0102	Find contemporary art and a community-minded spirit at this non-profit art center.
Transitions Bookplace	1000 W North Ave	312-951-7323	Books on spirituality, health, etc. Has a café.
Vintage Pine	904 W Blackhawk St	312-943-9303	Custom-made furniture from the English and French countrysides.

Map 23 • West Town / Near West Side

Alcala's Western Wear	1733 W Chicago Ave	312-226-0152	Western-wear emporium sells boots, jeans and cowboy hats.
Donofrio's Double Corona Cigars	2058 W Chicago Ave	773-342-7820	Brian Donofrio sells very fine imported cigars.
Guess Hookah	1829 W Chicago Ave	312-666-8801	Head shop meets the hookah trend with a lounge to show off your purchase.
H&R Sports	1739 W Chicago Ave	312-226-8737	Soccer gear.
Koi 8	1927 W Chicago Ave	312-846-6213	From locally designed buttons to silly stationery and chic attire.
Modern Times	2100 W Grand Ave	312-243-5706	Vintage mid-century modern funishings.
Painted Lady Organic Eatery	2018 W Chicago Ave	773-327-6931	Proof that politically-correct pastry—organic, sustainable—tastes good.
Permanent Records	1914 W Chicago Ave	773-278-1744	The place to head for vinyl.
Rotofugi	1953 W Chicago Ave	312-491-9501	Really cool toy store with urban vinyl figures.
Salvage One Architectural Elements	1840 W Hubbard St	312-733-0098	Warehouse of antique, vintage and salvaged architectural pieces for home/loft restoration.
Sprout Home	745 N Damen Ave	312-226-5950	Plants and gardening supplies meet modernism.
Tomato Tattoo	1855 W Chicago Ave	312-226-6660	Every hip strip needs a tattoo parlor.

Map 24 • River West / West Town

65Grand	1378 W Grand Ave	312-719-4325	Contemporary art comes at an affordable price by local and national artists.
Aesthetic Eye	1520 W Chicago Ave	312-243-1520	Art gallery, irregular hours.
Black Walnut/Robert Wayner Gallery	220 N Aberdeen St	312-286-2307	Handcrafted hardwood furniture along with modern art and accessories.
Brody's Balloons	1101 W Randolph St	800-652-7639	Piñatas and balloons!
Casati Gallery	949 W Fulton Market	312-421-9905	Mid-century Italian furniture and accessories.
Chicago Antique Market	W Randolph St & N Ogden Ave	312-951-9939	Leases space to a variety of vendors.
Chicago Avenue Discount	1637 W Chicago Ave	312-226-0004	Shoes for $1.93!
Design Inc	1359 W Grand Ave	312-243-4333	Architecturally centered home design.
Douglas Dawson Gallery	400 N Morgan St	312-226-7975	Fancy artifacts from around the world.
duchess	1043 W Grand Ave	312-933-5317	Two young curators turn their living room into a contemporary gallery.

Green Grocer	1402 W Grand Ave	312-624-9508	Give the planet a high-five. Local, organic, awesome groceries.
Halo [For Men]	938 W Madison St	312-526-3260	Hip men's haircare.
Hoosier Mama Pie Company	1618 W Chicago Ave	312-243-4846	"Keep your fork, there's pie!"
Jan's Antiques	225 N Racine Ave	312-563-0275	Mind-boggling antique emporium.
J.P. Graziano Grocery Co.	901 W Randolph St	312-666-4587	Spices, pasta, and dried beans in bulk.
Lush Wine and Spirits	1412 W Chicago Ave	312-666-6900	Wine, microbrews, and booze!
Ouest	1063 W Madison St	312-421-2799	From Philip Lim to Rozae Nichols…need we say more?
Pet Care Plus	1328 W Lake St	312-397-9077	For the pet-obsessed.
The Realm	1430 W Chicago Ave	312-491-0999	Exotic furniture from far-away places.
Roots	1140 W Grand Ave	312-666-6466	Trendy hair salon.
RR#1 Chicago Apothecary	814 N Ashland Blvd	312-421-9079	Old-school pharmacy.
Snap	470 N Ogden Ave	312-226-5110	Hair and nail salon.
Terry's Toffee	1117 W Grand Ave	312-733-2700	Gourmet, house-made toffee, ice creams, and biscotti.
Tonya's Hush Boutique	34 S Ashland Ave	312-738-1090	Unique upscale retail for women.
Upgrade Cycle Works	1130 W Chicago Ave	312-226-8650	Bikes, accessories and servicing.
Xyloform	1423 W Chicago Ave	312-455-7949	Furniture store.

Map 25 • Illinois Medical District

Accents Flowers and Gifts	2246 W Taylor St	312-850-4438	Flower shop conveniently located near major hospitals.
Salvation Army Thrift Store	2024 S Western Ave	773-254-1127	Good 'ol fashioned thrifting.
Symmetry	715 S Western Ave	773-645-0502	Upscale/modern furniture and décor featuring Tibetan rugs.

Map 26 • University Village / Little Italy / Pilsen

Barbara's Bookstore	1218 S Halsted St	312-666-3161	Catch a book signing or get a student discount.
Conte Di Savoia	1438 W Taylor St	312-666-3471	European and Italian specialties.
Lush Wine and Spirits	1306 S Halsted St	312-738-1900	Wine, microbrews, and booze
Mario's Italian Lemonade	1068 W Taylor St		The best summer treat in the city. Prepare to wait.
Scafuri Bakery	1337 W Taylor St	312-733-8881	The secret's in the bread.

Map 27 • Logan Square

Boulevard Bikes	2535 N Kedzie Blvd	773-235-9109	Friendly neighborhood bike shop.
Dill Pickle Food Co-op	3039 W Fullerton Ave	773-252-2667	Tiny as an organic kumquat, but with a dense food selection.
Disco City Records No. 6	2630 N Milwaukee Ave	773-486-1495	Latin music emporium.
Fleur	3149 W Logan Blvd	773-395-2770	Not your mother's floral arrangements, plus handmade goods from locals.
Provenance Food and Wine	2528 N California Ave	773-384-0699	Reasonably priced wines and unreasonably priced groceries.
Threads, Etc	2327 N Milwaukee Ave	773-276-6411	Resale clothes and furniture.
Village Discount Outlet	2032 N Milwaukee Ave	866-545-3836	Tons of clothes and weekly specials.
Wolfbait & B-Girls	3131 W Logan Blvd	312-698-8685	Two young designers showcase funky wares by dozens of locals.

Map 28 • Bucktown

Beta Boutique	2016 W Concord Pl	773-276-0905	Everything you'd find at your favorite sample sale.
Cynthia Rowley	1653 N Damen Ave	773-276-9209	Cute feminine designs that flatter the body.
European Imports	2475 N Elston Ave	773-227-0600	Get all the meat, cheese and pastries you've been craving.
G Boutique	2131 N Damen Ave	773-235-1234	Lingerie and bedroom accessories.
The Goddess and Grocer	1646 N Damen Ave	773-342-3200	Gourmet groceries and take-out.
Halo [For Men]	1655 N Damen Ave	773-342-4256	Hip men's haircare.
Intermix	1633 N Damen Ave	773-292-0894	The NYC shopper's mecca.
Jean Alan	2134 N Damen Ave	773-278-2345	House and home.
Lululemon	1627 N Damen Ave	773-227-1869	Canadian-based yoga wear brand brings soft-as-cashmere soy clothes and sleek attire.
Mark Shale Outlet	2593 N Elston Ave	773-772-9600	Great deals on grown-up clothes.
Micro Center	2645 N Elston Ave	773-292-1700	Department store chain full of electronics.
The Needle Shop	2054 W Charleston St		Fabric store that offers classes.
p.45	1643 N Damen Ave	773-862-4523	Edgy women's boutique.
Pagoda Red	1714 N Damen Ave	773-235-1188	Fine Asian antiques.
Pavilion Antiques	2055 N Damen Ave	773-645-0924	Antique furniture.
Psycho Baby	1630 N Damen Ave	773-772-2815	Hip gear for the urban baby.
The Red Balloon Company	2060 N Damen Ave	773-489-9800	A unique store for children—toys, clothes and furniture.
Robin Richman	2108 N Damen Ave	773-278-6150	Arty, indie boutique.
Scoop NYC	1702 N Milwaukee Ave	773-227-9930	On top of the trends.

Soutache	2125 N Damen Ave	773-292-9110	A treasure trove of ribbons, buttons and trim.
T-Shirt Deli	1739 N Damen Ave	773-276-6266	Pricey—but quality—custom-made t-shirts.
Tangerine	1719 N Damen Ave	773-772-0505	Feminine women's boutique.
Veruca Salt	1937 N Damen Ave	773-276-3888	Flirty ladies fashions.
Vienna Beef Factory Store	2501 N Damen Ave	773-278-7800	Here's the beef.
Village Discount Outlet	2032 N Milwaukee Ave	866-545-3866	Tons of clothes and weekly specials.
Vive La Femme	2115 N Damen Ave	773-772-7429	Style beyond size.
Vosges Haut Chocolat	2211 N Elston Ave	773-388-5560	Delicious exotic gourmet chocolates flavored with Indian spices, whiskey, etc.
White Attic	1842 N Damen Ave	773-252-8844	Clean home furnishings and art work.

Map 29 • DePaul / Wrightwood / Sheffield

Active Endeavors	853 W Armitage Ave	773-281-8100	Playing sports or heading into the great outdoors? This is your place for gear.
Art Effect	934 W Armitage Ave	773-929-3600	"A modern day general store" for everything fabulous.
Balance Health + Wellness	1901 N Clybourn Ave	773-472-0560	Striving to help clients return to a state of balance.
Crate & Barrel Outlet Store	1864 N Clybourn Ave	312-787-4775	What you wish you could furnish your home with.
Dirk's Fish	2070 N Clybourn Ave	773-404-3475	Carry out fresh fish and seafood spot.
Eclectica	1006 W Armitage Ave	773-697-9929	Boutique by local designers.
Intermix	841 W Armitage Ave	773-404-8766	The NYC shopper's mecca.
Isabella Fine Lingerie	1101 W Webster Ave	773-281-2352	Fine after-hours wear.
Jayson Home & Garden	1885 N Clybourn Ave	773-248-8180	Dedicated to making sure you live beautifully.
Kaveri	1211 W Webster Ave	773-296-2141	Boutique lines by designers like Trovata and Ulla Johnson.
The Left Bank	1155 W Webster Ave	773-929-7422	Jewelry and home décor.
Lush Cosmetics	859 W Armitage Ave	773-281-5874	Handmade soaps and natural cosmetics—too bad they aren't edible!
Mint	2150 N Seminary Ave	773-322-2944	Boutique featuring Midwestern artists.
Tabula Tua	1015 W Armitage Ave	773-525-3500	Housewares.
Uncle Dan's Great Outdoor Store	2440 N Lincoln Ave	773-477-1918	One-stop shopping for survivalists.
Wine Discount Center	1826 N Elston Ave	773-489-3454	Wine warehouse—free tastings every Saturday.

Map 30 • Lincoln Park

A New Leaf	1818 N Wells St	312-642-8553	Perhaps the most elegantly designed flower shop in Chicago.
Art + Science Hair Salon	1971 N Halsted St	312-787-4247	Beakers bring you back to science class. Student discounts available.
Barneys New York Co-Op	2209 N Halsted St	773-248-0426	Barney's "affordable" sister.
BCBGMAXAZRIA	2140 N Halsted St	773-287-2224	Upscale chic women's fashion.
Buy Popular Demand	2629 N Halsted St	773-868-0404	Consignment shop offering affordable fashions.
Club Monaco	2206 N Halsted St	773-528-2031	Fashion-forward clothing that doesn't try too hard.
Cynthia Rowley	808 W Armitage Ave	773-528-6160	Apparel and accessories.
Crossroads Trading Co.	2711 N Clark St	773-296-1000	Hip styles, thrift store prices.
Dave's Records	2604 N Clark St	773-929-6325	All LPs, from Janacek to Jay-Z.
Ethan Allen	1700 N Halsted St	312-573-2500	Furniture store.
Francesca's Collections	2012 N Halsted St	773-244-4075	Forever 21 in terms of price, something stylish in terms of style.
Lori's - The Sole of Chicago	824 W Armitage Ave	773-281-5655	Designer shoes.
Lululemon	2104 N Halsted St	773-883-8860	Canadian-based yoga wear brand brings soft-as-cashmere soy clothes and sleek attire.
McShane's	815 W Armitage Ave	773-525-0282	Designer resale. Head on upstairs for some serious markdowns.
Nau	2118 N Halsted St	773-281-1363	Eco-friendly attire for the athetic set.
Old Town Triangle	1763 N North Park Ave	312-337-1938	Don't miss their openings.
Sally Beauty Supply	2727 N Clark St	773-477-6222	Wholesale for stylists, but open to the public.
Smart Optical	2730 N Clark St	773-868-9189	As if eyewear wasn't cool enough.
Untitled	2707 N Clark St	773-404-9225	Uber hipster clothing.
Urban Outfitters	2352 N Clark St	773-549-1711	Retro fun clothing, nifty gifts, silly t-shirts.
White Elephant	2300 Childrens Plz	773-880-4031	Resale shop at the Children's Memorial Hospital.

Map 31 • Old Town / Near North

Crate & Barrel Outlet Store	1864 N Clybourn Ave	312-787-4775	Housewares.
Fleet Feet Sports	210 W North Ave	312-587-3338	The staff watches you run to make sure the shoes fit.
Fudge Pot	1532 N Wells St	312-943-1777	A chocolate institution.
Irv's Luggage Warehouse	820 W North Ave	312-787-4787	Carries some discounted luggage and briefcases.
Jumbalia	1429 N Wells St	312-335-9082	Great gift store.
Nicole Miller	1419 N Wells St	312-664-3532	The high-end designer sells her wares—from lingerie to bridal and formal attire—to the ladies who can afford to look this good.

Old Town Gardens	1555 N Wells St	312-266-6300	Beautiful plants and flowers.
Quiltology	2625 N Halsted St	773-880-5994	Make quilt, keep self warm.
String a Strand on Wells	4632 N Lincoln Ave	773-275-1233	Make your own jewelry.
The Spice House	1512 N Wells St	312-274-0378	Spice up your cooking.
Twisted Sister Bakery	1543 N Wells St	312-932-1128	And you thought they just served pleasing melodies... Try ice box cookies!
Up Down Tobacco	1550 N Wells St	312-337-8025	Great selection of cigars, cigarettes, and accessories.
Village Cycle Center	1337 N Wells St	312-751-2488	Good urban cycling store.

Map 32 • Gold Coast / Mag Mile

Agent Provocateur	47 E Oak St	312-335-0229	A British lingerie invasion in the Gold Coast.
900 North Michigan Shops	900 N Michigan Ave	312-915-3916	Hi-end mall stores.
Barney's New York	25 E Oak St	312-587-1700	Upscale boutique, clothing and accessories.
BCBGMAXAZRIA	113 E Oak St	312-475-0053	Upscale chic women's fashion.
Bravco Beauty Center	43 E Oak St	312-943-4305	For those who like to be pampered.
Chanel at the Drake Hotel	935 N Michigan Ave	312-787-5000	Classic, expensive clothing, accessories, and fragrances.
Club Monaco	900 N Michigan Ave	312-787-8757	Fashion-forward clothing that doesn't try too hard.
Elements	102 E Oak St	312-642-6574	Cool house-y stuff.
Europa Books	832 N State St	312-335-9677	International magazines.
Flight 001	1133 N State St	312-944-1001	Modern retro-style travel gear.
Frette	41 E Oak St	312-649-3744	European furniture and accessories.
Gucci	900 N Michigan Ave	312-664-5504	Tom Ford's alluring and provocative clothes and accessories.
H&M	840 N Michigan Ave	312-640-0060	European department store taking Chicago by storm.
Halo [For Men]	21 W Elm St	312-642-4256	Hip men's haircare.
Hermes	110 E Oak St	312-787-8175	Fancy scarves and more.
Hershey's Chicago	822 N Michigan Ave	312-337-7711	Dumb and fun chocoholic tourist trap.
Ikram	873 N Rush St	312-587-1000	The First Lady's favorite boutique.
Intermix	40 E Delaware Pl	312-640-2922	The NYC shoppers' mecca.
Jake	939 N Rush St	312-664-5553	Fashionista favorite for men and women.
Lululemon	930 N Rush St	312-915-0627	Canadian-based yoga wear brand brings soft-as-cashmere soy clothes and sleek attire.
More Cupcakes	1 E Delaware Pl	312-951-0001	The BLT cupcake is exactly what it sounds like.
Paul Stuart X/S	875 N Michigan Ave	312-640-2650	Located on the second floor, one of only two Paul Stuart outlets in the world. So far.
Prada	30 E Oak St	312-951-1113	Expensive, but delightful, clothing and accessories.
Pratesi	67 E Oak St	312-943-8422	Linens.
skinstinct	845 N Michigan Ave	312-202-0708	Tiny boutique featuring bamboo and organic clothing.
Tod's	121 E Oak St	312-943-0070	Italian luxury leather goods.
Ultimate Bride	106 E Oak St	312-337-6300	Bridal gear.
Ultimo	114 E Oak St	312-787-1171	Apparel and accessories.
Urban Outfitters	935 N Rush St	312-640-1919	Retro clothing, nifty gifts, and cool accessories.
Water Tower	835 N Michigan Ave	312-440-3166	Marshall Fields, er, Macy's.

Map 33 • Rogers Park / West Ridge

Argo Georgian Bakery	2812 W Devon Ave	773-764-6322	Some Russian baked goods for your trouble?
AutoZone	2555 W Touhy Ave	773-764-5277	Stuff for your car.
Cheesecakes by JR	2841 W Howard St	773-465-6733	Over 20 flavors of cheesecakes.
Chicago Harley Davidson	6868 N Western Ave	773-338-6868	Hogs, gear, etc.
Levinson's Bakery	2856 W Devon Ave	773-761-3174	Always fresh!
Office Mart	2801 W Touhy Ave	773-262-3924	Combination office supply store and and Internet coffee shop.
Raj Jewels	2652 W Devon Ave	773-465-5755	For all your Indian wedding needs.
Resham's	2540 W Devon Ave	773-764-9692	Saris and fabric fill the store.
Taj Sari Palace	2553 W Devon Ave	773-338-0177	Beautiful Indian clothing and accessories.
Tel-Aviv Kosher Bakery	2944 W Devon Ave	773-764-8877	Under the supervision of Rabbi Chaim Goldzweig!
Three Sisters Deli	2854 W Devon Ave	773-973-1919	Russian deli with fresh herring, smoked meats, and caviar.

Map 34 • East Rogers Park

Armadillo's Pillow	6753 N Sheridan Rd	773-761-2558	Score some paperbacks for cheap.
Flatts & Sharpe Music Company	6749 N Sheridan Rd	773-465-5233	Cheap guitars ($150), offering lessons and music accessories.
Mar-Jen Discount Furniture	1536 W Devon Ave	773-338-6636	Cheap futons, dorm furniture.
New Leaf Natural Grocery	1261 W Loyola Ave	773-743-0400	Adorable, horribly expensive organic grocery, as per usual.
Romanian Kosher Sausage Co	7200 N Clark St	773-761-4141	Kosher meat and poultry.

Map 35 • Arcadia Terrace / Peterson Park

Grazer's Gourmet	5333 N Lincoln Ave	773-561-5500	Homemade granola minus the macramé.

Map 36 • Bryn Mawr / Bowmanville

Target	2112 W Peterson Ave	773-761-3001	All you need, under one roof.

Map 37 • Edgewater / Andersonville

Alamo Shoes	5321 N Clark St	773-334-6100	Large selection for the soles from local retailer.
Andersonville Galleria	5247 N Clark St	773-878-8570	Indie mall with over 90 vendors.
Blue Hydrangea	1113 W Berwyn Ave	773-293-1113	Friendly flower shop.
Bon Bon	5410 N Clark St	773-784-9882	Sweet handmade chocolate boutique.
Brimfield	5219 N Clark St	773-271-3501	Eclectic design sensibility favoring plaid.
Broadway Antique Market	6130 N Broadway St	773-743-5444	BAM! Calling all mallrats and antique freaks—one of America's most reviewed antique stores.
Brownstone Antiques	5234 N Clark St	773-878-9800	Cluttered estate sale finds.
The Brown Elephant	5404 N Clark St	773-271-9382	Resale shop benefits local HIV clinic.
Cassona	5241 N Clark St	773-506-7882	Gorgeous home furnishings.
Early to Bed	5232 N Sheridan Rd	773-271-1219	Woman-oriented grown-up toys. Boy friendly.
Edgewater Antique Mall	6314 N Broadway St	773-262-2525	20th century antiques and vintage.
Elda de la Rosa	5555 N Sheridan Rd	773-769-3128	Custom gowns and dresses.
Erickson Jewelers	5304 N Clark St	773-275-2010	Large selection of jewelry.
Gethsemane Garden Center	5739 N Clark St	773-878-5915	Like mini-trip to a botanical garden; but you can take it home.
Hip Fit	1513 W Foster Ave	773-878-4447	Funky jeans shop.
Johnny Sprockets	1052 W Bryn Mawr Ave	773-293-1695	Caters to all your bicycle needs.
Kate the Great Bookstore	5550 N Broadway St	773-561-1932	Friendly staff actually knows something about books.
Middle East Bakery	1512 W Foster Ave	773-561-2224	So good, so cheap.
Mr. & Mrs. Digz	5668 N Clark St	773-447-8527	Funky used clothes boutique.
Par's Persian Store	5260 N Clark St	773-769-6635	$1/lb for curry powder. Enough curry for Chicago's winterpocalypse.
Paper Trail	5309 N Clark St	773-275-2191	Paper boutique and cards galore.
Presence	5216 N Clark St	773-989-4420	Cool boutique for young women.
The Red Balloon Company	5407 N Clark St	773-989-8500	A unique store for children—toys, clothes and furniture.
Room Service	5438 N Clark St	773-878-5438	Mid-Century design.
Roost	5634 N Clark St	773-506-0406	Cute furniture for your cute home.
Scout	5221 N Clark St	773-275-5700	Beautiful urban antiques.
Soothe Your Senses Day Spa	6260 N Broadway St	773-262-4246	Bringing Southern charm to Chicago.
Toys Et Cetera	5311 N Clark St	773-769-5311	Educational toys and quality books for kids.
True Nature Foods Community Market	6034 N Broadway St	773-465-6400	Pick up your weekly CSA box of fruits and veggies from your local farmers.
Tulip Toy Gallery	1480 W Berwyn Ave	773-275-6110	Woman-owned, inviting sex paraphenalia shop.
Urbanest	5228 N Clark St	773-271-1000	Sustainable-minded furniture design.
\White Attic	5408 N Clark St	773-907-9800	Clean home furnishings and art work.
Wickstrom's Swedish Deli	5247 N Clark St	773-275-6100	The Swedish epicenter of Andersonville.
Women & Children First	5233 N Clark St	773-769-9299	World's biggest feminist book and music store.

Map 38 • Ravenswood / Albany Park

Lincoln Antique Mall	3115 W Irving Park Rd	773-604-4700	Mid-sized antique mall.
The Music Store	3121 W Irving Park Rd	773-478-7400	Guitars and other musical instruments.
Odin Tatu	3313 W Irving Park Rd	773-442-8288	Get inked.
Rave Sports	3346 W Lawrence Ave	773-588-7176	Athletic shoes and clothing.
Scents & Sensibility	4654 N Rockwell St	773-267-3838	Cards. And things to put your cards and candles and flowers into.
Village Discount Outlet	4027 N Kedzie Ave	866-545-3866	Tons of clothes and weekly specials.

Map 39 • Ravenswood / North Center

Arcadia Knitting	1613 W Lawrence Ave	773-293-1211	Cozy knitting store. Sells good, cheap yarns and offers classes
Architectural Artifacts	4325 N Ravenswood Ave	773-348-0622	Renovator's dream.
Book Cellar	4736 N Lincoln Ave	773-293-2665	Book store/coffee shop/wine bar. Also has sandwiches.
Angel Food Bakery	1636 W Montrose Ave	773-728-1512	Whimsical bakery with interesting sandwiches to go.
Arcadia Knitting	1613 W Lawrence Ave	773-293-1211	Cozy knitting store. Sells good, cheap yarns and offers classes.
The Cheese Stands Alone	4547 N Western Ave	773-293-3870	Artisinal cheeses from Europe and America in this delightfully stinky shop.
The Chopping Block	4747 N Lincoln Ave	773-472-6700	Gourmet cooking utensils and cooking classes.
Different Strummer	4544 N Lincoln Ave	773-728-6000	Guitars and such.
East Meets West	2118 W Lawrence Ave	773-275-1976	Handpicked fair-trade global wares; totally boring.
European Import Center	4752 N Lincoln Ave	773-561-8281	Beer steins and other gifts from Bavaria.
Fleet Feet Sports	4555 N Lincoln Ave	773-271-3338	Runner's mecca.
Gallimaufry Gallery	4712 N Lincoln Ave	773-728-3600	Artisan crafts including instruments, incense, stone fountains.
Glass Art & Decorative Studio	4507 N Lincoln Ave	773-561-9008	Stained glass and gifts.
Griffins & Gargoyles Antiques	2140 W Lawrence Ave	773-769-1255	Pine furniture from Europe.
Happy Food Spot	4631 N Lincoln Ave	773-334-4002	Corner store has Mexican candy, German kraut, the works!
Hazel	1902 W Montrose Ave	773-769-2227	Stylish gifts and jewelry, plus an extensive stationery section.
Laurie's Planet of Sound	4639 N Lincoln Ave	773-271-3569	Funky CD shop with unpretentious service.
Margie's Candies	1813 W Montrose Ave	773-348-0400	Second generation of a Chicago classic.
Merz Apothecary	4716 N Lincoln Ave	773-989-0900	German and other imported toiletries, herbal supplements, etc. The original.
Nadeau	4433 N Ravenswood Ave	773-728-3497	This furniture warehouse may change your life.
Provenance Food and Wine	2312 W Leland Ave	773-784-2314	Selct offerings of wine, cheese, olives & other gourmet fare.
Quake Collectibles	4628 N Lincoln Ave	773-878-4288	Vintage toys and fun!
Timeless Toys	4749 N Lincoln Ave	773-334-4445	Old-fashioned toys.
Rock N Roll Vintage Inc	4740 N Lincoln Ave	773-878-8616	Guitars galore.

Map 40 • Uptown

Baan Home	5053 N Clark St	773-905-1228	Thai home decor and art.
Eagle Leathers	5015 N Clark St	773-728-7228	Come to daddy.
Foursided	5061 N Clark St	773-506-8300	Framing and more at this funky shop.
La Patisserie P	1052 W Argyle St	773-878-3226	The EuroAsian bakery of your dreams.
Patina Antiques	5137 N Clark St	773-334-0400	VIntage designer furniture.
Play It Again Sports	3939 N Ashland Ave	773-463-9900	Sporting goods.
Salvation Army Thrift Store	4315 N Broadway St	773-348-1401	Good 'ol fashioned thrifting.
Shake Rattle and Read Book Box	4812 N Broadway St	773-334-5311	Funky used bookstore, great finds, but cluttered.
skinstinct	5135 N Clark St	773-506-7343	Tiny boutique featuring bamboo and organic clothing.
Tai Nam Market Center	4925 N Broadway St	773-275-5666	Vietnamese. Very good.
Tattoo Factory	4441 N Broadway St	773-989-4077	High-profile place to get inked.
Transistor	5045 N Clark St	312-863-1375	Electronic music CDs & equipment, art books, sleek and shiny.
Unique Thrift Store	4445 N Sheridan Rd	773-275-8623	Half-price Mondays.
Uptown Bikes	4653 N Broadway St	773-728-5212	Cool, grungy bike shop.
Village Discount Outlet	4898 N Clark St	866-545-3836	Tons of clothes and weekly specials.
Wilson Broadway Mall	1114 W Wilson Ave	773-561-0300	Socks, shoes, ethnic shopping, music, luggage—it's all here.
Wooden Spoon	5047 N Clark St	773-293-3190	Heaven for foodies.

Map 42 • North Center / Roscoe Village / West Lakeview

Antique Resources	1741 W Belmont Ave	773-871-4242	Large inventory of antique furniture.
Andy's Music	2300 W Belmont Ave	773-868-1234	Knock yourself out browsing all the exotic musical instruments sold here.
Avenue	3322 N Western Ave	773-296-9387	Modern plus-size clothes.
Be Bye Baby	1654 W Roscoe St	773-404-2229	Unique maternity wear and eco-friendly toys, clothes and accessories for moms.
Caravan Beads	3361 N Lincoln Ave	773-248-9555	Loads of beads for all your beady needs.
Carlos and Sarah's Surplus of Options	3664 N Lincoln Ave		Everything you wanted that grandma gave up.
A Cooler Planet	2211 W Roscoe St	773.248.1110	A neat shop full of eco-friendly things for your home.
Father Time Antiques	2108 W Belmont Ave	773-880-5599	A plethora of timepieces.

Glam to Go	2002 W Roscoe St	773-525-7004	Girly-girls get pampered.
Good Old Days Antiques	2138 W Belmont Ave	773-472-8837	Antiques and treasures.
Jazze Junque	3419 N Lincoln Ave	773-472-6450	An entire store devoted to cookie jars.
Lula's at the Belle Kay	3862 N Lincoln Ave	773-404-5858	Beautiful vintage served by the dress nazi. Seriously.
Lush Wine and Spirits	2232 W Roscoe St	773-281-8888	Wine, microbrews, and booze.
Lynn's Hallmark	3353 N Lincoln Ave	773-281-8108	Cards, stationery, and gift wrap.
My Closet	3350 N Paulina St	773-388-9851	Marked-down designer wear from Bloomingdale's and Macy's.
The Pleasure Chest	3436 N Lincoln Ave	773-525-7151	Sextastic adult store.
Sacred Art	2040 W Roscoe St	773-404-8790	Featuring up and coming local designers.
Scooter's Frozen Custard	1658 W Belmont Ave	773-244-6415	The tastiest custard this side of St. Louis.
Shangri-La Vintage	1952 W Roscoe St	773-348-5090	Funky pleather jackets, plenty o' accessories, nylon shirts galore.

Map 43 • Wrigleyville / East Lakeview

The Alley	3228 N Clark St	773-883-1800	Skulls, tattoos, big boots.
Belmont Army Surplus Store	855 W Belmont Ave	773-549-1038	Mostly fashion; little bit of military.
Beyond the Wall	935 W Belmont Ave	773-871-5827	Cheap art for your walls.
Bittersweet Pastry Shop and Cafe	1114 W Belmont Ave	773-929-1100	Cookies as big as your head.
Bookworks	3444 N Clark St	773-871-5318	Friendly, well-organized used books.
Borrow a Dress Couture (BADC)	3221 N Sheffield Ave	773-904-8735	Rent a dress for the Grammys.
Fashion Tomato	937 W Belmont Ave	773-281-2921	Cheap, trendy clothes for girls who go to clubs and like to "party."
J. Toguri Mercantile Co	851 W Belmont Av	773-929-3500	Find Japanese books, paper, and foodstuffs here.
Krista K	3458 N Southport Ave	773-248-1967	For pregnant women. And babies.
Leahy & LaDue Consignment	3753 N Southport Ave	773-929-4865	Classy resale shop, mostly expensive, but good buys on the sale rack.
Midwest Pro Sound and Lighting	1613 W Belmont Ave	773-975-4250	DJ equipment, fog machines, strobe lights.
Namaskar Boutique	3950 N Southport Ave	773-472-0930	Yoga accessories.
Never Mind	953 W Belmont Ave	773-472-4922	Trendy accessories and clothes for trixie girls.
Paper Boy	1351 W Belmont Ave	773-399-8811	Hip Hallmark.
Play It Again Sports	3939 N Ashland Ave	773-305-9900	Sporting goods.
Powell's Bookstores	2850 N Lincoln Ave	773-248-1444	Remainders and off-price books. Mostly scholarly. Famous bookstore.
Saturday Audio Exchange	1021 W Belmont Ave	773-935-4434	Great bargains on name brand audio.
Strange Cargo	3448 N Clark St	773-327-8090	Hip affordable threads for the 20-somethings.
Thousand Waves Spa	1212 W Belmont Ave	773-549-0700	Get away from it all at this female-only spa.
Trousseau Lingerie	3543 N Southport Ave	773-472-2727	Beautiful and unique lingerie—tres chic.
Tula	3738 N Southport Ave	773-549-2876	Modern classics boutique.
Uncle Dan's Great Outdoor Store	3551 N Southport Ave	773-348-5800	Camping gear with a granola, Grateful Dead kind of feel.
Uncle Fun	1338 W Belmont Ave	773-477-8223	Cramped and crazy retro toys and novelties.
Yellow Jacket	2959 N Lincoln Ave	773-248-1996	Funky vintage shop with great window displays.

Map 44 • East Lakeview

Addendum	3341 N Broadway St	773-404-9222	Spectacularly ornamental.
Akira	643 W Diversey Pkwy	773-649-9257	High fashion for wanna-be Eurotrash.
borderline MUSIC	3333 N Broadway St	773-975-9533	Dance music store named after Madonna song.
The Brown Elephant	3651 N. Halsted St	773-549-5943	Resale boutique benefits Howard Brown Health Center.
Buffalo Exchange	2875 N Broadway St	773-549-1999	Sell or trade your old duds here.
Century Shopping Centre	2828 N Clark St	773-929-8100	Most notable occupants include the cinema and Bally's Fitness.
Clothes Optional	2918 N Clark St	773-296-6630	Funky thrift store.
Cupcakes	613 W Briar Pl	866-525-0817	Just fancy cupcakes.
GayMart	3459 N Halsted St	773-929-4272	Gay Barbie and other homo kitsch and gifts.
Gramaphone Records	2843 N Clark St	773-472-3683	DJ's shop here for the latest wax.
He Who Eats Mud	3247 N Broadway St	773-525-0616	Cards, cards, and more cards.
Hollywood Mirror	812 W Belmont Ave	773-404-2044	Vintage clothes and kitschy doo-dads.
Johnny Sprockets	3001 N Broadway	773-224-1079	Catering to all your bicycle needs.
Land of the Lost	614 W Belmont Ave	773-529-4966	Tubular vintage. 80s heavy.
P&L	2956 N Clark St	773-248-3758	The latest from Bangkok designers.
Pastoral Artisan Cheese, Bread & Wine	2945 N Broadway St	773-472-4781	One of Chicago's favorite cheese shops. Start your picnic here.
Phoebe's Cupcakes	3327 N Broadway Ave	773-868-4000	Cupcakes as light as air.
Ragstock	812 W Belmont Ave	773-868-9263	Vintage resale and trendy off-price clothes.
Reckless Records	3126 N Broadway St	773-404-5080	Oldies and new releases on vinyl.

Spare Parts	2947 N Broadway St	773-525-4242	Cool bags, purses, and man purses.
Tulip Toy Gallery	3448 N Halsted St	773-975-1515	Woman-owned, inviting sex paraphenalia shop.
Unabridged Bookstore	3251 N Broadway St	773-883-9119	Helpful bookstore with great travel, kids and gay sections.
Windy City Sweets	3308 N Broadway St	773-477-6100	Old-fashioned candy shop with homemade fudge.

Northwest

Albany Office Supply	3419 W Lawrence Ave	773-267-6000	A substantial portion of the store is devoted to Hello Kitty. Some other stuff too, but who cares about that?
American Science & Surplus	5316 N Milwaukee Ave	773-763-0313	Your one-stop obscure gizmo shop.
Fishguy	4423 N Elston Ave	773-283-7400	Get your local caviar here.
Harlem Irving Plaza	Irving Park Rd & Forest Preserve Ave	773-625-3036	Every tacky, low-end, wholesale-to-public you could ever want.
NY Shoes Imports	3546 W Lawrence Ave	773-509-9903	Has slightly fetishistic edge; interesting lingerie in back.
Perfumes R' Us	3608 W Lawrence Ave	773-463-9575	Well-known name brand perfumes including Nina Ricci, Chanel, DNKY, etc., discounted and wholesale.
Rolling Stone Records	7300 W Irving Park Rd	708-456-0861	The place to rock, with lots of big-haired in-store appearances.
Salvation Army Thrift Store	3837 W Fullerton Ave	773-276-1955	Good 'ol fashioned thrifting.
Srpska Tradicija	3615 W Lawrence Ave	773-588-7372	Music, books, religious icons, and gifts from Serbia and Montenegro.
Sweden Shop	3304 W Foster Ave	773-478-0327	Gifts from Scandinavia.
Village Discount Outlet	4635 N Elston Ave	866-545-3866	Tons of clothes and weekly specials.

West

Buyer's Flea Market	4545 W Division St	773-227-1889	A weekend bargain hunter's dream.
Family Dollar	5410 W Chicago Ave	773-287-7050	All your convenient(ce) store needs for under a dollar.
Moo & Oink	4848 W Madison St	773-473-4800	A barbeque enthusiast's Mecca.
Village Discount Outlet	4020 W 26th St	866-545-3866	Tons of clothes and weekly specials.
Village Discount Outlet	2514 W 26th St	866-545-3866	Tons of clothes and weekly specials.

Southwest

African American Images Bookstore	1909 W 95th St	800-552-1991	Books, art, and jewelry with an African-American theme.
Beverly & Novelty Costume Shop	11626 S Western Ave	773-779-0068	Lifeline of trick-or-treaters and masquerade ballers on Far Southwest Side.
The Beverly Cigar Company	10513 S Western Ave	773-239-3264	More than 65 types of stogies, including a Honduras-rolled house brand.
Beverly Records	11612 S Western Ave	773-779-0066	Flip through actual vinyl here. Remember that stuff?
Bobak's	5275 S Archer Ave	773-735-5334	A melange of Polish buffet and supermarket, Chicago style.
Calabria Imports	1905 W 103rd St	773-396-5800	Italian deli foodstuffs.
County Fair	10800 S Western Ave	773-238-5576	Classic family-owned market with produce, organics, butcher, and deli!
Ford City Shopping Center	7601 S Cicero Ave	773-767-6400	One-stop shopping for everyone on the Southwest Side and Suburbs. Multiplex cinema shows blockbusters.
Grich Antiques	10857 S Western Ave	773-233-8734	Furniture, housewares, and vintage electronics.
Izzy Rizzy's House of Tricks	6356 S Pulaski Rd	773-735-7370	Where to get your whoopy cushions, hand-buzzers, and fake puke.
Mr Peabody Records	11832 S Western Ave	773-881-9299	One of two black-owned, thriving retailers of rare vinyl in the world.
Ms Priss	9915 S Walden Pkwy	773-233-7747	Clubby young woman's fashion haven.
My Sisters' Knits	9907 S Walden Pkwy	773-238-4555	Beverly stitch and bitch knitter's paradise.
Optimo Hat	10215 S Western Ave	773-238-2999	Custom-made men's hats.
Village Discount Outlet	6419 S Kedzie Ave	866-545-3866	Tons of clothes and weekly specials.
Village Discount Outlet	7443 S Racine Ave	866-545-3866	Tons of clothes and weekly specials.
World Folk Music	1808 W 103rd St	773-779-7059	Weird instruments and lessons for kids and adults.

South

African Hedonist	8501 S Cottage Grove Ave	773-651-8511	Disc store features African and Caribbean tunage.

Halsted Indoor Mall	11444 S Halsted St	773-995-0265	Lots of bargains under one roof in historically black Morgan Park, on site of former golf course.
Underground Afrocentric Bookstore	1727 E 87th St	773-768-8869	New and used books of African-American interest.

Evanston

Active Endeavors	901 Church St	847-869-7070	New Evanston location for casual chic clothing.
Art & Science Hair Salon	811 Church St	847-864-4247	Beakers bring you back to science class. Student discounts available.
Asinamali Women's Boutique	1722 Sherman Ave	847-866-6219	Great clothes in a reasonable price range.
Bookman's Alley	1712 Sherman Ave	847-869-6999	Great selection of used books in good condition.
Campus Gear	1717 Sherman Ave	847-869-7033	Cheaper than the campus bookstore for Northwestern apparel. If that's your thing.
Uncle Dan's Great Outdoors	700 Church St	847-475-7100	Camping gear with a granola, Grateful Dead kind of feel.
William's Shoes	710 Church St	847-328-0527	Great boot and sneaker selection.

Oak Park

Antiques, Etc	125 N Marion St	708-386-9194	30+ dealers in one spot. Beautiful furniture, art, jewelry, rugs, and more.
Fly Bird	719 Lake St	708-383-3330	Warmly off-beat housewares and treats, 5-armed plush monsters to lemon-lychee candles.
Magic Tree Bookstore	141 N Oak Park Ave	708-848-0770	Welcoming children's bookstore that also has music, puzzles, and gifts.
Pumpkin Moon	1028 North Blvd	708-524-8144	The place for nostalgic collectables. Includes toys, T-shirts, and candy. Super fun.

Chicago's status as a city of neighborhoods extends to its arts scene, which can be grouped into several notable gallery districts:

River North **(Map 2)**—a scary industrial district in the 1970s—has grown into a glitzy nightlife district that's home to scores of Chicago's most established art dealers. **Jean Albano, Mary Bell, Catherine Edelman, Byron Roche, the Vale Craft Gallery, Zg,** and **Zolla/Lieberman** are just a few places where you can count on finding splendid original—and costly—works from recognized artists. The area hosts a variety of gallery walks and art fairs, such as a gala fall opening night and the annual River North Rendezvous and Feast of the Senses festivals, which pair art spaces with local chefs.

In search of larger, cheaper, and more contemporary spaces, many River North dealers have removed to the burgeoning West Loop **(Map 24),** turning it into a nexus of cutting-edge galleries. **Carrie Secrist** and **Kavi Gupta** are good starting points, while a gaggle of smaller spaces, such as **Bucket Rider, Packer Schopf, Peter Miller, ThreeWalls,** and **Tony Wight Bodybuilder & Sportsman,** to name a few standouts, also showcase quality art.

Wicker Park/Bucktown has been a focal point of progressive and experimental work for nearly 20 years, centering on the historic Flatiron Arts Building at the intersection of North, Damen, and Milwaukee avenues, although to find the art you may have to climb stairs—most of the gallery space is in lower-rent digs above street level. Look for promising artists at such galleries as **AllRise (Map 21), Around the Coyote (Map 21), Heaven (Map 21),** and **Johnsonese (Map 28)**. The district teems with art events, most notably the semi-annual Around the Coyote festivals.

Pilsen **(Map 26)** became the next haven for young artists priced out of the gentrifying Bucktown/Wicker Park, as well as a focal point of Latino art. Collectives like the **Chicago Arts District** and **Polvo Art (Map 26)** and galleries such as **Metzli (Map 10)** and **Vespine (Map 26)** showcase a broad array of emerging artists. The area hosts several annual open-studios events as well as coordinated Second Friday openings. Go to www.chicagoartsdistrict.org for an up-to-date calendar of openings and events.

Fine art can be found in many parts of the city, and it's worth seeking out more isolated showcases as well as **Gallery Guichard (Map 11),** which exhibits artists from the African diaspora, **Woman Made (Map 24),** whose focus is obvious; **R.H. Love (Map 2),** which deals in museum-quality American masterpieces; and the studios and galleries in the historic **Fine Arts Building (Map 6).** Finally, for the most adventurous, be sure to try some of the many alternative gallery spaces in the city. Chicago's reputation as an incubator for start-ups is well-deserved—there are more unorthodox galleries than ever before. Though they are a little dicier as far as exhibition schedules and locations, they often pay off with some of the most unusual and thought-provoking work Chicago has to offer: **Deadtech (Map 27)** and **Dogmatic (Map 24)** are examples.

Check www.chicagoart.net or www.chicagogallerynews.com for more info on galleries in the city, as well as details on openings. The opening celebrations of new exhibits usually take place on Friday evenings. A great web resource for working artists is www.chicagoartistsresource.org.

Map 1 • River North / Fulton Market District

Northeastern Illinois University Fine Arts Center Gallery	5500 N St Louis Ave	773-442-4944
Stuart-Rodgers Gallery	375 W Erie St	312-787-8696

Map 2 • Near North / River North

Alan Koppel Gallery	210 W Chicago Ave	312-640-0730
Aldo Castillo Gallery	675 N Frankin St	312-337-2536
Andrew Bae Gallery	300 W Superior St	312-335-8601
Ann Nathan Gallery	212 W Superior St	312-664-6622
Belloc Lowndes Fine Art	226 W Superior St	312-266-2222
Byron Roche Gallery	750 N Franklin St, Ste 105	312-654-0144
Carl Hammer Gallery	740 N Wells St	312-266-8512
Catherine Edelman Gallery	300 W Superior St	312-266-2350
Gwenda Jay/Addington Gallery	704 N Wells St	312-664-3406
Habatat Galleries	222 W Superior St	312-440-0288
Hildt Galleries	617 N State St	312-255-0005
I Space	230 W Superior St	312-587-9976
Jean Albano Gallery	215 W Superior St	312-440-0770
Judy A Saslow Gallery	300 W Superior St	312-943-0530
Kass Meridian Gallery	325 W Huron St	312-266-5999
Lydon Fine Art	309 W Superior St	312-943-1133
Marx-Saunders Gallery	230 W Superior St	312-573-1400
Mary Bell Gallery	740 N Franklin St	312-642-0202
Maya Polsky Gallery	215 W Superior St	312-440-0055
Melanee Cooper Gallery	740 N Franklin St	312-202-9305
Mongerson Gallery	704 N Wells St	312-943-2354
Nicole Gallery	230 W Huron St	312-787-7716
Oskar Friedl Gallery	1029 W 35th St	312-493-4330
Perimeter Gallery	210 W Superior St	312-266-9473
Peter Bartlow Gallery	226 W Superior St	312-337-1782
Portals	742 N Wells St	312-642-1066
Printworks	311 W Superior St	312-664-9407
RH Love Galleries	645 N Michigan Ave	800-437-7568
Richard Norton Gallery	612 Merchandise Mart Plz	312-644-8855
Rita Bucheit Fine Art & Antiques	449 N Wells St	312-527-4080
Robert Henry Adams Fine Art	715 N Franklin St	312-642-8700
Rosenthal Fine Art	3 E Huron St	312-475-0700
Roy Boyd Gallery	739 N Wells St	312-642-1606
Russell Bowman Art Advisory	311 W Superior St, Ste 115	312-751-9500
Schneider Gallery	230 W Superior St	312-988-4033
Spencer Weisz Galleries	46 E Superior St	312-527-9420
Stephen Daiter Gallery	311 W Superior St	312-787-3350
Trowbridge Gallery	703 N Wells St	312-587-9575
Vale Craft Gallery	230 W Superior St	312-337-3525
Zg Gallery	300 W Superior St	312-654-9900

Map 2 • Near North / River North—*continued*

Zolla/Lieberman Gallery	325 W Huron St	312-944-1990
Zygman Voss Gallery	222 W Superior St	312-787-3300

Map 3 • Streeterville / Mag Mile

The Arts Club of Chicago	201 E Ontario St	312-787-3997
City Gallery	806 N Michigan Ave	312-742-0808
Inspire Fine Art	435 E Illinois St, Ste 131	312-595-9475
Joel Oppenheimer Gallery	410 N Michigan Ave	312-642-5300
Lora D Art Gallery	435 E Illinois St	312-245-9005
Ogilvie/Pertl Gallery	435 E Illinois St, Ste 151	312-321-0750
RS Johnson Fine Art	645 N Michigan Ave, Ste 234	312-943-1661
Worthington Gallery	645 N Michigan Ave	312-266-2424

Map 4 • West Loop Gate / Greek Town

Gallery 2	847 W Jackson Blvd	312-563-5162
Primitive Art Works	130 N Jefferson St	312-575-9600
Thomas McCormick Gallery	835 W Washington Blvd	312-226-6800

Map 5 • The Loop

Donald Young Gallery	933 W Washington Blvd	312-455-0100
Illinois State Museum Chicago Gallery	100 W Randolph St, 2nd Fl	312-814-5322

Map 6 • The Loop / Grant Park

Beacon Street Gallery	410 S Michigan Ave	312-212-1323
Cliff Dwellers Gallery	200 S Michigan Ave	312-922-8080
Hilligoss Gallery	520 N Michigan Ave	312-755-0300

Map 10 • East Pilsen / Chinatown

Metzli Gallery & Cultural Organization	556 W 18th St	312-738-0860
Meztli Gallery	556 W 18th St	312-738-0860
Rogeramsay Gallery	711 N Milwaukee Ave	312-491-1400

Map 11 • South Loop / McCormick Place

Framing Mode	1526 S Wabash Ave	312-566-0027
Gallery Guichard	3521 S Dr Martin Luther King Jr Dr	773-373-8000

Map 13 • Bridgeport (East)

MN Gallery	3524 S Halsted St	773-847-0573

Map 16 • Bronzeville

Nicole Gallery II	4653 S King Dr	312-787-7716

Map 19 • Hyde Park

Artisans 21	5225 S Harper Ave	773-288-7450

Map 20 • East Hyde Park / Jackson Park

Hyde Park Art Center	5020 S Cornell Ave	773-324-5520

Map 21 • Wicker Park / Ukrainian Village

AllRise Gallery	1542 N Milwaukee Ave, Third Floor	773-292-9255
Around the Coyote Gallery	1935 1/2 W North Ave	773-342-6777
Carlos E Jimenez Gallery	2301 W North Ave	773-235-5328
David Leonardis Gallery	1346 N Paulina St	773-278-3058
Gallery 203	1579 N Milwaukee Ave	773-252-1952
Heaven Gallery	1550 N Milwaukee Ave, 2nd Fl	773-342-4597
JoJo's Closet	1579 N Milwaukee Ave, Ste 206	773-862-5656

Map 22 • Noble Square / Goose Island

1112 Gallery	1112 N Milwaukee Ave	773-486-9612
Madron LLC	1000 W North Ave, 3rd Fl	312-640-1302

Map 23 • West Town / Near West Side

Open-End Art Gallery	2000 W Fulton St	312-738-2140

Map 24 • River West / West Town

ARC Gallery	832 W Superior St	312-733-2787
Bucket Rider Gallery	835 W Washington Blvd	312-421-6993
Carrie Secrist Gallery	835 W Washington Blvd	312-491-0917
Dogmatic	1319 W Lake St	312-375-7757
Douglas Dawson Gallery	400 N Morgan St	312-226-7975
Flatfile Galleries	217 N Carpenter St	312-491-1190
Frederick Baker Gallery	1230 W Jackson Blvd	312-243-2980
Function + Art	1046 W Fulton Market	312-243-2780
Gallery 400	400 S Peoria St	312-996-6114
Gallery 40000	119 N Peoria St	312-738-0179
Gescheidle	1039 W Lake St	312-226-3500
Giola Gallery	118 N Peoria St	312-850-4487
GR N'Namdi Gallery	110 N Peoria St	312-563-9240
International Center For Documentary Arts	1303 W Chicago Ave	312-226-5902
Kasia Kay Art Projects Gallery	1044 W Fulton Market	312-492-8828
Kavi Gupta Gallery	835 W Washington Blvd	312-432-0708
Linda Warren Gallery	1052 W Fulton Market	312-432-9500
Lisa Boyle Gallery	1821 W Hubbard St	773-655-5475
Monique Meloche Gallery	118 N Peoria St	312-455-0299
NavtaSchulz Gallery	1039 W Lake St	312-421-5506
Packer Schopf Gallery	942 W Lake St	312-226-8984
Peter Miller Gallery	118 N Peoria St	312-951-1700
Rhona Hoffman Gallery	118 N Peoria St	312-455-1990
Rowland Contemporary	1118 W Fulton Market	312-421-6275
Rowley Kennerk Gallery	119 N Peoria St	773-983-0077
Shane Campbell Gallery	1431 W Chicago Ave	312-226-2223
Skestos Gabriele Gallery	212 N Peoria St	312-243-1112
ThreeWalls	119 N Peoria St	312-432-3972

Tony Wight Bodybuilder & Sportsman Gallery	119 N Peoria St, #2C	312-492-7261
Walsh Gallery	118 N Peoria St, 2nd Fl	312-829-3312
Western Exhibitions	1821 West Hubbard St	312-307-4685
Woman Made Gallery	685 N Milwaukee Ave	312-738-0400

Map 26 • University Village / Little Italy / Pilsen

Polvo Art Studio	1458 W 18th St	773-344-1940
Vespine Gallery & Studios	1907 S Halsted St	312-962-5850

Map 27 • Logan Square

Deadtech	3321 W Fullerton Ave	n/a

Map 28 • Bucktown

Johnsonese Gallery	2149 W Armitage Ave	773-252-8750
Morlen Sinoway-Atelier	1052 W Fulton Market	312-432-0100

Map 29 • DePaul / Wrightwood / Sheffield

Chicago Art Source/ 2nd Floor Gallery	1871 N Clybourn Ave	773-248-3100
Chicago Center for the Print	1509 W Fullerton Ave	773-477-1585
DePaul University Art Museum	2350 N Kenmore Ave	773-325-7506
Havana Gallery	1139 W Webster Ave	773-549-2492
La Llorona Gallery	1474 W Webster Ave	773-281-8460

Map 30 • Lincoln Park

Contemporary Art Workshop	542 W Grant Pl	773-472-4004
Triangle Gallery of Old Town	1763 N North Park Ave	312-337-1938

Map 31 • Old Town / Near North

Thomas Masters Gallery	245 W North Ave	312-440-2322

Map 32 • Gold Coast / Mag Mile

Armstrong Fine Arts	200 E Walton St	312-664-9312
Colletti Gallery	67 E Oak St	312-664-6767
FL Braswell Fine Art	73 E Elm St	312-636-4399
Galleries Maurice Sternberg	875 N Michigan Ave	312-642-1700
Richard Gray Gallery	875 N Michigan Ave, Ste 2503	312-642-8877
Valerie Carberry Gallery	875 N Michigan Ave, Ste 2510	312-397-9990

Map 37 • Edgewater / Andersonville

Las Manos Gallery	5220 N Clark St	773-728-8910

Map 39 • Ravenswood / North Center

Peter Jones Gallery	1806 W Cuyler Ave	773-472-6725

Map 42 • North Center / Roscoe Village / West Lakeview

August House Studio	2113 W Roscoe St	773-327-5644
Chicago Photography Center	3301 N Lincoln Ave	773-549-1631

Map 43 • Wrigleyville/ East Lakeview

Bell Studio	3428 N Southport Ave	773-281-2172
Fourth World Artisans	3727 N Southport Ave	773-404-5200

Map 44 • East Lakeview

Billy Hork Galleries	3033 N Clark St	773-528-9090
Leigh Gallery	3306 N Halsted St	773-472-1865

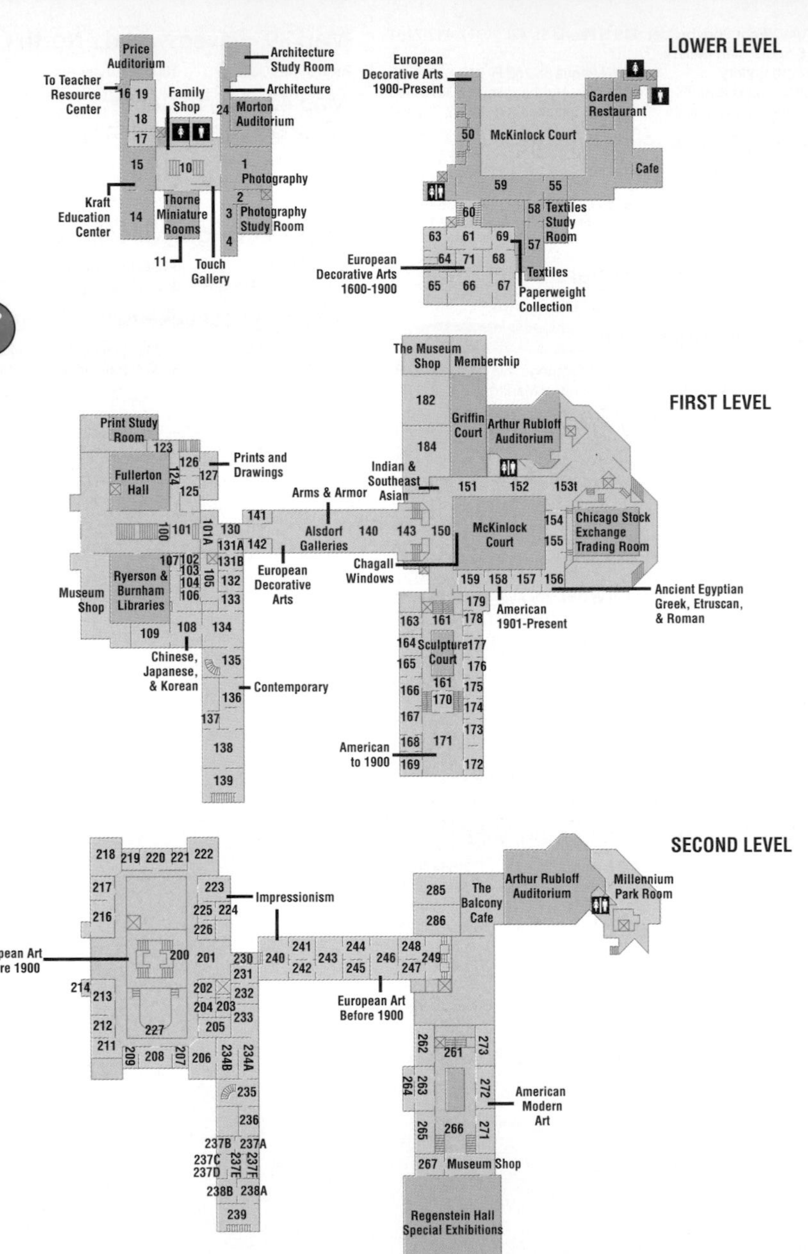
LOWER LEVEL
Price Auditorium
To Teacher Resource Center
Family Shop
Architecture Study Room
Architecture
Morton Auditorium
Photography
Photography Study Room
Kraft Education Center
Thorne Miniature Rooms
Touch Gallery
European Decorative Arts 1900-Present
McKinlock Court
Garden Restaurant
Cafe
Textiles Study Room
Textiles
European Decorative Arts 1600-1900
Paperweight Collection
MAP 6
FIRST LEVEL
The Museum Shop
Membership
Griffin Court
Arthur Rubloff Auditorium
Print Study Room
Prints and Drawings
Fullerton Hall
Indian & Southeast Asian
Arms & Armor
Alsdorf Galleries
McKinlock Court
Chicago Stock Exchange Trading Room
European Decorative Arts
Chagall Windows
Museum Shop
Ryerson & Burnham Libraries
Chinese, Japanese, & Korean
Contemporary
American 1901-Present
Ancient Egyptian Greek, Etruscan, & Roman
Sculpture Court
American to 1900
SECOND LEVEL
Impressionism
European Art Before 1900
The Balcony Cafe
Arthur Rubloff Auditorium
Millennium Park Room
American Modern Art
Museum Shop
Regenstein Hall Special Exhibitions

General Information

NFT Map: 6
Address: 111 S Michigan Ave
Chicago, IL 60603
Phone: 312-443-3600
Website: www.artic.edu
Hours: Mon–Wed & Fri: 10:30 am–5 pm;
Thurs: 10:30 am–8 pm;
Sat & Sun: 10 am–5 pm; Thanksgiving, Christmas, & New Year's Days: closed
Summer hours: Memorial Day through Labor Day open till 9pm on Thursdays and Fridays (free from 5–9 pm)
Admission: $16 for adults ($14 for Chicago residents), $7 for students/children/seniors, free for children aged 14 and under, free for all on Thursday evenings 5– 8pm

Overview

Built in 1892 as the only permanent structure of the 1893 Columbian Exposition, the Classical Revival-style Allerton Wing of the Art Institute of Chicago began life as the "Palace of Culture" for the World's Fair. (The lions were added two years later.) Today the Art Institute is one of the preeminent art museums in the country, housing the largest collection of 19th Century French art outside of Paris (and its modern art collection isn't anything to sneeze at, either). Walking up the grand staircase in the main entrance, visitors are presented with an eclectic collection of architectural fragments wrenched from Chicago buildings that were standing in the way of, well, you know: "progress." There are also impressive exhibitions such as the Japanese wood block prints, the Touch Gallery designed specifically for the visually impaired, as well as really, really old vases and things, but who are we kidding? Everyone comes here for an up-close and personal look at such celebrated paintings as Caillebotte's *Paris Street; Rainy Day,* Seurat's *Grand Jatte,* Grant Wood's *American Gothic,* and Hopper's *Nighthawks,* along with their impressive collection of Monets, Manets, Van Goghs, and Picassos.

The completion of Renzo Piano's Modern Wing in 2009 makes the Art Institute the nation's second largest art museum (we're gaining on you, Metropolitan Museum of Art!). The $300 million addition, which makes great use of filtered natural light thanks to Piano's "magic carpet" floating roof, includes a first floor gallery of film and electronic media, and an impressive exhibition of the museum's Surrealist collection, with many pieces new, reframed, or on display for the first time. A pedestrian bridge connects the new wing's third floor to Millennium Park, across the street.

Restaurants and Services

The Café, on the lower-level of the Rubloff Building, offers self-service dining with burgers, pizza, and deli sandwiches at reasonable prices 11 am–4 pm daily (11 am–7 pm on Thursdays). For a more elegant lunch, dine next door at the Garden Restaurant. Now open year-round from11:30 am to 3 pm daily, the restaurant features patio dining with seasonal cuisine and a full bar. The museum also offers free jazz concerts for Garden diners with their Jazz in the Garden program on Thursday evenings from July to September.

While postcards, books, and magnets may be purchased at kiosks throughout the museum, the Museum Shop, just off the main lobby, offers an extensive collection of art-oriented gifts and souvenirs (and you don't have to pay admission to shop there!). The lower-level Woman's Board Family Shop, adjacent to the Kraft Education Center and the Touch Gallery, hawks kid-oriented goodies. In the Modern Wing, the balcony café offers coffee and light fare with a view overlooking the wing's dramatic Griffith Court entrance.

In the Modern Wing, the balcony café offers coffee and light fare with a view overlooking the wing's dramatic Griffith Court entrance.

School of the Art Institute of Chicago

Boasting such illustrious alumni as Georgia O'Keefe, Claes Oldenburg, Laurie Anderson, and David Sedaris, the School of the Art Institute of Chicago (SAIC) offers a fine art higher education for tomorrow's budding Renoirs.

Gene Siskel Film Center

160 N State St, 312-846-2600;
www.siskelfilmcenter.org

The film branch of the Art Institute offers art house, foreign films, and revivals, with frequent lectures by academics and industry professionals. Highlights include an Annual European Union Film Festival, and Oscar Night America, Chicago's only Academy-sanctioned party.

How to Get There

By Car: The Art Institute is located on Michigan Avenue between Monroe and Jackson. From I-90/94 N (the Dan Ryan), exit to Congress East (Loop exit). From I-90/94 S (Kennedy Expressway), exit Monroe Steet East. Affordable parking is located underground at Millennium Park garages (enter at Columbus and Monroe) and Grant Park garages (enter on Michigan, either between Madison and Randolph or between Van Buren and Adams).

By Metra: Nearest stops are the Randolph and Van Buren stations served by the Metra Electric and South Shore Lines. For other Metra lines, transfer to the 151 Sheridan Avenue bus at Union Station.

By Bus: Numerous lines serve this strip of Michigan Avenue. Important buses include (from the south) the 3 King Drive, the 4 Collage Grove, and the 6 Jackson Park Express, (from the west) the 126 Jackson and 20 Madison, and (from the north) the 151 Sheridan, the 145 Wilson-Michigan Express, and the 146 Inner Drive/Michigan Express.

By L: From the Red and Blue lines, exit at Monroe. Brown, Orange, Purple and Green exit at Adams and Wabash.

Chicago has always been a bookish city and even so seems to be experiencing a literary renaissance of sorts. Great local authors, plentiful reading series, and the emergence of some notable small presses such as Featherproof Books and OV Books are all evidence of a thriving literary culture, augmented by the existence of several outstanding indie bookshops and a healthy smattering of big box stores.

Independent Bookstores

Printer's Row (Map 8), a section of Dearborn Street in the South Loop, was once the epicenter of Chicago's print and publishing trade. While most of that industry has shuttered or moved on, the two remaining stalwart indie bookstores: **Sandemeyer's (Map 8)** and **Printer's Row (Map 8)** are worth visits for bibliophiles—the latter specializes in rare and fine titles.

For general, all–purpose bookshops, **Barbara's (Map 3, 5)** is a Chicago Institution, as is **Unabridged Books (Map 44)** with its specialties in literary fiction, kids' books, travel, cookbooks, and gay and lesbian titles. Down by the University of Chicago campus, **57th Street Books (Map 19)** and **Seminary Co-op Bookstore (Map 19)** both appeal to the brainiac set. Up north **Book Cellar (Map 39)** is a super-friendly Lincoln Square indie with a cute wine bar. Get lit while getting lit.

Specialty Bookstores

Specialty stores abound in the city. We think **Women & Children First (Map 37)** may have the largest selection of feminist and woman–focused books in the country, and their children's section is also top-notch. **Afrocentric Bookstore (Map 16)** specializes in black literature and culture. **The Occult Bookstore (Map 21)** on Milwaukee Avenue offers everything a budding witch or warlock could desire. And you can overthrow your repressed bookshelf with works by Marx and Mao from **Revolution Books (Map 22)** on Ashland. Old Town's **Europa Books (Map 32)** features foreign language titles. **Quimby's (Map 21)**, in Wicker Park, specializes in esoteric small–press books and 'zines with a marked counter–culture feel. You'll find your John Fante, Kathy Acker, and Georges Bataille here.

Used Bookstores

Shuffle through the used stacks at **Bookworks (Map 43)** on North Clark or **Myopic (Map 21)** in Wicker Park. **Selected Works (Map 44)** on Broadway sells used books and sheet music. **Ravenswood Used Books (Map 39)** is as chaotically crammed with books as a used bookshop should be.

Comics

Chicago Comics (Map 43) is such a pleasant store that it's easy to forget about any comic-nerd stigma (don't fool yourself—you're still a dweeb). **Dark Tower (Map 39)** and **Variety Comic Book Store (Map 39)** serves Lincoln Square fanboys. In Wicker Park they head to **Brainstorm (Map 21)**, in Lincoln Park, **Graham Crackers Comics (Map 30)** is full of Marvels...

Reading Series and Literary Happenings

Several Chicago bookstores are known for their active reading series. Most of **Barbara's Bookstore's (Map 3, 5)** regularly scheduled event stake place in their UIC and Oak Park stores. Catering to the University of Chicago community, Hyde Park's **Seminary Co-op Bookstore (Map 19)** features theorists, philosophers, and literary authors, **Women & Children First's (Map 37)** active schedule favors top name women writers and feminists, as well as lots of local talent, **Quimby's (Map 21)** attracts the indie-press and alt-lit crowd, and **Book Cellar (Map 39)** hosts a monthly popular local authors night, and **Myopic (Map 21)** has a renowned poetry series.

The Harold Washington Library (Map 5) is another great place to catch free author readings and literary events. Furthermore, Chicago is host to a plethora of fun and dynamic literary series that occur on a regular basis at bars and cafes all around town. Of them, the Sunday night Uptown Poetry Slam at the **Green Mill (Map 40)** is one of the most enduring.The raucous RUI (Reading Under the Influence), which takes place the first Wednesday of the week at **Sheffield's (Map 43)** celebrates the connection between writers and booze, The first-rate, first-person stories of Second Story, which takes place at **Webster's Wine Bar (Map 29)** and other venues throughout the city, are scored with a live deejay, or occasionally, a live band. At **Innertown Pub (Map 21)**, the Quickies series features readings of complete stories of four minutes or less. Other enduring series include the Reconstruction Room (monthly at the **Black Rock Bar (Map 42)**), The Parlor reading series at **The Green Lantern Gallery (Map 21)**, and the Dollar Store series, which, in 2009, took their show on the road. The Danny's Reading Series, at **Danny's Tavern (Map 28)**, has justly earned a devoted audience of fans; the Windy City Story Slam and the Literary Death Match add a competitive edge to the shenanigans, and for the GLBT community, Homolatte (twice a month at **Big Chicks (Map 40)**) and Pints & Prose at the Pug (monthly at **The Wild Pug (Map 40)**) feature queer voices. Sappho's Salon, which occurs the third Saturday of each month at **Women & Children First Bookstore (Map 39)**, celebrates lesbian creative expression. The Guild Literary Complex (www.GuildComplex.org) hosts literary readings, series and events.

The Pilcrow Literary Festival, which takes place in October, offers a weekend's worth of readings and panel discussions featuring top local talent. In late July, the Newberry Library Bookfair is a used book lover and value hunters dream, featuring thousands of used books at rock bottom prices. Combining the best of both festivals, The Printer's Row Book Fair, which occurs in early June, showcases hundreds of vendors along with an active reading series featuring local and internationally known talent, as well as several topical panels on topics ranging from self-promotion to the future of the book.

A great way to keep on top of it all is through the Chicago Lit website Literago (www.literago.org).

Map 2 • Near North / River North

Abraham Lincoln Book Shop	357 W Chicago Ave	312-944-3085	History and military specialty store.
After-Words	23 E Illinois St	312-464-1110	New and used.
Beck's Book Store	50 E Chicago Ave	312-944-7685	Where there's a Beck's, there's a campus.

Map 3 • Streeterville / Mag Mile

Abbott Hall Book Center	710 N Lake Shore Dr	312-503-8486	Textbooks.
Barbara's	201 E Huron St	312-926-2665	Branch of local chain.
University of Chicago Graduate School of Business	450 N Cityfront Plz Dr	312-464-8650	Textbooks.

Map 4 • West Loop Gate / Greek Town

Waldenbooks	500 W Madison St	312-627-8334	Chain.

Map 5 • The Loop

Barbara's	111 N State St	312-781-3033	Branch of local chain.
Barbara's	233 S Wacker Dr	312-466-0223	Branch of local chain.
Barnes & Noble	1 E Jackson Blvd	312-362-8792	Chain.
Beck's Book Store	60 E Lake St	312-630-9113	Where there's a Beck's, there's a campus.
Beck's Book Store	315 S Plymouth Ct	312-913-0650	Where there's a Beck's, there's a campus.
Books-a-Million	144 S Clark St	312-857-0613	Chain.
Borders	150 N State St	312-606-0750	State Street books.
Graham Crackers Comics	77 E Madison St	312-629-1810	Comics.
Selected Works Bookstore	410 S Michigan Ave	312-447-0068	Quirky, junky used book store.

Map 6 • The Loop / Grant Park

Art Institute of Chicago	111 S Michigan Ave	312-443-3583	Art books and souvenirs.
Chicago Architecture Foundation	224 S Michigan Ave	312-922-3432	Lots of pretty pictures.

Map 8 • South Loop / Printers Row / Dearborn Park

Books In The City	545 S State St	312-291-1111	Textbooks.
Printers Row Fine & Rare Books	715 S Dearborn St	312-583-1800	The name says it all.
Sandmeyer's Book Store	714 S Dearborn St	312-922-2104	General.

Map 9 • South Loop / South Michigan Ave

Columbia College	624 S Michigan Ave	312-427-4860	Some general books, mostly textbooks.

Map 10 • East Pilsen / Chinatown

Chinese Champion Book & Gift	2167 S China Pl	312-326-3577	Chinese books.
World Journal	2116 S Archer Ave	312-842-8005	A world of Chinese books.

Map 11 • South Loop / McCormick Place

Paragon Book Gallery	1507 S Michigan Ave	312-663-5155	Asian arts.

Map 14 • Prairie Shores / Lake Meadows

Matthews Illinois College of Optometry Bookstore	3241 S Michigan Ave	312-949-7471	Textbooks.

Map 16 • Bronzeville

Afrocentric Bookstore	4655 S King Dr	773-924-3966	Celebrates the African-American literary tradition.

Map 19 • Hyde Park

57th Street Books	1301 E 57th St	773-684-1300	Frequented by U of C brainiacs.
Borders	1539 E 53rd St	773-752-8663	General/chain.
Frontline Books & Crafts & Crystal Power	5206 S Harper Ave	773-288-7718	New age.

O'Gara & Wilson	1448 E 57th St	773-363-0993	Used books.
Powell's	1501 E 57th St	773-955-7780	Remainders and off-price books. Mostly scholarly.
Seminary Co-op Bookstore	5757 S University Ave	773-752-4381	Underground trove of scholarly books for all.
University of Chicago Bookstore	970 E 58th St	773-702-7712	Textbooks.

Map 21 • Wicker Park / Ukrainian Village

Brainstorm	1648 W North Ave	773-384-8721	Comic books.
Myopic Books	1564 N Milwaukee Ave	773-862-4882	Rare and collectable books.
Quimby's Bookstore	1854 W North Ave	773-342-0910	Edgy, counter-culture bookshop.

Map 22 • Noble Square / Goose Island

N Fagin Books	917 N Ashland Ave	312-330-5699	Social sciences.
Occult Bookstore	1164 N Milwaukee Ave	773-292-0995	I put a spell on you.
Revolution Books	1103 N Ashland Ave	773-489-0930	Radical and revolutionary books.
Transitions Bookplace	1000 W North Ave	312-951-7323	Heal thyself.

Map 24 • River West / West Town

Joyce & Company	400 N Racine Ave	312-738-1933	Out of print books.

Map 25 • Illinois Medical District

UIC Medical Bookstore	828 S Wolcott Ave	312-413-5550	Reading material for when you're laid up.

Map 26 • University Village / Little Italy / Pilsen

Barbara's	1218 S Halsted St	312-413-2665	Branch of local chain.
Chicago Textbook	1076 W Taylor St	312-733-8398	Textbooks.
Libreria Giron	1443 W 18th St	312-226-2086	Spanish.

Map 28 • Bucktown

Libreria Nazareth De Lourves	1907 N Milwaukee Ave	773-342-8890	Spanish books.
Micro Center	2645 N Elston Ave	773-292-1700	Department store chain.

Map 29 • DePaul / Wrightwood / Sheffield

Barnes & Noble	1441 W Webster Ave	773-871-3610	Convenient for the run-in-and-grab-something shopper.
Transitions Bookplace	1000 W North Ave	312-951-7232	New Age.

Map 30 • Lincoln Park

Books in the City	2428 N Lincoln Ave	773-472-2665	Textbooks.
Graham Crackers Comics	2562 N Clark St	773-665-2010	Where good and evil meet.

Map 32 • Gold Coast / Mag Mile

Barnes & Noble	1130 N State St	312-280-8155	Chain.
Europa Books	832 N State St	312-335-9677	Foreign language books.
The Newberry's A.C. McClurg Bookstore	60 W Walton St	312-255-3520	Connected to the cultural library.
Rosenblum's World of Judaica	2906 W Devon Ave	773-262-1700	Your source for quality Judaica and Books.

Map 33 • Rogers Park / West Ridge

India Book House & Journals	2551 W Devon Ave	773-764-6567	Spiritual/cultural.
Iqra Book Center	2751 W Devon Ave	773-274-2665	Islamic books.
Russian American Book Store	2746 W Devon Ave	773-761-3233	Floor to ceiling with musty books, as it should be.

Map 34 • East Rogers Park

Armadillos Pillow	6753 N Sheridan Rd	773-761-2558	General used.
Beck's Book Store	6550 N Sheridan Rd	773-743-2281	Where there's a Beck's, there's a campus.

Map 35 • Arcadia Terrace / Peterson Park

Chicago Christian Book Center	5786 N Lincoln Ave	773-561-0055	Thou shalt not buy bibles from Amazon.
Korean Books	5773 N Lincoln Ave	773-769-1010	Korean books.

Map 37 • Edgewater / Andersonville

Ginkgo Leaf Books	1759 W Rosehill Dr	773-989-2200	Rare and collectable books.
Kate the Great Bookstore	5550 N Broadway St	773-561-1932	Used and New.
Stern's Psychology Book Store	1256 W Victoria St	773-506-0683	Psychology books.
Women & Children First	5233 N Clark St	773-769-9299	Spacious feminist bookshop.

Map 39 • Ravenswood / North Center

Book Cellar	4736 N Lincoln Ave	773-293-2665	General books and café.
Darktower Comics	4835 N Western Ave	773-506-0400	Comics.
Ravenwood Used Books	4626 N Lincoln Ave	773-593-9166	General used. Classic literature.
Variety Comic Book Store	4602 N Western Ave	773-334-2550	Comic books.

Map 40 • Uptown

Beck's Book Store	4520 N Broadway St	773-784-7963	Where there's a Beck's, there's a campus.
Shake Rattle and Read Book Box	4812 N Broadway St	773-334-5311	Weird little store. Mostly used, some new.
Stern's Psychology Book Store	1256 W Victoria St	773-506-0683	Psychology books.

Map 41 • Avondale / Old Irving

Devry University Chicago Bookstore	3300 N Campbell Ave	773-477-2600	Textbooks, etc.

Map 42 • North Center / Roscoe Village / West Lakeview

Casa de Carina	2834 N Western Ave	773-395-2834	Spanish language self-help and personal growth.
Galaxy Comic Zone	3804 N Western Ave	773-267-1043	Comic books.

Map 43 • Wrigleyville/ East Lakeview

Beasley Books	1533 W Oakdale Ave, 2nd Fl	773-472-4528	Jazz/Blues, Labor History.
Bookworks	3444 N Clark St	773-871-5318	Used and rare books.
Chicago Comics	3244 N Clark St	773-528-1983	Fun! Not geeky, really. . .
The Gallery Bookstore	923 W Belmont Ave	773-281-9999	Used books.
Hanley's	923 W Belmont Ave	773-975-8200	Mystery, sci-fi, and horror genre shop.
Powell's	2850 N Lincoln Ave	773-248-1444	Remainders and off-price books. Large art, architecture, photography and rare departments.

Map 44 • East Lakeview

Bookleggers Used Books	2907 N Broadway St	773-404-8780	Used books.
Selected Works Bookstore	3510 N Broadway St	773-975-0002	Quirky, junky used book store.
Unabridged Bookstore	3251 N Broadway St	773-883-9119	Great literary bookshop, best gay selection in town.

The Grande Dames of Chicago's museum scene, **The Art Institute of Chicago (Map 6)**, the **Museum of Science and Industry (Map 20)**, and the Museum Campus's **Adler Planetarium (Map 11)**, **Field Museum (Map 11)**, and **Shedd Aquarium (Map 9)**, may offer a lifetime of wonder, speculation, and enrichment; but impressive as they are, these cultural epicenters are only the tip of the iceberg when it comes to our city's museum offerings.

Art Museums

Although the Art Institute's collection *is* undeniably impressive (see p385), Chicago's true art lovers know to look past the lions to some of Chicago's less-celebrated treasures.

Columbia College's **Museum of Contemporary Photography (Map 9)** is one of two accredited photography museums in the nation. Other campus–linked art museums include University of Chicago's **Smart Museum (Map 19)**, where the collection spans some 5,000 years. Catch the Lunch at **Loyola University Museum of Art (Map 34)** series for a quick bite with artists and experts on exhibits. Artwork created by and commemorating veterans (from both sides) of the Vietnam War hangs on the walls of the **National Vietnam Veterans Art Museum (Map 11)**.

One of the country's largest collections of art post–1945 is housed at the always eye–opening **Museum of Contemporary Art (Map 3)**. The first Friday of the month, hundreds of twenty–something singles converge here for cocktails, live entertainment, and friendly flirtation.

History

The **Chicago History Museum (Map 32)** (previously the Chicago Historical Society) is a tremendous archive of the city's past and present. African–American history is celebrated at the nation's oldest museum focusing on the black experience, the **DuSable Museum of African–American History (Map 18)**. The **Oriental Institute (Map 19)** specializes in artifacts from the ancient Near–East, including Persia, Mesopotamia, and Egypt. Nobel Prize–winning sociologist **Jane Addams's Hull–House (Map 26)** examines Chicago's history of immigration, ethnic relations, and social work. "Artifacts" such as a John Lennon guitar and song lyrics by Bono are highlights of the collection at **The Peace Museum (West)**. Exhibits focus on individual peacemakers and artists, human rights, women's leadership, and the horrors of war.

Science and Technology

As if the aforementioned **Adler Planetarium (Map 11)**, **Shedd Aquarium (Map 9)**, and **Field Museum (Map 11)** (all of which get special treatment within the Parks & Places listings under "Museum Campus") and the **Museum of Science and Industry (Map 20)** (listed with "Jackson Park") weren't enough to satisfy your inner nerd, Chicago is also home to a handful of quirky, smaller science museums. The **International Museum of Surgical Science (Map 32)** offers a window to the world of questionable surgical practices of yore. The **Museum of Holography (Map 24)** examines the art and technology of making things appear 3–D. For kids, the **Children's Museum (Navy Pier)** presents a hands–on approach to learning about science and geography. Conservation and the environment are the focus of the **Peggy Notebaert Nature Museum (Map 30)**, which also features a butterfly haven, delighting the child in us all.

Architecture

The city itself is perhaps one of the best architecture museums in the world. Examine it by embarking on one of the tours offered by the **Chicago Architecture Foundation (Map 6)**. Frank Lloyd Wright's influence on Chicago architecture can be examined at the **Robie House (Map 19)** in Hyde Park and the Frank Lloyd Wright Home and Studio in Oak Park. Chicago's Prairie Avenue District offers an architectural glimpse at Chicago's Victorian Golden Age. Joint tours of the oldest house in Chicago, the **Clarke House (Map 11)** (c. 1836), and the neighboring **Glessner House (Map 11)** offer the curious an interesting inside peek.

Ethnic Museums

Immigration made Chicago into the "City of Neighborhoods." The **Swedish American Museum Center (Map 37)**, the **Chinese Historical Society of America (Map 10)**, the **Balzekas Museum of Lithuanian Culture (Map 53)**, and the **Polish Museum of America (Map 22)** all explore the impact of immigration on Chicago. The **Hellenic Museum and Cultural Center (Map 6)** is a celebration of all things Greek. The **Mexican Fine Arts Center (Map 25)** is the largest such museum in the country, and examines the Mexican experience through art and culture. The **Spertus Museum (Map 9)**, now in their fancy new building, specializes in Jewish history and heritage.

Miscellaneous

Housed in the former home of the legendary, influential blues label, Chess Records, Willie Dixon's **Blues Heaven Foundation (Map 11)** offers tours of where Chuck Berry, Muddy Waters, and even the Rolling Stones once recorded. (The site is memorialized in the Stones' song "2120 South Michigan.")

For the darker side of sightseeing, the **Leather Archives and Museum (Map 34)** exhibits eight galleries of fetish, bondage, and S&M artifacts including photographs, clothing, toys, and more. The **Antiques Fabricare Museum (Map 48)** offers a seemingly "cleaner" afternoon out with the chance to view antique irons, washing machines, and decades–old washing powders.

The **Museum of Broadcast Communications (Map 2)**, one of only three broadcast museums and home to the only Radio Hall of Fame in the nation, recently moved from the Chicago Cultural Center to its own space on State Street.

Museum	Address	Phone	Map
A Philip Randolph Pullman Porter Museum	10406 S Maryland Ave	773-928-3935	South
ABA Museum of Law	321 N Clark St	312-988-6222	32
Adler Planetarium & Astronomy Museum	1300 S Lake Shore Dr	312-922-7827	11
Antiques Fabricare Museum	4213 W Irving Park Rd	773-282-6216	South
Art Institute of Chicago	111 S Michigan Ave	312-443-3600	6
Balzekas Museum of Lithuanian Culture	6500 S Pulaski Rd	773-582-6500	SW
Bronzeville Children's Museum	9600 S Western Ave	708-636-9504	SW
Charnley-Persky House	1365 N Astor St	312-915-0105	32
Chicago Architecture Foundation	224 S Michigan Ave	312-922-3432	6
Chicago Blues Museum	3636 S Iron St	773-828-8118	12
Chicago Children's Museum	700 E Grand Ave, Navy Pier	312-527-1000	p234
Chicago History Museum	1601 N Clark St	312-642-4600	32
Chicago Maritime Society	310 S Racine Ave	312-421-9096	24
Chinese Historical Society of America	238 W 23rd St	312-949-1000	10
Clarke House Museum	1827 S Indiana Ave	312-745-0040	11
Columbia College Center for Book & Paper Arts	1104 S Wabash Ave	312-344-6630	8
DePaul University Art Museum	2350 N Kenmore Ave	773-325-7506	29
DL Moody Museum	820 N La Salle Dr	312-329-4000	32
DuSable Museum of African-American History	740 E 56th Pl	773-947-0600	18
The Field Museum	1400 S Lake Shore Dr	312-922-9410	11
Frank Lloyd Wright Home and Studio	951 Chicago Ave, Oak Park	708-848-1976	p236
Glessner House Museum	1800 S Prairie Ave	312-326-1480	11
Hellenic Museum and Cultural Center	801 W Adams St	312-655-1234	6
Holocaust Memorial Foundation of Illinois	4255 Main St, Skokie	847- 677-4640	p240
Hyde Park Historical Society	5529 S Lake Park Ave	773-493-1893	19
International Museum of Surgical Science	1524 N Lake Shore Dr	312-642-6502	32
Intuit: Center for Intuitive and Outsider Art	756 N Milwaukee Ave	312-243-9088	24
Irish-American Heritage Center	4642 N Knox Ave	773-282-7035	NW
Jane Addams Hull-House Museum	800 S Halsted St	312-413-5353	26
Jazz Institute of Chicago	410 S Michigan Ave	312-427-1676	6
Leather Archives & Museum	6418 N Greenview Ave	773-761-9200	34
Loyola University Museum of Art	820 N Michigan Ave	312-915-7600	32
Mexican Fine Arts Center	1852 W 19th St	312-738-1503	25
The Museum of Broadcast Communications	400 N State St	312-245-8200	2
Museum of Contemporary Art	220 E Chicago Ave	312-280-2660	3
Museum of Contemporary Photography	600 S Michigan Ave - Columbia College	312-663-5554	9
Museum of Holography Chicago	1134 W Washington Blvd	312-226-1007	24
Museum of Science and Industry	5700 S Lake Shore Dr	773-684-1414	20
National Vietnam Veterans Art Museum	1801 S Indiana Ave	312-326-0270	11
The Newberry Library	60 W Walton St	312-943-9090	32
Oriental Institute Museum	1155 E 58th St	773-702-9514	19
The Peace Museum	100 N Central Park Ave	773-638-6450	West
Peggy Notebaert Nature Museum	2430 N Cannon Dr	773-755-5100	30
Polish Museum of America	984 N Milwaukee Ave	773-384-3352	22
Ridge Historical Society	10621 S Seeley Ave	773-881-1675	SW
Robie House	5757 S Woodlawn Ave	773-834-1847	19
Rogers Park/West Ridge Historical Society	7344 N Western Ave	773-764-4078	33
Shedd Aquarium, John G	1200 S Lake Shore Dr	312-939-2438	9
Skokie Heritage Museum	8031 Floral Ave, Skokie	847-677-6672	p240
Smart Museum of Art	5550 S Greenwood Ave	773-702-0200	19
Smith Museum of Stained Glass	700 E Grand Ave, Navy Pier	312-595-5024	p234
Spertus Museum	610 S Michigan Ave	312-322-1700	9
Swedish American Museum	5211 N Clark St	773-728-8111	37
Ukrainian Institute of Modern Art	2320 W Chicago Ave	773-227-5522	23
Ukrainian National Museum	2249 W Superior St	312-421-8020	23
Willie Dixon's Blues Heaven Foundation	2120 S Michigan Ave	312-808-1286	11

The impeccably restored **Music Box Theatre (Map 43)**, built in 1929, features fantastic Moorish architecture, floating clouds on the ceilings, and live organ music at many weekend screenings. Specialties include the latest art house and international releases, as well as restored classics and weekend matinee double–features that follow monthly themes. Holiday season sing–alongs of White Christmas are huge hits that sell out in advance. The Music Box is also the major screening ground for International Film Festival and Gay and Lesbian Film Festival releases.

Other worthy art–house screening rooms include the **Landmark Century Centre Cinema (Map 44)** at the Century Mall and **Lowes Piper's Alley Theater (Map 31)** in Old Town. For even more refined or esoteric options, pick up schedules for the **Gene Siskel Film Center (Map 5)** of the Art Institute, **Facets Multimedia (Map 29)** in the DePaul neighborhood, **Chicago Filmmakers (Map 37)** in Andersonville and the **LaSalle Bank Cinema (Northwest)** on Irving Park Road.

The latest action features should be seen at **Loews (Map 29)** at Webster Place, **ICE Chatham (South)** off of 87th & the Dan Ryan, and Streeterville's **AMC River East (Map 3)**, which offer ample theaters and show times. Cheap seats on relatively new releases can be had at Lincoln Square's **Davis Cinema (Map 39)** and the **Village Art Theater (Map 32)** in the Gold Coast. The legendary **University of Chicago Doc Films (Map 19)** in Hyde Park has the perfect balance of historical, contemporary and international films. This student-run film society boasts cheap shows and seduces the intellectual crowd.

One of Chicago's most notorious places to catch a flick is **The Vic's "Brew and View," (Map 43)** where the drunken frat boy audiences are almost as annoying as the movies that they show.

Movie Theaters	*Address*	*Phone*	*Map*	
The Alliance Francaise	810 N Dearborn St	312-337-1070	32	Sparse, almost free French films.
AMC Ford City 14	7601 S Cicero Ave	773-582-1839	SW	Mainly teeny-boppers & families coming from the mall.
AMC Loews 600	600 N Michigan Ave	312-255-9347	3	Good concession options, limited times, expensive parking.
AMC Loews Gardens 1/6	175 Old Orchard Ctr, Skokie	847-674-0072	p240	Standard Megaplex.
AMC Loews Norridge 10	4520 N Harlem Ave	708-452-6677	NW	Megaplex suburbanite hell, unless you're a suburbanite.
AMC Loews Pipers Alley 4	1608 N Wells St	312-642-6275	31	Gorgeous backdrop & great independent films.
AMC River East	322 E Illinois St	312-596-0333	3	Blockbuster flicks, billiards, bar & bowling.
Brew & View	3145 N Sheffield Ave	312-618-8439	43	For the lush who likes old movies.
Chicago Cultural Center	78 E Washington St	312-744-6630	5	Free, cultural films and docs.
Chicago Filmmakers	5243 N Clark St	773-293-1447	37	Classes and films, no mainstream mess & no pretense.
Davis Theater	4614 N Lincoln Ave	773-784-0893	39	Four screens. Old, cute, cash-only, homie.
Facets Multimedia	1517 W Fullerton Ave	773-281-4114	29	Obscure independent films anyone?
Gene Siskel Film Center	164 N State St	312-846-2800	5	Tasty smorgasbord of international films.
Henry Crown MSI Omnimax	5700 S Lake Shore Dr	773-684-1414	20	Bring kids, 3-D glasses, and loot, cuz it ain't cheap.
ICE Chatham 14	210 87th St	773-783-8711	South	Mega-theater with comfy seats and fab parking.
Kerasotes Chicago City North 14	2600 N Western Ave	773-394-1600	28	Multiple spacious theaters, diverse crowd, plenty of parking.
Kerasotes Chicago Webster	1471 W Webster Ave	773-327-1314	29	Huge crowds, common date spot, latest movies.
Landmark Century Centre Cinema	2828 N Clark St	773-248-7759	44	Get stimulated by international films, then go shopping at mall.
LaSalle Bank Cinema	4901 W Irving Park Rd	312-904-9442	NW	Cheap vintage films, great parking, cash only.
Logan Theater	2646 N Milwaukee Ave	773-252-0628	27	Charming neighborhood spot, second-run, $3 flicks.
Museum of Contemporary Art Movie Theater	220 E Chicago Ave	312-397-4010	3	Few films, more live performance art.
Music Box Theatre	3733 N Southport Ave	773-871-6604	43	Antiquated theater with character, bad seats & great films.
Navy Pier IMAX Theatre	600 E Grand Ave, Navy Pier	312-595-5629	p234	Expensive, but cute spot for families with youngens.
University of Chicago Doc Films	1212 E 59th St	773-702-8575	19	Student-run film society, kickass variety of films, dirt cheap.
Village Art Theater	1548 N Clark St	312-642-2403	32	Small and dank, but cheap price for slightly old flicks.

If you live in Chicago, you know a few things for sure: hot dogs should have sweet relish, pickles, tomato, onion, sport peppers, and yellow mustard; the Cubs always lose; deep-dish is the best kind of pizza; and Chicago is a *theater* town. You can't swing Mrs. O'Leary's cow without hitting a tiny, struggling off-Loop storefront theater. The storefront theaters are so prevalent here that the city's Department of Cultural Affairs, in its effort to bring smaller productions to the newly revitalized "theater district" (more on that later), named its new downtown venue after them (**Storefront Theater (Map 5)**).

General Tips

The Theater section of the *Chicago Reader*, a free weekly available citywide in bookstores, cafés, bars, and in boxes on street corners (or online at www.chicagoreader.com) is the best friend of the Chicago theatergoer-in-the-know. Turn to the Short List, look for "Highly Recommended" status, or search for Critic's Choices to ferret out your best bets. Another source is the *New City*'s "Top Five Shows to See Now" list. Look for free copies of *New City* in the same places as the *Reader*. Hottix (www.hottix.org), a program of the League of Chicago Theaters, offers half-price tickets to same-day shows on a first-come-first-served basis. Most small theatres, however, won't charge you more than $15 or $20 for a seat—and the larger houses tend to have day-of and student rush tickets available in person at the box office. Also, if you are new in town and want to break into the biz, drop by any theater in your 'hood and pick up a copy of *PerformInk*, the Chicago trade paper for theater and the performing arts, or check 'em out online at www.performink.com. Many auditions and theatre-related gigs are also listed at www.chicagoplays.com via the "industry" link. Also, for the budget conscious, The Saints (a volunteer usher program used by most of the large and medium-sized theaters in Chicago) offers opportunities to usher and see multiple plays for free. You have to join their ranks for an annual $55 fee, but think of how much you'll save on theater tickets. Check out www.saintschicago.org for more information.

Let's get this out of the way. If you want to see a big, traveling Broadway show, check out www.broadwayinchicago.com. There you can find the listings for **Cadillac Palace Theatre (Map 5)**, **Ford Center for the Performing Arts/Oriental Theatre (Map 5)**, the **LaSalle Bank Theatre (Map 5)**, or the beautiful and historic **Auditorium Theatre (Map 5)** (designed by Louis Sullivan). When in doubt, the city will always have *Wicked* (at least it seems that way). But Chicago, my friends, offers so much more than just second runs…

Downtown Theaters a.k.a. "The Downtown Theater District"

There are many large theaters producing quality work in downtown Chicago. One of the oldest theaters in Chicago, **The Goodman Theatre (Map 5)** is a stalwart of the downtown theater scene. Now in its new location at 170 North Dearborn, the Goodman is a professional theater featuring high-quality plays by well-known and lesser-known playwrights. One of the classic Chicago theaters, **Steppenwolf Theatre Co. (Map 30)** in Old Town, produces wonderful ensemble productions with notable Chicago actors. Among their famous ensemble members are John Mahoney, John Malkovich, Laurie Metcalf, Martha Plimpton, and Gary Sinise. Similarly, **Lookingglass Theatre (Map 43)** (known for ensemble member David Schwimmer of *Friends* fame) creates productions that incorporate skills and acts you might otherwise find in the circus. Their new location (in Chicago's Water Tower Water Works building, one of the few structures to survive the famous 1871 Chicago fire) is well worth a trip downtown. Known as a playwright's theater, **Victory Gardens Theater (Map 30)** produces original works by contemporary, living playwrights in a newly renovated space in the historic Biograph Theatre on Lincoln Avenue. On Navy Pier, you'll find **Chicago Shakespeare Theater (Map 3)**, which offers up classy (but pricey) stagings of the Bard. Another Chicago theatre staple is *Blue Man Group*, which has completely taken over **Briar Street Theatre (Map 44)** with paint, drums, and marshmallows. Finally, the **Storefront Theater (Map 5)**, at the Chicago Department of Cultural Affairs, remounts the best of the neighborhood theater productions in its state of the art venue at 66 E Randolph.

Medium-Sized Neighborhood Theaters

Really amazing productions can be found at medium-sized neighborhood theaters. Some of the best picks include the longest running show in Chicago today, *Too Much Light Makes the Baby Go Blind* (at **The Neo-Futurarium (Map 37)**). Proclaiming to perform thirty plays in sixty minutes, the show ends when one or the other is over. Other good bets include **Stage Left Theatre (Map 43)** (whose work has cultivated some of the best national playwrights), **Live Bait Theater (Map 43)** (first-run plays), **About Face Theatre (Map 44)** (high-quality gay/lesbian/bisexual works), **Famous Door Theatre (Map 43)** (original and "seldom-produced" works), and **Redmoon Theater (Map 24)** (highly unique large-scale puppetry productions).

Improv

Chicago is also well known for its improv scene. The original, **The Second City (Map 31)** (the famed training ground for most of *Saturday Night Live*'s original cast) keeps on going with its many shows at four venues in Chicago. Check out www.secondcity.com for show times. Other improv venues include **The Playground Theater (Map 42)**, **ImprovOlympic Theater (Map 43)** (with its free Friday and Saturday midnight "Cage Match"), **Annoyance Theatre (Map 40)**, **Comedy Sportz (Map 44),** and **WNEP Theater (Map 39)**. Most of these venues feature improv teams battling against one another for audience approval. Information about all venues can be found on www.improvchicago.com.

Fringe/Performance Art/Other

At the **Museum of Contemporary Art (Map 3)** (www.mcachicago.org), a new theatre built of concrete offers a stage for a variety of theatre, dance, performance art, and readings of all ilks.

But if you don't catch the bigger shows (read: more expensive) at the MCA, some of Chicago's best productions occur in alternative spaces. They are created by smaller companies who don't have a venue (whether by choice or by size). These are the tiny, glittering gems of the Chicago theater scene. Find these productions in the Performance Listings in the *Reader*. Don't shy away from a theater company you've never heard of producing at a rented venue. You might just find your new favorite group of artists—and it's fun to latch onto a company, watch them grow, and then say "I knew them when." We can't list them all here (for they are too numerous), but here are some of our favorites.

For girl-on-girl combat action, check out *Babes with Blades* (www.babeswithblades.com) in semi-regular productions at various venues. 500 Clown (www.500clown.com) produces loose adaptations of classic tales (*Frankenstein, Macbeth*) in original, dangerous clown theater that the authors wouldn't recognize. *Defiant Theatre* (www.defianttheatre.org) subverts the social, moral, and aesthetic expectations of the theater with edgy productions at varied venues. At Strawdog, you'll find fresh takes on everything from classics to contemporary works to radio plays presented by a cohesive ensemble (www.strawdog.org). Collaboraction (known mainly for its *Sketchbook* series of ultra-short new plays) is a collective comprising cross-disciplinary artists presenting unique works in all media. Check them out at www.collaboraction.org. The House Theatre of Chicago (www.thehousetheatre.org) has drawn major critical praise (and major audiences) with its smart, witty adaptations and new works that incorporate dance, music, and magic. For super-intellectual takes on classic plays, seek out the Hypocrites (www.the-hypocrites.com). Uma (www.umaproductions.org) offers interesting, thought-provoking productions in a variety of styles. At Theater Oobleck (www.theateroobleck.com), you can expect to find quirky plays written by the ensemble and rehearsed without the help of a director. Drawing from diverse sources, Goat Island Performance Ensemble (www.goatislandperformance.org) offers up heady movement-based performance created in a lengthy ensemble process. *Plasticene* (www.plasticene.com) confronts audiences with rare physical theater. In the summer, look for remounts of favorite local productions at **Theater on the Lake (Map 30)** (www.chicagoparkdistrict.com), a screened-in theater venue (and former TB sanitarium) situated near Fullerton Avenue on Chicago's lakefront. Curious Theater Branch (www.curioustheaterbranch.com) has presented original, engaging theater for the last eleven years.

Out of Town

There also are some fantastic theatrical adventures just beyond the borders of our fair city. For outstanding productions of plays that focus on writing and language, check out Writer's Theatre in Glencoe. A little bit closer to home, Evanston offers some quality productions by Next Theatre, Light Opera Works, and acclaimed theater department at Northwestern University. West of the City, Oak Park offers up gems at the Village Players and the Oak Park Festival Theatre (which offers outdoor plays and musicals during the summer months). In Wilmette, an annual musical production is presented at the Wallace Bowl, in Gillson Park, just across the street from the Bahai temple.

All told, Chicago boasts somewhere in the neighborhood of 250 theatre companies—all of which believe they have something new and different to offer to the city. Any given weekend is likely to offer scores of theatrical options—so make it your business to get out to see some of them.

Theater	*Address*	*Phone*	*Map*
A Red Orchid Theatre	1531 N Wells St	312-943-8722	31
About Face Theatre	1222 W Wilson Ave	773-784-8565	44
American Girl Place	111 E Chicago Ave	877-247-5223	2
American Theater Company	1909 W Byron St	773-929-1031	42
Angel Island Theater	735 W Sheridan Rd	773-871-0442	44
Annoyance Productions	4840 N Broadway St	773-561-4665	40
Apollo Theater Chicago	2540 N Lincoln Ave	773-935-6100	29
Arie Crown Theatre	2301 S Lake Shore Dr	312-791-6190	11
Athenaeum Theatre	2936 N Southport Ave	773-935-6860	43
Auditorium Theatre	50 E Congress Pkwy	312-922-2110	5
Black Ensemble Theater	4520 N Beacon St	773-769-4451	40
Briar Street Theatre	3133 N Halsted St	773-348-4000	44
Cadillac Palace Theatre	151 W Randolph St	312-977-1700	5
Casa Aztlan	1831 S Racine Ave	312-666-5508	26
Chase Park	4701 N Ashland Ave	312-742-7518	40
Chicago Center for the Performing Arts	777 N Green St	312-733-6000	1
Chicago Cultural Center	78 E Washington St	312-744-6630	5
Chicago Dramatists	1105 W Chicago Ave	312-633-0630	24
Chicago Opera Theater	70 E Lake St	312-704-8414	5
Chicago Shakespeare Theater	800 E Grand Ave	312-595-5600	3
The Chicago Theatre	175 N State St	312-462-6363	5

Theater	*Address*	*Phone*	*Map*
Chopin Theater	1543 W Division St	773-278-1500	22
Civic Opera House	20 N Wacker Dr	312-419-0033	5
Cornservatory	4210 N Lincoln Ave	312-409-6435	39
Court Theatre	5535 S Ellis Ave	773-753-4472	19
Dance Center of Columbia College	1306 S Michigan Ave	312-344-8300	11
Drury Lane Theatre at Water Tower Place	175 E Chestnut St	312-642-2000	32
Ford Center for the Performing Arts/Oriental Theatre	24 W Randolph St	312-782-2004	5
Free Street Theater	1419 W Blackhawk St	773-772-7248	22
Getz Theater (Columbia College)	72 E 11th St	312-344-6126	8
The Goodman Theatre	170 N Dearborn St	312-443-3800	5
Gorilla Tango Theatre	1919 N Milwaukee Ave	773-598-4549	28
Harold Washington Cultural Center	4701 S Dr Martin L King Jr Dr	773-373-1900	16
Harris Theater for Music and Dance	205 E Randolph St	312-334-7777	5
The Heartland Café Studio Theater	7016 N Glenwood Ave	773-465-8005	34
Improv Olympic	3541 N Clark St	773-880-0199	43
Kathleen Mullady Memorial Theatre	1125 W Loyola Ave	773-508-3847	34
Lakeshore Theatre	3175 N Broadway St	773-472-3492	44
LaSalle Bank Theatre	22 W Monroe St	312-977-1710	5
Lifeline Theatre	6912 N Glenwood Ave	773-761-4477	34
Links Hall Studio	3435 N Sheffield Ave	773-281-0824	43
Live Bait Theater	3914 N Clark St	773-871-1212	43
Lookingglass Theatre	821 N Michigan Ave	312-337-0665	43
Mercury Theater	3745 N Southport Ave	773-325-1700	43
Merle Reskin Theatre	60 E Balbo Ave	312-922-1999	8
Museum of Contemporary Art	220 E Chicago Ave	312-280-2660	3
National Pastime Theater	4139 N Broadway St	773-327-7077	40
The Neo-Futurarium	5153 N Ashland Ave	773-275-5255	37
North Shore Center for the Performing Arts	9501 Skokie Blvd, Skokie	847-673-6300	p240
O'Malley Theater-Roosevelt University	430 S Michigan Ave	312-341-3831	6
O'Rourke Center for the Performing Arts	1145 W Wilson Ave	773-878-9761	40
Piccolo Theater	600 Main St, Evanston	847-424-0089	p214
The Playground Theater	3209 N Halsted St	773-871-3793	42
Profiles Theatre	4147 N Broadway St	773-549-1815	40
Prop Theatre	3504 N Elston Ave	773-539-7838	39
Raven Theatre	6157 N Clark St	773-338-2177	33
Redmoon Theater Co	1463 W Hubbard St	312-850-8440	24
Royal George Theatre Center	1641 N Halsted St	312-988-9000	30
Ruth Page Center Theater	1016 N Dearborn St	312-337-6543	32
The Second City	1616 N Wells St	312-664-4032	30
The Second City e.t.c./Donny's Skybox	1608 N Wells St	312-337-3992	31
The Side Project	1439 W Jarvis Ave	773-973-2105	34
Stage Left Theatre	3408 N Sheffield Ave	773-883-8830	43
Steep Theatre	3902 N Sheridan Rd	312-458-0722	43
Steppenwolf Theatre	1650 N Halsted St	312-335-1650	31
Storefront Theater	66 E Randolph St	312-742-8497	5
Strawdog Theatre	3829 N Broadway St	773-528-9696	44
Theater on the Lake	2400 N Lake Shore Dr	312-742-7994	30
Theatre Building	1225 W Belmont Ave	773-327-5252	43
TimeLine Theatre Co	615 W Wellington Ave	773-281-8463	44
Trap Door Productions	1655 W Cortland St	773-384-0494	28
UIC Theatre	1044 W Harrison St	312-996-2939	26
Viaduct Theater	3111 N Western Ave	773-296-6024	42
Victory Gardens	2257 N Lincoln Ave	773-871-3000	30
Vittum Theater	1012 N Noble St	773-342-4141	22

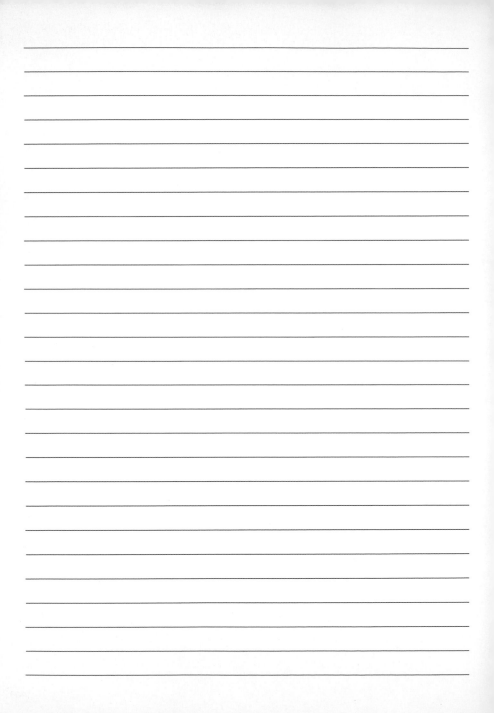

Street Index

Some of the townships and communities immediately adjoining Chicago proper thought it would be a fun joke to restart street numbering at their borders—or name a street exactly the same name as an entirely unrelated Chicago street. These cases are designated with an asterisk.*

B

C

D

E

H

I

Street Index

L

N

O

P

S

T

U

V

Y

General

All emergencies **911**
AIDS Hotline 800-342-AIDS
Animal Anti-Cruelty Society 312-644-8338
Chicago Dental Referral Service 312-836-7305
Chicago Department of Housing 773-285-5800
City of Chicago Board of Elections 312-269-7900
Dog License (City Clerk) 312-744-6875
Driver's Licenses 312-793-1010
Emergency Services 312-747-7247
Employment Discrimination 312-744-7584
Gas Leaks 312-240-7000
Income Tax (Illinois) 800-732-8866
Income Tax (Federal) 800-829-3676
Legal Assistance 312-332-1624
Mayor's Office 312-744-4000
Parking (City Stickers) 312-742-9200
Parking Ticket Inquiries 312-744-7275
Report Crime in Your Neighborhood 312-372-0101
Passports 312-341-6020
Police Assistance (non-emergency) 311
Social Security 773-890-2492
Streets and Sanitation 312-744-5000
Telephone Repair Service 888-611-4466
Voter Information 312-269-7900
Water Main Leaks 312-744-7038

Helplines

Alcoholics Anonymous 312-346-1475
Alcohol, Drug and Abuse Helpline 800-234-0420
Alcoholism and Substance Abuse 312-988-7900
Domestic Violence Hotline 800-799-7233
Drug Care, St. Elizabeth's 773-278-5015
Gamblers Anonymous 312-346-1588
Illinois Child Abuse Hotline 800-252-2873
Narcotics Anonymous 708-848-4884
Parental Stress Services 312-372-7368
Runaway Switchboard 800-621-4000
Sexual Assault Hotline 888-293-2080
United Way Community Information
and Referral 312-876-0010
Violence – Anti-Violence Project 773-871-CARE

Complaints

Better Business Bureau of Chicago 312-832-0500
Consumer Fraud Division (Attorney General's Office) 312-814-3000
Chicago Department of Consumer Services 312-744-9400
Citizen's Utility Board 800-669-5556
Department of Housing Inspection Complaints 312-747-9000
Mayor's Office 312-744-4000
Postal Service Complaints 312-983-8400